Studies of Economic Growth in Industrialized Countries

British Economic Growth

Studies of Economic Growth in
Industrialized Countries

MOSES ABRAMOVITZ & SIMON KUZNETS, EDITORS

British Economic Growth 1856-1973

R. C. O. Matthews, C. H. Feinstein, and
J. C. Odling-Smee

Stanford University Press, Stanford, California   1982

Stanford University Press
Stanford, California
© 1982 by the Board of Trustees of the
Leland Stanford Junior University
Printed in the United States of America
ISBN 0-8047-1110-0
LC 80-53222

Preface

This book owes its origin to the initiative of the Social Science Research Council, which, through the agency of Moses Abramovitz and Simon Kuznets, launched in the early 1960's a series of parallel historical studies of growth in seven industrial countries. Like our colleagues in the other countries, we have found that the task has taken us very much longer than we expected, and the work has been set aside from time to time as each of the three of us became drawn into other duties. The delay has had some offsetting advantages. It has enabled us to include within our compass the whole of the period of rapid postwar growth, setting a clear terminus to our story in 1973. It has also enabled us to take advantage of major revisions to the statistics relating to investment and the capital stock before 1914 undertaken by Charles Feinstein since the publication of his *National Income, Expenditure and Output of the United Kingdom, 1855-1964*. The core of our statistical data comes from that book, and it may be regarded as a statistical companion volume to the present one.

We have incorporated — with many changes — some material from earlier articles by one or other of us, listed in the references. What is said in this book should be taken to replace our earlier treatments in any places where they are discrepant.

All three authors have participated fully in the successive stages of the work, but two of us would like to put on record that it was the third, Robin Matthews, who made by far the most significant contributions to the design of the investigation, the analysis of the material, and the writing of the final text.

In the course of our work, we have incurred obligations to more people than we can here mention. Our particular thanks are due to Moses Abramovitz and Simon Kuznets for their encouragement, patience, and kind but discriminating comments on the draft; to those who helped us at various stages as research assistants, particularly Pat Yudkin and Ann Duncan, and also Rosemary Braddon, Keith Norris, Jennifer Phillips, Stephen Powell, and Joy Selby-Smith; to official statisticians and others who supplied us with material; to Belinda Powell, who bore the largest part of the heavy secretarial burden, and also to Hazel Griffin and Jo Hall; to the computing staff, typists, and librarians of the Oxford University Institute of Economics and Statistics and the Cambridge Department of Applied Economics; to Alan Harris, who drew the charts; and to Barbara Mnookin, as editor for Stanford University Press.

Financial assistance is gratefully acknowledged from the (American) Social Science Research Council and the Ford Foundation, who initiated the project, and from the (British) Social Science Research Council for a grant to help in its completion. We are indebted to the Oxford University Institute of Economics and Statistics, for allowing us to draw heavily on its facilities, and we also had much help from the Cambridge Department of Applied Economics.

In the matter of arrangement, we have tried to be mindful of the needs of different classes of readers. This is a long book, and our path will traverse some dense statistical thickets. Our hope, naturally, is that readers will accompany us throughout the journey. But realism teaches us that many will prefer to be selective. Accordingly, each of the central chapters (3–15) is prefaced by a synopsis, to enable the reader to pass lightly over topics that he is not especially interested in and is willing to take on trust. Readers whose interest is in the general picture rather than in the parts that make it up may find it most convenient to turn straight from Chapter 1 to the concluding chapters, 16 and 17. Those chapters are not a complete summary of the book, but they have been written so as to be self-contained.

R. C. O. MATTHEWS
C. H. FEINSTEIN
J. C. ODLING-SMEE

Contents

Figures

Tables

A Note on Conventions and Abbreviations

Footnotes contain material necessary for the understanding of the text; *back-notes* (numbered) contain additional or supporting material.

The *geographical coverage* is, unless otherwise indicated, the United Kingdom of Great Britain (England, Wales, and Scotland) and Ireland until 1920 and the United Kingdom of Great Britain and Northern Ireland after 1920. Series relating to the two areas are spliced at 1920 for the calculation of growth rates.

Successive *phases* are defined as follows:

Pre-1914 period	1856–1913
Trans–World War I period	1913–1924
Interwar period	1924–1937
Trans–World War II period	1937–1951
Postwar period	1951–1973

When *averages of annual data* are calculated for overlapping periods, the bridge year is included in the earlier period only; thus averages for 1937–51 and 1951–73 are the averages of the observations for 1938 through 1951 and for 1952 through 1973, respectively.

A circumflex (^) over a variable denotes its *growth rate*. Growth rates are annual compound-interest percentage rates of growth between end-years of a period.

Rounding of data in tables. Where totals and their components were calculated from unrounded data, they were rounded separately. An adjustment was then made if necessary, sometimes in a component and sometimes in the total, to ensure that the components added to the total. The adjustment was chosen so as to minimize the percentage error in the adjusted figures.

Parentheses around figures in tables means that the figures are not reliable.

A *dash* (–) in a table means not available or not applicable.

Data sources. A consistent set of basic statistical series was prepared for this study. Their sources are described in Appendix N. Where additional data were used in tables and figures, their sources are noted. Adjustments were often made to the published data, to bring them into line with the required concepts or to link them to other series. The data shown here are therefore not necessarily identical to those shown in the sources quoted.

Capital is gross domestic reproducible capital stock, unless otherwise indicated.

Commerce is used for the sector comprising the distributive trades, banking, insurance, and finance, and miscellaneous services.

The following *abbreviations* are used, in addition to familiar ones:

TFI (or f in algebraic expressions): Total factor input

TFP (or x in algebraic expressions): Total factor productivity

TF_YI, TF_HI, TF_QI: Alternative measures of TFI, in which labor input is measured respectively in man-years, man-hours, and man-hours adjusted for quality

TF_YP, TF_HP, TF_QP: Corresponding alternative measures of TFP

AYS: Average number of years of schooling

MEI: Marginal efficiency of investment

SPOF: Supply price of finance

PART ONE

The Method, the Problems, and the Profile

CHAPTER ONE

A Quantitative-Historical Approach to British Economic Growth

The subject of this book is the course and causes of British economic growth from the middle of the nineteenth century till 1973. More particularly, our aim is to view in their historical context the years between World War II and 1973. Those were years of unparalleled growth in Britain, as in other countries.

Certain of the questions about British economic growth are questions that can be asked about growth in any country. What was its time pattern? What was the relative importance of the various contributory causes, on the supply side and on the demand side? How did those causes interact with one another and with the process of growth itself? Other questions are particularly important in the British case. Principal among these are questions about the causes and consequences of changes in Britain's relative standing among industrial countries and in its competitive position in international trade, and questions about the effects of wars.

The features of the approach to British economic growth adopted in this book are that it is historical — a study of trends over a long period, not a comparison with other countries' growth in a particular period — and that it is set in quantitative national-accounting terms.

This chapter explains the scope, method, and arrangement of the book. In the process, it introduces some of the main substantive questions about British economic growth. It discusses the implications of the historical and quantitative national-accounting aspects of the approach adopted, the plan of the book, and the underlying conceptual framework, and describes some of the main features of British economic growth.

THE HISTORICAL ASPECT OF THE APPROACH

The history of past events may be studied either as a prerequisite for understanding the present or as a way of understanding the past itself.

Our purpose is to do both. We are especially interested in the postwar period,* because it is nearest to us and leads into the present. We shall therefore treat it more fully than earlier periods. In this respect we have not followed the precept of Ranke, that every age is equal in the sight of God. In the spirit of that precept, however, we have regarded earlier periods as being of interest in their own right, as well as for their relevance to the postwar period and to the present. Our interests are thus partly those of the economist, partly those of the historian.†

The period we cover runs from 1856 to 1973. The starting date, 1856, was chosen for statistical reasons, not because that specific year is to be regarded as a watershed. From that date annual statistics on national income and on inputs of labor and capital are available that are in principle internally consistent and comparable with those available from official sources on the postwar period (see Feinstein 1972; Feinstein forthcoming). The availability of such statistics is essential for a quantitative approach in national-accounting terms.

However, the middle of the nineteenth century also makes sense as a starting point for historical reasons. It corresponds roughly to the end of one phase of British economic development: the phase of industrialization, based principally on textiles. From the 1850's onward — in fact probably from a decade or so earlier — there was no significant trend increase in the proportion of the labor force engaged in manufacturing. This is in contrast with the steep rise that occurred in earlier decades of the nineteenth century. It is in contrast also with the rise that occurred in later periods in most of the other advanced countries.[1]

By 1856 Britain, with nearly a third of its labor force in manufacturing and with the framework of its railway system completed, had already become a mature industrial country in many respects. It had (probably) the world's highest income per head. The history of British economic growth in the next century and a quarter is the history of the development of the economy from that stage on.

*Throughout this book this expression will be used to refer to the years 1951–73 (the period 1945–51 being regarded as one of postwar recovery). Where "postwar" is used more generally for the periods after both world wars, the context will make that clear.

†"The historian is concerned with the past, in its relation to the present; the economist is concerned with the present, and for the sake of the present with the past" (Hicks 1979: 4). Some historians would regard even the first part of that sentence as conceding too much concern with the present. "The historian . . . is concerned with the later event only in so far as it throws light on the part of the past he is studying. It is the cardinal error to reverse this process and study the past for the light it throws on the present" (Elton 1967: 66).

The reason why we do not take the story back before the middle of the nineteenth century is not that the events of the previous century are irrelevant to the present, far less that they lack intrinsic interest. On the contrary. Britain's early start on the path of industrialization can with good reason be held responsible for many features of its later development, including features that are still with us. This early start — earlier than other countries by about half a century — took place in the latter half of the eighteenth century and the first half of the nineteenth. Some references to that period will be made at various points in ensuing chapters. However, as we go back in time, data limitations diminish the contribution that can be made by the quantitative national-accounting method to economic history relative to the contribution that can be made by other methods.[2]

Phases in the century and a quarter after 1856 have been variously characterized by economists and historians. Some have seen the whole period, crudely, in terms of continuous (relative) decline, at least after 1870; others have distinguished Kondratieff cycles; all have agreed that the two world wars ushered in major changes. The characterization that emerges from the following pages is indeed one of nearly continuous decline relative to other industrial countries. But as far as the British rate of growth itself is concerned, the pattern is a different one. It is best described as U-shaped. The rate of growth declined to a low point some time before or around World War I, then increased up to 1973.

The first part of the period, from 1856 to 1913, consists of two phases. The earlier phase culminated in what seemed at the time to be the high-water mark of Britain's industrial prosperity in the boom of 1872–73. The subsequent 40 years have been commonly regarded as a period of retardation — retardation relative to the growth rate that had been achieved earlier and retardation also relative to what was currently being achieved by the other countries whose competition was increasingly being felt. The timing and extent of this retardation are still unclear. But there is no doubt that the rate of growth of productivity was low, at least after 1900. And there is no doubt also that the 1870's saw a fall in the rate of return on capital that was never subsequently fully made good.

World War I and the years immediately after it were in many respects critical in the history of British economic growth. On the one hand, there took place in 1919–21 the greatest setback to real GDP that the country had experienced since the industrial revolution. On the other hand, those years marked also the beginning of a phase of increase in the rate of growth of productivity that persisted for the next half century. It is unfortunate that the statistics for the years 1914–21 are less satisfactory than for any other years within our period, and we shall not be able to analyze the immediate aftermath of World War I as fully as we would have wished.* We have taken 1924 and 1937 as the first and last years of what we normally refer to as the interwar period. This gives us two years that are broadly comparable in terms of the level of activity, and excludes the statistically uncertain and economically abnormal events of 1919–20.

In the interwar period economic growth was not a major topic of public discussion. Unemployment after 1920 never fell below 9 percent, there were violent divergences between the experience of different industries and regions, and international economic relations were in a state of turmoil. Recovery and the restoration of normalcy were the objectives of policy, rather than growth. Not for the first time or the last, however, the preoccupations of public men did not accurately mirror the importance of events. The period was certainly an abnormal one—so much so that for many purposes (e.g. the study of trends in investment) it does not provide a very helpful basis of comparison with the postwar period. But, as is now well known, real income per head of population rose considerably more rapidly than in the prewar years. The contributory causes—industrial, international, and demographic—will be discussed in later chapters. Straight reversal of the causes that had made for the setback of 1919–21 was not paramount among them.

We come finally to the postwar period, 1951–73. Our terminal date, 1973, marks the end of the great secular postwar boom, in Britain as in other countries. We do not carry the story into the long recession that began in that year. Naturally, certain of our remarks on the postwar period will be colored by an awareness of the doubts cast by the recession on whether the previous rate of growth will in the long run be capable of being restored, let alone improved.

In the postwar period the rate of growth of GDP was higher than in earlier periods. This was notwithstanding that the rate of growth of the labor force was considerably lower than in earlier periods. The rate of growth of GDP per worker was thus *much* higher than in any previous period (not excluding periods before 1856). "There is little doubt that

---

*There are also statistical problems with the years 1939–47, but these matter less because the behavior of the British economy was not so peculiar in the aftermath of World War II as it was in the aftermath of World War I. The periods of the two wars themselves are deliberately not much discussed in this book, as being obviously *sui generis*.

the British people would have regarded the post-war record of their economy as highly satisfactory if the United Kingdom had been an isolated state. But, while British growth was above its earlier rates, growth rates of the other large countries of Western Europe were much higher still" (Denison 1968: 232). Hence arises the persistent dilemma in the study of British economic growth in the postwar period: is the task to explain why Britain did so well or to explain why it did so badly?

The historical approach causes the first of these two questions to bulk more largely in this book than it does in most discussion of Britain's postwar economic performance: our subject is trends in the British economy over time, not comparison of those trends with trends in other countries. The latter would require an entirely different array of evidence; but we hope that our findings, in conjunction with research on other countries, will prove indirectly relevant to the second question. Comparisons between periods and comparisons between countries are complementary. Why, say, Britain's growth rate in the 1960's differed from Germany's is one question, and why Britain's growth rate in the 1960's differed from its growth rate in the 1930's is quite another. Ideally it should be possible to embrace the answers to both questions in a single grand model of economic behavior. As an intermediate enterprise, both types of question are worth asking. Which type of question is more helpful toward a better general understanding or toward the resolution of questions of policy is not self-evident. Much depends on the specific question at issue. Some of the underlying patterns of behavior are likely to be more nearly constant over time, others over space. On the one hand, different countries at the same date will have access to the same pool of knowledge and be subject to the same world economic environment. On the other hand, a given country at dates separated by a generation will have many of the same people in the labor force — to say nothing of the children they have brought up and molded — and it will have some of the same stock of physical capital. More important, perhaps, there will be continuity in its institutions, economic, social and political, and this continuity will persist over periods longer than a generation.

THE QUANTITATIVE ASPECT OF THE APPROACH

This book is economic history based on the national accounts and on data on inputs. The advantages of the national-accounting approach do not need to be labored. Gross national product (GNP) and its related measures are in principle comprehensive and at the same time susceptible of disaggregation, by sector and in other ways. They describe the performance of the economy as a whole, not just those aspects of it on which we happen to have particularly good information. They provide a unifying basis for the study of economic change. Being quantitative, they give a clear meaning to the concepts of growth or decline.*

The corresponding disadvantage is that the statistical data are by no means fully reliable. It is important to bear this in mind. In general it is our belief that the data are adequate for the purposes for which we have used them. But the possibility cannot be ruled out that future data revisions will alter some of our conclusions qualitatively, not just in detail. This possibility exists with all types of evidence.

A reminder of the fallibility of the data is provided by the imperfect consilience of the three indicators of GDP (income, expenditure, and output). Experience in handling the data reveals that the choice between such alternative indicators usually makes more difference to the results than is made by the choice of ways to manipulate them. In the particular case of the three GDP indicators, we avoid the problem by taking as benchmarks only years where the discrepancies are unimportant, and by using a geometric mean of the three indicators wherever possible.

In general the output statistics are more reliable for goods than for services, and all series are more reliable for recent times than for earlier times. The absolute margin of error in some series is large.† Margins of error in growth rates are probably less, insofar as the same sources of statistical error persist over time. But small differences between periods or sectors in growth rates cannot be regarded as significant. This is a particularly important matter in the case of the United Kingdom, where average growth rates have been fairly low, so that a small

---

*In the 19th century the word more commonly used was progress, with its vaguer and more debatable connotations. Thus the title of G. R. Porter's great statistical compendium, published in 1851, was *Progress of the Nation*. The word growth does not appear in the index of Marshall's *Priniciples*. Still more comprehensive indicators than GNP can, of course, be devised, taking account of leisure, environmental quality, and so on. The work done on such indicators suggests that although their actual growth rates are quite different from those of GNP, they do not make a great difference to *relative* growth rates (Nordhaus & Tobin 1972; Beckerman 1980). These enlargements of the GNP concept still rest on the same theoretical basis, which is ultimately that of revealed preference. For some purposes this basis is inadequate: neither GNP nor enlarged versions of it purport to measure such larger concepts as happiness or social harmony.

†See Appendix N for further discussion. Reference to the greater or lesser reliability of particular series or calculations is made throughout the text.

difference in growth rates may be sizable relative to the average growth rate. For example, the much-bruited slowdown in the rate of growth of output per man-year between 1856–73 and 1873–1913 was only a slowdown from an annual growth rate of 1.3 percent to an annual rate of 0.9 percent.* This *is* to be regarded as a significant difference; a difference of 0.4 percent in the annual growth rate, compounded over the 40 years between 1873 and 1913, would have made a difference of 17 percent in the level in the final year. Hence this is a phenomenon that *is* worth trying to explain. But it is not sensible to get excited by differences of one- or two-tenths of a percentage point. This is a warning we pronounce here once and for all: it might be desirable but would be tedious to reiterate it at frequent intervals throughout the book. Our own practice may sometimes seem to disregard the point. The chief reason for doing so is in connection with decomposition. If an annual percentage growth rate (or a difference between growth rates) of, say, 1.0 is to be decomposed additively into half a dozen sources, most of them are likely to turn out to be pretty small numbers. In such contexts we sometimes follow the practice of giving percentage growth rates to two decimal points, for purposes of comparison, while recognizing that they have no pretense to that degree of accuracy.

The problem just described is that the data may be inaccurate indicators of what they purport to measure. It may also happen that what they purport to measure is not exactly what would be appropriate from a theoretical point of view. An example is provided by statistics on the capital stock, where the gross measure and the net measure both have conceptual deficiencies (to some extent in opposite directions; see Appendix F). In this instance we give both measures when dealing with the economy as a whole, but only the gross measure when dealing with sectors (because net series are less reliable *statistically* and indeed, for that reason, are not published at all for individual sectors in official statistics for the postwar period).

In order to try to understand trends in the variables measured in the national accounts, it is necessary to have regard also to many other kinds of information. This we have done. However, the quantitative national-accounting approach has inevitably affected the scale on which different aspects of British economic growth are here treated. We shall have a great deal to say about investment, sectoral shifts, and international trade, but less about topics that are in principle at least as

---

*Throughout the book, growth rates are annual percentage compound rates calculated between peak years of business cycles, unless otherwise stated.

important, such as technology, entrepreneurship, and industrial relations. These are the subject of a gigantic literature at a very micro level, in industry studies, in business histories, and so on. But much of it is lacking in the historical dimension, and all of it is difficult to translate into overall measures in national-accounting terms. Discussion of these topics is included at various points, and we have not fought shy of drawing conclusions necessary for the formation of a view about what was important and what was not. However, much that relates to them has had to remain in unallocated residual sources of growth.

Quantitative economic history may imply to some people the use of sophisticated statistical or econometric methods. There are a number of reasons why these are not to be found here.

First, we are interested in trends over periods, not in cycles. It is as easy to see the relationship between the trend growth rates of a number of associated variables by writing them down in a table or plotting them on a chart, as by estimating a regression equation. And it does not misleadingly suggest a precise relationship.

Second, the number of degrees of freedom for estimating trends as opposed to cycles is small. It would be increased if we were to assume that the structural model was the same in each period. But it does not strike us as a plausible assumption that the same relationships between observable variables persisted over the period of 117 years from 1856 to 1973, or even that they changed over time in a way that could be captured in a single econometric model. Though there is continuity between successive periods, we view them as phases in a dynamic process, not as samples from a universe of observations.

Third, it is difficult to have much confidence in econometrically estimated relationships. This is partly because of data inadequacies and the well-known problems of linear regression.[3] But it is also because econometrics cannot always distinguish between two (or more) theoretically distinct models with markedly different implications; they may both (or all) be consistent with the data.[4] Econometrics can shed considerable light on economic relationships; but it can also mislead. A less formal approach to the data reduces the risk that all the emphasis is placed on a single explanation, which may in reality be false.

Our quantitative techniques are essentially very simple. We compare trends over time in related variables by examining growth rates and changes in percentage shares. These are usually calculated between cyclically comparable years. For many series annual data are also shown in charts. One device we have frequently found illuminating is to decompose variables into constituent parts (in the manner of $MV = PT$). Such tautological decomposition does not as such identify causal elements, any more than the estimation of regression equations does. Its usefulness depends on its appropriateness as a basis for decomposition.

To sum up on both historical and quantitative aspects, our treatment is heavily statistical and, we trust, well grounded in economic theory. It is more in the intellectual spirit of the economic historian than in that of the econometrician in accepting that there may be changes in the structural model between periods. Indeed, a major concern throughout is to identify and explain differences between periods. Throughout, we are conscious of those unavoidable limitations of our knowledge that Lundberg referred to in his characterization of the work of Kuznets: "All sets of findings necessitate more exact knowledge of the 'mechanism' involved than that which lies at hand. Hence the explanations do not turn out to be much more than 'suggestions,' e.g. in regard to those factors that have determined observed trends or fluctuations in the development: 'The result is, at best, a sketch of a possible but untested association between the findings'" (Lundberg 1971: 460, quoting Kuznets 1961a: 6).

PLAN OF THE BOOK

The book is arranged in five parts, as follows.

Part One is introductory. The present chapter reviews methods and issues. Chapter 2 describes the movement over time of the central variable, real national income.

The structure of Parts Two and Three is based on the foundation of the growth-accounting method first made familiar by the work of such writers as Abramovitz (1956), Kendrick (1961), and Denison (1962) on the empirical side and Solow (1957) on the theoretical side. (This method is further discussed in the next section.)

Part Two (Chapters 3–7) is concerned with the economy as a whole. The sources of growth of real national income are decomposed, by the growth-accounting method, into the growth of factor inputs and the growth of factor productivity. Chapters 3–5 describe the growth of factor inputs. They deal respectively with the growth of labor input measured in man-hours, the growth of labor quality, and the growth of the capital stock. The rate of growth of total factor input (TFI) is defined as the weighted average of the rates of growth of labor and capital, where the weights are the distributive shares of the factors in national income. Distributive shares are therefore dealt with next, in Chapter 6. The rate of growth of total factor productivity (TFP), equal to the excess of the rate of growth of GDP over the rate of growth of TFI, is discussed in Chapter 7.

Part Three (Chapters 8 and 9) deals with TFI and TFP by sector. Chapter 8 studies the growth of TFI and TFP in the principal sectors of the British economy and Chapter 9 the effects of the shifts over time in the relative importance of the different sectors.

The decomposition of the sources of growth yielded by the growth-accounting method is a decomposition into proximate sources only. It does not as such explain what caused factor inputs and productivity to move as they did. Parts Two and Three contain a full description of the trends in the proximate sources and discuss *some* of the underlying causes. The remaining causes are discussed in Part Four. The principle of arrangement has been broadly to include in Parts Two and Three analytical matter relating to topics that can reasonably be treated on their own and to postpone to Part Four matters where everything interacts. Thus the treatment of labor input in Chapters 3 and 4 in Part Two includes almost all we have to say on that subject; but since the rate of growth of the capital stock was, in our view, endogenous to the growth process, and moreover, affected demand as well as supply, we have confined the treatment in Part Two (Chapter 5) largely to a description of trends and have postponed the main discussion of underlying causal relationships to Part Four (Chapters 11–13). Part Four also deals with demand (Chapter 10) and with international trade and payments (Chapters 14 and 15). These are two related classes of consideration that cut across the growth-accounting categories and are liable to affect both inputs and output; more will be said about their relation to the growth-accounting approach in the final section of the present chapter.

Part Five (Chapters 16 and 17) draws together conclusions.

The above outline is designed merely to make clear to the reader the *logic* of the book's arrangement. A fuller indication of the ground covered may be had from the synopses that we have prefixed to each chapter.

CAUSATION AND EXPLANATION

We have been bandying about such expressions as source, proximate source, cause, and explanation. Everyone uses such expressions. But they are not free from ambiguities. The ambiguities matter. They affect the questions it is sensible to ask, and they can affect the answers — not least statistical answers. So a few further remarks are needed here.

If one could draw a complete deterministic map of knowledge, no *event* would be an ultimate cause — each event could be traced back to something else. The search for causes would then be the attempt to draw the map; it would be the search for the laws of motion of the entire system. Only very foolhardy persons set themselves such an objective. What economists usually do is try to set up a *limited* model of the system's laws of motion, embracing some aspects only and relegating the rest to the category of exogenous (most historians regard even that as too ambitious). Matters may be exogenous because they fall outside the confines of the model in time (initial conditions), in space (overseas events), or in scope (technological, political, or sociocultural aspects). Exogeneity is an attribute of the chosen framework of thought, not an attribute of the events themselves.*

The search for causes thus amounts to (1) identification of the behavioral relationships in the system, within the chosen limits of the model; and (2) identification of relevant exogenous events. Given the structure of the model, and given the fact of a certain exogenous event, the consequences of that event are determined; the consequences are the *joint* result of the exogenous event and the structure of the system.

The most fundamental source of disagreements about explanations of economic growth is disagreement about the structure of the system — which relationships were weak, which strong, and so on. Disagreement on this point may imply disagreement about the appropriate scope of the model as well, that is to say, about which classes of event can reasonably be treated as exogenous (e.g. sociocultural changes).

Even if a model is agreed on, there are a number of different types of questions that may be asked of it. This was noted above in connection with comparisons of periods as opposed to comparisons of countries; even supposing the same model of behavior is valid for all relevant countries and periods, the points of difference between countries regarding initial conditions and other exogenous influences will not be the same as the points of difference between periods. Questions about

---

*There may admittedly be events that any reasonable model would have to treat as exogenous, like the want of the horseshoe nail that led to the loss of an empire. Such events are not likely to be important for long-run economic growth, though they can certainly be significant for short-term economic movements (harvest variations, for example).

differences between countries and between periods, moreover, are not the only possible ones. Two other types are commonly asked:

(1) Counterfactual questions can be asked about the effects of hypothetical events that did not occur in any time or place. If one lists six causes of growth over a particular period and gives them quantitative magnitudes, one is implicitly making six counterfactual assertions about what the rate of growth would have been had only one cause been present at a time. This procedure creates no problems of principle if the causes are exogenous events. If the causes postulated are not wholly exogenous, serious difficulties can arise. One cannot postulate counterfactual assumptions that are inconsistent with the logic of the system. No quantitative answer is possible to the question "What would have happened to the rate of growth if investment had been higher and everything else had remained unchanged," because if literally everything else had remained unchanged, investment would not have *been* higher. In order to consider counterfactually the consequences of an endogenous variable like investment having been different from what it was, it is necessary to specify the supposed circumstances that would have led it to be different. Hence the need to go behind the proximate sources of growth, whether on the supply side or on the demand side.

(2) Entirely different again are questions relating to current policy. What steps the government could now take to alter the rate of growth (or for that matter the level of unemployment or the rate of inflation) is quite a different question from how the present state of affairs came about. Questions about the effects of *past* government policies are a particular kind of counterfactual question. We shall generally follow the practice of treating government policies as exogenous, while recognizing that on a broader definition of the scope of the model the actions of governments are no less endogenous than those of other economic agents.

The foregoing remarks have been made in order to indicate some of the pitfalls to be avoided and in order to explain the notions of causation that have been in our minds in writing this book. These remarks may appear to promise a program that is more ambitious and more rigorous than anything we shall actually carry out. We shall not produce a formal model of the working of the British economy over time, nor shall we define our scope so sharply as to make a firm distinction between what is exogenous and what is not. However, in Chapter 15 we do try to isolate the effects of influences that were exogenous in the sense of originating from abroad. Chapter 17 contains an outline (not in formal terms) of the underlying model of causal interactions that appears to us appropriate, though the area of our ignorance is one of the chief features we are conscious of.

GROWTH ACCOUNTING

The growth-accounting method used in Parts Two and Three is a way of carrying further the familiar breakdown of the growth of output into the growth of labor input and the growth of labor productivity. To this end it takes account of the contribution to the growth of output made by increases in capital input, as well as by increases in labor input. It also seeks to take into account the contribution made by improvement in the quality of the labor force, though this is more difficult to measure. The relative contributions made by the various inputs are estimated on the assumption that the remuneration of the factors of production is in proportion (not necessarily equal) to their marginal products — hence the weighting by distributive shares. (This assumption can be relaxed when there are specific reasons for doing so.) The rate of growth of TFP is then the contribution to the growth of output that comes from sources other than increases in measured inputs. Often referred to as "the residual," it includes any contribution that may arise from increasing returns to scale and from the effects of technical progress and advances in knowledge, of shifts in resources between sectors, and of changes in the extent of obstacles to more efficient use of resources (e.g. restrictive practices on the part of management or trade unions). It will also reflect any errors in the measurement of inputs and output, and in the specification of the relationship between them.

The growth-accounting approach has been subject to a number of criticisms. Some of the more technical problems are referred to in Chapter 7, where the underlying logic and the procedures are discussed more fully. More general objections have also been raised by some economists. Some see it as a futile attempt to cut up a seamless robe; this seems to us obscurantist. Whether it is the best way to cut up the robe is more fairly debatable. Our view is that the approach is useful, but only as a first step. It cannot be relied on to give answers to counterfactual questions. However, it is an orderly way of arraying the facts, and that is an important part of the job.

Ours are not the first estimates to have been published of rates of growth of TFI and TFP in the British economy. We do not claim that our results are necessarily to be preferred to those of other authors, though we have tried to make them as well based as possible. Some writers have carried out (chiefly for the postwar period) more detailed sectoral breakdowns than we have, and others have made international comparisons that are outside our scope.[5] The estimates here presented are, to the best of our belief, the first that have been published for such a long period as 1856–1973, covering both the economy as a whole and its sectors.

One of the main questions that has been asked in the literature of growth accounting is the relative importance of increases in factor input (TFI) on the one hand and of improvements in the way factors are used (TFP) on the other.[6] Where the distinction is drawn between the two is to some extent arbitrary (the matter is further discussed in Chapter 7). We shall see, however, that when account is taken of all elements of factor input that can reasonably be quantified, the rate of growth of TFP was far more important in the British case than the rate of growth of TFI as a source of *differences between periods* in the rate of growth of GDP. In particular, the faster-than-previous growth of GDP in the postwar period was more than wholly accounted for by a faster-than-previous growth of TFP (the rate of growth of TFI being lower than in earlier periods). On the other hand *over the average of the whole period 1856–1973* TFI made a considerably larger contribution to growth than TFP (1.4 percent compared with 0.5 percent). Between 1873 and 1913 there was no increase in TFP at all. Since technological advance (not directly or indirectly included in TFI) was plainly taking place in some sectors at that time, it follows that there was actual retrogression in other sources of TFP. This gives some prima facie support to the hypothesis of failures in entrepreneurship or in industrial relations put forward by such writers as Phelps Brown and Browne (1968) and Landes (1969), but disputed by econometric historians such as McCloskey and Sandberg (1971).

It is no surprise to find that the rate of growth of TFP was persistently higher in some sectors than in others. More interesting is the finding that in certain periods changes in the rate of growth of TFP in some untypical sectors had important effects on the rate of growth of TFP in the economy as a whole (commerce in the interwar period and across World War II, agriculture in the last quarter of the nineteenth century). However, the main conclusion that emerges from the sectoral data is that changes between periods in the rate of growth of TFP were usually similar throughout the economy. The causes making for these changes were evidently pervasive. In a sense, therefore, the study of the sectoral data leads to negative conclusions.

Also negative are the findings about the effects on the growth of TFP of changes in the relative weights of different sectors — manufacturing, agriculture, services (including government), and so on. Insofar as we are able to measure these effects, they turn out to be relatively small in most periods. This may, of course, be related to the fact that, as mentioned at the beginning of this chapter, the net shift of labor into manufacturing had already taken place by the middle of the nineteenth century. It is conceivable that, by comparison with other countries, the very absence in the United Kingdom of large effects of structural shifts was itself a matter of importance.

SUPPLY, DEMAND, AND FOREIGN TRADE AND PAYMENTS

The problem of distinguishing proximate from underlying causes perhaps arises most prominently in connection with the question of the relative importance of supply-side forces and demand-side forces in determining the rate of economic growth in the United Kingdom. Was growth in the postwar period faster than in the earlier periods because demand was stronger or because technology was advancing more rapidly? Was postwar growth in Britain slower than in other countries because of a government-imposed stop-go cycle in demand or because of the attitudes of management and labor? Closely related is the question of the role of foreign trade and payments.

One extreme position is that expressed by Say's Law, that the supply of labor and of know-how is exogenous and creates its own demand (at least apart from cycles). This is what is assumed in the elementary neoclassical growth model. The opposite extreme position is that factor inputs and/or productivity adjust themselves so as to permit the production of whatever is demanded (at least within reason). Intermediate positions are possible, and more appealing, in which interaction is allowed for between forces on the supply side and forces on the demand side.

The use of the growth-accounting framework may appear to prejudge the issue in favor of the primacy of exogenous forces on the supply side. However, this is not the case. As far as that framework is concerned, demand is one of a number of possible influences on trends in factor input and in TFP, and its importance relative to other influences is a matter for study.

An alternative framework is to decompose the growth of income into the growth of the constituent elements of expenditure: $C + I + G + X - M$. (This is done in Chapter 10.) The use of such a framework might appear to prejudge the issue in favor of the primacy of exogenous causes on the demand side; but that too is not the case. It leaves entirely open the question *why* the constitutents of expenditure moved over time in the way that they did. The underlying explanation could be either on the demand side or on the supply side, or a mixture of the two.

We shall be concerned with demand only insofar as it affected *trends* in real GDP or in inputs and productivity. Business cycles as such do not come within our purview, nor do movements in the general price level, though we shall find it necessary to say a certain amount about both of them. Our standard method of abstracting from cyclical movements will be to focus attention on growth rates between cyclical peaks. The treatment of demand will be in a Keynesian framework, but this framework will not be used in such a way as to preclude the recognition of influences or processes commonly regarded as non-Keynesian, such as crowding-out and the level of real wages.

In the British economy foreign trade and payments have been among the most important influences on the level of demand and also on its composition. Many authors have regarded the country's international position as crucial in determining its rate of growth. They have pointed to the retardation of growth in the face of foreign competition in 1873–1913; to the absolute fall in income across World War I associated with the fall in exports; to the failure after the return to gold in 1925 to achieve a boom comparable to America's or Germany's; and to the constraints imposed by the stop-go cycle in the postwar period. Kaldor (1966) and W. A. Lewis (1978) have seen the problems of the British economy as resembling the problems of a region, dependent for its prosperity on attracting an adequate share of the world demand for manufactures. Others have reached similar conclusions from rather simpler premises, unconnected with the *composition* of demand: they have seen growth as demand-constrained and demand as balance-of-payments-constrained. This view, expanded into the doctrine of vicious and virtuous circles (Lamfalussy 1963; Beckerman et al. 1965), was especially popular in the early 1960's and had some influence on the National Plan of 1965.

Opposed to all these is the doctrine, espoused broadly speaking by the Brookings Report (Caves et al. 1968), that the problems experienced by the United Kingdom in its foreign trade and payments have been principally a manifestation of supply-side constraints.

The conclusions that will emerge in later chapters, both on foreign trade and on demand more generally, are of an eclectic kind. The facts cannot be accommodated to monocausal explanations. Exogenous influences on growth from the side of demand or foreign trade *were* important, but they were not all-important, and they were more important in some periods than in others (for example, they contributed more to the improvement in the rate of growth of TFP that occurred after World War II than they did to the improvement that occurred after World War I). Eclecticism on this point, as on others, is not indecision. Nor does eclecticism amount to the implausible hypothesis that there were lots of exogenous forces all accidentally pulling in the same direction. It is a recognition of the complexity of the interactions within the system, both between periods and between Britain and the rest of the world.

Events on the demand side that may be treated as exogenous in consideration of economic growth in a single country include such matters as government policy, growth in other countries, and international economic arrangements. Though exogenous from one point of view, these are all firmly economic. Hence demand-dominated theories of growth can be fairly self-sufficient within the discipline of economics. Exogenous events on the supply side include a larger proportion of matters commonly regarded as outside the scope of economics, or at best on its fringe—demographic, technological, institutional, and attitudinal. Moreover, such matters affect the *structure* of the system as well as being a source of exogenous shocks. This is why treatments of British economic growth that emphasize the supply side tend to lapse into what has been called "a welter of amateur sociology." The amateurishness is not entirely the fault of the economists, since their colleagues the professional sociologists have tended not to be very interested in these questions.

Institutions and attitudes that affect TFP do not come into existence or change for arbitrary reasons. Though they may be influenced in part by wars and other events that can fairly be regarded as exogenous, they are likely to be strongly influenced by long-run economic developments. To treat them as fully exogenous is not satisfactory. Unfortunately, even the relevant taxonomy is still in its infancy, though attention is increasingly converging on it (Leibenstein 1979). The prospects of measurement or of a theory in historical terms are even more distant. We do believe that these supply-side forces were important in the British case, but for the reasons just stated we lack the means to deal with them adequately. Our discussion is therefore necessarily incomplete. Proper treatment of the missing topics must await a Volume II, which we hope may someday be written by other hands.

CHAPTER TWO

The Rate of Growth of Total Output

Rates of growth of GDP and GDP per man-year are shown for the following periods: pre–World War I, which is divided into 1856–73 and 1873–1913 (statistical problems hamper what would be a desirable further division at 1899); trans–World War I, 1913–24; interwar, 1924–37; trans–World War II, 1937–51; and postwar, 1951–73, which is further divided into five peak-to-peak cycles, 1951–55, 1955–60, 1960–64, 1964–68, and 1968–73. This division of periods is used throughout the book. Southern Ireland is included only up to 1920.

The rate of growth of GDP was highest in the postwar period, but differences in growth rates between periods were not enormous. The postwar period surpassed earlier periods in rate of growth of GDP per man-year by more than it did in rate of growth of GDP. Demarcation of long-run trends is obscured by the war periods, when growth was relatively slow, but broadly speaking the pattern was U-shaped, with deceleration up till World War I and acceleration thereafter.

GDP measures the performance of the domestic economy from the production side. For welfare comparisons, allowance must be made also for income from abroad and for the terms of trade, and adjustment must be made to a market-price basis. The period when these adjustments make most difference (for the worse) is across World War II.

INTERNATIONAL COMPARISONS

After 1870 Britain's rate of growth of GDP per man-year was persistently below that of the United States, France, Germany, Italy, Sweden, and Japan, the average shortfall being about 1 percent a year. In the postwar period there ceased to be a shortfall by comparison with the United States, but the shortfall compared with other countries was greater than previously. In level of productivity the United Kingdom *was at the top in 1870. It was overtaken by the United States soon after that, but remained ahead of most other countries until the postwar period. The tendency to convergence in productivity levels between most countries over time is marked, but the United Kingdom is anomalous in that it showed little tendency to converge toward the U.S. level once the United States had got ahead, and no tendency to converge toward the levels of other countries once they had got ahead.*

PRODUCTION AND PRODUCTION PER MAN-YEAR

The central concept of production that will be used in this study is gross domestic product at constant factor cost. GDP is adopted for this purpose as being the most appropriate measure of the productive performance of the domestic economy.[1]

The movement over time of GDP is shown in Table 2.1, along with the movement over time of GDP per employed worker (productivity).[2] Annual percentage growth rates in the postwar period, 1951–73, are here compared with growth rates in earlier phases of the period since 1856.* For this purpose the period 1856–1951 is divided into five phases. This phase division will be used throughout the study. The two wartime phases are shown separately, to facilitate the comparison of the postwar period with earlier peacetime periods.† The pre-1914 period is divided into two to give a mid-Victorian period of fairly rapid growth followed by a late-Victorian period of slower growth. It has been a subject of debate among economic historians whether the "climacteric" occurred in the 1870's or the 1890's. By choosing 1873 as the division between our two pre-1914 periods we are not implying that it was in the 1870's. Our concern is merely to ensure that our second period includes all the years of slower growth.‡ For most purposes we shall treat the period 1873–1913 as the pre-1914 datum period for mak-

---

*The growth rates are the compound rates of growth between the first and last years of each phase. For a justification for measuring average rates of growth in this way, and for a comparison with the growth of exponential trends fitted by least squares, see Appendix B.

†The estimates of changes in the main economic series across the two world wars are generally much less reliable than those referring to peacetime periods. This should be borne in mind when interpreting tables of growth rates.

‡The rate of growth slowed down after 1873 and more sharply after 1899, but the retardation was not continuous. The situation is obscured by discrepancies between the three different estimates of GDP. See Appendix L for further discussion.

TABLE 2.1

Growth of Gross Domestic Product and Gross Domestic Product per Man-Year
in the United Kingdom and in Great Britain and Northern Ireland, 1856–1973

(Annual percentage growth rates)

Period	United Kingdom		Great Britain and Northern Ireland	
	GDP	GDP per man-year	GDP	GDP per man-year
Peacetime phases:				
1856–1873	2.2%	1.3%	2.4%	1.2%
1873–1913	1.8	0.9	2.0	0.9
1924–1937	2.2	1.0	2.2	1.0
1951–1973	2.8	2.4	2.8	2.4
Wartime phases:				
1913–1924	– 0.1	0.3	– 0.1	0.3
1937–1951	1.8	1.0	1.8	1.0
1856–1973	1.9%	1.2%	2.0%	1.2%

Source: Basic statistics (Appendix N) and, for Great Britain and Northern Ireland in 1856–1913, Feinstein 1972: Tables 11.10, 54, 57.

Note: All data in the tables in this study are for the UK unless otherwise specified (as here) in the table title. We include Southern Ireland in the data through 1920. Growth in periods including 1920 is therefore a weighted geometric mean of growth in the larger area before 1920 and growth in the present area (Great Britain and Northern Ireland) from 1920 onward. This is the method adopted throughout this study except where it is stated otherwise.

The method of estimating the data for Great Britain and Northern Ireland in 1856–1913 was as follows. On the assumption that unemployment and participation rates moved in the same way in the north as in the south of Ireland between 1851 and 1911, estimates of the growth of employment were found for three areas: Great Britain, Great Britain and Northern Ireland, and Great Britain and all Ireland. We also have estimates of the growth of GDP in Great Britain, and in Great Britain and all Ireland, and so productivity growth in these two areas could be calculated. Productivity growth in Great Britain and Northern Ireland was estimated by interpolating on the basis of the growth of employment between the rates for Great Britain and the rates for the UK (including all Ireland).

ing comparisons with the interwar and postwar periods. Data relating to 1856–73 will also be shown whenever possible, but less significance is to be attached to differences between that period and the post–World War I periods.[3] Wartime phases are defined as 1913–24 and 1937–51 to include periods of postwar recovery. The exact choice of dates to define the periods is inevitably to some extent arbitrary; those chosen make the end-years of peacetime periods comparable from the cyclical point of view.[4]

The data on which Figure 2.1 and the first two columns of Table 2.1 are based relate to the political area of the United Kingdom, that is to say, Great Britain and Ireland through 1920 and Great Britain and Northern Ireland from 1920 onward, the series for the two geographical areas being spliced at 1920 in calculating growth rates across that date.[5] This is how data are always presented in this study, unless otherwise indicated. Comparisons of growth in post–World War I periods with growth in pre-1914 periods are therefore not strictly valid because of the change in boundary. Though Southern Ireland was never a large part of the United Kingdom, its experience during the nineteenth century was so different from Great Britain's that it is important to bear this break in comparability in mind.[6] In most cases it is not possible to say what was happening to the United Kingdom (present area) before 1920, but rough estimates of the pre-1921 rates of growth of GDP and GDP per man-year for Great Britain and Northern Ireland are shown in the last two columns of Table 2.1. The exclusion of Southern Ireland affects the growth rate of GDP to a small extent for the two pre–World War I periods, and the result is that the growth rate over the whole 1856–1973 period is 0.1 percent higher for the constant area than for the political area. The extent of the break between the postwar period and long-run experience thus appears fractionally less on this basis. However, this is not true of GDP per man-year, since the exclusion of Southern Ireland reduces its growth rate by about 0.05 percent over the 1856–1913 period; this occurs because the benefit to measured productively growth of a progressive shift in weight away from low productivity Southern Ireland toward higher productivity Great Britain is no longer included.

What are the main conclusions that emerge from the figures shown? GDP shows a higher rate of growth in the postwar period than in previous peacetime phases. But the difference is not very great, especially when the adjustment is made to give uniform geographical coverage.

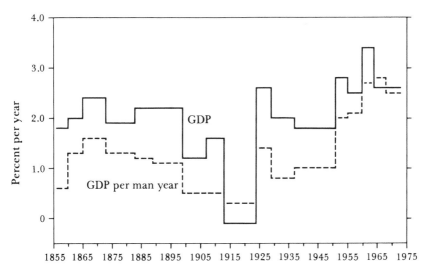

Fig. 2.1. Growth of gross domestic product and gross domestic product per man-year between cycle peaks, 1856–1973

TABLE 2.2

Growth of Gross Domestic Product and
Gross Domestic Product per Man-Year over Periods
Including Wars, 1873–1973

(Annual percentage growth rates)

Period	GDP	GDP per man-year
1873–1913	1.8%	0.9%
1913–1937	1.1	0.7
1924–1937	2.2	1.0
1937–1973	2.4	1.9

Within the various periods distinguished, moreover, there are no great differences in growth rates; the peacetime rate of growth of GDP over the course of 100 years varied within only quite a narrow margin,[7] and it does not show any of the spectacular spurts found in the history of certain other countries, such as Japan and the United States.

GDP grew more slowly in the two wartime phases than in the peacetime phases — in the case of World War I very much so. Hence the 1951–73 growth rate exceeds the average for the whole period 1856–1973 by a clearer margin than it exceeds the growth rate of earlier peacetime periods.

The slow growth during the two wartime phases suggests that for some purposes it might be appropriate to combine each wartime phase with its ensuing peacetime phase, to see how far the arrears of growth across the war were subsequently made good (Table 2.2). GDP grew somewhat more rapidly in the interwar period than in the years 1873–1913; but the difference was not enough to make good the ground lost across World War I, so the growth rate over the combined period 1913–37 was lower than the pre-1914 rate. The experience with World War II was different; the higher-than-previous growth rate in the postwar period more than wiped out the effects of relatively slow growth across World War II. The growth across the combined period 1937–73 was much higher than over the period 1913–37 and also higher, though only by a slight margin, than in previous peacetime periods.

Turning now to GDP per man-year (productivity), we find a rather more pronounced difference between the postwar period and earlier peacetime periods. The growth rate in productivity was significantly higher in the postwar period than in any previous period of comparable length. With the exception of 1913–24, the average annual rate of growth of productivity was close to 1.0 percent in every period up to 1951. Thereafter it was more than twice as great. It makes only a slight difference whether the postwar period is compared with earlier peacetime periods or with all earlier periods; the greater difference in this respect noted in the case of production arose because employment rose at a less-than-average rate in both wartime phases.

These comparisons take their starting point from the 1850's, when Britain was already far on the road to being an industrial country. Estimates for the early nineteenth century show higher growth rates, but not by a large margin (Feinstein 1978: 84, based chiefly on estimates in Deane & Cole 1962: 278-85 and Deane 1968). It is estimated that between 1800 and 1830 and between 1830 and 1860 the rates of growth of national output were 2.7 percent and 2.5 percent, respectively, and the rates of growth of national product per head of employed population were 1.3 percent and 1.3 percent, respectively. Even over this longer period, therefore, the conclusions stand (1) that the variations in the rate of growth of production have been over a fairly narrow range, and (2) that the rate of growth of productivity in the period after World War II compares favorably with that achieved in the past.[8]

We have so far been comparing the postwar period as a whole with earlier periods, broadly defined. It is interesting also to look at growth rates over shorter periods. Table 2.3 shows the rates between successive cyclical peaks within the postwar period, 1951, 1955, 1960, 1964, 1968, and 1973,[9] and Figure 2.1 shows the rates between cycle peaks over the whole period. Within the postwar period there is no obvious trend in the growth rate of GDP, but the growth rate of productivity rises up to 1968. This tendency to acceleration within the postwar

TABLE 2.3

Growth of Gross Domestic Product and
Gross Domestic Product per Man-Year Between
Postwar Cycle Peaks, 1951–1973

(Annual percentage growth rates)

Period	GDP	GDP per man-year
1951–1955	2.8%	2.0%
1955–1960	2.5	2.1
1960–1964	3.4	2.7
1964–1968	2.6	2.8
1968–1973	2.6	2.5

period appears in a number of other series, notably capital formation, and will be further discussed later on in this study. It suggests that the more rapid growth in productivity in the postwar period was not just a temporary phenomenon brought about, say, by making up for the low level of capital accumulation during World War II. If that were the case one would expect to find deceleration rather than acceleration.

The breaks caused by the two wars and by the higher level of unemployment in the interwar period make it difficult to identify long-run phases in the country's economic performance with any confidence. They also make it difficult to apply the hypothesis of "long swings" of approximately 20-year duration to British twentieth-century experience. The movements of GDP (and still more the movements of industrial production) between 1856 and 1913 do show some signs of long swings in growth rates, with a peak in the 1870's, a trough in the 1880's, another peak around 1900, and a trough in 1913. This parallels the well-known and better-attested inverse long swings in home and overseas investment. After 1913 the chief retardations come with the wars, and it would not be sensible to treat them as recessions in a long swing. Our knowledge of the historical background might possibly provide some justification for regarding the high unemployment of the 1920's, and hence the relatively low output in that period compared with 1913, as in some sense a continuation in a different form of the long swing recession of 1900–1913. The movement of output and productivity within the post–World War II period has some resemblance to a long swing, with a peak in the 1960's (the falling off after that would be more pronounced if the figures were carried beyond 1973); however, even after the middle of the 1960's the growth rate of output and (still more) of productivity remained higher than before World War II.

Perhaps the only long fluctuation that emerges from the GDP and GDP per man-year series discussed in this section is a division of the whole period into three very broad phases: a short first phase of fairly fast growth; a second long phase of deceleration; and a third long phase of acceleration, tailing off at the very end into growth at a rate that was still high by historical standards in the case of output and was still very high by historical standards in the case of productivity. The initial phase was centered on the third quarter of the nineteenth century and was one of fairly rapid growth in which the impetus of the growth of Britain's traditional industries — coal, textiles, and iron and steel — though perhaps diminishing, was still quite strong. The division between the first and second phases came some time in the last quarter of the nineteenth century, but aggregate series do not show exactly when the "climacteric" occurred.[10] The period from 1873 up to World War I saw a gradual decline in the growth of GDP and GDP per man-year, particularly after 1899. This second phase of deceleration continued across the war and its immediate aftermath in the early 1920's. It was a phase in which the country had not yet succeeded in adjusting to changes in the environment in international competition, technology, and industrial relations.

The interwar period was one of considerable adjustments to the changes that occurred before 1924; and as these adjustments began to have effect, the economy entered the third phase of faster growth, which, after an interruption in World War II, brought rates of growth higher than in either of the two previous phases. The readjustments resulted first in an improved growth performance in manufacturing industry in the interwar period, which continued into the postwar period. The distributive trades and services, which suffered a decline in productivity in 1924–37, then improved their performance in the postwar period.

Gross domestic product at constant prices, the concept of output we have been using so far, is a measure of the productive performance of the domestic economy. Two alternative concepts may be referred to which bring into account different aspects of the United Kingdom's international position. Use of these concepts has some effect on the results but does not alter the broad conclusions. Growth rates between benchmark years are given in Table 2.4, alongside those of GDP for comparison.

Gross national product (GNP) is equal to GDP plus net property income from abroad.[11] The inclusion of property income from abroad serves to raise the annual percentage growth rate by 0.1 over the period 1856–1913, when Britain's overseas investments were being built up, and to depress it by about 0.2 in the two wartime phases, when overseas investments were run down. It makes no difference to the rate of growth in the postwar period. Nor does it make any difference to the rate of growth over the period 1856–1973 taken as a whole. The series in column 6 of Table 2.4 (GNP, disposable income concept) involves a different sort of adjustment. The GNP series so far used measures the value at constant prices of national output; in principle, imports do not enter in at all, and exports are valued at their prices in the base year. GNP so measured (as it has traditionally been in official British national-income statistics) thus does not take into account changes in the purchasing power of exports due to changes in the terms of trade. It

TABLE 2.4

Alternative Concepts of the Growth of Output, 1856–1973

(Annual percentage growth rates)

Period	GDP (1)	Contribution of:			GNP (1) + (2) (5)	GNP (disposable income concept) (5) + (3) + (4) (6)
		Income from abroad (2)	Terms of trade (3)	Reweighting at market prices (4)		
Peacetime phases:						
1856–1873	2.2%	0.1%	0.2%	0.0%	2.3%	2.5%
1873–1913	1.8	0.1	0.0	0.0	1.9	1.9
1924–1937	2.2	0.0	0.3	−0.1	2.2	2.4
1951–1973	2.8	0.0	0.1	0.1	2.8	3.0
Wartime phases:						
1913–1924	−0.1	−0.1	0.3	0.0	−0.2	0.1
1937–1951	1.8	−0.3	−0.3	0.0	1.5	1.2
War and postwar phases:						
1913–1937	1.1	0.0	0.3	−0.1	1.1	1.3
1937–1973	2.4	−0.1	0.0	0.0	2.3	2.3
Post-WWII cycles:						
1951–1955	2.8	−0.2	0.5	0.0	2.6	3.1
1955–1960	2.5	0.0	0.3	0.2	2.5	3.0
1960–1964	3.4	0.1	0.0	0.0	3.5	3.5
1964–1968	2.6	−0.1	0.0	−0.1	2.5	2.4
1968–1973	2.6	0.3	−0.2	0.2	2.9	2.9
1856–1973	1.9%	0.0%	0.1%	0.0%	1.9%	2.0%

therefore does not exactly correspond to the measure of income relevant from the welfare point of view. For this purpose it is necessary to deflate exports at current prices not by the prices of exports, but by the prices of imports. The difference between the resulting real product measure and GNP measures the effects of changes in the terms of trade.[12]

A further adjustment has been made to obtain this series. If disposable income is to be a measure of welfare, it should be at market prices rather than at factor cost. The effect on the growth rate of reweighting the components of GNP at market prices amounts to as much as 0.1 percent a year in only 1924–37 and 1951–73 of the main periods.

The long-run movement in the terms of trade has been in Britain's favor, and the rate of growth of GNP (disposable income concept) over the entire period 1856–1973 was 2.0 percent as compared with 1.9 percent for GNP. Improvement in the terms of trade thus made a small but significant contribution to the growth in real incomes over the period. If the growth rate of GNP between 1856 and 1973 had been as it was, and the terms of trade had remained unchanged instead of improving, GNP (disposable income concept) in 1973 would have been about 7½ percent lower than it was.

The rate of growth of GNP (disposable income concept) exceeded that of GNP in all the major peacetime phases we have distinguished except 1873–1913, and also across World War I. But the terms of trade moved against Britain during World War II and the early postwar years, culminating in the exceptional rises in commodity prices during the Korean War. Between 1951 and 1973 the excess of the annual growth rate of GNP (disposable income concept) over that of GNP was about the same as it was in 1856–73 and 1924–37. However, all of the benefit came in the earlier part of the postwar period, and after 1960 the terms of trade actually moved against the United Kingdom. The improvement after 1951 was not quite enough to compensate for the deterioration between 1937 and 1951, so that the growth rate of GNP (disposable income concept) is fractionally less than that of GNP if we consider the period 1937–73 as a whole.

INTERNATIONAL COMPARISONS

In general, international comparisons lie outside the scope of our study. But one of the most prominent features of British economic performance in the postwar period is that the growth rate of productivity, though high by historical standards, was a good deal lower than in most other advanced countries. In viewing the postwar period in its historical perspective, therefore, it is important to ask to what extent this was a new phenomenon and to what extent a continuation of a longer-established trend. Did other countries' growth rates exceed the United Kingdom's in the past? And if so, was the gap in growth rates greater or less than in the postwar period?

Growth rates of GDP per man-year in the United Kingdom, the major European countries, Sweden, Japan, and the United States are shown in the top half of Table 2.5. The bottom half of the table gives the excess over the British growth rate in the corresponding period. The periods chosen for other countries correspond as nearly as possible to those used earlier in this chapter for the United Kingdom. The actual benchmark years differ because it was necessary to choose years of approximate cyclical comparability within each country, and these do not always coincide across countries.

Caution is needed in the use of these figures. The estimates given by different investigators differ in some periods to an important extent, and the basis of some of the estimates is far from satisfactory.[13] Moreover, our own estimates for the United Kingdom show some significant differences from those of other authorities (as discussed in Feinstein 1972: 11–12, 23–29). The comparative results are therefore not in all respects the same as those reached by other authors who have performed a similar exercise (see Kuznets 1956, 1966; Clark 1957; Paige 1961; Knapp & Lomax 1964; Maddison 1967, 1977, 1979). The qualitative conclusions can, however, be regarded as well established for long periods, if not for the subperiods here distinguished.

The answer to the first question posed above is now well known. The shortfall in the British growth rate of productivity relative to other countries was not a new post–World War II phenomenon but was clearly in evidence earlier. This is apparent from the bottom three rows of the table. It is noteworthy that out of the 42 country-period cases shown, there were only six in which the British growth rate was higher. The tendency for other countries to grow faster has thus been pretty general.[14]

The answer to the second question is less simple. All the countries experienced a faster rate of growth in the postwar period than they had done previously; but the extent of the increase in the growth rate varied considerably, being greatest in France, Germany, Italy, and Japan, and least in the United States and Sweden, with the United Kingdom in between. Thus the shortfall in the British growth rates was greater in the postwar period than earlier when the comparison is made with Germany, France, Italy, and Japan, but less than earlier when the comparison is with the United States or Sweden, the two countries relatively least affected by the war. Indeed productivity grew faster in the United Kingdom than in the United States in the postwar period as a whole, mainly because of a deceleration in the United States in the latter part of the period.

Table 2.5 shows a fair amount of variety in the timing of growth in the various countries. The periods during which they gained ground most rapidly relative to the United Kingdom were not the same in all cases. The United States, as is well known, gained ground relative to other countries chiefly in wartime phases; apart from 1873–99, its peacetime growth rate was lower than that of the continental countries and Japan. Between World War I and 1973 the U.S. average peacetime rate of growth was the same as the United Kingdom (1.9). The nineteenth century and transwar periods stand out as ones in which the United Kingdom lost relatively little ground to countries other than the United States (except for Japan in World War I and Sweden in World War II). Twentieth-century peacetime periods were less successful,

TABLE 2.5

Growth of Gross Domestic Product per Man-Year in the United Kingdom Compared with Six Other Industrial Countries, 1873–1973

Period	UK	U.S.	Sweden	France	Germany	Italy	Japan
Annual percentage growth rates							
1873–1899	1.2%	1.9%	1.5%	1.3%	1.5%	0.3%	1.1%
1899–1913	0.5	1.3	2.1	1.6	1.5	2.5	1.8
1913–1924	0.3	1.7	0.3	0.8	−0.9	−0.1	3.2
1924–1937	1.0	1.4	1.7	1.4	3.0	1.8	2.7
1937–1951	1.0	2.3	2.6	1.7	1.0	1.4	−1.3
1951–1964	2.3	2.5	3.3	4.3	5.1	5.6	7.6
1964–1973	2.6	1.6	2.7	4.6	4.4	5.0	8.4
1873–1951	0.9	1.7	1.7	1.4	1.3	1.3	1.4
1951–1973	2.4	2.3	3.0	4.4	4.8	5.5	7.9
1873–1973	1.2%	1.8%	1.9%	2.0%	2.0%	2.4%	2.6%
Excess over UK growth rate							
1873–1899	—	0.7%	0.3%	0.1%	0.3%	−0.9%	−0.1%
1899–1913	—	0.8	1.6	1.1	1.0	2.0	1.3
1913–1924	—	1.4	0.0	0.5	−1.2	−0.4	2.9
1924–1937	—	0.4	0.7	0.4	2.0	0.8	1.7
1937–1951	—	1.3	1.6	0.7	0.0	0.4	−2.3
1951–1964	—	0.2	1.0	2.0	2.8	3.3	5.3
1964–1973	—	−1.0	0.1	2.0	1.8	2.4	5.8
1873–1951	—	0.8	0.8	0.5	0.4	0.4	0.5
1951–1973	—	−0.1	0.6	2.0	2.4	3.1	5.5
1873–1973	—	0.6%	0.7%	0.8%	0.8%	1.2%	1.4%

Source: France, 1873–1964, communication from E. Malinvaud (estimates broadly consistent with those in Carré et al. 1975); 1965–73, OECD [6], [10]. *Germany*, 1871–1964, communication from H. Gerfin; 1965–73, OECD [6], [10]. *Italy*, 1881–1967, Fuà 1972; 1968–73, OECD [6], [10]. *Japan*, 1872–1953, Bairoch et al. 1968, Ohkawa & Rosovsky 1973, Maddison 1977; 1953–73, OECD [6], [10]. *Sweden*, 1870–1973, communication from R. Bentzel. *U.S.*, 1871–1967, communication from M. Abramovitz; 1968–73, OECD [6], [10]. *UK*, basic statistics (Appendix N).

Note: The desired concept of output is GDP at factor cost. In practice this was not available for all countries. The main exceptions are Germany 1871–1913 (NDP); U.S. 1871–1967 (GNP); and most countries post–World War II (market prices). The dates shown relate to the U.K. The benchmark years for other countries between which growth rates are calculated are:

US, 1871, 1890, 1905, 1921, 1939, 1949, 1967, 1973
Sweden, 1870, 1900, 1913, 1923, 1938, 1954, 1964, 1973
France, 1873, 1896, 1913, 1924, 1938, 1951, 1964, 1973
Germany, 1871, 1900, 1913, 1925, 1937, 1951, 1964, 1973
Italy, 1881, 1897, 1913, 1921, 1938, 1951, 1964, 1973
Japan, 1872, 1900, 1913, 1921, 1937, 1953, 1964, 1973

The underlying estimates for Italy for 1881–1967 are 3-year averages centered on the years shown; those for the U.S. for 1871–1967 are centered 5-year averages. Adjustments were made whenever contemporary boundaries changed between 2 benchmark years.

again except by comparison with the United States, though in the interwar period the UK growth rates fell below those of France and Italy by less than usual.

International comparisons may be made not only of growth rates, but also of absolute levels of GDP per man-year. As has often been

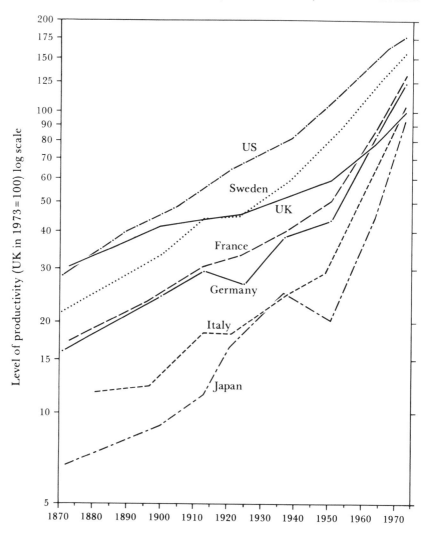

Fig. 2.2. Gross domestic product per man-year in the United Kingdom compared with six other industrial countries, 1873–1973. For the method used to compute these indexes, see note 15 to Chapter 2.

pointed out, the United Kingdom's slower growth rate has to be viewed against the background of the fact that for most of the period its absolute level of GDP per man-year exceeded that of most other countries. This fact, which may be seen from Figure 2.2,[15] has led people to suggest that other countries were able to achieve more rapid growth in some way *because* their absolute level was lower. The United Kingdom appears as the leader at the beginning of the period, but is overtaken by the United States in the next decade, by Sweden between the wars, by France and Germany around 1960, by Italy around 1970, and by Japan probably in the late 1970's.* The index-number problems involved in this sort of comparison are great. A better basis of calculation might alter the figures considerably, but it would probably not invalidate the statements just made.[16]

Figure 2.2 clearly demonstrates the remarkable convergence in GDP per man-year in the seven countries over the 100-year period.[17] In the 1870's productivity in the leading country (the UK) was more than four times as high as in the bottom one (Japan). By 1973 the level of productivity in the leading country (the U.S.) was less than twice that of Japan, still (but only just) at the bottom. Closer inspection shows that the great bulk of the catching up occurred in the postwar period. As Table 2.5 shows, France, Germany, Italy, and Japan grew more slowly than the United States and Sweden up to 1951, but this is partly a consequence of the greater setback that World War II represented for these four countries.

The United Kingdom is the anomaly in all this. Though it showed slight signs of convergence with the United States in the 1960's and 1970's, this followed three-quarters of a century or so of divergence. Moreover, it did not show any signs of catching up the ground that had been lost to other countries in the shorter period since *they* overtook it. Its performance was in these respects anomalous both before and after World War II. If there are forces tending to bring about the convergence of absolute output per man-year, the British experience (supported, incidentally, by the experience of one or two other countries, such as Australia and Belgium) suggests that they may work in a different way for countries that have fallen from a leading position than for countries that have always been behind.

---

*Agriculture was a much smaller part of the British economy than of other economies throughout most of the 100-year period. Since output per man-year is usually lower in that sector than in others in all countries, a comparison of output per man-year in the nonfarm economy, and especially in industry, would probably show the UK falling below the other countries earlier than the whole-economy cross-over points in Figure 2.2.

PART TWO

The Proximate Sources of Growth in the Economy as a Whole

CHAPTER THREE

Labor: Quantity

This chapter describes the course and causes of trends in labor input in man-hours. Quantitative measures are given in turn of the contributions made by changes in population, participation rates, unemployment, and hours of work. The chapter ends with a discussion, relevant to later chapters, of the extent to which labor (skilled and unskilled) was a bottleneck in the various periods, and of the relation between cyclical fluctuations and the average pressure of demand in the labor market.

POPULATION

The rate of increase of population underwent a step-wise decline from about 0.9 before 1914 to about 0.5 thereafter. Fertility and mortality had qualitatively similar trends: both fell from 1870 until World War II (apart from a temporary rise in mortality across World War I) and then flattened out; but fertility declined more than mortality. The economic and other causes of these movements are surprisingly obscure. Net migration was more directly influenced by economic forces, but its effects were relatively minor.

THE WORKING POPULATION

The main decline in the rate of growth of the population of working age did not occur until World War II because of favorable changes in age composition in the interwar period. After World War II, however, age composition changed, so that the population of working age grew less rapidly than total population. Throughout the period age-specific participation rates declined among the elderly and among young people (especially among the latter in the late postwar period). This reflected increases in real income and in social provision. But the participation rate of married women began to rise in the interwar period *and continued to do so much more strongly in the postwar period. This probably reflected forces on both demand and supply sides.*

EMPLOYMENT AND UNEMPLOYMENT

Changes in unemployment did not have a significant effect on the trend rate of growth of labor input except across the two world wars.

HOURS OF WORK

Hours worked by full-timers declined in infrequent large steps — in the early 1870's, in 1919, and in 1947–48 — and then more steadily from 1955 onward. The timing of these steps was related to the bargaining power of labor. In the postwar period there was an increase in part-time working among women; this canceled out a significant part of the effect of the increase in the participation rate of married women.

LABOR INPUT: QUANTITATIVE SUMMARY

The sources of growth in labor input in man-hours are summarized in Table 3.17. Labor input was stationary from 1856 to 1873, rose at about the same rate as population between 1873 and 1913, and then fell steeply across World War I. In the interwar period it rose much more rapidly than it had done before 1914. It had a level trend from 1937 to 1964 and then declined, quite steeply. The postwar period was thus unique among peacetime periods in having a decline in labor input. Demographic causes (including changes in age composition) and changes in hours of work were much the most important sources of difference in the rate of growth of labor input between periods. This is true even of the transwar periods. Demographic changes reflected economic forces, doubtless, but only in a very broad way, apart from migration. High demand increased labor's bargaining power, which in certain well-defined periods led to a major reduction in hours: an unexpectedly perverse response of labor input to demand. Age-specific participation rates were affected by a variety of economic forces, but they largely canceled out. In total they had little net effect on the trend rate of growth of labor input in any period.

UNEMPLOYMENT AND THE STATE OF THE LABOR MARKET

Before 1914 unskilled labor was subject to chronic non-Keynesian underutilization, especially in London, manifested in casual work. There was probably a downward trend in this chronic surplus in the pre-1914 period that does not show up in the statistics of total hours worked. The surplus was largely eliminated by 1914, but the interwar period was dominated by demand deficiency. There was a high demand for labor after World War II but with a downward trend within the postwar period, especially from the mid-1960's. Even at the end of the period there were still acute shortages of labor at cyclical peaks.

We now turn from output to inputs.

The basic measure of labor as an input in production is employment in man-hours. This is related to population as follows:

Working population = population × participation rate

Employment in man-years = working population × (1 − unemployment ratio)

Employment in man-hours = employment in man-years × average hours worked per year

We shall accordingly discuss in turn total population, the participation rate, unemployment, and hours of work.

The above breakdown is, as such, a purely arithmetical one. It is significant analytically insofar as movements in the four elements are affected by different causes. In practice the causes affecting them were sufficiently different to make the breakdown more than just an arithmetical one. But the separation of causal influences is not complete, and to that extent the breakdown has arbitrary elements from the analytical point of view.

The most important analytical distinction is between causes affecting the supply of labor and causes affecting the demand for labor. But when we are considering absolute magnitudes (population, participation rate, unemployment, hours of work), we cannot say that the movement over time in any one item is due wholly to demand or wholly to supply unless either the supply curve or the demand curve is completely inelastic. All four variables have in practice been affected by causes on both sides, though to different degrees. It is obvious that participation rates and hours of work are influenced both by demand and by supply. Population comes nearer to being wholly supply-determined, but demand comes in too, at least through migration. Unemployment, as normally measured, comes near to being wholly demand-determined, though it may be influenced to some degree by the availability of unemployment benefit or other financial reserves. More important, however, is the fact that unemployment, in the sense of willingness to work more hours at the current hourly wage than are actually worked, is not fully measured by the usual unemployment figures and is present in part in participation rates and hours of work.

The breakdown into the four elements therefore corresponds only partly to a causal breakdown. The breakdown does, however, represent a fairly clear-cut division of the *manifestations* of demand and supply in the labor market.

POPULATION

The Rate of Increase of the Population and Its Sources

The chief characteristic of the course of population growth in Great Britain in our period (Table 3.1, column 2) was the once-and-for-all fall in the rate of growth between the first and second decades of the twentieth century. The annual rate of growth averaged 1.1 percent from 1850 to 1910, and only 0.5 percent thereafter. Variations within the two periods were relatively small compared with the difference between them.

TABLE 3.1

Intercensal Growth of Population in Great Britain, Ireland, and the United Kingdom, 1851–1971

(Annual percentage growth rates)

Period	Rate of natural increase, Great Britain (1)	Actual growth rate		
		Great Britain (2)	Ireland (3)	UK (4)
1851–1861	—	1.0%	− 1.2%	0.6%
1861–1871	1.3%	1.2	− 0.7	0.9
1871–1881	1.4	1.3	− 0.4	1.0
1881–1891	1.3	1.1	− 0.9	0.8
1891–1901	1.2	1.1	− 0.5	1.0
1901–1911	1.2	1.0	− 0.2	0.9
1911–1921	0.7	0.5	− 0.1	0.4
1911–1921[a]	0.7	0.5	0.1	0.5
1921–1931	0.6	0.5	− 0.1	0.5
1931–1939	0.3	0.5	0.5	0.5
1939–1951	0.4	0.4	0.5	0.4
1951–1961	0.5	0.5	0.4	0.5
1961–1971	0.6	0.5	0.8	0.5

Source: Annual Abstract, UK [10]; *Census of Population*, UK [52]; Feinstein 1972: Table 55. Calculated from census population estimates in all years except 1939, for which a mid-year estimate was used.
    [a]The figures in columns 3 and 4 from this row on exclude Southern Ireland.

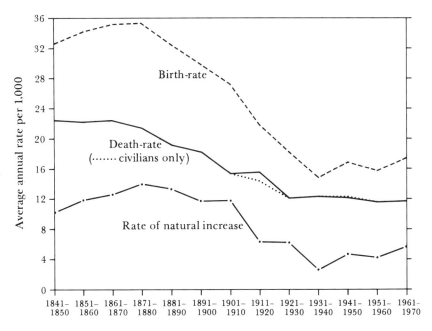

Fig. 3.1. Birth-rate, death-rate, and rate of natural increase by decade in England and Wales, 1841–1970. (*Source: Annual Abstract*, UK [53], *1972:* Table 18; *Registrar General's Statistical Review*, UK [54])

This step-wise pattern was influenced by migration. The rate of natural increase (Table 3.1, column 1) shows a rather more continuous decline, to a low point in the 1930's, followed by a rise in the postwar period. It remained at the end of the period still much below its pre-1911 level.

The foregoing relates to Great Britain. The United Kingdom had a significantly lower rate of population growth than Great Britain before 1914, because in Ireland net emigration persistently exceeded natural increase by a large margin (Table 3.1, columns 3 and 4). The United Kingdom's pattern of actual increase over time is, however, qualitatively similar to Great Britain's, namely, a once-for-all shift to a lower rate of increase in the decade 1911–21.

In discussing population trends we shall in general confine ourselves to Great Britain because of the peculiar nature of the Irish experience. Moreover, in the following discussion of natural increase, births and deaths, we shall deal only with England and Wales, since many of the data are more easily available for that area alone. Since the area accounts for 85–90 percent of the United Kingdom, nothing of substance is lost.

Figure 3.1 shows that the movements of the birth-rate and the death-rate had a broadly similar pattern, with the fall from around 1870 until the interwar period the dominant feature. The behavior over time of the rate of natural increase therefore depended on the relative magnitudes of the movements in births and deaths. Up to the 1870's the birth-rate was rising somewhat, and there was little change in the death-rate, so the rate of natural increase rose. From then until the 1900's the birth-rate began to fall, but so did the death-rate, so there was only a slight fall in the rate of natural increase. During World War I the birth-rate fell drastically, and the effects of this were not compensated for in the rest of the decade 1911–20; and in the two following decades the birth-rate continued to fall more rapidly than it had done before World War I. Meanwhile, the death-rate rose in 1911–20 on account of military casualties,* and after 1930 it ceased to fall significantly. Consequently, there were sharp falls in the rate of natural increase in 1911–20 and in 1931–40. After World War II there was some recovery in the birth-rate and hence in the rate of natural increase. The rate of natural increase in the postwar period remained much lower than the rate in the latter half of the nineteenth century, because the birth-rate had fallen more than the death-rate.

The Death-Rate

The history of the crude death-rate after the middle of the nineteenth century falls into three phases: little change between 1841–50 and 1861–70; steady decline from 1861–70 until 1921–30; and little change after 1921–30.

The crude death-rate is affected by the age distribution of the population. The standardized mortality ratio (SMR), which corrects for changing age distribution, is a better measure of underlying trends in mortality (Fig. 3.2). Like the crude death-rate, the SMR fell little between 1841–50 and 1861–70. There then came a long period of decline, with an acceleration in the rate of decline after 1900 that does not show up in the crude death-rate. The SMR continued to decline after the 1920's, unlike the crude death-rate, though there was some slowing

---

*Military casualties (defined as deaths of non-civilians outside the country) were 577,000 in 1911–21 and 240,000 in 1939–51. The effects on death-rates are shown in Figure 3.1. It will be noted that in 1939–51 the civilian death-rate was fractionally higher than the total death-rate, war casualties being insufficient to offset the normal tendency for those of military age to have lower mortality than the population as a whole.

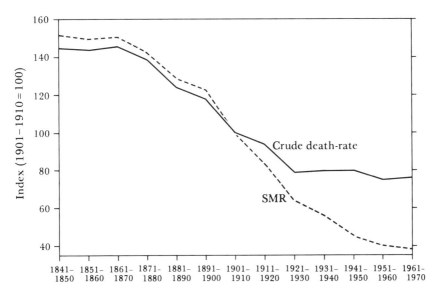

Fig. 3.2. Crude death-rate and SMR (Standardized Mortality Rate) by decade in England and Wales, 1841–1970. The SMR measures the number of deaths in a given period as a percentage of the deaths that would have been expected had the sex and age mortality of a standard period (1950–52) been experienced in that period. *(Source: Registrar General's Statistical Review, UK [54])*

down in the rate, especially in the postwar period. The absence of fall in the crude death-rate after the 1920's reflected an increase in the average age of the population, which in turn was caused partly by the fall in mortality itself, but partly also by a reduction in the absolute number of births after the beginning of the twentieth century.[1]

To the economic historian, the principal question about the decline in the death-rate is how far it was brought about by improvements in the standard of living in general and how far by medical advances in particular. There has been a major debate on this issue in relation to the fall in the death-rate in the eighteenth century. The upshot of that debate has been unsatisfactorily inconclusive (see Habakkuk 1972). We have a great deal more information about events in the period we are concerned with, but much is still unclear.

An abundance of data exists on the causes of death at different dates.[2] The picture is clear in general outline. The 100-year fall in mortality came about because diseases due to pathogenic micro-organisms were progressively reduced until they had become a relatively minor cause of mortality, leaving heart disease, cancer, and other degenerative diseases as the chief causes of death at the end of our period.

The timing of the decline differed greatly between individual diseases and between age groups. McKeown and Record (1962) show that
nearly half (47 percent) of the decline in the SMR between 1851–60
and 1891–1900 was due to a fall in deaths from tuberculosis, the remainder being accounted for by only four other groups of diseases.[3]
The decline in mortality chiefly affected those in the 3–34 age group.
From the 1840's up till 1900 the mortality rate of infants under one was
remarkably steady and showed no decline; thereafter it fell at a steady
rate. The decline in infant mortality[4] was largely responsible for the
acceleration in the decline in the SMR after 1900. The continuing
decline in mortality in other age groups after 1900 was due to more
varied causes than before 1900; declines continued in the old infectious
diseases but to these were added important declines in bronchitis and
pneumonia.

The possible underlying causes of these declines are (1) strictly
economic causes, chiefly improved diet but also improved housing; (2)
strictly medical causes, in the form of better clinical treatment, and
possibly also long-run immunological changes in man; and (3) causes
that combine elements of both: public health, sanitation, improved
water supply, and personal cleanliness.

It is generally agreed that with the exception of vaccination against
smallpox, improvements in prevention or therapeutic treatment did
not contribute in an important way to the fall in mortality until the introduction of effective chemotherapy in the 1930's. By that time the
greater part of the reduction had already been achieved. McKeown
and Record (1962) conclude, on the basis of an analysis of mortality
from individual diseases, that the decline in mortality before 1900 was
due 50 percent to improvement in living standards and 25 percent to
sanitary improvements (the remainder being accounted for by changes
essentially independent of human intervention, viz. the diminished
virulence of certain diseases, chiefly scarlet fever). The causes of the
decline in mortality after 1900 were more various and complicated,
but McKeown, Brown, and Record (1972) and McKeown, Record, and
Turner (1975) suggest that improvements in living standards, particularly nutrition, were the most important factors, as they had been
earlier.

Though improvements in living standards clearly contributed to the
reduction in mortality, much remains unclear about how exactly the
two were associated.[5] Evidently it was not that people were formerly
dying of starvation, but that with better living conditions people were

less prey to infectious diseases. But it is rather troublesome to note that the timing of the fall in mortality — the fall becoming pronounced from about 1875 and being particularly rapid in the early years of the twentieth century — seems to have been common to most Western countries, notwithstanding the differences in the levels and rates of change of their living standards (Stolnitz 1955). Certainly improvements in public health have to be brought into the picture, and some of these owed more to medical progress than to general economic growth (e.g. the pasteurization of milk). But as earlier suggested, much longer-run immunological changes may have played a significant part.[6]

The reasons for the exact timing of the fall in mortality in the United Kingdom are also unclear. The standard of living was rising between the 1840's and the 1870's, so why did mortality start to decline only after 1870?* And why did infant mortality only begin to decline in the twentieth century — the decline beginning in a period when the standard of living was rising less rapidly than before? The one point that *is* reasonably clear is that the decline in mortality flattened out in the postwar period because mortality from the principal diseases caused by pathogenic micro-organisms had been reduced to the point where further reductions were relatively unimportant.

The general conclusion, on the evidence available, is that economic growth, in its broadest sense, was a major cause of the decline in mortality, but that the relationship was not simple. Improvements in living standards and other factors interacted, probably multiplicatively rather than additively and no doubt subject to lags. The mediating mechanisms between improving living standards and falling mortality were various and complicated. Hence no clear consilience in timing between the rate of economic growth and the rate of reduction in mortality is to be found, nor is it to be expected.[7]

The Birth-Rate

Some similar difficulties in assessing the importance of economic and noneconomic causes arise with the birth-rate.

There was some downward tendency in the earlier part of the nineteenth century (not shown in Fig. 3.1). This was followed by a slight rise in the 1870's. The steep fall from then until the 1930's is the domi-

---

*One possible explanation is that in that period any beneficial effect on mortality that may have been exercised by rising living standards was offset by the ill-effects of increasing urbanization. The rate of urbanization slowed considerably in the last quarter of the 19th century.

nant feature. The trough in the birth-rate was reached in 1941, and the trend thereafter was upward, with some irregularity, until the mid-1960's. Data on average completed family size (Table 3.2, first column) show a similar picture.*

The fall in the birth-rate from the 1870's to the 1930's was common to most countries of northwest Europe, with relatively minor variations in timing. An exception was France, where the decline went back at least to the beginning of the nineteenth century. A decline from the beginning of the nineteenth century also occurred in the United States. In Britain and also in other countries the fall in the birth-rate occurred earliest and was greatest in the higher socioeconomic groups.

The decline in the birth-rate in economically advanced countries is one of the best-known and most studied of all demographic phenomena.[8] Because it was spread over so long a period and so wide an area, it cannot be explained by events confined to particular countries or periods, though these no doubt affected the details of its timing and extent. It is easy to make a list of possible contributing factors, but it is by no means clear what their relative importance was or how they interacted.

The decline was a decline in fertility within marriage, not a decline in nuptiality. Moreover, though there was some increase in the average age at marriage in the later part of the nineteenth century, it was not enough to account for more than a small part of the decline. Hence there must have been an increased or more effective use of family limitation within marriage. But technological improvements in contraception cannot have been responsible, since it is well established that contraceptive appliances were used only by a small minority of married couples until the interwar period, by which time the chief decline in the birth-rate had already occurred (Lewis-Faning 1949; similar evidence exists for other countries). The principal methods of birth control in use were withdrawal and (presumably) abstinence. Family limitation by such means had been known and practiced for centuries. Indeed, there have probably been few periods or countries in which reproduction within marriage has been entirely uncontrolled. The question is, therefore, why family limitation by traditional means became so much more prevalent in the last quarter of the nineteenth century.

*After the mid-1960's the birth-rate turned down sharply. This was, of course, not yet relevant to the labor force in the period with which we are concerned. For similar reasons we do not show completed family size for the more recent marriage cohorts in Table 3.2. It in fact rose to 2.3 and 2.4 for the marriage cohorts of 1950–54 and 1955–59, respectively.

TABLE 3.2

Average Completed Family Size and Completed Surviving
Family Size in England and Wales, 1861-1945

Date of marriage	Number of live births in family (1)	Number of children surviving to 5 years [a] (2)	Number of children surviving to 20 years [b] (3)
1861–1869	6.2	—	—
1871	5.9	—	—
1876	5.6	—	—
1881	5.3	4.0	3.8
1886	4.8	—	—
1890–1899	4.1	3.3	3.2
1900–1909	3.3	2.7	2.6
1910–1919	2.6	2.3	2.2
1920	2.5	2.2	2.1
1925	2.2	2.0	1.9
1930	2.1	1.9	1.9
1935	2.0	1.9	1.9
1940	2.0	1.9	1.9
1945	2.2	2.1	2.1

Source: Census of Population, UK [52], *1951: Fertility Report; Registrar General's Statistical Review,* UK [54]; Glass & Grebenik 1954: Table 9.

[a]The total number of live births in column 1 was first allocated to 5-year periods succeeding the date of marriage, according to estimates of live births by duration of marriage. Then the number of births in a 5-year period was multiplied by $(1 - m_1)^5$, where m_1 is the average mortality rate during that period of children aged 0–4. The number of children surviving to 5 years was then summed across all 5-year periods containing births resulting from marriages in a particular year.

[b]The exercise in column 2 was continued by multiplying the number of children surviving to 5 years in a particular year by $(1 - m_2)^5(1 - m_3)^5(1 - m_4)^5$, where m_2, m_3, and m_4 are the average mortality rates of children aged 5–9 in the next 5 years, of children aged 10–14 in the 5 years after that, and of persons aged 15–19 in the 5 years after that, respectively. The number of children surviving to 20 years was then summed as for children surviving to 5 years.

The most specific explanation that has been offered is that people were induced to limit births because the reduction in child mortality (including after 1900 a reduction in infant mortality) increased the size of the surviving family that resulted from a given number of births. This hypothesis helps to explain the rather striking coincidence in timing between the fall in the death-rate and the fall in the birth-rate.[9] It is also consistent with the class differential, since the death-rate, like the birth-rate, declined first at the upper end of the social scale. It is not, however, a complete explanation, since the fall in the birth-rate did more than compensate for the fall in the death-rate. There was a substantial fall in the surviving completed family size, as well as in family size, over the whole of the period that we can trace, viz. after the marriage cohort of 1881; and it is likely that there was also a fall in completed family size in the marriage cohorts of the previous decade or so (Table 3.2).[10] Moreover, though a similar parallelism between birth-rate and death-rate is found in some other countries, the pattern is not universal.[11]

The other explanations that have been offered are mostly of a general kind: improvements in education, leading to a rise in aspirations relative to attainments *or* to more widespread adoption (and more consistent implementation) of deliberate decisions on the size and spacing of families; improvements in living standards, with similar effects; urbanization; and the greater cost of children because of diminished employment opportunities and increased educational requirements. A more specific suggestion is that the distribution of real income moved in the last quarter of the nineteenth century to the disadvantage of the upper and middle classes, who then proceeded to give the lead in family limitation to the rest of the community. Another specific, and relatively uncontroversial, explanation is that World War I and the depression of the interwar years carried the long-term trend further than it would otherwise have gone. Finally, since the birth-rate was falling in the early part of the nineteenth century, it can be argued that what needs explaining is not so much the fall after 1870 as the absence of a fall between 1840 and 1870.

To say that the causes of the decline lay in the general character of socioeconomic change is not a very satisfying conclusion. But the evidence does not really permit us to go further or to identify the aspects of socioeconomic change that were chiefly responsible. It seems clear, moreover, that the decline had an epidemic character, whatever may have been its exogenous causes. Social imitation applied both to the notion of family limitation itself and to the size of family considered desirable—the distinction between the two being important conceptually but difficult to make in practice.

Declines in birth-rates had occurred during some phases in earlier centuries; but, typically, these declines did not prove permanent. It is here, perhaps, that improved techniques of contraception are significant and mark a break from the past. Traditional methods of limiting births, whether by the postponement of marriage or by family limitation within marriage, were irksome and required persistent restraint. They were therefore likely to be relaxed when the immediate inducement had disappeared. By World War II effective appliance methods, free from the disadvantages of traditional methods, had become available and were beginning to be widely used. They were made possible by improvements in technology and increases in income; and their diffusion surely owed much to the strains created by the very extensive use of non-appliance methods.[12] Improvements in contraceptive techniques, though not themselves the cause of the fall in the birth-rate, thus had a ratchet effect, in some respects similar to the effect of

medical improvements on the death-rate. When the special circumstances of the 1920's and 1930's had disappeared, family size did rise,
but not to anything like its old level (see Glass 1970). This rise in the
birth-rate after World War II was plainly due not to any slowdown in
the improvement of contraceptive techniques, but rather to an increase
in the size of the desired family.[13] However, the renewed fall in the
birth-rate after the mid-1960's may well have been partly due to further advances in contraception.

How, then, should the effects of economic factors on the birth-rate
be summed up? The decline in the birth-rate can be related in the most
general sense to the process of economic growth and its social concom-
itants through a variety of channels. More specifically, it is not surprising that families were particularly small in the depressed interwar
period and somewhat larger in the postwar period. But the central
phenomenon — the decline in the birth-rate between the 1870's and the
1930's — cannot readily be traced to economic circumstances that
distinguished that period from other periods.

Migration

The effect of migration on the growth of population is shown by the
differences between columns 1 and 2 in Table 3.1. There was a net loss
through migration from Great Britain in each decade from 1861 to
1931. Annual net emigration averaged 0.15 percent of the population.
Before 1914 there were long swings in net emigration closely related to
movements of foreign investment: the two major booms in emigration — 1879-93 and 1899-1914 — were both associated with rising export of capital and falling home investment (see Cairncross 1953; B.
Thomas 1973).

In the 1930's the outflow was reversed, and there was net immigration, the annual net inflow being of the same order of magnitude as the
average net outflow of the earlier decades. In the postwar period, taken
as a whole, there was little net migration.

The change from net emigration in the 1920's to net immigration in
the 1930's canceled the effect of the decline between those two decades
in the rate of natural increase, making the actual rate of population increase about the same in the two decades. A similar canceling out, in
the opposite direction, of changes in net migration and in the rate of
natural increase took place between the 1930's and the 1940's.

The fall in net emigration between the pre-1914 period and the postwar period was not, of course, sufficient to offset the decline in the rate
of natural increase; but it meant that the fall between the two phases in

the annual rate of population increase was between 0.1 percent and 0.2 percent less than it would otherwise have been, a significant offset.

The net emigration of the period 1861–1931 was part of the grand (though not steady) movement of population from the Old World to the New, and there is no need to discuss its causes here. The reversal of the movement in the 1930's resembled the trough phases of the old long swings in migration, but in more extreme form. Not only did the depression in primary producing countries and in the United States lead to a fall in emigration to them from Great Britain: it also led to a substantial amount of return migration to Great Britain. The return of Britons from abroad was the major explanation of the sharp rise in immigration in the 1930's (R.C. on Population, UK [80]: para 45). To this were added a relatively small number of political refugees from Europe and an only slightly larger number of migrants from Ireland. Insofar as the return migration took place because Britain was relatively less depressed than other countries, it was the same as what had happened in the pre-1914 long-swing troughs of emigration. But the severity of the depression probably also introduced a rather different considera-tion—that it is better to be unemployed at home than abroad if there is unemployment everywhere.

In the postwar period there was net emigration in most years. Emigration to Australia, Canada, and southern Africa occurred at much the same pace as in the 1920's. But for a brief period it was more than offset by immigration from the New Commonwealth. This immigration was concentrated chiefly in the years 1959–62, diminishing sharply after the introduction of restrictions under the Commonwealth Immigrants Act of July 1, 1962. In the preceding four years, it is estimated that the gross total of immigrants "is likely to have approached a million" (Registrar General's Statistical Review, UK [54], 1962: Part 3, p. 4). Immigration from the New Commonwealth, together with immigration on a smaller scale from Ireland and southern Europe, resulted in an annual growth rate of over 3 percent in the non-native-born population of Great Britain between 1951 and 1966.[14] If restrictions had not been imposed, the immigration would no doubt have continued longer and been on a still larger scale.

It is not surprising to find that economic factors affected migration more directly than they affected births and deaths. In the short run, the level of net emigration varied in response to relative opportunities in Britain and abroad; in the postwar period it was also greatly influenced by legislation. In the long run, there was a persistent net movement of the British-born to the countries of recent European settlement. In the postwar period only, there was for a while heavy immigration from less-developed countries (paralleled in northwest Europe by a great influx of workers from southern Europe, Turkey, and North Africa). This movement from less-developed countries had the epidemic characteristics of all major migration and to that extent cannot be explained exclusively in terms of current economic conditions. But the existence of full employment in the receiving countries was obviously the prime condition, and it was the main explanation of why the movement did not assume large dimensions until the postwar period.* It is better to think of the immigration as induced by full employment than as a compensation for the slow rate of natural increase; the prospect of jobs was the direct impelling agent, and the slow rate of natural increase was only one of the factors influencing the prospect of jobs, if indeed it affected it at all.

THE WORKING POPULATION

The Average Participation Rate

The working population is defined as the total number of persons working for pay or gain, or registered as available for such work. It therefore differs from the employed labor force (or the total in employment), which excludes those out of work and which is considered in the next section.†

In Table 3.3 growth rates for the working population are set alongside the growth rates for the total population. Annual data for the working population are plotted in Figure 3.3.

As with total population, there was a marked contrast between the decline of the Irish working population before 1911 and the growth of Great Britain's. The rate of growth of the United Kingdom working population was thus about 0.3 percent per year below Great Britain's

*Other factors operating to encourage immigration to Britain in the postwar period were the increasingly tight restrictions on migration of West Indians to the U.S. and the presence of large numbers of Indians and West Indians in Britain during World War II as members of the armed forces or as factory workers (Jones & Smith 1970: 11–14).

†U.K. official sources contain data on two different concepts of the labor force: the "working" population, as given by the Department of Employment, and the "economically active" (formerly "occupied") population, as given in population censuses. Furthermore, some significant changes were introduced in 1966 in the definition of the working population. There are resulting differences in definitions of participation rates. Details are given in Appendix C. The central concept of the labor force used in this study corresponds to the working population. We are obliged, however, to use the "economically active" concept in places where more detailed analysis has to be based on census materials. We have indicated in table headings where the data relate to the economically active population, while retaining working population as the general term in the text. Discrepancies between alternative concepts are minimized by focusing attention in the postwar period on 1966 (or where appropriate 1964) and 1973, rather than on 1961 and 1971, and this is accordingly what we have done.

TABLE 3.3

Growth of the Working Population in the United Kingdom, Great Britain, and Ireland, 1851-1973

(Annual percentage growth rates)

Period	Total population, UK[a] (1)	Working population		
		UK (2)	Great Britain (3)	Ireland (4)
1851-1861	0.6%	0.8%	1.2%	-0.5%
1861-1871	0.8	0.7	1.0	-0.7
1871-1881	1.0	0.7	1.1	-1.4
1881-1891	0.8	1.0	1.2	-0.5
1891-1901	1.0	1.2	1.4	-0.5
1901-1911	0.8	0.9	1.1	-0.8
1911-1921	0.4	0.4	0.4	0.7
1921-1931	0.4	0.9	0.9	0.0
1931-1939	0.5	1.1	1.1	-0.4
1939-1951	0.4	0.1	0.1	0.3
1951-1966	0.5	0.6	0.6	0.2
1966-1973	0.4	0.0	0.0	0.0

Source: Feinstein 1972; Annual Abstract, UK [10]; British Labour Statistics Historical Abstract, UK [48]; Population Projections, UK [78]; Dept. of Employment Gazette, May 1975; basic statistics (Appendix N).
Note: The figures exclude Southern Ireland from 1911 on.
[a]The data in this column differ slightly from those in Table 3.1 for comparability with the estimates of the working population. The figures here include members of the armed forces, seamen, and fisherm abroad on the day of the census (Table 3.1 refers to the de facto or home population); and those from 1921 on are based on mid-year estimates rather than census estimates to accord with the basis on which the working population was counted after 1920 (see Feinstein 1972: Chapter 11).

in this period. After 1911 the working population of Northern Ireland did not grow as rapidly on average as Great Britain's, but it was too small a part of the total (about 2½ percent in 1951) to affect UK growth rates to the nearest tenth of a percentage point.

The rate of growth of the working population is determined by the rate of growth of the total population, changes in the age distribution of the population, and changes in age- and sex-specific participation rates. From the 1850's to the 1920's the growth rates of the working population and the total population moved broadly together (Table 3.3); there was no significant trend in the average participation rate (Table 3.4). During the interwar period the total population grew at about half its pre–World War I rate, but the UK working population was able to continue to grow nearly as rapidly as before the war because of a large rise in the average participation rate. The participation rate fell across World War II, rose between 1951 and 1966, and then fell again. The net result was that from the end of the 1930's the working population grew more slowly than total population, and also more irregularly.

It is necessary to look in a little more detail at the separate causes of changes in the average participation rate in order to understand the reasons for divergences between the growth of total population and the growth of the working population in general, and in particular for the lag between the deceleration of total population and its transmission to the working population. The average participation rate may change on account of (1) changes in age distribution that alter the proportion of population of working age to total population or (2) changes in participation rates within particular age groups. The first of these is a demographic factor, closely connected with the rate of growth of total population; the second is not. A rough indication of the relative importance of the two factors and of total population growth is provided by the figures in Table 3.5.[15]

Until 1921 the contribution of total population growth to the growth of the working population was fairly stable in the range 80–95 percent. This was partly because of opposite age-distribution and specific-participation-rate effects. Movements thereafter were more complicated. Taking the four successive phases 1921–39, 1939–51, 1951–66, and 1966–73, there were alternate up and down movements in specific participation rates, and these were matched by corresponding movements in the effects of changes in age distribution (in 1951–66 the

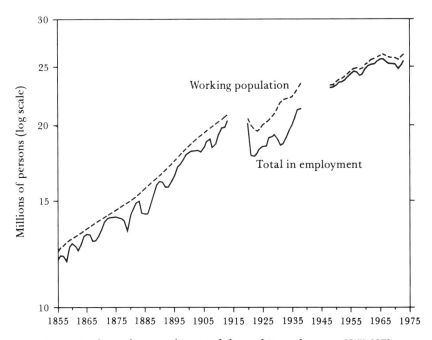

Fig. 3.3. The working population and the total in employment, 1855–1973

TABLE 3.4
Average Participation Rates in the United Kingdom and
Great Britain, 1851–1973
(Percent)

Year	UK: working population	GB: economically active population[a]
1851	44.0%	43.9%
1861	45.0	44.4
1871	44.4	43.9
1881	43.0	42.9
1891	43.9	43.6
1901	44.6	44.0
1911	44.8	44.8
1911[b]	45.1	44.8
1921	45.0	45.3
1931	47.1	47.0
1939	49.6	49.3
1951	47.5	46.3
1966	48.2	47.6
1973	47.0	46.1

Source: Tables 3.3, C.1, C.2.
Note: There is a break in comparability in the first column between 1939 and 1951 and again at 1966 because of changes in the definition of the working population. The 1951–73 figures have been spliced to give a continuous series on the same basis as those through 1939. By the current definitions, the UK participation rates were as follows: 1951, 47.2; 1966 (old), 47.9; 1966 (new), 47.0; 1973, 45.7.
[a]As defined in the Census of Population. This population differs from the working population in several respects, but chiefly in omitting members of the armed forces, seamen, and fishermen abroad on the day of the census. It also underestimates the working population in the postwar period because it does not include all irregular workers (see Feinstein 1972: Chapter 11).
[b]The UK figures from this row on exclude Southern Ireland.

effect of the changes in age distribution was of the same sign as in the adjacent periods but smaller). This synchronization of the effects of changes in age distribution and in specific participation rates appears to have been accidental. It produced quite significant alternations in the growth rate of the working population, notwithstanding near constancy in the rate of population growth. In the interwar period, when both effects were positive, they between them accounted for about half of the growth of the working population. Taking the postwar period 1951–73 as a whole, the opposite movements in the overall participation rate in the two phases 1951–66 and 1966–73 nearly canceled out, and the working population grew at a rate only very slightly less than the total population.

The age composition of the total population of Great Britain was very stable during the second half of the nineteenth century up to 1881 (Table 3.6). From the 1880's until World War II, on the other hand, age composition altered persistently in such a way as to increase the proportion of the working population in the total. This was because of

TABLE 3.5
Sources of Growth of the Economically Active Population of Great Britain, 1881–1973

(Percentage changes per decade)[a]

Period	Total population growth (1)	Changes in age distribution[b] (2)	Changes in age- and sex-specific participation rates[b] (3)	Interaction effects[b] (4)	Economically active population growth (5)
1881–1891	11.2%	1.7%	0.0%	0.1%	13.0%
1891–1901	12.0	3.4	−2.4	0.1	13.1
1901–1911	10.4	1.2	0.5	0.2	12.3
1911–1921	4.7	2.1	−1.0	0.1	5.9
1921–1931	4.7	3.8	0.2	0.1	8.8
1931–1939[c]	4.7	4.2	2.0	0.1	11.0
1939–1951[c]	4.3	−3.4	−1.6	−0.4	−1.1
1951–1966	5.5	−1.0	3.6	−0.5	7.6
1966–1973	4.1	−3.0	−1.4	−0.3	−0.6

Source: Tables C.1–C.3; H. Frankel 1945: Table 41.

Note: For sources of growth, let P_i, p_i, and N be the total population in the ith age-sex group, the participation rate of the ith age-sex group, and the total economically active population in all age-sex groups in the first year of a period. If $P = \Sigma P_i$ and the operate Δ indicates changes between the first and last years of the period, then the growth of the economically active population is given by

Economically active population growth $\dfrac{\Delta N}{N} =$

Total population growth $\dfrac{\Delta P}{P}$

Change in age distribution $+ \dfrac{P}{N} \sum p_i \Delta \dfrac{P_i}{P}$

Change in age-sex participation rates $+ \dfrac{P}{N} \sum \dfrac{P_i}{P} \Delta p_i$

Interaction effect $+ \dfrac{P}{N} \left\{ \dfrac{\Delta P}{P} \sum \Delta \left(p_i \dfrac{P_i}{P} \right) + \sum \Delta p_i \Delta \dfrac{P_i}{P} \right\}$

[a] For 1881–91 through 1921–31 the percentage change between end years; for 1931–39 the percentage change between 1931 and 1939 divided by 0.8; for 1939–51 the percentage change between 1939 and 1951 divided by 1.2; for 1951–66 the percentage change between 1951 and 1966 divided by 1.5; for 1966–73 the percentage change between 1966 and 1973 divided by 0.7.

[b] For all periods except 1931–39 and 1939–51, 8 age and sex groups were distinguished in the calculations. There were 4 age groups for each sex: 0–14, 15–24, 25–64, and 65 and over. For 1931–39 and 1939–51 only 6 groups were distinguished, 3 for each sex: 0–14, 15–64, and 65 and over.

[c] The division of sources of growth between columns 2, 3, and 4 differs for 1931–39 and 1939–51 because fewer age groups were distinguished in the calculations. The consequences of reducing the number of age groups can be seen from the following estimates for 1931–51 on both bases:

	(1)	(2)	(3)	(4)	(5)
1931–51 (8 groups)	4.6	−1.0	0.3	−0.2	3.7
1931–51 (6 groups)	4.6	−0.3	−0.2	−0.4	3.7

TABLE 3.6

Age Composition of the Population of Great Britain, 1851-1973

(Percent)

Year	Ages 0–14	Ages 15–24	Ages 25–64	Ages 65 and over	All ages
1851	35.5%	19.2%	40.6%	4.7%	100.0%
1861	35.7	18.8	40.8	4.7	100.0
1871	36.2	18.5	40.5	4.8	100.0
1881	36.5	18.8	40.1	4.6	100.0
1891	35.1	19.3	40.8	4.8	100.0
1901	32.5	19.6	43.2	4.7	100.0
1911	30.8	18.1	45.9	5.2	100.0
1921	27.9	17.7	48.4	6.0	100.0
1931	24.2	17.4	51.0	7.4	100.0
1939	21.4	15.9	53.7	9.0	100.0
1951	22.4	13.0	53.7	10.9	100.0
1966	23.3	14.5	49.9	12.3	100.0
1973	23.8	14.1	48.5	13.6	100.0

Source: Table C.1; R.C. on Population, UK [80]: 190–91, 203–4; H. Frankel 1945: Table 41.

the fall in the proportion of children in the population. This fall did not occur at a perfectly steady rate, being affected by a diversity of complicated factors including migration;[16] but its general tendency was to accelerate. The effect of the fall in the proportion of children more than offset the rise in the proportion of the elderly, which began after 1900 and reflected the consequences of reduced mortality.

The fall in the birth-rate stopped by World War II, and the proportion of children in the population then began to rise. At the same time, the proportion of the elderly continued to increase. These two forces were now pulling together, instead of against each other. The consequence was a sharp fall in the proportion of the population of working age, reversing the trend of the previous 60 years. The fall was steeper in 1939–51 and 1966–73 than in 1951–66.

Thus the decline in the rate of growth of total population did not work its way through to the growth of the working population until World War II. After World War II, on the other hand, changes in age distribution tended to make the working population grow less rapidly than the total population. But these changes were offset by increases in specific participation rates, to which we now turn.

Age- and Sex-Specific Participation Rates

The specific participation rates for each age and sex group did not always change in the same way (Table 3.7). Indeed the diversity of behavior of participation rates makes it difficult to summarize the main trends. The following points seem to emerge from an examination of the estimated contributions to the growth of the working population (Table 3.7) and the specific participation rates themselves (Appendix C).[17]

(1) The continuous decline in the participation of children (aged 14 and less) in the labor force, from an 8.1 percent rate for boys in 1891 and a 5.0 percent rate for girls, to zero when the school-leaving age was raised to 15 after World War II, tended to reduce the growth of the working population. Increased education in terms both of the numbers affected and of the length of schooling is the sole explanation for this.

(2) There was also a fairly steady decline in participation rates among the elderly: the male rate fell from 73.6 percent in 1881 to 23.5 percent in 1966, and the female rate from 18.0 percent to 6.7 percent.* This presumably reflects the growth of state and private pension schemes.[18]

(3) Changes in participation rates among males of working age (15–64) were not striking. The rate for males aged 25–64 was the same in 1973 as in 1881 (96 percent), and it never fell below that level, nor rose above 98 percent in intervening census years. Among young men (aged 15–24), however, there was a fall in participation in the labor force after the 1930's as a result of the expansion of full-time secondary, higher, technical, and vocational education. Between 1881 and 1931 the participation rate for young men was in the range 93–95 percent. Thereafter it fell increasingly rapidly, reaching 71 percent in 1973. This was another factor tending to reduce the growth of the working population (Table 3.7, row 2).

(4) Young women (aged 15–24) also began to take advantage of more full-time educational opportunities as they became available, but this did not bring about a reduction in their participation rates until the 1950's. The lag between the falls in the participation rates for young men and young unmarried women was the result partly of the earlier provision of additional educational opportunities for men than for women, and partly of other forces tending to raise the participation rates of young women. The decline in the participation rate of young women, as also with young men, was particularly rapid in 1966–73, when there was a great expansion of higher and further education.

(5) The most striking changes in participation rates in terms of their impact on the growth of the working population were the increases in the participation of females of working age throughout the twentieth

*However, the female participation rate did rise slightly within the postwar period, from 5.2% in 1951 to 5.4% in 1961 and 6.7% in 1966, falling to 6.5% in 1973.

TABLE 3-7

Contributions of Intercensal Changes in Specific Participation Rates of the Economically Active Population of Great Britain, 1881–1973

(Percentage changes per decade)[a]

Row	Age, sex, and marital status	1881–1891	1891–1901	1901–1911	1911–1921	1921–1931	1931–1951	1951–1966	1966–1973
(1)	0–14, males and females	0.89%	−1.03%	−0.71%	−0.48%	−0.46%	−0.74%	—	—
(2)	15–24, males	−0.01	0.16	−0.09	−0.21	−0.04	−0.32	−0.82%	−2.08%
(3)	15–24, females (total)	−0.14	−0.17	0.74	0.40	0.89	0.11	−0.73	−2.08
(4)	Married				0.02	0.17	0.23	0.18	0.21
(5)	Unmarried[b]				0.57	0.70	0.45	−0.78	−2.22
(6)	Marriage effect[c]				−0.19	0.02	−0.57	−0.13	−0.07
(7)	25–64, males	−0.05	0.09	0.22	−0.18	0.01	0.08	−0.11	−0.35
(8)	25–64, females (total)	−0.17	−1.15	0.68	−0.58	0.51	1.89	5.60	3.85
(9)	Married				−0.36	0.51	2.46	5.79	4.19
(10)	Unmarried[b]				−0.10	0.32	0.23	0.41	−0.23
(11)	Marriage effect[c]				−0.12	−0.32	−0.80	−0.60	−0.11
(12)	65 and over, males and females	−0.52	−0.35	−0.32	0.01	−0.76	−0.70	−0.35	−0.75
(13)	All groups	0.00	−2.45	0.52	−1.04	0.15	0.32	3.59	−1.41
(14)	Economically active population growth	13.0%	13.1%	12.3%	5.9%	8.8%	3.7%	7.6%	−0.6%

Source: Tables C.1–C.3.

Note: As indicated in the note to Table 3.5, changes in the total age- and sex-specific participation rates (row 13) can be written as

$$\frac{P}{N}\sum \frac{P_i}{P}\Delta p_i$$

The 8 groups (Table 3.5, note b) over which the summation was made in estimating row 13 (and Table 3.5, column 3) correspond to the age-sex groups in this table, provided the males and females are added together for the 0–14 and 65 and over groups. Hence in 4 cases (rows 1, 2, 7, and 12) the calculations for Table 3.5 provide the necessary information. In the case of women, for the 2 age groups 15–24 and 25–64 the terms $(P/N)(P_i/P)\,\Delta p_i$ have to be decomposed into changes in married women participation rates, changes in unmarried women participation rates, changes in marriage rates, and interaction effects as follows:

Change in specific participation rates $\quad \dfrac{P}{N}\sum \dfrac{P_i}{P}\Delta p_i =$

Change in married women participation rate $\quad \dfrac{P}{N}\dfrac{P_i}{P}m_i\,\Delta p_{im}$

Change in unmarried women [participation rate]

Change in marriage rate $\quad +\dfrac{P}{N}\dfrac{P_i}{P}(p_{im}-p_{iu})\,\Delta m_i,$

Interaction effect $\quad +\dfrac{P}{N}\dfrac{P_i}{P}\Delta m_i\,(\Delta p_{im}-\Delta p_{iu})$

where p_{im} and p_{iu} are the participation rates for married and unmarried women, respectively, in the ith age group, m_i is the proportion of women in the ith age group who were married in the first year, and the operator Δ indicates changes between the first and last years of the period.

[a] For 1881–91 through 1921–31 the percentage change between end years; for 1931–51 the percentage change between 1931 and 1951 divided by 2.0; for 1951–66 the percentage change between 1951 and 1966 divided by 1.5; for 1966–73 the percentage change between 1966 and 1973 divided by 0.7.

[b] Includes the widowed and divorced, as well as the never married.

[c] The sum of the change in the marriage-rate effect and the interaction effect (see table note above). In 1911–21 and 1921–31 the interaction effect was 5% or less of the marriage-rate effect; in later periods it was about 20% and usually of the opposite sign.

century (with the exceptions of the trans–World War I period and of young unmarried women in the postwar period, as just noted). Without this sizable increase in the participation of women, the overall effect of participation-rate changes on labor force growth (Table 3.5, column 3, and Table 3.7, row 13) would have been negative, and in the postwar period there would have been very little growth in the working population at all. As we will see later in the chapter, the significance of the rise in the female participation rate is considerably altered when account is taken of hours of work. Leaving that aside for the present, however, we note that the most significant increase in participation was among married women aged 25–64. The increase began already in the 1920's and was particularly rapid in the period 1951–66. The increase slowed down somewhat after 1966, but still remained rapid. The contribution from this source to the growth of the working population was very substantial (Table 3.7, row 9).[19] This growth in female participation was more than enough to offset the effects on average participation rates of the steady increase throughout the twentieth century in the proportion of women who were married (Table 3.7, rows 6 and 11).

Reasons for the Rise in Female Participation Rates

It is much easier to trace the effects of increases in female participation rates on the growth of the working population than to explain their causes.[20] These seem to fall into two classes, those operating on the supply side and those operating on the demand side. On the supply side there was an increase in the willingness of women to work outside the home because of (1) the fall in family size, which may have released on to the labor market older unmarried daughters who would otherwise have helped to bring up the younger children (probably most important near the beginning of the twentieth century; see Table 3.2), as well as allowing the mothers to return to work after the children reached a certain age; (2) a fall in the average age of marriage, which freed married women from childbearing at a relatively young age; (3) an increase in family income aspirations* and the tendency for goods and services that would formerly have been produced in the household to become cheaper and easier to acquire in the market; (4) changes in

---

*The emphasis here is on aspirations. One would expect increases in family income itself to lead to a decrease in participation. There was probably also an increase in the desire of women to have a source of income independent of their husband's (in the case of married women) or of their father's (in the case of young unmarried women).

social attitudes toward working women and changes in women's own perception of their role. The two wars no doubt hastened this process by showing that women could do work as efficiently as men,[21] and by overcoming the notion that it was "improper" for woman to work or to take certain jobs.[22]

On the demand side the most important factor was an increase in the proportion of jobs available to women. There were three elements in this. (1) Occupational shifts: an increased proportion of clerical jobs and a decreased proportion of skilled manual jobs favored female employment because women were often preferred for the former and not qualified for the latter. (2) Industrial shifts: female employment was more favorably placed than male employment in the interwar period when industries employing a relatively large proportion of women, especially the distributive trades and services, became relatively more important; this trend was reversed across World War II but continued during the postwar period. And (3) labor shortages during the wars and in the postwar period: employers took more trouble to employ female labor, as is suggested by the more rapid increase in average earnings of women in manual work compared with men in manual work across World War II,[23] and the increasing willingness of employers to make arrangements so that married women could work part-time.[24] This is consistent with the slackening in the rate of growth in the participation rate of married women after 1966, when the pressure of demand in the labor market was less strong.

The forces on the supply and demand sides interacted to a certain extent. As the proportion of women in the labor force rose, women became more familiar and acceptable as workers because significant changes in working arrangements and attitudes no longer had to be made. The observed occupational and industrial shifts may also to some extent have been the *result* as well as the cause of the increase in female employment. Thus an increased relative supply of women who were prepared to work for lower wages than men made it profitable for employers to accommodate them by altering occupational and industrial patterns. At the same time on the supply side, women became more willing to work as it became less common for them to stay at home except when family commitments required it.[25]

Because of the interactions (some of them subject to lags) between supply and demand factors, it is not possible to say conclusively which of the two is the more important. We would put more emphasis on the demand factors, at least as far as the timing of changes is concerned, noting the critical role of the wartime periods of high demand in accelerating female participation and also the signs of falling off after 1966. However, the increase in female participation that occurred within the postwar period cannot be attributed to a current increase in demand, since it is not possible to argue that the demand for labor was greater at the end of the period than at the beginning. Probably there was a lag between when the demand became apparent and when the increased female labor was forthcoming because of slowly changing attitudes. The falling age of marriage also contributed to the increase in female participation within the postwar period.[26]

Summary

By way of summarizing this section, let us consider the main features of postwar experience compared with earlier periods.

(1) In the postwar period the UK working population grew considerably more slowly than in earlier peacetime periods. The contrast between the postwar period and the pre-1914 period was even more marked in the case of Great Britain, or Great Britain and Northern Ireland together, because the contraction of the Irish population before World War I pulled down the rate of growth of the UK working population.

(2) The chief reason why the working population grew less rapidly in the postwar period than in the pre-1914 period was that the total population was growing less rapidly. But the growth of the working population was much less rapid in the postwar period than in the interwar period, despite a similar rate of growth in total population in the two periods. This was because of changes in age distribution, which had an unfavorable effect on working population growth in the postwar period and a favorable effect in the interwar period.

(3) The rate of growth of the working population in the postwar period would have been even lower than it was, had it not been for the historically unparalleled increase in participation rates among married women aged 25–64. Though female participation rates had been rising since the beginning of the century (apart from a decline in World War I), the rate of increase among married women moved sharply upward across World War II and remained high during the postwar period. Both demand and supply factors were responsible for this trend.

(4) Participation rates among the elderly continued to fall in the postwar period as they had in earlier periods. Among young men and unmarried women aged 15–24 they fell more steeply than before

TABLE 3.8

Distribution of the Economically Active Population of Great Britain by
Age, Sex, and (Females Only) Marital Status, 1881–1973

(Percent)

Age, sex, and marital status	1881	1921	1951	1966	1973
0–14, males and females	4.7%	2.2%	0.0%	0.0%	0.0%
15–24, males	20.2	17.4	12.3	12.3	11.0
15–24, females (total)	14.1	13.6	10.3	9.6	8.2
Married	—	0.4	1.4	2.0	2.4
Unmarried	—	13.2	8.9	7.6	5.8
25–64, males	42.9	48.4	54.0	49.7	50.0
25–64, females (total)	13.5	14.3	19.7	25.0	27.5
Married	—	3.3	10.2	18.1	21.1
Unmarried	—	11.0	9.5	6.9	6.4
65 and over, males and females	4.6	4.1	3.7	3.4	3.3
All ages, males	69.5	70.5	69.2	64.3	63.1
All ages, females	30.5	29.5	30.8	35.7	36.9
Married	—	3.8	11.8	20.4	23.9
Unmarried	—	25.7	19.0	15.3	13.0
All groups	100.0%	100.0%	100.0%	100.0%	100.0%

Source: Table C.2.

because of the rapid spread of secondary, higher, technical, and vocational education. But children aged 14 or less were now in full-time
education, so their steady withdrawal from the working population
had come to an end by 1951.

(5) Most of the principal postwar trends (the decline in the proportion of the population of working age, the fairly rapid increase in married women's participation rates, the decline in young men's participation rates, and the increase in the female marriage rate) were already
apparent in the immediate postwar years. However, the growth in the
working population in 1939–51 was not as great as during the 1951–73
period because the unfavorable factors (the changing age distribution
and the increase in the female marriage rate) were relatively more important than the favorable increase in participation rates among married women.

(6) Compared with earlier periods, the postwar labor force contained low proportions of men, unmarried women, young persons aged
15–24, and elderly persons (and contained no children under 15).
There was a high proportion of married women, especially in the 25–64
age group (Table 3.8).

(7) The working population ceased to grow altogether in 1966–73.

The two chief sources of the difference compared with 1951–66 were (a) demographic trends (both slower population growth and a stronger adverse trend in age distribution) and (b) a more rapid extension of education in the 15–24 age group.

EMPLOYMENT AND UNEMPLOYMENT: THE RATE OF
GROWTH OF THE EMPLOYED LABOR FORCE

The working population was not utilized to the same extent in all periods. Year-to-year movements during peacetime periods in the working population and in the total in employment are plotted in Figure 3.3 (p. 53). The gap between the two lines represents unemployment. The contrast between the three major peacetime periods is striking, and no less so for being well known. Of all the major variables surveyed in this study, none displays so clear a contrast between periods as measured unemployment. Unemployment is discussed in greater detail later in the chapter; here we confine ourselves to noting differences between the growth rates of the total in employment and the working population. The comparison is made, between our usual benchmark years, in Table 3.9.

TABLE 3.9
*Growth of the Total in Employment and the
Working Population, 1856–1973*
(Annual percentage growth rates)

Period	Total in employment	Working population
Peacetime phases:		
1856–1873	0.9%	0.8%
1873–1913	0.9	0.9
1924–1937	1.2	1.2
1951–1973	0.4	0.4
Wartime phases:		
1913–1924	−0.4	0.1
1937–1951	0.8	0.3
War and postwar phases:		
1913–1937	0.4	0.7
1937–1973	0.5	0.4
Post-WWII cycles:		
1951–1955	0.8	0.8
1955–1960	0.4	0.5
1960–1964	0.7	0.7
1964–1968	−0.2	0.0
1968–1973	0.1	0.1
1856–1973	0.7%	0.7%

The only significant differences occur in the transwar periods. This is the result of the high level of unemployment in the interwar period. The benchmark years were chosen so that secular growth in peacetime periods could be measured by the growth between years in which the level of economic activity, of which the unemployment rate is a manifestation, was approximately the same. Thus employment and the labor force grew at the same rate on this basis. Across the two wars, however, it is impossible to make comparisons in this way because unemployment was so much higher in the interwar period than before 1914 or after World War II. The transition across World War I to a lower level of activity pulled the growth of employment below that of the labor force; and the reversion to a higher level of activity across World War II raised the growth of employment above that of the labor force. The two effects canceled out, and over the whole 1856–1973 period employment grew at the same rate as the labor force.

HOURS OF WORK

The annual input of labor, in man-hours, depends on the number of persons in employment and on the average number of hours worked per year per person in employment.* Table 3.10 compares the growth of total hours worked per year in the United Kingdom over our usual periods with the growth of the total in employment. The average number of hours worked in benchmark years is given in Table 3.11.

There was a long-term reduction in the average number of hours worked a year: between 1856 and 1973 the hours declined at an annual rate of about 0.5 percent. As a result total hours worked grew very slowly, at only 0.2 percent. A reduction in average hours occurred in four periods, 1856–73, the two transwar phases, and the postwar period. Throughout the long 1873–1913 period there was little change in average hours, and they actually increased slightly in the interwar period. After 1873, those periods that experienced a relatively rapid growth in employment, namely 1873–1913 and 1924–37, were also those when average hours were not reduced. Total hours therefore declined or grew relatively slowly in the other periods (the transwar and postwar periods) for two reasons: because of the slower growth in employment and because of the reductions in average hours. Across World War I and after 1964 the fall in total hours worked was large,

---

*See Appendix D for a precise definition of average hours, and for details of the sources and methods of the statistics.

TABLE 3.10

Growth of Hours Worked per Year and the Total in Employment, 1856–1973

(Annual percentage growth rates)

Period	Total hours worked	Total in employment	Difference[a]
Peacetime phases:			
1856–1873	0.0%	0.9%	− 0.9%
1873–1913	0.9	0.9	0.0
1924–1937	1.5	1.2	0.3
1951–1973	− 0.5	0.4	− 0.9
Wartime phases:			
1913–1924	− 2.3	− 0.4	− 1.9
1937–1951	0.1	0.8	− 0.7
War and postwar phases:			
1913–1937	− 0.3	0.4	− 0.7
1937–1973	− 0.3	0.5	− 0.8
Post-WWII cycles:			
1951–1955	0.5	0.8	− 0.3
1955–1960	− 0.4	0.4	− 0.8
1960–1964	− 0.2	0.7	− 0.9
1964–1968	− 1.5	− 0.2	− 1.3
1968–1973	− 0.9	0.1	− 1.0
1856–1973	0.2%	0.7%	− 0.5%

[a]Approximately equal to the rate of growth of the average number of hours worked per year.

TABLE 3.11

Average Hours Worked per Year, 1856–1973

Year	Hours per year	Hours per week	Weeks per year
1856	3,185	65.0	49.0
1873	2,744	56.0	49.0
1913	2,753	56.4	48.8
1924	2,219	46.6	47.6
1937	2,293	48.2	47.5
1951	2,071	44.6	46.4
1964	1,904	41.2	46.1
1973	1,715	38.1	45.0

Note: The averages are taken over the total in employment.

because demographic factors, the change in the level of activity, and the reduction in average hours all worked in the same direction. The all-time peak in total hours, i.e. in labor input, was reached in 1913. The average number of hours worked per year can fall for a variety of reasons (e.g., a fall in the weekly hours worked by full-time workers, an increase in the proportion of part-time workers, an increase in holidays or in time lost through sickness). Some of these factors affect the average number of hours worked per week, and others (holidays, sickness, and strikes) affect the average number of weeks worked per year. It can be seen from Table 3.11 that the long-term decline in average hours per year derives from decreases in both average hours per week and average weeks per year. However, the change in weekly hours was much more substantial.*

The sources of changes in the average number of hours worked per year are quantified in Table 3.12 for the periods from 1913 to 1973. The most important source of changes in average weekly hours was the changes among full-time workers (for brevity referred to as full-time hours). However, after 1937 and especially after 1951, the increase in the proportion of part-time workers became an important source of the decline in average hours per week. In 1937 only 1.5 percent of the total in employment were part-timers; in 1973 the proportion was 15.6 percent.

Additional details of the sources of postwar changes in average hours worked per year are provided in Table 3.13. One interesting finding is that over the period 1951–73 as a whole females contributed rather more to the total change than males, though they formed only about a third of the total in employment. The decline in full-time hours was greater for females than for males, and the contribution of the change in the proportion of part-timers was larger for females than for males. In addition, a small contribution to the total change in average hours was derived from the changed sex breakdown of employment, since females worked fewer hours per year than males.

The quantitative identification of the sources of changes in average hours leads naturally to a consideration of the causes of the changes. There are three relatively independent sources requiring further examination: the decline in full-time hours, the increase in the proportion of part-timers after 1937, and the decrease in the number of weeks worked per year.

*These estimates, especially those relating to pre-1914 when it was crudely assumed that the average number of weeks worked per year was constant, are very rough.

TABLE 3.12

Sources of Changes in Average Hours Worked per Year, 1913–1973

(Absolute changes between benchmark years)

Source of change	1913–1924	1924–1937	1937–1951	1951–1964	1964–1973	1913–1973[a]
Changes in full-time hours per week	– 459	71	– 137	– 78	– 101	– 704
Changes in part-time hours per week	–	1	– 4	0	0	– 3
Changes in proportion of part-timers	–	4	– 28	– 84	– 51	– 159
Total changes in hours per week	– 478	76	– 172	– 158	– 147	– 879
Total changes in weeks per year	– 67	– 3	– 55	– 13	– 46	– 184
Total changes in average hours per year	– 534	74	– 222	– 170	– 189	– 1,041

Note: The sources of changes in average hours worked per year are measured as follows:

Change in full-time hours	$W(1-p)\,\Delta h_f$
Change in part-time hours	$Wp\Delta h_p$
Change in proportion of part-timers	$W(h_p - h_f)\,\Delta p$
Total change in hours per week	$W\Delta h$
Total change in weeks per year	$h\Delta W$

The sum of the changes in full-time hours per week, part-time hours per week, and the proportion of part-timers is not exactly equal to the total changes in hours per week because of an interaction term, $W\Delta p\,(\Delta h_p - \Delta h_f)$:

$$W(1-p)\Delta h_f + Wp\Delta h_p + W(h_p - h_f)\Delta p + W\Delta p(\Delta h_p - \Delta h_f) = W\Delta h$$

Similarly, the sum of the changes in total hours per week and total weeks per year is not exactly equal to the changes in average hours per year, $\Delta\Sigma w_i h_i W_i$, both because of an interaction term, $\Delta h\Delta W$, and because total hours worked per year were estimated on an industry basis, which procedure introduces a covariance term:

$$\Delta\sum_i w_i\left(h_i - \sum_i w_i h_i\right)\left(W_i - \sum_i w_i W_i\right)$$

Thus:

$$W\Delta h + h\Delta W + \Delta h\Delta W + \Delta\sum_i w_i\left(h_i - \sum_i w_i h_i\right)\left(W_i - \sum_i w_i W_i\right) = \Delta\sum_i w_i h_i W_i$$

Notation:

w_i	the weight of industry i in total employment
h_i	average hours worked per week in industry i
$h = \sum_i w_i h_i$	average hours worked per week in all industries
h_f	average hours worked per week by full-time workers in all industries
h_p	average hours worked per week by part-time workers in all industries
W_i	average weeks worked per year in industry i
$W = \sum_i w_i W_i$	average weeks worked per year in all industries
p	proportion of part-time workers in all industries

The operator Δ refers to absolute differences between the first and last year of a period, and variables without the operator Δ always refer to the first year.

[a] Obtained by summing the figures for the five component periods, rather than by applying the method used for the other columns.

TABLE 3.13
Sources of Changes in Average Hours Worked per Year, 1951–1973
(Absolute changes between benchmark years)

Source of change	1951–1955	1955–1960	1960–1964	1964–1968	1968–1973	1951–1973[a]
Changes in full-time hours per week:						
Males	17	−33	−23	−43	−24	−106
Females	−6	−18	−14	−25	−5	−68
Changes in part-time hours per week, males and females	0	2	−4	0	0	−2
Changes in proportion of part-timers:						
Males	−2	−3	−7	−8	−10	−30
Females	−17	−21	−17	−8	−10	−73
Changes in weeks per year:						
Males	−2	−8	−1	−8	−23	−42
Females	−6	1	2	−4	−9	−16
Changes in proportion of females	−3	−4	−4	−6	−10	−27
Interaction and covariance effects	−1	2	0	2	2	5
Total changes in average hours per year	−20	−82	−68	−100	−89	−359

Note: The sources of changes in average hours worked per year are measured as follows:

Change in full-time hours, males	$(1-f)W^m(1-p^m)\Delta h_f^m$
Change in full-time hours, females	$fW^f(1-p^f)\Delta h_f^f$
Change in part-time hours, males and females	$(1-f)W^m p^m \Delta h_p^m + fW^f p^f \Delta h_p^f$
Change in proportion of part-timers, males	$(1-f)W^m(h_p^m - h_f^m)\Delta p^m$
Change in proportion of part-timers, females	$fW^f(h_p^f - h_f^f)\Delta p^f$
Change in weeks per year, males	$(1-f)h^m \Delta W^m$
Change in weeks per year, females	$fh^f \Delta W^f$
Change in proportion of females	$\left(\sum_i w_i^f h_i^f W_i^f - \sum_i w_i^m h_i^m W_i^m\right)\Delta f$
Interaction and covariance effects	$\left(\sum_i w_i^f h_i^f W_i^f - \Delta \sum_i w_i^m h_i^m W_i^m\right)\Delta f$

$$+ (1-f)W^m \Delta p^m(\Delta h_p^m - \Delta h_f^m) + fW^f \Delta p^f(\Delta h_p^f - \Delta h_f^f) + (1-f)\Delta h^m \Delta W^m$$
$$+ f\Delta h^f \Delta W^f + (1-f)\Delta \sum_i w_i^m \left(h_i^m - \sum_i w_i^m h_i^m\right)\left(W_i^m - \sum_i w_i^m W_i^m\right)$$
$$+ f\Delta \sum_i w_i^f \left(h_i^f - \sum_i w_i^f h_i^f\right)\left(W_i^f - \sum_i w_i^f W_i^f\right)$$

The notation is exactly as defined in the note to Table 3.12 with the addition of superscripts m and f to denote males and females, and a new variable, f, which is the proportion of females in the total in employment. It can be shown that the sum of the above rows is equal to

$$\Delta \sum_i \sum_i w_i^f h_i^f W_i^f,$$

the change in average hours worked per year for all industries and both sexes.
[a]Obtained by summing the figures for the five component periods.

Full-Time Hours

Changes in the average number of hours worked by full-time workers (Table 3.14, column 1) can result either from changes in hours worked within given occupational groups or from changes in the relative importance in the labor force of occupational groups with different working hours. We shall consider intra-occupational changes first.

Satisfactory data do not exist to enable us to study changes in hours of work for each occupational and industrial group. However, estimates are available for manual workers in certain industries and services, covering about half of the total in employment. Since it appears that changes in manual workers' hours were soon reflected in other workers' hours, it is probably sufficient to concentrate on that group.

Changes in actual hours worked by full-time manual workers can in turn be divided into those that result from changes in normal hours and those that result from changes in net overtime (overtime net of short-time).* This is a conventional distinction. It may or may not correspond to the economically significant distinction — i.e. the distinction between changes in the hours that workers and employers agree should be worked as the standard practice and changes in hours due to short-term variations in the demand for labor (analogous to changes in unemployment). We shall refer to the first as changes in "standard" hours to distinguish the concept from the conventional statistical one of "normal" hours.

The variations in the amount of net overtime worked between benchmark years in Table 3.14 up to and including 1951 were probably due chiefly to variations in demand for labor. Over this period normal hours can therefore be taken as an indicator of standard hours.

It is worth noting, incidentally, that the amount of net overtime was much the same in all benchmark years before 1951 except 1924, when there was negative net overtime. The rise in overtime, and hence in actual hours, between then and 1937 can thus be taken to indicate that there was some increase in the demand for labor, notwithstanding the lack of significant change in the unemployment percentage.

After 1951 the situation was different. The upward trend in overtime hours worked owed little or nothing to increases in the level of

---

*Normal weekly hours represent the period recognized, by contract or by custom, as the basis for the payment of the weekly wage rate. Overtime or short-time is the difference between actual hours worked and normal hours.

TABLE 3.14

Average Hours Worked per Week by Full-Time Manual Workers in the
Production Industries, Transport and Communications,
and Public Administration, 1856–1973

Year	Actual hours of total in employment (1)	Manual workers			
		Actual hours (2)	Normal hours (3)	Net over-time (4)	"Standard" hours[a] (5)
1856	65.0	65.0	63.0	2.0	63.0
1873	56.0	56.0	54.0	2.0	54.0
1913	56.4	56.0	54.0	2.0	54.0
1924	47.0	45.8	47.0[b]	– 1.2[c]	47.0
1937	48.6	48.5	47.1	1.4	47.1
1951	45.6	46.3	44.4	1.9	44.4
1955	45.9	47.0	44.4	2.6	45.1
1960	44.8	46.2	43.1	3.1	44.3
1964	43.9	45.8	42.0	3.8	43.9
1968	41.7	44.5	40.2	4.3	42.6
1973	41.0	43.9	40.0	3.9	42.0

Source: Basic statistics (Appendix N); Labour Statistics Year Book, UK [39], 1973: Table 42; British Labour Statistics
Historical Abstract, UK [48]: Table 84.
[a]Defined as normal hours of manual workers in 1856–1951, as their actual hours minus 1.9 in 1955–73 (see text).
[b]Figure refers to the normal hours worked by all manual workers whose hours were fixed by those national collective
agreements and statutory wages regulations orders used in compiling the official index of normal weekly hours (see
Ministry of Labor Gazette, Sept. 1957, pp. 330–31).
[c]Negative figure indicates short-time working.

activity.[27] Rather it reflected the tendency for unions to seek to obtain
higher wages by increasing the proportion of the working week classified as overtime, and therefore paid at a higher hourly rate, as well as
by altering the wage rate itself. Once overtime becomes habitual, even
if the provision of overtime is not actually specified in the contract, the
distinction between normal hours and overtime hours becomes
blurred. In these circumstances the concept of standard hours that
enters into collective bargaining, along with wage rates and other
fringe benefits, is the total number of hours worked in a typical week.
Standard hours then consist of both normal hours and the average
amount of overtime as conventionally defined.

We shall now consider the course and causes of changes in standard
hours. In accordance with what has been said above, we take standard
hours as equal to the normal hours of manual workers up to 1951, and
as equal to their actual hours minus overtime in 1951 (1.9 hours) in
1955–73. No precision is claimed for the figures so derived, and they
are included in Table 3.14 merely as a rough guide.

The remarkable feature of standard hours during the whole period
from 1856 to 1973 is that they were significantly altered in only four

periods, and, in three of these, reductions covering a wide range of industries were concentrated into a few years. The first change occurred in the early 1870's, when there was a move from a week of about 63 hours to a nine-hour day and a six-day week (54 hours). During the next 50 years occasional and fairly small reductions in hours were made in a few industries (e.g. engineering in England and Wales, coal mining, some building trades, and printing). Clapham (1938: 477–79) puts the average reduction in all industries between the 1880's and 1914 in the range 2.5–5 percent.[28] No allowance for this has been made in our figures, and so our estimate of hours worked per year in 1913 may be slightly too high.*

The next major change in hours came during the short-lived boom following World War I. Then, in the single year 1919, more than 6,000,000 workers had their working week shortened by some seven hours, most commonly by starting work at 8:30 A.M., and so abandoning the old practice of working one hour before breakfast. For the whole of the interwar period the standard week was typically 47 hours, in most cases spread over five and a half days. Further reduction again came in the aftermath of war: in 1947 and 1948 there was a decrease of about three hours a week. At this stage a five-day week became popular, with the interesting consequence that from Monday to Friday many manual workers were actually reverting to the old nine-hour day, as opposed to the eight or eight and a half hours that had constituted the typical working day between the wars. The last of the four reductions came after the mid-1950's and did not have the discontinuous character of the previous reductions. The reduction gradually achieved over the 18 years 1955–73 was three hours, the same as had been achieved in the two years 1947–48.

The pattern by which hours of work were reduced in infrequent large steps contrasts with the more of less steady rise in real wages over time. The contrast is not what would be predicted by the usual analysis of the worker's choice between leisure and real income. Indeed, the step-wise reduction in hours does not lend itself to explanation by marginalist economic theory of the usual type at all. A number of valuable suggestions are made in the thorough investigations of Bienefeld (1972), but the phenomenon remains something of a mystery.

Bienefeld points out that because reductions in hours normally involve reductions in the degree of utilization of capital, employers

---

*If we assume the maximum reduction suggested by Clapham for the preceding 40 years, the growth of total hours worked would be 0.8% (instead of 0.9%) in 1873–1913 and −1.9% (instead of −2.3%) in 1913–24.

attach a greater value to maintaining hours than employees attach to reducing them. The least-cost, or maximum-gain, resolution of the conflict of interests therefore lies in changes in wages and other fringe benefits, but not in changes in hours. In itself this would tend to explain why the reductions in hours were small, not why they occurred in steps. It could be argued, however, that in face of employers' reluctance to reduce hours, the balance between pay and leisure gets progressively out of line with workers' preferences until such time as they are able and willing to apply strong pressure for a change.

The four periods of reductions in hours have several points in common. They were all periods of boom, when labor's bargaining power was strong. They were all periods of rapid increases of money wages; this could be taken as a further indicator of labor's bargaining power, or it could be taken to mean that workers, suffering from money illusion, put a lower priority on further increases in pay than on reductions in hours. In the 1870's and in the aftermath of the two wars, though hardly in 1955–73, there were fears of an impending decline in activity, and a desire to share out the available work by shorter hours. A special factor in the aftermath of the two wars was the combination of warweariness (very long hours had been worked in wartime) and a hopeful determination to make a radical improvement in the condition of the worker. It is noteworthy that the especially large reduction in hours immediately after World War I was common to most European countries (Phelps Brown & Browne 1968: 206–7). The more protracted reduction in hours after 1955 may betoken a change in the pattern and reflect a situation in which great union power ceased to be an exceptional occurrence. An analogy may be found here with the trend in money wages, which in former times as a rule rose much faster than productivity only in exceptional periods, chiefly across wars, but in the postwar period did so persistently.

Changes in the occupational and industrial structure of the labor force in our period tended to be such as to reduce the average number of full-time hours worked. The trend was away from areas, such as agriculture, railways, retailing, and domestic service, where long hours were worked. The most rapidly growing group was clerical and professional workers, who worked relatively short hours. Structural changes of this kind accounted for 10–20 percent of the total fall in full-time hours between 1913 and 1924, and for 30–40 percent of the decline between 1951 and 1973; they were relatively unimportant in the other two twentieth-century periods, 1924–37 and 1937–51. These structural changes naturally occurred gradually, not in steps. They were no doubt chiefly due to circumstances unconnected with hours of work; but to some extent they probably reflected an increasing reluctance of workers to take on jobs with long hours, and in this way gave expression to the increase in leisure-preference associated with the long-term rise in income.

Part-Time Working

The increase in part-time working became an important phenomenon only after the beginning of World War II (Table 3.12). Though the proportion of working females in part-time jobs remained very much larger than the proportion of working males (Table 3.15), the increase in the male proportion during the postwar period contributed almost 30 percent to the change in average hours worked per year that was due to part-time working (Table 3.13). We consider males and females in turn.

It may be assumed that almost all the transwar increase in the proportion of part-timers came from the female side.[29] For males, it is necessary to explain the rise in the proportion of part-timers during the postwar period. There was an increase in part-timers among all age groups. Up to 1964 the increase was greatest for the very young and the very old; after 1964 it was greatest for those in the middle-range age groups, 25–54. The contribution of the increase in the proportion of part-timers among males of working age (from 0.1 percent in 1951 to 0.7 percent in 1964 and 2.6 percent in 1973) was about half of that among males aged 65 or over up to 1964, but more than twice as much after 1964.[30] The main causes of the rise in the importance of male part-time working were (1) the extension of part-time educational courses; (2) the growth of real hourly earnings, which enabled those with a relatively high preference for leisure, including those (especially

TABLE 3.15
*Proportion of Part-Timers in the Total in
Employment, 1937–1973*
(Percent)

Year	Males	Females	Both sexes
1937	—	—	1.5%
1951	0.3%	12.1%	4.1
1964	1.9	28.6	10.9
1973	4.3	34.6	15.6

among the elderly) whose physical capacity for long hours of work was limited, to afford to work only part-time; (3) the growth of the real value of pensions, permitting the retired to work only part-time; and (4) the spread of occupational pension schemes.

The rise in the proportion of part-timers among female workers began with World War II. This trend has to be viewed in relation to the rise in the female participation rate, which as we have seen, was predominantly among married women, and which (together with the increased proportion of married to unmarried women in the population as a whole) led a spectacular rise in the percentage of working women who were married: from 15.2 percent in 1931 to 38.2 percent in 1951 and again to 64.8 percent in 1973. This is clearly the chief explanation on the supply side of the rise in the proportion of part-timers among women workers. It was aided by changes on the demand side that were largely induced by the change in supply and by the overall shortage of labor. The labor shortage, especially during World War II, induced employers to introduce organizational arrangements that would accommodate part-time workers; had (full-time) labor been more abundant, they might have been more reluctant to make the necessary changes.

The growth of the proportion of part-time workers in the total tends to be cumulative. The more there are, the easier society finds it to make appropriate arrangements for them. Workplace organizations, career structures, pre-school day-care centers, and other institutions, all adapt themselves to more part-time workers, and this in turn stimulates others to do part-time jobs. There was probably also some decline of an autonomous nature in the importance of the jobs traditionally organized on a full-time basis (e.g. machine operators in manufacturing industries) compared with jobs where part-time workers could be more easily assimilated (e.g. typing, cleaning, and shop-assisting).

The move toward part-time was a substantial offset to the effects of the increase in the female participation rate (see Table 3.17, below). At the same time full-time hours declined proportionately more for women than for men (Table 3.13, above); it is possible that this too was indirectly the result of the fact that so many more of the women workers were married. The net result is the surprising one that, despite the great increase in the female participation rate in the postwar period, the ratio of total hours worked by women to total hours worked by men rose by only a small amount over the whole of the postwar period and actually declined fractionally up till 1964.[31]

Weeks per Year

Time is lost through holidays, sickness, and industrial disputes.* The relative importance of the three sources is shown in Table 3.16. Industrial disputes are unimportant compared with the other two. Holidays accounted for the greatest part of the growth in time lost over the period, though the contribution of sickness increased significantly across World War I and slightly across World War II.

Before World War I 10 to 11 days' holiday was typical. (Both paid and unpaid holidays are included.) In 1924 most manual workers received one week's holiday plus six public holidays, and by the end of the interwar period this had risen to about a week and a half plus public holidays. In 1951 many manual workers had two weeks plus public holidays; by 1964 all had at least two weeks, and some had more; and by 1973 about three-quarters had three or more weeks. Nonmanual workers had always had longer holidays than manual workers. Here, as with the trend to shorter normal hours, the main changes were concentrated in a few periods (across the two wars and in 1968–73); and for long periods of time no lengthening of holidays occurred, though the diffusion throughout the labor force of arrangements made by the pace-setters was spread over a longer period of time than in the case of normal hours (see Cameron 1965). In the interwar period much of the pressure was devoted not to the achievement of longer holidays, but to the introduction of legislation aimed at forcing employers to pay their employees during holidays. Though holiday pay never became a statutory obligation (except in Wages Council Industries), by 1945 there were very few workers who were not entitled to at least one week's paid holiday plus public holidays. It may be noted that the substantial extension of holiday entitlement in 1968–73, combined with the fall in weekly hours, accounts for the unusually rapid reduction in hours per year in that period.

The increase that took place in time lost owing to sickness could have been due to an increase in the incidence of ill-health or to an increase in the propensity to stay away from work in response to a given degree of ill-health. The second of these probably accounts for all or nearly all of the observed increase. The reasons for supposing this are:

(1) The improvements in nutrition, public health measures, and

*Absenteeism, which is also a source of lost time, is in principle allowed for in the estimates of the number of hours worked per week. Except in the case of coal mining, it cannot be measured separately.

TABLE 3.16

Average Weeks of Work Lost per Year Through Holidays, Sickness, and Industrial Disputes, 1913–1973

Year	Holidays	Sickness	Industrial disputes	Total
1913	1.4	1.7	0.07	3.2
1924	2.1	2.2	0.08	4.4
1937	2.3	2.1	0.03	4.5
1951	3.1	2.5	0.01	5.6
1955	3.5	2.3	0.02	5.8
1960	3.6	2.3	0.02	5.9
1964	3.5	2.4	0.01	5.9
1968	3.8	2.3	0.03	6.2
1973	4.7	2.3	0.06	7.0

treatment of morbidity are such as to make it unlikely that the growth of more modern forms of ill-health (e.g. obesity and depression) were great enough to offset them.

(2) The expansion of coverage under the National Insurance acts and of the number of private sick pay schemes decreased the average cost to the employee of taking time off work because of ill-health.

(3) The institution of the National Health Service, charging (from 1952) only nominal fees for prescriptions, reduced the cost of medical treatment.

The second point was particularly important after each of the two wars, when the numbers covered by National Insurance schemes took a step upward; and the third point was relevant from the late 1940's. It is not surprising, therefore, to find that all increases in time lost through sickness occurred across the two wars.

An implication of the foregoing is that there was a decline over time in the number of those actually at work who were suffering from poor health. The average productivity of those at work was presumably less when it included some who, in more modern times, would be classified as sick. There is therefore a source of productivity growth here that we shall return to in the next chapter.

LABOR INPUT: QUANTITATIVE SUMMARY

The sources of changes in labor input between benchmark years are summarized in Table 3.17.

Labor input fell steeply across World War I, then grew in the inter-war period at a rate exceeding the pre-1914 rate. It underwent little change across World War II. In the postwar period it was at first constant, then declined. The net result was a negative growth rate (– 0.3 percent) over the 60 years from 1913 to 1973, compared with a positive growth rate (0.6 percent) over the 57 years from 1856 to 1913.

It is apparent from Table 3.17 that both the downward trend in the rate of growth of labor input and its variations between periods were chiefly due to two sources: demographic changes and changes in hours of work. The net effect of changes in age- and sex-specific participation rates was small. Changes in unemployment were quantitatively important only across the two wars.

We suggested at the beginning of this chapter that the most important analytical distinction between the various causes of change in the labor force is between supply and demand. We shall now look at the various statistically defined sources of change with this distinction in mind, while remembering at the same time that the forces of supply and demand are liable to interact, possibly in complicated ways and with long lags.

Demographic forces. Differences between periods in the growth of the labor input cannot, with the exception of differences between 1873–1913 and later periods, be directly attributed to differences in population growth, which occurred at a constant rate of 0.4–0.5 per-

TABLE 3.17
Sources of Growth of the Labor Input, 1856–1973
(Annual percentage growth rates)

Source of change	1856– 1873	1873– 1913	1913– 1924	1924– 1937	1937– 1951	1951– 1964	1964– 1973
Population growth	0.8%	0.9%	0.5%	0.4%	0.5%	0.5%	0.4%
Changes in age distribution	–	0.1	–	0.7	–	– 0.1	– 0.3
Changes in male age-specific participation rates	–	0.0	–	– 0.1	–	– 0.2	– 0.3
Changes in female age-specific rates and proportion of female part-timers	–	0.0	–	0.2	–	0.2	0.2
Changes in unemployment	0.1	0.0	– 0.5	0.0	0.5	0.0	– 0.1
Changes in full-time hours (including holidays)	– 0.9	0.0	– 1.8	0.2	– 0.6	– 0.4	– 0.9
Other[a]	0.0[b]	– 0.1	– 0.5[b]	0.1	– 0.3[b]	0.0	– 0.1
Growth of labor input	0.0%	0.9%	– 2.3%	1.5%	0.1%	0.0%	– 1.1%

Source: Tables 3.5, 3.7, 3.9, 3.10, 3.12, and 3.13, roughly adjusted to different periods where necessary.
Note: The measures in this table correspond in principle to those used to estimate the sources of working-population growth (Tables 3.5 and 3.7) and the sources of changes in average hours worked per year (Tables 3.12 and 3.13). However, converting the breakdown of the working population sources from a Great Britain intercensal basis to a UK benchmark-year basis inevitably introduces an element of imprecision.
[a] Includes interaction and rounding effects.
[b] Includes changes in age distribution (positive in 1913–24, negative in 1937–51) and in sex- and age-specific participation rates (negative in 1913–24, positive in 1937–51).

cent from 1913. But indirectly population growth was important in later periods too, operating through changes in age distribution.

We suggested earlier that, of the factors influencing the labor supply, the growth of population came nearest to being supply-determined. This does not mean that it was not influenced by economic forces. Some of the economic influences on the size of the population were direct and relatively immediate: those operating through migration, in particular, and also the influence of the depression in the interwar years on the birth-rate. Indeed, superficial observation of the time-pattern of population change, with its once-for-all fall in the growth rate in the second decade of the twentieth century, might suggest that the immediate influences were the most important ones. But this would be a wrong conclusion. The immediate influences affected the timing and the extent of the movement, but the underlying causes of the trend were more deep-seated. Both the long-run decline in mortality and the (greater) long-run decline in fertility began long before the actual rate of population growth declined. They appear to have owed much to the general course of socioeconomic change and, as such, were endogenous to the growth process, though possibly operating with very long lags. But there remains much that is obscure about the exact nature of the relationship. There was a further lag, of a more obvious kind, of movements in the working population after movements in population. The changes in age distribution, referred to in the previous paragraph, were essentially reflections of earlier movements in fertility and mortality.

Migration is the demographic channel on which the demand for labor might be expected to operate most directly. It contributed + 0.2 to the difference in the annual percentage increase in labor input in the interwar period compared with pre-1914, and + 0.1 to the difference between the postwar period and pre-1914. This was certainly due primarily to economic forces. But in the interwar period the effect was in a perverse direction in respect to the domestic demand for labor: the world depression led to net immigration, chiefly through return migration. In the postwar period high demand for labor led to immigration (from the New Commonwealth) in the orthodox fashion. However, the curtailment of this immigration after the early 1960's was due to social policy rather than economic forces.

Hours of work. This was the most important single source of interperiod differences in labor input. It had its greatest impact in 1856–73, in the two transwar periods, and in 1964–73. The causes of the changes that occurred in hours of work may be taken to have been predominantly economic, operating on both the supply side and the demand side.

On the supply side, one would expect rises in real income to increase the utility attached to leisure. This is consistent both with the long-run decline in hours and with the more than usually rapid decline in the postwar period, when real incomes were rising more rapidly than in earlier peacetime phases.

On the demand side, it is well known that, in the short run, hours worked rise and fall with the cycle. A direct demand-induced effect of this kind was responsible for the slight increase in hours of work between 1924 and 1937. In the longer run, however, it appears that the effect of demand pressure on hours was perverse, and subject also to a lag. Declines in hours occurred chiefly on a relatively small number of occasions, when trade union bargaining power was particularly strong; and the strength of trade union bargaining power was in turn largely connected with the strength of the demand for labor. It took some time for the reductions in hours thus achieved to spread through all industries, so reductions in average hours tended to continue for a while after the demand for labor had ceased to be particularly strong. The forces that determined this timing of reductions in hours are not, admittedly, entirely clear, and the above account does not explain (save possibly in very general terms of union bargaining power) why hours fell more rapidly in 1964–73 than in 1951–64. It is possible that in 1964–73 the state of the demand for labor had some effect in the orthodox direction, inasmuch as an awareness of slacker demand influenced unions to use their bargaining power increasingly in the pursuit of longer holidays. However, there can be little doubt that there was in the long run a predominantly perverse relationship between hours and pressure of demand for labor.

Unemployment. The direct relation between demand for labor and unemployment is obvious and requires no comment. Changes in the amount of unemployment were not, however, important sources of change in labor input in the peacetime periods under consideration (apart from cycles).

Participation rates. These were subject to a variety of forces, largely canceling out in net. There was a trend rise from World War I onward in the participation rate of married women (and in the interwar period of unmarried women too), partly but not wholly offset in the postwar period by the rise in the proportion of women working part-time.*

---

*And also, in the period 1951–64, by the more rapid decline in female than male full-time hours. The effect of this appears in Table 3.17 in hours of work.

We discussed above the interaction of supply and demand forces responsible for this trend. Supply factors (the fall in family size and the
average age of marriage and the need to maintain family incomes in
the face of heavy unemployment) may have dominated in the interwar
period, whereas demand factors, possibly operating with a lag and interacting with supply-side factors, may have been relatively (though
perhaps not absolutely) more important in the postwar period.[32]

In the case of men, there was a significant decline in the participation rate in the postwar period, attributable chiefly to the extension of
education and to a lesser extent to earlier retirement — both supply-side
phenomena, the latter related to better public and private pension arrangements. The extension of education applied also to young women.
The decline in participation rates among young men and young women
aged 15–24 reduced the labor force in the period 1964–73 at an annual
rate of 0.4 percent (compared with 0.2 percent in 1951–64).

Conclusions on the roles of supply and demand. The long-run
tendency for the rate of growth of labor input to decline, apart from a
brief interruption in the interwar period, was due chiefly to supply-side
forces affecting population growth, hours of work, and to a lesser extent education and retirement. All these reflected more or less directly
the long-run effects of economic growth.

Apart from the long-run trend, there were significant variations between periods. The orthodox effect of changes in the pressure of demand in eliciting changes in the labor force in the same direction was
manifested in a number of ways: through changes in unemployment,
through an increase in hours of work within the interwar period,
through changes in the participation rate of married women in the
postwar period, and possibly through holidays in 1964–73. Quantitatively, however, the net effect of all these changes except the last
was relatively unimportant in peacetime periods, apart from cycles.
More important were variations in the impact of domestic demographic forces; these were influenced, among other complex causes, by
the demand for labor 20 or so years earlier, insofar as that was one of
the determinants of variations in the birth-rate. Most important of all
were variations in the rate of reduction in standard hours of work.
These did reflect changes in the demand for labor, but predominantly
in the perverse direction. In net, therefore, again abstracting from
cycles, it appears that the positive effect of demand pressure on the supply of labor was either relatively small or else subject to extremely long
lags, and that the most important medium-run effect was in the
perverse direction.

UNEMPLOYMENT AND THE STATE OF THE LABOR MARKET

Change in unemployment, as noted, did not have a significant effect on the rate of growth of labor input between the end-years of any of our standard peacetime periods. However, the balance of supply and demand in the labor market has more general implications for the character of the various periods and therefore merits further discussion.

Labor is heterogeneous and jobs are heterogeneous. So a gross excess supply of labor (unemployment) always coexists to some extent with a gross excess demand for labor (unfilled vacancies). It is only for the first of these that we have statistics stretching over a long period. However, the broad characterization of the different peacetime periods given by the unemployment percentage is not likely to be disputed as a general indicator of the relative state of the labor market in the three periods shown in Table 3.18. Unemployment in the postwar period was much lower than in earlier periods, both at cyclical peaks and over the average of all years (especially the latter). The interwar period was much worse than the pre-1914 period. We shall now proceed to look at these three periods more closely.

The Pre-1914 and Interwar Periods

There were two types of unemployment before 1914, cyclical and chronic. Cyclical unemployment affected chiefly industrial workers, especially those in the capital goods and export industries. As a counterpart to it, there were in most cyclical peaks some shortages of labor in industries particularly affected by the boom. The shortage of coal miners in 1872 is the best-known late-nineteenth-century example; other examples reported in contemporary sources (e.g. the annual

TABLE 3.18
Proportion of Unemployed Workers in the
Civilian Working Population: Period Averages and
Cycle Peaks, 1857–1973
(Percent)

Period	Period averages	Cycle peaks
1857–1913	4.4%	2.1%
1920–1938	10.6	6.1
1951–1973	1.9	1.6

Note: For 1920–38 the term unemployed includes the temporarily stopped; for the other periods it refers to the wholly unemployed only.

Commercial History and Review of *The Economist*) were in the building trades in the late 1870's, in ship-building in 1889, and in coal mining again in 1900. But in all cases the shortages were brief, and came to an end either because the demand fell off or because new labor was quickly recruited.

There is no significant trend up or down in the trade union unemployment statistics before 1914. These statistics relate chiefly to skilled workers, who were not necessarily typical. Unemployment among skilled workers is in some ways comparable to the underutilization of capital equipment. The number of skilled workers, like the amount of capital, is likely to be regulated in the long run chiefly by the expected demand for their services, not by exogenous population growth. So it is not too surprising that unemployment among skilled workers should have had no clear trend up or down in this period, and that their unemployment should have been low at cyclical peaks, as was the underutilization of capital equipment.

There is fairly abundant qualitative evidence that even in boom years before 1914 there was a chronic surplus of unskilled urban labor.[33] It is doubtful whether at cyclical peaks there was much general underutilization of capital capacity (see pp. 157–58); hence a general increase in demand for final output would not have permitted this surplus labor to be absorbed unless there had been at the same time a shift in the structure of demand toward labor-intensive products. It follows therefore that the chronic labor surplus was not of the Keynesian type. It more resembled that found in underdeveloped countries. Limited supplies of capital to cooperate with the labor, and lack of human capital in the form of skills, meant that there was not enough for the labor to do. At full employment, its marginal product could have been at or near zero; to put it another way, an intermittent use of labor was the most efficient available use of labor.

In the nineteenth century this kind of unemployment particularly manifested itself in the British economy in casual working. Chronic unemployment made it easy for employers in industries with an irregular demand for labor to pick it up on a casual basis. The classic examples of unemployment and underemployment associated with casual working were in the docks and in the building trades.[34] But there were many other industries where workers were engaged by the day or even by the hour. The surplus labor crowded into occupations where there was a chance of *some* employment, and employers lacked inducement to arrange work on a less casual basis because of the general excess supply. In regarding this as simply a fault in organization, to be corrected

TABLE 3.19
Regional Rates of Unemployment as a Percentage of
the United Kingdom Rate, 1913–1973

Region[a]	1913–14	1929	1937	1951	1964	1973
London	192%	50%	52%	⎧	⎧	56%[b]
South East and East				⎨ 69%	⎨ 59%	
Anglia	105	52	65	⎩	⎩	70[c]
South West	134	77	70	92	88	89
West Midlands	87	⎧ 86	⎧ 61	31	53	81
East Midlands	71	⎨	⎨	⎧ 54	⎧ 65	78
Yorkshire and Humberside	71	132	99	⎩	⎩	107
North West	87	126	125	92	123	133
North	63	—[d]	169	169	194	174
Wales	60	187	210	207	153	130
Scotland	55	115	151	192	212	170
Northern Ireland	184[e]	131	214	469	389	237

Source: Beveridge 1944: Table 12; *Labour Statistics Year Book*, UK [39], *1973*; *Labour Statistics Historical Abstract*, UK [48]: Tables 110, 162, 168.
   Note: The unemployment rates are calculated as the averages of the monthly statistics of the total registered unemployed (including the temporarily stopped) as a percentage of the mid-year estimates of total insured employees. The underlying insurance statistics did not cover the whole labor force for pre–World War II years, and hence figures for these years are not entirely representative. The bias is probably not serious for 1929 and 1937, but it might be for 1913–14, since only about 13% of employees were insured.
   [a]The definitions of the regions are not constant through the period, but they are sufficiently similar to allow broad conclusions to be drawn from the table. For details of the definitions, see UK [48], cited above, Appendix E. The nomenclature in the table is that of the Standard Regions for statistical purposes introduced in 1966.
   [b]South East and London combined.
   [c]East Anglia.
   [d]Included in Yorkshire and Humberside, and the North West.
   [e]In principle includes Southern Ireland. In practice the bulk of the Irish insured workers in 1913–14 were in the north.

by decasualization schemes, contemporaries like the Webbs overlooked the more deep-seated problem that there would not have been enough work for everyone to be engaged on a full-time basis.
   As industrial development proceeded in the latter half of the century, there was a downward trend in the proportion of labor hired on a casual basis and a progressive increase in the proportion of workers more or less permanently attached to a single employer; this was noted by contemporaries as one of the chief forces tending to reduce unemployment in the course of the century.[35] There were thus elements of the "dual labor market," and the proportion of workers in the "organized" sector increased over time (as has happened in Japan). It did not manifest itself in any downward trend in the recorded unemployment figures because most casual workers fell outside the scope of these figures and also because the urban surplus continued to be replenished by the immigration of rural surplus labor.
   The regional pattern of unemployment casts an interesting sidelight on these long-run trends and provides a transition to our discussion of the interwar period.

TABLE 3.20
Regional Male Participation Rates as a Percentage of
the United Kingdom Rate, 1881–1961

Region[a]	1881	1921	1961
South East	98.8%	98.7%	101.7%
East Anglia	100.4	99.4	99.3
South West	98.6	99.1	98.1
West Midlands	98.6	100.2	103.2
East Midlands	100.8	102.0	101.7
Yorkshire and			
Humberside	102.1	103.8	101.0
North West	102.3	103.4	100.0
North	98.3	97.7	98.1
Wales	100.7	99.1	98.8
Scotland	100.0	98.4	97.7
Northern Ireland	101.9	96.1	83.1

Source: Census of Population, UK [52], 1881, 1921, 1926 (Northern Ireland), 1961.
Note: The UK rate here excludes Southern Ireland even in 1881.
[a]The regions are consistently defined throughout, and they approximate to the Standard Regions for statistical purposes introduced in 1966. The regions of England are defined as follows:
South East: Bedfordshire, Berkshire, Buckinghamshire, Essex, Hampshire and Isle of Wight, Hertfordshire, Kent, London, Middlesex, Oxfordshire, Surrey, Sussex.
East Anglia: Cambridgeshire, Huntingdonshire, Norfolk, Suffolk.
South West: Cornwall, Devon, Dorset, Gloucestershire, Somerset, Wiltshire.
West Midlands: Herefordshire, Shropshire, Staffordshire, Warwickshire, Worcestershire.
East Midlands: Derbyshire, Leicestershire, Lincolnshire, Northamptonshire, Nottinghamshire, Rutland.
Yorkshire and Humberside: Yorkshire East and West Ridings.
North West: Cheshire, Lancashire.
North: Cumberland, Durham, Northumberland, Westmoreland, Yorkshire North Riding.
Wales is defined to include Monmouthshire.

The extent of differences in unemployment rates between regions
(Table 3.19) was of the same order of magnitude before World War I
as after. But the ranking was almost exactly the opposite (except for
Northern Ireland). The highest unemployment was in London, and the
lowest in the regions that later became the depressed areas.* In the
postwar period the ranking was not greatly different from what it had
been in 1937, nor did it alter much in the course of the period.
The relative male participation rates tell the same story (Table
3.20).[36] In 1881 and 1921 (before the effects of the interwar depression
had set in) participation rates were low in the South East (including
London), and high in the East Midlands, Yorkshire, the North West,
and Wales. By 1961 the South East and the West Midlands had the
highest participation rates, and the old industrial areas (especially
Wales and Scotland) had low rates. The relatively high level of demand for labor in the North of England as compared with the South

*This holds for individual industries as well as for the total (Beveridge 1944: 74).

before 1914 is confirmed by regional data on pauperism and agricultural wages.[37]

The broad pattern of regional development is clear. Before 1914 the areas of high unemployment and low participation were those in which industrial development had proceeded least rapidly in relation to population. London acted as a magnet for labor but was not able to absorb it in industry; indeed, manufacturing industry in London was tending to decline.* After World War I the industrial development of the London area accelerated, and the regions of high unemployment and low participation were those with old established declining industries rather than those that had never been heavily industrialized. Northern Ireland remained the exception, the one major region still suffering from unemployment of the old labor-surplus type.[38]

By 1914 the elimination of rural surplus was largely completed, and the stage was set for a more rapid elimination of urban surplus. But the long-run tendency for labor to become more scarce as capital accumulates was entirely overshadowed in the interwar period by the demand deficiency brought about by the collapse in the demand for traditional staple industrial products in the 1920's, followed by the world slump in the early 1930's. In the late 1930's some significant shortages of special types of labor were experienced because of the requirements of the rearmament program; otherwise, as would be expected, labor shortages were not common in the interwar period (Beveridge 1937; Richardson 1967: 285).

The Postwar Period

The high demand for labor in the postwar period may be regarded as reflecting both a long-run increase in the scarcity of labor, associated with the process of economic growth and capital accumulation, and an unusually high level of demand for final output in the Keynesian sense. There was, however, a distinct downward trend in the demand for labor, at least as measured by unemployment, within the postwar period (Table 3.21). This trend was at first mild but became much more pronounced in the mid-1960's. It will therefore be convenient to treat separately the subperiods 1951–64 and 1965–73.

*Much of the evidence relating to the chronic excess supply of urban unskilled labor before 1914 comes from London. There is therefore some danger of forming an exaggerated picture of the extent of the problem in the country as a whole and in particular inferring from the London evidence that the problem was getting worse over time (G. S. Jones 1971: Tables 5, 6, and Chapter 1; in this book Jones provides a detailed treatment of the problem of casual labor in London).

TABLE 3.21

*Proportion of Unemployed Workers in the
Civilian Working Population: Period Averages and
Cycle Peaks, 1948-1973*

(Percent)

Period	Period averages	Cycle peaks
1948–1951	1.2%	1.1%
1952–1955	1.3	1.0
1956–1961	1.5	1.4
1962–1965	1.7	1.3
1966–1969	2.1	2.3
1970–1973	2.9	2.4

Note: Cycles are here defined as running from the year following a cyclical minimum in unemployment through the year with the next cyclical minimum. The figure in the second column is for the end year of the period. Because of the upward trend in unemployment, the figure in the second column in 1966–69 is higher than the figure in the first column.

1951-64. There is no shortage of evidence to support the conclusion that unemployment in the postwar period was very low by any earlier standards. The unemployment percentage even in recession years was only a little above the level it had reached at the tops of booms in the nineteenth century. In certain regions, especially Northern Ireland, some unemployment problem persisted, but for the most part the amount of unemployment was small, and those who did become unemployed had little difficulty in finding new jobs (Gillion & Black 1966).

We cannot infer the absolute amount of *net* excess demand for labor by comparing registered unemployment with the official vacancy data (vacancies reported to Employment Exchanges and unfilled by the end of the month), since neither is a comprehensive measure. The unemployment rate does not take into account demand-induced variations in participation rates (see below), and not all vacancies are filled through Employment Exchanges. However, in this period the movements in the vacancy statistics are more or less a mirror-image of those in unemployment, so the two are consistent. More directly relevant to the excess demand for labor are the survey data collected by the Confederation of British Industries (CBI) on the factors expected by firms to limit their output. These are summarized in Table 3.22. About a third of manufacturing firms expected a shortage of skilled labor to be the most important factor or one of the most important factors in limiting output in the booms of 1960 and 1964; the returns for individual industries in some cases show much higher proportions. A considerably smaller proportion of firms, but still over 10 percent, cited the shortage of other labor as the bottleneck. There are objections to interpreting these data at their face value,[39] but they suggest that labor shortages imposed a significant brake on the growth of output at cyclical peaks. Even in the peak year 1964, however, over half the firms still cited a shortage of orders or sales as among the most likely constraints on output. At cyclical troughs, orders or sales were the dominant limitation on output; a shortage of skilled labor remained of some importance, but very few firms were troubled by a shortage of other labor.

On this basis we may infer that at cyclical peaks there was significant net excess demand for labor, especially skilled labor, and that excess demand for some types of labor persisted throughout the cycle. It does not appear that there was chronic *net* excess demand for labor as a whole throughout the cycle, as there was in the years immediately following the war (until 1951). However, the CBI data probably understate the general tendency to excess demand for labor, since they relate only to manufacturing, which on the whole had less trouble with labor recruitment in the postwar period than other sectors.

TABLE 3.22

Survey Data on Factors Expected to Limit Output, 1960–1973

(Percent of firms surveyed)

Year	Orders or sales	Skilled labor	Other labor	Plant capacity	Credit	Materials or components	Other
1960	18%	29%	11%	13%	2%	12%	—
1961	34	28	8	9	4	4	—
1962	68	15	5	7	4	2	—
1963	71	11	3	9	3	3	—
1964	50	30	13	22	2	9	4
1965	50	39	17	19	4	9	3
1966	60	35	13	13	7	7	3
1967	79	19	4	9	6	3	2
1968	66	27	9	18	5	5	2
1969	56	31	12	24	8	11	4
1970	58	27	8	22	11	17	4
1971	80	12	2	13	8	5	3
1972	78	12	3	15	3	6	5
1973	41	37	19	28	3	28	5

Source: CBI, *Industrial Trends Survey* for the years shown. The figures here are the averages for all the surveys conducted during the year.

Note: The 1960–63 figures are not directly comparable with the ones for 1964–73. The question asked for 1960–63 was "If your output is likely to be limited in the next four months by shortage of any of the following, please tick the most important." The question asked for 1964–73 was "What factors are likely to limit your output over the next four months? Please tick the most important factor or factors." The change in the form of the question is responsible for the absence of "other" in 1960–63, and for the totals adding to less than 100 in that period and more than 100 in 1964–73.

The smallness of the average unemployment rate in the 1951–64 period owed much to the smallness of its cyclical fluctuations.* In the interwar and pre-1914 periods the amplitude of fluctuations in employment was not greatly different from that of GDP. But in 1951–64 they were proportionately very much smaller than in GDP. The reduction in fluctuations in employment in the postwar period compared with the pre-1914 periods owed more to the reduction in the output-elasticity of employment than it did to the reduction in the amplitude of fluctuations in output. Compared with the interwar period, the reduction in the amplitude of output fluctuations was the more important force, but reduction in the output-elasticity of employment was also substantial.

Fluctuations in employment are reflected in fluctuations in participation rates as well as in unemployment. In the interwar period 95 percent of the amplitude of the employment cycles was taken up by fluctuations in unemployment, and only 7 percent by fluctuations in participation rates.[40] In 1951–64, by contrast, unemployment and participation rates accounted for about equal parts. The distinction between a decrease in participation and an increase in unemployment may not be very meaningful. The married women, the elderly, and the other marginal workers who accounted for the fall in participation rates in recessions were not eligible for unemployment benefits. Consequently, they had little incentive to register as unemployed at Employment Exchanges, and they did not appear in the unemployment statistics when they lost their jobs. Cyclical reductions in participation rates should probably be regarded as mainly involuntary. This means that the magnitude of the true cyclical movement in involuntary unemployment was larger than the official unemployment figures suggest (see Hunter 1963; Galambos 1967; Corry & Roberts 1970; J. Taylor 1971). It also means that rather more of the burden of cyclical variations in the demand for labor fell on marginal workers than in former times. However, even if the whole of the fluctuations in participation rates in 1951–64 were taken to reflect unrecorded involuntary unemployment, the amplitude of true employment fluctuations would still be much less than in earlier periods.[41] This is because the amplitude of the employment cycle was so small in the postwar period.

Account must also be taken of cyclical fluctuations in hours of work. We do not have quantitative evidence on this for earlier times; but in

---

*Cyclical fluctuations are further discussed in Chapter 10. The following remarks draw on the statistics given there (Table 10.1) and use the same definition of cyclical amplitude.

the cotton industry, for example, it is well known that organized short-time working in response to slack demand was already an established practice before the middle of the nineteenth century. In the postwar period short-time working was less important than variations in the amount of overtime.

Figure 3.4 shows that the weekly hours worked by full-time manual workers in trough years in 1951–64 were on average about half an hour below the peak-to-peak trend. The amplitude of this series is (for both sexes together) 0.6.* Fluctuations in the hours worked by nonmanual workers were probably less marked, and hence the amplitude of average hours worked per year by all workers would be less than 0.6. If cycles in average hours coincided with cycles in employment, one might guess that the amplitude of fluctuations in total hours worked (number of workers times hours per worker) in 1951–64 was about 1.0. But it appears from Figure 3.4 that cycles in hours coincided with those in output and anticipated those in employment; fluctuations in output were immediately transmitted to hours, but to employment only after a lag, reflecting the gradual adjustment to a new equilibrium level of employment. The amplitude of fluctuations in total hours in the postwar period was therefore probably less than 1.0.

Allowance for average hours worked would also increase the prewar measures of cyclical amplitudes of labor input, to an extent possibly greater than in the postwar period. It follows that in total labor input, as well as in employment, cyclical fluctuations were much smaller in 1951–64 than formerly, both absolutely and relative to the amplitude of cyclical fluctuations in output. An interesting further implication is that productivity *per man-hour* must have tended to move counter-cyclically in former times (since the cyclical amplitudes of employment and output were about the same). This is as would be expected if the least efficient plant or workers were the most prone to go out of employment in the slump. After World War II that was outweighed by the treatment of labor as an overhead.

The tendency to treat labor as an overhead, and the consequent stability of employment over the cycle, is a phenomenon related to the long-run decline in casual working referred to earlier. It was, in effect,

---

*Measured over the specific cycles in average hours worked by full-time manual workers. These cycles are the same as those in GDP. (Actually, Figure 3.4 shows that 1959 rather than 1960 was the peak. We have chosen the latter, however, on the grounds that the large fall in normal hours between 1959 and 1960 conceals the *increase* in overtime hours that was occurring for cyclical reasons.)

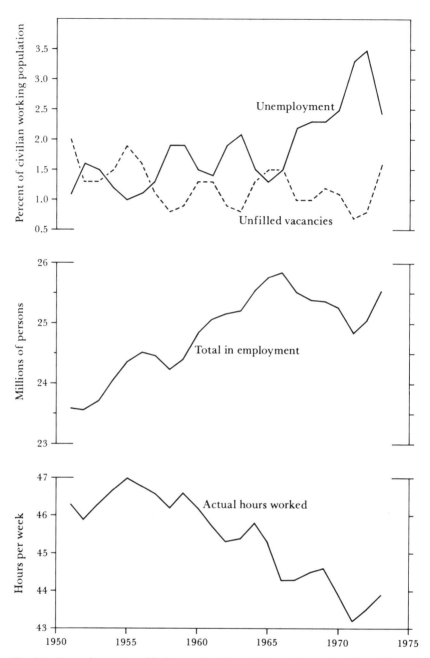

Fig. 3.4. Unemployment, unfilled vacancies, the total in employment, and actual hours worked by manual workers, 1951–1973. (*Source:* Basic statistics [Appendix N]; *Annual Abstract*, UK [10]; *Labour Statistics Year Book*, UK [39], *1973*; *British Labour Statistics Historical Abstract*, UK [48]; *Northern Ireland Digest of Statistics*, UK [62])

a continuation of that trend. As labor became scarcer, the costs of hiring and firing increased and the de facto period of engagement became longer. In this way the high *average* level of demand for labor in 1951–64 contributed to making the demand for labor *stable*. Within the period 1951–64 there was a mild but downward trend in the pressure of demand for labor, as measured by both unemployment and vacancies (Fig. 3.4). After the mid-1960's this trend became stronger, and employment also became less stable.

1965–73. It is more difficult to generalize about the demand for labor in this period than in 1951–64, partly because the cycle lost its regularity. The boom of 1968 was unusually feeble. The upswing of 1972–73, on the other hand, was a strong one. It was followed, outside the period of our concern, by the worst recession of the postwar period. There has been very extensive debate about the meaning of the steep rise in unemployment that accompanied these developments (see Worswick 1976). All we attempt to do here is to summarize the conclusions we draw from this debate, in the light of our findings on earlier periods.

The rise in unemployment was not matched by a comparable fall in vacancies. The CBI survey data indicate that in 1973–74 the labor market was for a short period even tighter than in earlier booms, though unemployment was still quite high. Hence it has been widely believed that the unemployment data changed their meaning, in particular that the unemployment they measure was really voluntary. On the other hand there is little in the unemployment data themselves to indicate a change in meaning: analysis by age, sex, duration, region, and so forth does not reveal any special points of difference from earlier years. The arguments for regarding the unemployment as voluntary could equally well be applied to the 1930's — as indeed they have been.

The explanation of events seems to lie chiefly in an increase in the output-elasticity of employment, together with an increase in the degree of mismatch in the labor market, and possibly a continuation of a trend weakening in the demand for labor relative to the supply.

It is not disputed that the demand for labor relative to the supply was weaker *on the average* in the years after 1966 than it was earlier;[42] the years 1973–74 were a flash in the pan. Even the vacancy data indicate this, and it is further attested by the endogenous elements in the decline in participation rates.

The increase in the output-elasticity of employment represented a reversion to more nearly the prewar pattern. The cyclical movements in employment in 1966–74 were almost as large as those in output. Moreover, cyclical movements in hours per worker were larger than in 1951–64 (Fig. 3.4). In recessions after 1964, employers, it has been said, increasingly reverted to holding their labor reserves "externally" in the form of unemployment and shorter-time working, rather than internally, in the form of underemployment (A. J. Brown 1976). In earlier periods (as argued above) a trend *strengthening* in the demand for labor led to a trend increase in the *stability* in the demand for labor. After 1966 this process went into reverse. The long period without a strong boom weakened confidence in future prospects. Increased cyclical instability of employment was thus both a consequence and a cause of the weaker demand for labor. At the same time the hoarding of labor was discouraged by an increase in its cost (see pp. 315, below); other reasons can also be cited.* One consequence was that a given amount of net excess supply of labor was associated with more registered unemployment than would otherwise have been the case, especially in recession phases. To this extent there *was* a change in the meaning of the unemployment data. A further consequence, which has been less often perceived, was that the number of vacancies tended to rise, especially in booms, insofar as employers had to look outside when they wanted to increase their labor force rather than merely reactivate the force they already had. So if the strong upward trend in the number of unemployed overstates the rise in the excess supply of labor, the roughly steady trend in vacancies understates it, and for much the same reason.

The greater cyclical sensitivity of employment goes a long way to ex-

*Notably the higher proportion of two-earner households, which made redundancies less traumatic, and higher social security benefits, which had the same effect. The new benefits are often cited as a cause of voluntary withdrawal from the labor force and hence as an explanation of high recorded unemployment generally. It is likely *a priori* that this should have happened to some degree, but it does not help to explain the long period from 1967 to 1971 when unemployment was high *and* vacancies also relatively low. Insofar as improved social security benefits and higher unemployment were related, there is also room for debate about the direction of the causation. Account of this is taken in Maki & Spindler 1975 and Cubbin & Foley 1977, but without a systematic modeling of the political processes involved. "The economic Ministers decided (in December 1965) that graduated unemployment benefits, plus redundancy payments were essential . . . to deal with (what was then not a remote possibility) mass unemployment" (Crossman 1975: 396). Laslett (1978) points out that the distribution of the unemployed by period out of work points to a shake-out in 1966 and concurs in the estimate of the Department of Employment that the maximum combined effect of the introduction of earnings-related supplement and redundancy grants was 0.35% ("Changed relationship between unemployment and vacancies," UK [40]).

plain the situation in 1973–74.* Employers in manufacturing, in particular, having reduced employment by some 7 percent between 1969 and 1972, naturally found when demand recovered in 1972–73 that they had a lot of vacancies and had difficulty in filling them all quickly. The unusually large structural changes that had taken place since the previous full-bodied boom and a less-close synchronization of fluctuations between industries (p. 296, below) probably also contributed to mismatches in the labor market, and hence to the coincidence of gross excess demand and gross excess supply at the peak.

Our conclusions on the years after 1965 may be summed up as follows. Up to the year 1974 the demand for labor remained strong by pre–World War II standards. It was on average less strong than earlier in the postwar period. This was largely because employers were less willing or able to hold on to their labor force through recessions, so that there was more unemployment relative to underemployment than before. As a consequence, when a strong recovery in demand did come, it was difficult to expand labor input quickly in the places where it was needed. Hence there was an acute shortage of labor in 1973 and 1974 even though unemployment was then twice as high as at former cyclical peaks.

International Comparisons

To what extent were the broad differences between periods in the degree of pressure on the labor market peculiar to the United Kingdom? This question is relevant in connection with the effect of demand pressure on the balance of payments, among other things, and so for the answer let us turn to some comparative international data (Table 3.23). It is important to note that the postwar figures in the table are the only ones that are adjusted so as to put all countries on the same basis.[43] Bearing this in mind, we can make the following observations.

---

*Part of the large movement in employment over the 1968–73 cycle, however, was due to the Selective Employment Tax (S.E.T.). This tax was put into effect in 1966, doubled in 1968, then halved in 1971, and finally abolished in 1973. Reflecting this, employment in the distributive trades and miscellaneous services fell from 1966 to 1971 and rose from 1971 to 1973, thus exhibiting a much larger movement than usual. The overall data for output and employment thus exaggerate to some extent the increase in the sensitivity of employment to the cycle as such. Not all of the apparent increase in the cyclical sensitivity of employment can be explained in this way, though, since the increase occurred also in manufacturing, which was not subject to S.E.T. and might therefore have been expected to be affected, if anything, in the opposite direction. In manufacturing the ratio of the cyclical amplitude of employment to the cyclical amplitude of output rose from 0.34 in 1951–64 to 0.63 in 1964–73.

TABLE 3.23

*Average Unemployment in the United Kingdom Compared with
Six Other Industrial Countries, 1874–1973*

(Percent of civilian labor force)

Country	Pre-1914[a]	1925–1929	1930–1937	1952–1964	1965–1973
United Kingdom	4.7%	8.4%	13.9%	2.5%[b]	3.2%[b]
United States	4.2	3.5	18.3	5.0	4.5
Sweden	—	11.2[c]	16.4[c]	1.7	2.0
France	—	—	—	1.7	2.4
Germany	3.6	11.1[c]	24.1[c]	2.7	0.8
Italy	—	—	—	5.9	3.4
Japan	—	—	5.0[d]	1.9	1.3

Source: Galenson & Zellner 1957: 455–56, Table 1; OECD [7]; Maddison 1964: Appendix E, especially Table E.1; U.S. 1960, 1979; *Monthly Labor Review*, May 1979; basic statistics (Appendix N).

[a] 1874–1913 for the UK, 1900–1913 for the U.S., 1903–13 for Germany.

[b] Figure differs from the official figure used elsewhere in this book because unemployment here is measured according to the concepts used in the U.S. These include many marginal categories of unemployed, such as students and housewives, who in UK statistics are not included in the labor force at all. An adjustment of this sort has not been made for earlier periods.

[c] These estimates are from Galenson & Zellner. The figures refer only to trade union members, among whom unemployment was probably greater than in the working population as a whole. Maddison has tried to estimate unemployment rates for the whole working population, but it would appear that he has underestimated unemployment among non-union members. His figures are *Sweden*, 1925–29, 2.6%, 1930–37, 5.7%; *Germany*, 1925–29, 4.9%, 1930–37, 9.7%.

[d] 1929–37.

(1) The average level of unemployment in the United Kingdom in the postwar period was rather above that in France, Germany (except in the period 1952–64), Japan, and Sweden, though lower than the level in Italy and the United States.

(2) In all countries for which historical data are available, unemployment was lower in the postwar period than in either the pre-1914 or the interwar period, with the conspicuous exception of the United States.

(3) Unemployment was high in the interwar period in all countries for which data are available. In all countries unemployment was higher in 1930–37 than in 1925–29; but in Germany and Sweden, as in the United Kingdom, unemployment in 1925–29 was already very high.

(4) The United Kingdom differed from most other countries in having an upward trend in unemployment within the postwar period. This trend is not only apparent in Table 3.23, but borne out by annual OECD data not here reproduced. In the 1960's, in particular, Germany, Italy, and the United States experienced falling unemployment, and in fact by the late 1960's average unemployment rates were much the same in Italy and the United States as in the United Kingdom; in

Germany they were lower. In North America, Germany, and Japan the rise in unemployment to historically high levels did not occur till 1974. Only in France, and to a lesser extent Sweden and the Netherlands, was the pattern broadly like the British one, with the rise beginning in the middle of the 1960's.

CHAPTER FOUR

Labor: Quality

The rate of growth of quality-adjusted labor input equals the rate of growth of man-hours plus the rate of improvement in labor quality. Estimates, albeit rough ones, can be devised for trends in some of the dimensions of labor quality, enumerated below.

THE AGE-SEX-NATIONALITY DISTRIBUTION OF THE LABOR INPUT

A steady small improvement in labor quality came from the reduction in the proportion of young people in the labor force. A reduction in Ireland's share in the UK labor force was a significant source of improvement before 1914. Changes in sex-composition were not important.

THE INTENSITY OF WORK

There is good reason to suppose that reductions in hours of work lead to increases in the intensity of work, at least up to a certain point, and that they do so to a particularly great extent if hours of work are initially very high. To disregard this offset to reductions in hours of work would be misleading, but the extent of the offset is largely guesswork. It is postulated that the offset was complete before 1914 and diminished thereafter till it was zero after World War II.

EDUCATION

The average years of formal schooling that had been received by the labor force rose by about 0.6–0.7 of a year per decade until 1931 and a little more slowly thereafter. Improvements in the standards of technical education, on the other hand, appear to have been rather more rapid after 1931 than before. Taking formal and technical education together, the overall improvement was at a fairly steady rate throughout the period.

LABOR INPUT: QUANTITATIVE AND QUALITATIVE SUMMARY

Qualitative improvement from the above sources, taken together, was on average a much larger source of increase in quality-adjusted labor input than the increase in man-hours (Table 4.7). Allowance for quality does not alter the conclusion that the rate of growth of labor input was much lower in the postwar period than in earlier peacetime periods.

LABOR ATTITUDES AND THE QUALITY OF ENTREPRENEURSHIP

These can be regarded either as aspects of labor quality or as aspects of general economic efficiency. The evidence on neither is quantifiable, but it does suggest certain tentative conclusions. There was a trend toward labor attitudes more favorable to productivity in the nineteenth century and in the interwar period, but this trend was interrupted between the 1890's and 1920 and with a few exceptions did not continue after World War II. The trend in the quality of entrepreneurship is broadly similar to the observed trend in the rate of growth of productivity, with signs of deterioration up to World War I and signs of improvement in the interwar and postwar periods.

The productivity—average or marginal—of a man-hour of labor is affected by the ability and effort of the labor concerned. The data on labor input, measured in man-hours, that were offered in the previous chapter must therefore be supplemented by measures of labor quality.

Labor quality has many dimensions. It has to be defined, moreover, in relation to prevailing circumstances. Thus, women workers may be potentially no less productive than men, but if conventions prevent women from using their talents to the full, then an extra female worker adds less to the effective labor force than an extra male worker.

In this chapter we shall offer rough measures of the effect on labor quality of the following:

(1) Age-sex-nationality composition of the labor force.

(2) Changes in intensity of work associated with changes in hours of work. Allowance for these has the effect of reducing the importance of the changes in hours of work described in the previous chapter. The appropriate size of the allowance is subject to a large margin of error.

(3) Education. This is the aspect of labor quality most familiar in the literature.

There are other aspects of labor quality that are clearly relevant in principle but have to be excluded because their effects are not measurable (e.g. changes in health due to changes in nutrition standards). The line between labor quality and the general efficiency of the economy is not a hard and fast one. If workers are alienated and uncooperative, is this to be called poor labor quality or is it to be called general inefficiency in the system? In the last section we review some of the evidence relating to the two major matters that come under this head, the attitudes of labor and the quality of entrepreneurship. No quantification of these is attempted, nor is account taken of them in the overall measures of labor quality used later in the book.

THE AGE-SEX-NATIONALITY DISTRIBUTION OF
THE LABOR INPUT

The most important long-term change in the age-sex distribution of the labor input in our period was the decline in the proportion of young persons in the labor force. Changes in sex composition were unimportant. In 1881 23 percent of the working population in Great Britain were under 20 years of age; the proportion fell to 19 percent in 1921, to 11 percent in 1951, and to 8 percent in 1973. The proportion of females in the working population was approximately the same in 1951 (30.8 percent) as in 1881 (30.5 percent), though it had fallen (to 29.3 percent in 1911) and risen again in the intervening years. In the postwar period, as we have seen, the large increase in the proportion of females in the labor force was at first neutralized in its impact on labor input growth by the move toward part-time work, but an increase (from 28.0 percent to 30.4 percent) occurred in females' contribution to measured labor input (i.e. total hours worked) between 1964 and 1973.

To convert information about the age-sex composition of the labor input into a measure of the average quality of labor associated with the age-sex distribution requires data on the marginal productivity of labor of each sex and age group. No direct estimates of marginal productivity exist, and so it is necessary to measure it indirectly. We do this by assuming that marginal productivity is proportional to average earnings; relative earnings for different age-sex groups therefore reflect relative marginal productivities.

An obvious objection to this procedure is that differences in age-sex specific earnings may result in part from factors other than differences in marginal productivity. In particular, there may be institutional factors that distort the structure of relative earnings. It may be argued, for example, that the apprenticeship system makes the earnings of young people fall below the average by more than the amount due to marginal productivity differences; and pay discrimination against women widens the gap between male and female earnings. Both these examples suggest that relative earnings may exaggerate the actual differences in marginal productivity between age-sex groups. No correction is made for this possible error, but its effects on the results are unlikely to be significant.[1]

The correct procedure would be to use the relative earnings of a particular period to weight the different age-sex groups in that period, but historical information on relative earnings is not available in sufficient detail to permit that. However, such data as we do have suggest that little change in the age-sex structure of relative earnings took place, apart from a slight tendency for the earnings of young people to catch up with adult earnings.[2] This provides a justification for the use in all periods a single set of relative earnings weights, which are based on median hourly earnings of all workers (manual and nonmanual in September 1968; Table 4.1).[3]

Data limitations also introduce errors into the measures of the age-sex structure of the labor input. For years up to 1951 the total number of man-hours worked cannot be broken down by age-sex group. For 1951 and 1964 separate estimates for males and females are available, but we have not attempted to break down the within-sex totals into age groups.[4] For 1881–1951 and for age-groups in 1951–64, the estimation of the change in quality of labor is therefore based on the working population and not on man-hours worked (in addition, the figures relate to Great Britain only). This approximation will in general result in an error if the change in the average number of hours worked per year over a period was significantly different for different age-sex groups. In general it is unlikely that this occurred, though the shift in

TABLE 4.1

Earnings of Males and Females by Age Group as a Percentage of Earnings of Males 21 and Over, September 1968

Age	Males	Females
15–19	46%	41%
20–24	85	63
25–44	106	66
45–64	98	61
65 and over	78	55

Source: *New Earnings Survey*, UK [47], *1968*: Table 40B, and estimates.

recent periods toward more part-time working by females and elderly persons does imply that we have overestimated the extent to which lower-paid age-sex groups were becoming important. The correction of this error would therefore lead to a higher estimate of the increase in age and sex quality, especially in the trans–World War II period, when the move toward female part-time working was fairly pronounced.[5]

We can now consider the estimated changes in the quality of the labor input resulting from changes in age-sex composition, bearing in mind these statistical reservations.

Age-Sex Changes

As noted earlier, the most important long-term change in the age-sex distribution of the labor input was the decline in the proportion of young people in the labor force. Since their earnings are relatively low, this implies a secular improvement in measured age quality. The growth rates (in Table 4.2, column 1) of quality resulting from changes in age composition reflect this trend, though other less important changes in age composition also played a role.

TABLE 4.2

Growth in Labor Quality Resulting from Changes in
Age-Sex Composition, 1881–1973

(Annual percentage growth rates)

Period	Age[a] (1)	Sex (2)	Age & sex (3)
1881–1911	0.1%	0.0%	0.1%
1911–1921	0.0	0.0	0.0
1921–1931	0.1	0.0	0.1
1931–1951	0.2	0.0	0.2
1951–1964	0.0	0.0	0.0
1964–1973	0.2	−0.1	0.1

Source: Tables 4.1, C.2; Chapter 3, note 31.

Note: The total age-sex-quality measure is (except in 1951–73)

$$\sum_i w_i n_i / \sum_i n_i$$

where w_i is relative earnings in age-sex group i, and n_i is the labor input in age-sex group i. The age-quality measure is the weighted average of the age-quality measure for each sex calculated according to the same formula (but with the summation only over all age groups for the particular sex); the weights are the shares of the sexes in total labor input in a base year (1911 for 1881–1921 quality indexes, and 1951 for 1921–73). The sex-quality measure is (except in 1951–73) the ratio of the total age- and sex-quality measure to the age-quality measure.

Relative earnings (the w_i) are as in Table 4.1. The labor input (n_i) refers to the working population in 1881–1951; in 1951–73 the age-quality measure is also based on the working population but the sex-quality index is estimated separately from total man-hours data. The total age- and sex-quality measure in 1951–73 is the product of the age- and sex-quality measures.

[a] 6 age groups were employed for the 1881–1921 indexes, corresponding to those in Table 4.1 and the under-15 group. For the 1921–73 estimates an additional three were created by splitting the 15–19, 25–44, and 45–64 groups into 15–17 and 18–19, 25–34 and 35–44, and 45–54 and 55–64 groups.

Though the improvement in age quality was fairly steady, it was never great, averaging 0.1 percent per year. It was most marked in 1931–51 and 1964–73. On both occasions there was a substantial drop in the proportion of young people in the labor force, brought about by the prolongation of education and, in 1931–51, by a fall in the proportion of the young in the population as a whole.

These changes, though small, must nevertheless be regarded as genuine offsets to the reduction in the growth of the labor force brought about by increases in the duration of education. The effect of those increases is exaggerated if account is not taken of the fact that the workers taken out of the labor force by education had below-average productivity, as measured by their wages.

Over the whole period, and within each of the periods distinguished in Table 4.2 except 1964–73, the change in sex quality never amounted in absolute terms to as much as 0.05 percent per year.

Nationality Changes

This heading refers to an adjustment for Ireland. The calculation here is much rougher than for age and sex, but the direction of the effect is clear. Ireland accounted for 21 percent of the population of the United Kingdom in 1856 and only 9 percent in 1913. This diminution may be regarded as a source of "quality improvement" in the labor force, inasmuch as the average product of labor was lower in Ireland than in Great Britain. Essentially the same point arose earlier when it was noted that GDP per head grew somewhat faster in the United Kingdom than in Great Britain and Northern Ireland (Table 2.1).

This effect could be treated not as an improvement in the quality of the labor force, but simply as a form of productivity increase (mainly associated with a structural shift away from agriculture). However, since it was a source of productivity gain no longer available after the separation of the 26 counties from the United Kingdom in 1922, it is useful in comparing the rate of growth of the labor force and productivity before and after the territorial change to know what difference it made.

The magnitude of the effect cannot be estimated with any precision. Output per man in Ireland can be estimated at a little over a half of output per man in Britain. The difference between the two countries in labor income per head was probably less than this.[6] However, the ratio of marginal to average product of labor was undoubtedly lower in Ireland than in Great Britain, both because Ireland was more over-populated and because peasant proprietors were more numerous relative to hired laborers in Irish agriculture than in British agriculture. We have therefore weighted a unit of Irish labor as equal to 0.5 of a unit of British labor — rather lower than the ratio of average products. These assumptions yield a contribution of 0.2 in both 1856–73 and 1873–1913 to the annual percentage increase in the quality of the UK labor force. The labor force in Ireland declined more rapidly in 1873–1913 than in 1856–73, but this was offset by the smaller weight that Ireland had in the United Kingdom in the second period. The weight was, of course, very much smaller by 1913, so that the effect does not show at the first decimal place in later periods.[7]

THE INTENSITY OF WORK

This section is concerned only with those changes in the intensity of work that are associated with changes in average hours worked per year. Changes in intensity caused by other factors, such as improved nutrition and improved working conditions, are not considered.

It is often argued that major reductions in average hours of work do not result in equivalent reductions in the effective labor input, because the intensity of work increases. In the case of reductions in the average weekly hours of full-time workers, there will be less fatigue and hence greater intensity of work, implying fewer mistakes, better quality, and higher output per man-hour. Moreover, the compression of a given amount of work into a shorter time may in itself increase the intensity of work. In many occupations, especially of the personal service type (e.g. shop assistants, switchboard operators), work is not continous and more can be fitted into an hour if there is a demand for it. Thus if a shop is open for a reduced number of hours per week, it may maintain the same turnover with the same staff, whose intensity of work has therefore increased. Reductions in the number of weeks worked per year will similarly lead to increased intensity of work. If the fall in weeks worked is because of longer holidays, then again one would ex-pect less fatigue — mental perhaps as much as physical fatigue — to be the chief factor. If it is the result of more time being taken off because of sickness, then, as was argued in Chapter 3 (p. 76), output per man-hour will increase. Finally, reductions in hours may induce employers to seek more efficient methods of working. In principle this should be regarded as an improvement in organizational efficiency rather than an improvement in the quality of the labor force. In practice, however, it is difficult to separate the two, and induced improvements in organiza-tion no doubt account in part for the empirical findings of industrial psychologists about the effects of hours on productivity.

The most appropriate way within our analytical framework to handle increases in the intensity of work, and hence in output per manhour, resulting from changes in average hours worked per year, is to view them as improvements in the quality of labor. If the labor input were measured in such a way as to take account of its quality as well as its quantity (in man-hours), reductions in average hours of work per year would lower the total quantity of man-hours, but raise the quality of labor because of increased intensity. The ratio of the increase in quality to the decrease in quantity has been called the productivity offset or the efficiency offset of the reduction in hours (see, e.g., Denison 1967: 60). The offset can range from zero, when no increase in intensity occurs and the quantitative measure of total man-hours is the correct one, to unity, when intensity rises to exactly compensate for the reduction in average hours, and output is maintained at the old level.[8] In this section we wish to measure this efficiency offset, and hence the increase in the quality of labor resulting from increased intensity.*

It is exceptionally difficult in practice to make any quantitative statement regarding improvements in the quality of labor resulting from increased intensity. This is partly because the changeover to a shorter week has usually been the opportunity — or the motivation — for the introduction of other changes in organization or equipment, and partly because, as is invariably the case, other conditions change at the same time, and it is impossible to isolate the effects of the reduced hours. To simplify the problem, we confine our attention to the four periods when major reductions in average hours occurred: 1856–73, 1913–24, 1937–51, and 1951–73. The same efficiency offset is assumed to apply to all reductions in hours, whatever their causes (reduction in full-time weekly hours, increase in holidays, increase in sickness, etc.). The task is then to estimate efficiency offset factors to apply to the rate of decline of average hours worked per year (Table 3.10, column 3).

In the nineteenth century, when the hours of work were long, the case for a shorter working week was often made on the grounds that it would not lead to any fall in output.[9] Moreover, studies of industrial fatigue and efficiency, especially the ones on munitions workers stimulated by the two world wars suggest that when the number of hours of work is *increased*, a critical level is reached beyond which output does not rise.[10] However, there is not much agreement about what this level

---

*One possible consequence of a reduction in average hours of work, namely a reduction in absenteeism, should not be included in this measure of the increase in the quality of labor. It is in principle already taken into account in the measure of total man-hours, since the estimates of average hours worked per week exclude the hours missed through absenteeism.

TABLE 4.3

Growth in Labor Quality Resulting from Changes in the
Intensity of Work, 1856–1973

Period	Reduction in average annual hours[a] (annual percentage growth rates)	Efficiency offset[b] (percent)	Growth in labor quality[c] (annual percentage growth rates)
1856–1873	0.9%	100%	0.9%
1913–1924	1.9	70	1.4
1937–1951	0.7	30	0.2
1951–1973	0.9	0	0.0

Source: Table 3.10 and estimates in the text.
[a]The difference between the annual percentage growth rates of total hours worked and the total in employment.
[b]The ratio of the increase in labor quality to the decrease in labor quantity.
[c]The product of columns 1 and 2 divided by 100.

is. Some writers suggest 48 hours per week (e.g. Florence 1924; Reynolds 1954: 255–56; Denison 1962); others prefer a higher figure (e.g. Verdoorn, as cited by Hartog 1956). Nor are the conclusions drawn by different writers about the extent to which the efficiency offset is lower at lower levels of average hours at all uniform. Thus Godley and Shepherd (1964) put the UK offset in the early postwar period at a third; yet, in other studies, values of between 20 percent and 100 percent have been assumed for various industrial counties in which the average hours worked were not markedly different from those in the United Kingdom.[11] In the light of these remarks, any assumptions that are adopted here for the United Kingdom can only indicate the broad orders of magnitude involved. The relevant figures for the four periods when major reductions in average hours occurred are shown in Table 4.3. The efficiency offset is assumed to fall from 100 percent in 1856–73 to zero in the postwar period. It is assumed to be 70 percent in 1913–24 and 30 percent in 1937–51.* At equivalent levels of average hours worked, it is lower than Denison's and Reynolds' assumed efficiency offsets, but not very different from Verdoorn's, except in the postwar period.

We have not thought it necessary to make any (negative) efficiency offset for the small *increase* in hours in the interwar period, an increase due largely to the unusually large amount of short-time working in 1924 (Table 3.14), since eliminating short-time working would not necessarily have effects of the kind that the efficiency offset is designed

---

*The assumption of 100% offset in 1856–73 implies that employers had previously been irrational or ill-informed in insisting on longer hours. We do not regard this as an objection to the assumption.

to measure. (It is possible that our estimate of the efficiency offset to the decline in hours between 1913 and 1924 is slightly too high for the same reason.)

Applying these assumed efficiency offsets to the growth rates of average hours worked per year, yields the growth in labor quality resulting from changes in the intensity of work (Table 4.3, column 3). Growth in quality was rapid in 1856–73 and 1913–24, slow in 1937–51, and nonexistent in 1951–73. This reflects the larger efficiency offsets assumed for pre-1924 reductions in average hours and also the fact that the trans–World War I decline in average hours was particularly steep. The arbitrary nature of these calculations must be emphasized; they can do no more than indicate general orders of magnitude. One broad conclusion, however, would probably survive the adoption of any alternative reasonable assumption (e.g. of an offset of 0.2 or 0.3 in the postwar period), namely that there was a considerable improvement in quality in the two periods 1856–73 and 1913–24, and only a small or negligible improvement after 1937.

EDUCATION

The educational qualifications of the labor force will be considered under three headings: total formal education, university education, and technical education.

The Amount of Formal Education Received

The educational standard of the labor force in a given year depends, not on the standard of schooling given to children in that year, but on the average standard of schooling received in their day by all those currently in the labor force. It is thus affected by the standards of education over a long past period, going back more than 50 years. In Figure 4.1 we show, first, the average number of years' formal schooling (AYS) estimated to have been received by age-cohorts born at different dates between 1801 and 1939 and, second, the AYS of the whole labor force at census years between 1871 and 1961.[12] The second set of figures is derived by multiplying each cohort's AYS by the proportion of that cohort in the labor force, and summing for all cohorts. The details of the estimates are discussed in Appendix E. The number of years of schooling has been adjusted for incomplete attendance, but not for the number of schooldays per year.*

*Except for Sunday schools, which were an important element in the educational system during much of the 19th century and have therefore been taken account of separately in the calculations.

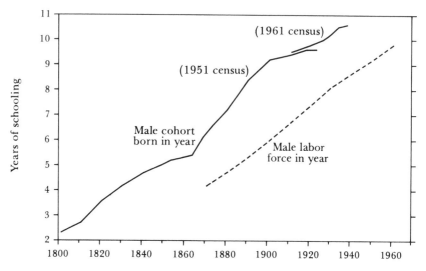

Fig. 4.1. Average number of years schooling of males by birth cohort and representation in the labor force, 1801–1961. (*Source:* Tables E.1 and E.2)

The curve showing the AYS of successive cohorts increases continuously, but not smoothly, over time. The rate of improvement appears to have been rapid in the early nineteenth century but was tending to tail off until it was sharply revived with the institution of the School Board system and compulsory education in the 1870's. The renewed slowing down for cohorts born after 1900 reflects mainly the fact that attendance rates had by then become nearly complete, improved attendance rates having made a substantial contribution to the overall increase in the preceding two decades. The AYS of cohorts born after 1900 went on increasing at much the same (relatively slow) rate, until a renewed acceleration appears as we reach the cohorts affected by the 1944 Education Act.

These fluctuations in the cohort curve are interesting, but they turn out to have relatively little effect on the rate of growth of the AYS of the total labor force. The process of averaging over all cohorts damps them out and leaves a nearly smoothly rising curve after 1881 (the rise was probably rather slower before that). The AYS of the labor force increases by around 0.6 or 0.7 of a year per decade from 1881 to 1931 and at a slightly lower rate—between 0.5 and 0.6 of a year per decade—between 1931 and 1961.

The customary way of deriving from such data an index of quality-adjusted labor force is to infer the marginal productivity of schooling from cross-section data on earnings of workers with differing educational attainments. Leaving aside the general issues about the validity of this type of inference,[13] the data needed to do it over any substantial length of time are not available.[14] We may, however, illustrate the orders of magnitude involved on customary assumptions. The "European weights" used by Denison (1967: 85) show in increase in earnings[15] by an average of about 8 percent for each year of schooling completed in excess of eight, and a smaller rate of increase, about 5 percent, for each extra year of schooling below the number of eight. If we take 6 percent as the relevant figure for the United Kingdom, we find that the increase in AYS served to raise the quality-adjusted labor force at a rate of between 0.3 percent and 0.4 percent a year averaged over the period 1871–1973.[16] Using an alternative figure for the 6 percent would proportionately alter the results.

An increase in AYS can come about either from an increase in the compulsory minimum leaving age or from an increase in the proportion of students staying at school beyond that age. The effects of the two on the dispersion around the mean AYS are quite different, and the effects on productivity are likely to be different also. We have not made a systematic breakdown in these terms of the sources of the increase in the AYS; but it is clear that the contribution made by increased voluntary schooling is much the smaller component. This is notwithstanding the fact that the proportion of children staying beyond the minimum leaving age began to increase very rapidly after World War II,[17] and moreover that these cohorts are now becoming a larger and larger proportion of the labor force. For this reason it may be conjectured that the 6 percent figure, derived from cross-section data, for the increase in earnings attributable to one year's extra schooling errs on the high side when applied to British time-series data. In a cross-section, those with above average schooling are relatively scarce, and the earning differential in their favor reflects this. But when there is an increase in the minimum leaving age, the skills acquired through the additional year's schooling cease to be scarce in that generation. An estimate of their marginal productivity based on a situation in which they are scarce will therefore tend to be too high. In addition, it is reasonable to suppose that children who voluntarily stay in school beyond the compulsory period benefit from the additional schooling more, on average, than do those who stay longer only because they are obliged to by an increase in the compulsory minimum leaving age.

University Education

The effect of university education on the AYS of the labor force in the past has been almost negligible, because of the very small proportion of

108 GROWTH IN THE ECONOMY AS A WHOLE

TABLE 4.4
Proportion of University Graduates in Male Birth Cohorts
and Labor Force, 1886–1971

Proportion of male birth cohort attaining degree		Proportion of graduates in male labor force	
Birth year	Percent	Year	Percent
1886 or before	0.9%	1931	0.7%
1887–1896	0.8	1951	1.4
1897–1906	1.2	1961	1.9
1907–1916	2.2	1971	3.6
1917–1931	2.7		
1932–1941	4.4		
1942–1951	6.9		

Source: Appendix E.

the population involved. But income differentials in favor of graduates have commonly been found to be particularly large, and it is often held that the importance of their numbers is not accurately reflected in the effect of university education on AYS. Figures relating to graduates have therefore been calculated separately and are shown in Table 4.4 (the details of the calculation are given in Appendix E). Though a lack of data on older cohorts makes it impossible to calculate the proportion of graduates in the labor force before 1931, it is evident that the big change came after that. Since the contribution to earnings of a year's extra schooling is greatest at the university level,[18] this will have served to offset to some degree the slight slowing down after 1931 in the rate of increase of overall AYS noted below.[19] The proportion of graduates in the labor force in 1961 and 1971 was much lower than the proportion of new graduates in those years to their age cohorts. So a major further increase in the proportion of graduates in the labor force is bound to take place in the future, unless in the decades after 1971 there is a drastic decline in the number of those graduating as a proportion of their age cohorts.

Technical Education

Technical training in its various forms is directly and deliberately aimed at increasing productivity in a way that formal school education is not. But it is inherently almost impossible to measure the contribution of on-the-job training, especially where comparisons over time are concerned. This is a more serious deficiency in AYS as a measure of educational quality in Britain than it is in some other countries, because technical education has traditionally been given largely, and in some cases exclusively, on a part-time basis after leaving school. This is true not only of the training of craftsmen and technicians, but also of the training of some classes of professionals or semiprofessionals (e.g. engineers, accountants, surveyors, and ancillary medical staff). The system of technical education in Britain is extremely complicated, with a wide variety of types and places of training and types of qualification, and it is impossible to derive summary measures from published data.[20]

The chief means of training for skilled manual workers is and has always been the apprentice system. This system has often been criticized for failing to provide a guarantee of proper training, for serving as a cloak for restrictions on entry, and for creating rigidities in the labor force. But it is the system under which, for better or worse, most training has been given. The apprentice receives practical instruction on the job, which may be supplemented by more formal instruction in evening classes, by day-release, or in a firm's own apprentice school. In the postwar period the proportion of male school-leavers aged 15–17 entering apprenticeships was about 35 percent, without much trend.[21] Data are not available for the prewar years, but the proportion then is believed to have been considerably lower — below 20 percent (Liepmann 1960).

In the absence of long-run data on apprenticeship and other forms of training for manual workers, the results may be inferred from the numbers of skilled workers. The absolute number of skilled manual workers was practically unchanged at each census year from 1911 to 1951; from 1951 to 1961 the number increased by about 2 percent, a considerably slower rate than for the labor force as a whole, and between 1961 and 1971 it fell by 11 percent. The ratio of skilled manual workers to total labor force therefore fell steadily, the fall being particularly rapid in the postwar period, as shown in Table 4.5. This has to be viewed in conjunction with the general decline in the proportion of manual workers in the labor force. But from 1911 to 1931 the ratio of skilled to total manual also fell. It rose from 1931 to 1961, then fell again, returning by 1971 to just about the same level as in 1931.*

Routh has constructed an index of the average amount of post-school training (including university and other full-time training) embodied

---

*The rise during World War II was due partly to the admission of "dilutees" (unapprenticed men) to jobs ranked as skilled. The shortage of skilled workers in the postwar period led to the retention of dilutees in these jobs. An increase in the effective supply of skilled labor from this source contributed to the growth of productivity by relaxing a restrictive practice relating to the classes of worker to whom on-the-job training was available.

TABLE 4.5

Proportion of Skilled Manual and Total Manual Workers in the
Labor Forces of Great Britain, 1911–1951, and the
United Kingdom, 1951–1971

(Percent)

Year	Total manual	Skilled manual	Ratio of skilled to total manual
1911	79.7%	30.6%	38.3%
1921	76.9	28.8	37.3
1931	76.5	26.7	34.9
1951	69.6	25.0	35.9
1951	71.1	26.3	37.0
1961	65.9	24.9	37.9
1971	59.9	21.8	36.2

Source: Routh 1965; *Changes in the Occupational Distribution of the Labour Force in Great Britain*, UK [42]; *Occupational Changes, 1951–61*, UK [65].
Note: The break in the series at 1951 is partly because of changed definitions and partly because of geographical coverage (the estimates for the first 4 rows relate to Great Britain, those for the last 3 to the UK). There was also a break in the underlying series in 1961, but it has been removed by rough splicing.

in the labor force on the basis of occupational distribution.[22] This shows no significant change in the period between 1911 and 1931, when the adverse effects of a decline in the proportion of skilled manual workers were just balanced by an increase in the proportion of nonmanual workers (credited with more training time). From 1931 to 1951 the training time increased from 1.60 years per worker to 1.77 years, because unskilled and semiskilled manual workers declined in numbers faster than skilled workers, and there was a correspondingly faster increase in the number of nonmanual workers. Increases of about the same absolute amount for the index emerge from the application of Routh's method to the periods 1951–61 and 1961–71.[23]

Whether the reasons for these trends lie mainly on the demand side or on the supply side, it is apparent that technical training did not make steady progress over the years. Within the manual class, in fact, there was actually retrogression between 1911 and 1931, between 1961 and 1971, and over the period 1911–71 as a whole.

This leaves out of account the quality of the training given. This has no doubt been subject to some trend improvement, but it appears that progress was considerably more rapid after World War II than before. Extensive improvements in the provision of technical training of a more systematic kind than is provided by apprenticeship as such were brought about after the war by the action of government, and by employers, employers' associations, and trade unions. This is reflected in an extremely fast increase in the number of workers acquiring formal technical qualifications, and though this was partly because the scope of these qualifications increased and more store came to be set on acquiring them, it must also indicate to a considerable extent an improvement in standards.[24]

We may sum up on technical education as follows. Quantitative information is lacking for years earlier than 1911. From then until 1931 it is doubtful whether there was much increase in the amount of technical training embodied in the labor force, though there was no doubt some improvement in its quality. In the postwar period both the quantity and the quality increased a good deal more rapidly, though the increase in quantity did not apply to manual workers. The improvements affected mainly new entrants to the labor force, and their effect on the average standard of the labor force was smaller, but significant.

To indicate the broad orders of magnitude involved, the improvement in the quality of the labor force resulting from technical education is estimated at a rate of 0.2 percent a year during World War II and the postwar period, and at an annual rate of 0.1 percent in earlier periods.[25]

Conclusions

Table 4.6 shows our estimates of how education, in all its forms, improved the quality of the labor force.[26] These estimates are very rough, and it would not be surprising if they were subject to errors of 50 percent or more. As far as formal education is concerned, the error is

TABLE 4.6
Growth in Labor Quality Resulting from Improvements in Education, 1856–1973
(Annual percentage growth rates)

Period	Growth	Period	Growth
Peacetime phases:		Wartime phases:	
1856–1873	0.3%	1913–1924	0.5%
1873–1913	0.5	1937–1951	0.6
1924–1937	0.5		
1951–1964	0.6	1856–1973	0.5%
1964–1973	0.5		

Source: Calculated as follows from estimates in the text:

Period	Formal education	University education	Technical education
1856–1873	0.2%	0.0	0.1%
1873–1937	0.4	0.0	0.1
1937–1964	0.4	<0.05	0.2
1964–1973	0.3	<0.05	0.2

most likely to be on the side of overestimation, because of the bias resulting from the use of cross-section data on income differentials. Comparisons between periods are subject to a smaller margin of error, and we can therefore conclude that the contribution to growth made by improvements in educational standards did not differ greatly between periods.

LABOR INPUT: QUANTITATIVE AND QUALITATIVE SUMMARY

The growth in the quality of the labor input resulting from the three sources studied in this section is summarized in Table 4.7. We must once again draw attention to the unsatisfactory nature of these measures, and urge the reader to take to heart the many qualifications attached to the estimates when they were introduced.[27] Further, we have attempted to measure only three of the many possible sources of quality improvement (and in the case of one of those sources, the intensity of work, only changes relating from one particular cause, namely changes in the number of hours worked per week). Though these are perhaps the most important sources, it is likely that over the whole period under review there were significant unmeasured changes in the intensity of work resulting from, for example, improvements in nutrition, improvements in the working environment (e.g. quieter machines, heated and air-conditioned factories and offices), and, with the opposite effect, a fall in the proportion of self-employed in the labor force.[28]

Subject to these qualifications, the conclusions that emerge are the following.

(1) Over the period 1856–1973 as a whole the improvement in quality, as here measured, was at a substantially greater rate than the increase in quantity (man-hours). It accounted for most of the increase in quality-adjusted man-hours.

(2) The most important source of the improvement in quality was education. On the assumptions here made, education alone contributed more to the growth of quality-adjusted man-hours than did the increase in man-hours. It contributed practically nothing, however, to differences between periods in the rate of the improvement of quality.

(3) Changes in the intensity of work resulting from changes in the hours of work were the main source of differences between periods in the rate of the improvement of quality. This reflects the discontinuous process by which hours of work were reduced. The periods chiefly affected were 1856–73 and 1913–24. Peacetime periods other than 1856–73 were not affected. Allowance for this factor naturally dimin-

TABLE 4.7

Growth in the Quality of the Labor Input, 1856–1973

(Annual percentage growth rates)

Period	Growth in quality associated with: Age, sex, nation-ality	Intensity of work	Educa-tion	All identified sources	Growth in man-hours	Growth in man-hours ad-justed for quality
Peacetime phases:						
1856–1873	0.2%	0.9%	0.3%	1.4%	0.0%	1.4%
1873–1913	0.3	0.0	0.5	0.8	0.9	1.7
1924–1937	0.1	0.0	0.5	0.6	1.5	2.1
1951–1964	0.0	0.0	0.6	0.6	0.0	0.6
1964–1973	0.1	0.0	0.5	0.6	-1.1	-0.5
Wartime phases:						
1913–1924	0.0	1.4	0.5	1.9	-2.3	-0.4
1937–1951	0.2	0.2	0.6	1.0	0.1	1.1
1856–1973	0.2%	0.3%	0.5%	1.0%	0.2%	1.2%

Source: Tables 3.10, 4.2, 4.3, 4.6, and text, p. 102.

ishes the effects of changes in hours on labor input, and brings the pattern of movements of quality-adjusted labor input to somewhere between that of man-years and that of man-hours.

(4) The effects of changes in the age-sex distribution of the labor force were positive but small. They were highest in 1937–51. They were due chiefly to reductions in the proportion of juveniles in the labor force.

LABOR ATTITUDES AND THE QUALITY OF ENTREPRENEURSHIP

We turn finally to two important matters that do not lend themselves to quantitative measurement and on which we confine ourselves to the review of the work of others.

Labor Attitudes and Restrictive Practices

Labor attitudes may affect the quality of labor input and productivity through the presence (or absence) of overtly restrictive practices: demarcation barriers, restrictions on entry to an occupation, resistance to technical innovation, overmanning requirements, and so on. They may also have more general and diffused effects, through a greater or lesser degree of cooperation, effort, and initiative on the part of labor. The effects may be on the level of productivity or else, insofar as they obstruct change, on its rate of growth.

Neither labor attitudes nor specific restrictive practices are easily measured, and we cannot hope for anything like a simple statistical indicator measuring trends over time. But some picture can be had from the qualitative literature.[29]

Already in the nineteenth century British workers were thought to be more restrictive in their attitudes and more resistant to change than workers abroad, especially in America and Germany (Marshall 1919: 136–37; Phelps-Brown & Browne 1968: 186–88). One contributing cause may have been the craft tradition, embodied in craft unions, and reflecting the *gradual* historical evolution from workshop to factory in Britain, in contrast to the more sudden arrival of modern manufacturing in countries that were later starters industrially. There was apparently some improvement in the course of the nineteenth century, principally in the form of less resistance to improved machinery once an industry had passed its first phase of mechanization (Webb & Webb 1902; Marshall 1919: 213). However, in the period from the 1890's to 1914 and again in 1919–20 the climate of industrial relations deteriorated and the prevalence of restrictive practices increased in certain industries. In the interwar period the general tendency was toward a diminution of restrictive practices; contemporaries regarded this as a long-run trend.[30] During World War II, also, a number of restrictive practices were dropped and were not resumed (Zweig 1951: 21).

When we come to the post–World War II period, the literature no longer conveys an impression of continuing general improvement. In the 1950's and early 1960's the combination of unexpectedly fast-rising real wages, full employment, and political consensus may admittedly have produced a more cooperative attitude toward innovation in some parts of the labor force. Improvements are thought to have taken place in some industries, for example in agriculture, where more cordial relations between farmers and laborers were brought about by the reduction in the number of laborers per farm. On the other hand, with the rapid spread of trade unionism, restrictive practices were noted in some sectors where they had never existed before. Restrictions on the efficient use of labor continued to be regarded as a major source of low productivity and of the gap (possibly increasing) between the manpower requirements on identical equipment in British industry and in industry abroad. It is arguable, too, that the shortage of skilled labor, often a bottleneck at postwar cyclical peaks, was partly due to labor's resistance to a reorganization of work methods or a change in standards of recruitment that would have eased the bottleneck.

The general picture suggested is thus one of some trend improvement, interrupted or reversed between the 1890's and 1920, and not continued in the postwar period. If this is correct, the effect was to depress further, relative to other periods, the low (in fact negative) growth rates of effective labor input across World War I and in the postwar period.

Impressionistic evidence of the kind we have referred to is inevitably extremely unreliable, even in relation to a single industry, and it does not take proper account of the effects of changes in industrial structure. Moreover, since technical change was more rapid in the postwar period than in earlier times, more *manifestations* of resistance to change would be expected, even if the propensity to resist change remained unaltered.

The Quality of Entrepreneurship

The quality of entrepreneurship is usually classified as part of the "residual" element in the sources of growth, rather than as an element in the quality of labor input. However, some of the considerations that have been raised in the literature are related to those already discussed, and it is convenient to refer to them briefly here.

For almost (not quite) as long as the deficiencies of British workers have been complained of, so have those of British entrepreneurs and managers: their inferiority in motivation to Americans, in training to Germans, and in recruitment to both. Apart from chronic deficiencies, it has generally been held that matters got worse in the late nineteenth century and better in the postwar period, with more doubt about the direction of change in the interwar period. This belief has been prompted partly by the observation of trends in the economy at large[31] and partly by direct evidence on motivation, training, and recruitment.[32]

Not all that has been said about late-nineteenth-century deterioration stands up to examiniation.* But a good deal of it has the ring of truth.

(1) In established industries the age distribution of the trees in the Marshallian forest was unfavorably affected by the combination of rapid earlier growth, independently originating sources of slowdown, and obstacles to new entry created by increased scale. There was a hiatus in the transition from the original entrepreneurial firm to the meritocratic one. During this hiatus firms were controlled by descend-

---

*There is no evidence that the social prestige of business *declined* during the 19th century, or that the sons of business men were *increasingly* deflected to the life-style of the landed gentry, nor is it clear that the traditional professions absorbed an *increasing* proportion of the labor force.

ants of the founder who lacked his ambition to make good and who regressed to the mean in talent. The decline in entrepreneurial energy and the increase in risk-aversion were expressed and reinforced by the marked growth of cartels and restrictive practices toward the end of the nineteenth century (and were perhaps also symbolized by the rapid development of the insurance industry at that time). The growth of monopolistic practices in turn in some cases restricted the entry or growth of new firms.

(2) The Empire opened up increasing employment opportunities, commercial as well as governmental, to the educated classes and was a drain on resources. Less often emphasized, but perhaps equally important, a rapidly expanding demand for clerks and schoolteachers brought new employment opportunities to the lower-middle classes, the source that had supplied most of the first-generation entrepreneurs. The diversion of talent away from business into public and professional service at home and in the Empire raises the same question as capital export. A shortage of engineers, like a shortage of finance, was not much complained of before World War I. Engineers trained in Scotland, where educational arrangements were different, found employment all over the world, not just in Britain. On the other hand, in at least some of the more promising fields, like retailing and newspapers, new entrepreneurs did not fail to come forward. This suggests that much of the trouble came from demand. Were people pulled away from business by attractions elsewhere, or were they pushed away because business openings did not expand enough to absorb the increased supply of educated manpower? As with capital export, it was probably a bit of both.

(3) Ever since the seventeenth century the ambitious Englishman had aspired to the status of gentleman (a status historically connected with position in the state) as much as to financial success. This was reflected in the educational system. An increase in middle-class incomes led in the nineteenth century to the rapid growth of the public school system, which was not geared to preparation for business (let alone industry), and which, in addition, had certain peculiarities of its own traceable to its clerical origins and to its internal evolution. This kind of education was not necessarily worse than what had been available before, but its neglect of engineering and chemistry, and professionalism in general, mattered more as technology became more sophisticated and affected not only entrepreneurs themselves but also the kind of person they were predisposed to employ. Likewise the anti-commercial aversion to salesmanship mattered more as world compe-

tition increased. The expansion of education at the upper end (not quantitatively important in the AYS measure, however) had thus a substantial "screening" element. At the same time, the predominance of apprenticeship in the training not only of craftsmen but also of the growing numbers of professionals in business (engineers and accountants) produced a conservative bias a little lower down in the social scale, which likewise mattered more as the tempo of change increased.

The attitudes and institutions affecting the supply and quality of entrepreneurship in the Edwardian age outlived the circumstances of their origin. But they did gradually change, assisted by the jolts administered by the two wars. In the interwar period an increasing number of ex-public-schoolboys (and university graduates) went into business (especially finance, but also industry). This was not necessarily an unmixed blessing in itself. But public school education itself was also becoming less narrow. At the same time, state secondary education was made available in 1902, affording a new ladder, and the influx of refugees in the 1930's added an additional source of entrepreneurial talent. After World War II the whole system opened up considerably. Recruitment became more broadly based, and in most respects education became more relevant to economic needs. For all that, however, complaints about the old weaknesses did not cease to be heard.

CHAPTER FIVE

Capital

DEFINITION AND MEASUREMENT

The central concept of the capital stock (K) here used is domestic reproducible capital at constant prices. For certain purposes attention is confined to fixed capital. Both gross and net measures are used; the net measures give more weight to the more modern parts of K. Total real assets are defined as K + net overseas assets (current price values divided by GDP-price-deflator).

THE CAPITAL STOCK AND ITS GROWTH: AGGREGATE MEASURES

The rate of growth of K (especially net K) was markedly higher in the postwar period than previously. Moreover, it increased within the postwar period up to 1968. This increase was accompanied by some fall in the average age of capital. There was a pronounced long swing in the rate of growth of K from 1870 to 1914 and indeed up to the end of the period, if wars are included in the reckoning (peaks in 1877, 1900, 1937, and 1968; troughs in 1886, World War I, and World War II). The inventory-output ratio tended to fall in peacetime periods, but inventories do not significantly affect the rate of growth of total K.

Net overseas assets grew steeply until 1914 and then declined, mainly across the wars. Their level in constant prices was the same in 1973 as in 1973. The wartime declines occurred because the prices of overseas assets did not keep pace with inflation and because in World War II the current balance of payments was in deficit. There was no significant adverse balance in World War I, but this proved illusory: Britain sold assets and borrowed, and in return acquired claims on its allies that were repudiated in 1931. The rundown of overseas assets was so large that total assets increased scarcely at all between 1913 and 1951. In the postwar period the ratio of net overseas assets to GNP changed little.

CAPITAL STOCK GROWTH AND INVESTMENT:
HARROD IDENTITIES

The measure of capital accumulation appropriate to growth accounting is the rate of growth of K. It is related to the investment-income ratio by the Harrod identity, which in the case of gross K is

$$\frac{\Delta K}{K} = \frac{Ip_I}{Yp_Y} \div \frac{Kp_I}{Yp_Y}$$

where I is investment net of retirements and p_I and p_Y are the prices of investment goods and of GDP. Differences between periods in the rate of growth of K were due much more to differences in the investment-income ratio than to differences in the capital-output ratio. The gross capital-output ratio at current prices rose from about 3.2 before 1914 to 3.5 in the interwar period, because of excess capacity. It rose again to around 4.0 in the postwar period for a different reason, a big rise in the relative prices of investment goods (p_I/p_Y). The capital-output ratio at constant prices remained at much the same level (a little over 4.0 at 1958 prices) from 1856 to 1973, apart from the interwar period.

A similar calculation can be made for total assets. A steep fall in the savings-income ratio and a rise in the assets/income ratio both contributed to a decline in the rate of growth of total assets from 2.7 percent a year in 1856–73 to 1.4 percent a year in the interwar period. In the postwar period the savings-income ratio rose sharply to almost twice the interwar level, and there was also a fall in the assets-income ratio, with the result that the rate of growth of total assets rose to 3.3 percent a year, the highest rate in the period considered.

SAVINGS

Gross savings equal gross domestic investment plus overseas investment. Net savings equal gross savings minus depreciation (not retirements). The net savings ratio was somewhat higher in the postwar period than before 1914, but not by such a large margin as either the gross savings ratio or the domestic investment ratio: depreciation was a larger fraction of GNP, and overseas investment a much smaller fraction, in the postwar period than before 1914. The pre-1914 long swing in domestic investment was not matched in the savings ratio. The savings ratio was abnormally low in the interwar period. It rose steeply within the postwar period.

The increase of two percentage points in the savings ratio between 1874–1913 and 1952–73 was rather more than wholly accounted for by an increase in government savings. The private sector, however, was responsible for the fall in the savings ratio across World War I, for part of its rise across World War II (corporate savings), and for almost the whole of its rise in the postwar period up to 1968 (personal savings). Causes of these trends in private savings included changes in the level of demand and in depreciation needs. Various explanations can be offered for the rise in the personal savings ratio in the postwar period; their relative importance is unclear.

THE UTILIZATION OF CAPITAL

Effective capital input depends not only on the size of the capital stock, but also on the intensity of its utilization. There is no presumption that short-run changes in utilization due to the pressure of demand will have any persistent trend. The pressure of demand on capital capacity does not appear to have been felt more acutely in the postwar period than before 1914, nor do survey data indicate any clear trend within the postwar period. Even at postwar cyclical peaks, capital capacity was not the main bottleneck. In the longer run, utilization is affected by changes in methods of production. Data relating to electric motors indicate a substantial trend increase in the utilization of equipment in manufacturing from 1924 to 1964 (but not thereafter). Its extent was such as to imply an increase in effective capital input in that sector as great as was brought about in the increase in the capital stock. It is most unlikely, however, that there was such a large increase in the utilization of the capital stock in the economy as a whole. Long-run increases in utilization are best regarded as a form of increase in productivity. For this reason, measures of capital input used later in this book are not adjusted for utilization.

DEFINITION AND MEASUREMENT

The central measure of physical capital input used in this study is the gross stock of domestic reproducible capital, measured at constant prices. Wherever possible movements in the net stock are also considered. The gross capital stock is defined as accumulated gross investment minus retirements. The net capital stock is defined as accumulated gross investment minus depreciation. The net stock is thus lower than the gross stock. More important, it gives greater relative weight to investment of more recent date. As a consequence, the ratio of net to gross tends to be relatively high following periods of high investment. The relation between the two concepts is further considered in Appendix F, where they are compared with other possible measures of capital as an input into production.

The measures of the capital stock in this chapter are not adjusted for variations in the degree of utilization. Changes in utilization are discussed in the last section.

The terms domestic and reproducible indicate that coverage is limited to assets in the United Kingdom (irrespective of their ownership); that land and mineral wealth are excluded; and that both fixed capital and inventories are included. Two types of assets within the defined area are excluded: consumer durables and military installations and equipment.

Since total output is defined as GDP, the domestic stock of capital is the appropriate input. But for some purposes the accumulation of net overseas assets is also relevant to our study and the available data on this are reviewed below, and related to GNP.

Land is omitted for lack of data. The inclusion of a figure obtained on the assumption of a constant ratio of land to structures (see Goldsmith 1962) would give a better total but would not significantly alter the rate of growth of total capital, which is our main concern in estimating productivity. Estimates of the level of the rate of return on capital are, however, affected by the omission of land, since rents from land are included (but not separately distinguished) in the estimates of income from property.

The estimates of fixed capital stock both gross and net are those presented and explained in Feinstein 1972, for 1938–64, continued to 1973 from the Central Statistical Office series in the Blue Book;[1] and in Feinstein (forthcoming) for 1856–1938.[2] Reference should be made to these studies for further details of sources and methods. Estimates of the stocks at constant prices were generally made by extrapolating backwards or forwards from a benchmark year according to the perpetual-inventory method. In the case of the gross measure, the stock at the end of any year was derived from the stock at the end of the previous year by adding gross fixed capital formation at constant prices and subtracting an estimate at constant prices of scrapping or retirements. For the net stock, depreciation or capital consumption instead of scrapping was subtracted. The postwar estimates of the benchmark-year stocks were built up by aggregating gross fixed capital formation at constant prices over the assumed average lives of the assets in the stock and, in the case of the net measure, subtracting depreciation at constant prices similarly aggregated. For pre-World War II estimates, the benchmarks were obtained from a variety of sources (including published and unpublished company accounts, physical capacity statistics, and tax assessments), and for the earliest year involve a large degree of approximation and conjecture. Scrapping and depreciation in postwar years were estimated from historical statistics of gross fixed capital formation, together with assumptions about the average lives of various types of assets.[3] Depreciation was calculated on a straight-line basis throughout.

The resulting series have a substantial margin of error, especially for the earlier years.[4] However, the errors are likely to operate in the same direction in different years, so that the growth rate of the capital stock is probably more accurately measured than its absolute level. There is a discrepancy between the two estimates available for 1938 (the first one, comparable with other interwar and earlier years, is lower by 2 percent in the case of the gross fixed stock and higher by almost 6 percent in the case of the net fixed stock than the second estimate, which is comparable with postwar years). In the calculations of growth rates that follow this has been dealt with by chaining the two series together in 1938. However, where the absolute level is important, the break in the series has been retained.[5]

Statistics of inventories (i.e. stocks of raw materials and finished products, and work in progress) in 1920–38 and 1948–73, based on the book value of stocks held, are available in Feinstein 1965 (Tables 2.80, 5.10, 5.20), the Blue Book (yearly changes), and *Economic Trends* (benchmark years at current and constant prices). In principle two series for each period are required, one in which end-year inventories are valued at the average prices of the year and another in which end-year inventories are valued at the average price of a constant base year. These are both available for the interwar years, as is a constant price series in the postwar period, but the nearest to a current price series for postwar years is an estimate of the book value of stocks (which is typically the lower of the original cost and the market value). In practice, unless prices change very rapidly between the time of addition to stocks and the end of the year, book values are not likely to be markedly different from current prices.[6]

An examination of the estimates of inventories for each industry in 1938 and 1948 suggested that they were broadly consistent in all cases except agriculture. We therefore made new estimates of end-1938 inventories in agriculture consistent with postwar estimates, thus introducing an additional discrepancy between pre-1938 and post-1938 capital statistics.[7] Satisfactory data on pre-1920 inventories do not exist. Rough estimates were made for agricultural inventories (livestock and crops; see Feinstein forthcoming for details), and for non-farm inventories it was assumed that the ratio of inventories to total final expenditure at current prices as 25 percent throughout. The resulting series for current-price inventories was converted to constant prices using a wholesale price index.[8]

The estimates of net overseas assets are census-type estimates based on data from various sources, such as official returns, company balance sheets, and returns by banks and other financial institutions. The valuation underlying the figures is mixed and comprises face or nominal values (for gold, short-term assets and liabilities, and intergovernmental loans), market values (for portfolio investments), and book values (for direct investments). The usefulness of figures of overseas assets and liabilities is further reduced because the value of certain components is not known and so rough estimates have to be made. Nevertheless, the estimates are probably of the correct order of magnitude to indicate the broad changes that have taken place over time.[9]

THE CAPITAL STOCK AND ITS GROWTH:
AGGREGATE MEASURES

Annual data relating to gross and net reproducible domestic fixed capital are charted in Figure 5.1 (1938 break eliminated), and the corresponding annual growth rates in Figure 5.2. Growth rates between benchmark years are given in Table 5.1. Columns 3 and 4 of the table refer to fixed capital, gross and net; column 2 refers to gross fixed capital together with inventories; and in column 1 net overseas assets are also added in.

It can be seen that the inclusion of the inventories makes no significant difference to the growth rate of the gross capital stock. There was a slight tendency for inventories to grow less rapidly than fixed capital in the postwar period, but only sufficient to show up as a difference of one-tenth of a percentage point in the growth rates of the gross stock including and excluding inventories. The ratio of inventories to output at constant (1938) prices moved as follows:[10]

Year	%	Year	%	Year	%
1873	40	1924	38	1951	39
1913	34	1937	34	1973	34

The fall in each of the peacetime periods was thus quite large, but was partially offset by the rise in the transwar periods. If both inventories

and output are measured at current prices, the ratio starts at a much
higher level (for 1873 it is 71 percent) and falls more steeply in each of
the peacetime periods. This reflects the fact that the average price of
inventories was falling relative to all prices in each period and was no
doubt associated with the relative decline in import prices, which are
important determinants of inventory prices.

Because of the poor quality of the pre-1920 and trans–World War II
inventory estimates, the emphasis in most of this chapter will be on the
growth of fixed capital,[11] but the remarks about differences in growth
between periods also apply to total domestic capital (fixed capital plus
inventories), as can be seen from columns 2 and 3 of Table 5.1. The
growth of total reproducible assets including net overseas assets as well
as inventories (column 1 of Table 5.1) will be discussed later in this
section.

A comparison of the postwar period with earlier periods yields two
outstanding conclusions: (1) the growth rate of the fixed capital stock in
the postwar period, whether measured gross or net, was higher than in

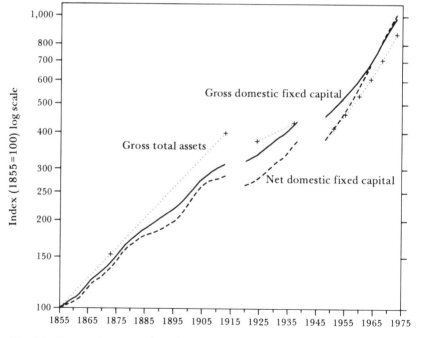

Fig. 5.1. Gross and net capital stock at constant prices, 1855–1973. Estimates of total
assets are only available for benchmark years, which are indicated by crosses.

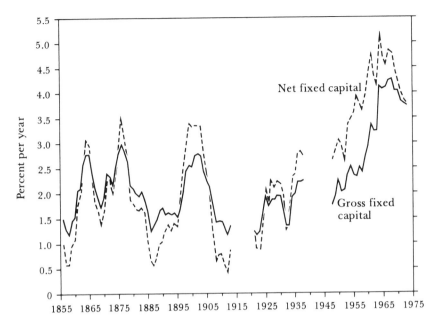

Fig. 5.2. Growth of gross and net domestic reproducible fixed capital, 1856–1973

any previous period, and (2), within the postwar period, there was a pronounced acceleration from 1951–55 to 1964–68, and despite a slight slowing in 1968–73, the growth rate in that final cycle was still very rapid by past standards, though the trend was downward.

The high rate of growth postwar has to be viewed against the background of World War II, when investment was low. However, if we take the entire period 1937–73, the growth rate of the gross stock remains higher than in earlier periods. Moreover, the acceleration within the postwar years up to 1968 (1964 for the net stock) suggests that this was not merely a catching-up phenomenon. It has only one historical parallel, the period 1886–1902 (when the high rate of growth was followed by a precipitous decline).

Up to 1914 a long swing is clearly apparent in the rate of growth of the capital stock, and with the decline in the rate of growth in the final cycle (1968–73),* another is evident in the postwar period. Both the long swing and the relatively low average rate of domestic capital ac-

*The annual rate of growth of the gross stock continued to decline after 1973, falling to 2.7% in 1978, compared with a peak of 4.3% in 1968. For the net stock the peak was 5.2% in 1964, and the figure fell to 3.8% in 1973 and 2.3% in 1978.

TABLE 5.1
Growth of the Capital Stock, 1856–1973
(Annual percentage growth rates)

Period	Total gross reproducible assets (1)	Domestic gross reproducible assets (2)	Domestic reproducible fixed assets	
			Gross (3)	Net (4)
Peacetime phases:				
1856–1873	2.5%	1.9%	2.0%	1.8%
1873–1913	2.4	1.9	2.0	1.8
1924–1937	1.1	1.8	1.9	2.1
1951–1973	3.4	3.2	3.3	4.1
Wartime phases:				
1913–1924	−0.4	0.9	0.9	0.0
1937–1951	−0.1	1.1	0.9	0.9
War and postwar phases:				
1913–1937	0.4	1.4	1.4	1.2
1937–1973	2.0	2.4	2.4	2.9
Post-WWII cycles:				
1951–1955	2.7	2.3	2.3	3.3
1955–1960	2.8	2.6	2.6	3.9
1960–1964	3.4	3.4	3.4	4.6
1964–1968	4.0	4.1	4.2	4.7
1968–1973	4.0	3.7	3.9	4.1
1856–1973	1.9%	2.0%	2.0%	2.0%

Note: The 1938 break in the capital series has been eliminated.

cumulation before 1914 have to be viewed in conjunction with overseas capital formation, discussed below.

The net stock and the gross stock exhibit the same general features in their behavior, but the net stock exhibits them in a higher degree: its postwar rate of growth exceeded earlier rates by more; its acceleration within the postwar period was faster; and its long cycles before 1914 were more pronounced. The reason for this is that generally speaking the ratio of net to gross is high when the growth rate is high, as explained in Appendix F. In periods when the growth rate of the gross stock was rapid, such as the upswing phases of pre-1914 long swings and the period after World War II, the net stock rose relative to the gross stock, so that the net stock's growth rate was high on two counts.

This is more than merely an arithmetic phenomenon, because the gross and net stocks measure slightly different economic concepts in giving different weights to different vintages of capital. As explained above, the use of the net measure of capital is a method (albeit an imperfect one) of giving more weight to capital of lower age, which may be assumed to be more efficient. It follows that the rate of growth and acceleration of the capital stock in efficiency units in the postwar period exceeded the rate in former periods by an even greater extent than the gross stock series indicates.*

The limited direct evidence available on the average age of the capital stock gives some confirmation that the average age fell in the postwar period, as suggested by the rise in the ratio of net to gross stock. The evidence is described in Appendix G. The extent of the fall is significant in proportional terms, though it may not seem very great absolutely. In the case of manufacturing and construction (excluding textiles), the estimated average age of the gross capital stock (weighted at constant-price values, without allowance for depreciation) was 20.2 years in 1948 and 17.4 years in 1962. A change of this order is consistent with what has been found in other countries.[12]

We have so far been concerned with domestic capital. Account must be taken of net overseas assets in order to extend the discussion to national reproductive capital. Estimates of Britain's overseas assets and liabilities, as well as the accumulated sum of annual net investment abroad, all at current prices, are shown in Table 5.2 for certain benchmark years. The ratio of net assets to GDP is shown in column 8. It corresponds to the crosses in Figure 14.8.

Changes in the value of overseas assets over time come about not only from net overseas investment, but also from defaults and changes in the valuation of existing assets and liabilities. These are shown in columns 6 and 7 respectively of Table 5.2, though column 7 also picks up any residual errors. Defaults and changes in valuation appear here as relatively small except in 1924–37 and in the postwar period. The negative item under this heading in 1937 largely reflects the repudiation of war debts after 1931. The positive items in the postwar period reflect the general rise in the price level.

Our information is not sufficient to allow the presentation of annual series of overseas assets and hence of total reproducible capital at constant prices. Instead, figures for benchmark years are given in Figure 5.1 and Table 5.3. Growth rates of total gross reproducible assets are given in the first column of Table 5.1.

The rate of growth of total reproducible assets over the entire period 1856–1973 is the same as the rate of growth of domestic capital. Britain's net overseas assets were small in 1856, and they were small again in 1973. Likewise, within the post–World War II period the rate of

---

*For the economy as a whole, the ratio of net to gross fixed capital was 52% at the end of 1951 and 60% at the end of 1964 (Feinstein 1972: Table 44). From 1964 to 1973 the ratio increased more slowly, rising by just two percentage points.

TABLE 5.2

Overseas Assets and Liabilities, 1856–1973

(£ billion at current prices)[a]

Year	Values at end of year				Changes between successive years			Ratio of net assets to GDP (8)
	Assets (1)	Liabilities (2)	Net assets (3)	Accumulated net investment abroad[b] (4)	Net assets (5)	Accumulated net investment abroad (6)	Difference (5) − (6) (7)	
1856	0.3	0.0	0.3	0.3	—	—	—	0.4
1873	1.1	0.1	1.0	1.0	0.7	0.7	0.0	0.8
1913	4.6	0.4	4.2	4.1	3.2	3.1	0.1	1.8
1924	6.8	1.6	5.2	5.0	1.0	0.9	0.1	1.3
1937[c]	5.3	1.3	4.0	5.1	−1.2	0.1	−1.3	0.9
1951	6.9	7.6	−0.7	0.2	−4.7	−4.9	0.3	−0.05
1964	14.8	13.0	1.8	1.0	2.5	0.8	1.7	0.06
1973	67.8	60.4	7.4	1.9	5.6	0.9	4.7	0.12

Note: The change in territory in 1920 does not create a significant break in comparability in these series.
[a] It is not strictly correct to say that these estimates are at current prices. In fact different components of total assets and liabilities are subject to a variety of valuations, notably face or nominal value (short-term assets and liabilities, including gold; long-term official assets and liabilities; until 1924, portfolio investments), market value (from 1937, portfolio investments), and book value (direct investments). It is unlikely, however, that before World War II this mixture of valuations gave a total that was very different from the current market valuation; after World War II the increasing importance of direct investments valued at historical cost (book values) means that the present estimates would tend to underestimate the current market valuation, but the error is not very large, as can be seen from the comparison between these estimates for 1964 (£14.8 billion assets and £13.0 billion liabilities) and current market price estimates given in Revell & Roe 1971: £15.9 billion assets and £14.6 billion liabilities.
[b] The starting point was the figure for 1856 in column 3: £0.28 billion.
[c] In 1931 all intergovernment loans incurred during and after World War I were repudiated, and this accounts for a large part of the difference (column 7) between the two estimates of the change in net assets between 1924 and 1937. In 1924 the assets and liabilities arising in this way were £1.8 billion and £1.1 billion, respectively.

growth of total reproducible assets was not very different from that of domestic capital, because overseas assets were too small a proportion of the total to make much difference. Similarly, total reproducible assets exhibited the same acceleration in rate of growth within the postwar period as domestic fixed capital, though the pace was slightly slower, and there was no decline in the rate of growth in the final cycle (1968–73).

But though the growth rates of total assets and domestic fixed capital were thus similar in the postwar period and over the entire span 1856–1973, the enormous rise and fall of net overseas assets in the intervening period shows up in some major effects on the rate of growth of total assets.

Before 1914 the increase in overseas assets was much greater proportionally than the increase in domestic assets, and indeed was almost as great in absolute terms. Consequently, between 1856 and 1913 total assets grew at 2.4 percent a year, compared with only 1.9 percent for the domestic capital stock. This has to be borne in mind when one compares the postwar rate of growth of domestic fixed capital with the rate in earlier times. Nevertheless, the pre-1914 rate of growth of total assets was still considerably below the postwar rate in the case of gross assets, and hence *a fortiori* in the case of net assets. The rapid capital accumulation of the postwar period followed a long spell of years in which the growth of total assets was extremely slow. The reduction in the real value of overseas assets is estimated to have wiped out over 15 percent of the Britain's total net assets during World War I and nearly 28 percent during World War II. The domestic capital stock, by contrast, merely suffered a retardation in its rate of growth during these periods. It is easier to run down paper assets, whether as a deliberate means of war financing or as a result of uncontrollable outside circumstances, than it is to reduce the stock of real domestic capital. So great was the decline in overseas assets as a result

TABLE 5·3

Gross Reproducible Assets, 1856–1973

(£ billion at 1938 prices)

End of year	Gross domestic fixed assets	Inventories	Net overseas assets[a]	Total[b]
1856	4.22	0.6	0.5	5.4
1873	5.92	0.7	1.5	8.2
1913	12.86	1.3	7.3	21.5
1924	13.79	1.39	4.9	20.1
1937	17.49	1.66	4.1	23.3
1951	20.37	2.39	−0.3	22.4
1955	22.33	2.56	0.1	25.0
1960	25.37	2.98	0.5	28.8
1964	29.07	3.35	0.6	33.0
1968	34.22	3.46	0.6	38.3
1973	41.40	3.88	1.5	46.8

Note: There are 2 breaks in comparability. The first arises from the change in territory: post-1920 estimates exclude Southern Ireland. The estimates for the respective areas at the end of 1920 are:

	Gross domestic fixed assets	Inventories
Including Southern Ireland	13.44	1.50
Excluding Southern Ireland	13.09	1.45

(Net overseas assets are assumed to be unchanged.)
The second break in comparability arises from the 2 estimates for the end of 1938:

	Gross domestic fixed assets	Inventories
Comparable with earlier years	17.88	1.74
Comparable with later years	18.25	1.59

[a] The figures for net overseas assets derive from the estimated current-price value of assets net of liabilities (with some allowance for appreciation and depreciation) deflated by the implicit GDP price-deflator.
[b] Growth rates calculated from these data will not agree exactly with those in Table 5.1, column 1, which were calculated from a series in which the separate assets were weighted at 4 different sets of prices (1900 prices for 1856–1913, 1938 prices for 1913–38, 1958 prices for 1938–64, and 1970 prices for 1964–73) rather than all at 1938 prices.

of the two wars that over a period of nearly 40 years from the beginning of World War I the total real wealth of the United Kingdom
scarcely increased at all — a phenomenon that must have few parallels
in the history of an advanced economy.

Over the years of World War I taken as a whole, the current account
was broadly in balance. Income from shipping, overseas assets, and
other invisibles was about sufficient to offset both the increased deficit
on visible trade and the government's expenditure abroad. However,
the government was also a substantial net lender, and there was a small
amount of private investment abroad. This was financed by the sale of
some £550,000,000 in overseas securities (Morgan 1952: 331) and by a
net deterioration in Britain's short-term credit position. From 1920 to
1924 the current account was again in surplus, and this financed renewed private investment (making the total for the period 1914–24
some £770,000,000), further government lending, and a recovery in
the short-term position.

Net overseas assets thus rose in current prices between 1913 and
1924, but though real GDP did not grow between these years, the ratio
of net assets to GDP fell (see Table 5.2) because of a rapid rise in
general prices.[13] However, the longer-term effect of World War I on
net overseas assets was more adverse than so far indicated because of
the repudiation of all intergovernment war debts in 1931. This represented a further loss of assets arising from the war and amounting to
some £700,000,000.[14]

The effect of World War II on the capital account was much worse,
and there was a substantial fall in net assets. In contrast to the period
before 1914, there was this time no cushion in the form of an initial
favorable current balance, so that the wartime deterioration caused
adverse current balances of enormous size throughout the war.* Wartime disinvestment was financed by making military-related purchases
in India, Egypt, and other countries and not paying the bills; by selling
some $1.1 billion in foreign investments (mainly those in the United
States); and by running down short-term dollar assets. In contrast to
World War I, net intergovernment loans were zero.

The switch from being a net creditor before World War II to being a
net debtor afterwards was mainly the result of incurring very large
liabilities. Gross overseas assets actually rose, despite the sale of foreign
investments. Appreciation in the prices of overseas assets was apparently on the order of 20 percent of the end-1937 value over the 1937–51

*Net disinvestment abroad amounted to some £4.61 billion over the years 1939–45
(Sayers 1956: 499).

period—much less than the rise in general prices.[15] So, as in World War I, the ratio of net overseas assets to GDP fell because of the failure of gross overseas assets to appreciate sufficiently, as well as because of the needs of war finance.

Though it is useful to view the rapid postwar increase in total assets against the background of the stagnation of the preceding 40 years, it would be misleading to regard the stagnation as in any direct sense a cause of that increase. A long period of low investment in domestic fixed assets tends to create arrears of investment opportunities and prepares the way for a swing back. But the same does not apply to overseas assets, the rundown of which was the main reason why total assets increased so little from 1913 to 1951. The loss of income from abroad admittedly makes foreign exchange more scarce and thereby enhances the real value of the return from new foreign investment; but new foreign assets have also to be acquired with scarce foreign exchange, and the two effects tend to cancel out. This canceling out does not apply with domestic capital, where a high rate of return is not *ipso facto* accompanied by a correspondingly high cost of capital goods.

In Chapter 2 we noted a broad three-phase division of the growth pattern of output in the United Kingdom over our 100-year period: first reasonably rapid growth, then retardation, then more rapid growth again. From what has just been said, it is apparent that a similar three-phase division applies even more strongly to the growth of total assets. But the timing is rather different in the two cases, and the causal connection between them is not simple, the output pattern having been due mainly to movements in domestic productivity, and the asset pattern to wars.

CAPITAL STOCK GROWTH AND INVESTMENT: HARROD IDENTITIES

In most discussions of capital accumulation in the United Kingdom and other European countries since World War II, attention has been focused on the level of gross fixed capital formation, or the ratio of this to national income, rather than on the rate of growth of the fixed capital stock. The difference between the ratio of gross fixed capital formation to income and the rate of growth of the capital stock is, of course, twofold: the growth rate of the capital stock involves (1) the deduction of retirements (or depreciation) in the numerator, and (2) the use of the capital stock rather than income as the denominator. There would be general agreement that a deduction of retirements (or depreciation) should in principle be made if it is statistically feasible. The use of the

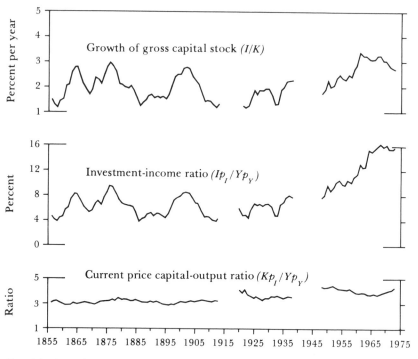

Fig. 5.3. Gross domestic fixed capital accumulation, 1856–1973: Harrod identities. (For the notation, see Table 5.4.)

capital stock as a denominator is more controversial. The unreliability of the estimates of the capital stock seriously increases the margin of error in the resulting measures. Moreover, there are theoretical difficulties in the whole concept of an aggregative measure of capital, and these do not apply so strongly to measures of capital formation and income (especially if these are measured in current prices, as they are when considering the investment-income ratio). But the rate of growth of the capital stock is the measure of capital accumulation that is relevant for considering the rate of increase of factor inputs over time.

As it happens, the broad conclusions about the United Kingdom's domestic capital accumulation in the postwar period compared with earlier times come out pretty similar, whether we look at the rate of growth of the capital stock or the proportion of national income devoted to capital accumulation.*

*This is not true if a comparison is being made between different countries, an exercise of a different kind from the one we are engaged in. The two measures then give some substantially different results. (See Denison 1967: 138.)

TABLE 5.4

Gross Domestic Fixed Capital Accumulation, 1856–1973: Harrod Identities

Period	I/K Growth of gross capital stock (% per year)	Ip_I/Yp_Y Investment-income ratio (%)	Kp_I/Yp_Y Current-price capital-output ratio	K/Y Constant-price capital-output ratio	p_I/p_Y Relative capital price (1958 = 100)
Peacetime phases:					
1856–1873	2.0%	6.1%	3.0	4.0	75
1873–1913	2.0	6.2	3.2	4.1	78
1924–1937	1.9	6.6	3.5	4.8	74
1951–1973	3.3	13.1	4.0	4.1	97
Wartime phases:					
1913–1924	0.9	3.3	3.6	4.4	83
1937–1951[a]	0.9	3.9	3.8	4.2	90
Post-WWII cycles:					
1951–1955	2.3	10.0	4.3	4.1	105
1955–1960	2.6	10.6	4.1	4.1	100
1960–1964	3.4	13.3	3.9	4.0	96
1964–1968	4.2	15.7	3.7	4.0	93
1968–1973	3.9	15.7	4.0	4.3	93
1856–1973[a]	2.0%	7.0%	3.5	4.2	83

Note: In order to preserve the identity, the current-price capital-output ratio was measured as the ratio of gross fixed capital at the beginning of the year valued at average investment prices of the year to GDP at current prices during the year:

$$\frac{I}{K} = \frac{Ip_I}{Yp_Y} \div \frac{Kp_I}{Yp_Y}$$

where I = investment (net of retirements) at constant prices during the year; K = gross capital stock at constant prices at the beginning of the year; Y = GDP at constant prices during the year; p_I = average price of investment goods during the year; and p_Y = average price of GDP during the year. This differs from measures of the capital-output ratio elsewhere in this study (e.g. Chapter 6, Fig. 6.3), in which capital at the *end* of the year valued at the average *capital* prices of the year is expressed as a ratio of output at current prices during the year. (The difference between average investment prices and capital prices is unimportant since it results only from different weights given to the component assets: the prices of the individual assets are assumed to be the same whether the assets are being added to, retired from, or left in the stock.)

In averaging the component terms of the Harrod equality over a number of years for the figures in this table the exact identity is lost. For convenience, unweighted arithmetic averages of the investment-income and capital-output ratios were taken, and the growth of capital was measured as the annual rate of growth between the first and last years of the period. The left-hand side of the "identity" can then be expressed as:

$$\left(\prod_n \frac{K+I}{K} \right)^{1/n} - 1$$

and the right-hand side as:

$$\frac{1}{n} \left(\sum_n w \frac{K+I}{K} \right) - 1$$

where

$$w = \frac{Kp_I / Yp_Y}{\sum_n Kp_I/Yp_Y}$$

and n = number of years between the first and last years. The averages exclude the first year of the periods shown in the table (e.g. they refer to 1857–73 inclusive). The two sides will not necessarily be the same because of the different averaging method (one geometric and one arithmetic) and because of the capital-output ratio weights that appear on one side but not on the other. In practice the discrepancy is small (not exceeding 0.05% a year).

[a] The 1938 break has been left unadjusted so as to maintain the validity of the Harrod identity.

The relationship between the two can conveniently be expressed in terms of the well-known Harrod identity, that the growth rate of the capital stock equals the ratio of savings to income, s, divided by the ratio of capital to output, v ($\Delta K/K = s/v$). The ratio of savings to income has to be defined in the present context as gross domestic fixed capital formation, less retirements, divided by GDP. It is natural to measure it in current prices so that it indicates the proportion of current-valued output devoted to domestic fixed capital formation; for this reason it is referred to below as the investment-income ratio. The capital-output ratio has therefore also to be measured in current prices, that is to say, it is the capital-output ratio at constant prices multiplied by the ratio of capital goods prices to GDP prices. The series for the gross capital stock are shown year by year in Figure 5.3 and over benchmark periods in Table 5.4. A corresponding calculation could be made using the net stock and net domestic fixed capital formation, but this has not been done because rough calculations indicated that it would not yield significantly different conclusions from the gross stock exercise.

We consider the investment-income ratio and the capital-output ratio in turn.

The Investment-Income Ratio

The main movements in the growth rate of gross fixed capital were due to movements in the ratio of net investment (gross investment less retirements) to GDP, rather than to movements in the capital-output ratio. Inspection of the series in Figure 5.3 shows that the movements in the investment-income ratio were similar to those in the rate of growth of the gross capital stock. In both cases the postwar period stands out both for its high level and its acceleration. However, the growth of the capital stock exceeded its rate in earlier periods by a smaller margin than did the investment-income ratio, since the current-price capital-output ratio was higher. Long cycles are prominent in the period before 1914, and reappear in the postwar period.

The investment-income series in Figure 5.3 relates to gross fixed capital formation less retirements. Figure 5.4 shows separately the ratio to GDP of gross fixed investment (I/Y) and of retirements (R/Y). (The third series on this figure, S/Y, gross savings, will be discussed later.) R/Y was at a marginally higher average level in the interwar period than before 1914, and at a considerably higher level in the postwar period. This was due partly to an increase in the proportion of the capital stock consisting of machinery and vehicles (which have a

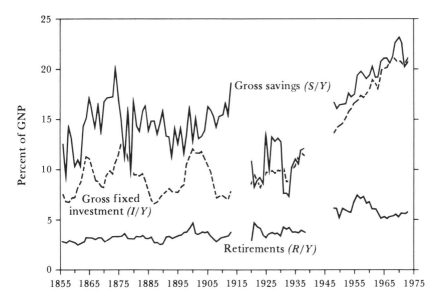

Fig. 5.4. Gross savings, gross fixed investment, and retirements as a percentage of gross national product, 1856–1973

shorter life than buildings and thus a higher rate of replacement) and partly to the upward trend in the value-capital-output ratio (Fig. 5.5), since a higher capital-output ratio means that a given proportional retirement of the capital stock amounts to a greater proportion of the national income. A consequence is that gross I/Y rose to an even greater extent across World War II than the investment-income ratio did. Similarly, gross I/Y in the interwar period was on average significantly higher than before 1914, whereas the ratios net of retirements were not very different between the two periods. Within the postwar period the hump in the rate of retirements in the late 1950's is mainly explained by a large-scale scrapping of equipment in the cotton and man-made fibers sectors of the textile industry (see Dean 1964: 337).

The Capital-Output Ratio

The behavior of the capital-output ratio will be more fully discussed in Chapter 11. At this stage we shall comment only on the broad movements.

The series of gross capital-output at current prices given in Figure 5.3 is broken down into price and quantity components in Figure 5.5 (in both figures the 1938 break has been eliminated by chaining).

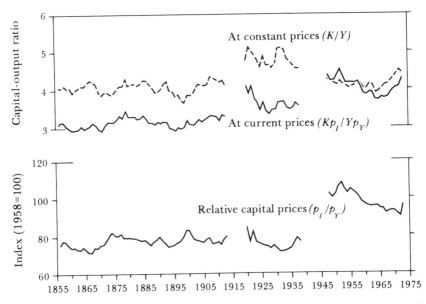

Fig. 5.5. Capital-output ratio at constant and current prices, and relative price of capital goods, 1856–1973

The dominant feature of the price series is the enormous rise in the ratio of the price of capital goods to general prices across World War II. Though there is evidence from other countries, especially the United States, of a trend rise in this ratio (see Gordon 1961), such a large discontinuous rise must create suspicions of some statistical bias, due, for example, to inadequate allowance for improvement in quality of capital goods. However, there are a number of factors that between them appear to explain most, if not all, of the rise (see Appendix H). Though the basis of the price data is admittedly rough and unsatisfactory, there is no clear evidence of a statistical bias significant enough to warrant adjusting the figures.

The largest movements in the volume capital-output ratio are the rise across World War I and the reversal across World War II. The high capital-output ratio shown for the interwar period is influenced by the general unemployment and below-capacity working of that time (the capital figures are, of course, not corrected to allow for the degree of utilization); this consideration is of about the right order of magnitude to account for the higher level of the ratio in the interwar period compared with the periods before and after.

Throughout the whole period the constant-price capital-output ratio varied only within a fairly narrow range — roughly from 4 to 5 — which is hardly larger than the margin of error in the capital stock statistics, and if allowance is made for below-capacity working in the interwar period the ratio might reasonably be regarded as a long-run constant at a level of just over 4. The decline across the period of World War II is a good deal less pronounced than in the United States, where the capital-output ratio in the postwar period was about only two-thirds of the 1929 value; and this notwithstanding that there was a greater change in the level of activity in the United Kingdom after 1929 than there was in the United States. There is thus no evidence of a long-run downward tendency in the capital-output ratio in the United Kingdom.

The Growth of Total Assets

The rate of growth of total assets, A (including inventories and overseas assets), can likewise be broken down into the elements of the Harrod identity. This is done, for peacetime periods, in Table 5.5. The first column differs slightly from the growth rates of total assets shown in Table 5.1, because, in order to make the values conceptually consistent with the savings-income ratio, total assets are here defined exclusive of appreciation of existing overseas assets. The procedure underlying the calculations is unavoidably arbitrary in some respects, and the figures should not be regarded as indicating more than orders of magnitude.

TABLE 5.5

Total Asset Accumulation, 1856–1973: Harrod Identities

Period	$\Delta A/A$ Growth rate of total assets (percent per year)	S/Y Savings- income ratio (percent)	A/Y Assets-income ratio
1856–1873	2.7%	11.3%	4.1
1873–1913	2.4	11.3	4.7
1924–1937	1.4	7.2	5.0
1951–1973	3.3	14.3	4.3

Note: $\Delta A/A$ is the annual rate of growth in A between the first and last years of each period. For this purpose, the level of A at the beginning of each period is taken as that shown in Table 5.3; the level of A at the end of each period is also as in Table 5.3 in the case of domestic fixed capital and inventories, but in the case of overseas assets it is arrived at by adding the sum of annual overseas investment (deflated by the GDP price deflator) to the opening stock. The measure thus takes account of changes in the valuation of overseas assets prior to each period but not of changes in valuation within the period. S/Y is the average of annual values within each period of the percentage to GNP of the sum of gross domestic fixed investment, minus retirements, plus inventory investment, plus overseas investment. A/Y (at current prices) is obtained as a residual.

Figure 5.4 shows annual movements in the gross savings ratio (S/Y; the sum of gross domestic fixed investment, plus inventory investment, plus net overseas investment as a proportion of GNP), alongside the domestic gross fixed investment ratio (I/Y) for comparison. S/Y in the postwar period, whether measured net of retirements (as in Table 5.5) or gross (as in Fig. 5.4), exceeded the pre-1914 level by a much smaller margin that I/Y did. S/Y (unlike I/Y) was exceptionally low in the interwar period.* Note also, in Figure 5.4, that because of the inversion of home and overseas investments, the long swings that were so prominent in I/Y before 1914 were not nearly so apparent in S/Y. The two periods around 1872 and 1913 can possibly be interpreted as long cycle peaks, but the long cycle cannot be identified in the same unmistakable way as it can for I/Y.

The total capital-output ratio at current prices (A/Y) was higher in the period 1873-1913 than it was in the postwar period, though the corresponding ratio for domestic fixed assets (Kp_K/Yp_Y) was lower. This reflects the higher ratio of overseas assets to total assets before 1913. The capital-output ratio for overseas assets is the ratio of overseas assets to net income from abroad, that is to say, the reciprocal of the rate of return on overseas assets. It is therefore much higher than the domestic capital-output ratio. Inclusion of overseas assets in total assets and income from abroad in total output thus raises the overall capital-outut ratio, and increasingly so, as the ratio of overseas assets to domestic assets rises. Before 1914 a large proportion of UK assets were overseas, and a higher savings-income ratio was therefore needed to bring about a given rate of increase of total assets than would otherwise have been the case.

One way of looking at this is that from the national point of view, overseas investment is the most capital-intensive of all forms of investment, since it yields its fruit in the form of income from abroad, without the cooperation of any national labor at all. As a result, the fruit is not very large — the capital-output ratio is high. So a nation with much of its total assets abroad, as Britain was in 1913, has to devote a large proportion of its national income to savings in order to achieve a given rate of increase of these assets.

*The contrast between the 1920's and the 1930's appears in rather a different light, however: I/Y was on average higher in the 1930's than in the 1920's, but the opposite is true of S/Y. The increase in the proportion of the national income devoted to domestic investment in the 1930's was thus associated with a diversion of savings from overseas to home investment rather than an increase in the propensity to save.

Conclusions

We may conclude as follows. As far as *domestic* capital is concerned, its rate of growth was higher in the postwar period than before because there was an increase in the proportion of the national income devoted to domestic capital accumulation. This increase reflects the fact that compared with the interwar period, a higher proportion of income was saved. Compared with 1856–1914, it reflects not so much an increase in the proportion of national income saved (though there was some increase) as a diversion of savings away from overseas investment toward domestic investment. The increase in the investment-income ratio in the postwar period, compared with earlier times, more than compensated for an increase in the current-price capital-output ratio brought about by a rise in the relative price of capital goods across World War II.

As far as *total* assets are concerned, the main reason why the rate of increase was faster in the postwar period than earlier was that the savings-income ratio was higher. The effect of this was augmented by the asset-income ratio being lower (except by comparison with 1856–73).

SAVINGS

In the last section, the ratio of capital formation to income was looked at in connection with its effects on the growth rate of the capital stock. We will now consider it from the point of view of the propensity to save of the households, companies, and government that comprise the economy.

For this purpose gross savings may be defined as before, as the sum of gross domestic fixed capital formation, inventory investment, and net overseas investment. Net savings, from the saver's point of view can, however, be more appropriately measured as gross investment minus depreciation, rather than gross investment minus retirements (used in Table 5.5 to conform with the gross stock measure of capital).

The movements of the gross and net savings ratios (S/Y) are summarized in Table 5.6. Reference may also be made to the annual figures of gross S/Y depicted in Figure 5.4. The low level of S/Y in the interwar period stands out as abnormal, and the much higher rates prevailing in the postwar period are evidently in large part a reversion to a more normal state of affairs. But they are more than just that, because the ratio, whether measured gross or net, was above the pre-1914 level, not merely above the interwar level. However, a large

TABLE 5.6

Gross and Net Savings as a Percentage of Gross National Product, 1856–1973

Period or year	Gross savings	Depreciation	Net savings
Annual averages			
1857–1873	15.7%	5.2%	10.5%
1874–1913	14.6	5.6	9.0
1925–1937	10.9	6.0	4.9
1952–1973[a]	20.4	9.1	11.2
1952–1964[a]	18.9	8.6	10.3
1965–1973[a]	22.4	9.8	12.6
Benchmark years			
1856	12.6	5.2	7.4
1874[b]	20.4	5.5	14.9
1913	18.7	6.0	12.7
1924	10.9	6.2	4.7
1937	12.0	6.1	5.9
1951	16.5	8.1	8.4
1964[a]	20.8	8.5	12.3
1973	21.7	10.7	10.9

Note: Savings equal gross domestic fixed capital formation, plus inventory investment, plus net overseas investment.
[a]The estimates for 1964–73 are based on the 1975 Blue Book and have not been linked to those for 1951–64, which are based on the 1968 Blue Book. The estimates for 1964 consistent with the figures for 1965 onward are gross savings, 21.7%; depreciation, 9.0%; and net savings, 12.7%.
[b]1874 is shown rather than the usual benchmark 1873 because it was the peak year for savings and hence more comparable with later benchmark years. The 1873 figures are gross savings, 17.2%; depreciation, 5.5%; and net savings, 11.7%.

part of the increase in gross S/Y compared with pre-1914 is associated with an increase in depreciation. Though net S/Y was higher in the postwar period than the average rate for 1856–1913, it was only a little higher than the rate in the decade or so before World War I. In the early postwar years net S/Y was lower than it was on average in 1873–1913: the very rapid rise within the postwar period (much more rapid than any upward trend before 1914) carried it well above the 1873–1913 average, though not above the high-water marks of the years 1874 and 1913.

The steep rise in the savings-income ratio within the postwar period makes it difficult to speak of the postwar period as a whole. The rise can best be investigated by looking at the three sources of savings: the personal, corporate, and government sectors.* The proportion in GNP of total savings, corporate savings, personal savings, and government savings (all measured gross) are shown for 1933–38 and for the postwar

*The personal sector consists of households, unincorporated businesses, and private non-profit-making concerns. Public corporations are included with companies in the corporate sector. Government savings comprise savings by the central government and local authorities.

period in Figure 5.6. Provided that savings are measured net of stock appreciation, as they are in Figure 5.6 for the postwar years though not for the prewar years,[16] the sum of personal savings, corporate savings, and government savings is conceptually equivalent to total savings and investment, as shown in Figure 5.4, for example, except in 1948–55 when investment exceeded the sum of sectoral savings because of capital tranfers from abroad.[17] But in practice the residual in the national accounts is not zero, and so the sum of estimated sectoral savings is not exactly equal to estimated total investment. For the late 1930's and the postwar period, the difference between the income and expenditure sides of the national accounts is not large enough to invalidate conclusions based on comparing sectoral savings with total investment, but in 1920–32 the residual error averaged 4.2 percent of GNP, and the sum of sectoral savings shows a significant upward trend relative to GNP between the 1920's and 1930's, whereas total investment shows none. In these circumstances an examination of sectoral savings is not

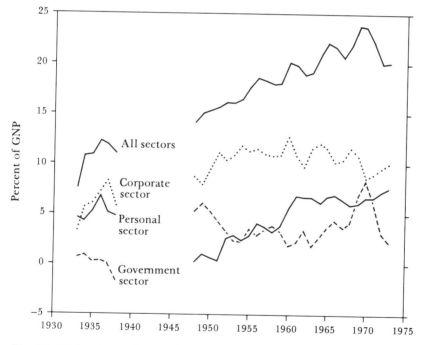

Fig. 5.6. Total savings and savings by sector as a percentage of gross national product, 1933–1973. Stock appreciation is included in the corporate and personal sectors for 1933–38 only.

TABLE 5.7
Gross Savings by Sector as a Percentage of Gross National Product, 1935–1973
(Annual averages)

Period	Personal sector (1)	Corporate sector (2)	Government sector (3)	All sectors[a] (4)	Total savings[a] (5)
1935–1938	5.6%[b]	6.8%[b]	−0.3%[b]	11.6%	11.4%
1948–1951	0.5	9.3	5.2	15.0	16.5
1952–1973[c]	5.3	10.9	3.6	19.8	20.4
1952–1955	2.7	11.1	2.8	16.6	17.2
1956–1960	4.1	11.4	3.1	18.6	19.5
1961–1964	6.1	11.1	2.6	19.8	19.9
1965–1968[c]	6.6	11.0	3.9	21.5	21.9
1969–1973[c]	7.1	10.1	5.3	22.5	22.8

[a]The difference between columns 5 and 4 is the national accounts residual error plus (in 1948–51 and 1952–55 only) capital transfers from abroad. The latter averaged 1.5% of GNP in 1948–51 and 0.1% in 1952–55.
[b]Including stock appreciation. Stock appreciation is not available by sector in this period. It averaged in total 0.5% of GNP and relates almost entirely to the personal and corporate sectors.
[c]For the years during which investment grants were paid (1967–73), we have increased the private sector savings as defined in the national accounts by the amount of the investment grants received, and reduced government savings by the same amount, so that the institutional change from subsidizing investment via tax relief to subsidizing investment via grants would not affect our measure of savings. (In the national accounts, tax relief enters the current account and so raises savings, but investment grants appear in the capital account and so do not affect measured savings.)

very illuminating, and it is for this reason that the series plotted in Figures 5.6–5.8 begin in 1933, though data for earlier years are available. The averages of the relevant ratios over the cycles between 1935 and 1973 are shown in Table 5.7.*

Two important conclusions are suggested by the data in Figure 5.6 and Table 5.7: (1) the rise in the overall savings ratio *within* the postwar period was almost entirely due to the rise in personal savings;† (2) on the other hand, the rise in the overall savings ratio in the postwar period as a whole compared with the 1930's was due entirely to the rise in corporate and government savings.

The ratio to GNP of the savings of the personal and corporate sectors can in turn be broken down into the products of the ratio of the sector's

*One serious statistical reservation must be made about the sectoral savings estimates. They are derived as the (small) difference between two (large) estimates of the income and expenditure of the sector, and they are therefore subject to wide margins of error. For the postwar period, alternative estimates of sectoral savings built up by aggregating identified outlets for savings, both real (capital formation) and financial (net acquisition of financial assets), give a markedly different picture. For example, the rise in the ratio of personal savings to GNP apparent in Figure 5.6 is insignificant when the alternative estimate is used. Clearly, not too much weight should be attached to the sectoral savings statistics discussed in this section. See Odling-Smee 1973 for a further discussion of this point.

†This is true for the period as a whole. In the years 1969–71 the ratio of personal savings to GNP increased more slowly, and the increase in the ratio of GNP of government savings, especially by the central government, made a more important contribution to the growth of the overall savings ratio.

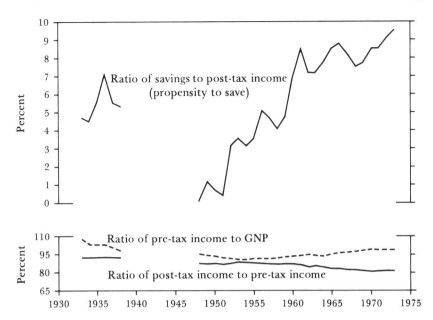

Fig. 5.7. Personal income and savings, 1933–1973. Stock appreciation is included in income and savings for 1933–38 only.

savings to its post-tax income, the ratio of its post-tax income to its pre-tax income, and the ratio of its pre-tax income to GNP. This is done in Figures 5.7 and 5.8.

Personal Savings

The dominant feature in the postwar period was the movement in the ratio of personal savings to personal disposable income (the propensity to save). The proportional changes in the personal sector's share in GNP and in its tax payments are unimportant by comparison.* The personal propensity to save showed a strong upward trend in the

---

*Personal pre-tax income is defined as the sum of income from employment; income from self-employment, rent, dividends, and net interest; national insurance benefits and other current grants from public authorities; and current transfers from abroad and to charities from companies. Personal disposable income is defined as pre-tax income, less payments of UK tax, less taxes paid abroad. Personal savings are defined as disposable income, less consumers' expenditure, less transfers abroad. In the 1933–38 period stock appreciation is included in income and savings, and in the postwar period it is excluded. The treatment of stock appreciation and transfers from abroad makes these definitions slightly different from those in Feinstein 1972: Table 10 and in the Blue Book (e.g. *National Income and Expenditure*, UK [21], *1975:* Table 21).

1950's, stabilized in the 1960's and resumed its upward movement in the early 1970's (see Fig. 5.7).*

Three factors combined to bring about the transwar fall in the ratio of personal savings to GNP: (1) the propensity to save fell; (2) taxation increased, so that personal disposable income was a lower proportion of pre-tax income after the war than before; and (3) the share of pre-tax income in GNP fell. The last point is at first sight surprising, since there was a transwar increase in the share in GNP of income from employment (see Chapter 6). The explanation is to be found in the much greater decline in the share of income from self-employment and rent, dividends, and interests, reflecting among other things the diminution of the unincorporated sector and the higher retention ratios of companies.[18] Moreover, since there is a greater prospensity to save out of these two types of personal savings than out of income from employment, part of the explanation for the fall in the ratio of savings to disposable income is to be found in the changed structure of personal income.

As a result of the transwar fall in the personal propensity to save, and its postwar rise, the level established by the early 1960's was not greatly different (slightly higher) from that of the late 1920's. But it was rather lower than the level in most other advanced economies, and this remained true even at the high level of 1973.[19] Changes in the distribution of income between self-employment and property income and other income do not explain the *rise* in the UK personal savings rate within the postwar period. The shares of rent, dividends, and interest and of income from self-employment fluctuated a little during the postwar period, but in total remained broadly stable at around one-fifth of personal income.[20]

No generally accepted explanation exists for the rise in the personal savings ratio in the 1950's and 1960's, which is one of the curiosities of British economic statistics. The order of magnitude of the rise is not altered if one redefines personal savings to include purchases (less depreciation) of consumer durables. It was to be expected that there would be a recovery in personal savings from the very low levels of the early 1950's; what is surprising is that the rise should have continued for so long and been so gradual.

Brief reference may be made to some of the explanations that have been offered for the rise, assuming for the moment that the observed

---

*The personal savings ratio continued to rise strongly after 1973 and reached an unprecedented level. This has commonly been attributed to the acceleration of inflation, though there is less agreement about the precise mechanism.

statistical rise correctly reflects reality. Increases in contractual savings in the form of pension contributions and repayment of mortgages on owner-occupied houses amounted to about half of the total rise that had occurred by the mid-1960's.* These may be attributed partly to institutional reasons, particularly the encouragement given to owner occupation through tax privileges and rent controls. After 1964, however, the main forms of contractual savings remained fairly stable as a proportion of personal disposable income, and the sharp rise in the personal savings ratio in the early 1970's resulted mainly from noncontractual savings (see *BEQB* 1977: 27).

There was a shift in the age structure of the population toward the 45–59 age group, which has the highest savings ratio (Lydall 1955: 142–43), and this would account for part, though not much, of the rise in the average savings propensity.[21] The extremely liquid position of the personal sector in the immediate postwar period helps to account for low savings at that time, though it can scarcely explain the continued rise in the savings ratio during the whole ensuing period. A gradual rise in disposable income relative to consumer aspirations may be conjectured to have occurred during the 1950's in association with the (historically) rapid rate of increase of real incomes; but if this was one of the factors responsible for the earlier rise in the savings ratio, it cannot have helped to bring about the further rise in the 1970's, when real incomes clearly lagged behind aspirations. Increased *awareness* of inflation and of the need to safeguard real assets may also have been a significant element, even during the earlier phase when inflation itself was not accelerating.

In the absence of any more satisfactory explanation, these factors may be regarded as the chief explanations of the rise.[22] The question is in need of further research; but the unreliability of the basic data to be explained is an obstacle to any decisive conclusion.[23]

Corporate Savings

The proportion of corporate savings to GNP increased across World War II.[24] Within the postwar period it was roughly constant. The reasons for the transwar increase will be discussed below. The con-

---

*Whether they *explain* half the rise depends on whether one considers the non-contractual savings of households independent of their contractual savings. Non-contractual savings in 1964 were probably still below the 1933–38 level. This has to be viewed in relation not only to the increase in contractual savings, which households may regard as a substitute, but also to the increase in corporate savings (which serves the same function by increasing the real value of shareholdings). (See Berman 1967.)

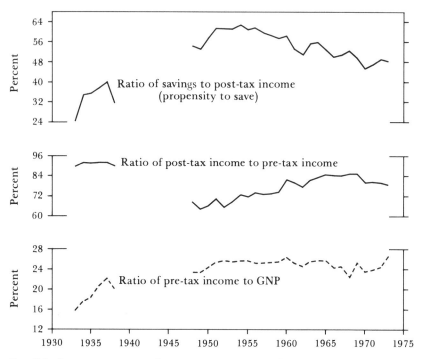

Fig. 5.8. Corporate income and savings, 1933–1973. Stock appreciation is included in income and savings for 1933–38 only.

stancy within the postwar period was the result of two opposite trends (Fig. 5.8). Until 1968 the proportion of profits taken in tax tended to fall, but the proportion of post-tax corporate income saved also fell. After 1968 there was a reversal in the trend toward reduced taxation and hence, as the propensity to save out of post-tax income continued to fall, corporate savings as a proportion of GNP declined slightly. The proportion of corporate income to GNP did not change significantly.[25]

These two opposite trends are not entirely independent of each other, because though taxation may influence corporate dividend policy, under the tax laws prevailing during this period, the proportion of profits distributed by a company helped determine its tax obligation.[26] The standard-rate income tax paid on undistributed profits entered into corporate tax payments, but the income tax on distributed profits paid by companies on behalf of their shareholders did not; in addition, profits tax was levied at a higher rate on distributed than on undistributed profits for part of the period. The reduction in the proportion of corporate income paid in tax during the postwar period was therefore partly the consequence of the declining propensity to save out of post-tax income: by increasing distributions, companies passed part of the income tax burden on to shareholders and reduced their own tax liability. The relationship between the corporate propensity to save and the tax ratio also worked the other way around. In order to end up with the same amount of internal finance after tax and distributions, a lower retention ratio was required given that the tax ratio was falling.

Tax changes, however, were not the only factors operating on the tax ratio and the savings propensity. The most important cause of the fall in the proportion of corporate income taken in tax was the increase in depreciation allowances, resulting from a number of factors, among them the rising ratio of fixed investment to income, higher rates of allowance, and the gradual diffusion of more generous rules relating to allowances as an increasing proportion of the capital stock was covered by them. Similarly, the fear of take-over bids has often been cited as a deterrent to low distribution policies because of the established tendency for the market valuation of shares to be more influenced by dividends than by undistributed profits. The growing threat of take-overs in the late 1950's and the 1960's therefore persuaded some companies to increase their distributions. The relative fall in tax liabilities must in this context be viewed as a factor enabling companies to increase distributions without reducing savings. Had there not been the favorable change in taxation, companies might not have been prepared to reduce savings as a proportion of pre-tax income, thereby either becoming more dependent on outside sources of finance or having to curtail their investment programs. Finally, the high level of savings in the early postwar period reflects in part the general policy of "dividend restraint" urged by the government and in part the business community's lack of confidence that prosperity would persist and companies' desire to have a financial cushion should economic activity decline. These factors became less important during the course of the 1950's.*

The significant transwar rise in the proportion of corporate savings to GNP was largely the result of the 50 percent increase in the corporate propensity to save out of post-tax income, and it occurred despite much heavier tax payments after the war. In terms of the pro-

*Again, it should be noted that the allocation of total savings by sector might not be quite as the statistics suggest. If they overestimate the upward trend in the personal sector, then the counterpart of that error might be the overestimation of the downward trend in the corporate propensity to save (see Odling-Smee 1973).

portion of pre-tax income to GNP, the corporate sector also rose in relative importance because of a relative rise in both the trading profits of never-public industries and company income from abroad (see Chapter 6).

The increase in tax payments between the late 1930's and the early postwar period reflects three things: (1) an increase in tax rates;[27] (2) an increase in corporate retentions, and hence a greater proportion of income subject to income tax after the war than before; and (3) a relatively low level of tax payments compared with tax accruals in the late 1930's. The transwar rise in the corporate propensity to save had a number of causes, several of which have already been mentioned. The higher level of investment in the postwar period obviously induced more corporate savings. The big inroads into company income made by taxation implied that the propensity to save out of post-tax income had to be even higher and the increased cost of external finance (see pp. 348–49) also worked in the same direction. Finally, the increase in capital consumption (Table 5.6) required more gross savings if the net savings rate was not to decline.[28]

Government Savings

Savings by the central government and local authorities were close to zero in the interwar period and then rose substantially across World War II. Local authority savings were always positive and fluctuated within a range of 0.6–1.4 percent of GNP, falling across the war and rising gradually in the postwar period to a level similar to that of the late 1930's. The central government dissaved in the interwar period when it found it difficult to balance its budget in the face of depression. Its savings rose to a very high level in 1948–51 owing to the use of fiscal policy to contain demand. The fall in central government savings from 1948–51 to 1961–64 reflects partly the greater reliance on monetary policy to control demand, and partly the rise in private savings, which made it possible to reduce government savings without creating excess demand. The return to a high level of government savings in the late 1960's and early 1970's was again the consequence of the extensive use of fiscal policy to restrain demand. By 1969–73 the ratio of government savings to GNP was back at the 1948–51 level and almost double the average for 1952–64.

The breakdown into sectoral share of GNP and sectoral savings propensity does not, of course, have the same significance for the government sector as it has for the personal and corporate sectors. The transwar rise in government savings relative to GNP was arithmetically the result of both an increase in government income (basically tax receipts, together with some trading income, rent, and interest) as a proportion of GNP, reflecting the widened scope of government activity in the postwar period and an increase in the proportion of this income saved by the government. Within the postwar period both ratios fell slightly until 1964, at which date the government's "propensity to save" was almost the same as the personal sector's, and then began to rise again, with the proportion of government income saved increasing from 7 percent in 1961–64 to 11½ percent in 1969–73.

Summary

The ratio of gross savings to GNP was higher in the postwar period than in either the interwar or pre–1914 years, and within the postwar period the ratio rose rapidly. The higher postwar ratio is partly attributable to the increase in depreciation, but savings net of depreciation in the postwar period were also higher than before 1914. Sectoral savings estimates are not available for pre–World War I years, but government data for 1900–1913 (see Feinstein 1972: Table 14) suggest that nearly all the savings that took place in the early period were private (personal and business). Thus comparing net savings in the postwar period with net savings in 1874–1913, the increase in government savings (from approximately zero to some 3½ percent of GNP in 1952–73) more than accounts for the rise of two percentage points in the total (Table 5.6).

Turning to the comparison of the postwar period with the interwar period, and to movements within the postwar period, it is clear that changes in government savings account for part of the rise in the total after World War II, but not for the upward trend within the postwar period. Attention must therefore be directed to the private sector's savings to explain the three chief features of the 60-year period from 1913 to 1973: the fall across World War I; (part of) the excess of the post–World War II average; and the rise within the postwar period (Tables 5.6 and 5.7). These movements cannot all be explained in the same terms. A number of influences appear to have been at work, no one of which is a complete explanation. Three broad factors may be listed that have commonly been held to influence the propensity to save:

(1) The level of demand, in a Keynesian sense. (High demand stimulates saving (a) by raising measured income relative to subjective assessments of "permanent" income and (b) by creating good investment opportunities and thereby encouraging business savings.) This

was probably largely responsible for the low level of savings in the interwar period. It is also in the right direction to help explain the high postwar level of gross savings compared with before 1914. It does not contribute to the explanation of the rise within the postwar period.

(2) The distribution of income (the hypothesis of Kaldor and others that there is a greater propensity to save out of profits than out of wages.) The fall in profits' share across World War I is in the right direction to explain the concurrent fall in the propensity to save. Across World War II the overall share of property income fell, which is in the wrong direction to explain the rise in savings. This fall, however, was due to the fall in rents and non-corporate net income from abroad, recipients of which may reasonably be supposed to have a lower propensity to save than other profit earners. The share of corporate profits in national income rose — a contribution in the right direction. But as seen above, the major part of the increase in corporate savings was not due to this, but to the increased proportion of corporate profits saved. There were no changes in distribution within the postwar period that might account for the rise in savings; on the contrary, there was a fall in the share of property income in GNP and in private income, whether measured before or after direct taxation. Comparing postwar with pre-1914, there was a rise in the (gross) propensity to save, notwithstanding a substantial fall in profits' share (however measured).[29]

The distribution-of-income hypothesis can be regarded as a special case of a more general Kaldorian-Keynesian hypothesis: that investment determines savings (whether through changes in the distribution of income or the level of income, or in some other way). As far as the postwar period is concerned, it is difficult to trace any direct causal connection between the increase in investment and the concomitant rise in the personal savings ratio. But one could argue that if the personal savings ratio had not risen, the pressure on demand would have tended to be stronger and fiscal policy would have been tightened to prevent excess demand. On this reckoning, the rise in investment *would have* stimulated a rise in government savings if private savings had not, coincidentally, also been rising. This would be consistent with the Kaldorian-Keynesian approach and is a defensible position. But it is also possible that if personal savings had not risen, the government might then have either restricted public sector investment or adopted a monetary policy that would have inhibited private investment. So it cannot be taken as established that the investment-income ratio was the cause and the savings-income ratio the effect, rather than the other way around.

(3) Depreciation needs provide a clearer instance of (gross) invest-ment-determining savings. They go a good way to explain the high level of gross savings in the postwar period, but not the fall across World War I or the rise within the postwar period.

Between them, these three elements are sufficient to account for the differences between the average savings propensities shown for the pre-1914, interwar, and postwar periods. But they do not help to ex-plain the rise in the savings ratio, originating mainly in the personal sector, within the postwar period. Possible explanations for this have already been discussed. Private gross savings in this period were higher than in any previous period. Taking the period 1874–1913 as a stand-ard of comparison, the increase in private gross savings was more than accounted for by the greater provision for depreciation. The factors tending to increase the ratio of private net savings to income – such as the high level of demand, social and institutional developments en-couraging contractual savings (probably), a long-run tendency for rises in real income as such to increase the average propensity to save (possibly) – appear to have been slightly outweighed by factors that operated in the opposite direction – such as the fall in profits' share in national income and the reduction in the need for private savings brought about by social security legislation.

THE UTILIZATION OF CAPITAL

In the preceding sections the measure of the stock of fixed capital has been the capital in existence rather than the capital actually used. This would apply also to the use of these series as indicators of capital input, and they thus differ in this respect from our measure of labor input, which is based on actual hours worked. The purpose of this section is to consider the evidence on the degree of utilization of the available capital. We begin with a review of the relevant concepts.

Two concepts of capital utilization may be distinguished. The first, which we call *economic utilization*, is the relation between the hours actually worked and the level of capital-hours employers see as the nor-mal maximum that can be profitably achieved. This is the concept rele-vant to the pressure of demand on the capital in existence. The second concept, which we call *physical utilization*, is the relation between ac-tual capital-hours and the amount of capital in existence (or 168-hours-a-week working, which comes to the same thing). Changes over time in physical utilization include changes in economic utilization, but they include other elements as well.

Changes over time in economic utilization are largely unplanned; changes over time in physical utilization include also planned changes in utilization connected with changes in organization or in the hours of labor. Long-run improvements in technique and in organization, permitting more nearly continuous working, may raise utilization. The expansion of the economy in general may permit fuller utilization of indivisible overhead facilities, such as railways and roads. On the other hand, decreases in hours worked by labor will tend to reduce utilization. It is not clear, therefore, whether on balance one would expect planned utilization to increase or decrease in the long run.

Two theoretical considerations lead one to expect there to be no long run trend in economic utilization.

In the first place, capital is brought into existence with the conscious intention that it should be profitably used. Entrepreneurs, in installing new equipment, will recognize that 24-hour working is not normally feasible, and they may be prepared on the basis of past experience for cyclical and seasonal fluctuations. But a demand for final output that is *persistently* insufficient to keep the capacity in use at the planned intensity implies a defect in foresight at the time when the capacity was installed. One would not expect any systematic trend in the degree to which foresight is defective.

In the second place, capital, unlike labor, can be scrapped when it is clear there will be no further demand for its services. This adds an extra dimension to utilization. If there is more capital than can be manned with the existing labor force, the older and less efficient capital can be scrapped and will then pass out of the measured gross capital stock. If there were a long-run tendency toward decreased capital utilization in the economic sense, it would probably be reflected in earlier scrapping rather than increased underutilization.

There are no continuous statistical series on the degree of utilization comparable to the unemployment percentage for labor. In this section the very limited and perhaps rather unrepresentative information that is available is reviewed in an attempt to form a general impression of the extent to which the degree of utilization of capital in both senses has varied over time.

Electricity Consumption, 1924–1968

The relationship between the horsepower of electric motors in industry and the electric power actually consumed has been suggested by Foss 1963 as a useful indicator of the degree of physical utilization of capital equipment. Census data permitting such a calculation for the United Kingdom are available for three years, 1924, 1930, and 1951.

TABLE 5.8

Ratio of Actual to Potential Electricity Consumption in
Manufacturing, 1924–1968

(Percent)

Industry	1924	1930	1951	1955	1960	1964	1968
Food, drink, tobacco	57.6%	55.1%	66.6%	58.2%	64.8%	68.5%	65.2%
Chemicals	68.0	68.0	134.3	149.0	166.2	187.4	202.4
Iron and steel	27.9	31.5	61.2	77.0	82.2	83.0	85.5
Other metal-users	23.9	22.5	30.1	35.7	41.8	45.5	44.9
Textiles, leather, clothing	44.3	45.8	59.0	53.4	67.7	59.8	51.6
Paper, printing, publishing	52.6	59.5	88.5	80.3	82.0	75.0	67.4
Other manufacturing	42.9	48.7	59.9	–	–	–	–
Total manufacturing	34.4%	37.4%	53.6%	59.0%	67.0%	71.4%	72.0%
Annual growth rate since previous date	–	1.4%	1.7%	2.8%	2.6%	1.6%	0.2%

Source: Census of Production, UK [4], 1924, 1930, 1951; Heathfield 1972 and private communication.

Note: Total electricity consumption is expressed as a percentage of potential electricity consumption, assuming a 46-hour week and a 50-week year. Potential electricity consumption in each industry is estimated by multiplying the total power (expressed in watts) of installed electric motors by a grossing-up factor, taken from the 1961 survey, to obtain the total installed wattage in all uses (heating, lighting, motive power, electrolysis, etc.); the total installed wattage is then multiplied by 2,300 to obtain potential electricity consumption (expressed in kilowatt hours). The totals for 1955–68 exclude other manufacturing industries; the comparable total figure for 1951 is 52.9%.

In addition, Heathfield (1972: 208–20), working with the 1951 census data and information from an unpublished 1961 sample survey by the Electricity Council, has provided annual estimates of capital utilization for 1955–68. The ratio of electricity consumption to electric motors installed is shown in Table 5.8 for 1924, 1930, and the postwar peak years (unfortunately excluding 1973).

These figures suggest that capital utilization rose significantly between 1924 and 1930 and between 1930 and 1951 and rose still more rapidly in the 1950's. The rise slowed down somewhat in the 1960's and virtually ceased between 1964 and the feeble cyclical peak 1968. The big trans–World War II increase occurred in all the industry groups distinguished in Table 5.8, and indeed in nearly all the individual trades that can be compared using census figures. The rise within the postwar period was confined to chemicals, iron and steel, and other metal-using industries. Some of the postwar increase in these industries may have been the result of structural changes in the composition of output, in the direction of processes with a high ratio of actual to potential consumption (high because they work on two- or three-shift systems, or because they have a high ratio of installed wattage to electric motor wattage). But the order of magnitude of such structural changes could not account for much of the increase.[30]

The rates of increase shown in Table 5.8 are substantial. Up till 1960 they are of the same order of magnitude as the rates of increase in the national capital stock. If they could be taken to apply to all capital, they would imply that capital input into production increased nearly twice as fast as the capital stock. However, this would certainly be an exaggeration, probably a great one. The findings relate to electric equipment in manufacturing. There are difficulties in extending it even to the rest of the capital stock in manufacturing. There are elements of the manufacturing capital stock — buildings and works and road vehicles — whose utilization is only very indirectly related to the utilization of electric equipment. It would be still less appropriate to extend the findings to the capital stock outside manufacturing. The electricity data therefore do not enable us to put a figure on the degree of utilization of the capital stock as a whole. However, they do indicate a marked upward trend in the physical utilization of one part of the capital stock.

Confederation of British Industry Survey Data, 1958–1973

For the period 1958–73, the degree of utilization can be inferred from the answers to the following CBI survey item: "Excluding seasonal factors, is your present level of output below capacity (i.e are you working below a satisfactorily full rate of operation)?" The results are dominated by the cycle (Fig. 5.9, top curve). The proportion of firms reporting below-capacity output fluctuates in a smooth cycle from about 40 percent at peaks to 70 or 80 percent at troughs. No trend is apparent.[31] The form of the question asked is such that the replies reflect changes in utilization in the economic sense. Changes in utilization due to causes (such as increased shift working) that led manufacturers to alter their idea of what constitutes a satisfactory rate of utilization would not affect the figure.

This curve may be compared with the others in Figure 5.9, also derived from the CBI survey, regarding factors expected to limit output. The proportion of firms reporting that they expected their output to be limited by plant capacity fluctuates closely in step with the proportion replying that they were not operating below capacity, but the proportion of firms limited by plant capacity is always much lower, indicating that "capacity working" is not interpreted to mean that output is at an absolute limit. Even at cyclical peaks, plant capacity appears as a much less important limitation on output than either skilled labor or orders and sales; it is of about the same importance as unskilled labor. This conclusion is consistent with that of other survey evidence.[32]

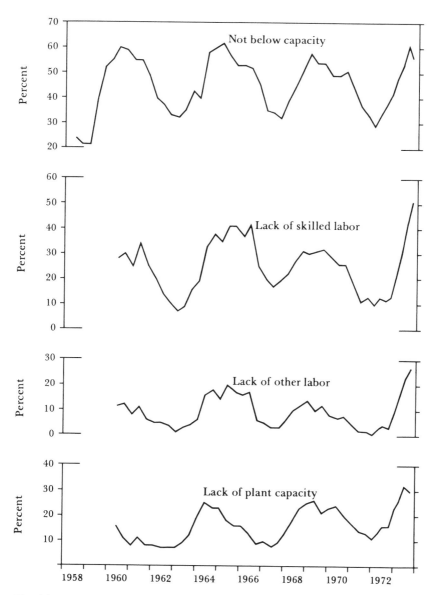

Fig. 5.9. Percentage of firms operating at full capacity and percentages expecting output to be limited by lack of skilled labor, other labor, or plant capacity, 1958–1973. *(Source: Confederation of British Industry, Industrial Trends Survey)*

TABLE 5·9

Proportion of Shift Workers in Manufacturing, 1951–1973

(Percent of all operatives)

Industry	September 1951[a]	April 1954[b]	October 1964[b]	April 1973[c]
Food, drink, tobacco	12%	13%	19%	21%
Chemicals	24	24	29	29
Metal manufacture	40	42	44	45
Engineering and shipbuilding	22	6	11	11
Vehicles	17	13	33	26
Metal goods n.e.s.	12	8	14	15
Textiles	10	11	22	18
Leather, clothing, timber, furniture	1	0	1	2
Bricks, etc.	17	17	23	22
Paper, printing, publishing	10	14	24	15
Rubber and other manufacturing	21	21	27	30
Total manufacturing	16%	12%	20%	18%

Source: Census of Production, UK [4], 1951; Ministry of Labour Gazette, April 1965; New Earnings Survey, UK [47], 1973.

[a]Based on all establishments in Great Britain employing more than 10 persons.

[b]Based on a sample of establishments in the UK (covering 75% of wage-earners in 1954 and 70% in 1964). Because the sample was biased toward large firms, in which it may be presumed that shift-working was more prevalent, these figures may be regarded as upper limits. The lower limit would be given by the assumption that there were no shift workers in establishments not covered by the samples. This would give proportions of 5% in 1954 and 14% in 1964 for total manufacturing. The year 1954 is not exactly cyclically comparable with 1951 and 1964, especially in the case of engineering and shipbuilding, where the big decline between 1951 and 1954 is attributable largely to the cyclical decline in demand (see Marris 1964: 155–58).

[c]The percentage of all manual adult employees in Great Britain who received premium payments for shift work, night work, or weekend work not paid as overtime. This definition of shift workers is probably slightly wider than that used for the estimates for earlier years.

There were certain much-publicized examples of output being limited by plant capacity, notably steel in the boom of 1955, bricks in 1960, and chemicals on several occasions, but in industry in general plant capacity was not usually felt as the chief short-run limitation to output in the postwar period.*

The combination of an upward trend in physical utilization suggested by the electricity figures for chemicals, iron and steel, and other

*There are some interesting features about the behavior of the CBI data after 1965. In the two peak years 1968 and 1973 the proportion of firms reporting that they were not working below capacity was lower relative to past cyclical peaks than the proportion of firms expecting plant capacity to limit output. This could reflect mismatch, such as was also postulated for the labor market: some firms were pressing hard against capacity, but many others were below it. Moreover, in 1968 the electric motors data showed a less-than-trend increase, suggesting a not very high level of economic utilization, whereas the CBI returns, especially the responses relating to the proportion of firms expecting plant capacity to limit output, indicate a normal or nearly normal cyclical peak. This is not necessarily inconsistent. A significant *number* of firms may have been short of capacity in 1968 (perhaps because of shifts in the structure of demand associated with devaluation), even though the *average degree* of utilization for industry as a whole was relatively low.

metal-using industries, with no distinct trend in the pressure of demand on capacity as perceived by businessmen, implies an increase in planned utilization of capital. If capital is operating for longer hours each day, one would expect to find an increase in shift working, especially during a period when labor's average working week was shortening. Such evidence as there is on shift working does not refute this hypothesis, though it does not lend strong support to it (Table 5.9). The increase between 1951 and 1964 in shift working in chemicals and metal manufacture (which includes nonferrous metals as well as iron and steel) was in the right direction but not large; in other metal-using industries there was a big fall in shift working in engineering and shipbuilding, and the rise in vehicles, a smaller industry, can barely have made up for it. The figures for 1973 are very similar to those for 1964. There was a marked increase in shift working in food, drink, and tobacco in the postwar period, but no significant increase in capital utilization is suggested by the electricity figures. This is a puzzle, and again we must remind ourselves that both the electricity and the shift-working figures are only very approximate measures of the concepts that we are here concerned with.*

Evidence on the Pre-1914 Period

None of the evidence so far examined goes back before 1924. We have little quantitative information on the degree of utilization in the pre-1914 period or how it compared with the interwar period. Hours worked by labor fell in the early 1870's and immediately after World War I, and this must have tended to reduce the degree of utilization of capital, but we do not know how far this was offset by improvements in organization, less frequent breakdowns, etc. Likewise, it is obvious that the general deficiency of demand in the interwar period would have tended to reduce utilization substantially compared with pre-1914.

In the business annals of the pre-1914 period, such as *The Economist's Annual Commercial History and Review*, reports of industry being unable to meet demand because of capacity limitations were relatively infrequent, though the problem was not unheard-of, notably in engineering; and most of the leading industries were reported to be at or near full capacity at all cyclical peaks between

---

*The main problem in interpreting shift-working data arises from differing capital intensities; large changes in capital utilization in capital-intensive plants will have only a small impact on the number of shift workers, whereas similar changes in labor-intensive plants will lead to large changes in shift working. The picture is further confused by the correlation between shift working and capital intensity (Marris 1964).

1870 and 1914 except that of 1882–83.* The general impression derived from these publications is that the pressure on capital capacity was little if at all less in pre-1914 booms than it was in booms after World War II. Combining this (admittedly impressionistic) conclusion with the finding that the amplitude of fluctuations in output was only moderately greater in 1879–1914 than in the postwar period, it would appear that the *average* degree of pressure of capacity over the cycle cannot have been very much less in the pre-1914 period that it was in the postwar period.

An indirect piece of evidence points to capital capacity having been actually more of a bottleneck at pre-1914 peaks. If capital rather than demand is the main limit on output at the top of the boom, *increases* in output may be expected to be a function (possibly lagged) of the *level* of additions to capital capacity. If there is a smooth (sine curve) cycle in investment, the peak in capacity (relative to trend) will lag by a quarter of a cycle after the peak in investment (or more, if there is a lag between investment and the new capacity becoming available for use). Capacity continues to rise strongly after investment has passed its peak because the rate of additions to capacity, though declining, is still high. In a context where demand exceeds capacity, so that capacity sets the limit on output, output will go on rising for a while even after demand has begun to fall, so long as capacity continues to increase. In postwar cycles this was not the pattern; investment (especially in manufacturing) lagged after output rather than the other way around. In most of the cyclical peaks of the half century before 1914, however, output did reach its peak a year later than investment in machinery and other equipment (the class of investment most directly relevant to short-run bottlenecks).† There are of course other explanations that would be consistent with these patterns, besides the hypothesis of capacity being the bottleneck, so it is not a strong test. But at least it tends in that direction.

Summary and Conclusions

We refer first to capital utilization in the economic sense, and then to capital utilization in the physical sense.

The underutilization of capital due to cyclical or other deficiency of demand for the final product appears to have been much less in the

---

*Even in this notoriously feeble boom, there were exceptions: in engineering there were reports in 1882 that orders could not be met on time.
†The exception is 1883. But this could be taken as the exception that proves the rule, since it was noted as an exceptionally poor cyclical peak from entrepreneurs' point of view, i.e. in respect of intensity of use of capacity.

postwar period than in the interwar period, but probably not much less than it was before 1914. At the beginning of the postwar period there may have been some increase in average utilization as the most serious bottlenecks were eliminated, and major sectors of industry were no longer operating below capacity because of shortages of materials. But after the middle 1950's there was no trend in capital utilization in the economic sense.

We have been unable to find satisfactory evidence on physical utilization before World War I. There was, however, almost certainly an increase between the interwar and postwar periods and, in some industries at least, within the postwar period. It is reasonable to expect a trend increase in the physical utilization of capital to be associated with the process of economic growth. Advances in technology and organization that permit such an increase are one aspect of technical progress.* On the other hand, the long-run fall in hours worked by labor is a factor operating in the opposite direction, though with less force, at least from the interwar period onward.

Utilization in the economic sense and utilization in the physical sense are not of course entirely independent. In particular, changes in the former may affect the latter. Thus the pressure of demand on capital capacity in the early postwar period in certain industries (e.g. iron and steel, and machine tools) may have led to attempts to increase the physical utilization of existing capital, as well as to the growth of the capital stock in place.

We have decided not to make any attempt to adjust our measures of total factor input for changes in capital utilization. Such adjustment would be appropriate in principle for changes in economic utilization, but accurate data are lacking. Changes in economic utilization between cyclical peaks within the three main peacetime periods do not appear to have been great, though account needs to be taken of them in transwar movements. Other sources of change in physical utilization are better regarded as affecting total factor productivity rather than total factor input.

*Technical progress might be expected in the same way to permit a fuller and more intensive utilization of labor. There is, however, a major offsetting factor (absent in the case of capital) in the desire for less arduous conditions of work as living standards rise.

CHAPTER SIX

Factor Shares

The distributive shares of labor and property in national income serve as weights in the calculation of total factor output. Trends in distributive shares are also a major topic in their own right in the study of economic growth.

THE FUNCTIONAL DISTRIBUTION OF INCOME

Labor's share in GNP showed a substantial long-run increase, from 54 percent in 1873 to 73 percent in 1973. Earlier it had fallen somewhat, dropping from 58 percent in 1856 to its lowest point of 51 percent in 1871.

LABOR'S SHARE

The share of wages, narrowly defined, altered little. The long-run increase in labor's share took the form mainly of an increase in the share of salaries, reflecting an increase in the number of salary-earners relative to wage-earners. There was also some increase, mainly in the postwar period, in the share of employers' insurance contributions. There was a small decline in the labor component of self-employment income.

PROPERTY'S SHARE

The fall in property's share occurred mainly across the two wars. But the sources of the transwar falls were not the same as the sources of the long-run fall.

Property's share may be divided into four components: income from abroad, rent, farm property income, and profits.

The share of income from abroad rose till 1913, then fell, chiefly across the wars. The rise and the fall were of about equal extent, so that income from abroad did not make a significant contribution to the fall in property's share between 1856 and 1973. Income from abroad did, however, account for over a third of the fall between 1913 and 1973.

The share of rent, defined as rent (actual and imputed) of dwellings and of government non-trading property, fell across both wars (especially the second) and rose in peacetime phases. These movements roughly canceled out in the long run.

The share of farm property income fell enormously between the 1870's and World War I. This was chiefly the result of the reduction in agriculture's weight in the economy and as such was not in itself a cause of decline in property's share in GNP.

Profits (non-farm non-rent domestic property income) are the most important category of property income. Profits are most usefully measured not as a share in GNP but as a share of the corresponding class of income ("trading income"). The fall in this share was the main source of the long-run fall in property's share in GNP. The fall in profits' share in trading income took place chiefly in the 1870's and 1880's, across World War I, to a lesser extent across World War II (the fall occurred in services and in the sometime-public sector, not in manufacturing), and in the postwar period (especially after 1968 and especially in the never-public sector). The fall across World War I owed much to the interwar depression. By the same token a rise was to be expected across World War II but did not happen. Various special explanations for this can be invoked. The implication of these explanations, and also of certain considerations relating to the postwar period, is that the underlying downward trend in profits' share was more continuous that the statistics suggest.

The decline in the profit rate (the percentage of the property component of nonfarm trading income to the capital employed in earning it) was broadly similar in amount and timing to the decline in profits' share. The chief exception was across World War II, when the profit rate fell by considerably more than profits' share. This fall was matched by a rise in the relative price of capital goods; measured at constant prices, the profit rate rose somewhat. Within the postwar period, up to 1972 the relative price of capital goods fell, and the constant price profit rate therefore fell more than the current price profit rate.

The foregoing relates to gross measures. There was a long-run upward trend in capital consumption as a proportion of national income, so property's net share fell more than its gross share, particularly across World War II. The decline in the net profit rate within the postwar period was much greater than the decline in the gross profit rate, partly because of the increase in capital consumption and partly because the net capital stock grew more rapidly than the gross capital stock.

THE DISTRIBUTION OF PRIVATE AND PERSONAL INCOME

The functional distribution of income, so far discussed, is not the same thing as the distribution of private income or personal income. Differences arise from government debt-interest, taxation, grants, and corporate income retention. The rise in government debt-interest across World War I significantly softened the impact of the fall in property's functional share on property's share in private income. Across World War II property's share in post-tax personal income fell much more than property's functional share, on account of an increase in corporate income retention and a shift in the burden of taxation to property income. Within the postwar period, on the other hand, the burden of taxation was shifted back to labor income, and as a result property's share in post-tax personal income scarcely fell at all.

EXPLANATIONS

Market power phenomena and international competition help explain the timing, at least, of the decline in property's functional share. However, they would probably not have been sufficient to bring about the sustained decline that occurred had there not also been trends unfavorable to capital of the kind analyzed in neoclassical theory, viz. a capital-saving bias in technical progress or a less-than-unit elasticity of substitution between labor and capital. Capital export helped to sustain property's share in GNP during the period 1873–1913, when domestic property's share in GDP was already declining.

The rates of growth of labor and capital, dealt with in the three preceding chapters, may be amalgamated into a measure of the rate of growth of total factor input (TFI). This in turn leads to measures of the rate of growth of total factor productivity (TFP), defined as the excess of the rate of growth of output over the rate of growth of TFI.

The rate of growth of TFI is defined as the weighted average of the rate of growth of labor input and the rate of growth of capital input, where the weights are respectively the distributive shares of labor and capital income.* The next step is accordingly to discuss trends in these distributive shares.

Trends in distributive shares have, however, a wider significance than their use as weights in TFI.[1] They are of interest in themselves and as possible causes and consequences of the course of economic growth. They are therefore treated here in more detail than would be required if the purpose were merely to devise weights for the calculation of TFI.

The most usual theoretical model of economic growth shows no change over time in the distribution of income between labor and capital. This does not conform to the experience of the United Kingdom, which exhibited a quite marked shift over time in favor of labor.

THE FUNCTIONAL DISTRIBUTION OF INCOME

We are concerned with the distribution of income between the two factors of production, labor and property. All income that cannot be classified as labor income is attributed to property. Thus property's share includes profits, rent, and income from abroad. (All data unless otherwise indicated are exclusive of stock appreciation, before allowance for capital consumption, and before tax.) Income from self-employment is divided between labor and property components as described below. Movements over time in labor's and property's shares in GNP are shown in Figures 6.1 and 6.2, respectively; and Table 6.1 gives data for benchmark years.†

Over the whole period 1856–1973 there was a significant shift of income from property to labor. Labor's share increased from 58 percent in 1856 to 73 percent in 1973. The whole of this substantial rise is ac-

---

*In simplest terms the rationale is as follows (it is more fully discussed and its limitations considered in the next chapter). The rate of growth of TFI is equal to the rate of growth of output that would have occurred in consequence of increases of input only, given constant returns to scale:

$$\hat{f} = \frac{1}{q} \left(\frac{\partial q}{\partial n} \frac{dn}{dt} + \frac{\partial q}{\partial k} \frac{dk}{dt} \right)$$

where f = TFI, q = output, n = labor, k = capital, t = time, and the circumflex denotes proportional date of change over time. On the assumption of marginal productivity factor pricing, the wage, w, equals $\partial q/\partial n$, and the profit rate, ϱ, equals $\partial q/\partial k$. Hence

$$\hat{f} = \gamma \hat{n} + (1 - \gamma) \hat{k}$$

where $\gamma = wn/q$ (labor's distributive share) and $(1 - \gamma) = \varrho k/q$ (capital's distributive share).

†These data are given so as to provide an indicator of the order of magnitude of the changes involved, but any choice of benchmark years (or even averages of years) is liable to be misleading in series like these when the fluctuations are sizable relative to trend movements. The reader's main attention should therefore be given to Figures 6.1 and 6.2 rather than the tables. In Table 6.1 and in some of the other tables in this chapter, 1953 is given in addition to our standard benchmark year 1951, because the distribution of income in 1951 was not representative.

TABLE 6.1

Factor Shares as a Percentage of Gross National Product at Current Prices, 1856–1973

Category	1856	1873	1913	1924	1937	1951	1953	1964	1973
Wages	43.5%	41.4%	36.6%	40.6%	38.6%	41.9%	41.2%	38.2%	34.4%
Salaries	6.9	6.3	11.9	17.3	18.1	20.0	19.8	23.8	26.5
Employers' contributions, etc.	0.0	0.0	1.0	2.1	2.5	3.8	3.9	5.0	6.6
Labor income from self-employment	7.4	6.7	6.5	6.6	5.9	5.2	5.1	4.4	5.3
Total labor income	57.8%	54.4%	56.0%	66.6%	65.1%	70.9%	70.0%	71.4%	72.8%
Income from abroad	2.2	4.4	8.5	5.0	4.2	2.7	1.5	1.4	2.3
Rent	4.8	5.2	6.4	5.3	6.4	3.4	3.6	5.0	6.6
Farm property income	10.1	7.2	2.4	1.8	1.1	1.9	2.0	1.3	1.1
Profits	25.1	28.8	26.7	21.3	23.2	21.1	22.9	20.9	17.2
Total property income	42.2%	45.6%	44.0%	33.4%	34.9%	29.1%	30.0%	28.6%	27.2%
Capital consumption	5.6	5.7	6.3	6.4	6.1	8.5	8.7	8.5	10.1
Net non-farm profits	22.1%	25.3%	22.2%	16.6%	18.9%	15.1%	16.6%	14.4%	9.4%

Note: All tables in this chapter exclude stock appreciation unless otherwise indicated. For definitions, see text. There are 2 breaks in the series in 1920; neither seriously affects comparability between pre-1914 and post-1914 data. One is caused by the exclusion of Southern Ireland, and the other by the use of a slightly higher GNP estimate for comparisons with post-1920 years. The latter includes estimates of income from small holdings (£10 million) and bank interest payments (£67 million), and a small addition to wages to cover income from subsidiary jobs (£47 million), but excludes some interest received by financial companies (£97 million). (See Feinstein 1972: 157, especially Tables 1.4 and 7.12.) The shares in GNP in 1920 are affected as follows:

Category	Pre-1920 estimation basis: Including Southern Ireland	Pre-1920 estimation basis: Excluding Southern Ireland	Post-1920 estimation basis: excluding Southern Ireland
Wages	46.1%	45.8%	46.5%
Salaries	14.9	15.2	15.1
Employers' contributions, etc.	1.0	1.0	1.0
Labor income from self-employment	6.3	6.0	6.0
Total labor income	68.3	68.1	68.6
Income from abroad	4.5	4.5	4.5

Category	Pre-1920 estimation basis: Including Southern Ireland	Pre-1920 estimation basis: Excluding Southern Ireland	Post-1920 estimation basis: excluding Southern Ireland
Rent	2.9%	2.9%	2.9%
Farm property income	3.0	2.6	2.8
Profits	21.3	21.9	21.2
Total property income	31.7	31.9	31.4
Capital consumption	7.9	7.9	7.3
Net non-farm profits	15.6	16.2	15.8

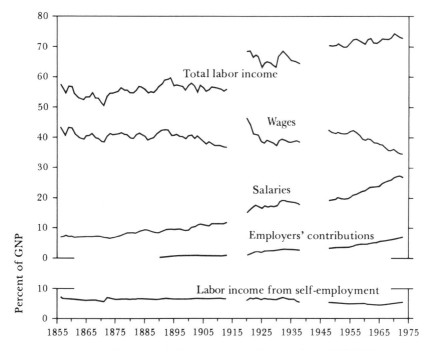

Fig. 6.1. Labor income's shares in gross national product, 1856–1973

counted for by two abrupt jumps during and immediately after each of the two world wars. The shift across World War I was larger than across World War II. The long-run trends that occurred within peacetime periods (down in the interwar period, up after World War II) were small by comparison. There were, in addition, in peacetime periods, cyclical movements and some erratic movements, and also one and a half very long swings from 1856 to 1913, with labor's share falling up till 1871, rising till the early 1890's, and then falling (slightly) up till 1913. In general, movements within peacetime periods were much less important than changes between periods: labor's share rose from a range of 50–59 percent before World War I to 63–68 percent in the interwar period and 70–73 percent after World War II.

LABOR'S SHARE

Movements in labor's share can be looked at in terms of its four component parts: (1) wages (including pay of armed forces); (2) salaries; (3) the part of the income of the self-employed that is a reward for their labor rather than their capital; and (4) employers' contributions to National Insurance, private pension schemes, and so forth.

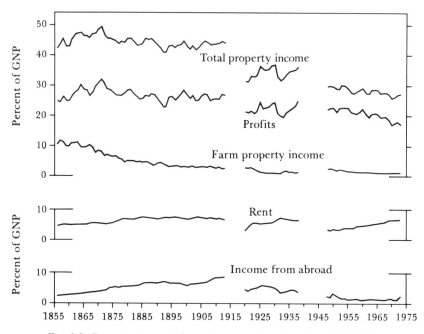

Fig. 6.2. Property income's shares in gross national product, 1856–1973

Wages and Salaries

The distinction between wages and salaries does not have much relevance to the distribution of income between labor and capital, but it
does represent a division between broad occupational groups of
workers that is meaningful for certain social and economic purposes.
Administrative, technical, and clerical employees are classified as
salary-earners; all other employees are classified as wage-earners.[2]
Salary-earners' share of the national income expanded persistently,
from nearly 7 percent in 1860–69 to 17 percent in 1921–24 and 27 percent in 1970–73. By contrast, the long-run share of wage-earners was
remarkably constant: the trend, though mildly downward, remained
within a few percentage points of 40 percent of GNP in all peacetime
years up till the late 1960's.

It is this overall stability in the share of wages before 1938 that
originally attracted the attention of Kalecki (1938) and Keynes (1939a:
48) and was subsequently investigated by Phelps Brown and Hart
(1952), who pointed out the changes in the proportion of wage-earners
in the working population. It is evident from the above data that the

TABLE 6.2
*Wage- and Salary-Earners: Numbers in Employment and
Average Earnings, 1911–1971*

Year	Numbers in employment (millions)		Average annual earnings (£)		Wage-earners as percent of total employees	Ratio of average salaries to average wages
	Wage-earners	Salary-earners	Wage-earners	Salary-earners		
1911	15.42	1.98	52	126	88.6%	2.4
1921	13.13	2.75	122	249	82.7	2.0
1931	13.43	3.13	115	237	81.1	2.0
1938	15.44	3.80	126	240	80.2	1.9
1951	16.84	4.95	322	523	77.3	1.6
1961	16.51	6.80	585	821	70.8	1.4
1971	14.23	8.16	1193	1650	63.6	1.4

Source: Feinstein 1972: Tables 11.10, 57; *Census of Population*, UK [52], *1971:* Economic Activity Tables, Part 4; basic statistics (Appendix N).
Note: Part-time workers are counted as full-time, and so the estimates of wages and salaries are averages of part-time and full-time earnings. Wage-earners include the armed forces. The 1911 figures include Southern Ireland; the total of wage- and salary-earners in Great Britain and Northern Ireland alone in that year was 16.5 million.

seemingly miraculous "stability of the proportion of the national dividend accruing to labour" (Keynes 1939a: 48–49) depends on the exclusion from the definition of labor of both salary-earners – the large category of administrative, technical, and clerical workers – and the self-employed.

The increase in aggregate salaries relative to aggregate wages came about because the number of salary-earners increased relatively to the number of wage-earners, not because the average salary increased relatively to the average wage (Table 6.2). On the contrary, the ratio of the average salary to the average wage fell from 2.0 in 1921 to 1.4 in 1961 (with no futher change between 1961 and 1971). This was more than offset in its impact on the ratio of aggregate salaries to aggregate wages by the fall in the share of wage-earners in total employees from 83 percent in 1921 to 64 percent in 1971.[3] Over half of the increase in total employees in the 50 years up to 1971 went into salaried occupations, though only 17 percent of employees held such positions in 1921. Many of the additional salary-earners after 1938 must have gone into the lower-paid occupations, such as clerical work,[4] thus slowing down the rate of increase of average salaries and contributing to the fall in the ratio of average salaries to average wages.[5]

Employers' Contributions

This item covers both employers' contributions to private pension and retirement programs and employers' compulsory contributions under National Insurance and earlier state schemes. It grew from a small proportion of national income before 1914 to a very substantial one by 1973. Its rise was an element, but a relatively minor one, in the rise in labor's share across the two wars. Its big rise between 1951 and 1973 accounted, arithmetically, for the *whole* of the increase in labor's share during that period.

Employers' contributions under state programs and under private schemes were of a similar order of magnitude, contributions to private schemes being always slightly the larger but growing at a rather slower rate proportionally. The rise in each contributed just about equally, both in amount and in timing, to the rise in the total.[6]

It is obviously right to treat employers' contributions under private schemes as part of the remuneration of labor. More doubts may be felt about employers' national insurance contributions. Most employees would not regard them as part of their remuneration. They are only loosely related to benefits received and are in many respects more like a tax on employment. However, for the analysis of the functional distribution of income, it is right to include them in labor's share, since they are part of the cost of employing labor. Economic theory suggests that, in the absence of forces tending in the other direction, a rise in employers' contributions would be accompanied by a reduction in the share in national income of the other constituents of labor remuneration, as indeed it was in the postwar period. So though it is a fact worth noting that the rise in labor's share within the postwar period all came in the form of employers' contributions, it would be misleading to conclude, on that account, that labor's share in some more fundamental sense did not really rise. The case for including all employers' contributions as part of labor income is, moreover, made more intuitively appealing by the closely parallel trends in the contributions to public and private schemes.

Labor Income from Self-Employment

Income from self-employment covers the income of farmers, independent professional persons and other sole traders or partnerships. This third, and largest, segment is itself very varied in composition, ranging from the small tradesman working without assistance to the owner of a large but unincorporated business employing many workers.

The income of the self-employed (employers and workers on own account) combines both the remuneration for their labor and the return on capital invested. We have therefore attempted to apportion the income from self-employment between labor and property, though any such division is inherently arbitrary. The method that had been adopted is to assume that the labor component of a self-employed person's total income is the amount which he would have received as a paid employee in the same broad sector of the economy, and then to regard the difference between total income and estimated labor income as the return on capital. Twelve sectors were distinguished for the years after World War I; the estimates for earlier years are much less reliable, being based on assumptions about the constancy of the ratios of the self-employed to total manpower and of relative average earnings over the years 1861–1911 in all sectors other than agriculture.[7]

An alternative method of allocating income from self-employment would be to assume that the return on capital was the same for unincorporated business as for the corporate sector, thus leaving the labor component as the residual. The reason for preferring the former method is primarily statistical: satisfactory data do not exist for capital in corporate and unincorporated enterprises separately for the years before World War II and even those for the postwar period have a large margin of error, so any estimates of the property component of self-employment income would be extremely rough.[8]

The long-run downward trend in the share of labor income from self-employment in GNP was the result of a steady fall in the share of total self-employment income in GNP, partially offset by a rise in labor's share of total self-employment income (Table 6.3). All these trends became more marked after World War II; but there was a reversal in the late 1960's, possibly induced by the structure of taxation. The declining importance of the unincorporated sector was associated in the nineteenth century with the agricultural depression and the fall in the number of farmers, especially in Ireland.[9] Labor income from nonfarm self-employment actually rose as a percentage of GNP from 3.9 percent in 1856 to 5.3 percent in 1913, but the increase was not sufficient to offset the farmers' declining share. The fall in the number of self-employed outside agriculture relative to the number of wage-and salary-earners took place almost wholly across World War II (Table 6.4). Average income from self-employment (labor and property components combined) also fell relative to average employee income in nonfarm sectors, from nearly three times as much in 1911 to only one and a half times in 1964. There was no downward trend in the ratio of average farmer's income to average farmworker's income, and in the

TABLE 6.3
Income from Self-Employment, 1913–1973

Year	Labor income from self-employment as percent of GNP	Total income from self-employment as percent of GNP	Labor income from self-employment as percent of total income
1913[a]	6.5%	15.7%	41.1%
1924	6.6	16.0	41.4
1937	5.9	12.8	46.1
1951	5.2	11.1	47.4
1964	4.4	7.9	56.0
1973	5.3	10.6	50.2

[a]Including Southern Ireland.

TABLE 6.4
The Self-Employed and Wage- and Salary-Earners:
Numbers in Employment and Average Earnings, 1911–1973

Year	Ratio of the number of self-employed to the number of wage- and salary-earners			Ratio of average income from self-employment to average income of wage- and salary-earners[a]		
	Agriculture	Other sectors	Total	Agriculture	Other sectors	Total
1911[b]	0.36	0.11	0.12	2.9	2.8	2.6
1924	0.45	0.11	0.13	2.6	2.3	2.1
1937	0.54	0.10	0.11	2.0	2.1	1.9
1951	0.61	0.07	0.08	2.8	1.9	2.0
1964	0.72	0.06	0.07	2.6	1.5	1.6
1973	0.68[c]	0.07	0.08	3.6[c]	1.7	1.8

[a]Before providing for depreciation and stock appreciation.
[b]Excluding Southern Ireland. These are rough estimates only, to permit comparisons with later years.
[c]These figures are not comparable with those for 1964 and earlier years because of a change in the concept of employment in agriculture. The comparable 1964 figures are 0.54, for the ratio of numbers, and 3.2, for the ratio of incomes.

postwar period it was actually higher than before World War II. Labor income from self-employment outside agriculture fell proportionately less than these figures on numbers and average earnings suggest, because of the increase referred to above in the labor element in total income from self-employment.

The Price of Labor

The price of labor is the average payment that has to be made to labor. Average labor income, in the context of the aggregates being considered in this chapter, can be defined as total labor income (wages, salaries, employers' contributions, etc., and labor income from self-employment) per member of the employed labor force. Average labor

TABLE 6.5

Growth of Real Wages and Real Income, 1856–1973

(Annual percentage growth rates)

Period	Per man-year		Per man-hour	
	Real wages	Real income	Real wages	Real income
Peacetime phases:				
1856–1873	1.0%	1.4%	1.9%	2.3%
1873–1913	1.1	1.0	1.1	1.0
1924–1937	1.1	1.2	0.9	1.0
1951–1973	2.6	2.5	3.5	3.4
Wartime phases:				
1913–1924	1.3	0.2	3.2	2.1
1937–1951	1.4	0.8	2.2	1.6
Post-WWII cycles:				
1951–1955	2.0	1.9	2.2	2.1
1955–1960	2.1	2.2	2.9	3.0
1960–1964	3.1	2.9	4.0	3.8
1964–1968	3.1	2.8	4.4	4.1
1968–1973	2.8	2.6	3.8	3.6
1856–1973	1.4%	1.3%	1.9%	1.8%

Note: Real income is GNP at current factor cost estimated from the income side, deflated by the price index implied by GNP expenditure-side estimates.

income, deflated by a general GDP deflator, we shall here call the real wage, and it can be considered to be the cost of labor for making comparisons with the cost of capital. Tautologically, labor's share is equal to the real wage divided by real income per head (i.e. per member of the employed labor force). Thus differences between the rates of growth of real wages and of income per head betoken changes in the distribution of income.

The rates of growth of real wages between benchmark years, on a per-year and a per-hour basis, are given in Table 6.5 alongside the corresponding GNP growth rates.

Over the period 1856–1973 as a whole real wages grew faster than real income (by 0.1 of a percentage point). It is sometimes said that the contribution made by changes in distribution to the long-term growth of real wages is negligible compared with the contribution of general economic growth. This was broadly true in the United Kingdom, though the contribution of such changes to the annual rate of growth of real wages was not *entirely* negligible. The excess of the rate of growth of real wages over the rate of growth of income per head was concentrated in the two war periods, as follows from what has already been said about shares.

The long-run rate of growth of real wages per man-year was remarkably constant, except for the post–World War II period. In other periods, *including* the two war phases, the rate of growth of real wages per man-year lay within the range 1.0–1.4 percent. The growth of real wages is thus unlike the growth of most other variables in that the war phases do not stand out as exceptional. The constancy of the growth rate is naturally somewhat less if the periods are broken up into shorter units. In particular, real wages grew at a faster rate between 1873 and 1889 (1.7 percent) than between 1889 and 1913 (0.7 percent).

If one looks at the real wage as a measure of the cost of labor as a factor of production, the hourly wage is more relevant than the yearly wage. The hourly wage does not show the same constancy of growth rates between periods as the annual wage. This difference reflects the irregularity in the rate of reduction of hours of work. The war periods stand out as showing a substantially more rapid rate of growth of hourly real wages than the average of the peacetime periods before World War II.

Within the postwar period the rate of growth of the real wage (both per year and per hour) was significantly higher after 1960 than in the 1950's. This reflected chiefly the higher rate of growth of income per man. But it also reflected a tendency after 1960, not present in the 1950's, for real wages to grow faster than real income. The 1870's and 1880's are the only other peacetime period of comparable duration when this happened. The excess of the rate of growth of real wages over the rate of growth of real incomes between 1960 and 1973 was rather more than 0.2 percent a year — a significant amount, though not nearly as great as the excess in the two transwar periods.[10]

PROPERTY'S SHARE

We divide property's share in GNP into four components, as follows. The definitions differ in certain respects from those usually used, and the reader is asked to note them carefully.

(1) *Income from abroad:* net property income from abroad.

(2) *Rent:* rent from dwellings, *plus* rent from non-trading property (offices, schools, etc.) owned and occupied by the central government and local authorities. Agricultural rent and rent from business premises are *not* included under this heading.

(3) *Farm property income:* all non-labor income generated in agriculture, consisting of rent on farmland and farm buildings *plus* farm profits (chiefly the property component of the incomes of self-employed farmers).

(4) *Profits:* all other property income, consisting of the gross trading profits of companies, *plus* the gross trading surpluses of the public sector, *plus* rent paid by trading concerns and public authorities, *plus* the property component of income from nonagricultural self-employment.

Both farm property income and profits thus include components normally included under rent. The chief reason for using the present definitions is that the division between rent and profits (both in industry and commerce and in agriculture) is pointless analytically unless rent is confined to land rent, as opposed to rent on buildings, and this breakdown is not statistically feasible; indeed the data are unsatisfactory even for rent on land and buildings taken together.[11]

The division of property income into these four components is much more important analytically, and also more complicated, than the division of labor income into wages, salaries, and self-employment income. The influences affecting each component and the consequent movements in their shares in GNP have been different. Net property income from abroad is determined by past movements in capital export and is not part of domestic product. Rent as here defined has been greatly influenced by government controls on rented dwellings and by the imputation procedures used for measuring rent of owner-occupied dwellings; imputation procedures also largely determine the rent from non-trading properties owned and occupied by public authorities. Movements in farm property income reflect the special forces affecting agriculture's position in the economy, especially its steep decline in the agricultural depression of the last quarter of the nineteenth century. Finally, profits — the earnings of domestic non-farm trading capital — correspond most closely to the economist's usual concept of profit as a class of income. Profits, as the largest part of property income, received the most attention below.

The main features of the movements in the overall property share in GNP were the step-wise declines across the two wars, especially World War I, corresponding to the increase in the overall labor share (Fig. 6.2 and Table 6.1). It is therefore natural, though in fact misleading, to look at the sources of the transwar declines in order to discover the sources of the long-run decline. Declines in the shares of income from abroad and rent together accounted for nearly half the decline across World War I and totaled more than the whole of the decline across World War II (see Table 6.6). One might therefore conclude that the long-run decline in property's share was due to these two items, both of which stand rather apart from the normal forces determining the distribution of national income.

TABLE 6.6

Changes in Percentage Shares in Gross National Product of Property Income and
Its Components, 1856–1973

Period	Income from abroad	Rent	Farm property income	Profits	Total
1856–1913	6.3	1.6	– 7.7	1.6	1.8
1913–1924	– 3.5	– 1.1	– 0.4	– 5.3	– 10.3
1924–1937	– 0.8	1.1	– 0.7	1.9	1.5
1937–1953	– 2.7	– 2.8	0.9	– 0.3	– 4.9
1953–1964	– 0.1	1.4	– 0.7	– 2.0	– 1.4
1964–1973	0.9	1.6	– 0.2	– 3.7	– 1.4
1856–1973	0.1	1.8	– 8.8	– 7.8	– 14.7

Note: The 1913–24 figures allow for the effects of the changes in geographical area and in the basis of the GNP estimates in
that period, and hence do not exactly correspond to the difference between the relevant columns in Table 6.1.

But this conclusion would be erroneous. For the wartime falls in the
shares of these two items were more than matched by peacetime rises.
Over the entire period 1856–1973 the decline in property's share came
from the other two items, farm property income and profits.

The different classes of property income will now be examined in
turn.

Income from Abroad

This class of income was small in 1856, and it was small again in
1973. At its peak, in 1913, however, it accounted for 8½ percent of
GNP. The subsequent decline in its share, chiefly across the two wars,
explains in an arithmetic sense nearly two-fifths of the fall in property's
overall share between 1913 and 1973. It is further discussed in Chapters 14 and 15.

Rent

The movements in the shares in GNP of the two types of non-farm
rent, rent from dwellings and the non-trading rent of the government,
were similar. They both rose up to 1913, fell across each of the two
wars, and recovered during the subsequent peacetime periods. The
1913 share of rent had been regained by 1937; and the 1937 share had
been rather more than regained by 1973. Government non-trading
rent was much the less important of the two,[12] and it behaved in the
same way because both series reflect the same movements in ratable
values. It is, of course, an imputed figure. The same is true of an increasing proportion (viz. the owner-occupier part) of the rent from
dwellings.

The change in the share of rent from dwellings can be explained primarily by movements in relative prices. Broadly speaking, house rents rose more rapidly than other prices during peacetime periods, but they hardly increased at all across the wars when other prices were moving up sharply. Rent-control legislation was largely responsible for these fluctuations.[13] Rents were frozen in 1915 and again in 1939. The recovery in rents, relative to other prices, took place more quickly after World War I than after World War II. Increases in rents were permitted by the legislation of 1919, 1920, and 1923, so that already by 1924 the share of rents from dwellings in GNP was only slightly lower than it had been in 1913 (4.6 percent compared with 5.5 percent). After World War II, by contrast, no significant measure of decontrol was enacted until 1957. At that date rent from dwellings accounted for only 3.3 percent of GNP. Thereafter, however, rent's share in GNP rose as a result of the more rapid increase in house rents than in other prices. The impulse toward rising rents came partly from rises in interest rates and in the relative cost of house-building.

Only houses rented from private landlords were subject to rent control legislation, and in Great Britain these accounted for just 17 percent of the housing stock at the end of 1973, compared with 88 percent in 1913 (Hemming & Duffy 1964; *Social Trends*, UK [24], *1974*: 162). However, movements in the imputed rents of owner-occupied houses (11 percent of the total stock in 1914 and 52 percent in 1973) also reflected movements in the rents of controlled property to some extent.[14] The share of rents from the third class of housing, houses owned by local authorities (and by the central government, on a much smaller scale), rose steadily as these houses became more important in the stock.[15]

Farm Property Income

The long-run secular decline in the share of farm property income in GNP, especially before World War I, reflected the declining importance of agriculture in the economy rather than declining profitability of agriculture (Table 6.7). Though the low point of agriculture was not reached until the late 1920's,* most of the falls in the shares in GNP of farm property income and of total agricultural income occurred before 1913.

There are three points of interest to note about the pre-1914 period. (1) The decline in the share of agricultural income in GNP between

---

*In 1927 farm rent and profits accounted for 1% of GNP, and total agricultural income for 2.7%. The share of farm rent and profits in total agricultural income was 36%.

TABLE 6.7
Agricultural Income and Farm Property Income,
1856–1973

Year	Farm property income as percent of GNP	Agricultural income as percent of GNP	Farm property income as percent of agricultural income
1856	10.1%	22.5%	45%
1873	7.2	14.7	49
1913	2.4	6.1	39
1924	1.8	4.3	43
1937	1.1	3.2	35
1951	1.9	5.1	38
1964	1.3	3.2	40
1973	1.1	2.7	41

Note: The changes in geographical coverage and in the basis of GNP estimates affect comparability between 1913 and earlier years on the one hand and 1924 and later years on the other. The 1920 estimates comparable with 1913 are, respectively, 3.0%, 6.7%, and 44%; and the 1920 estimates comparable with 1924 are 2.8%, 5.6%, and 50%.

1856 and 1913 was mainly a decline in agriculture's share in real output. It did not owe much to the fall in agricultural prices from the late 1870's onward.[16] Of course the ultimate cause of both the stagnant agricultural output and the fall in prices was the same, namely, the combination of a slower growth of demand with an increased availability of imports. (2) Ireland was an important part of the United Kingdom as far as agriculture was concerned, but its experience does not appear to have been significantly different from Great Britain's, at least after the 1870's.[17] (3) Both agricultural rent and the property component of farmers' self-employment income fell relative to GNP as landlords shared the burden of falling prices and stagnant output with their tenants.[18] Rent remained about 30% of total agricultural income throughout the half century before World War I.

The fall in the share of farm property income in GNP, due chiefly, as just shown, to the decline in agriculture's importance in the economy, accounts arithmetically for well over half the total fall in the share of property income between 1856 and 1973. It would be wrong, however, to infer that the decline in agriculture's importance was a major force in diminishing property's share in GNP. Property's share in agricultural output in 1856 was in fact only fractionally higher than property's share in GNP (or the share of domestic property in GDP).[19] The decline in the relative importance of agriculture, taken by itself, would therefore have done little more than alter the sector of the economy where property income was earned; it would have resulted in an increase in other property income's share in GNP nearly equal to the fall in farm property income's share.

The effect on distribution between land and other capital is a different matter. Data do not exist on income from land as such. But it is obvious that the land-capital ratio is higher in agriculture than in the rest of the economy.[20] So the shift away from agriculture, though approximately neutral for labor, was unfavorable to land and favorable to capital. The shift away from agriculture, and the resulting fall in the the return from land, was largely the consequence of the increased availability of the output of the land-abundant countries of the New World in international trade, in conformity with the factor-price-equalization theorem. The theoretically distinctive attribute of land, that it is in fixed supply, does not necessarily tend to make its share in GNP fall. This depends on the elasticity of substitution. It is by no means obvious that land's share in GNP did decline after World War I. By that time *agricultural* land had ceased to be a major source of income, and the use of land had come to be increasingly in the production of non-tradables.

Profits

The share of profits in GNP (Tables 6.1 and 6.6) fell by 11.6 percentage points over the 100 years 1873–1973. Almost the whole of this fall was accounted for by the falls across World War I (5.3 points) and in the postwar period (5.7 points). Movements in other periods were small by comparison.

The movement over time in the share of profits in GNP reflected, among other things, the change in the shares in GNP of income from abroad, rent, and farm property income. When one share falls, all other shares tend as a result to rise. Consequently, profits' share in GNP does not exactly measure the distribution of domestic non-rent non-farm income between the factors labor and capital. It is therefore useful also to look at shares in a different way, successively taking out net income from abroad, rent, and agriculture from the denominator as well as from the numerator.

The first four rows of Table 6.8 adopt this alternative way of presenting some of the data already considered. Row 5 introduces a different element, to be explained in a moment. The last row deducts depreciation. The table shows property's shares in alternative measures of national income in benchmark years; the corresponding labor shares are the difference between 100 and the figures shown.

TABLE 6.8

Property's Share in Alternative Measures of National Product, 1856–1973

(Percent)

Category	Comparable with 1913	Comparable with 1924	1856	1873	1913	1924	1937	1951	1953	1964	1973
(1) Property income as per cent of GNP	31.7%	31.4%	42.2%	45.6%	44.0%	33.4%	34.9%	29.1%	30.0%	28.6%	27.2%
(2) Domestic property income as percent of GDP	28.5	28.2	40.9	43.1	38.8	29.9	32.1	27.1	29.0	27.6	25.5
(3) Domestic non-rent property income as percent of non-rent GDP	26.2	25.9	37.8	39.8	34.2	25.8	27.2	24.5	26.2	23.7	20.1
(4) Profits (domestic non-rent non-farm property income) as percent of trading income (non-rent non-farm GDP)			35.6	38.1	33.8	24.9	27.0	23.8	25.4	23.2	19.6
(5) Profits as percent of "non-public" trading income			—	—	35.8	27.1	29.3	26.6	28.5	26.0	22.6
(6) Net profits as percent of net trading income			32.7	35.1	29.8	20.5	23.0	18.2	19.9	17.2	11.4

Source: Basic statistics (Appendix N); A. L. Chapman 1952; Deane & Cole 1962; Routh 1965; *National Income and Expenditure, UK* [21], 1968, 1964–74.

Note: The changes in geographical coverage and in the basis of the GNP estimates in 1920 (see Table 6.1) affect comparability between 1913 and earlier years on the one hand and 1924 and later years on the other. Estimates for 1920 on comparable bases are:

Category	Comparable with 1913	Comparable with 1924
Profits as % category of trading income	24.8%	24.4%
Profits as % of "non-public" trading income	27.0	26.6
Net profits as % of net trading income	19.4	19.3

The first row is the same as the total property income row of Table 6.1 and shows property's share in GNP. In row 2 income from abroad has been excluded. Income from abroad grew as a proportion of GNP up till 1913. Hence, though property's share in GNP rose between 1856 and 1913, its share in GDP fell. On the other hand, after 1913, and especially across the two world wars, income from abroad fell, so property's share decreased less in GDP than in GNP.

The exclusion of rent from domestic income (row 3) further reduces the fall in property's share across the wars, especially across World War II. But it intensifies the fall between 1856 and 1913 that appears in row 2, because the share of rent in GNP increased almost continuously over that period. When agriculture is removed (row 4), the fall between 1856 and 1913 is reduced again, but movements after 1913 are not much affected. Profits' share of non-farm GDP (row 4) contrasts with its share of GNP (Table 6.1) chiefly in its much larger fall between 1856 and 1924.

Row 4 of Table 6.8 compares profits with non-farm non-rent GDP (henceforward referred to as trading income); that is to say, it compares profits with output in the main productive sector of the economy. Of the measures so far considered, it thus comes nearest to the economist's usual notion of the proportion of the product of industry going to capital.[21] Its annual movements are shown in Figure 6.3. The long-run downward trend after 1870 is striking. It occurs in the period 1870–90, across the two wars, and in the postwar period, especially after 1968.* It is arrested but not reversed in 1890–1913 and in the interwar period (when the large cyclical movements make trends difficult to discern).

The concept of trading income here used includes income earned in the public sector from the provision of certain public goods, such as defense, education, and health services, on which no profit element is recorded in the national accounts. This means that property's share will decrease if these services increase their share relative to other items in the national product, as they in fact did. Row 5 of Table 6.8 shows property's share in domestic non-rent non-farm income when incomes earned in public nonprofit-making activities are excluded from the denominator (incomes earned in nationalized industries are not excluded, nor are incomes earned in the private sector from the sale of goods and services to the public sector). The data do not permit

---

*As a statistical point, it may be noted that the inclusion in profits of rent paid by trading concerns, which was justified on p. 173, above, contributes significantly to the fall in profits' share across World War II. The share in non-rent non-farm GDP of rent paid by trading concerns fell by slightly over one percentage point in that period.

estimates for before 1913. Despite a rise in the importance of public nonprofit-making activities,* from less than 5 percent of GNP in 1913 to over 15 percent in 1973, the absolute magnitude of this sector turns out not to be large enough for its expansion to have made more than a fractional contribution to lowering property's share. We therefore continue henceforward to use trading income as previously defined without making this deduction on account of the public sector.

The final row of Table 6.8 shows that when depreciation is deducted from both numerator and denominator, profits' share in trading income fell by significantly more than the gross measures indicate.

The profits data we have so far been discussing include the estimated property element in non-farm self-employment income, and also the trading surpluses of public corporations and other public enterprises. They thus differ from the data on company profits' share, often used as a measure of distributive shares in the postwar period. Figures for the company sector and the other two sectors (the unincorporated and public sectors) are available for 1935–38 and for postwar years, and are shown in Table 6.9. In this table, and in the following tables where we are concerned chiefly with movements within the postwar period, we take cycle averages in order to avoid giving undue prominence to individual years. In view of the peculiarities of 1950 and 1951, we take 1952–55 as representing "early postwar."

We consider first the movement across World War II, i.e. between 1935–38 and 1952–55. Table 6.9 shows that the public sector's share of profits in trading income rose. This result is affected, however, by the increase in the size of the public sector. In Table 6.10 the data are reclassified into sectors of constant coverage; the "sometime-public sector" comprises industries that were in the public sector for either all or part of the period 1935–73.[22] This table shows that the share in trading income of the profits of the industries in the sometime-public sector fell substantially across the war.[23] This accounts for the whole of the transwar fall in profits' share in trading income; the share in trading income of the profits of the never-public sector rose fractionally, and within the never-public sector there was a steep fall in the unincorporated sector's share, so the share of never-public company profits in trading income rose significantly. Since the division between companies and unincorporated business is chiefly an institutional matter, however, the trend in profits' share in the never-public sector as a

---

*In the sense of public today. Before World War II some nonprofit educational and health services were in the private sector, but they are treated as being in the public sector for this calculation.

TABLE 6.9
Gross Profits by Sector, 1935–1973
(Percent of trading income; annual averages)

Period	Unincorporated sector	Company sector	Public sector	Total
1935–1938	25.0% [a]		1.7%	26.7%
1948–1951	4.8%	17.6%	1.9	24.3
1952–1955	3.9	18.3	2.9	25.1
1956–1960	3.0	17.5	2.8	23.3
1961–1964	2.6	16.4	3.1	22.1
1965–1968	2.5	14.9	3.5	20.9
1969–1973	3.0	12.2	3.3	18.5

Note: Subsidies to the public corporations are excluded, so that the total gross profits are lower than those in Table 6.8 and Figure 6.3.
[a] Combined figure for unincorporated and company sectors excluding stock appreciation; the data do not allow a breakdown between the two. The figures for the two sectors including stock appreciation are 8% and 17.6%, respectively.

TABLE 6.10
Gross Profits by Sectors of Constant Coverage, 1935–1973
(Percent of trading income; annual averages)

Period	Never-public sector		Sometime-public sector [a]	Total
	Unincorporated sector	Other		
1935–1938	21.4% [b]		5.3%	26.7%
1948–1951	4.8%	17.2%	2.3	24.3
1952–1955	3.9	18.1	3.1	25.1
1956–1960	3.0	16.8	3.5	23.3
1961–1964	2.6	15.9	3.6	22.1
1965–1968	2.5	14.6	3.8	20.9
1969–1973	3.0	12.2	3.3	18.5

Note: See note to Table 6.9.
[a] The sometime-public sector consists of those industries that were in public ownership at some stage during the postwar period. The allocation of stock appreciation between this sector and the never-public sector is rough. We have assumed that stock appreciation in this sector was zero in 1935–38 and the same as in the contemporary public sector in 1948–73.
[b] Combined figure for unincorporated and company sectors excluding stock appreciation. The figures for the two sectors including stock appreciation are 8% and 14%, respectively.

whole is more significant analytically, and this, as stated, showed little change across the war.

In interpreting the movements of distributive shares across World War II, and in interpreting the timing of movements in shares after 1914 more generally, it is important to bear in mind the effect of variations in the level of activity. There is a general tendency for profits' share to be below trend in cyclical slumps. The whole of the interwar period had some of the characteristics of a cyclical slump, and the decline in profits' share across World War I undoubtedly owed a significant amount to the fall in the level of activity. By the same token, a substantial rise in profits' share was to be expected across World War II as the economy passed from its interwar depression to its postwar high activity. On this reckoning the near-constancy in the share of profits in the output of the never-public sector across World War II is no less remarkable than the fall in profits' share across World War I.

Three special factors contributed to the movement — or lack of movement — across World War II.

(1) Though there was still much unemployment in the late 1930's, the amount of surplus capital capacity was probably a good deal less than it had been in the 1920's (see pp. 152–54, above). Since it is surplus capacity that is responsible for profits' share being low in cyclical slumps, the late 1930's may not have been such a severe cyclical slump from that point of view.

(2) The growth of cartels in the 1930's, especially in the industries where excess capacity remained most acute, probably kept profits' share at a higher level than would normally be associated with a low rate of activity.

(3) In the early postwar years many items (besides rents) remained subject to price controls, and this must have served to keep down profits' share.

These considerations help to explain why there was not a rise in profits' share across World War II. The first and second points carry the implication that an underlying tendency to a falling profits' share may have operated *within* the interwar period, though it does not show in the statistics. The third suggests that the underlying tendency to a decline in profits' share *within* the early postwar period was larger than the statistics indicate, insofar as the lifting of price controls served to increase profits' share as the postwar period progressed.

The general effect of the foregoing considerations is thus to show the decline in profits' share since 1914 as a smoother and more continuous process than the statistics at first sight suggest.

Within the postwar period the share of profits in the public sector rose up till the late 1960's, whether reckoned on a "public" basis (Table 6.9) or on a "sometime-public" basis (Table 6.10).[24] The fall in the share of profits in the never-public sector was accordingly more severe than the fall in the share of profits in the economy as a whole; and it became more rapid after 1969. Two rather special considerations are relevant here. (1) The reintroduction of some controls over prices probably influenced profits' share, as the relaxation of price controls had done, in the opposite sense, in the 1950's: prices rose very fast, but not as fast as costs. (2) The fast price rise from 1969 was the source of stock appreciation, and if this is added back into profits, their fall becomes

TABLE 6.11

Gross Profits' Shares by Main Industry Group, 1935–1973

(Percent of trading income; annual averages)

Period	Never-public industries			Sometime-public industries			Average all industries
	Manufacturing	Construction	Commerce	Mining, quarrying	Gas, electricity, water	Transport, communications	
1935–1938	27.8%	12.5%	39.3%	17.2%	54.9%	29.3%	26.7%
1948–1951	33.3	11.5	32.5	10.5	39.2	26.4	24.4
1952–1955	32.8	12.8	34.3	10.4	44.4	27.3	25.1
1956–1960	31.3	12.1	32.5	12.7	48.9	25.5	23.4
1961–1964	29.4	13.6	31.4	19.1	54.1	27.3	22.6
1965–1968	27.7	16.8	31.1	18.0	56.4	27.6	22.0
1969–1973	21.9	21.7	30.9	17.1	57.2	26.7	19.8

Note: Subsidies to the public corporations have not been deducted in this table, as they were in Tables 6.9 and 6.10. The profits' share for all industries is therefore consistent with the data in Table 6.8 and Figure 6.3. The industry groups shown do not always fall completely into either the never-public or the sometime-public category. In those cases where parts of an industry were never public and parts were sometime public, the industry is classified according to the category into which the bulk falls. The industries most affected are manufacturing (iron and steel was sometime public), mining and quarrying (non–coal mining was never public), and transport and communications (shipping and parts of road transport were never public). The average for all industries includes not only the industries shown, but also forestry, fishing, professional services, and (denominator only) labor income in public administration and defense; profits have been adjusted for financial services.

much less pronounced. This is not normally considered the right procedure theoretically; but the paper profits from stock appreciation may have been partly responsible for the incomplete adjustment of prices to costs, as they had apparently been on earlier occasions.* Allowance for these two considerations suggests that other forces tending to depress profits' share may not have been very much stronger after 1969 than they had been up to then.

To conclude our discussion of profits' shares, we show in Table 6.11 the trends in the principal industry groups in the never-public and sometime-public sectors. The main point of interest here is the difference between manufacturing and services. The absence of any substantial change in profits' share across World War II in the never-public sector as a whole emerges as having been the result of sizable opposite movements in the two principal component industries: profits' share rose in manufacturing and fell in services. In the course of the postwar period the trend was downward in both sectors, but the fall was much

*As a rule, property's share tended to rise in cyclical upswings and fall in cyclical downswings. Prominent exceptions are the years 1920 and 1951, both cyclical peaks in which property's share was low relative to trend. Both were years of an exceptionally rapid price increase. There appears to be some tendency for the exclusion of stock appreciation to overcorrect for the effects of price changes and hence to show systematic falls (rises) in profits in years when stock appreciation (depreciation) is larger (Neild 1963: 44–45). This may reflect a tendency for firms' price decisions to respond only after a lag to changes in costs and is a plausible explanation for the anomalous movements in profits' share in 1920 and in 1951.

greater in manufacturing, especially at the end of the period. The net outcome was that the proportional fall in profits' share between 1935–38 and 1969–73 was almost the same in the two sectors.

The reasons for these differences are not altogether obvious, especially in respect of the changes across World War II.[25] Explanations may be sought on the side of labor supply and on the side of demand.

On the side of labor supply, average wages rose more in services than in manufacturing across the war. In the 1930's services had enjoyed unusual access to cheap labor because of the high unemployment. Moreover, the rise in the school-leaving age after the war reduced the supply of cheap juvenile labor, previously much used in services.

On the side of demand, output rose considerably across the war in manufacturing but fell in services; and the export boom, associated with the devaluation of 1949, may have made it easier to raise the price of manufactures relative to costs than to raise the price of services in the conditions of early postwar austerity in the home market. The greater decline in the share of profits in manufacturing than in services in the course of the postwar period may be regarded as the result of the progressive reversal of some of the above circumstances.

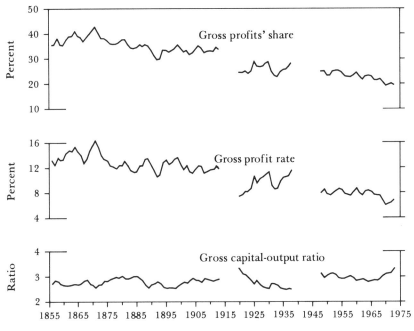

Fig. 6.3. Gross profits' share in trading income, gross profit rate, and gross capital-output ratio, 1856–1973. Trading income is non-farm, non-rent GDP.

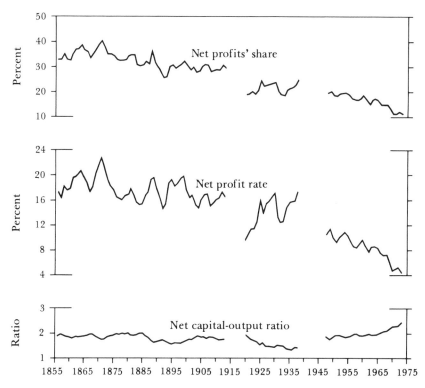

Fig. 6.4. Net profits' share in net trading income, net profit rate, and net capital-output ratio, 1856–1973. Net trading income is non-farm, non-rent NDP. The net profit rate and the net capital-output series for years up to 1938 have been multiplied by constant adjustment factors so as to eliminate the sudden breaks in 1938 caused by the discrepancy between the capital stock estimates consistent with earlier years and the capital stock estimates consistent with later years.

The Profit Rate

The share of profits in trading income can be decomposed into the profit rate per unit of capital and the capital-output ratio (at current prices). This decomposition raises a number of points of interest, though the resulting figures are less firmly based than those relating to profits' share, inasmuch as the measurement of the capital stock is subject to more conceptual and statistical difficulties than the measurement of income or profits. Gross and net profits' shares, profit rates, and capital-output ratios (all for the trading sector, that is, excluding dwellings, other non-trading rent, and agriculture) are plotted in Figures 6.3 and 6.4, respectively.[26] Data for benchmark years are given in Tables 6.12 and 6.13. The gross profit rate is defined as the ratio of

TABLE 6.12

Gross Profits' Share in Trading Income, Gross Profit Rate, and
Gross Capital-Output Ratio, 1856–1973

Year	Profits' share (percent)	Profit rate (percent)	Capital-out-put ratio
1856	35.6%	13.2%	2.70
1873	38.1	14.0	2.71
1913	33.8	11.8	2.86
1924	24.9	8.7	2.86
1937	27.0	10.6	2.55
1951	23.8	7.7	3.10
1953	25.4	8.3	3.06
1964	23.2	8.3	2.79
1973	19.6	5.8	3.33

Note: The changes in geographical coverage and in the basis of the GNP estimates in 1920 (see Table 6.1) have a minor effect on comparability between 1913 and 1924.

TABLE 6.13

Net Profits' Share in Trading Income, Net Profit Rate, and
Net Capital-Output Ratio, 1856–1973

Year	Profits' share (percent)	Profit rate (percent)	Capital-out-put ratio
1856	32.7%	15.6%	2.10
1873	35.1	17.3	2.03
1913	29.8	14.9	1.99
1924	20.5	11.2	1.84
1937	23.0	14.2	1.62
1951	18.2	9.3	1.96
1953	19.9	10.5	1.89
1964	17.2	8.7	1.96
1973	11.4	4.6	2.45

Note: The changes in geographical coverage and in the basis of the GNP estimates in 1920 (see Table 6.1) have a minor effect on comparability between 1913 and 1924. The change in the basis of the net capital stock estimates in 1937 affect comparability between 1937 and 1951. The comparable 1937 figures are 23% for profits' share, 15.9% for profit rate, and 1.45 for the capital-output ratio.

gross profits to gross capital stock. The net profit rate is the ratio of profits net of depreciation to net capital stock. In the net measure both the numerator and denominator are thus lower than they are in the gross measure: whether the net measure is higher or lower than the gross measure depends on the length of life of the capital stock, its age distribution, the rate of growth, and so forth. In practice, however, as shown in Tables 6.12 and 6.13, the net rate was always higher up till just before the end of the period.

TABLE 6.14

Gross Profit Rates by Sector, 1935–1973

(Percent; annual averages)

Period	Never-public sector		Sometime-public sector	All sectors
	Unincorporated sector	Other		
1935–1938	15.3%[a]		4.6%	10.4%
1948–1951	20.4%	10.3%	2.0	7.9
1952–1955	17.4	10.8	2.8	8.3
1956–1960	16.1	10.1	3.2	7.9
1961–1964	16.6	9.7	3.4	7.8
1965–1968	15.2	9.1	3.6	7.5
1969–1973	17.4	6.9	2.9	6.0

Note: Subsidies to the public corporations have been deducted, so that the profit rate for all sectors is lower than that in Table 6.12 and Figure 6.3.

[a]Combined figure for the never-public sector excluding stock appreciation. The total with stock appreciation is 15.7%, within which the Unincorporated sector is 35.1% and Other is 11.9%.

Movements in the capital-output ratio were in most phases smaller than movements in profits' share, so that the profit rate generally moved in the same direction as profits' share. In the case of the net measures, the capital-output ratio fell all the way up till 1937 and rose thereafter; hence the profit rate tended to fall less rapidly than profits' share through 1937 and more rapidly than profits' share thereafter. In the gross measures the relation between share and rate in the interwar period and from 1937 onward was similar to that in the net measures, though less pronounced. Before 1914, however, the gross capital-output ratio rose, instead of falling like the net capital-output ratio, so the fall in the gross profit rate was larger then the fall in gross profits' share.

Gross profit rates in the late 1930's and the postwar period are shown by sector in Table 6.14 and by main industry group in Table 6.15. The transwar fall was particularly severe in the unincorporated sector.* The fall in the profit rate in the rest of the never-public sector was of

*In contrast to the sharp fall in the share of unincorporated profits in total trading income, this fall is not to be explained by the relative contraction in the size of the sector, since in principle that would affect equally both numerator and denominator in the profit rate. The explanation appears in part to lie in the above-average decline in the profit rate in the distributive trades, services, and construction (see Table 6.15), where unincorporated businesses are largely concentrated. This is not sufficient to provide the whole explanation, however, and the figures imply that within industries the profit rate fell considerably more in the unincorporated sector than in companies. A further implication is that there was a substantial rise in the capital-output ratio across the war in the unincorporated sector, since it is impossible to reconcile the data in Table 6.3 with the supposition that the profit-output ratio in the unincorporated sector fell to anything like the same extent as the profit rate.

TABLE 6.15

Gross Profit Rates by Main Industry Group, 1935–1973

(Percent; annual averages)

Period	Never-public industries			Sometime-public industries			
	Manufac-turing	Construc-tion	Commerce	Mining, quarrying	Gas, electri-city, water	Transport, communi-cations	All industries
1935–1938	11.1%	26.8%	26.8%	8.4%	4.9%	4.3%	10.4%
1948–1951	9.8	20.4	17.5	5.6	2.3	3.4	8.0
1952–1955	10.0	20.0	19.1	5.5	2.9	3.7	8.3
1956–1960	9.4	18.0	19.2	5.9	3.5	3.7	8.0
1961–1964	8.8	20.8	18.0	6.2	4.5	4.5	8.0
1965–1968	8.1	23.9	16.8	6.1	4.7	5.1	7.7
1969–1973	5.7	26.3	14.5	4.5	4.2	4.2	6.2

Note: Subsidies to the public corporations have not been deducted in this table, as they were in Table 6.14. The profit rate for all industries is therefore consistent with the data in Table 6.12 and Figure 6.3. The industry groups shown do not always fall completely into either the never-public or the sometime-public category. In those cases where parts of an industry were never public and parts were sometime public, the industry is classified according to the category into which the bulk falls. The industries most affected are manufacturing (iron and steel was sometime public), mining and quarrying (non–coal mining was never public), and transport and communications (shipping and parts of road transport were never public). The average for all industries includes not only the industry groups shown, but also forestry, fishing, and private professional services.

the order of one percentage point between 1935–38 and 1952–55, from 12 percent to 11 percent. The fall was much greater in the distributive trades and services and in construction than in manufacturing (Table 6.15); this is consistent with the above-average fall in the unincorporated sector. The fall in the profit rate in the sometime-public sector was from about 4½ percent to about 2 percent.[27]

Within the postwar period the fall in the overall gross profit rate was small up till the late 1960's. That in the net profit rate was significantly greater. In the incorporated never-public sector the gross profit rate fell by about one percentage point between the early 1950's and the mid-1960's, as it had done across World War II. The gross profit rate rose in the public sector, and ceased to fall significantly in the unincorporated sector.

The decline in the profit rate speeded up very considerably after the late 1960's. As may be seen from Tables 6.12 and 6.13, the gross profit rate fell by nearly a third between 1964 and 1973, and the net profit rate by nearly a half. The speeding-up of the decline was more marked than it was in the case of profits' share because the capital-output ratio rose. The more rapid fall in the net rate than in the gross rate reflected both a more rapid fall in the net share than in the gross share and a more rapid rise in the net capital-output ratio than in the gross capital-output ratio. Both these sources of difference between net and gross were due to the long-continued rise within the postwar period in the investment-output ratio and the increase in investment in plant and machinery relative to investment in buildings, both of which tended to increase capital consumption and to reduce the average age of capital. The fall in the profit rate was felt both in manufacturing and in the service industries, though not in construction, and it also occurred, though to a less extent, in the public sector (Table 6.15).

The Profit Rate at Constant Prices

The concept of the profit rate so far used is profits (gross or net) at current prices divided by the value of capital stock (gross or net) at current prices. This is what is relevant in the consideration of the rate of return to the owner of capital at a given time and also in the consideration of profits as a potential source of finance for new investment. But the concept of the profit rate appropriate for measuring the price of capital as a factor of production, analogous to the price of labor as measured by the real wage,[28] is a different one, namely the profit rate at current prices divided by the ratio of the price of capital goods to the price of output (p_k/p_y).* The price of capital to the user depends not only on the money rate of return on the sum invested (the current price profit rate), but also on the price of capital goods. Under marginal productivity factor pricing, moreover, changes in the profit rate at constant prices can be taken to measure changes in the marginal product (at constant prices) of the capital stock (at constant prices). Profit rates at constant prices are thus the more relevant concept in considering the production function.

Constant price profit rates for benchmark years are given in Table 6.16, together with current price profit rates and p_k/p_y ratios. The movements in the constant and current rates were very similar up to World War II, because p_k/p_y was fairly constant. From World War II onward, the situation changed. There was a very large rise in p_k/p_y

---

*The real wage (w/p_y) is total labor income (W) divided by the total in employment (N) and deflated by a GNP price deflator (p_y); or alternatively it is labor's share in GNP (W/Yp_y) multiplied by real GNP per member of the labor force (Y/N):

$$\frac{w}{p_y} = \frac{W/N}{p_y} = \frac{W}{Yp_y} \times \frac{Y}{N}$$

Similarly for capital, profits (P) divided by constant price capital (K) and deflated by a GNP price deflator (or profits' share $[P/Yp_y]$ divided by the real capital-output ratio) gives the current price profit rate multiplied by the ratio of capital goods to output prices, i.e. the real profit rate:

$$\frac{P/K}{p_y} = \frac{P}{Yp_y} \div \frac{K}{Y} = \frac{P}{Kp_k} \times \frac{p_k}{p_y}$$

TABLE 6.16

Real Profit Rates, 1856–1973

Year	Current price profit rates (percent)		Price ratios: p_K/p_Y (1938 = 100)		Real profit rates (percent; 1938 prices)	
	Gross	Net	Gross	Net	Gross	Net
1856	13.2%	15.6%	106	109	14.0%	16.9%
1873	14.0	17.3	104	107	14.6	18.5
1913	11.8	14.9	104	107	12.3	16.0
1924	8.7	11.2	98	101	8.6	11.3
1937	10.6	14.2	102	103	10.8	14.7
1951	7.7	9.3	135	139	10.3	12.9
1953	8.3	10.5	132	132	11.0	13.8
1964	8.3	8.7	122	122	10.1	10.6
1973	5.8	4.6	128	129	7.5	6.0

Note: There are breaks in comparability at both wars; see notes to Tables 6.12 and 6.13. For the net current price profit rate, the 1937 estimate comparable to 1951 is 15.9%, and for the net constant rate, the comparable estimate is 16.4%. The other figures for 1937 are comparable with those for 1951.

TABLE 6.17

Gross Profits' Share in Trading Income, Gross Profit Rate,
and Gross Capital-Output Ratio in the Never-Public Sector at Constant
and Current Prices, 1935–1973

(Annual averages)

Period	Profits' share (percent)	Profit rate (percent)		Capital-output ratio	
		Current prices	Constant (1938) prices	Current prices	Constant (1938) prices
1935–1938	21.4%	15.3%	15.2%	1.4	1.4
1952–1955	22.0	11.4	15.9	1.9	1.4
1961–1964	18.5	10.3	12.9	1.8	1.4
1968–1973	15.2	7.8	9.6	2.0	1.6

across World War II (see p. 136 and Appendix H). It had the effect of almost totally wiping out, in the constant price measure of the gross profit rate, the transwar fall that occurred in the current price measure. In the case of the net profit rate, the fall in the constant price series was still significant, but it was very much reduced in size. During the postwar period p_k/p_y fell up till the final year 1973; in consequence there were larger falls in profit rates at constant prices than at current prices.

Table 6.17 shows data on the profit rate at constant and current prices for the never-public sector. At constant prices neither the profit rate nor the capital-output ratio shows much change between 1935–38 and 1952–55. The opposite movements in those two variables in the current price series are thus due almost wholly to the transwar rise in p_k/p_y. Between 1952–55 and 1960–64, however, the moderate fall in the current price profit rate becomes a much more substantial fall in the constant price profit rate because of the fall in p_k/p_y. Measured at constant prices, the profit rate in the never-public sector fell only slightly less rapidly between 1952–55 and 1960–64 than it did between 1960–64 and 1969–73. The current-price profit rate fell more rapidly in the latter periods, but the effect on the constant-price profit rate was no longer being augmented by a fall in p_k/p_y. Alternatively, one may prefer to put it the other way around and say that in the later part of the postwar period the effect of the fall in the constant-price profit rate on the current-price profit rate was no longer relieved by a fall in p_k/p_y.

THE DISTRIBUTION OF PRIVATE AND PERSONAL INCOME

So far in this chapter we have been concerned with the functional distribution of income between labor and capital. In the context of a study of economic growth, this is the most relevant concept of income distribution, as indicating the relative contribution made by the factors of production to GNP. But it differs from the concepts of income distribution relevant from the social point of view because it takes no account of transfers and taxation.

Table 6.18 sets forth the relevant data for benchmark years. Rows 7 and 8 are the functional shares, already discussed. The remainder of the table shows how these shares are altered by allowing for the payments shown in rows 1–6. Rows 9–11 show the percentage shares of labor, property (including debt interest received), and grants in private income before tax, that is to say, in GNP plus public sector debt interest payments (less interest received) and current grants minus public sector property income. Rows 12–14 show for the period from 1924 on the percentage shares of labor, property (including debt interest received), and grants in personal income after tax. Rows 9–11 will be referred to as private shares and rows 12–14 as personal shares: we shall compare their movements over time with those of the functional shares.

The increases in the importance of grants (row 3) and public-sector property income (row 1) stand out as persistent trends over the whole period. By contrast, the importance of debt interest fluctuated greatly (row 2). The shares in private property income before tax of undistributed profits and taxation (rows 4 and 5) show large movements, especially across World War II.

The main feature of the period before 1914 was the decline in the importance of debt interest as GNP grew and the national debt fell

TABLE 6.18

Shares in Private and Personal Incomes, 1856–1973

(Percent)

Category	1856	1873	1913	1924	1937	1951	1964	1973
Public sector income and transfers (as percent of GNP):								
(1) Property income	0.3%	0.4%	1.8%	1.9%	2.9%	2.9%	5.5%	5.8%
(2) Net debt interest	4.5	2.6	1.7	8.2	5.3	4.8	4.0	3.8
(3) Current grants	0.4	0.3	1.0	4.4	5.4	6.1	8.1	10.5
Distribution of private profits (as percent of private property income before tax):								
(4) Undistributed post-tax company income	–	–	–	10.8	19.0	32.0	37.6	34.7[a]
(5) Direct property taxes	–	–	–	19.2	14.6	31.4	21.7	22.2[a]
Taxation of labor income (as percent of labor income before tax):								
(6) Direct labor taxes	–	–	–	4.2	5.1	12.0	15.4	21.3
Functional share in GNP (percent):								
(7) Labor	57.8	54.4	56.0	66.6	65.1	70.9	71.4	72.8
(8) Property	42.2	45.6	44.0	33.4	34.9	29.1	28.6	27.2
Shares in private income including transfers before tax:								
(9) Labor	55.2	53.0	55.5	60.2	60.4	65.7	67.0	67.2
(10) Property	44.3	46.6	43.5	35.8	34.6	28.7	25.4	23.1
(11) Grants	0.4	0.3	1.0	4.0	5.0	5.6	7.6	9.7
Shares in personal income including transfers after tax:								
(12) Labor	–	–	–	66.5	67.2	78.3	76.0	73.0
(13) Property	–	–	–	28.9	26.9	14.2	13.9	13.8
(14) Grants	–	–	–	4.6	5.9	7.5	10.1	13.2

Source: Basic statistics (Appendix N); Mitchell & Deane 1962.
Note: These data refer to the contemporary area of the UK. The changes in territory and in the basis of the GNP estimates in the early 1920's had insignificant effects on shares (0.3 of a percentage point at the most).
[a]Investment grants have been treated as a negative direct property tax, so as to make the 1973 figures comparable to those for 1964, when all investment subsidies operated through the tax system.

somewhat. Property's private share (row 10) therefore fell by more than its functional share (row 8) from the 1870's onward, and there was a slight decline over the whole period from 1856 to 1913 in the private share, in contrast to a rise in the functional share. World War I very greatly increased the burden of debt interest and significantly softened the impact of the fall in property's functional share on property's private share. In the 1920's debt interest was about the same percentage of GNP as income from abroad was on the eve of World War I; the rise in the one served to offset the fall in the other.[29]

Within the interwar period the share of debt interest fell, mainly because of the rise in GNP and the reduction in interest rates, but it remained much above the 1913 level. From 1924 we can bring into the picture the effects of taxation and undistributed profits, and so trace the movement of shares in personal income as well as shares in private income. The burden of property taxation fell between 1924 and 1937, but the increase in company retentions more than offset this fall. Consequently, the share of personal posttax property income in total personal income declined by more than property's private share.

World War II was financed with a larger amount of taxation relative to borrowing than World War I and with lower interest rates (see Morgan 1952; Sayers 1956). This, combined with the effects of inflation on the real value of outstanding debt, prevented the war from leading to any increase in the proportion of debt interest to GNP. Grants became a somewhat larger item, but the movements of private shares across World War II were not very different from the movements of functional shares.[30] Shares in personal income, however, are quite a different story. The burden of direct taxation increased by a much larger amount for property income (including company income) than for labor income (rows 5 and 6). At the same time there was a big increase in undistributed profits.[31] As a result, property's share in personal income after tax fell drastically, much more than its private or functional share.

Some of the transwar changes continued within the postwar period, but others were reversed. Grants continued to rise. Public-sector property income also rose (partly because of the increase in the profits of nationalized industries, and partly because of the increase in the proportion of the housing stock owned by local authorities). Debt interest declined and became for the first time less than public-sector property income. For these reasons, property's private share fell significantly more than its functional share.

Notwithstanding this, property's share in personal income after tax remained remarkably constant within the postwar period, as a result of a drastic reversal of the transwar trend in favor of labor in the incidence of direct taxation.* The increase within the postwar period in the share of grants in personal income after tax was thus at the expense of labor income. The proportion of property income taken in direct taxation declined, whereas that of labor income continued to increase,[32] so that there was a very great increase in the proportion of direct-tax revenue that came from labor income. By 1973 the *rate* of direct taxation had become almost as high on labor income as on property income.

*The abolition in 1963 of Schedule A taxation on the imputed rent from owner-occupied dwellings and the increasingly unrealistic assessment of Schedule A tax liability before 1963 also contributed to the reduced tax burden on private property income.

It was the increase in undistributed profits rather than changes in taxation that was chiefly responsible for property's personal share falling so much more than property's functional share between the interwar and postwar periods. Within the postwar period there would have been a significant shift in favor of property's personal share if companies had not retained in undistributed profits much of the benefit they derived from lower taxation. (This is notwithstanding that the proportion of *post-tax* company income retained fell within the postwar period.) Insofar as undistributed profits raised share values, they brought a benefit not shown in the present statistics to persons owning capital.

Property's functional share fell much more steeply across World War I than across World War II, and it continued to decline somewhat in the postwar period. This may appear in some conflict with the observation of the sources of personal income suggested by casual empiricism. Most people would probably hold that World War II was more of a setback to capital-owners than World War I, and, on the other hand, that the relative position of capital-owners improved in the course of the postwar period until the late 1960's. The effects of debt interest across World War I, of taxation and undistributed profits across World War II, and of taxation and capital gains within the postwar period go most of the way to resolve this apparent conflict.

We started by looking at functional shares and then went on to look at the effects of taxation. This procedure was not meant to imply that functional distribution is necessarily independent of taxation. Taxation may to some extent be passed on. The chief relevance of this consideration is to trends within the postwar period. It is possible that the shift in the tax burden away from capital toward labor was partly passed on and thus contributed to the decline in capital's functional share before tax.* The shift of the tax burden in the opposite direction across World War II did not, however, have any observable effect in *raising* capital's functional share.

EXPLANATIONS

The increase in labor's share over the period 1856–1973 was considerable. Since this movement occurred chiefly across the wars, it is tempting to regard it as largely institutional in origin. But on closer in-

---

*Most economists would agree that straightforward income tax will not be passed on. However, a significant part of direct taxation on labor and capital in the postwar period consisted of other taxes, about which there is more scope for argument: profits tax and corporation tax, net of investment allowances, etc., in the case of profits, and national insurance contributions in the case of labor.

spection, it emerges that the most plainly institutional phenomena, namely rent control and the loss of income from abroad, though important in the transwar changes, did not contribute much to the long-run shift toward labor. The tendency to a fall in property's share therefore appears to have been more deep-seated. It was also more spread out in its timing. Excluding rents and income from abroad (from both numerator and denominator), we find falls in profits' share not only across the two wars (chiefly World War I), but also in the 1870's and 1880's and in the postwar period; and when allowance is made for special features of the 1930's (p. 182, above), it is possible that there was also an underlying downward trend in profits' share within the interwar period.

In considering trends in the total share of property income in GNP, one major point is clear. Export of capital, which generates property income but no labor income (in the lending country), helped to sustain property's share in GNP before 1914 in face of a decline in its share in GDP. After 1914 the decline in overseas assets made property's share in GNP fall faster than its share in GDP. The explanation for the decline in property's share in GDP is, however, not so clear.

There are two broad types of explanation. One is based on the production function (the neoclassical approach). The other is based on changes in market power.

The neoclassical explanation is that the bias of technical progress (taken in conjunction with the supply of investment and the elasticity of substitution) tended to be unfavorable to capital from 1870 onward. (The growth of salaries could be taken to suggest that the bias was not away from capital as such, but away from nonhuman capital toward human capital.) The existence of some kind of neoclassical relationship, involving movement along the production function, receives support from the tendency for movements in the real capital-output ratio and the real profit rate to be inversely related to each other between most phases.[33] If the elasticity of substitution between labor and capital is less than one, as is usually supposed, one would expect to find labor's share rising most in periods when the capital-output ratio was rising relative to its trend. Some such tendency is apparent, but it is not clear-cut, and the neoclassical explanation requires supplementation (by reference to changes in the average level of activity and possibly also to varying degrees of capital-saving bias between periods) in order to explain the exact timing of the shift to labor.

Any market-power explanation is bound to be complicated, since it has to take account of both the product market and the labor market.[34] In the labor market, there plainly took place a long-run increase in the strength and bargaining power of trade unions. Moreover, union membership increased particularly during and immediately after the two wars (*British Labour Statistics Historical Abstract*, UK [48]: 395), and this accords well with the movement in income distribution.

Unionization raises labor's share if it reduces the effective degree of employer monopsony in the labor market, i.e. if it causes the employer to be presented with a flatter supply curve of labor than before (J. Robinson 1933: 292–304). It is likely that some such effect was felt from the growth of unionization in the course of the twentieth century, not least during World War II; and a similar consequence followed from the simulation of the results of collective bargaining in non-unionized industries through the Wages Council system. It does not help to account for the decline in profits' share in 1870–90; nor would it account for any possible underlying tendency to decline in the interwar period.

In an industry where wages are already determined by collective bargaining, the main effect of labor militancy will prima facie be to raise prices rather than to alter distributive shares. Thus it is for the explanation of the rate of growth of money wages that union militancy has been adduced by writers such as Hines (1964, 1969). For militancy to be relevant to shares, we have to suppose that there are obstacles to increasing prices. This is where reference to market power in the labor market is inadequate and needs to be supplemented by consideration of the product market.

It is hardly plausible to suggest that there was a long-run decline in the degree of monopoly in the British economy, though within the postwar period some tendency in this direction may have come about because of legislation against restrictive practices (including the repeal of Resale Price Maintenance). But there is a hypothesis about the product market that can be adduced to explain a falling profit share, namely foreign competition. Growing foreign competition presses on product prices, and wages can be adjusted only with a lag if at all, so prices are reduced relative to prime costs. There is good reason to suppose that this force did operate in several of the relevant periods: in the 1870's and 1880's (both in industry and in agriculture), across World War I, and within the postwar period. This hypothesis can be stated independently of the hypothesis of increasing labor bargaining power, or it can be combined with it to suggest that the squeeze on the margin between wages and prices came from both sides.

The foreign-competition hypothesis does not explain the fall in profits' share that took place in sectors other than manufacturing across World War II. A more general difficulty is that the hypothesis describes essentially a disequilibrium situation and is not therefore easily invoked to explain the sort of maintained and cumulative decline in profits' share that occurred.

We are not able to resolve these issues here (see pp. 393–94, 529) for further discussion. Our conjectural conclusion is as follows. Market-power phenomena did affect the distribution of income in a number of phases in our period. They thus affected at least the timing of the shift toward labor. Moreover, changes in market power probably had some long-run tendency to increase labor's share, if only by reducing the degree of employer monopsony. In this respect the neoclassical explanation, which disregards monopolistic and disequilibrium elements, is defective. On the other hand, market power alone could not have been sufficient to bring about the sustained increase in labor's share that took place had there not been a capital-saving bias in technical progress of the kind postulated by the neoclassical hypothesis.

How should the shift to labor within the postwar period be viewed against this long-run background? Both market-power and neoclassical effects can be discerned, and possible also the passing on of some of the effects of taxation. There was certainly an increase in foreign competition, and in some sectors an increase in domestic competition as well. The importance of *increasing* union strength or militancy is doubtful, at least till the late 1960's, but the high absolute level of union strength limited employers' room for maneuver in face of foreign competition. The very rapid rise in money wages after 1969 may well have tended to reduce capital's share, not only because price increases were inhibited by foreign competition (wage escalation occurred abroad also), but because of lags in price adjustment, themselves partly due to government restrictions and partly to historic cost pricing conventions. On the other side the postwar rise in the capital-output ratio at constant prices is consistent, in neoclassical terms, with the fall in the profit rate and also (assuming less-than-unit elasticity of substitution) with the fall in capital's share.

CHAPTER SEVEN

Total Factor Productivity

THE CONCEPT AND ITS MEASUREMENT

A fully comprehensive measure of TFI would include inputs of all scarce resources, weighted according to their base-year marginal products, direct and indirect. The rate of growth of TFI, so defined, would be little if at all lower than the rate of growth of output, at least for the world as a whole. Feasible measures of TFI are not comprehensive in this sense. The measured rate of growth of TFP therefore consists of the part of the growth of output that either is not due to the growth of domestic inputs or is not properly captured by the chosen measure of those inputs. Despite its inexactness, the growth of TFP is a convenient category for study, provided that the limitations of the concept are recognized. The base-year valuation of inputs makes it an unreliable guide to counterfactual questions relating to long periods. TFI and TFP are the "sources" of growth only in a proximate sense.

THE MEASUREMENT OF THE INPUTS

In the measures of TFI and TFP given below, gross and net measures of capital stock are both used, as alternatives. So are measures of labor input with and without allowance for quality change. Weights are shares in GDP, not NDP.

THE GROWTH OF INPUTS AND OF TFP

The growth rates of TFI and TFP, on alternative bases of calculation, are given in Table 7.4. If labor input is measured in man-hours, TFP appears as a more important source of growth than TFI over the period 1856–1973 as a whole. If labor input is measured with allowance for estimated quality change, this conclusion is reversed. On any reckoning, the rate of growth of TFI was lower in the postwar period than in earlier peacetime periods, and the rate of growth of TFP *substantially higher. The rate of growth of TFP was notably low in the period 1873–1913. The large fall in hours of work after World War I makes the estimate of the growth of TFP in 1913–24 very sensitive to the inclusion or exclusion of the estimated consequential improvement in labor quality, which is inevitably an uncertain estimate. The estimates adopted show a decline in the rate of growth of TFP, after allowance for labor quality change, between each period up to and including 1913–24, and a rise between each period thereafter.*

THE CONCEPT AND ITS MEASUREMENT

In earlier chapters we discussed the movement over time of measures of total labor input and total capital input. From these, together with measures of output, can be derived measures of labor productivity — the original meaning of the word productivity — and of capital-productivity (output-capital ratio).

The concept of total factor productivity (TFP), or output per unit of input, pioneered by Abramovitz (1956), Solow (1957), and Kendrick (1961), and given its most elaborate use by Denison (1967), carries the notion of productivity a stage further.[1] Labor and capital are aggregated into a measure of total factor input (TFI), just as skilled and unskilled labor are aggregated in the measure of labor input and machinery and buildings are aggregated in the measure of capital. Comparison of the growth rates of output and of TFI yields the growth rate of TFP.

The abbreviations TFI and TFP are used where general reference is made to the concepts of total factor input and total factor productivity. Where a more precise indication is required, the following abbreviations are used:

TF_YI or TF_YP: the labor input measured in man-years

TF_HI or TF_HP: the labor input measured in man-hours

TF_QI or TF_QP: the labor input measured in man-hours and adjusted for quality changes as defined in Chapter 4.

TF_YP and TF_HP thus include the effects of the quality changes in the measure of productivity, but TF_QP does not.

The decomposition of the sources of output growth into the growth of TFI (and its various components) and the growth of TFP (and its various components) has been called growth accounting. It can be regarded as a descriptive device, useful for posing matters for study. Alternatively, it can be regarded as a device for measuring the parameters in a particular theoretical model of growth — a model that may or may not be empirically correct. We regard it in the first way. But it would not be useful even for this purpose if it did not bear some relation to a theoretical model. A brief discussion is therefore needed of its theoretical implications and its limitations.

Taken in its most rigorous sense, growth in TFP must mean growth in output due to causes other than growth in the quantity or quality of input of scarce resources, including capital, non-human and human, in all its forms. That is to say, it is growth due to causes that resemble, in the stock phrase, manna from heaven. However, human activity is a scarce resource; and almost all economic change is ultimately due to human activity in one form or another (the only exception comes from exogenous changes in climate or other aspects of the natural environment). So in the last analysis TFI change must account for almost all of the change in output, and the residual attributable to change in TFP is as likely to be negative as positive. On this reckoning, the large positive figures for growth in TFP yielded by conventional calculations must be held to be due to errors of measurement.[2] It should be noted that this relates to the world as a whole. For a single country, manna from abroad is likely to be significant, even if manna from heaven is not; that is to say, increases in output may be due to the borrowing of innovations that were, indeed, ultimately traceable to inputs of scarce resources, but not to inputs in the country in question.

For ideally correct measurement, each factor input would need to be weighted by its marginal social net product, embracing all externalities and unintended by-products (insofar as they affected measured output); and every activity that had an effect beyond the present period would have to be taken into account in reckoning capital formation. Thus capital formation would have to include not only investment in physical capital and education, research and medical care, but also, for example, the effect of agricultural inputs on standards of nutrition and hence on labor productivity in the present and later generations; the effect of investment in dwellings on attitudes and lifestyles affecting motivation to work; the effect of industrial capital formation on occupational distribution and hence on political and social attitudes and hence on government policies (or civil disturbances) affecting output; and innumerable other effects that are equally indirect but not on that account necessarily unimportant.

It is obvious that a statistical estimation of TFI in its fullest sense is not a practical proposition. More restricted measures of TFI have to be used, and the lines of demarcation between TFI and TFP are bound to be to some extent arbitrary.

The measure of change in TFP that we use is a simple one: it corresponds to that used by Solow (1957), adapted for changes in discrete time instead of instantaneous rates of change. This is expressed in the equations

$$\hat{x} = \hat{q} - \hat{f} \tag{1}$$

$$\hat{f} = \alpha \hat{n} + (1 - \alpha)\hat{k}, \tag{2}$$

where the circumflexes denote the average annual rate of change between two benchmark years, x is TFP, f is TFI, q is output, n is labor, k is non-human capital, and α is a weighting term, taken as equal to the share of labor in income in the first year.

The increase in TFP, so defined, in a given country is tautologically equal to that part of the increase in output that is due to (1) causes other than increases in all that country's factor inputs, *plus* (2) any excess of the effects on output of increases in factor inputs over those measured by this method (viz. the method of aggregating factor inputs into k and n according to certain conventions and weighting k and n by the respective average base-year rates of remuneration).

If TFI were ideally measured and factors were paid according to their marginal social products, (2) would be near to zero for the world as a whole. As it is, it will not be equal to zero for four reasons: because no account is taken of divergence between marginal social product and rate of remuneration, brought about by externalities (including nonconstant returns to scale) and market imperfections; because capital formation is restricted to physical capital formation and inputs into education, research, etc. are treated as current inputs; because factors are aggregated into two groups, k and n, and the average rate of remuneration of k and n is not necessarily equal to the rate of remuneration of those types of k and n that increased (even apart from the first reason); and finally, because we are dealing with a single country.

The pragmatic justification for the procedure is that (1) and (2) taken together form a convenient category for study. For practical research purposes, the exact division between TFI and TFP may not matter much; for example, if the effects of education on growth are to be separately estimated anyway, it is not important whether they are classed as TFP growth or as capital formation.

The above method weights factor inputs by base-year prices. A fundamentally different alternative is the direct estimation of a production function by econometric techniques. Though this method has its advantages (especially for individual industries), we have chosen not to adopt it. Our chief reason is that direct estimation requires a specific mathematical form of the production function. In the absence of any convincing evidence in favor of one type of production function rather than another, it is desirable to be as unspecific as possible* The method here used involves saying "let us see what remains unexplained if we assume that in the base year the factors of production, as defined, are paid the value of their marginal product." At least at the macroeconomic level, this seems a more interesting and appropriate question in the present state of knowledge than such a question as "what remains unexplained if we assume that the production function at any time is $q = (0.25k^{-0.7} + 0.75n^{-0.7})^{-1.4}$?" The results of the econometric fitting of production functions have exhibited marked instability in the face of minor modifications in data, specification, observation period, and estimation method (for survey articles, see Nerlove 1967a, 1967b; Nadiri 1970; Kennedy & Thirlwall 1972). In the absence of firm views about each of these aspects, the results could be presented only in the form of rather wide-interval estimates and not as point estimates, thus making interpretation difficult.

The proposed method of measuring growth in TFP has the great advantage of simplicity and ease of interpretation. In making comparisons between periods it can readily be seen whether differences in TFP growth are the result (in a purely arithmetic sense) of differences in output growth, or in the growth of one or more of the inputs, or in first-year factor shares. This would not be true of a more complicated system.

Enough has been said to indicate that, in offering measures of increases in TFI and TFP, we are not postulating the existence in reality of a particular production function. Mention may be made, however, of the kind of production function that would be necessary for the method to give a fully correct measure of the relative contributions to growth made by increased factor input and other causes. The require-

---

*Of course a number of different specifications can be estimated econometrically. But then the problem of choosing between them arises, and since statistical tests are generally not helpful in such circumstances, the issue of an *a priori* preference for a particular production function cannot really be avoided.

ments are constant returns to scale; homogeneous labor and capital; growth in TFI and in TFP mutually independent; marginal productivity pricing; and no discontinuities.* On these assumptions, growth in TFI and TFP would be exactly measured, over periods of time sufficiently short for second-order terms to be neglected. For changes over longer periods there would be biases depending in size and sign on the specific production function; this is further discussed, for the sake of completeness, in Appendix I.

We deal throughout in annual compound interest rates of growth. This raises a point of some importance. Our standard subperiods are of significant duration, 13 years or more, and our entire period is 117 years. When we say between 1856 and 1973 TFI rose by 0.8 percent per year and TFP by 1.1 percent per year, this is a shorthand. What it means is that the movement between 1856 and 1973 is *as if*, between each successive pair of years within that period, TFI (as measured) had risen by 0.8 percent and TFP by 1.1 percent. We are not actually making a comparison between the two end-years; for if we did that, second-order effects would not necessarily be negligible. We shall use the customary shorthand referred to, because it would be tedious continually to repeat the "as if" formula; but the meaning must be borne in mind.

Not all the problems are, of course, resolved by this way of looking at the findings. We are entitled to say, for example, that during the period 1924–37 growth of output in manufacturing proceeded as if there were an interannual growth of 1.9 percent in x and 1.3 percent in f, the latter being made up of a weighted average of $\hat{k}$ of 1.0 percent and $\hat{n}$ of 1.4 percent. If *in one single year* $\hat{k}$ had instead been, say, 2.0 percent, it is not too bad an approximation to say that $\hat{f}$ in that year would have been 1.6 percent (α being 0.74), that $\hat{x}$ would have remained 1.9 percent, and that, with a constant degree of utilization of resources, $\hat{q}$ would therefore have been 3.5 percent. But we cannot say that if $\hat{k}$ had been 2.0 percent *throughout the period*, the same conclusion would necessarily hold. For in that case, by the end of the period the capital intensity of production would have moved into a realm substantially different from that actually observed, and a change might have taken place in the weighting of k and n required to indicate their relative marginal products. So when in Chapter 13 we come to consider the effects of investment in different periods, we shall not be able

---

*The Cobb-Douglas production function does *not* have to be assumed. This assumption is involved only if α is held constant through time.

simply to infer from the figures given by the decomposition of sources of growth what the growth of potential output would have been if $\hat{k}$ had been different. This has to be considered on the basis of more general evidence, and the results are necessarily tentative.*

There remains to be noted one further general point of importance. Growth accounting separates the sources of growth into growth in TFI and growth in TFP, and each of these may be further divided into constituent elements.[3] But the "sources of growth" so identified are not to be regarded as the ultimate independent variables determining the rate of economic growth. Least of all is it implied that the ultimate determinants of growth can be reduced to the three elements population growth, propensity to save, and technical progress. The different "sources" do not necessarily correspond to prime independent variables, nor are they even necessarily independent of one another. (For example, the rate of capital accumulation may well be affected by present or past technical progress, and vice versa). Growth accounting is only a starting point. Having identified the "sources," it remains to be considered how they are related to each other and to other profounder causes. This would, moreover, still be true even if we had ideal measures of TFI such that TFP growth was largely or wholly eliminated; it would remain to consider what had caused the various constituents of TFI to grow as they did.

THE MEASUREMENT OF THE INPUTS

Before outlining the method used to measure the inputs that enter into the calculation of growth in TFI, we briefly consider why we did not include as inputs two factors of production, raw materials and land, that crop up in the theoretical literature.

The case of raw materials is straightforward in principle. If the measure of output is gross of raw materials, then raw materials should be included as an input, but if output is measured net of raw materials, they should be excluded. The output measures we use for individual industries and hence for the economy as a whole are in principle defined net of raw materials, and so it is not appropriate to treat raw materials as part of TFI. It would, of course, be of interest to ask whether raw

---

*Thus in the example cited, two extreme hypotheses are (1) that in the interwar period technical progress was very capital-saving, so that if $\hat{k}$ had been much higher there would have been severely diminishing returns; and (2) that there was nothing special about the character of technical progress, more $\hat{k}$ could have been used to great advantage, but investment was held down by the depression. Decomposition of the sources of growth does not distinguish between these hypotheses.

materials are being used more efficiently or not, that is, whether value-added (new output) per unit of raw materials input is rising or falling. Unfortunately, reliable measures cannot be made for lack of appropriate data.[4] However, for the whole economy, and also for all manufacturing industries together, the rates of growth of gross output and intermediate inputs in the early postwar period do not appear to have been greatly different. For 1954 to 1963 the annual growth rates of gross output and intermediate inputs in all sectors of the economy were, respectively, 2.7 percent and 2.8 percent; for manufacturing industry, the corresponding rates were 2.6 percent and 2.3 percent.[5] This suggests that there may have been an approximate canceling out of the opposing forces of material-saving through technical progress on the one hand and the substitution of materials (made relatively cheaper through technical progress in the supplying industry) for labor on the other.*

In principle land should be included along with capital and be weighted according to its price in the appropriate benchmark year. As was explained in Chapter 5, it is not possible to estimate the amount of land in use by sector. Even in the cases of agricultural and forest land, where the total acreage is known, it is difficult to establish an appropriate price. This is because the market price refers to improvements to the land (drainage, ditches, farm roads, etc.) as well as to the land itself, whereas we want the price of the unimproved land, because the improvements have in principle already been included in the capital stock for agriculture and forestry. It is practically impossible to estimate directly the amount of land in use in other sectors. Rough estimates for the interwar years are available in Feinstein 1965. However, they are not very satisfactory for the purpose of providing an independent estimate of the growth of land input in the interwar period because in nearly all industries except agriculture and forestry the value of land

---

*The differences between the rates of growth of gross output and intermediate inputs cannot be attributed entirely to changes in the efficiency of utilization of raw materials. There are two other possible causes. (1) The structure of an industry, in the sense of the product-mix, might have changed. If, for example, there had been a shift toward those products with a relatively high raw material content, gross output would have grown less rapidly than intermediate inputs. (2) There might have been a change in the extent to which activities were integrated. For example, there might have been an increasing tendency for manufacturing plants to subcontract various service functions (e.g. advertising, cleaning, transport) to specialist firms; or there might have been a change in the extent to which processes were vertically integrated. Given both the shortage of data and the problems of interpretation, there is not much point in pursuing a productivity measure that incorporates changes in the efficiency of utilization of raw materials.

is assumed to be a fixed proportion of the value of the capital stock in buildings and works. We have not therefore made use of them.

The omission of land from TFI tends to lead to an overestimate of the growth of TFI in the economy as a whole, because the amount of land in existence in all sectors does not grow. The Feinstein interwar figures, for what they are worth, show that in 1924 land represented about 9 percent of total domestic assets (including fixed reproducible assets, inventories, and land). Assuming no change in land between 1924 and 1937, the true growth of total assets over the period should be about 91 percent of our measured growth rate, and the true growth of TFI about 97 percent of the measured rate. The error is therefore small.

The basic measure of the labor input is the total number of man-hours worked per year. This is derived from the total number in employment and average hours worked, allowing for part-time workers, sickness, holidays, and strikes, as described in Chapter 3. The effects of changes in the composition of the labor force by age, sex, and nationality, changes in the intensity of work resulting from changes in hours worked per week, and changes in the educational qualifications of the labor force (all discussed in Chapter 4) are included in TFP, except when otherwise stated. Separate estimates of the effects of changes in the allocation of labor between industries and occupations are discussed in Chapter 9, but they are always classified as part of the growth of TFP.

The alternative measures of the capital input were presented in Chapter 5. These are the gross capital stock and the net capital stock, including both domestic fixed assets and inventories, and excluding overseas assets. The gross and net stocks measure slightly different concepts, and it is not clear which is the more relevant. The net-stock measure gives a higher weight to newer assets than the gross-stock measure does, and so it is better if there is much physical deterioration or technical obsolescence. Net stock grows more rapidly than gross stock when the growth rate is high, because then the average age of the stock decreases. In this chapter we use both gross and net stocks as the capital input for the economy as a whole, but it is not possible to do this for the estimates in Chapter 8 because we do not have data on net stock by industry in postwar years.

Finally, the weights that are used to combine the growth rates of the labor and capital inputs according to equation 2 (p. 201) are in general the shares of labor and property, respectively, in gross domestic income in the first year of the period. Property's share therefore includes capital consumption, and capital receives a relatively larger weight than it would if shares in net domestic income were used. The use of shares in gross rather than net domestic income is consistent with the measurement of output as gross rather than net domestic product. From a theoretical point of view, it would be preferable to measure NDP, and hence to use shares in net domestic income, but this has not been done for statistical reasons.[6] The net measures are calculated for the economy as a whole, however (see the next section), and they can be compared with the gross measures.

In estimating labor and property shares, income from self-employment is separated into labor and property components by the method described in Chapter 6, and rental income is included in total property income.

THE GROWTH OF INPUTS AND OF TOTAL FACTOR PRODUCTIVITY

Labor Measured in Man-Hours

It is convenient to look at the growth of total factor input first before turning to the growth of total factor productivity. Table 7.1 accordingly presents growth rates of labor, capital, and TF_HI, together with the weights (factor shares) used to derive the growth rates of TF_HI. The trends in labor and capital and in the weights have already been discussed in Chapters 3–6.

Comparing the postwar period with the earlier peacetime periods, capital grew more rapidly, and labor declined. The more rapid capital growth was not sufficient to offset the decline in labor growth, so that the rate of growth of TF_HI in the postwar period was lower than in earlier peacetime periods. The annual percentage rate of growth of TF_HI in the postwar period was below the average of the earlier peacetime periods by 0.7 of a percentage point.* Part of this reduction (using a geometric mean of Paasche and Laspeyres indexes, about a half) is due to the fact that a lower weight is accorded, on the basis of income shares, to the faster-growing input, capital, in the postwar period than in earlier periods.

Both factor inputs grew more slowly across the two wars, especially World War I, than during the preceding peacetime periods — in the case of capital because of the diversion of resources to the war effort, in the case of labor because of the various causes discussed in Chapter 3, of which war casualties were not the most important.

---

*References in the text to TFI and TFP relate, unless otherwise indicated, to the measure of TFI based on gross capital.

TABLE 7.1
Growth of Inputs, 1856–1973
(Annual percentage growth rates)

Period	Labor (Total man-hours)	Capital Gross	Capital Net	Weights in $TF_H I$ [a] Labor	Weights in $TF_H I$ [a] Capital	$TF_H I$ [a] Gross capital	$TF_H I$ [a] Net capital
Peacetime phases:							
1856–1873	0.0%	1.9%	1.7%	0.59%	0.41%	0.8%	0.7%
1873–1913	0.9	1.9	1.8	0.57	0.43	1.3	1.3
1924–1937	1.5	1.8	2.0	0.70	0.30	1.5	1.6
1951–1973	−0.5	3.2	3.9	0.73	0.27	0.5	0.7
Wartime phases:							
1913–1924	−2.3	0.9	0.2	0.62	0.38	−1.1	−1.4
1937–1951	0.1	1.1	1.3	0.68	0.32	0.4	0.5
Post-WWII cycles:							
1951–1955	0.5	2.3	3.0	0.73	0.27	1.0	1.2
1955–1960	−0.4	2.6	3.8	0.72	0.28	0.4	0.8
1960–1964	−0.2	3.4	4.3	0.72	0.28	0.9	1.1
1964–1968	−1.5	4.1	4.5	0.72	0.28	0.1	0.2
1968–1973	−0.9	3.7	3.8	0.73	0.27	0.4	0.4
1856–1973	0.2%	2.0%	2.0%	—[b]	—[b]	0.8%	0.8%

[a] The subscript H indicates that the labor input is measured in man-hours.
[b] No explicit estimate was made for the 1856–1973 period, the rate of growth of $TF_H I$ being derived from the rates for the components periods.

TABLE 7.2
Growth of Output, Inputs, and Total Factor Productivity, 1856–1973
(Annual percentage growth rates)

Period	Output[a]	$TF_H I$ [b] Gross capital	$TF_H I$ [b] Net capital	$TF_H P$ [b] Gross capital	$TF_H P$ [b] Net capital
Peacetime phases:					
1856–1873	2.2%	0.8%	0.7%	1.4%	1.5%
1873–1913	1.8	1.3	1.3	0.5	0.5
1924–1937	2.2	1.5	1.6	0.7	0.6
1951–1973	2.8	0.5	0.7	2.3	2.1
War-time phases					
1913–1924	−0.1	−1.1	−1.4	1.0	1.3
1937–1951	1.8	0.4	0.5	1.4	1.3
Post-WWII cycles:					
1951–1955	2.8	1.0	1.2	1.8	1.6
1955–1960	2.5	0.4	0.8	2.1	1.7
1960–1964	3.4	0.9	1.1	2.5	2.3
1964–1968	2.6	0.1	0.2	2.5	2.4
1968–1973	2.6	0.4	0.4	2.2	2.2
1856–1973	1.9%	0.8%	0.8%	1.1%	1.1%

[a] GDP at factor cost; average of estimates from the expenditure, income, and output sides (see Appendix A).
[b] The subscript H indicates that the labor input is measured in man-hours.

Within the postwar period there was marked (though not regular) deceleration in the labor input. This was partly but not completely offset by the clear acceleration in the capital input until 1968 or so. The rate of growth of TF_HI was lower in the latter part of the postwar period, 1964–73, than in the earlier part, 1951–64. Over the period 1951–73 as a whole the rate of growth of TF_HI was much the same as it was in 1937–51.

Turning to the growth of total factor productivity (Table 7.2), the postwar period experienced considerably more rapid growth than earlier periods. This reflects both more rapid growth in output and less rapid growth in TF_HI. The rate of growth of output per man-hour exceeded that of former times by a still larger margin, since such growth as there was in TF_HI all came on the capital side.

A striking feature of Table 7.2 is the low rate of growth of TF_HP in 1873–1913 — much lower than in 1856–73.* There is, moreover, some indication that within the period 1873–1913 the rate of growth of TF_HP took a change for the worse around the turn of the century, but quantifying this is hampered by cyclical fluctuations and by the unusually large discrepancy that exists between the alternative measures of GDP at that time (see Appendix L). The rate of growth of TF_HP was relatively high in both of the transwar periods. These comparisons between periods will be somewhat altered when we have taken account below of possible changes in the intensity of work associated with changes in hours, which particularly affect the periods 1856–73 and 1913–24. In addition, consideration of sectoral performance (Chapter 8) will show the interwar period in a rather more favorable light.[7]

Over the whole period 1856–1973 a larger part of the growth of output was accounted for by growth in TF_HP than by growth in TF_HI (1.1 percent compared with 0.8 percent). However, the relative contributions from the two sides differed greatly between periods. In the postwar period and in the two transwar periods, the preponderant contribution was from TF_HP growth; in 1873–1913 it was from TF_HI growth.

TF_HP accelerated within the postwar period up till the early 1960's. Thereafter, the high rate of growth was more or less maintained but not increased. This is much the same pattern as was noted in Chapter 2 in regard to output per man, though the acceleration in TF_HP is of

*Allowance for possible reductions in hours of work between 1873 and 1913, not reflected in our data (see p. 71), would raise the estimate of the rate of growth of TF_HP fractionally. However, even at the outside the difference amounts to less than 0.1 of a percentage point.

TABLE 7.3

Growth of Net Output, Inputs, and Total Factor Productivity, 1856–1973

(Annual percentage growth rates)

Period	Net output[a]	Weights in TF_HI[b] Labor	Weights in TF_HI[b] Capital	TF_HI[b] (net capital)	TF_HP[b] (net capital)
Peacetime phases:					
1856–1873	2.2%	0.62%	0.38%	0.7%	1.5%
1873–1913	1.8	0.60	0.40	1.2	0.6
1924–1937	2.2	0.75	0.25	1.6	0.6
1951–1973	2.6	0.80	0.20	0.4	2.2
Wartime phases:					
1913–1924	– 0.2	0.66	0.34	– 1.5	1.3
1937–1951	1.8	0.75	0.27	0.4	1.4
1856–1973	1.9%	–[c]	–[c]	0.7%	1.2%

[a]NDP at factor cost; average of estimates from the expenditure, income, and output sides (see Appendix A).
[b]The subscript H indicates that the labor input is measured in man-hours.
[c]No explicit estimate was made for the 1856–1973 period, the rate of growth of TF_HI being derived from the rates for the component periods.

somewhat smaller extent, reflecting the acceleration in capital input in the course of the period.

The net output measures that correspond to the gross-output measures in Tables 7.1 and 7.2 are shown in Table 7.3.* The estimated growth of output over the whole period 1856–1973 is the same whether the net or gross measure of output is used. In some of the individual periods the growth of net output is slightly different from that of gross output, and in some the higher share of labor in net income than in gross income leads to slightly different estimates of the growth of TF_HP. Thus in the postwar period the lower weight according to capital relative to labor by the net measure reduces the rate of growth of TF_HI and somewhat increases that of TF_HP. But the broad conclusions about the differences between periods in the growth of output, TF_HI, and TF_HP are the same whichever set of measures is used. We can therefore with an easy conscience continue to concentrate on gross output and shares in gross income, and to ignore the equivalent net measures.†

*Capital is also measured net in Table 7.3, though it is a different, but related, concept of netness. It would not be incorrect to use the gross measure of capital (any more than it is incorrect to use net capital with gross output and shares in gross income), but it is perhaps less confusing if the net measure is used. The conclusions are unaffected by the choice of capital measure.

†But not the net-capital measure, where the netness is conceptually different. Moreover, the differences between the growth rates of gross and net capital are sufficiently interesting to warrant examination wherever the data permit it.

Labor Adjusted for Quality Change

Finally, we consider what happens to the measures of TFI and TFP growth when the measure of labor input is adjusted to allow for the improvements in quality identified in Table 4.7. This adjustment has the effect of shifting part of the residual TFP growth to identified TFI growth, and the series are referred to as $TF_Q I$ and $TF_Q P$, respectively. The resulting estimates are shown in Table 7.4. The margin of error attached to some of the estimates of improvements in the quality of labor is very wide (see Chapter 4), and the following remarks must be read with this in mind.

The sources of improvement in labor quality were, in order of importance over the period as a whole, the rise in educational standards, the increased intensity of work consequent on reduced hours (referred to below as the hours-offset), and the change in age-sex distribution (chiefly in the proportion of young workers). The reduction in Ireland's weight in total was significant before 1914 but not after. The effect of education was much the same in all periods, and allowance for it therefore serves to depress the rate of growth of $TF_Q P$ and raise that of $TF_Q I$ throughout, without much affecting comparisons between periods. On the other hand, the effect of the hours-offset is almost entirely concentrated in the periods 1856–73 and 1913–24. Allowance for it goes some way toward putting the labor input measure on a man-

TABLE 7.4

Growth of Inputs and Total Factor Productivity with Labor Quality
Improvements Reallocated to Inputs, 1856–1973

(Annual percentage growth rates)

Period	Labor quality in TFP		Labor quality in TFI	
	$TF_H I^a$	$TF_H P^a$	$TF_Q I^a$	$TF_Q P^a$
Peacetime phases:				
1856–1873	0.8%	1.4%	1.6%	0.6%
1873–1913	1.3	0.5	1.8	0.0
1924–1937	1.5	0.7	2.0	0.2
1951–1973	0.5	2.3	1.0	1.8
Wartime phases:				
1913–1924	– 1.1	1.0	0.1	– 0.2
1937–1951	0.4	1.4	1.1	0.7
1856–1973	0.8%	1.1%	1.4%	0.5%

Source: Basic statistics (Appendix N); Table 4.7.
[a] Based on the gross capital measure. The subscript H indicates that the labor input is measured in man-hours. The subscript Q indicates that the labor input measured in man-hours is adjusted to include changes in quality.

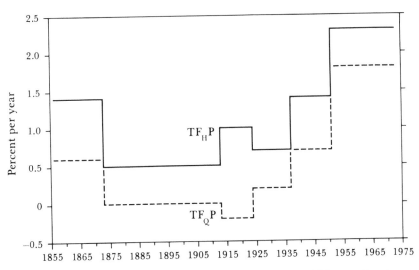

Fig. 7.1. Growth of total factor productivity including effects of labor quality change ($TF_H P$) and excluding them ($TF_Q P$), six standard periods, 1856–1973. (*Source:* Table 7.4)

years' basis rather than a man-hours' basis, but with the difference that the assumed offset to reductions in hours on account of increased intensity of work diminishes over time as hours of work fall. The change in age-sex distribution is a relatively unimportant item.

Allowance for changes in labor quality due to these causes adds 0.6 of a percentage point to the rate of growth of TFI over the period 1856– 1973 as a whole and consequently deducts 0.6 of a point from the rate of growth of TFP, which is thereby reduced by more than a half. Growth of $TF_Q I$ appears as the source of nearly three-quarters of the growth in output. This is in contrast to the result without allowance for labor quality, which shows growth in $TF_H P$ more important than growth in $TF_H I$.

The low rate of growth of $TF_H P$ between 1873 and 1913 has already been noted. When allowance is made for labor quality, that period emerges with no growth in $TF_Q P$ at all. Allowance for labor quality reduces the growth of TFP in 1856–73 by an even larger amount (because of the hours-offset); the falling-off between that period and 1873–1913 remains on the $TF_Q P$ measure, but not such a great falling-off as on the $TF_H P$ measure. The period most affected by allowances for labor quality is 1913–24, which emerges with negative growth in $TF_Q P$; the magnitude of the adjustment in this period is again due to the hours-offset. The historically high rate of TFP growth in the postwar period stands out more prominently than ever by contrast. Indeed, on the present reckoning there was no significant net increase at all in TF_QP over the two-thirds of a century comprised by the period 1873–1937; there was no increase in output per man-hour between the start and finish of that period over and above what was attributable to increases in the capital stock and improvements in the quality of the labor input. This rather startling conclusion (which is subject to the statistical caveat already noted) implies that in some sectors TF_QP must have actually declined. This is confirmed by the sectoral data in the following chapter, if an allowance for labor quality is introduced.

Figure 7.1 presents the TFP data in Table 7.4 in pictorial form. The general trend in the rate of growth of TF_QP over time, after allowance for changes in labor quality, was at first steadily downward, to a low point around World War I (or possibly in 1899–1913). Thereafter it was steadily upward, at a rate more rapid than the previous decline. The difference from the rather more irregular timepattern shown by TF_HP growth is almost entirely due to the hours-offset. Though its exact magnitude is conjectural, some offset certainly existed, and the lower of the two curves in Figure 7.1 therefore probably gives the truer picture of the underlying pattern of change between periods. The difference between the *average* heights of the two curves is largely due to education.

The downward tendency in the rate of growth of TFP on either measure in the first part of the period appears to have been a continuation of a trend that occurred earlier in the nineteenth century. Feinstein (1978: 86) gives the following estimates for the average annual rate of growth in TF_rP in Great Britain (not the United Kingdom): 1800–1830, 1.4 percent; 1830–60, 0.8 percent. Our estimate of the rate of growth of TF_rP in Great Britain in 1856–73 is 0.8 percent. This is not perfectly comparable with the figures for the earlier periods on account of differences in the basis of the estimates of GDP. The figures suggest, however, that there was no substantial phase in the nineteenth century during which the trend in the rate of growth of TFP was upward.

PART THREE

Growth and Its Proximate Sources in the Principal Sectors of the Economy

CHAPTER EIGHT

Output, Inputs, and Productivity by Sector

The sectoral measures contained in this chapter are consistent with output-side estimates of GDP but not necessarily with expenditure-side or income-side estimates. Growth in output is measured by single indicators, not double deflation. Labor input is measured in man-hours. The capital stock is measured gross. Sectoral distributive shares are used as the weights in calculating TFI. Nine major sectors are studied: agriculture, forestry, fishing; mining, quarrying; manufacturing; contruction; gas, electricity, water; transport, communications; commerce; public and professional services; and dwellings.

THE COURSE OF STRUCTURAL CHANGE

Long-run changes in the relative importance of the nine major sectors are reviewed before looking at the sectoral growth rates for output, inputs, and productivity. The main findings are in Table 8.1, which shows each sector's share in inputs and output at benchmark years. The largest sectors are manufacturing and commerce, together with agriculture at the beginning of the period and public and professional services at the end. Agriculture's share in inputs fell at a fairly steady proportional rate (except for a rise in 1937–51), but the main absolute fall was over by 1914. Its share in output changed little after 1924, a reflection of its above-average growth of productivity. Manufacturing's share in labor input rose across World War II but otherwise had no upward trend; it was the only sector not to show a rise matching agriculture's loss before 1914. However, output and capital stock regularly grew faster in manufacturing than in the economy as a whole. The net change in the share of commerce in inputs over the entire period 1856–1973 was small. It rose steeply before 1914 and also rose in the interwar and postwar periods, but it fell steeply across World War II. Productivity in commerce, as measured, grew less than in the economy as a whole, and its share in output at constant prices had a downward trend. The proportion of the labor force in public and professional services rose in all periods but especially across World War II (measures of output in this sector are largely conventional). There was some tendency to convergence over time in sectoral capital-labor ratios.

THE GROWTH OF OUTPUT, INPUTS, AND TFP IN THE MAJOR SECTORS OF THE ECONOMY

Sectoral growth rates are given in Table 8.3. These data lead to six general findings.

(1) *The increase in* the rate of growth of output *between 1873–1913 and 1924–37 came almost entirely from industrial sectors, and that between 1924–37 and 1951–73 almost entirely from nonindustrial sectors.*

(2) *The most prominent single change in* the rate of growth of TFI *was common to all sectors, viz. the fall in the postwar period compared with previous peacetime periods.*

(3) *The U-shaped pattern in* the rate of growth of TFP *was general, but the timing and magnitude of the changes varied between sectors. The decline between 1856–73 and 1873–1913 was largest in agriculture, mining, and construction; there was also a fall in manufacturing. TFP grew more rapidly in 1924–37 than in 1873–1913 in every sector with the important exception of commerce (where it fell absolutely, reflecting concealed unemployment). It grew more rapidly in 1951–73 than in 1924–37 in every sector, the improvement being most pronounced in nonindustrial sectors in 1951–64 and in industrial sectors in 1964–73.*

(4) *The period 1937–51 stands apart. The shifts in TFI toward manufacturing, mining, and agriculture, and away from commerce, were accompanied by opposite trends in the rate of growth of TFP, suggesting a tendency to diminishing returns. There was a unique large absolute fall in TFP in construction, a sector where (in contrast to commerce) TFP was apparently adversely affected by the move to a full employment economy.*

(5) *The ranking of the nine sectors with respect to the rate of growth of TFP was in general more uniform between periods than their ranking with respect to the rates of growth of TFI and output. Differences between sectors in the rate of growth of TFP increased after World War I.*

(6) *Differences between periods in sectoral rates of growth of TFI did not closely match those in output. There was some tendency for*

variations between periods in sectoral rates of growth of TFI to be in the opposite direction from those in TFP.

THE GROWTH OF OUTPUT, INPUTS, AND TFP
IN SUBSECTORS OF THE ECONOMY

Rates of growth of output, inputs, and productivity can also be calculated (usually from 1924 only) for 21 subsectors: 13 in manufacturing, 3 in commerce, and 5 in transport and communications. There were, naturally, expanding and declining subsectors. However, differences between periods in the rate of growth of TFP in the respective sectors were in general pervasive through the constituent subsectors. Thus, the distributive trades, insurance, banking, and finance, and miscellaneous services all experienced absolute declines in TFP in the interwar period. In the distributive trades this happened also, though less markedly, before 1914, when the increase in numbers employed was particularly large. A cross-industry correlation for the 13 industries in manufacturing is undertaken in Appendix J, with broadly similar results to those obtained by previous writers. The same manufacturing industries (mainly metal-using ones) tended to have high rates of growth of TFI in the periods 1924–37, 1937–51, and 1951–64, but not in 1964–73.

In Chapter 7 we considered the changes in TFI and TFP in the economy as a whole, and movements in aggregate output were reviewed in Chapter 2. In this chapter we examine the corresponding findings for the main sectors of the economy.

The measurement of output in the individual sectors is conceptually the same as that for the whole economy, but statistically, sectoral output can only be measured from output data. To maintain consistency with these sectoral estimates, the estimates for GDP given in this chapter are also the output series, not the average of output, expenditure, and income series used in Chapters 2 and 7. The change in output in all individual sectors and industries except agriculture is measured by single indicators rather than the conceptually preferable method of double deflation. Some implications of this and other aspects of the procedure are considered more fully in Appendix I.

The method of measuring the growth of TFP in individual sectors is the same as that used for the whole economy. The labor input is the number of man-hours worked per year, unadjusted for changes in the quality of labor. The approximate order of magnitude of such adjustments at the aggregate level was shown in the last section of the previous chapter, but though one may reasonably assume that similar improvements in labor quality occurred in most sectors, sector-specific information is lacking. The capital stock is measured gross of depreciation (but after allowing for retirements) because data on the net capital stock are not available by industry for the postwar years. For 1856–73 and 1873–1913 there are no data on inventories by sector, and the capital stock estimates for these periods therefore cover only fixed assets. The weights used to combine the growth rates of labor and capital are the shares of labor and capital in the total income of the particular sector in the first year of the period.[1]

Our calculations of TFI and TFP are made for nine major sectors of the economy: agriculture, forestry, fishing; mining, quarrying; manufacturing; construction; gas, electricity, water; transport, communications; commerce; public and professional services; and dwellings. However, for two of these sectors — public and professional services, and the ownership of dwellings — output and TFP are not very meaningful concepts, and they are included only for completeness.[2]

Before considering the sectoral growth rates, we look first at the changes over time that they brought about in the relative importance of sectors in the economy.

THE COURSE OF STRUCTURAL CHANGE

Changes in the Relative Importance of the Major Sectors

Table 8.1 shows the changes in the relative importance of the nine major sectors over the years 1856–1973 based on output at constant prices, output at current prices, labor input, and capital input at current prices. Table 8.2 gives supplementary information on shares in the labor force within services, on a more disaggregated basis.

Movements in industries' shares in the total may follow different courses according to the variable under discussion — a point that has often led to discussions at cross purposes.*

In the case of output, changes in relative prices are liable to lead to divergences between the trends in shares at constant and current prices

*For example, in discussions about "de-industrialization," conclusions based on trends in shares in the labor force have often been used as if they betokened trends in shares in output at constant prices.

(and the divergences would probably be even greater if the same constant price weights were used for all periods). This is most apparent in
manufacturing and in public and professional services. Between 1951
and 1973 manufacturing's current-price share fell and its constant-
price share rose, both by significant amounts. In the interwar period its
current-price share rose slightly, but its constant-price share rose substantially. In public and professional services the downward trend
found in the constant-price share in both peacetime periods is replaced
by an upward trend in the current-price share.

In general movements in labor-force shares correspond more closely
to those in current-price output shares than to those in constant-price
output shares. This is to be expected. Since wages are the major element in costs, the value of industries' output at current prices is likely
to exhibit similar trends to their labor input. These will not correspond
to constant-price trends if the rate of growth of productivity differs between industries. However, in some sectors there are systematic differences between the *levels* of the shares in current-price output and the
shares in labor. The extreme example is dwellings, which has no labor
force at all, but around a quarter of the entire capital stock. The other
most prominent example is utilities, whose share in the labor force has
always been much smaller than its share in the capital stock, and hence
also smaller than its share in output. In general the sectors that had
below-average or above-average capital-labor ratios at the beginning
of the period continued to do so 117 years later. However, there was
some tendency to converge: most sectors were nearer the mean in 1973
than in 1856.[3]

Trends in Individual Sectors

Let us now look briefly at the experience of the various sectors in
turn to see how their relative importance altered over time.

The series on manufacturing is of special interest and may be considered first. Its course is curious. The proportion of the labor force in
manufacturing was more or less constant from 1861 until 1911.[4] There
was a sharp rise across World War I to 1920 (not shown in Table 8.1),
but this was temporary and was not maintained in the face of the ensuing depression.[5] During the rest of the interwar period there was little
trend, and the level was about the same as in the nineteenth century.
Then across World War II and in the early postwar years there was
another steep rise. A peak was reached in 1960, and there was then a
decline.

What emerges, therefore, is that the rise from 1937 to 1960 should
not be regarded as a continuation of a long-standing trend, nor should

TABLE 8.1
Sectoral Shares of Output, Labor, and Capital in the Whole Economy, 1856–1973
(Percent)

Sector and variable	1856–1913			1913–1937			1937–1973			
	1856	1873	1913	1913	1924	1937	1937	1951	1964	1973
Agriculture, forestry, fishing:										
Output, constant prices	18.4%	13.5%	6.4%	5.3%	4.9%	4.4%	4.2%	4.5%	4.4%	4.4%
Output, current prices	—	—	—	—	4.9	3.5	3.5	5.5	3.4	3.0
Labor	29.6	21.4	11.5	(9.2)	8.1	5.8	5.3	5.6	4.1	2.9
Capital	19.1	15.4	6.2	(9.2)	8.2	6.1	5.7	5.4	4.4	3.9
Mining, quarrying:										
Output, constant prices	4.6	6.1	6.4	6.6	6.1	4.3	5.8	4.3	2.8	1.6
Output, current prices	—	—	—	—	6.1	3.7	3.7	3.5	2.5	1.5
Labor	3.6	4.1	6.5	(5.8)	6.2	4.0	4.1	3.7	2.6	1.5
Capital	1.6	2.2	2.1	(2.0)	2.2	1.9	1.8	1.3	1.5	1.2
Manufacturing:										
Output, constant prices	22.2	24.6	26.6	29.0	30.9	34.8	29.5	34.6	37.0	38.2
Output, current prices	—	—	—	—	30.9	31.3	29.5	35.7	33.6	30.1
Labor	32.5	33.5	32.1	(32.5)	32.9	32.9	30.4	35.1	36.1	34.7
Capital[a]	12.9	14.6	18.5	(20.4)	20.3	19.0	19.5	23.8	25.5	22.8
Construction:										
Output, constant prices	3.2	3.8	2.9	2.7	4.2	5.6	7.9	5.6	6.5	6.0
Output, current prices	—	—	—	—	4.2	5.0	5.1	5.4	7.1	7.8
Labor	4.0	4.8	4.9	(4.9)	4.5	5.9	6.0	6.9	8.5	8.7
Capital[a]	(0.8)	(0.8)	(0.6)	(0.6)	0.6	0.6	0.6	0.7	1.0	1.1
Gas, electricity, water:										
Output, constant prices	0.3	0.5	1.9	1.6	2.2	3.4	1.3	2.2	2.9	3.6
Output, current prices	—	—	—	—	2.2	2.7	2.7	2.0	3.2	3.2
Labor	0.1	0.2	0.6	(0.7)	1.1	1.3	1.3	1.6	1.7	1.4
Capital	1.7	2.7	4.8	(4.4)	4.5	7.0	7.8	6.8	8.4	8.6
Transport, communications:										
Output, constant prices	6.5	7.6	10.5	9.0	10.3	9.5	7.2	8.5	8.1	8.6
Output, current prices	—	—	—	—	10.3	9.7	9.6	8.9	8.4	8.9
Labor	4.1	5.6	7.8	(8.2)	8.6	7.7	7.6	8.1	7.5	7.4
Capital	18.5	22.6	23.4	(20.5)	19.5	16.5	15.8	12.6	10.9	9.9

Commerce:										
Output, constant prices	23.7	25.5	27.2	33.3	27.7	25.9	30.4	24.2	25.2	26.1
Output, current prices	—	—	—	—	27.7	29.4	30.4	23.7	25.5	27.0
Labor	20.8	24.7	28.5	(31.1)	29.2	32.6	35.4	23.4	24.5	25.4
Capital	12.4	11.2	9.8	(12.8)	12.7	12.0	11.0	9.7	10.5	11.4
Public and professional services:										
Output, constant prices	8.6	7.9	10.2	11.8	12.8	11.4	12.8	15.5	12.9	12.4
Output, current prices	—	—	—	—	12.8	13.1	13.9	14.8	15.6	18.0
Labor	5.3	5.7	8.1	(7.6)	9.4	9.8	9.9	15.6	15.0	18.0
Capital	6.5	6.2	11.1	(9.7)	9.5	10.0	11.4	10.8	11.2	13.2
Dwellings:										
Output, constant prices	12.5	10.5	7.9	4.5	4.8	4.6	4.2	3.9	3.5	3.5
Output, current prices	—	—	—	—	4.8	5.6	5.6	3.0	4.3	5.8
Capital	26.5	24.3	23.5	(20.4)	22.5	26.9	26.4	28.9	26.6	27.9
Adjustment for financial services:[b]										
Output, constant prices	0.0	0.0	0.0	-3.8	-3.9	-3.9	-3.3	-3.3	-3.3	-4.4
Output, current prices	—	—	—	—	-3.9	-4.0	-4.0	-2.5	-3.6	-5.3

Note: Figures in parentheses are rough estimates, either to provide a link across breaks in the data, as explained later in this note, or to fill gaps in the data, as explained in note a.

There are major breaks in all series in 1913 and 1937, and so comparisons should not be made between sets of figures in different periods. Two breaks are common to all series: (1) Southern Ireland is included in the 1856–1913 figures, excluded in the 1913–37 and 1937–73 figures; (2) the industrial classification is roughly consistent with the 1948 Standard Industrial Classification in the 1856–1913 and 1913–37 figures, but is based on the 1958 SIC in the 1937–73 figures.

Apart from these, the main breaks are as follows.

Output at constant prices: different price bases were used within periods; 1907 prices were used for 1856–1913, 1924 prices for 1913–37, and 1958 prices for 1937–73. The adjustment for financial services (see note b) was assumed to be zero in 1856–1913.

Labor: based on estimates of man-years up to 1913 (first figure) and man-hours from 1924. The second 1913 figure has been roughly linked to the 1924 figure to produce an approximate estimate, shown in parentheses, on a man-hours' basis.

Capital: based on the estimates of gross fixed capital only through 1920, on gross fixed capital and inventories thereafter, all at current prices. The second 1913 figure has been roughly linked to the 1924 figure to produce an approximate estimate, shown in parentheses, on a total capital basis. There is also a break in 1937 resulting from inconsistencies between the statistical series for earlier and later years.

A number of minor breaks resulting from statistical inconsistencies have been removed in all series by splicing within periods, and thereby concentrated in 1913 and 1937.

[a]Separate estimates for capital in manufacturing and construction in 1856–1920 do not exist. The share of capital in construction in 1913 was therefore assumed to be 0.6%, and the stock was assumed to have grown from 1856 to 1873 and from 1873 to 1913 at the same rate as output of construction; the share of manufacturing was found as a residual.

[b]This adjustment is necessary to exclude the services of the financial sector to other sectors, because statistical deficiencies prevent its being allocated. The output of other sectors is therefore overestimated.

TABLE 8.2

Shares of Service Industries in the Total Labor Input, 1856–1973

(Percent)

Year	Commerce			Public and professional services		
	Distribu-tive trades	Insurance, banking, and finance	Miscella-neous services	Armed forces[a]	Civil public admin-istration	Professional and scienti-fic services
1856	6.3%	0.1%	14.4%	1.9%	1.1%	2.3%
1873	7.8	0.3	16.6	1.7	1.2	2.8
1913	12.2	1.1	15.2	2.0	2.1	4.0
1913	(12.6)	(1.1)	(17.4)	(2.0)	(2.0)	(3.6)
1924	12.4	1.9	14.9	1.8	3.2	4.4
1937	14.3	2.0	16.3	1.7	3.5	4.6
1937	15.2	2.0	18.2	1.7	3.4	4.8
1951	11.2	1.8	10.4	3.5	5.5	6.6
1964	13.2	2.3	9.0	1.6	5.1	8.2
1973	12.4	3.3	9.7	1.4	6.1	10.5

Note: On the breaks in comparability at 1913 and 1937, see Table 8.1.
[a]Includes those stationed abroad and excludes members of the U.S. and other forces stationed in Britain.

the falling-off after that be regarded as a reversal of such a trend. The rise from 1937 to 1960 was an altogether exceptional phenomenon by historical standards. The data as they stand suggest that since the beginning of the nineteenth century, every substantial increase in the proportion of the labor force in manufacturing in Britain has occurred in or after a period of war (including possibly 1811–21), though we should not wish to press this as a causal relationship.[6]

The conclusion that in peacetime periods the proportion of the labor force in manufacturing was roughly constant up to World War II calls for one further comment. In the early nineteenth century, and indeed in the later nineteenth century too, a significant proportion of those in manufacturing were domestic workers or workers in very small work-shops rather than in factories. From the point of view of supply condi-tions, though not from the point of view of the structure of demand, it might be more relevant to consider the proportion engaged in "modern manufacturing industry," i.e. in factories. Taking the year 1841, the earliest with reasonably usable data, we may deduct, from the 2,700,000 engaged in manufacturing in Great Britain, about 600,000 in clothing (exclusively a non-factory industry, and much the largest one) and 250,000 hand-loom weavers in textiles. This reduces the number to 1,850,000, 22 percent of the labor force.[7] In 1924 the total number of manufacturing out-workers, most of them in clothing, amounted to only 0.16 percent of the total in employment; thus their exclusion would not alter significantly the proportion engaged in manufacturing. So whereas the overall proportion remained about constant between 1841 and 1924, the proportion in factories increased substantially. Moreover, the above adjustment understates the increase, because there were shifts from non-factory to factory employment in other manufacturing industries besides clothing and textiles.

The trend in manufacturing's share in output at constant prices was different from its share in the labor force: as already noted, its share in output at constant prices had a persistent tendency to rise in peacetime, as well as across wars, despite the absence of a similar trend in its share of the labor force. This reflects partly the tendency for productivity to rise faster in manufacturing than in the economy as a whole, and partly the rise in manufacturing's share in the national capital stock in certain phases, namely in the period before 1914 and across World War II.*

Trends in other major sectors may be more briefly treated. The proportion of the labor force in agriculture plunged down throughout the period. The main decline took place before 1914. After that the proportion declined at an even faster rate, as a percentage of itself, but the proportion itself had become so much smaller that such declines were much less significant in absolute terms than they had been earlier. The fall in agriculture's share in the capital stock followed a broadly similar pattern. In the period 1873–1913 its share of the capital stock actually fell faster, proportionately, than its share in the labor force. The decline in agriculture's place in the economy in this period was not merely the result of normal structural change and the elimination of rural surplus population; it was due also to foreign competition and the consequent agricultural depression. Agriculture's share in output at constant prices changed little after 1924, despite the continuing diminution of its share in factor inputs – a reflection of its good growth in productivity.

The other main declining sector, mining, differed from agriculture in that up to World War I its share of the labor force and output were increasing rapidly; the increase was particularly great in the first decade of the twentieth century.[8] Between 1924 and 1973 its share in the labor force declined absolutely by almost as much as agriculture's,

---

*It is striking that the fall in the share of manufacturing in output at current prices between 1951 (the peak was actually in 1955) and 1973 was substantially greater than the fall in its share in either labor input or capital input. This necessarily implies a fall in the wage rate or the profit rate (or both) in manufacturing relative to the rest of the economy. In fact the fall was entirely on the side of the profit rate. The decline in the relative profit rate in manufacturing was discussed in Chapter 6.

and proportionally it declined more. In contrast to agriculture, its share in output fell as much as its share in the labor force.

Like mining, transport and communications absorbed a rapidly increasing proportion of the labor force in the nineteenth century. After World War I its share in the labor force remained about constant, and its share in the capital stock declined.

Public and professional services was the great growth sector. It is made up of three principal components, the armed forces, public administration, and professional and scientific services, the trends in which were rather different. The armed forces' share in the labor force was much higher in 1951, where there was still conscription, than it was in 1937, but in the course of the postwar period it fell to a lower level than in earlier peacetime periods. Public administration increased its share in the labor force chiefly in two large steps across the wars. Within the postwar period it first fell, then rose. Professional and scientific services, of which health and education are the largest elements, increased its share in the labor force in all periods, peacetime as well as across the wars. Its increase in the postwar period was larger, absolutely and proportionally, than in earlier periods. In the sector as a whole, output at current prices is a more significant statistic than output at constant prices on account of the conventional basis on which the latter has to be measured. Between 1937 and 1951 (though not in the postwar period) the rise in the sector's share in output at current prices was much smaller than the rise in its share in labor input, owing to a very substantial fall in relative wages.

Trends in the share in the economy of commerce did not follow any simple pattern of rise or fall. That sector too is made up of rather heterogeneous elements. The substantial rise in the sector's share in the labor force up till World War I was due almost entirely to the distributive trades. There was no net change in the share of miscellaneous services before 1914,* and though there was a rapid proportional increase in insurance, banking, and finance, the absolute numbers involved were small. The distributive trades continued to give employment to an increasing proportion of the labor force in the interwar period. The proportion in miscellaneous services also increased in that period, but not enough to offset the fall across World War I. Two-thirds of the enormous fall in commerce's share in the labor force between 1937 and 1951 came from miscellaneous services, one-third from the distributive trades. Within the postwar period the proportion of the labor force in the distributive trades first rose (till 1964), then fell; the proportion in

*Miscellaneous services includes domestic service and also catering, hotel service, entertainment and sport, hairdressing, laundries, and photography.

miscellaneous services first fell (till 1960), then rose. The substantial rise in insurance, banking, and finance, which was particularly rapid in the late postwar period, resembled what happened in the other predominantly white-collar subsector, professional services. It accounted for most of the increase between 1951 and 1973 in the commerce sector taken as a whole.

Focusing attention on shares in the labor force, we may thus summarize as follows trends over the three periods 1856–1913, 1913–37, and 1937–73 (thus including the war periods with the subsequent peacetime periods). Between 1856 and 1913 the enormous decline in agriculture's share permitted increases in the share of all other sectors, except manufacturing; the largest increase was in the distributive trades. Between 1913 and 1937 no sector was releasing labor on anything like the same scale as agriculture had done before 1913. The continuing decline in agriculture, and now also a decline in mining, were matched by fairly general increases in the shares of other sectors, the largest gains (but on a much smaller scale than before 1913) being in the service industries. Between 1937 and 1973 there was a decline in the share of miscellaneous services and, to a lesser extent, the distributive trades, of an amount far greater than the change in any sector's share between 1913 and 1937; the decline in their share of total labor input over those 36 years was larger than the decline in agriculture's share in the 40 years between 1873 and 1913 (11.3 percentage points, compared with 9.9 points). Substantial declines also continued in the shares of agriculture and mining. The declines in these three sectors were matched, to rather more than half their extent, by the increase in the share of public and professional services. There was also, for the first time in over 100 years, a significant increase in the proportion in manufacturing. The main part of this increase, and of the big decline in miscellaneous services and the distributive trades, had already taken place by 1951. Between 1951 and 1973 the principal net changes were that declines in agriculture and mining were matched by increases in the service industries, a pattern resembling in some respects that of the period before 1914.

THE GROWTH OF OUTPUT, INPUTS, AND TOTAL FACTOR
PRODUCTIVITY IN THE MAJOR SECTORS OF THE ECONOMY

We now turn from the long-term trends in the relative importance of the major sectors to the underlying growth rates of their output, inputs, and TFP. The data for the nine sectors for all periods except 1913–21 (for which the inputs by sector are not available) are set out in Table 8.3. The postwar period is divided into two parts, 1951–64 and

TABLE 8.3
Growth of Output, Labor, Capital, Total Factor Input, Total Factor Productivity, and Weighted Total Factor Productivity by Sector, 1856–1973

(Annual percentage growth rates)

Variable and sector	1856–1873	1873–1913	1924–1937	1937–1951	1951–1964	1964–1973
Output:						
Agriculture, forestry, fishing	0.2%	−0.1%	1.4%	1.7%	2.6%	2.5%
Mining, quarrying	3.6	1.9	−0.4	−1.0	−0.7	−3.3
Manufacturing	2.6	2.0	3.2	2.5	3.2	3.0
Construction	3.1	1.1	4.6	−1.2	3.8	1.8
Gas, electricity, water	5.5	5.1	5.8	4.2	5.1	5.2
Transport, communications	2.9	2.7	1.5	2.4	2.2	3.5
Commerce	(2.4)	(2.0)	1.7	−0.2	3.0	3.0
Public and professional services	(1.4)	(2.5)	(1.3)	(2.7)	(1.5)	(2.2)
Ownership of dwellings	1.0	1.1	1.9	0.8	1.8	2.6
GDP	2.0	1.8	2.3	1.5	2.8	2.7
Labor:[a]						
Agriculture, forestry, fishing	−1.0	−0.6	−1.1	0.4	−2.4	−4.8
Mining, quarrying	1.7	2.1	−2.0	−0.6	−2.7	−7.2
Manufacturing	1.1	0.8	1.4	1.0	0.2	−1.6
Construction	2.0	1.0	3.5	1.1	1.6	−0.8
Gas, electricity, water	4.7	3.3	3.1	1.4	0.5	−3.4
Transport, communications	2.0	2.1	0.6	0.5	−0.7	−1.3
Commerce	1.9	1.3	2.3	−3.2	0.3	−0.7
Public and professional services	1.3	1.8	1.8	3.4	−0.4	0.9
GDP	0.9	0.9	1.5	0.1	0.0	−1.1
Capital:[b]						
Agriculture, forestry, fishing	0.3	−1.0	−0.1	0.8	1.5	3.3
Mining, quarrying	3.3	2.0	0.5	−0.4	3.3	1.6
Manufacturing	3.2	2.6	1.0	2.9	3.3	3.3
Construction	(3.1)[c]	(1.1)[c]	1.6	2.4	6.2	6.4
Gas, electricity, water	4.9	3.6	4.8	0.9	4.0	4.1
Transport, communications	3.2	2.0	0.2	−0.4	1.1	2.7
Commerce	1.6	1.6	2.0	1.2	3.7	6.0
Public and professional services	2.1	3.1	2.3	1.2	2.9	5.8
Ownership of dwellings	1.5	1.9	3.4	1.0	2.3	3.2
GDP	2.0	2.0	1.8	1.1	2.8	3.9

Note: The GDP figures for output differ from those in Table 7.2 because they are based on output-side estimates of GDP at factor cost to make them comparable to the sectoral output estimates, and not on the (geometric) mean of expenditure, income, and output estimates. The estimates of TFP are similarly affected. Output-based estimates are used in the rest of this chapter. The less reliable estimates are shown in parentheses. The problems with the output and weighted TFP estimates for commerce in 1856–1937 and with the output, TFI, and weighted TFP estimates for public and professional services are described in note 2 (pp. 646–47). The basis for the estimates of the capital stock in construction in 1856–1913 is explained in note c, below.

TABLE 8.3 *continued*

Variable and sector	1856–1873	1873–1913	1924–1937	1937–1951	1951–1964	1964–1973
TFI:						
Agriculture, forestry, fishing	−0.7%	−0.5%	−0.7%	0.5%	−0.9%	−1.0%
Mining, quarrying	2.2	2.0	−1.6	−0.6	−2.2	−5.5
Manufacturing	1.7	1.4	1.3	1.6	1.2	−0.1
Construction	(2.3)	(1.0)	3.3	1.3	2.0	0.2
Gas, electricity, water	4.9	3.5	4.0	1.1	1.8	0.9
Transport, communications	2.4	2.0	0.5	0.2	−0.2	−0.2
Commerce	1.8	1.5	2.2	−1.8	1.3	1.2
Public and professional services	(1.4)	(2.4)	(1.9)	(2.7)	(0.5)	(2.3)
Ownership of dwellings	1.5	1.9	3.4	1.0	2.3	3.2
GDP	1.4	1.4	1.6	0.4	0.7	0.3
TFP:						
Agriculture, forestry, fishing	0.9	0.4	2.1	1.2	3.5	3.5
Mining, quarrying	1.4	−0.1	1.2	−0.4	1.5	2.2
Manufacturing	0.9	0.6	1.9	0.9	2.0	3.1
Construction	(0.8)	(0.1)	1.3	−2.5	1.8	1.6
Gas, electricity, water	0.6	1.6	1.8	3.1	3.3	4.3
Transport, communications	0.5	0.7	1.0	2.2	2.4	3.7
Commerce	(0.6)	(0.5)	−0.5	1.6	1.7	1.8
GDP[d]	0.64	0.45	0.70	1.09	2.04	2.42
TFP weighted by sector's share in GDP:						
Agriculture, forestry, fishing	0.16	0.06	0.10	0.04	0.19	0.12
Mining, quarrying	0.06	−0.01	0.08	−0.02	0.05	0.06
Manufacturing	0.20	0.16	0.58	0.29	0.70	1.07
Construction	0.03	0.00	0.05	−0.12	0.10	0.11
Gas, electricity, water	0.00	0.01	0.04	0.08	0.07	0.14
Transport, communications	0.03	0.05	0.10	0.21	0.21	0.31
Commerce	(0.15)	(0.14)	−0.12	0.47	0.42	0.45
Total of above	0.63%	0.41%	0.83%	0.95%	1.74%	2.26%
Total intra-industry[d]	(0.55)	(0.35)	0.60	0.84	1.88	2.19
Residual	(0.09)	(0.10)	0.10	0.25	0.16	0.23
GDP[d]	0.64%	0.45%	0.70%	1.09%	2.04%	2.42%

[a]For 1856–1913, man-years; for other periods, man-hours. See also pp. 211–12, 230.
[b]Gross fixed capital, 1856–73 and 1873–1913; gross capital stock plus inventories, other periods.
[c]Capital stock in construction, 1856–73 and 1873–1913, assumed to grow at the same rate as output of construction.
[d]Includes public and professional services, ownership of dwellings, and an allowance for financial services. See also note 2 to this chapter.

1964–73. Comparable figures relating to the five postwar cycles are given in Appendix K. Labor input is measured in man-years for 1856–1913 and in man-hours thereafter. The quality of the labor supplied in the man-years or man-hours is thus included in TFP, not in TFI.*

The first four sections of Table 8.3 contain the sectoral data for the growth rates of output, labor, capital, and total factor input ($TF_H I$ or $TF_I I$) for each of the nine sectors. The growth rates of total factor productivity ($TF_H P$ or $TF_Y P$) are given in the fifth section for the seven sectors for which it is a meaningful concept.[9] The last section shows the same data weighted by the sector's share in total output; the weighted figures indicate the contributions of the sector to the overall growth of TFP, and their variations between periods therefore include the effects of changes in the weights of the sectors. The sum of weighted sectoral growth rates in TFP (intra-industry TFP growth) is less than the growth rate of TFP in the economy because of a structural element that will be discussed in Chapter 9.

We comment first on output, input, and TFP in the peacetime periods. Trends across World War II have certain special characteristics and will be discussed separately.

Output

The annual percentage rates of growth of total output in successive peacetime periods were 2.0, 1.8, 2.3, 2.8, and 2.7. This pattern of fall, rise, and fractional fall was reproduced in only one sector, that sector, curiously enough, being agriculture. Manufacturing differed in having no increase in the rate of growth between 1924–37 and 1951–64. The unreliable pre-1914 figures for the other largest sector, commerce, for what they are worth, indicate a lower growth rate in 1924–37 than before 1914, contrary to the aggregate pattern. The rate of growth of output in mining declined between each successive peacetime period. In utilities the rate was high and steady.

Comparing the sources of the changes in the overall rate of growth of output between successive periods, we note that the fall between 1856–73 and 1873–1913 was common to most sectors.† The increase between 1873–1913 and 1924–37 arose almost exclusively from the in-

---

*However, the use of the man-years' measure for 1856–1913 has the same effect (disregarding differences between sectors in changes in hours) as would result from taking a man-hours' measure adjusted for the hours-offset element in the change in the quality of an *hour* of labor. This is because the hours-offset in this period is assumed to have been 100% (see Table 4.7).

†This was also true of the further deceleration within the period 1873–1913. See Appendix L and Table L.2.

dustrial sectors (other than mining), viz. manufacturing, utilities, and construction, and from agriculture — a finding rather different from the normal stereotype of the interwar period. On the other hand, between 1924–37 and 1951–64 the increase came entirely from the nonindustrial sectors; output in manufacturing grew at about the same rate in the two periods, and mining, construction, and utilities showed a falling-off in the rate of growth. Between 1951–64 and 1964–73 neither the largest industrial sector, manufacturing, nor the largest nonindustrial sector, commerce, showed any significant change in the rate of growth of output, nor did agriculture and utilities. A falling-off in construction and a further falling-off in mining were about balanced by the increased rates in transport and communications and in public and professional services.

Inputs

There was no significant difference between 1856–73 and 1873–1913 in the rate of growth of labor, capital, and TFI in the economy as a whole. There was some increase between the two periods in the rate of growth of the labor force in mining, and some slowing down in the percentage rate of decline in the agricultural labor force (hence *a fortiori* in its absolute rate of decline); this was offset by a slight slowdown in the rate of increase of the labor force in the two largest sectors, manufacturing and commerce.

Labor input grew more rapidly in 1924–37 than in 1873–1913 and capital input less rapidly (considerably less rapidly if dwellings are excluded). TFI grew more rapidly, by a small margin. Sectoral trends were mixed. In the largest sectors, manufacturing and commerce, and also in agriculture, differences between the two periods in the growth rates of TFI did not conform to the differences noted above in the growth rates of output. In manufacturing, more rapid growth of labor input in 1924–37 than in 1873–1913 was outweighed by much less rapid growth in capital input, so that growth in TFI was slightly lower, despite the much faster growth of output. In commerce, on the other hand, where output grew less rapidly in 1924–37 than in 1873–1913, both labor input and capital input grew more rapidly.

Comparisons involving the postwar period show rather more uniformity in input trends. The rate of growth of labor input was lower in 1951–64 than in 1924–37 in every sector, and the rate of growth of capital input was higher in every sector except dwellings and utilities. The trend in labor outweighed the trend in capital, and the rate of growth of TFI fell in every sector without exception.

Comparing the two parts of the postwar period, we find that the rate of growth of labor input was lower in 1964–73 than in 1951–64 in every sector except public and professional services. Higher rates of growth of capital in 1964–73 than in 1951–64 were also fairly general, but there were important exceptions in utilities and manufacturing (with little or no change) and mining (which fell). The rate of growth of TFI was either lower or unchanged in 1964–73 compared with 1951–64 in all sectors except public and professional services. These net differences between 1951–64 and 1964–73 were the result in some cases of a long-swing type of movement within the five cycles of the postwar period. This was most pronounced in utilities and construction, where the rate of growth of TFI was at a peak in the 1960–64 cycle, and thereafter fell steeply. In manufacturing a similar pattern appeared, in less pronounced form and on the side of capital only, the rate of increase in capital being higher in the 1960–64 and 1964–68 cycles than either before or after.

Reference may also be made to the trends in the capital-labor ratio. One would expect the ratio to rise in the course of economic growth. And so it did in the economy as a whole and in every sector, in both parts of the postwar period and, to a much lesser extent, in 1873–1913 and (except for commerce) in 1856–73. In the interwar period, however, the rate of growth of the total capital stock excluding dwellings (1.3 percent) was actually less than the rate of growth of the labor input. The decline in the capital-labor ratio in that period was particularly great in manufacturing.

Total Factor Productivity

The rate of growth of TFP in the economy as a whole followed the U-shaped pattern discussed in the previous section. The downward phase of the U, as it appears in Table 8.3, is confined to the decline between the periods 1856–73 and 1873–1913. Sectoral data cannot be shown for the period 1913–24, which marks the low point for the economy as a whole in the rates of growth of TF_QP and TF_YP.

The U-shaped pattern is found fairly generally across sectors. It occurs in agriculture, mining, manufacturing, and construction. It occurs in commerce, but with the low point in 1924–37 instead of in 1873-1913. Transport and utilities lack the downward phase of the U and have instead a rising rate of TFP growth between each period. There was, however, in the various phases a considerable variety between sectors in the magnitude of the movements, as well as some variety in their timing.

Between 1856–73 and 1873–1913 there was a particularly large decline in the rate of TFP growth in agriculture, at that time one of the three largest sectors. Even larger were the declines in construction, where TFP barely grew at all between 1873 and 1913, and in mining, where it fell absolutely.[10]

The movements within the period 1873–1913 are considered in Appendix L. Until 1899 the main sources of slowing down in the rate of growth of TFP were agriculture and mining. After 1899 there was significant slowing down in manufacturing and also in construction (affected by the long swing in building). In a number of sectors there was a retardation in 1873–82, made good in the 1880's and 1890's. In manufacturing there was a similar retardation in the 1880's, made good in the 1890's.

TFP grew more rapidly in the interwar period than in 1873–1913 in every sector, with the important exception of commerce, where it fell absolutely. This is compatible with the generally held view that labor crowded into the distributive trades and miscellaneous services in the interwar period in face of the general unemployment. The fall in TFP was thus in a sense a measure of underemployment rather than an indication of an adverse shift in the production function. The improvement in commerce was, as may be seen from the final section of Table 8.3, much the largest single sectoral source of improvement in TFP growth between 1924–37 and 1951–64.* Allowance for the abnormal factors affecting the distributive trades and miscellaneous services in the interwar period would raise the overall figure for TFP growth in that period and make it more substantially in excess of the very low figure for 1873–1913, while leaving it much below the postwar rate. It would underline the pervasiveness of the upward trend in TFP growth in the interwar period compared with 1873–1913.

Productivity trends within the interwar period show considerable divergences between sectors (see Appendix M for a more detailed account). TFP in agriculture, mining, construction, and transport did substantially better in 1924–29, commerce and manufacturing in 1929–37 (Table M.2). The outcome for TFP in the economy as a whole was a better performance in 1924–29 than in 1929–37 (Table M.1).

Pervasive improvement continued in the postwar period. The rate of TFP growth was more rapid in 1951–64 than in 1924–37 in every sec-

---

*These conclusions appear to hold for those parts of the commerce sector, namely the distributive trades and insurance banking, and finance, where employment is not widely used as an indication of output. (Table 8.8 shows that labor productivity growth in the component sectors changed in the same way between periods as TFP growth in total commerce.) The interperiod differences are probably not therefore a statistical illusion.

TABLE 8.4

Growth of Total Factor Input and Total Factor
Productivity: Excess of Rates in Manufacturing over
Commerce, 1856–1973

(Annual percentage growth rates)

Period	TFI	TFP
1856–1873	– 0.1%	0.3%
1873–1913	– 0.1	0.1
1924–1937	– 0.9	2.4
1937–1951	3.4	– 0.7
1951–1964	– 0.1	0.3
1964–1973	– 1.3	1.3

Note: Labor is measured in man-years for 1856–1913, in man-hours for 1924–73.

tor. This includes the industrial sectors where, as already noted, output grew less rapidly in 1951–64 than in 1924–37. However, the extent of the difference in TFP growth between the periods was significantly less in the industrial sectors (except utilities) than in the nonindustrial sectors. Most important, the rate of growth of TFP in manufacturing in 1951–64 scarcely exceeded what it had been in 1924–37.*

These contrasts between sectors were to a large extent reversed between 1951–64 and 1964–73. The rate of growth of TFP in 1964–73 was substantially higher than in 1951–64 in manufacturing, mining, and utilities, but not in commerce or agriculture.

Between the two parts of the postwar period, the opposite trends in TFI growth and TFP growth in the two largest sectors, manufacturing and commerce, thus largely canceled out. In manufacturing TFI growth fell to an unusual extent,[11] and TFP growth rose to an unusual extent; in commerce there was no clear trend in either. In both, therefore, there was little trend change in the rate of growth of output. Some similar tendency to offset between TFI and TFP is observed also in the postwar period in some other sectors (agriculture, mining, utilities), where likewise a divergence from GDP-average in the trend of TFI growth was accompanied by a divergence in the opposite direction in the trend of TFP growth.

The tendency to offsetting sectoral movements over a larger period in the rates of TFI growth and TFP growth is brought out in relation to the two largest sectors in Table 8.4, which shows the differences be-

*This needs to be qualified by reference to the possibility discussed in Appendix I, namely that some of the large productivity growth attributed statistically to the service industries and agriculture in the postwar period may have really had its origin in improvements in the quality of intermediate manufactured inputs.

tween manufacturing and commerce in the rates of TFI growth and TFP growth. The change from one period to the next is almost always in opposite directions in the two columns, i.e. a change between successive periods in the extent of difference between the rates of growth of TFI in the two sectors was always (except for 1873–1913) accompanied by a change in the opposite direction in the extent of the difference between them in the rate of growth of TFP.

This opposition was most pronounced of all in the trans–World War II period, to which we now turn.

The Trans–World War II Period: 1937–1951

The pattern of growth in output, inputs, and TFP in 1937–51 was, not surprisingly, a good deal more uneven across the economy than in peacetime periods.

Total output grew less rapidly than in earlier peacetime periods. The fastest growth was in public and professional services (which includes defense) and in manufacturing; output in commerce fell. TFI in manufacturing grew fairly rapidly. TFI also grew in agriculture—the only period when this happened. TFI in mining declined at a much less rapid pace than in either 1924–37 or 1951–73. Agriculture and mining were both sectors where for strategic or balance-of-payments reasons (or both) the growth of inputs was encouraged. Most other sectors experienced relatively slow growth of TFI by comparison with other periods.

The overall rate of growth of TFP was slightly higher than in the interwar period; this was due chiefly to a structural change (discussed in Chapter 9), rather than to improved performance within industries. Intra-industry improvement in TFP growth compared with 1924–37 came chiefly in commerce, which shed the surplus labor it had acquired in the depression. On the other hand, the three sectors where TFI grew more rapidly (or declined less rapidly) than in other periods, namely agriculture, mining, and manufacturing, experienced much slower growth of TFP in the transwar period than in the peacetime periods. This suggests that the policy of pushing resources into these sectors in the transwar period may have brought them up against diminishing returns. In fact, of the seven sectors shown in the last section of Table 8.3, there was only one, construction, in which the changes between the interwar and transwar periods in the growth of TFI and the growth of TFP were not in opposite directions. We shall revert in Chapter 9 to the question of whether a more general inference of diminishing returns is justified by the opposite trends in TFI and TFP in other periods.

The trend in productivity in construction is unique and calls for special comment. The fall in productivity in 1937–51 was so great that notwithstanding a historically high growth rate during the postwar period, the *absolute* level of productivity in construction prevailing before World War II was not regained till near the end of the 1960's. (This is true whether it is measured as labor productivity or as TFP.) The absence of any net rise in productivity in construction between 1937 and the late 1960's, which has no parallel in any other sector, is the more remarkable in that technical advances in building materials and methods were more rapid than ever before (see, on this point and others that follow, Zweig 1951; Carter 1958; M. Bowley 1966, 1967; Richardson & Aldcroft 1968).

There were a number of special reasons for the fall in productivity in construction across World War II.* A major general reason, however, appears to have been the effect of full employment. Whereas in the distributive trades and miscellaneous services the move to full employment raised productivity, by drawing away surplus labor, the net effect in construction was in the opposite direction. High pressure of general demand can have unfavorable or favorable effects on productivity. There appear to be four reasons why the unfavorable effects predominated in the case of construction:

(1) Temporary holdups due to bad weather, delays in supplies, or intervals between jobs are more of a feature in construction than in other industries. When there was extensive general unemployment, such holdups led to labor being laid off, but under full employment this was discouraged by competition for labor.

(2) The industry always had more than its share of low-quality workers, and this became more pronounced under full employment, both because of a loss of men to other industries and because when there was substantial unemployment the lowest-quality workers had tended not to be in employment at all.

(3) Holdups due to delays in supplies tended to become more frequent when the pressure of demand was higher.

(4) Possibly, the threat of unemployment and the risk of failure were more important in construction than in other industries in maintaining the incentives of workers and employers.

It may be noted that though these aspects of full employment tended to lower productivity in construction, they did not necessarily repre-

---

*In particular the proportion of building done on contract increased relative to speculative building, a change that is thought to have made planning more difficult and reduced incentives to efficiency.

TABLE 8.5

Growth of Total Factor Productivity by Sector,
1856–1913 and 1924–1973

(Annual percentage growth rates)

Sector	1856–1913	1924–1973
Gas, water, electricity	1.3%	3.3%
Agriculture, forestry, fishing	0.6	2.6
Transport, communications	0.6	2.2
Manufacturing	0.7	1.8
Mining, quarrying	0.4	1.2
Commerce	(0.6)	1.2
Construction	(0.3)[a]	0.4

Note: Labor is measured in man-years for 1856–1913, in man-hours for 1924–73.
[a]Based on the assumption that the capital stock in construction grew at the same rate as output. The rate of growth of labor productivity was 0.35%.

sent any absolute loss to the economy as a whole. Rather they reflected a tendency to diminishing returns to total production from increasing pressure of demand.[12]

The statistics suggest that the very long-run trend in construction, as in other sectors, was for the rate of productivity growth to rise from World War I onward. However, this trend was subject to a very substantial offset across World War II on account of the transition to a full-employment economy, and it took a long time for the general upward trend to productivity to make that good.[13]

To conclude our discussion of TFP by sector, Table 8.5 shows rates of growth over the two long periods, each of about half a century, before and after World War I.

In every sector TFP grew more rapidly in 1924–73 than in 1856–1913. The sectors are ranked in Table 8.5 by their rate of growth of TFP in 1924-73. The 1856–1913 ranking is similar, to the extent that utilities come at the top and construction at the bottom. However, the differences between the remaining sectors in 1856–1913 are small and are well within the margin of statistical error (large for that period). From the data available to us, it thus appears that there was fanning-out between sectors in TFP in 1924–73 that had not occurred before World War I.

There is much less stability between the two periods in the way the sectors ranked in respect of growth of TFI and output, and except for utilities, their ranking in TFI growth does not bear any regular relationship to their ranking in TFP growth. This suggests that the relative stability of the ranking in TFP growth was the result of technical or other supply-side characteristics of the sectors.

THE GROWTH OF OUTPUT, INPUTS, AND TOTAL FACTOR
PRODUCTIVITY IN SUBSECTORS OF THE ECONOMY

Some of the sectors discussed in the last section are large or heterogeneous, and it is interesting to consider the movements in productivity
in industries within such sectors. Two sectors, manufacturing and commerce, accounted for about 60 percent of GDP. Sectors as large as these
two are not likely to be as homogeneous, in the sense of producing
related types of goods or services in a distinctive way, as the smaller
sectors. We therefore consider the growth of productivity in their component industries in this section. We shall also consider some of the industries in the transport and communications sector, partly because
this sector is also a fairly large one, but also because it is made up of
both declining and growth industries.

Discussion is confined almost exclusively to periods after World War
I for lack of sufficiently disaggregated data on earlier periods. There is
also a problem with the interwar capital stock data.[14]

Manufacturing

The manufacturing sector is divided into 13 industry groups that
correspond, with one or two minor adjustments, to the Standard Industrial Classification (SIC).* Most of them are still fairly heterogeneous, but less so than when aggregated. The largest industry groups
are food, drink, tobacco; mechanical engineering and shipbuilding;
and textiles. Chemicals, the other metal-using industries, and paper,
printing, publishing are also important (Table 8.6). The rates of
growth of output, labor, capital, and TFI in the 13 industry groups
over four post-1924 periods are shown in Table 8.7. As in the last section, labor is measured in man-hours, and capital is gross of depreciation (net of retirements); and the weights used to combine the growth
rates of labor and capital are their shares in total income in the first
years of each period.[15] Table 8.7 also shows the rates of growth of TFP
and TFP weighted by the industry's share in manufacturing.

As before, we first consider the interwar and postwar periods, leaving the wartime period for separate treatment; and again we divide the
postwar period into its earlier and later parts, 1951–64 and 1964–73.

There was, naturally, diversity in experience between industries.
But insofar as there were differences *between periods* in the rates of
growth of inputs and productivity in manufacturing as a whole, they

---

*See Appendix N for a precise definition of our industries in terms of the 1948 and 1958
Standard Industrial Classifications.

TABLE 8.6

Shares of Value-Added in Manufacturing, 1924–1973

(Percent)

Industry	1924	1937	1951	1964	1973
Food, drink, tobacco	15.0%	13.9%	9.5%	11.0%	10.8%
Chemicals	5.8	6.3	7.2	8.8	7.6
Iron and steel	6.2	7.4	7.5	6.6	5.0
Electrical engineering	3.6	5.5	7.4	9.2	10.0
Mechanical engineering and shipbuilding	11.5	11.8	15.4	15.8	16.9
Vehicles	6.2	9.3	8.7	10.8	10.7
Other metal industries	6.6	7.7	7.6	7.9	8.7
Textiles	16.0	10.5	12.6	7.2	5.9
Clothing	10.3	8.5	4.9	3.8	3.5
Bricks, pottery, glass, cement	3.4	4.5	4.2	4.3	4.4
Timber, furniture	3.8	3.7	3.4	2.9	3.7
Paper, printing, publishing	7.8	7.8	7.8	7.8	8.5
Leather and other manufacturing	3.8	3.1	3.8	4.0	4.3
Total manufacturing	100.0%	100.0%	100.0%	100.0%	100.0%

Note: The classification by industry in 1924 and 1937 is according to the 1948 SIC and that in 1951 and 1964 is according to the 1958 SIC. If the 1951 estimates were reclassified onto the 1948 SIC the most significant changes in shares would occur in food, drink, tobacco (+ 0.6), mechanical engineering and shipbuilding (– 1.8), vehicles (+ 1.0), other metals (+ 1.1), and textiles (– 0.6).

were pervasive. That is to say, they were the result of similar differences in the great majority of the 13 industries distinguished, rather than the result of extremely strong movements in a few.

In manufacturing as a whole output grew at almost the same rate in each of the three periods, 1924–37, 1951–64, and 1964–73. The rate of growth of labor was lower in 1951–64 than in 1924–37 (all 13 groups). The rate of growth of capital was higher in 1951–64 than in 1924–37 (11 groups).[16] As a result of these opposite movements in labor and capital, the rate of growth of TF_HI was about the same in 1924–37 and 1951–64 in manufacturing, and so was the rate of growth of TF_HP.

The rate of growth of labor was lower in 1964–73 than in 1951–64 (12 groups). The rate of growth of capital was on average the same in 1964–73 as in 1951–64; hence the rate of growth of TF_HI was lower in 1964–73 than in 1951–64 (10 groups). The rate of growth of TF_HP was higher in 1964–73 than in 1951–64 (11 groups); the two exceptions, vehicles and clothing, were both industries where there had been a falling off in the rate of growth of output. However, there were other industries, such as iron and steel, where the rate of TF_HP growth increased despite a substantial fall in the rate of growth of output.

The pervasiveness of these trends suggests strongly that the causal forces at work were of a general nature rather than particular innovations or other special factors affecting individual industries.

TABLE 8.7

Growth of Output, Labor, Capital, Total Factor Input, Total Factor Productivity, and Weighted Total Factor Productivity in Manufacturing, 1924–1973

(Annual percentage growth rates)

Industry	OUTPUT				LABOR				CAPITAL			
	1924–1937	1937–1951	1951–1964	1964–1973	1924–1937	1937–1951	1951–1964	1964–1973	1924–1937	1937–1951	1951–1964	1964–1973
Food, drink, tobacco	2.8%	1.7%	2.6%	2.7%	1.8%	0.2%	0.1%	−1.2%	0.7%	1.6%	3.7%	4.0%
Chemicals	3.1	4.8	5.8	6.2	1.7	3.9	0.3	−1.1	1.7	4.0	5.5	5.0
Iron and steel	3.0	1.7	2.5	−0.2	1.0	0.6	0.0	−3.1	0.6	0.1	4.8	2.0
Electrical engineering	6.2	5.6	6.0	5.7	5.4	3.1	3.1	−1.1	2.4	6.3	5.0	3.5
Mechanical engineering and ship-building	1.8	3.8	2.4	3.2	1.1	3.0	0.5	−1.6	0.7	6.6	4.0	3.7
Vehicles	6.3	3.6	4.9	0.7	3.2	3.7	1.0	−1.8	3.1	8.4	4.6	0.8
Other metal industries	4.5	2.8	2.0	0.9	2.3	1.8	0.6	−1.2	1.8	6.6	3.3	4.3
Textiles	1.6	0.2	0.1	2.9	−0.3	−1.2	−2.8	−3.5	−0.4	−0.1	−2.6	2.1
Clothing	2.1	−1.7	2.2	1.9	0.4	−1.6	−1.6	−2.4	2.1	2.2	0.5	2.0
Bricks, pottery, glass, cement	4.6	2.4	3.4	3.4	2.8	0.3	0.2	−2.0	0.1	1.0	4.9	5.0
Timber, furniture	4.8	−0.2	2.2	3.5	2.0	−0.4	−0.6	0.3	1.9	2.2	2.8	4.8
Paper, printing, publishing	2.8	2.6	4.1	2.7	2.0	−0.2	1.2	−1.4	2.1	2.1	3.1	3.3
Leather and other manufacturing	4.3	3.0	3.2	4.5	1.5	1.2	0.3	0.1	2.0	0.9	2.8	5.5
Total manufacturing	3.2%	2.5%	3.2%	3.0%	1.4%	1.0%	0.2%	−1.6%	0.9%	2.9%	3.3%	3.3%

	TF$_{H}$I				TF$_{H}$P				WEIGHTED TF$_{H}$P[a]			
Food, drink, tobacco	1.3%	0.8%	1.8%	1.1%	1.5%	0.9%	0.8%	1.6%	0.22%	0.12%	0.07%	0.17%
Chemicals	1.7	3.9	2.6	1.8	1.4	0.9	3.2	4.4	0.08	0.05	0.23	0.39
Iron and steel	1.0	0.4	2.0	-1.7	2.0	1.3	0.5	1.5	0.13	0.10	0.04	0.10
Electrical engineering	4.2	4.3	3.7	0.2	2.0	1.3	2.3	5.5	0.08	0.07	0.17	0.51
Mechanical engineering and ship-building	1.1	3.6	1.4	-0.2	0.7	0.2	1.0	3.4	0.08	0.02	0.15	0.54
Vehicles	3.2	4.9	1.8	-1.3	3.1	-1.3	3.1	2.0	0.19	-0.12	0.27	0.21
Other metal industries	2.2	3.4	1.5	0.3	2.3	-0.6	0.5	0.6	0.15	-0.04	0.04	0.05
Textiles	-0.3	-1.0	-2.7	-1.9	1.9	1.2	2.8	4.8	0.30	0.13	0.35	0.34
Clothing	0.7	-1.0	-1.2	-1.4	1.4	-0.7	3.4	3.3	0.15	-0.06	0.17	0.12
Bricks, pottery, glass, cement	2.1	0.5	1.7	0.5	2.5	1.9	1.7	2.9	0.09	0.08	0.07	0.12
Timber, furniture	2.0	-0.1	0.1	1.1	2.9	-0.1	2.1	2.4	0.11	0.00	0.07	0.07
Paper, printing, publishing	2.0	0.5	2.0	0.0	0.8	2.1	2.1	2.7	0.06	0.16	0.17	0.21
Leather and other manu-facturing	1.6	1.2	1.2	1.6	2.7	1.8	2.0	2.9	0.10	0.06	0.07	0.11
Residual	—	—	—	—	—	—	—	—	0.2	0.3	0.1	0.2
Total manu-facturing	1.3%	1.6%	1.2%	-0.1%	1.9%	0.9%	2.0%	3.1%	1.9%	0.9%	2.0%	3.1%

[a]The weights are the shares in total manufacturing output, as in Table 8.6, in the first year of each period.

In addition to considering the extent to which individual industries conformed to sector-wide trends, one may also analyze the relationships between the growth rates of inputs, output, and productivity in the individual industries. Correlations between and within periods for these and certain other variables are given and further discussed in Appendix J in relation to the periods 1924–37, 1951–64, and 1964–73. The following points emerge.[17]

As might be expected, there was a positive correlation between periods in the rate of growth of output by industry, reflecting changes in industrial structure. At the present level of aggregation the correlation is only fair, and in fact there were only two industries (electrical engineering and bricks, pottery, etc.) where output in all three periods grew faster than the average for manufacturing as a whole. Within each period there was a strong positive correlation between the rate of growth of output and the rate of growth of TF_HP, as has been found in many other such studies. There was also a strong positive correlation between the output and TF_HI rates. On the other hand, the growth rates of TF_HI and TF_HP were not correlated with each other at all in the postwar period, and were only weakly correlated in the interwar period.

In general, not surprisingly, the two parts of the postwar period showed more resemblance to each other than to the prewar period. This is especially notable in the rate of growth of TF_HP, where there was no correlation at all between interwar and postwar but a reasonable correlation between the two parts of the postwar period. However, the interwar period and 1951–64 were more alike than the two parts of the postwar period in one respect: there was a strong tendency for the same industry groups to experience a high rate of growth of labor input, and hence of TF_HI, in both periods. (To a considerable extent, these were the same industries that had rapid growth in TF_HI in 1937–51; see below). However, there was virtually no such tendency between 1951–64 and 1964–73. Thus the correlation in output growth between the first pair of periods was achieved mainly through correlation in TF_HI growth and in the second pair of periods mainly through correlation in TF_HP growth.

The contributions of the several industries to growth in TF_HP in manufacturing as a whole, shown in the last section of Table 8.7, are, of course, affected by changes in their weights over time. Three industry groups (chemicals, electrical engineering, and mechanical engineering, shipbuilding) between them account for almost the whole of the increase in the rate of growth of TF_HP in manufacturing between the first and last periods (1924-37 and 1964-73). Both the weights of these industries and their TFP growth rates increased. By contrast, the contribution made by textiles and clothing to the total remained about unchanged because the decline in their weights offset the substantial increases in their TF_HP growth rate. A further contrast is provided by vehicles, whose weight rose but whose TF_HP growth rate fell.

The trans-World War II period was marked by rapid growth in the output of and inputs into those industry groups that were essential for the war (metal-using industries and chemicals), and that were important in the postwar investment and export booms (broadly the same industries); other groups grew much less rapidly. The contrast was particularly noticeable on the input side: the "war" industries experienced very rapid input growth, involving both labor and capital, and TF_HI growth was more rapid in 1937-51 in these industries than in any of the peacetime periods. The metal-using industries continued to have above-average growth in TF_HI in 1951-64 but ceased to do so in 1964-73. The other industry groups generally experienced slower growth of TF_HI in 1937-51 than in the peacetime periods. This was the consequence of the wartime direction of labor policies and of the concentration of government-financed investment during the war years in chemicals and the engineering and allied industries.[18]

Growth in TF_HP in most manufacturing industries was slow (sometimes negative) in 1937-51 compared with the two peacetime periods; further, some of the rapidly growing engineering and metal-using industries experienced the slowest growth.

Commerce

After manufacturing, commerce is the largest of the nine major sectors. It would be interesting to examine the growth of output and inputs in each of the three component industry groups — distributive trades; insurance, banking, and finance; and miscellaneous services — but unfortunately we do not have sufficiently reliable capital-stock data for each industry group to calculate the growth rates of TFI and hence TFP separately. Output, labor and labor productivity growth rates are available, however. (Table 8.8).

Of the three groups, distributive trades is the largest (Table 8.9). It includes both wholesale and retail trades that are similar in size. The insurance, banking, and finance group is fairly large in terms of output and capital,[19] though not in terms of labor input. The most important

TABLE 8.8

Growth of Output, Labor, and Labor Productivity in Commerce, 1856–1973

(Annual percentage growth rates)

Variable and sector	1856–1873	1873–1913	1924–1937	1937–1951	1951–1964	1964–1973
Output:						
Distributive trades	2.7%	2.0%	1.9%	-0.2%	2.9%	2.8%
Insurance, banking, finance	–	–	1.6	0.6	4.1	5.2
Miscellaneous services	–	–	1.6	-1.4	2.3	1.5
Total commerce	(2.4)	(2.0)	1.7	-0.2	3.0	3.0
Labor:						
Distributive trades	2.1	2.1	2.6	-2.3	1.2	-1.9
Insurance, banking, finance	7.6	4.3	1.8	-0.8	2.0	2.3
Miscellaneous services	1.7	0.7	2.1	-4.5	-1.1	0.0
Total commerce	1.9	1.3	2.3	-3.2	0.3	-0.7
Labor productivity:						
Distributive trades	0.6	-0.1	-0.7	2.1	1.7	4.7
Insurance, banking, finance	–	–	-0.2	1.4	2.1	2.9
Miscellaneous services	–	–	-0.5	3.1	3.4	1.5
Total commerce	(0.5)	(0.7)	-0.6	3.0	2.7	3.7

Note: Labor is measured in man-years for 1856–1913, in man-hours for 1924–73.

TABLE 8.9

Shares of Gross Domestic Product at Current Prices in Commerce, 1924–1973

(Percent)

Sector	1924	1937	1951	1964	1973
Distributive trades	13.5%	13.7%	11.5%	11.5%	10.6%
Insurance, banking, and finance	7.1	8.3	5.3	6.3	8.7
Miscellaneous services	7.1	7.4	6.9	7.7	7.7

Note: The classification by sector in 1924 and 1937 is according to the 1948 SIC and that in 1951 and 1964 is according to the 1958 SIC. Reclassifying the estimates for 1951 onto the 1948 SIC would alter the distributive trades' share in GDP by – 0.4 and the miscellaneous services' share by – 0.6.

part of miscellaneous services until World War II was private domestic service, but in the postwar period both catering, hotels, and the like and vehicle repair shops and garages were relatively more important.

In the interwar period employment in each of the three industry groups grew rapidly, faster than output, so that labor productivity fell, suggesting diminishing returns and the underemployment of cheap labor. The same conclusion would probably apply if we could measure the growth of TF_HP as well as the growth of labor productivity: TF_HI in the sector as a whole grew at a rate of 2.2 percent, only slightly below the rate of growth of labor; and TF_HP growth was probably negative in each industry. It is interesting that in 1873–1913 the distributive trades also experienced a fall in labor productivity when labor was growing rapidly. This provides further evidence of their capacity to absorb excess labor.

The demands of the wartime and reconstruction economies reversed this trend. Between 1937 and 1951 labor left the commerce sector, and especially miscellaneous services, where the rundown in private domestic service, which had low productivity, was most marked.* The result was that productivity rose again to a level in 1951 that was higher than it had been in 1924. In the postwar period labor moved into the distributive trades in 1951–64 and out of them in 1964–73. Insurance, banking, and finance was one of the few industry groups showing a substantial increase in the labor input in 1964–73, greater even than in 1951–64, when it was also high. In the whole sector there was throughout the postwar period a rapid growth in output and by past standards in labor productivity. As has already been noted, this made an important contribution to the faster growth of output and productivity achieved in the postwar period compared with the interwar period.

Transport and Communications

Finally, we consider the growth of output and inputs in the industry groups in the transport and communications sector (Tables 8.10, 8.11). This sector is sharply divided into expanding and declining industries. The two historically largest groups, railways and water transport, declined relative to the economy as a whole. The contribution to GDP of the other groups, road transport, posts and telecommunications, and air and other transport and storage, increased.†

There is a marked contrast in both output and input between the declining industries and the growth industries in all four periods shown in Table 8.11.[20] In railways and water transport output grew only slowly, and inputs declined or grew only very slightly, whereas in the rest of the sector output and both inputs grew at rates above the average for the economy as a whole. The increase in output growth between 1924–37 and 1951–64 was brought about by a shift in the

*In 1937 miscellaneous services employed 3,059,000 persons, of whom about half were in private domestic service. By 1951 only 417,000 were in private domestic service out of a total of 1,945,000 (1948 SIC).

†Moreover, since private cars are not considered part of the road transport industry, the effects of the switch of passenger traffic from the railways to the roads is not fully reflected in the growth of road transport.

TABLE 8.10

Shares of Gross Domestic Product at Current Prices in Transport and Communications, 1938–1970

(Percent)

Sector	1938	1958	1970
Railways	2.9%	1.4%	1.2%
Road transport	2.5	2.7	2.4
Water transport	2.3	1.7	1.3
Posts and telecommunications	1.4	1.7	2.5
Other (including air and storage)	0.1	0.6	1.2

Note: The classification by sector in 1938 is according to the 1948 SIC and that in 1958 is according to the 1958 SIC. An additional 0.1% of GDP is included in transport and communications, probably mostly in road transport, under the 1948 SIC as compared with the 1958 SIC.

TABLE 8.11

Growth of Output, Labor, Capital, Total Factor Input, and Total Factor Productivity in Transport and Communications, 1924–1973

(Annual percentage growth rates)

Variable and sector	1924–1937	1937–1951	1951–1964	1964–1973
Output:				
Railways, water	0.2%	0.4%	0.3%	1.3%
Roads, posts, other	4.0	4.9	3.5	4.6
Total transport and communications	1.5	2.4	2.2	3.5
Labor:				
Railways, water	−1.0	−0.1	−2.1	−5.5
Roads, posts, other	2.8	1.1	0.2	0.5
Total transport and communications	0.6	0.5	−0.7	−1.3
Capital:				
Railways, water	−0.1	−0.9	0.2	0.7
Roads, posts, other	2.2	2.3	4.3	6.4
Total transport and communications	0.2	−0.4	1.1	2.7
$TF_H I$:[a]				
Railways, water	−0.8	−0.3	−1.4	−3.8
Roads, posts, other	2.7	1.5	1.4	2.2
Total transport and communications	0.5	0.2	−0.2	−0.2
$TF_H P$:				
Railways, water	1.0	0.7	1.7	5.1
Roads, post, other	1.3	3.4	2.1	2.4
Total transport and communications	1.0	2.2	2.4	3.7

Source: Basic statistics (Appendix N) and sources quoted there; Deakin & Seward 1969: Table A.1; communication from Deakin.
[a] The same weights for labor and capital were used for the subtotals as for total transport and communications.

structure of the sector toward the rapidly growing industries and not by any significant increase in intra-industry output growth (at a more disaggregated level, of course, there was some increase in output growth, e.g. in water transport). The increase in TF_HP growth between the interwar and postwar periods, noted earlier in the chapter, occurred among both declining industries and expanding industries. In 1964–73 the growth of TFP in the declining industries actually exceeded the growth in the expanding ones, as a result of a drastic reduction in labor input, along with some increases in their rate of growth of output.

CHAPTER NINE

The Effects of Structural Change

Changes over time in the relative importance of sectors may be due to changes in the structure of demand or to changes in factor supply. In general terms, they contribute to measured growth if they correct initial inequalities between marginal products, if they increase the weight in the economy of sectors with fast TFP growth, or if they raise TFP growth in individual sectors. More specifically, hypotheses that have been put forward about the United Kingdom have concerned the limited scope for movement out of agriculture; the belated interwar movement away from old staples toward new industries; interwar underemployment in services; the government's role in the increase of service employment; and the effect of international competition on the demand for manufactures.

SOME PARTICULAR FEATURES OF STRUCTURAL CHANGE

Light on some of these hypotheses may be cast by simple inspection of the course of structural change. (1) There was no relation over time between the rate of outflow of labor from agriculture and the rate of inflow into manufacturing. (2) The magnitude of structural change within manufacturing was indeed greater in the interwar period than before 1914; it was greater still in the postwar period. (3) A crude definition of certain industries as "new" leads to the conclusion that their increased contribution to the growth of GDP in the interwar and postwar periods, compared with before 1914, arose simply because of their increased weight in the economy and not because they were outstripping other industries more rapidly than before.

EFFECTS OF CHANGES OF WEIGHTS OF INDUSTRIES WITH DIFFERENT LEVELS OF TFP

The effects on growth of net movements of factors between sectors with different levels of productivity is measured by "quality-shift," *defined as the shortfall of the rate of growth of TFI below the rate of growth of weighted TFI, where the weights are* sectoral *rates of factor payment. TFP growth in the economy as a whole can be shown to be equal to the sum of (1) intra-industry TFP growth (the output-weighted sum of sectoral TFP growth rates) and (2) quality-shift. The line between the two depends on the sectoral breakdown adopted.*

Quality-shift has a labor component and a capital component. Labor quality-shift was lowest in 1924–37 and highest in 1937–51 (the movement into and out of low-wage miscellaneous services being largely responsible); it was intermediate between these extremes in the postwar period and (probably) before 1914. Capital quality-shift was greatest in the postwar period, when the rate of growth of the capital stock in manufacturing and commerce exceeded that in low-return dwellings and utilities by a greater amount than before.

Quality-shift is a genuine "structural" source of growth insofar as it reflects a correction of an initial inequality of marginal products between sectors. But it reflects other elements as well, in particular changes in the quality of labor and the durability of capital. Excluding these elements would probably not alter the main conclusions.

Quality-shift was much less important than intra-industry TFP growth, both absolutely and as a source of difference in total TFP growth between periods. It was, however, not much smaller than intra-industry TFP growth in 1937–51 and possibly also in 1873–1913.

EFFECTS OF CHANGES OF WEIGHTS OF INDUSTRIES WITH
DIFFERENT RATES OF GROWTH OF TFP

Changes over time in the weights of sectors with different rates of growth of TFP did not have quantitatively important effects.

EFFECTS OF STRUCTURAL CHANGE ON THE RATES OF
GROWTH OF TFP IN INDIVIDUAL INDUSTRIES

Structural change had certain effects on intra-industry TFP growth:

(1) The rate of growth of TFP in commerce was substantially lowered in 1924–37 and raised in 1937–51 by the inflow and outflow of labor — a kind of diminishing returns, though attributable to general demand conditions.

(2) The effects of classical diminishing returns were apparent in mining but not (except in 1937–51) in agriculture. TFP in mining fell absolutely in 1873–1913 and 1937–51, when the industry was expanding, but rose in 1924–37 and 1951–73, when it was contracting. In agriculture TFP suffered along with TFI in 1873–1913, but rose rapidly in the postwar period, when demand was strong.

(3) Dynamic increasing returns (the Verdoorn effect) may well have been present in manufacturing, but they can make only a limited contribution to the explanation of movements over time in TFP growth in that sector. They do not explain why TFP in manufacturing grew more rapidly in 1951–73 than in 1924–37, since output grew at the same rate in the two periods.

EFFECTS OF FOREIGN TRADE AND DOMESTIC ABSORPTION ON
MANUFACTURING'S SHARE IN OUTPUT

Foreign trade had an unfavorable effect on the trend in manufacturing's share in GDP in all periods except 1856–73 and 1937–54. The hypothesis that foreign competition was damaging to manufacturing is in that respect confirmed. However, changes between periods in manufacturing's share in GDP were mainly accounted for not by foreign trade, but by changes in the structure of domestic absorption, which were considerable.

CONCLUSIONS

The central conclusion of this chapter is that measurable structural effects on the rate of growth were relatively small. The firmness of this conclusion is qualified by the unreliability of some of the data. Thus the measurement of output in public and professional services is largely conventional. The growth of this sector (as of finance) appears as a positive contribution to growth. Some possible structural effects are difficult to isolate and measure. The effects of changes in the position of manufacturing are particularly elusive. They include effects through the balance of payments, discussed in a later chapter.

Structural change is here defined as change over time in the relative importance of different industries, in terms of resources employed. Its course, in regard to the main sectors of the economy, was described in the previous chapter (see Table 8.1).

Structural change has accompanied growth in GDP in all countries. Neither structural change nor growth in GDP is an exogenous variable; both result from a complex of interacting causes on the supply side and the demand side. It is therefore not meaningful to ask whether structural change is the cause or the consequence of growth in GDP, nor is it possible to measure the total effect of the one on the other. However, there are certain phenomena that can be regarded as more or less distinctly structural, and that may have an effect on the overall rate of growth. These phenomena are the subject of this chapter.

Broadly speaking, structural change is favorable to measured economic growth if it increases the relative weight in the economy of industries with good productivity performance. Good productivity performance is partly a matter of *level* of productivity and partly a matter of *rate of growth* of productivity; and changes in weight reflect both changes in the *demand for goods* produced by different industries and changes in the *supply of factors* to different industries.

The level of productivity. If there were perfect mobility of factors of production, the marginal productivity of factors, in value terms, would be equal in all industries. But it may happen that, for historical or other reasons, marginal productivities are not equal and that frictions prevent instantaneous adjustment. There is then, initially, a misallocation of resources, and a reduction of this misallocation will contribute to growth over the period. This will occur if there is a net shift of *factor supply* away from the industries where marginal productivity is low toward the industries where marginal productivity is high. A shift in *demand for output* toward the industry where the marginal productivity of factors is initially high will also contribute to growth in measured GDP (at constant base-year prices), since this will strengthen the forces making for a transfer of resources (assuming the resources are not totally immobile), and such a transfer brings about an increase in measured output.*

The rate of growth of productivity. Even if initially there is no misallocation and marginal productivities are everywhere equal, industries may differ in the rate at which productivity rises or is capable of rising. These differences may occur because industries differ in their susceptibility to technical progress in the strict sense or else in the extent to which they are subject to increasing (or diminishing) returns. Shifts in weight in favor of industries that are "progressive" in one or other of these senses are favorable to the overall rate of growth. Some increase over time in the weight of these progressive industries is to be expected from the normal working of the price system. So long as prices reflect costs, the prices of products of progressive industries will tend to

---

*This is notwithstanding the fact that such a switch in demand may actually lead to an increase in the disparity between the marginal productivities in the sectors. We speak here of the effect on measured output, rather than on welfare; it is not meaningful to compare the welfare consequences of alternative structures of demand, since these imply alternative tastes (unless the differences relate only to the structure of export demand).

fall relatively; and so long as demand is at all price-elastic, their weight at constant prices in total output will therefore tend to rise. Their weight in output at current prices may either rise or fall, depending on the elasticity of demand. In addition to these movements along demand and supply schedules, however, shifts in the schedules must also be considered. *On the supply side*, it will be favorable to growth if factors tend to move toward the progressive industries. *On the demand side*, it will be favorable to measured productivity growth (though not necessarily to welfare) if consumers develop an increased preference for the products of progressive industries or if these products have a high income-elasticity of demand. One important source of changes in the structure of demand arises from foreign trade; changes in the structure of demand from this side reflect not only changes in consumers' preferences at home and abroad, but also changes in the competitiveness of home and foreign industry.

The foregoing are general considerations, applicable in principle to any country. Let us now classify, in the same terms, the chief hypotheses that have been put forward in the literature about the role of structural change in the particular case of the British economy.

First, three hypotheses about the level of productivity:

(i) A decline in the proportion of the labor force engaged in agriculture is characteristic of economic development. Because industrial development in the United Kingdom has been going on for such a long time, the proportion of the labor force in agriculture was already low by the end of World War II, and in contrast to many other countries the productivity of the agricultural labor force was relatively high compared with other parts of the economy. Hence the United Kingdom was able to obtain less benefit in the postwar period than other countries did from the movement of labor out of agriculture into sectors with higher productivity. This is part of the reason why its growth has been slower than theirs.* The validity of this hypothesis is well established, and it is scarcely controversial. However, in this book we are concerned with comparisons over time rather than with comparisons between countries. The corresponding hypothesis for that purpose is that in recent times the United Kingdom has benefited less than it did formerly from the outflow of labor from agriculture.

(ii) In an old industrial country agriculture is not necessarily the only sector that, for historical reasons, absorbs an excessive amount of

_____

*The absence of a large low-productivity agricultural sector serves to make the *level* of income per head in the UK *higher* than it would otherwise be.

resources. Slowness to reallocate resources, both labor and capital, away from the old staples (cotton, shipbuilding, coal-mining) toward "new industries" (electricity, motor vehicles) was commonly blamed for retardation in the British economy in the late nineteenth century. Belated movement in the right direction has been regarded as a main source of the better features of the interwar experience, and movement in the same direction took place and contributed to growth in the postwar period.

(iii) In the interwar period general unemployment brought about a movement of labor into miscellaneous service industries, where jobs, albeit low-productivity jobs, were easier to find than elsewhere. This tended to reduce the average level of productivity in the economy. During World War II and in the early postwar period this process was reversed. Labor flowed out of the low-productivity service sectors into other sectors, and this contributed to the overall increase in productivity.

Next, two hypotheses about the rate of growth of productivity arising from the supply side:

(iv) The low level of productivity in agriculture compared with the rest of the economy is not the only reason why the outflow of labor from agriculture, especially to manufacturing, contributes to the growth of productivity. Further reasons are that manufacturing has in general an above-average rate of productivity increase, and that the flow of labor into manufacturing makes for a high rate of increase of productivity in manufacturing itself, since manufacturing is subject to increasing returns (other sectors are not, or not so much, hence there is not an offset there). These benefits were lost when the reserve army was exhausted and the British economy became "mature."

(v) The argument about "new industries" has a rate-of-growth aspect as well as a level aspect. These industries have been held to be more susceptible to productivity increase than the older industries, as well as being subject initially to underallocation of resources.

Finally, two hypotheses about the rate of growth of productivity arising from the demand side:

(vi) In the late postwar period there was some shift of demand away from manufactures toward services, induced at least in part by increases in government spending. It was also possibly encouraged by the relatively more favorable tax treatment of services (which the Selective Employment Tax was designed to correct). If services were not subject to increasing returns and manufacturing was, this shift was unfavorable to measured economic growth.

(vii) Changes in foreign trade restricted the rate of growth of demand for the output of manufacturing, held to be a key sector for economic growth on account of its susceptibility to technical progress and economies of scale. Britain's share in world manufacturing output has been falling since the last quarter of the nineteenth century. Because other countries developed later than Britain, this was inevitable. But it had an adverse effect on Britain's own performance (not merely its performance compared with that of other countries), because it meant that Britain's role as supplier of manufactures to the world was progressively eroded. The growth of output of manufactures was limited by increasing foreign competition, and this served to limit the rate of growth of GDP.

These hypotheses will be referred to in the course of the chapter, which is arranged as follows. We first deal with some particular features of structural change: the role of agriculture as a source of labor for manufacturing (hypothesis i), and the relative magnitude of structural change in different periods and the role of new industries (hypotheses ii and v), though both these subjects really require a much finer disaggregation than undertaken here. The following section measures the overall effect of movements of factors between sectors with different levels of productivity (hypotheses i, ii, and iii); this is shown to be the same in principle as the difference found in Chapter 8 between the overall rate of growth of TFP and the weighted sum of intra-industry rates of growth of TFP. The discussion then turns to the effects on the overall rate of growth of TFP of changes in the relative weights of industries with differing rates of growth of TFP (one aspect of hypotheses iv, v, and vi). This is followed by a discussion of the effects of changes in the relative weights of industries on their own rates of productivity growth (the other aspect of hypotheses iv, v, and vi). We then consider the extent to which foreign trade was responsible for changes in manufacturing's weight in the economy (relevant to hypothesis vii). The last section presents general conclusions on the significance of changes over time in the position of the principal sectors.

SOME PARTICULAR FEATURES OF STRUCTURAL CHANGE

Agriculture and Manufacturing

Simple inspection of the course of structural change, as shown in Table 8.1, enables us to dispose of one of the hypotheses just discussed. This is the hypothesis that the slowing down of the exodus from agriculture in the postwar period led to less rapid growth in the proportion of the labor force in manufacturing. In the period 1856–1914, when the big decline was taking place in agriculture's share in the labor force, manufacturing was the one sector that did *not* significantly increase its share. There was only one phase in the whole period 1856–1973 when manufacturing's share in the labor force increased substantially, and that was 1937–51. By then agriculture's share was already small; and it was, in fact, for the time being actually increasing! We have to go back to the first quarter of the nineteenth century in order to see in operation the classic model in which a big outflow from agriculture is matched by a big inflow into manufacturing. In subsequent periods, the size of the outflow from agriculture does not seem to have been a factor influencing in any direct way manufacturing's share in the labor force.

The Magnitude of Structural Change in Different Periods

Some writers consider the economy's flexibility in the face of changes in circumstances relevant to its growth performance. We may therefore ask how the *magnitude* of structural change has compared between periods. This can be measured in various ways. Table 9.1 gives a measure in terms of the weighted average dispersion of the rates of growth of output in individual industries around the overall growth rate. This is approximately equal to the difference between the weighted average growth rates of the industries that are growing faster than average and the industries that are growing more slowly than average.[1]

TABLE 9.1
Weighted Average Dispersion of the Rates of
Growth of Output, 1900–1973

Period	Manufacturing	GDP
1900–1913	0.8%	—
1913–1924	1.6	—
1924–1937	1.2	1.0%
1937–1951	1.5	1.4
1951–1964	1.4	0.9
1964–1973	1.4	0.5

Source: Basic statistics (Appendix N); Lomax 1959.
Note: The measures are based on a breakdown by Orders in the SIC. For manufacturing, the dispersion is that of 13 industries (11 in 1900–1924), which in most cases correspond to individual Orders, around the average for manufacturing. In the GDP calculation, manufacturing is treated as a single industry. A finer or otherwise different breakdown might lead to different results.

We consider first manufacturing. Dispersion was high in both war-time periods: the expansion of the metal-using industries at the expense of textiles and clothing was largely responsible in both cases. In view of the well-known misfortunes of the old staples and the rise of new industries in the interwar period, it is not surprising to find that dispersion was a good deal greater in 1924–37 than in 1900–1913. It is rather more surprising to find that in the postwar period dispersion was somewhat higher again than in 1924–37. The generally high rate of expansion and pressure of demand in the postwar period made structural changes less conspicuous and less disturbing than they were in the interwar period.

In GDP, in contrast, dispersion was slightly less in 1951–64 than in 1924–37 and distinctly less in 1964–73. This is, perhaps, less relevant to the question of flexibility than is the measure of dispersion within manufacturing, since the very large size of some of the sectors compared may conceal considerable intrasectoral dispersion.

"New" Industries

It is commonly held that the slow development of new industries in the United Kingdom in the decades preceding World War I was an important source of the decline in the rate of growth compared with earlier in the nineteenth century and represented the chief shortcoming compared with other countries, especially Germany. It is likewise a familiar idea that much of the growth of the interwar period was due to the more rapid, if belated, rise of new industries. The question may be asked, what was the contribution of new industries to overall growth, and in particular, how important was it in the postwar period compared with earlier periods?

This is a rather elusive question to try to answer statistically. It is not clear how a new industry should be defined, or how, having defined it, its contribution to growth should be measured. If all industries followed a regular life-cycle (e.g. growth along a logistic path), we could define a new industry in terms of the stage it had reached in its life-cycle (e.g. in the logistic case an industry could be regarded as new until it reached the point of inflection). However, industries do not in fact exhibit a regular life-cycle pattern.

The data already given on dispersion provide some indication of the growth of new industries; but though new industries are a source of the structural change measured by dispersion, they are not the only one, since old industries may also grow at an abnormally rapid rate for a while, as the building industry did in the 1930's, and the coal industry

TABLE 9.2

Contribution of Three "New" Industries to the Growth of Output
in Manufacturing, 1900–1973

Category	1900–1913	1913–1924	1924–1937	1937–1951	1951–1964	1964–1973
(1) Annual percentage growth rate of output in new industries $(\hat{q}_n)$	3.8%	4.0%	5.2%	4.5%	5.5%	4.0%
(2) Annual percentage growth rate of output in manufacturing $(\hat{q})$	2.0%	0.7%	3.2%	2.5%	3.2%	3.0%
(3) Ratio of "new" industries' growth rate to manufacturing growth rate $(\hat{q}_n/\hat{q})$	1.9	5.4	1.6	1.8	1.7	1.3
(4) "New" industries' share in manufacturing in base year (q_n/q)	8.8%	11.0%	15.6%	21.1%	23.3%	28.9%
(5) "New" industries' share in the growth of output in manufacturing $(\Delta q_n/\Delta q)$	18.6%	69.2%	28.8%	44.3%	46.8%	41.9%

Source: Basic statistics (Appendix N); Lomax 1959.

Note: The 3 industries, based on the SIC classification, are electrical engineering, chemicals and allied, and vehicles. 4 price weights are used: 1924 for 1900–1937; 1937 for 1937–51; 1951 for 1951–64; and 1964 for 1964–73. The need to use 1924 weights instead of initial-year weights for 1900–1913 and 1913–24 probably biases downward the figures for these periods in rows 4 and 5.

in the years before 1914. An alternative approach is simply to identify certain named industries on the basis of casual empiricism. In principle, this requires a high degree of disaggregation; and the same industries will not rank as new throughout the whole of a long period. In practice, however, a very large proportion of the manufacturing industries that would be thought of as new at any point in the period after 1900 fall under three SIC classifications — Electrical engineering, Chemicals and allied, and Vehicles (which includes aircraft) — industries where output has grown at a rate considerably above the average throughout. Of course different industries *within* these classifications were "new" in the different periods.

Writing a subscript n to denote the total of new industries, the contribution made by growth in these classifications to growth in total manufacturing, $\Delta q_n/\Delta q$ (row 5 in Table 9.2) is approximately equal to their share in output in the base year, q_n/q (row 4), multiplied by the ratio of their growth rate to that of total manufacturing, $\hat{q}_n/\hat{q}$ (row 3).*

*There would be strict equality if the growth rates measured the proportionate change over the period as a whole, rather than average annual changes (i.e. the total change decompounded).

The ratio does not vary widely between the periods, except for 1913–24, when it is much higher, and 1964–73, when it is rather lower. The high figure for 1913–24 reflects the poor performance of the rest of the manufacturing sector rather than an abnormally high rate of growth of output in the new industries (see rows 1 and 2). It does not increase, but it does not fall significantly either until 1964–73, as it might have been expected to do if the industries as a whole had lost their "new" status and become senescent. Meanwhile, their contribution to growth increased because of the increase in their weight in the total. The increase in the contributions of these new industries to growth in the interwar period compared with before World War I thus came about, not because they were outstripping other industries to a greater extent than formerly, but because they had become more important in the economy. The same process continued after World War II.[2] The fall in 1964–73 was the result of a slowdown in the output of vehicles, an industry that, as a whole, had by then lost its status of newness.

The main impression is of the steadiness of the process until near the end of the period.

The foregoing approach to the question of new industries is extremely crude. It concerns solely their contribution to the growth of *output*. Moreover, the data of the kind under discussion do not provide any indication of the indirect effect of the growth of new industries on output and productivity elsewhere in the economy. This may be important in the case of industries like electricity and electrical engineering, which produce mainly producers' goods.

Having surveyed in general terms the course of structural change, we return now to the main analytical framework described at the start of this chapter. We begin with effects arising from intersectoral differences in the *level* of productivity.

EFFECTS OF CHANGES OF WEIGHTS OF INDUSTRIES WITH
DIFFERENT LEVELS OF TOTAL FACTOR PRODUCTIVITY

As we saw in Chapter 8, the rate of growth of TFP in the economy as a whole regularly exceeded the sum of the weighted rates of growth of TFP in individual industries (Table 8.3). The reason for this discrepancy is that there was regularly an above-average rate of growth of inputs into industries with initially above-average levels of TFP, that is to say, above-average rates of remuneration of factors. The same has been found for other countries (Massell 1961). Possible sources of this positive covariance are (1) that there tended to be a net shift of factors of given quality toward industries with above-average earnings; and

(2) that improvements over time in the quality of factors permitted above-average growth of inputs in industries where earnings were above average. In recognition of these two possible sources, the contribution made by this covariance to the growth of TFP will be called, for short, quality-shift. Labor quality-shift is defined as the excess of the rate of growth of weighted labor input, where labor in each industry is weighted according to its rate of remuneration in the base year, over the rate of growth of unweighted labor input. Capital quality-shift is defined similarly. Overall quality-shift is defined as the sum of labor quality-shift and capital quality-shift, weighted by the distributive shares of labor and capital, respectively. It can be shown that the average annual rate of growth of TFP in the economy as a whole is in principle identically equal (apart from a small decompounding term, of no economic significance) to the output-weighted quality-shift.[3]

Quality-shift is a statistical measure whose size depends on the industry breakdown adopted. What is its economic significance? It constitutes a genuinely structural source of growth insofar as it reflects the correction of an initial misallocation of resources. The misallocation of resources means that marginal productivities differ between sectors. If factors are paid in proportion to their marginal products, this will mean differences in rates of factor-payments between sectors. Misallocation is diminished insofar as there is a net movement of factors to sectors with above-average rates of remuneration. The ultimate cause of this net movement may be growth in demand for the output of these sectors, creating opportunities for employment there; it may be growth in the supply of cooperating factors there; or it may be the removal of obstacles to mobility or simply the passage of time, necessary to iron out initial disequilibria. The plainest example is the movement of labor out of low-productivity peasant agriculture in the course of industrialization, but this is not the only possible example, or, as it happens, the most important one in the British case.

As a measure of the degree to which initial misallocation is corrected during a period, quality-shift is subject to two qualifications (in addition to its dependence on a particular industry breakdown): (1) differences in the rates of factor payments between industries are due partly to differences in the quality of the factors employed; and (2) factor payments may not be equal to marginal products, and the degree of inequality may differ between industries.

These qualifications are serious. They make it impossible to treat quality-shift as such as a measure of the correction of misallocation. However, we can try to devise approximate indications of the effects of

the correction of misallocation by deducting from it rough allowances
for other components of quality-shift. Notwithstanding the need for
these allowances, quality-shift, being in principle based on relative
marginal productivities, is better grounded in economic theory as an
indicator of the gains from reallocation than are measures based on
average labor productivity.

We shall consider in turn the measures for labor and capital. For the
measurement of labor quality-shift, the economy is disaggregated into
24 sectors, 11 nonmanufacturing and 13 manufacturing. For the measurement of capital quality-shift, the statistics permit only 8 nonmanufacturing sectors to be distinguished, making 21 sectors in all. We shall
also give measures of quality-shift within manufacturing. Throughout
this section, growth rates will be given to two decimal places, because
rounding leads to misleading results when we are concerned, as here,
with small figures; this is not to be taken as implying that the underlying data have that degree of accuracy.

Labor

Periods after World War I are the only ones for which adequate data
exist, and they will be considered first. The quality-shift for labor was
positive in all four periods (Table 9.3), as might be expected. It was
much larger in 1937–51 than in any of the peacetime periods. It was
larger in the postwar periods than in the interwar period, and rather
larger in the late part of the postwar period than in the early part.

The smallness of the quality-shift gain in the interwar period was
largely due to the increase in numbers of miscellaneous services, an industry with below-average labor earnings. Likewise, the large movement out of miscellaneous services was chiefly responsible for the large
net quality-shift in the period 1937–51. The other main source of the
large figure for 1937–51 comes from the increase in man-hours in
public administration and defense, a sector with above-average rates of
pay. The temporary reversal in 1937–51 of the long-run downward
trend in agriculture's share in the labor force was a factor tending to
depress quality-shift in that period. In both parts of the postwar period
the gain came chiefly from three sources: the decline in agriculture and
the rise in banking, insurance, and finance and in professional and
scientific services. The annual gain from each of these sources was
larger in 1964–73 than in 1951–64.

Manufacturing, taken as a single industry, did not contribute much
to total quality-shift in any period, because its wage is close to the
average wage. However, there was some favorable shift within manu-

TABLE 9.3

Quality-Shift in Labor, 1924–1973

(Annual percentage growth rates)

Period	Whole economy (24 sectors)	Manufacturing (13 sectors)
1924–1937	0.05%	0.09%
1937–1951	0.58	0.22
1951–1964	0.14	0.12
1964–1973	0.22	0.02

Note: Labor quality-shift is the excess of the annual percentage growth rate of man-hours weighted by the base-year industry rate of remuneration over the unweighted annual percentage growth rate of man-hours. Thus quality-shift in column 1 can be written:

$$\sum_i \frac{n_i}{n} \hat{n}_i \left(\frac{w_i}{w} - 1 \right)$$

where n_i and w_i are the initial number of man-hours and the wage, respectively, in industry i, n and w are the equivalent measures for all industries, and $\hat{n}_i$ is the annual percentage growth rate of man-hours in industry i. In the calculation of column 2, total man-hours in manufacturing (n_m) and the average wage in manufacturing (w_m) are used instead of n and w. The first year in each period is used as the base-year in calculating rates of remuneration. The 11 non-manufacturing sectors are those in Table 8.1, with commerce divided into 3 sectors (distributive trades; insurance, banking and finance; miscellaneous services) and public and professional services into 2 (professional and scientific services; public administration and defense). One sector, occupation of dwellings, employs no labor and therefore has a zero weight in the calculation of labor quality-shift. The 13 manufacturing sectors are those in Table 8.6.

facturing, and this made some contribution to the total for the whole economy.* The favorable shifts within manufacturing came chiefly from the sources that would have been expected, the largest contributions being the contraction of low-wage textiles and clothing and the expansion of high-wage vehicles. The 1937–51 shift exceeds that in the other periods largely because of a particularly rapid expansion in high-wage mechanical engineering and chemicals.

Relating these findings to the three "level" hypotheses referred to at the beginning of the chapter, we can say that the shift of labor out of miscellaneous services across World War II made an important contribution to productivity growth, and that the shift of labor out of agriculture and toward the newer manufacturing industries each made some contribution, but a relatively small one — smaller than that made by the increase in numbers in professional and financial services.

As noted earlier, positive quality-shift — a net movement of the labor force toward higher-paid industries — can be due either to forces concerned with the supply of labor or to forces concerned with the demand for the final product. The usual identification problem makes it diffi-

*The figures given for manufacturing in Table 9.3 refer to shifts within manufacturing and are calculated with reference to the average wage in manufacturing. They are not multiplied by manufacturing's share in the whole economy. For these reasons they do not directly enter as components of the figures given for the whole economy.

cult to separate the two statistically. However, to judge from the individual industries chiefly responsible, both elements were present. The movement of labor into miscellaneous services during the interwar period and out of them during the transwar period reflected mainly changes in the supply of labor to this sector, due to changes in the amount of excess supply of labor in the economy as a whole. The movement of labor out of agriculture in both peacetime periods also arose mainly from the side of labor supply, reflecting a familiar long-run tendency to excess supply of labor in that sector; the temporary halt of this movement across World War II, however, reflected the revival in the demand for the products of British agriculture. On the other hand, the reallocation of labor within the manufacturing sector reflected differences in the rates of growth of demand for final product, which were especially pronounced in 1937–51. The trend-increase in the numbers in professional and financial services reflects both supply and demand sides.*

We must now consider the qualifications arising out of (1) a possible inequality between wage and marginal product and (2) shifts reflecting quality-change rather than the correction of misallocation.

(1) It is commonly held that shifts of labor away from agriculture raise overall productivity to a greater extent than earnings differentials would suggest, because earnings in agriculture exceed labor's marginal product.[4] But it is doubtful whether this is true of Britain. The rationale of the hypothesis is that those leaving agriculture are farmers who work on inferior holdings, or members of farm families who share the product of their labor among themselves on the basis of average rather than marginal productivity. In Britain, however, the decline in the numbers in agriculture came about almost exclusively from a decline in the number of hired laborers, and hardly at all from a decline in the number of farmers. There is no presumption that hired laborers in agriculture are paid more than their marginal product.

Still, the corresponding argument does have some force as applied to miscellaneous services and also the distributive trades, where the number of self-employed is large. Allowance for it would increase the esti-

---

*It might appear that the movement into public and professional services ought not to be included as a source of growth in measured output, inasmuch as the output in this sector is measured largely by labor input. However, the valuation of the output of this sector in the national accounts relative to that of other sectors in fact reflects the high average rate of pay there, so that an increase in the proportion of the labor force in public and professional services does make for growth in measured national output. Moreover, because we are concerned here with the implied *level* of productivity, the procedure is less open to objection than if it depended on measures of *growth* in productivity in these sectors.

mate of the favorable effect of reallocation in the transwar period, and would produce a more unfavorable measure for the interwar period.

The case of coal-mining also requires comment. Coal-mining had above-average wages (to a greater extent in the postwar period than previously), and a movement of labor out of coal-mining therefore tended to reduce the rate of growth of the wage-weighted labor force. But in the postwar period, wages in the less efficient pits, which is where the labor force was most reduced, were plainly in excess of marginal product, for these pits were run at a loss and were subsidized by the more efficient ones. This tends to bias downward our measure of the favorable effect of reallocation in the postwar period.

(2) In part, inter-industry differences in wages reflect quality differences. Since some net quality improvement in the labor force is to be expected over time, and since the overall quality-shift turns out to have been relatively small in peacetime, the question arises whether there was any positive net effect of pure reallocation at all. To calculate the pure reallocation element, one may attempt to estimate the inter-industry part of quality improvement and deduct it from the overall effect of the inter-industry shifts already calculated. The inter-industry part of quality improvement is defined as that part of the overall improvement in labor quality that is reflected in above-average rates of increase in labor input in industries where the base-year quality of labor input is above average. It is distinguished from the intra-industry part of labor quality improvement — improvement in the quality of labor input *within* each industry — which is irrelevant to the present purpose.

Quality may be measured in terms of many attributes: in Chapter 4 measures of quality associated with age, sex, nationality, intensity of work, and education were presented. We will here take a measure based on three attributes: age, sex, and occupation.[5] This can be divided into inter-industry and intra-industry components in the postwar period, but for earlier periods the division can be made only very roughly.

Table 9.4 shows the excess over the unweighted labor growth rate of the growth rate obtained by weighting each age, sex, and occupation group by its rate of remuneration in a base-year. The estimates of age and sex quality are taken from Table 4.2, and the estimates of occupational quality were derived in a similar manner. The figures indicate very little change in the quality of the labor force from 1911 to 1931 and an improvement after 1931 due to improvements in occupational and age quality. A large part of the positive net figure recorded for the

TABLE 9.4

*Growth in Labor Quality Resulting from Changes in
Age, Sex, and Occupation, 1911–1971*

(Annual percentage growth rates)

Source of change	1911–1921	1921–1931	1931–1951	1951–1961	1961–1971
Age	0.04%	0.13%	0.18%	−0.05%	0.20%
Sex	0.00	−0.02	−0.02	0.00	−0.11
Occupation[a]	0.01	0.00	0.34	0.32	0.19
Total	0.05%	0.11%	0.50%	0.27%	0.28%

Source: Working papers for Table 4.2; Routh 1965: Tables 1, 48; *Labour Statistics Year Book*, UK [39], *1970; Changes in the Occupational Distribution of the Labour Force in Great Britain*, UK [42]; *Occupational Changes, 1951–61*, UK [67].
    Note: The total age-sex-occupation quality measure is the excess of the annual percentage growth rate of labor weighted by age-, sex-, or occupation-specific rates of remuneration over the unweighted annual percentage growth rate of labor. Thus for any type of quality (age, sex, or occupation) the measure can be written:

$$\sum_i \frac{n^j}{n} \hat{n}^j \left(\frac{w^j}{w} - 1 \right)$$

where superscript *j* refers to the *j*th quality class, *n* and *w* refer, respectively, to initial labor and initial wage, and *n* is the annual percentage growth rate of labor.
    [a]9 occupational groups were distinguished for 1911–51, 8 for 1951–61 (used instead of 1951–64), and 10 for 1961–71. The data for 1911–51 relate to the total labor force in Great Britain, and those for 1951–61 to the total employment in the UK. The base year, used for the relative rates of remuneration for each occupational group are: 1913 for 1911–21, 1922–24 for 1921–31, 1935–36 for 1931–51, 1955–56 for 1951–61, and 1970 for 1961–71.

growth in occupational quality in 1931–51 and 1951–71 derives from the relative increase in two classes: higher professionals and managers. These classes also increased before 1931, but to a lesser extent, and there was an offsetting unfavorable effect resulting from an increase in the unskilled (1911–21) and semiskilled (1921–31).
    In Table 9.5 the inter-industry elements in changes in age, sex, and occupation are shown, and the sum of these is deducted from quality-shift. The residual would measure the pure "correction of misallocation" if the measures of inter-industry quality improvement were perfect (which they obviously are not). In 1951–64 the inter-industry element in age-sex-occupational change accounted for half of the quality-shift, so the residual was less than 0.1 percent. In 1961–71, on the other hand, the inter-industry term was negative (on account of the above-average growth of employment in industries employing a high proportion of women). The residual in 1964–73 is therefore larger than the quality-shift.
    A breakdown like that in Table 9.5 cannot be carried out for previous periods. It appears from rough estimates that the inter-industry component of the total change in age, sex, and occupational quality was larger in the transwar period than in 1951–64, but was still less than a third of the total. If we put it at 0.15, and deduct this from

the total inter-industry effect of 0.58, we are still left with a substantial net effect in that period from the correction of misallocation. The inter-industry change in age, sex, and occupational quality in 1921–31 seems to have been near zero.

Finally, we may take account of the specific reasons referred to above for the divergence of wage from marginal product. As was noted, the effect of these is to lower somewhat the estimate for the "correction of misallocation" in the interwar period and to raise somewhat the estimate for the transwar and postwar periods. Guessing some allowance for these effects, and allowing also for the inter-industry element in the change in labor quality, we may estimate the addition to the annual percentage rate of growth of the weighted labor input due to the correction of misallocation, in the present sense, as follows, ignoring second decimal points: 1924–37, 0.0; 1937–51, 0.5; 1951–64, 0.1; 1964–73, 0.3.

We do not have much faith in these estimates. In particular, a more refined disaggregation of occupations might substantially alter the deduction to be made on account of occupational change (it might reduce the suspiciously large difference between 1951–64 and 1964–73). Moreover, we are dealing here with small figures that are very sensitive to errors in the underlying data. But we feel reasonably

TABLE 9.5

Quality-Shift in Labor and Inter-Industry Quality Effects, 1951–1973

(Annual percentage growth rates)

Source of change	1951–1964	1964–1973
Labor quality-shift	0.14%	0.22%
Inter-industry quality effects		
Age	0.00	0.00[a]
Sex	−0.01	−0.06[a]
Occupation	0.08	0.04[a]
Residual	0.07%	0.24%

Source: Basic statistics (Appendix N); *Changes in the Industrial Distribution of Employment, 1931 – 71*, UK [41]; *Changes in the Occupational Distribution of Employment*, UK [42]; *New Earnings Survey*, UK [47], 1968; *Census of Population*, UK [52], *1951*; *Occupational Changes, 1951 – 61*, UK [66]; Routh 1965: Table 48.

Note: Total quality-shift as in Table 9.3; total inter-industry and intra-industry age-sex-occupational effects as in Table 9.4. The inter-industry age-sex-occupational effects were calculated in the same way as the total of inter-industry and intra-industry effects, but on the assumption that the breakdown by quality class was the same at the end of each period as at the beginning. The measure for any type of quality can thus be written

$$\sum_i \sum_j \frac{n_i^j}{n} \dot{n}_i \left(\frac{w^j}{w} - 1 \right)$$

where subscript i refers to industry i and superscript j to quality class j, and the rest of the notation is as defined in Tables 9.3 and 9.4.

[a]1961–71.

confident in drawing two conclusions: (1) that in 1937–51 there was a significant gain from shifts to higher-paid industries, not accounted for by changes in age, sex, or occupation; and (2) that in peacetime periods the gains on this account were small.

Because of the lack of adequate data on industry wage rates before 1924, it is not possible to produce comparable measures of labor quality-shift for earlier periods. A fortiori, it is not possible to estimate that part of labor quality-shift due to the correction of misallocation. One would expect labor quality-shift to have been greater before World War I than it was in the interwar period, because there was not the abnormal shift into low-paid services;* no obvious presumptions exist about how labor quality-shift in earlier times compares with that in the postwar period.

We can derive some indications of orders of magnitude from the estimates given by Deane and Cole (1962) of earnings in five sectors.[6] These suggest that labor quality-shift was about 0.1 percent a year over the period 1871–1911 and higher — about 0.2 percent — over the period 1911–24.[7] These may be compared with our figures of 0.14 percent and 0.22 percent for the periods 1951–64 and 1964–73 and 0.05 for 1924–37. Labor quality-shift was thus probably a little higher before 1914 than in the interwar period and a little lower than in the post–World War II period. Comparing the two transwar periods, quality-shift appears to have been smaller in the first than in the second (about 0.2 percent a year against 0.5). Before 1914 the most important contribution to quality-shift came from the movement of labor into relatively high-paid public and professional services, with the movement out of agriculture also helping. Across World War I the large absolute decline in relatively low-paid domestic service was also an important factor.

*Judging from the British experience after World War I, one might also expect that the shortfall of average agricultural earnings below average earnings outside agriculture would become greater as one goes back in time, thus increasing the gain derived from the movement out of agriculture and making for higher quality-shift. This would also be in line with the tendency toward a narrowing of the inequality in productivity between the agricultural and nonagricultural sectors found in most countries as development proceeds. (Kuznets 1966: 213.) In Britain, however, any normal convergence tendency that there may have been from this source was interrupted by the agricultural depression of the late 19th century. In the 1850's agricultural wages were higher relative to wages elsewhere in the economy than in 1924. This possible source of increased quality-shift as one goes back in time cannot therefore be invoked in a comparison of the interwar period with 1856–1913 as a whole, though it probably did contribute to increasing quality-shift in the last quarter of the 19th century. For wage data, see Mitchell & Deane 1962: 349–51, based on estimates by A. L. Bowley.

Capital

The results here are markedly different. They are set out in Table 9.6.

The concept of shifts in resources does not apply to capital in the same way as to labor. Many physical assets cannot be transferred from one industry to another, though there are some that can be, e.g. vehicles or office buildings. Changes in the distribution of the capital stock between industries take place mainly through differences between industries in the rates of gross investment and retirements. However, since a large part of the changes in the distribution of the labor force also occurs through different rates of recruitment and wastage, the contrast is not all that fundamental.

Gross rates of return per unit of capital have differed much more widely between industries than wage rates. The chief distinction is between manufacturing and commerce, with high gross rates of return, and dwellings, utilities, and transport, with low ones. The size of the differences in the rates of return makes it likely that capital will show bigger differences between weighted and unweighted growth rates than labor. As may be seen from Table 9.6, quality-shift for capital was positive in all periods, being greatest in manufacturing in 1937–51, and in the economy as a whole in 1964–73. In the postwar period it was much larger than labor quality-shift. Capital quality-shift increased between each period shown. The high figure for capital quality-shift in the postwar period has to be viewed in relation to the rapid overall rate of capital accumulation, as reflected in the high level of the unweighted growth rate. The faster the rate of capital accumulation, the more scope there is for increasing the proportion of the capital stock in the sectors with above-average rates of return.

TABLE 9.6
Quality-Shift in Capital, 1924–1973
(Annual percentage growth rates)

Period	Whole economy (21 sectors)	Manufacturing (13 sectors)
1924–1937	0.37%	0.24%
1937–1951	0.47	0.94
1951–1964	0.56	0.10
1964–1973	0.92	0.37

Note: The method of calculation is the same as for Table 9.3, with gross capital stock and gross profit rate instead of n and w, respectively. The basis of disaggregation is that of Tables 8.1 and 8.3 (the available data do not permit the further disaggregation of the service sectors adopted in Table 9.3).

The relatively low capital quality-shift in the interwar period is partly the result of the concentration of investment on dwellings. But even if dwellings are excluded, quality-shift is lower than in the postwar period. This is largely because of the low interwar net investment in the high-profit manufacturing sector. In the transwar period an exceptionally large proportion of all investment was in manufacturing. In the postwar period the proportion of investment in manufacturing and (especially in the years 1964–73) in commerce, both high profit sectors, was much higher than in the interwar period, and the proportion in dwellings and utilities, both low profit sectors, was much lower.

We are not able to calculate capital quality-shift for the years before 1924, on account of lack of information on sectoral profit rates. However, we do know that the profit rate was lower in agriculture than in the economy as a whole, and that there was a major shift of capital away from agriculture. This alone may have contributed as much as 0.4 percent per year to the total capital quality-shift in 1873–1913 (and about 0.2 percent in 1856–73). Assuming that there was as usual a tendency for the rest of the economy to produce some positive quality-shift, though probably less than in later periods because the rates of growth of capital in the main sectors differed from one another to a lesser extent, total capital quality-shift in 1873–1913 was at least as great as in 1924–37 and 1937–51.

It should be noted that since inter-industry differences in gross profit rates are due to differences in the average durability of assets rather than to differences in net profit rates, quality-shift in the case of capital cannot be identified with the correction of misallocation. Suppose that the gross profit rate is higher in industry A than in industry B *solely* because A uses less long-lived assets, and that the profit rate net of depreciation is the same in the two industries. The investment of a given amount in industry A will increase GDP more than investment of the same amount in industry B. It is proper to take this effect into account in the explanation of the growth of measured GDP. But since investment in either industry will have the same effect on NDP, it is not reasonable to speak of a "correction of misallocation" if A's capital stock rises relative to B's. There is then reallocation, certainly, and it has an effect on measured GDP, but not the presumed welfare improvement implicit in the term "correction of misallocation."[8] It is a reallocation toward quicker-yielding investment rather than toward higher-yielding investment.

Our central concern is with the sources of the growth of measured GDP, and that is why we have used gross profit rates in calculating capital quality-shift. In order to get some indication of the extent to which capital quality-shift, so measured, was due to differences in depreciation and hence spurious from the welfare point of view, an estimate was obtained for the postwar period using net rather than gross profit rates in the quality-shift calculation. The resulting measure of capital quality-shift is not, in the event, very different from the one based on gross profit rates;* the reason is that there is much less inter-industry variance in depreciation rates than in gross profit rates.

The limitations of our measures of the gross rate of return have to be acknowledged. They relate to the average rate of return in the in-dustry, which may not be the same as the rate of return on new invest-ment. They are to some extent sensitive to the base year chosen. No distinction is drawn between a high rate of return that is due to the high profitability of an industry as such, and a high rate of return that is due to the capital stock in an industry being newer or better designed than average to an extent not fully measured in the price-deflator used (corresponding to the quality element in labor quality-shift). These limitations, however, can hardly affect the very large and consistent differences in rates of return found between the big sectors that dominate the total. The rates of return in individual manufacturing in-dustries are more doubtful and alter a good deal between periods. As may be seen from Table 9.6, this mainly affects 1937–51.

Total

In the preceding sections we considered labor quality-shift and capital quality-shift separately. We now bring the two together and see how much quality-shift as a whole contributed to the growth of TFP. The effects thereby measured of shifts of resources between industries will then be set alongside the contribution made by productivity growth within industries, already discussed in Chapter 8.

The contribution of the two elements, intra-industry growth and quality-shift, in the four periods 1924–37, 1937–51, 1951–64, and 1964–73 are shown in Table 9.7. Together with the decompounding term, they add up to the total shown in Table 8.3 for the rate of growth

---

*Quality-shift in 1951–73 in the whole economy (nine sectors only; manufacturing treated as a single sector), estimated on the basis of net profit rates (gross profit rates minus depreciation rates), yields 0.89% per year, which compares with 0.60% using gross profit rates (as in Table 9.6).

TABLE 9.7

Contribution of Intra-Industry Growth and Quality-Shift to the Growth of Total Factor Productivity, 1924–1973

(Annual percentage growth rates)

Source of change	Whole economy				Manufacturing			
	1924– 1937	1937– 1951	1951– 1964	1964– 1973	1924– 1937	1937– 1951	1951– 1964	1964– 1973
Intra-industry[a]	0.55%	0.64%	1.76%	2.06%	1.73%	0.57%	1.87%	2.94%
Quality-shift	0.15	0.55	0.26	0.41	0.13	0.43	0.12	0.12
Decompounding term	0.00	−0.10	0.02	−0.05	0.04	−0.09	−0.03	0.09
Total	0.70%	1.09%	2.04%	2.42%	1.90%	0.91%	1.96%	3.15%

Source: Basic statistics (Appendix N); Tables 8.7, 9.3, 9.6.

Note: See p. 259 and note 3 to this chapter for the definitions of the measures of the intra-industry and quality-shift contributions and the decompounding term.

[a]The estimates for the whole economy shown here differ from those in Table 8.3 for two reasons: (1) they exclude quality-shift and decompounding elements in manufacturing; and (2) they exclude some labor quality-shift in services. For TFP growth here and in the tables that follow, labor is measured in man-hours (TF_HP) unless otherwise indicated.

of TFP for GDP as a whole. The quality-shift shown in Table 9.7 includes, of course, the effects of inter-industry (though not intra-industry) quality improvements in inputs, as well as the effects of the correction of misallocation.

Since the industry TF_HP growth rates that enter into the intra-industry term themselves contain an element of quality-shift, namely, that resulting from changes in weights between sub-industries, a more detailed industry breakdown would move some (positive or negative) productivity growth from the intra-industry productivity term to the quality-shift term. In order to identify the quality-shift element as closely as possible, the figures for quality-shift and intra-industry TFP growth in Table 9.7 have been based on the 24-sector and 21-sector disaggregations used for calculating quality-shift in labor and in capital, not on the nine-sector disaggregation used in Table 8.3.[9] This causes the quality-shift element (together with the decompounding term) in Table 9.7 to be rather larger than the residual item in Table 8.3, and the intra-industry growth element to be correspondingly smaller.[10]

The contributions of labor quality-shift and capital quality-shift to the total were about the same. Capital quality-shift was the larger of the two, but labor had a greater weight in total input.

Table 9.7 shows that in peacetime periods quality-shift was, as might be expected, a much less important source of growth in TF_HP

than intra-industry growth. Quality-shift was less important than intra-industry growth in 1937–51, as well; but its proportional contribution to the total growth TFP was not negligible (about two-fifths). The *increase* between the two parts of the postwar period in the rate of growth of $TF_H P$ was due almost as much to the increase in quality-shift as to the increase in intra-industry TFP growth, the increase in quality-shift coming in about equal parts from the labor side and the capital side.

Quality-shift before 1914 can only be guessed.[11] The remarks made above about labor quality-shift and capital quality-shift in that period suggest that overall quality-shift was probably a little over 0.2 percent, and thus larger than in the interwar period but smaller than in 1937–51 or after World War II. As such, it would still have contributed significantly to the very low figure (0.4 percent) for total TFP growth in 1873–1913.

The effects of shifts of resources to industries where productivity was higher or growing more rapidly than elsewhere were thus positive but relatively small. They were much less important than intra-industry growth in productivity, both in absolute terms and in explaining differences between periods. It is, of course, possible to argue that the *persistent* smallness of these structural effects marks a point of weakness in the British economy over a long period compared with other economies; but consideration of that would take us beyond our scope.

EFFECTS OF CHANGES OF WEIGHTS OF INDUSTRIES
WITH DIFFERENT RATES OF GROWTH OF
TOTAL FACTOR PRODUCTIVITY

Changes over time in the weights of sectors with different rates of growth of TFP are a subject that can be dealt with briefly, because these changes turn out to have been unimportant.

An individual industry's contribution to total intra-industry TFP growth is the product of its weight q_i/q, and its own rate of TFP growth, $\hat{x}_i$. It can change over time as a consequence of a change in either of these terms. Likewise, total intra-industry TFP growth is equal to $\Sigma \hat{x}_i q_i / q$. An increase in it between periods can result either from a general preponderance of increases among the $\hat{x}_i$'s or from an increase in the weights, q_i/q, of the industries with above-average or increasing $\hat{x}_i$'s.

Effects of the latter sort were not in fact important, either in the economy as whole or in manufacturing. Table 9.8 shows the breakdown of the differences in intra-industry growth between 1924–37 and

TABLE 9.8

Contribution of Change in Industry Rates of Growth of Total Factor Productivity and Change in Weights to Change in the Intra-Industry Growth of Total Factor Productivity Between 1924–1937 and 1951–1964

(Annual percentage growth rates)

Category	Whole economy	Manufacturing
Change in industry $TF_H P$ growth rates	1.16[a]	0.20
Change in weights	0.14	0.04
Interaction	−0.09	−0.10
Total change in intra-industry $TF_H P$ growth	1.21	0.14

Note: The measures are:

(1) Change in intra-industry TF_H growth	$\Delta \sum (q_i/q)\hat{x}$	
(2) Change in industry $TF_H P$ growth rates	$\sum (q^i/q)(\Delta \hat{x}_i)$	
(3) Change in weights	$\sum [\Delta (q_i/q)]\hat{x}_i$	
(4) Interaction	$\sum [\Delta (q_i/q)](\Delta \hat{x}_i)$	

where the operator Δ defines changes between 1924–37 and 1951–64, and variables without Δ refer to 1924–37. A slightly different picture is obtained if the variables without Δ refer to 1951–64:

	Row 1	Row 2	Row 3	Row 4
Whole economy	1.08	0.04	0.09	1.21
Manufacturing	0.10	−0.06	0.10	0.14

[a] Includes the change in intra-services quality-shift (−0.09), which has to be deducted from the change in identified intra-industry TFP growth (1.30).

1951–64, the pair of periods between which the change in intra-industry growth was greatest. The effect of the industry TFP term is dominant. The same is true in the comparison of other pairs of periods. The smallness of the effect may seem surprising. Much is often made, for example, of the damage to the growth of total productivity supposedly brought about by the increase in the importance of public and professional services, a sector in which productivity growth, at least as measured, is small. Reflection shows, however, that really large changes in weights are needed for the effect to be important, especially if there is a relatively low rate of TFP growth in all sectors, and hence relatively small absolute differences in TFP growth between sectors. Thus suppose that TFP grows at 1.0 percent a year in sector A and at 2.5 percent a year in the rest of the economy. An increase in sector A's weight in GDP from 10 percent to 15 percent — a very large change — reduces the annual rate of TFP growth in the whole economy only a fraction, from 2.35 percent to 2.275 percent.

It is to be noted that we are dealing here with data of a chain-index type, in which q_i/q is measured for each period at the prices of the first year of that period. Changes in weights between periods therefore reflect relative price changes as well as volume changes. If we were using the same prices for all periods, it is likely that there would be a sizable positive $\Sigma(\Delta q_i/q)\hat{x}_i$ term, since industries with high $\hat{x}_i$ tend to have falling relative prices over time. However, that would not be an appropriate procedure for comparisons between periods of this length.

A further possible structural source of growth, which was referred to in the first section of the chapter, is the effect of shifts of factors *within a period* between industries with differing rates of growth of TFP. This is not statistically a separate component of TFP growth, because of the way TFP growth is defined for the economy as a whole and for individual sectors. Any interaction within a period between the growth of input and the growth of TFP is already incorporated into the measures of sectoral TFP growth.[12] This need not, however, prevent us from measuring it directly. It amounts to the weighted covariance across industries between the growth rates of TFI and TFP. This covariance turns out in fact to be completely negligible, its contribution to total intra-industry TFP growth lying between $+0.01$ point and -0.01 point in all periods. This particular structural effect can therefore be disregarded.

EFFECTS OF STRUCTURAL CHANGE ON THE RATES OF GROWTH OF TOTAL FACTOR PRODUCTIVITY IN INDIVIDUAL INDUSTRIES

We found in the last section that the effects of structural change arising from inter-industry differences in the rates of productivity growth were small between periods and negligible within periods. However, the importance attached by Kaldor (1966, 1967) and others to inter-industry differences in productivity growth in analyzing the effects of structural change does not rest mainly on exogenously given differences in productivity growth rates between industries. Rather, it depends on the effects of structural shifts, arising from forces on the demand side, on the rate of productivity growth *within* given sectors. Three types of effect may be distinguished under this head.

Underemployment in Certain Sectors

Suppose that for historical, institutional, or other reasons certain sectors, viz. services and agriculture, are the repositories of whatever underemployment there is in the economy. Then if demand expands for the output of other sectors, labor will be drawn off from the sectors where there is underemployment with little loss of output. The result will be an increase in productivity in the sectors with underemployment. There is thus a gain in intra-industry productivity growth, additional to the quality-shift gain from reallocation. Conversely, there will be a fall in productivity in the sectors with underemployment if demand for the output of other sectors declines.

The principal instance in the British experience was the absolute fall in TFP in commerce in the interwar period and its substantial rise in 1937–51. We do not know exactly how much of this was due to changes in the amount of underemployment, but it is likely that the effect was sizable. If, say, the rate of growth of TFP in commerce had been as high in 1924–37 as it was on average in the two periods 1924–37 and 1937–51 combined, the rate of growth of TFP in the economy as a whole in 1924–37 would have been higher by nearly 0.3 point. Likewise, faster growth in demand elsewhere in the economy might, counterfactually, have led to faster growth of TFP in commerce before 1914, though this is not such a strong proposition, since measured TFP in commerce did rise in that period, not fall absolutely as in the interwar period. The historically high rate of growth of measured TFP in commerce in the postwar period cannot be explained in quite the same way as for 1937–51, since in the postwar period commerce increased its share of labor input. However, an analogous effect was present, insofar as labor shortage experienced in the sector, as never before in peacetime, stimulated innovation as well as capital accumulation.[13] The same is partly true of agriculture in the postwar period.*

Diminishing Returns Due to Fixed Factors

An increase in the demand for the output of agriculture and mining might be expected, ceteris paribus, to be adverse to TFP on account of diminishing returns in the classical sense. In the British case there are more signs of this in mining than in agriculture. In mining, TFP fell absolutely in 1873–1913, when demand was causing a fast increase in output and inputs, and it fell again in 1937–51, when attempts were being made to revive the industry. By contrast, TFP in mining rose in the interwar and postwar periods, when the industry was being run down. This accounted for a difference of nearly 0.1 point in the rate of growth of TFP in the economy as a whole between the periods concerned. There is no reason to doubt that diminishing returns contributed to this result; however, the extent of the tendency to diminishing returns (and indeed even its existence) cannot be inferred simply from comparisons of the rates of growth of TFI and TFP, on account of an identification problem (see the next subsection).

*It is true of the innovative elements in the postwar mechanization of British agriculture. It is not true of the other element in the postwar agricultural revolution, the use of fertilizers and improved varieties, since this was landsaving rather than laborsaving.

In agriculture there were signs of the same pattern in 1937–51, when in response to wartime and early postwar needs TFI increased (the only period when this happened), and the rate of growth of TFP fell. On the other hand, it appears that in peacetime the favorable effects of high demand on innovation in agriculture (together with other forces) outweighed whatever tendency there was to diminishing returns. In the face of continuing strong demand in the postwar period, TFP grew faster than ever. By contrast, in the agricultural depression of the late nineteenth century, TFP in agriculture did very badly. This was an important matter quantitatively, accounting for about a third of the fall between 1856–73 and 1873–1913 in the rate of growth of TFP in the economy as a whole.[14] The agricultural depression led to an absolute decline in agricultural output between 1873 and 1913, and this was the principal cause of the slow growth in its TFP. (It was not, admittedly, the sole cause; there was also a slowdown in the rate of labor outflow from agriculture, especially after 1900, and for this other explanations must be sought, such as demand deficiency in other sectors of the economy.)

Dynamic Economies of Scale in Manufacturing

The hypothesis for consideration is that of Kaldor — that manufacturing enjoys economies of scale of a kind not enjoyed in other sectors. Consequently, it is held, an increase in manufacturing's weight in the economy raises the rate of growth of productivity in manufacturing without causing adverse effects on the rate of growth of productivity in other sectors. As advanced by Kaldor, the relevance of this hypothesis is largely counter factual: productivity would have benefited if foreign trade conditions had allowed the demand for British manufactures to grow faster than it did (or alternatively, if a large reserve of labor in agriculture had allowed faster growth of inputs into manufacturing). However, the hypothesis also has relevance to comparison between periods.

The theoretical basis of the hypothesis is not so much static economies of scale as economies of growth. If manufacturing is growing rapidly, there is scope for learning by doing, for embodied technical progress, for new entrepreneurs, and so on. The statistical basis of the hypothesis is the so-called Verdoorn Law, the observed correlation between the rate of growth of productivity and the rate of growth of production. In what follows, productivity will be understood in the sense of TFP, not labor productivity. We do this because in a growth-accounting framework the effects of output growth on labor productivity via capital accumulation are taken care of under the heading of capital accumulation. This means that some of the causal relationships considered important by Kaldor and his colleagues may be passed over here; however, in Chapter 13 we will deal with the causes and effects of capital accumulation.

A positive correlation between the rates of growth of production and productivity is a phenomenon that appears in many contexts.[15] It is the origin, for example, of the well-established tendency for output indexes to rise faster when weighted by base-year prices than by current-year prices (since trends in relative quantities are inversely related to trends in relative prices, and trends in relative prices to trends in productivity). In international trade, likewise, countries tend to have high production in industries where they have high productivity. Arithmetically, such a correlation must be found, unless there is a negative correlation between the rates of growth of productivity and inputs.

It has often been pointed out that observed relations between the rates of growth of productivity and production are liable to be affected by exogenous movements in both of them, and also in the rate of growth of inputs. The interpretation of the observed correlation is therefore ambiguous.[16] One interpretation is that of Kaldor, just mentioned: that the exogenous variable is production, and the correlation reflects increasing returns. Another interpretation is that the exogenous variable is productivity, and the correlation reflects, in the case of inter-industry comparisons, the effect of productivity on output demanded, via relative prices, or, in the case of intercountry or inter-period comparisons at the macro level, the effect of an exogenously given growth of labor input.

The hypothesis of dynamic economies of scale can itself be specified in a number of ways. The specification that translates them most simply from static into dynamic terms is that in manufacturing the rate of growth of TFP is an increasing function of the rate of growth of TFI.[17] However, a comparison of trends in British manufacturing over time shows not a positive correlation between the rates of growth of TFI and TFP, but a negative one (Table 9.9). In a simple comparison of periods it is always possible for an underlying relationship to be obscured by other forces; but results similarly unfavorable to the specification have also been found in cross-country and cross-industry studies (Rowthorn 1975; Wragg & Robertson 1978: 26). Some alternative specification is therefore required.[18] It is obvious, however, from Table 9.9 that the Verdoorn relationship itself, however specified in terms of underlying

TABLE 9.9

Growth of Output, Total Factor Input, and Total Factor
Productivity in Manufacturing, 1856–1973

(Annual percentage growth rates)

Period	Output	TFI	TFP
Peacetime phases:			
1856–1873	2.6%	1.7%	0.9%
1873–1913	2.0	1.4	0.6
1924–1937	3.2	1.3	1.9
1951–1973	3.2	0.8	2.4
WWII phase:			
1937–1951	2.5	1.6	0.9
Post-WWII cycles:			
1951–1955	3.8	2.0	1.8
1955–1960	2.8	0.8	2.0
1960–1964	3.1	0.8	2.3
1964–1968	2.9	0.0	2.9
1968–1973	3.1	−0.3	3.4

Note: Labor is measured in man-years for 1856–1913, in man-hours for 1924–73.

causation, cannot, to say the least, have been the sole explanation of changes over time in the rate of growth of TFP in British manufacturing. TFP grew more rapidly in the postwar period than in the interwar period, but output did not. The rate of growth of TFP rose in the course of the postwar period, but that of output did not. The rate of growth of TFP increased by a larger amount between 1873–1913 and 1924–37 than the rate of growth of output, so that to make the latter the cause of the former implausibly implies negative marginal costs. Only the comparison between 1856–73 and 1873–1913 is reasonably satisfactory.

This does not establish of course that dynamic (or static) economies of scale were not present; it merely shows that other causes must have made a major contribution to the observed rise in the rate of growth of TFP in manufacturing from its low point in 1873–1913. The *a priori* arguments for the presence of dynamic economies of scale are reasonably persuasive, to say nothing of the empirical evidence for static ones in manufacturing (see J. S. Bain 1965, and on the UK, Pratten et al. 1965; Pratten 1971). Their effect cannot be identified from a single-equation model; in principle what is required is a simultaneous model, though whether one could be constructed satisfactorily for comparisons over a long period of time is problematical.[19]

The evidence is manifestly too ambiguous to permit quantitative estimates of the importance, if any, of dynamic economies of scale in manufacturing. Our guess is that they did exist, though they were not the main causes of changes over time in the rate of growth of TFP. On this reckoning, they contributed to the decline in the rate of growth of TFP before World War I, and they contributed to the improvement in the interwar period. The failure of manufacturing output to grow faster in the postwar period than in the interwar period may help to explain why the rate of TFP growth increased less in that sector between the two periods than in some other sectors. Some doubts are raised by the trend within the postwar period and also by the period 1937–51, when demand was clearly strong (as evidenced by the rapid growth of TFI, as well as by common knowledge) and yet the rate of growth of TFP was poor.* This suggests that dynamic economies of scale were not universally in operation or reliable in all circumstances.

The possible significance of dynamic economies of scale goes rather beyond the context of structural change and its consequences. They could arise from changes in the rate of growth of demand for output as a whole, whether they resulted in shifts between sectors or not. This point will be taken up again in Chapter 17.

EFFECTS OF FOREIGN TRADE AND DOMESTIC ABSORPTION ON
MANUFACTURING'S SHARE IN OUTPUT

This section provides a link between the present chapter and Chapters 14 and 15 on the role of foreign trade and payments.

Those who hold that the place of manufacturing is crucial for a country's economic growth have commonly held also that ever since the 1870's foreign competition has been a brake on the growth of British manufacturing, on manufacturing's share in output, and hence on the growth of output as a whole. It is therefore relevant to ask how far changes in manufacturing's share in output were due to changes arising on the side of foreign trade. This is also relevant to the interpretation of the slowing-down since the mid-1950's in manufacturing's share in GDP, following its unusually sharp rise in the early postwar years. Was this slowdown due to a switch in demand in a direction relatively less favorable to manufactures, or did it reflect mainly the increased inroads of foreign competition?

A brief discussion is needed first of the principles involved. Write Q for output, A for absorption, and B for the foreign balance, all for the

---

*Moreover, the falling-off in 1937–51 was particularly great in two of the industry groups where the increase in TFI was greatest, vehicles and other metal-users (Table 8.7), suggesting a war-period tendency to diminishing returns similar to that noted above in mining and agriculture.

economy as a whole, and correspondingly, q, a, and b for output, absorption, and foreign balance of manufactures. By definition, then, $Q = A + B$ and $q = a + b$. Manufacturing's share in output is given by

$$\frac{q}{Q} = \frac{a}{Q} + \frac{b}{Q}$$

The contributions to the change in manufacturing's share in output made by domestic absorption and the foreign balance are measured respectively by the contributions of a/Q and b/Q:

$$\frac{\Delta(q/Q)}{q/Q} = \frac{\Delta(a/Q)}{q/Q} + \frac{\Delta(b/Q)}{q/Q}$$

The contribution of domestic absorption may be written, disregarding second-order terms, as

$$\frac{\Delta(a/Q)}{q/Q} = \frac{a}{q}(\hat{a} - \hat{A}) + \frac{a}{q}(\hat{A} - \hat{Q})$$

The first term here measures the effect on q/Q of changes in the composition of domestic absorption. The second term reflects the fact that the effect of domestic absorption on the composition of output increases if total absorption increases relative to total output.

The contribution of foreign trade can likewise be written as

$$\frac{\Delta(b/Q)}{q/Q} = \frac{b}{q}(\hat{b} - \hat{B}) + \frac{b}{q}(\hat{B} - \hat{Q})$$

The first term here relates to changes in the position of manufactures within the overall balance and the second to changes in the overall balance relative to output.[20]

Calculating the absorption of GDP is straightforward.* Calculating the absorption of manufactures is more difficult, because statistics on exports and imports of manufactures relate to the total value of the goods traded and cannot be compared directly to statistics on output, which relate to value-added in manufacturing. The following procedure was adopted. Exports of manufactures were allotted to the industry producing them, and imports of manufactures to the industry with which they compete, thus giving a balance of trade for each manufacturing industry. Regarding balances of trade as a form of final demand for industries' gross output, we used input-output tables to

---

*It is GDP, plus imports of goods and services, minus exports of goods and services (excluding net property income from abroad).

compute for benchmark years the value-added in each manufacturing industry that resulted from the balance of trade.* It was assumed that the input-output coefficients of an industry's exports and import-substitutes were the same as those of its total output. The results were then summed over all manufacturing industries to give the value-added in manufacturing due to the foreign balance. This was deducted from total value-added in manufacturing in order to give the absorption of manufactures in benchmark years at current prices. The proportion of output at current prices due to absorption in each benchmark year was then multiplied by output at constant prices for that year, and the growth rate, $\hat{a}$, was calculated from the figures so derived.

The foregoing method depends on the use of input-output tables. Such tables are available only for certain years (1907, 1935, 1954, 1963, 1972). Consequently, the periods in Table 9.10 are not identical to our standard periods. The 1935 input-output matrix was used to calculate absorption in 1924 and 1937; this is a source of inaccuracy, but probably not a major one. For the periods 1856–73 and 1873–1913 proper input-output calculations are not possible, and value-added due to the foreign balance was therefore derived by the much cruder and less reliable method of multiplying the total balance of payments in manufactures by half.[21]

The results shown in Table 9.10 are in some respects as expected, and in others surprising.

The behavior of the series relating to the contribution of the foreign balance, row 8, is much as expected. There is a positive effect in 1856–73 and then a small negative one in 1873–1913, a period in which Britain's competitive position in the world market for manufactures was being increasingly challenged. There were further and more substantial negative effects across World War I and in the interwar period. These resulted mainly from a fall in the overall balance, associated with a decline in capital exports. There was a substantial positive contribution in 1937–54, when there was a big expansion of exports of manufactures, which Britain *needed* to undertake because of the deterioration in the terms of trade and the decline in income from abroad, and which it was *able* to undertake because other European industrial countries and Japan had not yet recovered from the war. There was little effect in 1954–63, and then in 1963–72 the largest negative effect ever, reflecting the very rapid inroads of imported

*Including the value-added resulting indirectly from the balance of trade of other manufacturing industries, but not that resulting indirectly from the balance of trade in nonmanufacturing industries and services.

TABLE 9.10

Growth of Output and Absorption in the Whole Economy and
in Manufacturing, 1856–1972

(Annual percentage growth rates)

Category	1856–1873	1873–1913	1907–1924	1924–1937	1937–1954	1954–1963	1963–1972
Whole economy:							
(1) Output $(\hat{Q})^a$	1.98%	1.79%	0.38%	1.90%	1.94%	2.80%	2.70%
(2) Absorption $(\hat{A})$	2.08	1.81	0.75	2.30	1.51	2.98	2.76
Manufacturing:							
(3) Output $(\hat{q})$	2.63	2.02	1.23	3.21	2.54	2.77	3.07
(4) Absorption $(\hat{a})$	2.61	2.21	1.63	3.80	1.87	2.88	3.76
Manufacturing's share of total:							
(5) Output $(\hat{q} - \hat{Q})$	0.65	0.23	0.85	1.31	0.60	−0.03	0.37
(6) Absorption $(\hat{a} - \hat{A})$	0.53	0.40	0.88	1.50	0.36	−0.10	1.00
Sources of manufacturing's share of output (row 5):							
(7) Domestic absorption $(a/q)\,[(\hat{a} - \hat{A}) + (\hat{A} - \hat{Q})]$	0.45	0.33	1.12	1.85	−0.07	0.07	0.93
(8) Foreign trade (row 5 − row 7)	0.20	−0.10	−0.27	−0.54	0.67	−0.10	−0.56

Source: Basic statistics (Appendix N); *Annual Statement of Trade*, UK [2]; *Statistical Abstract*, UK [7]; Barna 1952; Schlote 1952; *Input-Output Tables for 1954, 1963, 1972*, UK [9], [16], [17]; Conrad & Meyer 1965.
Note: The percentage growth rates are shown to 2 decimal places because rounding leads to misleading results with such small figures; they are not necessarily accurate to the second decimal place.
[a] GDP at constant market prices (factor cost for 1856 – 73), estimated from the expenditure side.

manufactures. Over the whole period 1856–1972 the net effect was negative but extremely small, −0.05 percent (−0.10 percent for 1873–1972). The chief source of this small negative effect was the tendency over the period as a whole for total absorption to rise rather faster than total output.

It is also no surprise to find that the structure of domestic absorption moved substantially in favor of manufactures in almost all periods (row 6); and that this shift in the composition of domestic absorption was the main element in the effect (row 7) of domestic absorption on manufacturing's share in output. The $(\hat{a} - \hat{A})$ element was the predominant one in row 7 in all periods except 1937–54, when (as already mentioned) there was a big fall in total domestic absorption relative to GDP, and 1954–63, when all the figures were small.

What *is* surprising is how greatly the shift of the structure of domestic absorption toward manufactures differed from period to period.[22] These variations outweighed variations from period to period in the contribution from the foreign trade side, so that the course of $(\hat{q} - \hat{Q})$ over the period is dominated by the course of $(\hat{a} - \hat{A})$. It is also noteworthy that the absorption and foreign trade contributions moved in opposite directions between all successive pairs of periods except one.

Taking the periods in turn, we find that in 1873–1913, for the first and only time, the movement of absorption and foreign trade effects, compared with the previous period, were in the same direction, namely downward. Between 1907 and 1937 there were exceptionally large shifts in the structure of domestic absorption in favor of manufactures, so that despite adverse influences from the foreign trade side, manufacturing's share in output grew more rapidly than before. The period 1937–54 is more complicated. It seems likely that the small negative figure for the effect of domestic absorption (− 0.07 percent) was made up of a larger negative figure up till about 1948 and a positive figure thereafter.[23] At the same time, there was a substantial positive contribution from the foreign trade side, reflecting the postwar increase in exports of manufactures, already referred to. The increase in exports was itself probably responsible in part for the fall in the rate of increase of manufacturing's share in domestic absorption, by creating short supply on the home market. The net outcome of the absorption and foreign trade effects in this period was that manufacturing's share in output rose significantly *less* than it had done in the interwar period. In 1954–63 it actually declined, in consequence of a further adverse shift in the structure of domestic absorption (which export-induced domestic shortages cannot be invoked to explain). The final period, 1963–72, is in some ways the most striking of all. Despite the unprecedentedly large adverse foreign trade effect, manufacturing's share in output rose, in contrast to the previous period, on account of a major shift in the structure of domestic absorption in favor of manufactures.

The conclusions of this section are as follows.

The effects of foreign trade on manufacturing's share in output moved between periods in much the ways that might have been expected. The effect was unfavorable in all periods with the exception of 1856–73 and the major exception of 1937–54. The effect averaged over the whole period was unfavorable, though not by much. This was doubtless a point of contrast between Britain and a number of other countries, including those at an earlier stage of industrialization.

But it was not foreign trade that mainly determined changes from period to period in manufacturing's share in output; it was changes in the structure of domestic absorption. Their effects on the structure of output were much larger than the effects of foreign trade, with the single exception of the period 1937–54.

Domestic absorption likewise had in most instances a larger effect than foreign trade on second differences, that is to say, on changes between successive periods in the rate of change of manufacturing's share in output. The exceptions were the change between 1856–73 and 1873–1913 and the change between 1937–54 and 1954–63. The first of these is the only instance when absorption and foreign trade pulled in the same direction. The second is the only instance when the total moved in the opposite direction from absorption.

CONCLUSIONS

The central finding of this chapter is the smallness of those structural effects that we have been able to measure. They are small both in their net contribution to the overall rate of growth and in their net contribution to the explanation of differences in growth rates between periods. The chief exception is the period 1937–51, when the transition to a full-employment economy brought structural gains that accounted for perhaps half of the increase in TFP. The rate of growth of TFP in the interwar period was reduced by the structural changes that resulted from the depression; in their absence the improvement over 1873–1913 would have been more marked.

Since we have summed up the conclusions of each section of the chapter as we went along, we shall not recapitulate them here. Instead, we shall now sum up the various aspects of structural change in particular sectors that were, or might have been expected to be, of most importance for growth in the economy as a whole. Before doing so, however, we should repeat our warnings about the measurement problems and make clear that the conclusions should be interpreted only in relation to the particular statistics being used. The two major problems are these. (1) The size of the measured effects of structural change on growth depends on the particular industry breakdown being used. Some of the overall measures, such as the contribution to growth of quality-shift change might be very different if the industry breakdown were changed. (2) Throughout this chapter the objective has been to provide estimates of the contribution of structural change to the growth of GDP as measured by our statistics. To the extent that the statistics are inaccurate, the estimated contribution of structural change will also be incorrect. One possible source of inaccuracy lies in biases in measured output growth resulting from a failure to allow sufficiently for improvements in quality, and from the use of single indicators rather than double deflation. As is explained in Appendix I, there may be, as a result, a tendency to underestimate output and hence productivity growth in manufacturing, compared with other sectors. The structural benefits to be derived from shifting resources to manufacturing may therefore have been underestimated, but it is unlikely that the error is very large. A second source of inaccuracy is the use of employment indicators to measure output in public and professional services. Since this sector experienced rapid changes in employment and output shares, the use of a better measure of output (assuming one could be constructed) might lead to a different picture of the importance of structural effects.

Agriculture. Agriculture's share in factor input fell steadily, as in other countries. In the postwar period Britain clearly had less scope than other countries for increasing the national product by shifting resources out of agriculture. This was because agriculture already occupied so small a place in the economy and also because productivity was not much lower in agriculture than in other sectors. The small scope for gain by reducing excessive allocation of resources to agriculture is not a major point of difference between the postwar period and earlier periods, at least unless we go back very much earlier. Already by 1911 only 9 percent of the labor force of Great Britain and Northern Ireland was in agriculture, forestry, and fishing. As we go back into the nineteenth century the numbers become larger, and the absolute importance of agriculture's relative decline becomes greater. But in the latter half of the nineteenth century the marginal product of labor in agriculture, as measured by wages, was not vastly below that elsewhere, so the gain from reallocation was not all that great. In one respect, indeed, the gain may have been greater in the postwar period. One of the supposed advantages of the outflow of labor from agriculture is to raise productivity in agriculture itself. However, in the agricultural depression of the late nineteenth century, productivity in agriculture rose extremely slowly despite the exodus of labor. This made an important contribution to the overall decline in the rate of growth of TFP between 1856–73 and 1873–1913. In the postwar period, by contrast, productivity in agriculture rose faster than in almost any other sector. A number of possible explanations can be offered for this acceleration, unconnected with the labor supply. To some extent, however, it is likely that postwar agricultural improvements were stimulated by the accumulated effect of outflow over a long period, which meant that for the first time labor was in really short supply to farmers. Insofar as this was the case, the continuing outflow of labor from agriculture conduced more to productivity growth in the postwar period than it did earlier.

Mining. The decline in the labor force in mining after World War I was of the same order of magnitude as the decline in the labor force in agriculture. The correction of misallocation thereby involved was of about equal extent in the interwar and postwar periods. The pre–1914 experience of the two sectors is of course in no way comparable. The rapid increase in the numbers in mining before 1914 cannot be considered as producing misallocation in the static sense, since it reflected the rapid growth in the demand for coal, and the wages of miners were relatively high. Indeed the shift of labor toward mining at that time must itself be considered to have been a correction of misallocation. From this point of view, the gain from correcting misallocation in respect of mining does not mark a point of difference between the postwar period and earlier periods, though it was achieved in the opposite way. However, in the period when the labor force in mining was increasing, productivity rose much less rapidly than it did after the labor force started to decline. It seems probable, therefore, that the turnaround in mining's position after World War I had a favorable effect on productivity growth within the industry through the operation of diminishing returns. In this sense, the structural changes affecting mining had a more favorable effect on overall productivity growth in the interwar and postwar periods than they had before 1914.

Manufacturing. The effects on growth of changes in manufacturing's place in the economy are what have received most attention in discussions of the role of structural factors in Britain's economic growth. Yet the main conclusion that emerges from the data we have received is the comparative unimportance of these changes. They were unimportant for two reasons. First, changes in manufacturing's share in total inputs was not large. In the case of labor, the only major change between 1856 and 1973 was the increase between 1937 and 1955, partly but not wholly reversed between 1955 and 1973. The big decline in agriculture's share in the labor force before 1914 was not taken up by manufacturing. Second, even if the changes had been greater it is not clear that they would have made much difference to growth, since both the level and the rate of growth of TFP in manufacturing exceeded the average for the economy as a whole by only quite moderate amounts (the level by about 10 percent in most periods and the rate of growth by an average of about 0.4 percent a year).

The main identifiable effect was the once-for-all gain that resulted from the shift of resources to manufacturing between 1937 and 1951. Gains from shifts within manufacturing were also largest within that period.

As with structural effects generally, it is of course possible to argue that their very smallness is itself a point of great significance. Insofar as this is so, it is relevant for the comparison of the United Kingdom with other countries, rather than for the comparison of different periods, which is our main concern. It is also possible to argue that measures of the above type understate the strategic importance of manufacturing in growth on three grounds:

(1) Dynamic increasing returns to scale may be more important in manufacturing than elsewhere. It was found that dynamic increasing returns cannot provide the chief explanation for differences between periods in the rate of growth of TFP in British manufacturing. It does not follow that they do not exist.

(2) Manufacturing may have made a contribution, not properly reflected in the statistics, to the growth of TFP in other sectors that use manufactures as intermediate goods.

(3) Manufactures are important to the balance of payments. To the degree that the balance of payments affected the performance of the economy, through demand or in other ways, changes (or the lack of them) in manufacturing's place in the economy may have affected growth more than would appear from considerations of productivity alone.

If we were to assume that all these effects were present and important, some of the hypotheses mentioned at the start of the chapter would gain credence. We should then have to attribute more harm to the adverse effects of foreign trade on manufacturing's share in output in 1873–1913 and likewise to the failure of manufacturing to achieve a faster rate of TFP growth in the earlier part of the postwar period than it had between the wars. As regards the late postwar period, more importance would attach to the inroads of foreign competition in the domestic market for manufactures and to the outflow of labor from manufacturing, if that outflow is regarded as exogenous to manufacturing itself; but it has to be noted that despite this outflow of labor, faster productivity growth actually enabled manufacturing to increase its share in output at constant prices faster between 1964 and 1973 than between 1955 and 1964.

Of the three effects enumerated above, the existence of some tendency to dynamic increasing returns, even though not readily quantifiable, may be accepted as a reasonable conjecture, but it is not clear that the same tendencies do not apply outside manufacturing. The second effect, regarding inputs to nonmanufacturing, undoubtedly exists, but its quantitative importance is more questionable; moreover, it relates more to the productivity of the manufacturing sector than to the effects of changes in the sector's size. On the other hand, the argument about the balance of payments is obviously plausible, and we shall revert to it in Chapter 15.

The distributive trades and miscellaneous services. The abnormal absorption of labor into these sectors in the interwar period affected the growth of productivity unfavorably both by reducing the normal quality-shift gain and by reducing productivity in these sectors themselves. The combined effect was to reduce the interwar rate of growth of labor productivity in the economy as a whole, compared with 1873–1913, by about 0.3 percent a year. This was more than made good in the period 1937–51, when the reversal of the abnormal absorption was responsible for a substantial proportion of the overall growth of TFP. This reflected a shift in factor supply, in response to a change in the general availability of employment, rather than a shift in the structure of final demand. In the postwar period there was little net change in the proportion of labor input absorbed by these sectors. They increased their share of capital input. Statistically, this had a favorable effect on TFP growth, since the rate of return on capital was significantly higher than in the economy as a whole; in other words, the investment of capital there was well directed.

Public and professional services and finance. These sectors resemble each other. They are alike in exhibiting a long-term increase in importance in the national economy, particularly marked in the postwar period. They are alike too in that productivity in them is measured by largely conventional means, which probably underrate the upward trend. Finance differs from the others in that its output is chiefly sold to the private sector rather than to public authorities.

The much-complained-of shift of labor to these sectors in the postwar period does not appear as a source of loss to measured TFP growth, but rather the contrary. The reason is that the *level* of earnings in these sectors was higher than the average for the economy as a whole. The increase in the weight in the economy of a sector with a below-average measured rate of productivity growth did exercise some depressing effect; but larger changes in weights than occurred are needed for this kind of effect to be quantitatively important.

PART FOUR

Further Consideration of Some of the Forces Affecting the Rate of Growth

CHAPTER TEN

Demand

The pressure of demand relative to supply *may directly affect the comparison of rates of growth of TFI and TFP between benchmark years. In addition to this statistical point, the pressure of demand is important because it may affect the rate of growth of TFI or TFP during a period. A consideration of the sources of the* growth of demand *is a necessary counterpart to the consideration of the sources of growth of supply.*

THE LEVEL OF EXCESS DEMAND OR SUPPLY IN THE GOODS MARKET

The pressure of demand relative to supply in the goods market is not easy to measure, but it is plain from statistical evidence and contemporary annals that the pressure of demand was on average higher in the postwar period than before 1914, and higher before 1914 than in the interwar period after 1920. There was some downward trend in the pressure of demand in the course of the postwar period, and this probably contributed to the prominence of short-run bottlenecks (especially lack of materials) in the sudden strong cyclical upswing of 1972-73. Differences in cycle-amplitude partly accounted for the differences between periods in the pressure of demand. The average shortfall of activity below that in cycle peaks was greater before 1914 than in the postwar period—though not by an enormous amount—and it was greater still in the interwar period. By comparison with cycles in earlier periods, postwar cycles were distinguished by their short duration and also by a high degree of conformity between industries. By comparison with cycles in other countries, they were not more violent, but their downswing phases tended to be long relative to their upswing phases.

Price behavior is of only limited use as an indicator of the pressure of demand because it was much affected by world prices as well as by domestic influences. There was a systematic tendency for foreign trade prices to move in the same way as domestic prices, but by larger amounts. The exception was the postwar period, when domestic forces seem to have been more important in determining price movements than in other periods.

THE FORCES AFFECTING THE LEVEL OF
EXCESS SUPPLY OR DEMAND

A Keynesian decomposition of sources of demand indicates that foreign trade was the main proximate source of the lower level of demand in the interwar period, compared with the pre-1914 period. Investment was the main proximate source of the higher level of demand in the postwar period compared with the interwar period (and before 1914). The stability of exports was the principal reason why postwar cycles were smaller than pre-1914 cycles. Direct injection of demand by government was not responsible for the high average level of demand in the postwar period, but government policy may have contributed to high demand in other ways. There is some evidence — notably in relation to the 1920's and the period after 1966 — to support the hypothesis that unduly high wage costs are partly responsible for unemployment; but the largest single change in the level of activity, namely, its rise across World War II, is not to be explained in this way. Long-run trends in the money supply raise some points of interest, but they provide no shortcut to the explanation of differences between periods in demand pressure. The trend-rate of growth of the money supply, in periods when exchange rates were fixed, was surprisingly close to the trend-rate of growth in the volume of output. In these periods, which comprise the bulk of the period under study, the growth of the money supply cannot be treated as an exogenous variable.

THE COMPONENTS OF THE GROWTH OF DEMAND

A Keynesian decomposition can also be applied to the proximate sources of the growth of demand. Over the period 1856–1973 as a whole exports and investment on this reckoning contributed about equally to the growth of demand. The contribution of exports was the more spasmodic of the two, being greatest in 1856–73 and 1937–51. The contribution of investment was the greater of the two in both the interwar and the postwar period.

CONCLUSIONS

The final section of the chapter summarizes its conclusions by period, in chronological order. It thus serves as a pendant to the above synopsis, which summarizes the chapter's conclusions by topic.

The pressure of demand may be defined as the extent of the net excess of demand for goods and factors at current prices. In the output-per-unit-of-input approach to growth, the pressure of demand is relevant in two ways. In the first place, the pressure of demand in a given year affects the level of output and resource-allocation directly, so that comparison between two benchmark years will be affected if demand is stronger in one than in the other. The use of cycle peaks as benchmark years is an attempt to cope with this problem, but it may not do so completely. In the second place, the pressure of demand is likely to affect the rate of capital accumulation, and it may also affect the rates of growth of the labor force and TFP. This second class of effect depends on the pressure of demand over all years, not just at cycle peaks. It will therefore be necessary in this chapter to pay attention to the pressure of demand both in benchmark years (cycle peaks) and over the cycle as a whole.

This chapter is primarily concerned with the demand for goods — the demand for factors was considered in Chapters 3 and 5. Measuring the pressure of demand, as defined, raises a number of problems, both conceptual and practical. In the first place, trends in the net excess demand for goods, labor, and capital are not necessarily the same and need to be treated separately. In the second place, whatever the market under consideration, there is no unambiguous measure of net excess demand. In the case of labor (see pp. 81–93) we looked at both measures of gross excess supply (e.g. unemployment) and measures of gross excess demand (e.g. vacancies). In the case of capital (see pp. 151–59) we looked at utilization, while noting that observed changes in the degree of utilization can reflect planned changes in organization (e.g. through shift-working), which are not indicators of excess demand or supply, as well as unintended changes in excess capacity, which are. In the goods market, the concept of utilization does not apply, and excess demand and supply have to be measured more indirectly.

The main parts of this chapter are devoted to two questions: (1) how strong or weak was the pressure of demand in the goods market in different periods and (2) what were the proximate determinants of the pressure of demand in those periods?

All of the foregoing relates to the pressure of demand in the sense of the level of demand relative to supply — not the level of demand absolutely or its rate of growth. However, as was noted in Chapter 1, the whole process of growth can (and indeed must) be looked at from the demand side as well as from the supply side. The observed course of growth implies not only a growth in supply (composed of the growth of TFI and the growth of TFP) but also a corresponding growth in demand (composed of growth in the various categories of expenditure generating national income). The question of how demand came to grow as it did requires attention. Accordingly, we shall in the last section of this chapter consider the proximate causes of the growth in demand. A more thorough consideration will follow in Chapters 11–15 of the forces responsible for trends in the two main relevant categories of demand, investment and foreign trade, both in relation to the pressure of demand relative to supply and in relation to the growth of demand over time.

THE LEVEL OF EXCESS DEMAND OR SUPPLY IN THE GOODS MARKET

The Effect of Cycles

Throughout the whole of our period (indeed, from the 1790's, if not earlier), aggregate demand in the United Kingdom fluctuated in fairly regular cycles. If a comparison is made between two periods, each embracing several cycles, the average level of activity may differ either (1) because the level of activity at cycle peaks was higher in one period than the other or (2) because over the average of the cycle there was a smaller shortfall below the peak in one period than in the other, that is to say, because the amplitude of the cycle was less. It is much easier to measure (2) than (1), and we look at that in this section, before going on to consider the joint effects of the two.

The concept of the cycle is that it is a fluctuation of demand relative to productive potential. A cyclical depression year is a year in which output is low relative to potential, a year, that is to say, when there is a more than average amount of idle or underutilized productive resources. In accordance with this concept, we define a cyclical upswing (downswing) as consisting of those years in which the year-on-year rate of growth of GDP was above (below) trend. A cyclical peak (trough) is the last year of the upswing (downswing).

Table 10.1 shows the duration and amplitude of cycles in GDP and employment in various periods. Because the postwar cycles were shorter than earlier ones, it is important to have a measure of amplitude that takes proper account of duration. A given difference between the average annual growth rate in the upswing and the average annual growth rate in the downswing will lead to larger deviations from the trend line if the cycle is long than if it is short. Deviations from the trend will also be larger if the downswing and upswing are of equal duration than if they are of unequal duration. In Table 10.1 (and subsequently) we therefore measure amplitude by the difference be-

TABLE 10.1

Average Duration and Amplitude of Cycles in Gross Domestic Product and Employment, 1873–1974

Period	Average duration (years)		Annual percentage growth rates			Duration factor	Amplitude
	Downswing	Upswing	Downswing	Upswing	Difference		
GDP[a]							
1873–1913	3.8	4.2	−0.1%	3.1%	3.2%	0.90	2.8
1920–1937	2.0	6.5	−3.7	3.3	7.0	0.69	4.5
1951–1964	2.0	2.3	1.1	4.9	3.8	0.49	1.8
1964–1973	3.0	1.5	2.1	4.0	1.9	0.49	1.0
Total in employment							
1873–1913	3.8	4.2	−1.2%	2.6%	3.8%	0.90	3.1
1920–1937	2.0	6.5	−6.5	1.9	8.4	0.69	4.7
1951–1966[b]	2.3	2.3	0.1	1.1	1.0	0.60	0.6
1966–1974[b]	2.0	2.0	−1.0	0.5	1.5	0.46	0.8

Note: The duration factor for any cycle is defined as $t_u t_d / 2(t_u + t_d)$, where t_u and t_d are the durations in years of the upswing and downswing, respectively. The amplitude of any cycle is defined as the product of the duration factor and the difference between the growth rates in the upswing and the downswing. The growth rates here are simple, not compound as elsewhere in this study; they are measured by dividing the change between cyclical turning points expressed as a percentage of the initial peak level of the cycle by the duration of the downswing or upswing. The averages for each period in the table are the arithmetic averages of the measures for each cycle within the period; consequently, the duration factor cannot be derived from the first 2 columns, and the amplitude figure is not exactly equal to the product of the duration factor and the difference between the upswing and downswing growth rates. The downswing is measured from peak to trough and the upswing from trough to peak. The peaks and troughs are defined as follows (except for total in employment in the postwar period; see below):

Peaks: 1873, 1883, 1889, 1899, 1907, 1913; 1920, 1929, 1937; 1951, 1955, 1960, 1964, 1968, 1973
Troughs: 1879, 1886, 1893, 1904, 1908; 1921, 1932; 1952, 1958, 1962, 1967, 1971

Unless otherwise noted, all tables in this chapter dealing with the amplitude of cycles are calculated in this same manner and are based on the same cycles.
[a]GDP at constant market prices estimated from the expenditure side.
[b]Measured over cycles in employment. The peaks are 1951, 1956, 1961, 1966, 1969, and 1974; the troughs are 1953, 1959, 1963, 1968, and 1971.

tween upswing and downswing growth rates multiplied by a duration factor. The amplitude thus defined measures what would be the average percentage shortfall below the peak-to-peak trend if the cycle were a linear one (Matthews 1969).

As Table 10.1 shows, postwar cycles in constant price GDP were milder in amplitude than earlier ones. Within the postwar period, cycles were on average milder in 1964–73 than in 1951–64: this reflects the feebleness of the "boom" of 1968. The postwar cycles were distinguished by the persistence of some positive growth in downswing phases. The difference in amplitude compared with earlier periods was mainly by comparison with the exceptionally disturbed interwar period. The interwar period contained only two complete peak-to-peak cycles, both severe (amplitude measures 3.8 and 5.4). The difference in amplitude between 1951–64 and the pre-1914 period was not very great. The difference between upswing and downswing average annual growth rates was actually larger in 1951–64 than in 1873–1913, but the shorter durations of the 1951–64 cycles made their overall amplitude somewhat less. As far as real GDP is concerned, therefore, postwar fluctuations were not so very small by the standards of the more remote past, but they were much smaller than they were between the wars.[1]

The amplitude of fluctuations in *employment* was lower in 1951–64 than in earlier times by a much greater margin than was the amplitude of fluctuations in real GDP. This is less true of 1964–73.

The main conclusions can be expressed by asking what would have happened if the level of output relative to trend in peak years had been identical in the three periods (pre-1914, interwar, postwar) but the differences between the periods in the amplitude of fluctuations were as they actually were. The level of output relative to trend in the post-war period would then have averaged some 1¼ percent higher than pre-1914 and some 3 percent higher than in the interwar period. The corresponding figures for employment are 2½ percent and 4 percent. This gives a proximate indication of the effect of cycles taken by themselves, subject to the qualification that the amplitude of cycles cannot necessarily be assumed to be independent of the average level of activity relative to trend at peak years.

There is a further difference between the postwar cycles and earlier cycles that does not emerge from the aggregate data. Industries moved in step with each other over the cycle to a greater extent in the postwar period than formerly. The index of conformity between the fluctuations in the output of different industries is markedly higher in the postwar period, especially before 1964, than in previous periods (between which the differences are not significant).[2] This has two implications: (1) the amplitude of fluctuations in the output of the typical industry in the postwar period was less than in former periods by a greater extent than Table 10.1 suggests, and (2) the greater conformity presumably tended to diminish frictional unemployment, i.e. the coexistence of excess demand for labor in one sector with excess supply of labor in another; it thus contributed to making possible a lower average level of unemployment.

Wilson and others have made systematic comparisons of the relative amplitude and pattern of cycles in the United Kingdom and other countries in the postwar period (Wilson 1966, 1969; Lundberg 1968: Chapter 3; National Economic Development Office 1976). These comparisons are relevant to the familiar contention that growth in the United Kingdom was less rapid than elsewhere largely because of "stop-go." The main point emerging is that the amplitude of fluctuations (in the sense of the magnitude of deviations from the trend line) in the United Kingdom was not only not greater than elsewhere, but if anything less. There were also some differences in the pattern of cycles. Compared with the postwar cycles of most other countries, Britain's were unusually regular and of rather short duration. Moreover, its cycles tended either to have upswings and downswings of about equal duration or to have longer downswings than upswings. This is to be contrasted with a number of other countries, where the cycle often consisted of a long upswing followed by a short, sharp downswing. It appears, therefore, that if the hypothesis about the ill-effects of stop-go is to be sustained, it has to be based on the short duration of upswings rather than on the magnitude of fluctuations over the cycle as a whole. Thus it could be held that the short duration of upswings caused investment plans to be too often overtaken by the downswing before they had come to fruition, with consequent disappointment and disruption to orderly planning.

Comparison of Periods

Direct measures of excess demand and supply in the goods market are hard to come by. An excess supply of goods is typically potential rather than actual: in the absence of demand, the goods remain unproduced rather than being produced and left unsold. Excess demand for goods shows up in shortages and waiting lists that cannot be added up into a single measure.

The ratio of output to its trend output or to its level at the previous peak may be useful for comparing the level of demand in different years within any one cycle. But cycles as a whole cannot be compared with each other unless one is prepared to make bold assumptions about the level of supply in different cycles.[3] There is not enough information in a single output index to throw light on changes in the relationship between two variables, demand and supply. In the absence of direct information, we have to rely mainly on what can be inferred from factor markets. Excess *supply* in the goods market can exist only if there is excess supply in all the relevant factor markets, but excess *demand* for goods will result if there is excess demand for a single necessary factor.

No elaborate analysis is needed to establish that changes in the pressure of demand were not large enough to affect significantly the interpretation to be placed on observed rates of growth of TFI and TFP between benchmark years, with the exception of the transwar periods 1913–24 and 1937–51. But a bit more requires to be said about the characteristics of the successive periods.

In the pre-1914 period higher demand in the short run would certainly have elicited higher supply. Labor was rarely a bottleneck. Only in 1872–73 were there clear signs, including a shortage of labor, of pressure against the ceiling of productive potential. At other cycle peaks, the degree of underutilization of capital may not have been very great, but capacity was not completely at full stretch, and anyway cycle peaks accounted for only one year in eight.* In general, annals of the period, such as *The Economist*, suggest that the level of output in industry and trade was dominated by the state of demand.† Likewise, it is not difficult to conclude that there was excess supply of goods in most interwar years. This conclusion has to be qualified by evidence of excess demand in the late 1930's in particular industries affected by the recovery. The boom of 1919–20 stands apart from the rest of the interwar period. It had peculiar features. In 1920 there was nearly full employment (the unemployment rate was 2 percent), and in that year and in 1919 output was certainly constrained by supply bottlenecks. Yet output in 1920 was lower than in 1913, and so too was productivity. Between 1920 and 1924 output rose, but so, paradoxically, did unemployment (to 7.8 percent). Productivity rose steeply. A possible explanation for these events, apart from the general postwar disruption and recovery, is that in 1920 industry had not yet adapted to the great reduction in hours of work that took place in 1919, but did so over the next few years.

The pressure against the ceiling that was felt in 1919–20 appears thus to have been due more to the abnormally low level of the ceiling than to the abnormally high level of demand. In fact the forces making for low demand were already present, especially on the export side (see pp. 466–68). The pressure on the ceiling and the violent price movements associated with it probably aggravated the recession that occurred when the boom broke.

---

*This is not to imply that there was or was felt to be a chronic depression. The contention that "from 1870 the British economy moved from one deep slump to the next, punctuated only by brief booms" (W. A. Lewis 1978:127) does not appear to be well supported by the evidence. If the booms were so brief, one would expect to find that in the majority of years the level of unemployment was nearer to that in the adjacent cycle trough than to that in the adjacent cycle peak. But the reverse was the case: excluding the peak and trough years themselves, there were between 1870 and 1913 21 years when the level unemployment was nearer to the level in the adjacent peak and 11 years when it was nearer to the level in the adjacent trough.

†A literary expression of this dominance, interesting because not labored but taken for granted, is in Arnold Bennett's *The Old Wives' Tale*. Bennett's business-cycle chronology is very accurate.

We turn now to the postwar period. It saw a more persistent short-age of labor than earlier peacetime periods. In peak years there was also some excess demand for capital capacity. It is plain that had factor supplies not been limited in the short run, output at cycle peaks would have been higher.

There was certainly *more* excess demand in the postwar period than earlier. Whether there was an average *positive* net excess demand is a question not worth pressing, since, given heterogeneous products, the netting-out is a purely notional concept.* A more important question concerns the trend within the postwar period. The labor market in-dicators point to a downward trend in the pressure of demand. Did this also apply to the goods market?

It is fairly generally agreed, on the basis of impressions, that short-ages were more prevalent in the immediate postwar period than they later became. This is confirmed by evidence on the ratio of orders to output in the engineering and machine tool industries, which show a downward trend till as late as 1959.[4] There was no year between 1966 and 1972 when demand pressure was as high as at previous peaks, and in that sense a further downward trend in demand pressure in the goods market occurred in those years; on the other hand, the down-swing phases of the cycles in 1964–73 were milder than usual, so the average shortfall below the peak-to-peak trend in output was not greater than in earlier postwar cycles.

The boom of 1973 stood apart from this trend and had some unique features. In 1973 the proportion of firms in the CBI survey expecting orders or sales to limit output was much lower than in 1964 (Table 3.22). There is abundant impressionistic evidence that excess demand in the goods market in 1973–74 was exceptionally strong. Excess de-mand for labor and capital, on the other hand, was only moderately, if at all, greater than in previous booms. The boom of 1973–74 was ex-ceptional (at least after the immediate postwar period) in that shortage of materials featured prominently among the constraints on output.[5] One may interpret this by saying that the factor in shortest supply was not labor or fixed capital but inventories. An unusually rapid upswing impinged on a situation where stocks were initially low, and this was exacerbated by some special factors.[6] The stock output ratio thus con-

*One might argue that zero net excess demand would cause half of all firms to find their output limited by lack of demand. By this criterion there was on average excess sup-ply in the years covered on a uniform basis by the CBI survey (1964–74): the proportion of firms expecting to be so limited averaged 60%.

tinued abnormally low for some time after the recession had started. The low levels of stocks of materials at the end of 1971 probably reflected the same financial difficulties and lack of confidence among firms that had led them to cut their labor forces during the recession. Firms therefore started the recovery with unusually low reserves of both labor and inventories.

The supply-side obstacles to the expansion of output in 1973 were thus different from what they had been in 1964 and earlier postwar booms. They had a more short-run character. At the same time the pressure of demand was stronger. The net outcome was that output in 1973 was probably little if at all higher in relation to the trend of productive potential than it had been at previous peaks. Excess demand in the product market was greater, but shortages of inventories prevented this from being fully reflected in output or in excess demand for plant capacity or labor.

Price Movements and Their Implications

Movements in the general price level may provide further evidence about the pressure of demand in goods markets. This is therefore a convenient place to discuss them. The behavior of the general price level as such is only indirectly relevant to our main theme, the growth of real output, and we shall argue that it does not in fact provide much useful additional evidence on the pressure of demand. Our treatment will therefore be brief.

Annual GDP prices are shown in Figure 10.1 and growth rates between the usual benchmark years in Table 10.2. There was a trend increase in prices, but this was the result of rises in three phases only, World War I and its aftermath, World War II, and the postwar period. Much the most rapid price increase in the whole period 1856–1973 was during and immediately after World War I; prices increased between 1914 and 1920 at an annual rate of 17.9 percent.

The postwar period is unique in British history (since the time of James I) in having had a sustained and substantial rise in prices in peacetime. In most of the 1950's and 1960's the rate of price increase was slightly declining. A new phase of much faster price increase began in 1970 and continued in the years after 1973 (not shown in the figure). In most of the interwar period prices fell. Between 1856 and 1913 there were one-and-a-half long cycles in prices (with troughs in the 1850's and peaks in the 1870's and 1913) but no trend.

In broadest terms, these price trends are what might have been expected, given that the level of activity was high in the postwar period,

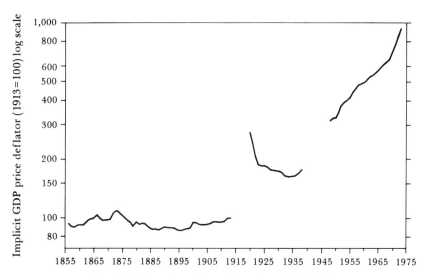

Fig. 10.1. Gross domestic product prices, 1856–1973

low in the interwar period, and middling before 1914. However, it is not really possible to infer anything more specific from price behavior about the pressure of demand in different periods. The nature of the relation between price movements and excess demand (for goods or labor) is the subject of dispute, and we cannot use evidence on prices both to infer what the pressure of demand must have been and to test alternative hypotheses about the relation between the pressure of demand and prices.

Few economists would now subscribe to a simple Phillips-type hypothesis that the pressure of demand is the *only* force affecting changes in the general price level.

In the first place, account must also in principle be taken of expectations, possibly based on the extrapolation of past trends. This is most relevant to the postwar period and has often been put forward as the explanation of the acceleration in prices in the 1970's, which is not easily explained by the straight Phillips hypothesis. It is more doubtful whether it was important in peacetime periods before World War II, since trends in prices were then very much milder.

In the second place, in an open economy under fixed exchange rates, domestic prices must be much influenced by world prices and hence by the forces that determine world prices. The question of the relation between world influences and domestic influences on British price levels

TABLE 10.2
Growth of Gross Domestic Product Prices, 1856–1973
(Annual percentage growth rates)

Period	Growth	Period	Growth
Peacetime phases:		Post-WWII cycles:	
1856–1873	0.9%	1951–1955	4.4%
1873–1913	– 0.2	1955–1960	3.6
1924–1937	– 0.6	1960–1964	2.6
1951–1973	4.6	1964–1968	3.6
Wartime phases:		1968–1973	8.2
1913–1924	5.7		
1937–1951	5.3	1856–1973	2.0%
War and postwar phases:			
1913–1937	2.2		
1937–1964	4.5		

Note: The prices are those implied by the 2 series, one at current prices and the other at constant prices, of GDP at factor cost, estimated from the expenditure side. The estimates for 1856–70 are rough because no satisfactory expenditure-side estimates exist for those years.

arises in all the peacetime periods under review and is discussed in Chapters 14 and 15. The conclusions may be summarized as follows:

(1) In the second half of the nineteenth century changes in domestic prices were associated with changes in both domestic demand and world prices. Since domestic demand was itself associated with world prices to some extent, it is not possible to disentangle the separate influence on British prices of external and purely domestic factors.

(2) From 1899 to 1913 domestic prices were more unambiguously determined by world prices. These tended to raise the British price level, despite the downward pressure on demand from investment and from the monetary impact of the rise in world prices itself.

(3) Again in the interwar period world prices had a major impact on domestic prices. The domestic depression and the return to a high exchange rate in 1925 also contributed.

(4) By contrast, domestic forces dominated in the postwar period, so that domestic prices rose notwithstanding a fall in the ratio of foreign trade prices to the GDP deflator. The tendency for domestic prices to decelerate up to the mid-1960's, however, may have owed something to the moderating influence of world prices. And the acceleration of domestic prices beginning in the late 1960's, though larger than the acceleration of foreign trade prices until 1972, was obviously partly the result of the 1967 devaluation and the acceleration of world prices.

Thus the domestic price level was affected both by the pressure of domestic demand and by world prices. Because of the independent

TABLE 10.3
Average Amplitude of Cycles in Gross Domestic
Product Prices, 1873–1964

Period	Implicit GDP prices	GDP at current prices[a]	GDP at constant prices[a]
1873–1913	1.2	3.9	2.7
1920–1937	2.3	6.4	4.5
1951–1964	-1.7	0.5	1.8

Note: Method of calculation as in Table 10.1. Data for the period 1965–73 are not included because the cyclical movements cannot be disentangled from the trend acceleration in prices.
[a] GDP at constant market prices estimated from the expenditure side.

effect of world prices, the pressure of demand cannot be inferred from the behavior of prices. A rise in world prices was, moreover, capable in some circumstances of having a deflationary effect on real demand in the United Kingdom. In the postwar period domestic as opposed to foreign influences on the price level were more preponderant than in earlier periods.

Reference may be made in conclusion to the cyclical behavior of prices. A glance at Figure 10.1 suggests that cycles in prices were larger in the pre-1914 and interwar periods than in the postwar period. This is confirmed by the amplitude measures shown in Table 10.3. Indeed, cycles in prices in 1951–64 tended to be *inversely* related to those in output, whereas in the other peacetime periods they were positively related. This could be reconciled with the pressure-of-demand hypothesis by postulating that in the postwar period there was a lag of two years or so between the pressure of demand and the resultant increase in prices, and that the lag was very much shorter in earlier periods.

THE FORCES AFFECTING THE LEVEL OF
EXCESS SUPPLY OR DEMAND

The Components of Demand: The Average Level of Activity

The first step is to consider, in terms of an elementary Keynesian model, the effects of the different components of demand on the level of activity. The level of activity is defined as $Y/\bar{Y}$, where Y is GDP and $\bar{Y}$ is "full-employment" GDP.[7] Including public authorities' current expenditure on goods and services as a form of consumption, we can write the familiar identity

$$Y = C + I + X - M$$

where Y is GDP at current market prices. Defining s and m as the ratios of savings (including government savings) and imports to GNP (rather than GDP), and A as net income from abroad (i.e. the difference between GNP and GDP), Y can be written as

$$Y = \frac{I + X + A(1 - s - m)}{s + m}$$

Likewise, the expression for the level of activity, $Y/\bar{Y}$, can be written as

$$\frac{Y}{\bar{Y}} = \left[\frac{I}{\bar{Y}} + \frac{X}{\bar{Y}} + \frac{A(1 - s - m)}{\bar{Y}} \right] / (s + m)$$

The level of $Y/\bar{Y}$ is thus shown as being determined by five variables, $I/\bar{Y}$, $X/\bar{Y}$, $A/\bar{Y}$, s, and m. (For an earlier similar presentation, see Matthews 1968; also C. T. Taylor 1978). The contributions of each of these five variables is shown in Table 10.4, for averages of all years

TABLE 10.4

Contribution of Components to the Pressure of Demand: Annual Averages for All Years and for Cycle Peaks, 1857–1973

	All years[a]				Cycle peaks[b]			
Component	1857– 1873	1874– 1913	1925– 1937	1952– 1973	1857– 1873	1874– 1913	1925– 1937	1952– 1973
(1) Level of activity $(Y/\bar{Y})$	96.3%	95.3%	88.3%	98.2%	98.4%	97.5%	91.8%	98.2%
Categories of expenditure as % of full employment:								
(2) Investment $(I/\bar{Y})$	8.3	8.8	8.8	17.3	8.6	8.9	9.7	18.0
(3) Exports $(X/\bar{Y})$	26.8	25.9	16.2	20.4	28.0	28.3	18.0	20.5
(4) Income from abroad, adjusted $[A(1 - s - m)/\bar{Y}]$	1.5	3.3	2.6	0.7	1.7	3.5	2.7	0.6
(5) $[I + X + A(1 - s - m)]/\bar{Y}$	36.6	38.0	27.6	38.4	38.3	40.7	30.4	39.1
Propensities:								
(6) Savings (s)	12.5	13.1	9.4	18.1	13.3	14.6	10.9	18.3
(7) Import (m)	25.5	26.8	21.7	21.0	25.6	27.1	22.2	21.6
(8) $s + m$	38.0	39.9	31.1	39.1	38.9	41.7	33.1	39.7

Note: $\bar{Y}$ is defined as $Y / (1 - u)$, where u is the unemployment rate. All underlying series are in current market prices. In the underlying annual series row 1 is identically equal to the ratio of row 5 to row 8. This identity is only approximately true of the annual averages given in the table. Investment is measured as gross domestic capital formation plus half stock-building, and imports are measured as imports of goods and services minus half stock-building. Stock-building is allocated in this way because it is estimated that about half of stock-building in postwar years consisted of stock-building of imports ("Short-Term Economic Forecasting," UK [95]: 9). The simpler procedure of including all stock-building in investment would give exaggerated figures for m and I, because of the well-known tendency of stock-building and imports to be abnormally high in cycle peak years.
[a]Unweighted averages of the values of the series in the years shown.
[b]Unweighted averages of the values of the series in the following cycle peaks: *1857 – 73*, 1857 – 73, 1860, 1865, 1873; *1874–1913*, 1883, 1889, 1907, 1913; *1925–37*, 1929, 1937; *1952–73*, 1955, 1960, 1964, 1968, 1973.

TABLE 10.5

Contribution of Components to Interperiod Changes in the Pressure of Demand: Annual Averages for All Years and for Cycle Peaks, 1857–1973

(Percentage points)

	Change between:					
	1857–1873 and 1874–1913		1874–1913 and 1925–1937		1925–1937 and 1952–1973	
Component	All years	Cycle peaks	All years	Cycle peaks	All years	Cycle peaks
(1) $I/\bar{Y}$	1.4	0.6	−0.1	2.3	24.6	22.9
(2) $X/\bar{Y}$	−2.3	0.9	−27.8	−28.0	12.1	6.9
(3) $[A(1-s-m)] / \bar{Y}$	4.5	4.4	−2.0	−2.0	−5.5	−5.8
(4) s	−1.3	−3.2	9.6	9.6	−23.0	−19.4
(5) m	−3.3	−3.6	13.7	12.5	1.9	1.6
(6) Total change in level of activity $(Y/\bar{Y})$	−1.0	−0.9	−6.6	−5.6	10.1	6.2

Note: The contributions were found by multiplying the interperiod differences in $I/\bar{Y}$, $X/\bar{Y}$ and $A(1-s-m) / \bar{Y}$ by the coefficient a_n, and those in s and m by the coefficient a_d. These coefficients represent the average contribution for the successive periods of a unit of each component of demand to the overall level of activity $Y/\bar{Y}$. Writing n for $[I + X + A(1-s-m)] / \bar{Y}$, d for $(s+m)$, subscripts 1 and 2 for the first and second periods in each pair, and the operator Δ for changes between periods, the calculations are as follows:

$$(1) = a_n\Delta \; (I/\bar{Y}) \qquad (3) = a_n\Delta \; [A(1-s-m)/\bar{Y}] \qquad (5) = a_d\Delta m$$

$$(2) = a_n\Delta \; (X/\bar{Y}) \qquad (4) = a_d\Delta s$$

where $a_n = (d_1 + d_2)/2d_1d_2$ and $a_d = (n_1 + n_2)/2d_1d_2$. Row 6 is the change between periods in the ratio between rows 5 and 8 in Table 10.4. This ratio is approximately equal to $Y/\bar{Y}$ shown in row 1 of Table 10.4. It can easily be shown that all contributions are additive.

within periods and for averages of cyclical peak years within periods. The chief interest lies not in the figures for a single period taken by itself, but in comparisons between periods. So first differences between successive periods are also shown in Table 10.5. They are multiplied by coefficients that represent the average contribution for the two periods being compared of a unit of each component of demand to the level of activity $(Y/\bar{Y})$. The rows of Table 10.5 add up to the actual interperiod change in the level of activity.

The following are the chief features revealed by the figures. Attention is focused on Table 10.5.

(1) There was no great change between *1857–73 and 1874–1913*, either in components or in total. *Fluctuations* in exports were more severe in the second of the two periods, as shown by the opposite signs for "all years" and cycle peaks in row 2 of Table 10.5, but this did not carry over to total demand to any significant degree.

(2) The decline between *1874–1913 and 1925–37* in the level of activity was due chiefly to exports and the concomitant fall in income

TABLE 10.6

Contribution of Components to the Pressure of Demand: Annual Averages for
Postwar Subperiods, 1952–1973

(Percent)

Component	1952–1955	1956–1960	1961–1964	1965–1968	1969–1973
(1) $Y/\bar{Y}$	98.7%	98.5%	98.3%	98.2%	97.2%
(2) $I/\bar{Y}$	14.7	16.4	17.6	19.1	18.5
(3) $X/\bar{Y}$	22.1	20.8	18.9	18.5	21.5
(4) $A(1-s-m)/\bar{Y}$	0.8	0.7	0.7	0.6	0.6
(5) $[I+X+A(1-s-m)]/\bar{Y}$	37.6	37.9	37.2	38.2	40.6
(6) s	15.0	17.5	18.1	19.5	19.9
(7) m	23.1	21.0	19.8	19.5	22.0
(8) $s+m$	38.1	38.5	37.9	39.0	41.9

Note: See Table 10.4 for method of calculation.

from abroad. The falls in m and s, especially s, and the resulting favorable effects on the level of activity, were no doubt partly induced by
the depression and to that extent were built-in stabilizers rather than
exogenous offsets.

(3) Much the largest contribution to the rise in activity between
1925–37 and 1952–73 came from investment. A smaller but still substantial contribution was made by exports. The contrast between the
two periods in the contribution of exports was much more substantial
for all years than for cycle peaks. The rise in the average propensity to
save was not very much less than the rise in $I/\bar{Y}$. If all five items are
regarded as fully exogenous, therefore, the foreign trade side (X, A,
and m) must be held to have contributed more than the domestic side
(I, s) to the rise in activity between the two periods for the average of
all years (though not for cycle peaks). It is misleading, however, to take
I and s together in this way, because the rise in s was to a considerable
extent, if not predominantly, induced by the rise in activity (see pp.
139–51).

Comparison may also be made between other periods. For example,
one may compare 1874–1913 and 1952–73. The net rise between these
two periods (all years) came from a big rise in investment, incompletely
offset by a rise in the propensity to save. On the foreign trade side, the
net change between these two periods was unfavorable, the decline in
$X/\bar{Y}$ and income from abroad more than outweighing the fall in m.

This general method of presentation can be extended to the comparison of shorter periods. Figures on post–World War II subperiods
are given in Table 10.6. The contribution of $I/\bar{Y}$ rises steadily until the
last cycle, then it falls. X/Y follows exactly the opposite pattern, as does

$m. s$ rises steadily throughout (a movement that cannot appropriately be regarded as simply induced by changes in the level of activity). The fall in $Y/\bar{Y}$ in 1969–73, compared with the preceding periods, appears as the result of a fall in $I/\bar{Y}$ accompanied by a continued rise in s.

The interwar period can likewise be divided into subperiods (figures not shown here). Great differences appear between the 1920's and the 1930's. By comparison with pre-1914, the 1930's were broadly speaking like the 1920's, only more so: there was a further fall in the contribution to $Y/\bar{Y}$ made by exports and income from abroad, and a further increase in the contributions from investment, savings, and imports. Consequently, when one is comparing the postwar period with the interwar period, the increase in exports appears as relatively more important, and the increase in investment as relatively less important, if the comparison is with the 1930's rather than with the 1920's or with the interwar period as a whole.

The Components of Demand: Cyclical Fluctuations

Reference has been made to implicit measures of cyclical amplitude contained in the foregoing data. We now give some explicit measures.

Measures of cyclical amplitude for the components of GDP, calculated in the same way as those already given in Tables 10.1 and 10.3 for GDP, employment, and prices, are shown in Table 10.7. The first two panels show the average amplitude of fluctuations over the GDP cycles defined earlier in each class of expenditure. The components are revalued at constant prices in the first panel and at current prices deflated by implicit GDP prices in the second. The first thus measures cyclical fluctuations in the *volume* of the expenditure of the class concerned, and the second the fluctuations in the total *cost* (in GDP prices) of that expenditure. Differences between the two arise from differences in the cyclical behavior of prices.

Though both types of measure are of interest, the cost measure has more relevance to the generation of demand, and we therefore focus on it. In panel 3 the amplitudes in panel 2 are multiplied by the weight of each component in GDP, to show the amount of fluctuation in GDP approximately due to each component; and in panel 4 these amounts are shown in percentage form.[8]

There were considerable differences between periods in the cyclical behavior of different classes of expenditure. The following are the principal points that emerge.

(1) In the interwar period all categories of expenditure (except stock-building, for which the data are unreliable) had cycles of larger amplitude than in other periods.

TABLE 10.7

Average Amplitude of Cycles in Components of
Gross Domestic Product, 1873–1973

Period	Consumers' expenditure	Public authorities' current expenditure	Gross domestic fixed capital formation	Stock-building[a]	Exports of goods and services	Imports of goods and services	GDP[b]
(1) Amplitude (constant market prices)							
1873–1913	1.4	– 0.7	4.2	–	5.9	3.5	2.8
1920–1937	2.8	2.3	4.1	–	12.0	6.6	4.5
1951–1964	1.6	– 0.9	3.4	–	1.8	4.6	1.8
1964–1973	1.3	0.3	0.3	–	2.0	4.1	1.0
(2) Amplitude (current market prices deflated by GDP prices)							
1873–1913	1.0	– 1.0	6.3	–	7.1	4.8	2.8
1920–1937	3.5	1.6	7.3	–	18.4	16.7	4.5
1951–1964	2.0	– 0.1	2.9	–	2.1	6.3	1.8
1964–1973	1.5	0.2	2.2	–	3.7	7.5	1.0
(3) Absolute contribution to the amplitude of GDP cycles[c]							
1873–1913	0.9	– 0.1	0.6	(0.8)	2.0	– 1.4	2.8
1920–1937	2.9	0.2	0.7	0.4	5.4	– 5.1	4.5
1951–1964	1.4	0.0	0.4	1.1	0.5	– 1.6	1.8
1964–1973	1.0	0.0	0.4	0.5	0.7	– 1.6	1.0
(4) Percentage contribution to the amplitude of GDP cycles[c]							
1873–1913	32%	– 3%	21%	(29%)	71%	50%	100%
1920–1937	66	4	15	8	121	– 114	100
1951–1964	76	– 1	24	63	26	– 88	100
1964–1973	94	4	40	46	68	– 152	100

Note: Amplitude is calculated according to the method explained in Table 10.1.
[a] The usual measure of amplitude is not in general meaningful in the case of stock-building because of the possibility of negative stock-building in certain years. However, the contribution of stock-building cycles to GDP cycles is a valid and measurable concept. (It is found as a residual.) Non-farm stock-building before 1914 is estimated as 40% of the change in GDP (see Feinstein [forthcoming]), and hence its measured contribution to GDP cycles in 1873–1913 is arbitrary.
[b] GDP at constant market prices, estimated from the expenditure side.
[c] Estimated by weighting the amplitudes of cycles in the second series by their shares in GDP in peak years.

(2) Exports accounted almost wholly for the relative smallness of the fluctuations in GDP in the postwar period compared with the pre-1914 period. The (absolute) contribution to the amplitude of GDP cycles made by other classes of expenditure was much the same in the two periods (panel 3).

(3) Consumers' expenditure actually fluctuated rather more in 1951–64 than in the pre-1914 period, and by almost as much in 1964–73 (panels 2 and 3), even though the fluctuations in GDP were smaller. The relative contribution (last panel) made by consumers' ex-

penditure to GDP cycles was therefore much greater in the postwar period than earlier.

(4) The contribution to the cycle made by gross domestic fixed capital formation in different periods was much affected by movements in its price relative to that of GDP. The amplitude of fluctuations in GDFCF measured at cost (panel 2) and hence its multiplier repercussions were less than half as great in 1951–64 as they had been before 1914. But measured in volume (panel 1) the amplitude was, rather surprisingly, only slightly less in 1951–64 than before 1914. By contrast in 1964–73 the volume measure shows very small fluctuations, but the cost measure shows fluctuations not much less than in 1951–64.

(5) The absolute contributions to the amplitude of GDP cycles made by the different classes of expenditure were very similar in the two parts of the postwar period, with one exception, stock-building. This reflects the absence in 1968 of a stock-building boom of comparable magnitude to the booms of earlier postwar peaks. Stock-building, along with consumption, appears as the source of diminished amplitude in GDP fluctuations in 1964–73 compared with 1951–64. In comparing the two parts of the postwar period, however, it must be remembered that the two cycles of 1964–73 were far less homogeneous than the three cycles of 1951–64. The measured amplitude of fluctuations in 1964–73 comes out low because both the peak of 1968 and the troughs on either side of it were mild. The period 1966–72 has some of the character of a long relatively low plateau separating the peaks of 1964 and 1973; and the cycle as a whole shows signs of reverting to the pre–World War II Juglar, instead of the Kitchin pattern characteristic of 1951–64.

The Role of Government

In the analysis by components of expenditure with which we began this section, government was not separately distinguished. A current-account surplus budget surplus appeared as part of the overall propensity to save, government investment appeared as part of investment, and the effects of monetary policy, exchange-rate policy, tariffs, controls, and other policy instruments appeared in whatever categories of expenditure they may have affected. When we come to consider in Chapters 11–15 the causes of trends in investment and the foreign balance, we shall have a good deal to say about the role of government actions. But we shall not have occasion to revert to the effects on demand of government actions as a whole, so some discussion is appropriate at this point.

Government actions affected demand even before the days when that became a conscious aim. But the chief channel was through wars, and the Boer War was the only important one falling within our period up till World War I. The question about the role of government in the determination of the level of demand in peacetime relates chiefly to the postwar period and, to a lesser extent, the interwar period. The most important question is whether the high average level of demand in the postwar period was attributable to government policy.

As far as fiscal policy is concerned, the facts on their face suggest that the answer is unequivocally no. Net government savings were substantial and positive throughout the postwar period, in contrast to the negligible savings of earlier periods (pp. 148–49). By that measure, fiscal policy was on average deflationary, not inflationary, in the postwar period. Some qualification is needed because of balanced budget multiplier effects and because of the effects of the level of activity on net government savings. It is not possible to calculate exactly the magnitude of those effects in comparing two periods covering such a wide span of time as the interwar and postwar periods. But fairly extreme assumptions would be needed to avoid the conclusion that the net effect of the budget on current account in the postwar period was, by comparison with the interwar period, deflationary in its net impact. Certainly it cannot have been inflationary to the extent required to provide the main explanation of the difference between the two periods in the level of activity.

This conclusion is not fundamentally altered by taking public-sector investment into account. Public-sector investment was indeed higher relative to GDP in the postwar period than in the interwar period. But investment in the sometime-public sector was a lower proportion of total (nonresidential) investment postwar than prewar (as we shall see in the next chapter). So though this class of investment played its part in the postwar rise in investment, it was not the leader. (Differences between the time path of public and private investment *within* the postwar period were significant and are referred to below.)

There is no ready criterion by which to determine whether monetary policy on average made for a higher level of expenditure in the postwar period than in earlier periods. In the 1970's the money supply grew exceptionally rapidly; its rate of growth was only slightly greater in the 1950's and 1960's than in the interwar period,[9] and was actually less in relation to the rise in output. However, this is a measure of monetary expansion from year to year and is therefore not exactly what is relevant to the question of the *average* degree of monetary ease. It is possible that on balance there *was* greater monetary ease in the postwar period than in the prewar period, but even this is by no means clear.

On the face of it, therefore, the evidence suggests that fiscal and monetary policies were not the main cause of the high average level of activity in the postwar period, and that they may even have pulled in the other direction.

However, this is not the whole story. In the first place, fiscal and monetary policies are not the only ways government affected demand. Exchange-rate policy was also important. The devaluations of 1949 and 1967 tended in themselves to increase demand (disregarding deliberate fiscal offsets that are already taken into account in measures of the overall fiscal impact). They were perhaps the most important point of difference from the economic policies followed by the government in the 1920's.

In the second place there is the question of timing. The net effect of a given government action on the average level of activity over the ensuing few years may depend on the state of the economy when it is done. Given that fiscal and monetary policy did not sustain demand by the injection of purchasing power over the average of all years, did it perhaps do so by injecting purchasing power at critical moments and hence reducing cyclical fluctuations? An affirmative answer would mean that attempts at "fine tuning" in the postwar period were on balance successful, or at least more successful than government action (or inaction) in earlier periods. Certainly, cycles were milder than in the past, and this had an important effect on the average level of activity. However, this was mainly due to a cause other than government action, namely that exports fluctuated much less than in the past (Table 10.7). Whether government action helped to reduce fluctuations or whether it made them worse has been much debated, with indecisive results.[10] There can be little doubt that government intervention had important effects on the *character* of the cycles, which differed considerably from cycles of earlier periods, notably in their shorter duration. One aspect of government policy was clearly destabilizing, namely the regular tendency to take further deflationary measures when a downswing was already well under way. However, this had its counterpart in similar action undertaken by the monetary authorities in earlier times and was not necessarily a turn for the worse. Stabilizing effects, on the other hand, might be expected from the policy adopted at the other phase of the cycle when government action was most prominent, namely the bottom of the trough. The tendency for government to stimulate spending, especially consumption, at this point may well have reduced the duration, and hence the magnitude, of the downswing. This aspect of postwar government policy has been criticized as tending to produce overloading or an adverse balance of payments, or both, and indeed has been regarded by some as the root of the whole stop-go cycle. But even if this sort of intervention did lead to overloading, it is arguable that allowing the downswing to go deeper would have made the cycle larger.

More significant perhaps than either continuous injection of demand or regular mitigation of fluctuations were certain more miscellaneous actions taken or avoided by government in consequence of its general commitment to full employment, particularly in the early postwar years. There was no repetition of the monetary contraction carried out in the early 1920's. On the fiscal side, a decline in government savings matched the rise in private savings in the years 1948-53 (Fig. 5.6). Joined with the admittedly much more favorable world environment, these actions not only directly prevented demand from falling off, but also established confidence that the maintenance of full employment was receiving more than lip service. It was not the direct operation of fiscal or monetary policy that kept employment at a higher level than in earlier periods, and this needs to be emphasized. But the investment that *was* the mainstay of the high demand over most of the postwar period may well have been encouraged by confidence that the government had a commitment to prevent deep slumps.

Not all the above is equally applicable to the whole of the postwar period. In particular, changes in government policy became much more violent after the devaluation of 1967. It would be different to deny that government policy in 1967-73 was destabilizing, whatever it may have been earlier.

There were also certain general trends within the postwar period in the effect of government policy on demand. Up to the mid-1960's, the general trend in demand management policies was increasingly expansionary. Government savings fell as a proportion of GNP; monetary restrictions and quantitative restrictions on private investment were eased (pp. 370-72); and investment in the sometime-public sector rose more rapidly than investment in the private sector (Fig. 11.2). These things did not all happen at the same time, but the general direction was clear. After 1967 the situation changed. Not only were there bigger changes from year to year, but also the different instruments of policy more frequently pulled in opposite directions. From 1968 onward the volume of public-sector investment ceased to rise at all. The fiscal position on current account over the years 1967-73 as a whole was substantially more deflationary than before (in part a deliberate compensation for the expansionary effects of the 1967 devaluation). In 1970 the money supply began to be expanded much more rapidly than earlier in the postwar period. It appears likely that the net outcome of these various forces was to halt and probably reverse the previous trend toward more expansionary policies, with the exception of the brief period 1972–73.

The conclusion may be summed up as follows. Direct injections of demand by fiscal or monetary policy or public-sector investment were not responsible for the unusually high average level of activity in the postwar period. It is possible, however, that government policy in a broader sense did contribute to the high average level of activity, partly on account of the devaluations of 1949 and 1967, partly by the timing of fiscal and monetary measures, partly by effects on confidence. Within the postwar period there was a trend toward more expansionary policies up to the mid-1960's. After 1967 this trend probably ceased, though the net outcome is difficult to discern because of the conflicting effects of different government actions and because of the much greater instability of policy compared with the earlier postwar years.

The Effects of Real Wage Rates

Pre-Keynesian theory, now revived, holds that the cause of unemployment is too-high real wage rates, i.e. real wage rates higher than the marginal product of labor at full employment. The effects can manifest themselves in any of the classes of expenditure generating national income. In this theory it is envisaged that too high a real wage may make certain activities absolutely unprofitable (e.g. the operation of the oldest machine in a vintage model) and so lead to low utilization of capital as well as labor, and thus to the symptoms of a general depression; alternatively, with different values for the relevant elasticities, it may make for more intensive use of capital and thus to excess supply in the labor market only. Also ambiguous is the effect on labor's distributive share, which depends on whether the elasticity of demand for labor is more or less than one.

Keynesian theory acknowledges that excessive real wages *could* lead to unemployment — who could deny it? — but it does not regard this as the main cause in practice. Our conclusions, which follow, are broadly consistent with that; but we do not write off the influence of real wage rates altogether. There is no *a priori* objection to involving both Keynesian and non-Keynesian influences in the explanation of unemployment.

The extreme version of the pre-Keynesian hypothesis, viz. that *all* major movements in unemployment are traceable to the behavior of real wage rates, is easily seen from the historical record to be erroneous.* It is hopeless as an explanation of the single most important change in unemployment in the course of the past century, namely its fall across World War II (when real wages and labor's share both *rose* to an unusual extent). Nor is it promising as an explanation for cyclical fluctuations, which have accounted for a major part of unemployment over the average of all years. However, there are certain historical phases in relation to which the hypothesis is more plausible.

(1) The first has already been discussed. Some of the unemployment experienced before 1914 arose because the minimum supply price of labor (as determined by the opportunity cost and disutility of work and by what could be had from private or public charity) exceeded its marginal product at full employment. The marginal product of some workers in those days, e.g. the elderly, must have been very near zero. This kind of unemployment cannot be described as a malfunctioning of labor markets, but neither was it Keynesian unemployment.

(2) Real wages (product-wages) per man-hour rose more rapidly between 1913 and 1924 than in any other phase before 1960 (Table 6.5); and their rate of growth exceeded that of output per man-hour by a larger margin than in any other phase at all. Weekly wage rates more than doubled between 1916 and 1920, and the effect on labor costs was greatly increased by the extremely large reductions in hours of work in 1919 (p. 71, above; see also Dowie 1975). The extreme labor militancy of 1919 that brought this about was the British counterpart of the unrest that had caused revolution in Russia and soon came near to causing it in Germany. There was thus a large shift in the distribution of income toward labor, a shift only partly reversed later in the interwar period.

Was the high cost of labor an independent (non-Keynesian) source of unemployment in the late 1920's? Or is it better regarded merely as an aspect of an unrealistic exchange rate that squeezed employers between domestic money wages and world prices? Certainly, reversion to the prewar exchange rate inhibited price rises and the restoration of profit

---

*We are disregarding here the near-tautological version of the hypothesis, according to which all unemployment and all changes in unemployment are traceable to the behavior of real wages because the effect of any other influences that might be at work could always be offset by a sufficient adjustment in the real wage. This version of the hypothesis is of some theoretical interest, but it is no use to the historian of actual events, whose task is to explain the origins of differences between periods.

margins. However, the shift to labor had already occurred in 1920, when the exchange rate was floating and the economy was not yet in depression. Indeed, labor's share of GNP was actually higher in 1920–24 than it was in the late 1920's (Fig. 6.1). To restore the profit margins of the early 1920's to the level of 1913 would have required prices to rise some 10 percent relative to wages. Weak as labor's bargaining position was in the 1920's, the social environment would surely have made this difficult to achieve, whatever the policy adopted on the exchange rate. It follows that the rise in labor costs immediately after World War I probably did play some independent part in reducing profitability and employment in the following years.

To the extent that the rise in labor costs on this occasion was due to the shortening of hours, it was of course accompanied by a reduction in the supply of labor, as well as a reduction in the demand for it. It is therefore only a possibility, not a necessary consequence, that it led to an increase in involuntary unemployment.

(3) It is interesting to note that the only other occasion before World War II when there was a major nationwide reduction in hours of work, namely the early 1870's, was also followed by above-average unemployment. On this occasion, as indeed in the 1920's, it is difficult to separate the effects of the reduction in hours from the effects of the ordinary cyclical reaction from a violent boom—a boom that had itself been partly responsible for the reduction in hours by increasing the bargaining power of labor.

(4) The final period for consideration is the most recent one, 1966–73. Real wages grew more rapidly in this period than in any other. Their rate of growth also exceeded the rate of growth of productivity by more than in any other peacetime period. As was seen in Chapter 6, the excess over productivity growth was partly accounted for by a rise in employers' National Insurance contributions—a tax on employment that in the circumstances of the time could not be fully passed on. The effect was augmented by S.E.T. during part of the period. It is reasonable to suppose that these imposts contributed to depressing the demand for labor in those years, partly by discouraging employers from retaining their labor force through recessions. Price control, delays in passing cost increases on in higher prices, and the absence of inflation accounting helped to ensure that the reduced demand for labor was more than just temporary. As far as S.E.T. is concerned, the effects on employment in the service industries were of course intended, but it was not foreseen that the outcome would be a reduction in *total* employment.

There is therefore some reason to suppose that in the 1920's, in the period after 1966, and possibly in the late 1870's and early 1880's rises in the real cost of labor contributed to increasing unemployment. On each of these occasions, however, the effects are difficult to separate from those of other influences tending in the same direction.

Money

No major school of economists holds that monetary factors are the chief determinants of the long-run rate of growth of real output. However, monetary factors are usually agreed to be among the forces affecting demand at current prices. The monetarist's view is that they are the paramount forces, and hence that the decomposition of demand into the national-accounting categories of expenditure is at best of secondary interest and at worst misleading.

We may distinguish three types of approaches to these matters.

(1) The orthodox Keynesian position: changes in the quantity of money (M) can be important, but their effects are much qualified by changes in the velocity of circulation (V), and in any case changes in M are largely induced not autonomous.

(2) The crude monetarist position: changes in M are autonomous and are the main determinant of changes in money income.

(3) The newer monetarist position, adapted to open economies: under fixed exchange rates, changes in M in an individual country cannot be treated as autonomous because they are affected by the balance of payments; however, the relationships involved are in principle regular and predictable.

A separate area of debate is the relative extent to which changes in money demand (however originating) impinge on prices and output. On all but the most extreme hypotheses, however, it is granted that variations in the degree of excess demand can persist for periods long enough to be significant.

Table 10.8 presents growth rates for our standard periods in the four elements in the equation of exchange $MV = PT$.* The results give some support to both the Keynesian and the newer monetarist positions.

Consider first the three periods 1891–1913, 1924–37, and 1951–64. In these three periods the movements in M were practically identical to those in T. This result is at first sight very surprising. Making the

---

*T is defined as total final expenditure at constant market prices, and P as the corresponding price deflator. If T is defined instead as real GDP, the results are broadly similar.

TABLE 10.8
Growth of Monetary Variables, 1891–1973
(Annual percentage growth rates)

Period	Money stock[a] (M)	Income-velocity[b] (V)	Price deflator (P)	Total final expenditure — At constant prices (T)
Peacetime phases:				
1891–1913[c]	2.2%	0.3%	0.5%	2.0%
1924–1937	2.0	– 1.2	– 1.0	1.8
1951–1964	2.9	2.9	2.7	3.1
1964–1973	6.3	3.2	6.2	3.3
Wartime phases:				
1913–1924	7.6	– 2.2	5.6	– 0.2
1937–1951	7.0	0.8	6.3	1.5

Source: Basic statistics (Appendix N); Sheppard 1971; Table (A) 3.3: Bank of England 1975.
[a]Currency in circulation with the public and deposits with UK banks, at current prices.
[b]Defined as a residual: $\hat{V} = \hat{P} + \hat{T} - \hat{M}$, where $\hat{V}$, $\hat{P}$, etc., are the average annual growth rates of V, P, etc.
[c]The standard pre-1914 periods cannot be used here because the data on the money stock before 1891 are unreliable.

money stock grow at the same rate as (potential) real output is the policy for price stability prescribed by the Chicago School. But no one has suggested it is a policy that the British monetary authorities deliberately followed in those periods. It is apparent, moreover, that insofar as they did follow it unwittingly, the promised price stability did not materialize. The difference between the annual percentage rates of growth of *M* and *T* in the three periods were 0.2, 0.2, and – 0.2. These give no hint of their quite divergent price movements: 0.5 percent, – 1.0 percent and 2.7 percent, respectively. Since *MV* = *PT*, the movements in *P* were nearly identical to those in *V*. Differences between the three periods in the rate of change of *V* were much larger than the differences between them in the rate of change of *M*.

A crude monetarist explanation of these data clearly does not get off the ground. But the findings are not quite so inconsistent with the newer version of monetarism. In all these periods there were fixed exchange rates. Under strict gold standard assumptions, there would be no room at all for autonomous changes in *M*; *M* would adjust itself in such a way as to keep prices in line with world prices. On this reckoning, the match between the movements of *M* and *T* would not be so surprising. If *T* were (exogenously) rising fast, there would have to be a correspondingly fast rise in *M*, to prevent prices from getting out of line with world levels. The conformity of the movements of *V* and *P* might (perhaps with some difficulty) be explained by the effect of expected price changes on *V*. The behavior of *P* would then fall to be explained by world forces, which might or might not be monetary in origin, rather than by domestic ones. Any differences between periods in the pressure of demand would have to be explained in some other way. The model is obviously oversimplified, as well as leaving important aspects unexplained: British prices and world prices did not move so closely together as the model implies, and the domestic pressure of demand did have some independent effect on prices, especially in the postwar period. With these qualifications, the model does have some plausibility as applied to the three periods in question.

The experience of the other three periods—the two wars and 1964–73—was much more in accord with the crude quantity theory, abnormally high increases in M being matched by abnormally high increases in P (though there were also some substantial differences in the behavior of V). M rose much faster between 1964 and 1973 than it had done earlier in the postwar period, and so did P, with relatively little apparent effect on T and without much change in the rate of increase of V. The monetary background of the 1964–73 and transwar price increases was thus altogether different from that of the price increase in the earlier postwar period.*

The contrast between the first set of periods (pre-1914, 1924–37, 1951–64) and the second (the two war periods and post-1964, to which the Napoleonic War might be added) can then naturally be attributed to the absence in the latter of fixed exchange rates. The ultimate reason why exchange rates were not fixed in these periods was, of course, that the pressure of circumstances gave the authorities little choice. But once exchange rates had ceased to be fixed, there was more scope for autonomous (i.e. discretionary) movements in the money supply and for effects on prices of the type predicted by the quantity theory. It does not, of course, necessarily follow that changes in M were in fact autonomous or can usefully be treated as an independent variable.

It would take us far from our main theme to explore these matters fully. Enough has been said to indicate that the behavior of the money supply does not provide a short-cut explanation to differences between periods in the pressure of demand or prices. In what follows (here and in later chapters) we shall, within the framework of a generally

*In comparing the two transwar periods, it should be noted that M actually fell between 1920 and 1924, as did P. There was no corresponding period of fall after World War II. Any monetary causes contributing to the opposite movement in the level of activity across the two wars are no doubt to be found in this contrasting experience, rather than in the minor difference in the rate of growth of M between the two periods 1913–24 and 1937–51 taken as a whole.

income-and-expenditure approach, endeavor to take account of monetary factors where they are relevant, without, we hope, thereby begging any theoretical questions.

So much, for the time being, on the pressure of demand relative to supply. We turn now to the rate of growth of demand.

THE COMPONENTS OF THE GROWTH OF DEMAND

The rates of growth of the major components of demand at constant prices between the usual benchmark years* are shown in Table 10.9. As one would expect, consumers' expenditure grew at much the same rate as GDP in all periods except across the two wars: it grew slightly more than GDP across World War I and considerably less than GDP across World War II. Within the shorter postwar cycles, there was, naturally, more irregularity: the variations between cycles in the rate of growth of consumption were rather less than those in GDP up to 1964 and rather more after 1964.

The volume of public authorities' current expenditure on goods and services (P.A.C.E.) grew more rapidly than GDP in all periods except the postwar period. Over the whole period from 1873 P.A.C.E. was the fastest growing component of GDP. In the postwar period, however, contrary to common belief, it grew consistently slower than GDP. This was mainly the result of falling military expenditure.[11] The volume of nonmilitary expenditure also grew less rapidly than GDP in 1951–64, but it grew more rapidly than GDP in 1964–73. The unit cost of P.A.C.E. rose relative to GDP prices in the postwar period to a greater extent than in earlier periods; this could represent in part a greater unrecorded quality improvement in P.A.C.E. than in previous periods and hence a greater underestimate than in the past of its growth in real terms. Hence the growth of P.A.C.E. measured at cost (i.e. deflated by GDP prices) was greater than its growth measured in volume (i.e. deflated by its own prices, as in Table 10.9). However, even measured at cost, its growth in 1951–64 was less than that of GDP. It grew more than GDP in 1964–73, but not by such a large margin as in 1873–1913 or 1924–37.[12]

We can take a step nearer to identifying the sources of changes in demand, without abandoning an essentially descriptive approach, by expressing the components of the growth of demand in the elementary

*Except 1856–73, because no satisfactory expenditure-side estimates of GDP exist for years before 1870. However, estimates for investment, imports, exports, and net income from abroad are available back to 1856 and, together with income-side estimates of GDP, they enable calculations for 1856–73 to be made for Tables 10.4, 10.5, and 10.10.

Keynesian terms used earlier in analyzing the sources of differences between periods in the level of $Y/\bar{Y}$. This is done in Table 10.10. As is appropriate in this context, all series are here expressed at current prices deflated by implicit GDP prices. The contribution of the growth in a particular item to GDP growth therefore includes the growth in its own price relative to average prices, as well as the growth in its volume. The contributions of the components in each row are additive.[13]

In a steady state, investment and exports, together with income from abroad if any, would be the only exogenous sources of growth, and their contributions would be in proportion to their shares in national income. In fact, over the period 1856–1973 as a whole, investment and exports contributed almost equally to the growth of GDP. Exports were in all periods larger absolutely, but investment had the faster growth rate.[14]

Investment and exports were important in different periods. Investment made a major contribution to GDP growth in all periods after 1924. The contribution of exports was more spasmodic; it was greatest in 1856–1913, 1937–51, and 1964–73.

Change in the propensity to save, s, had a small negative effect on GDP growth over the period as a whole (i.e. s rose). It was of impor-

TABLE 10.9

Growth of the Components of Demand at Constant Prices, 1873–1973

(Annual percentage growth rates)

Period	Consumers' expenditure	Public authorities' current expenditure	Gross domestic fixed capital formation	Exports of goods and services	Total final expenditure	Imports of goods and services	GDP[a]
Peacetime phases:							
1873–1913	1.7%	3.3%	1.5%	2.6%	1.9%	2.7%	1.8%
1924–1937	1.9	3.5	3.8	−1.0	1.8	1.2	1.9
1951–1973	2.8	1.9	4.9	4.3	3.1	4.6	2.9
Wartime phases:							
1913–1924	0.1	1.4	1.2	−2.1	−0.2	0.6	−0.4
1937–1951	0.6	4.3	1.2	2.1	1.5	−0.2	1.8
Post-WWII cycles:							
1951–1955	3.0	2.3	6.3	3.4	2.9	3.3	2.9
1955–1960	2.8	0.0	5.6	2.7	2.9	4.4	2.6
1960–1964	3.3	2.5	6.7	3.1	3.6	3.4	3.6
1964–1968	2.0	2.3	5.0	5.3	2.8	4.3	2.5
1968–1973	3.3	2.1	1.8	6.9	3.6	7.5	2.8
1873–1973	1.6%	2.9%	2.5%	1.9%	1.9%	2.2%	1.8%

[a]GDP at constant market prices, estimated from the expenditure side.

TABLE 10.10

Contribution of Exogenous Demand-Side Forces to the Growth of Gross Domestic Product, 1856–1973

(Annual percentage growth rates)

Period	Investment[a]	Exports	Income from abroad	Saving propensity	Import propensity[b]	Total GDP growth[c]
Peacetime phases:						
1856–1873	0.8%	2.8%	0.3%	−0.7%	−1.1%	2.1%
1873–1913	0.3	1.4	0.3	−0.1	−0.1	1.8
1924–1937	1.3	−1.4	0.2	−0.3	2.1	1.9
1951–1964	2.0	0.3	0.0	−0.9	1.6	3.0
1964–1973	1.5	2.7	0.1	0.1	−1.7	2.7
Wartime phases:						
1913–1924	−0.1	−1.9	−0.3	1.7	0.2	−0.4
1937–1951	1.4	3.0	−0.2	−0.8	−1.6	1.8
1856–1973	0.9%	1.1%	0.1%	−0.2%	0.0%	1.9%

Note: Writing $\hat{I}$, $\hat{X}$, $\hat{A}'$, $\hat{s}$, and $\hat{m}$ for the annual growth rates of I, X, A $(1 − s − m)$, s, and m, all as defined in the text, the sources of growth are measured as follows:

Investment	$w_I \hat{I}$		$w_I = a_I/(a_I + a_X + a_{A'})$
Exports	$w_X \hat{X}$		$w_X = a_X/(a_I + a_X + a_{A'})$
Income from abroad	$w_A \hat{A}$	where	$w_{A'} = a_{A'}/(a_I + a_X + a_{A'})$
Saving propensity	$-w_s \hat{s}$		$w_s = a_s/(a_s + a_m)$
Import propensity	$-w_m \hat{m}$		$w_m = a_m/(a_s + a_m)$

The a's are the geometric means of the values of the series in the first and last years of the period.
[a]Measured as gross domestic fixed capital formation plus half stock-building.
[b]Measured as imports of goods and services minus half stock-building.
[c]GDP at constant market prices estimated from the expenditure side.

tance in the trans–World War I period when s fell. In all other periods (except 1964–73) s rose to a greater or lesser extent, the largest rises begin in 1856–73, 1937–51, and 1961–64. The two transwar movements in s were in the opposite direction from those of other components of demand and thus had a stabilizing (and no doubt largely induced) character.

CONCLUSIONS

Let us summarize the main conclusions of this chapter in chronological order, taking account at the same time of what was said in Chapters 3 and 5 about the degree of utilization of labor and capital.
Pre-1914 period. At cyclical peaks, capital and skilled labor were both fairly fully utilized, but serious excess demand for these factors occurred rarely. Unskilled labor was chronically in excess supply (especially in London), though the excess supply had a long-run tendency to diminish. Foreign trade was the main proximate source of the growth of demand in 1856–73 and remained so, though somewhat diminished, in 1873–1913.

Interwar period. The pressure of demand, after 1920, was by every criterion lower on average than before 1914. Cycle peaks were at a lower level and the shortfall of troughs below peaks was greater. All classes of expenditure, except stock-building, fluctuated more than in either the pre-1914 period or the postwar period. The direct and multiplier effects of the fall in exports relative to full employment output, together with the fall in income from abroad, provide a full proximate explanation of why the level of activity was lower on average than before 1914. It is possible that one of the underlying contributory causes was the abnormally rapid rise in real wages relative to GDP between 1913 and 1924, though the effect of this factor is difficult to separate from others. Investment was a much larger proximate source of growth of demand within the interwar period than it had been before 1914, and foreign trade a much smaller one.

Postwar period. By every criterion the pressure of demand was higher than in earlier periods. This was much as in other industrial countries, though the tendency in Britain for the pressure of demand to fall somewhat within the postwar period was not shared abroad. For the first time labor shortages became regular. In manufacturing they were confined mainly to skilled labor and to cycle peaks; in other sectors they were probably more general. The amplitude of cycles in total output was only moderately less than before 1914, and the average extent of pressure on capital capacity was likewise only moderately greater than before 1914. Until toward the end of the 1960's, however, the cyclical fluctuations in employment were much smaller than those in output. This was a contrast to earlier periods, when the magnitude of the two had been much the same (and indeed, if hours of work are taken into account, probably greater in employment than in output). Prices, too, no longer fluctuated cyclically as they had formerly done — a change that may have made it easier for employers not to reduce employment so much in recessions. The timing of fluctuations in different industries was more uniform than it had been in earlier periods. There was a mild upward tendency in unemployment throughout the postwar period. After the mid-1960's a more pronounced reduction became apparent in the pressure of demand for labor, taking the form particularly of a reversion to a larger output-elasticity of employment over the cycle. There was probably also some structural mismatch.

Both exports and investment contributed to the higher level of demand in the postwar period compared with the interwar period, investment being the more important. Direct government injection of demand did not contribute, but government policy may have contributed in other ways to the maintenance of a higher average level of activity, by the devaluation of 1949, by the timing of fiscal and monetary measures, and by effects on confidence.

Fluctuations in exports were much smaller than in earlier periods and were no longer the mainstay of the cycle. Fluctuations in consumption played a much larger part in the cycle than they did before 1914.

Exports were the main proximate source of growth across World War II. Foreign trade contributed much more to the growth of demand within the postwar period than it had in the interwar period. Its contribution in the postwar period was not greatly different from what it had been before 1914. The reason why demand in total grew faster than before 1914 lay in the faster growth of investment.

It remains in the ensuing chapters to consider what caused investment and foreign trade to behave as they did. The behavior of investment is relevant both to the generation of demand and, directly, to the rate of growth of TFI. Trends in foreign trade and payments do not contribute directly to the growth of TFI (overseas assets are not included in TFI as here defined); but in addition to affecting demand, they had some indirect influence on the rates of growth of TFI and TFP.

CHAPTER ELEVEN

Investment: Introduction

THEORETICAL CONSIDERATIONS

This chapter and the next two are about the causes of trends in investment. The conceptual framework is that private investment (and public investment insofar as it is governed by economic considerations) is determined by the intersection of schedules of the marginal efficiency of investment (MEI) and the supply price of finance (SPOF). This is not inconsistent with investment functions based on the acceleration principle or on profitability. MEI is affected by expectations about demand, about absolute profitability, and about the relative profitability of alternative methods of production. Some variables, like labor supply, may have opposite effects on MEI through these several channels and hence have ambivalent effects overall.

THE PRINCIPAL TRENDS

This section shows the main trends in investment, disaggregated by broad industrial sectors, by types of assets, and by public and private sectors. Comparisons between periods are similar, though not identical, whether we take the ratio of investment to GNP as the measure or the rate of growth of the capital stock. The industrial and commercial sector was most largely responsible for investment being higher in the postwar period than earlier though the investment-GNP ratio was also higher than earlier in the other two broad sectors (utilities, transport, and public and professional services; dwellings). There was a smooth long swing in total fixed investment within the postwar period; it arose from sectoral movements of markedly different pattern and timing. Public-sector investment was a significantly larger proportion of the total in the postwar period than in the interwar period, but when correction is made for the changed coverage of the public sector, there is little difference between the two periods, and the sometime-public sec-

tor's share in nonresidential fixed investment was actually lower in the postwar period than in the interwar period. The flattening-out in investment at the end of the postwar period came mainly from the public sector.

THE CAPITAL-OUTPUT RATIO

There is no a priori *presumption about whether the secular movement of the constant-price capital-output ratio (K/Y) in the economy as a whole will be upward or downward. In fact it was slightly upward. On theoretical grounds it is to be expected that K/Y will in the long run fall (rise) relative to the average in sectors with above-average (below-average) TFP growth. This duly occurred. Since the growth of TFP and the growth of output were correlated, this produced in all periods a negative interaction component in the three items, into which change in overall K/Y may be composed sectorally:*

$$Intra\text{-}industry \quad = \quad \sum \frac{y}{Y} \, \Delta \frac{k}{y}$$

$$Structural \quad = \quad \sum \left(\frac{k}{y} - \frac{K}{Y} \right) \Delta \frac{y}{Y}$$

$$Interaction \quad = \quad \sum \Delta \frac{y}{Y} \, \Delta \frac{k}{y}$$

The structural component was positive in most periods (all periods if dwellings are excluded), reflecting the increasing weight to be expected of capital-intensive industries as the capital-labor ratio increases over time. Movements of the intra-industry component were the least systematic of the three and gave signs of being influenced by disequilibrium elements, as well as by responses to changes in the equilibrium capital-intensity and structural shifts within sectors.

In early chapters we have treated the level of capital accumulation as a given. In this chapter and the next two we consider what determined it.

Investment in the postwar period, though high by historical standards, was lower than in most other advanced countries. There has been much debate about whether this should be regarded as the cause or the consequence of the British growth rate having been lower than elsewhere. Denison (1967, 1968) has pushed the argument a stage further by suggesting that capital per worker was lower in Britain than in other advanced countries not only in 1964, but also early in the postwar period and hence, presumably, already before World War II. Such international comparisons raise the question of whether there *ought* to have been more investment in Britain, both in the postwar period and earlier; and they raise the question of whether the investment that was done was of the right kind. These questions are not easy to answer, and they are in principle difficult to separate from the question of residual efficiency. However, we shall give some attention to them, as well as to the "positive" question of what caused investment to behave as it did.

THEORETICAL CONSIDERATIONS

There is no generally agreed theoretical framework for analyzing and explaining long-run trends in capital accumulation. In the simple neoclassical growth model, capital accumulation is viewed as a more or less passive (though not necessarily unimportant) concomitant of growth. In this model the growth rate of output in the steady state is determined by the underlying forces of population growth and technical progress, augmented by capital accumulation to an extent that depends on the capital-elasticity of output in the production function. A certain proportion of income is saved, and so as income increases, investment and hence the capital stock grow too. If the growth rate and the propensity to save are constant, the capital stock grows at the same rate as output, and capital per worker grows at the same rate as output per worker. A further feature of this model is that if technical progress is neutral (in the sense of Harrod), the rate of profit remains constant over time, and so does the distribution of income between labor and capital. The steady state with constant capital-output ratio is taken as the "normal" case of economic growth, though it is recognized that there may be cyclical or other departures from it.

This model of steady-state growth is subject to many qualifications. Some of these give investment a more central role in growth.

In the first place, if the investment-income ratio is not constant over time, capital per worker will grow at a rate different from the steady-state rate. How much effect this will have on output will depend on the elasticities in the production function (understanding them in the broadest possible sense to allow for vintage effects, induced changes in technical progress, etc.). If these elasticities are high, changes in the investment-income ratio may have a major effect on the growth rate and may be more important than any exogenous changes in the rate of technical progress in explaining differences between periods in the growth rate of output.*

In the second place, it is obviously inappropriate in the study of British economic growth to assume full employment or even a constant proportion of unemployment.

In the third place, the propensity to save cannot be taken as exogenously given: it may, for example, be affected by investment opportunities. In the British case, capital export provides another important reason why domestic investment — our concern in this chapter — cannot be taken as determined by full-employment savings.

For such reasons as these, the level of investment cannot be taken to be wholly determined, as it is in the extreme neoclassical model, by an exogenously given propensity to save on the one hand and full-employment income on the other. The investment function has to be treated as something of importance in its own right, as do the expectations that enter into it. Unfortunately, the theory of the investment function, especially in the long run, is not one of the strongest points in economic theory.

The following remarks are framed with reference to nonresidential private investment. However, they are also applicable, with certain modifications, to private investment in dwellings, and they are relevant to public investment insofar as it is determined by economic rather than political considerations.

The most widely accepted investment function is the modified-acceleration principle (capital-stock-adjustment principle). This asserts that there exists a certain capital-output ratio that is optimal for the firm, this ratio being determined by technology (including the pattern of consumer demand) and factor prices. Investment is such as to bring the capital stock, possibly with a lag, into this desired ratio to expected output.† What determines the desired capital-output ratio and the expected output at any given time are then matters for study. The desired

---

*In the limiting case where there are no diminishing returns to investment, the model becomes completely capital-dominated and conforms to the Harrod model of warranted growth.

†There will also be an optimal rate of scrapping of old equipment. This will enter into the determination of gross investment.

capital-output ratio is not, of course, to be thought of in a purely engineering sense. There is scope for variation by varying the relative weights in the economy of industries with different capital intensity. Another aspect concerns risk. Expected output is not a fixed magnitude. It has a range of uncertainty. There is therefore scope for variation in the extent to which businesses find it worthwhile to run the risk of excess capacity and install enough capital to be able to meet the demand should demand turn out to be at the higher end of the possible range. It is to be noted, in this context, that expected output is itself a complicated concept (unless demand curves are supposed to be vertical): it is the output that the firm expects to be the most profitable to produce, and it is therefore affected by future costs, as well as by further demand. Uncertainty can therefore stem from the difficulty of predicting changes in relative prices, as well as from doubts about real demand.

The desired capital-output ratio and the expected level of output will be affected to a greater or lesser extent by the underlying real forces, including both population growth and technical progress and the propensity to save. If these dominate, a model based on the acceleration principle will conform closely to the neoclassical model. If, however, such forces as entrepreneurial psychology and monetary conditions are what mainly determine the expected output and the desired capital-output ratio, the result will be a more Harrodian one.

In what follows, we shall bear in mind the modified-acceleration principle as a general guideline. We have found it more convenient, however, to arrange our discussion in terms of an implicit investment function, regarding investment decisions as determined by the interaction of two schedules, one defining the marginal efficiency of investment (MEI) and the other the supply price of finance (SPOF). This corresponds to the Keynesian approach, with the more general notion of the supply price of finance substituted for Keynes's "rate of interest." An advantage of this approach is that the analysis of the forces affecting MEI is relevant not only to the determination of investment, but also to the consideration of its effects on output and to the counterfactual consideration of the hypothetical effects of alternative levels of investment.

The line between the forces affecting SPOF and the forces affecting MEI can be drawn in various ways. For example, a reduction in company taxation can be viewed as reducing SPOF or as increasing MEI (or both). The following conceptualization seems most appropriate in the context of a study of long-run growth.

The MEI on a single investment project is the rate at which the stream of quasi-rents expected by a firm's management to accrue from that project must be discounted in order to equal its cost (measuring both quasi-rents and cost at constant prices). It is defined regardless of how the expected quasi-rents will be distributed between the various parties with a claim on them (holders of existing equity, buyers of newly issued equities, creditors, the government as tax receiver) and regardless also of how the investment is financed. It thus measures the expected real return from an act of investment. The MEI *schedule* for the firm consists of the MEI from different amounts of investment, beginning with the most profitable.

SPOF is the minimum rate of return (as just defined) that an investment project must have in order that the project should not be expected by the firm's management to make the initial equity-holders worse off than they would otherwise have been. This definition includes in SPOF, rather than in MEI, all considerations regarding taxation and also (because of the definition in terms of constant prices) considerations regarding the relative prices of capital goods and final output. Both SPOF and MEI, as defined, are subjective concepts not susceptible to direct observation.

Since expectations enter into the definitions of MEI and SPOF, it is inherent that those definitions must strictly speaking relate to an individual firm. It is at this level that investment decisions are made. However, it is convenient for many purposes to think of MEI and SPOF schedules in the aggregate (whether for investment as a whole or for categories of investment). For this purpose one may take the MEI and SPOF schedules of a representative firm, appropriately scaled up, as the aggregate schedules.

The level of the MEI schedule is affected by (1) expectations about the level of demand for the final product of the representative firm; (2) expectations about profitability (quasi-rents) at any future level of output of the representative firm's product; and (3) expectations about the relative profitability of alternative methods (including more or less capital-intensive methods) of producing a given output. These expectations in turn may be determined to a greater or lesser extent by extrapolating the recent past, by correct foresight of future real trends, and by purely psychological considerations.

The direction in which certain forces will affect MEI is obvious. Unfavorable effects will flow from expectations of a low general level of final demand, the initial presence of excess capital capacity, a low rate

of embodied technical progress, a capital-saving bias in technical progress, or low profitability on account of, say, foreign competition; and
favorable effects from the opposite conditions. More ambivalent is the
effect of a high or rising real wage relative to the price of the product,
and of low or diminishing availability of labor (supposing that labor is
not in perfectly elastic supply to the representative firm). These will
tend to depress expected quasi-rents and hence to depress the level of
output that firms expect to be the most profitable. But they will tend to
increase the *relative* profitability of capital-intensive methods of production. The net effect on investment depends on which effect prepon-
derates.* The theoretical issues here are complicated. But the paramount importance of expectations is clear. If an existing labor shortage
does not adversely affect expectations about future output, it *will* at
least for the time being encourage investment. But if entrepreneurs
persist in the expectation of rapidly growing output in the face of labor
shortage and seek to achieve it by high investment, the profit rate is
liable to fall, unless of course a fully offsetting change in the pace or
bias of technical progress is induced; and the encouragement to investment may thus not be sustained.

The forces affecting the SPOF schedule can be more briefly enumerated. In the simplest neoclassical model, the SPOF schedule for the
economy as a whole is vertical, being given by the propensity to save.
In the simplest Keynesian model, it is horizontal, being given by a
monetarily determined rate of interest. In reality it is indeed likely to
be affected by the propensity to save (hence by profits' share) and by
monetary forces. But it is affected by other influences as well: stock
market expectations, financial institutions, taxation, the level of activity (affecting the supply of savings), the relative prices of capital
goods, and (for domestic capital formation) the attractions of net
capital export. The schedule is likely to be upward sloping.†

---

*This ambivalence appears in a number of contexts in economics. On the one hand we
have the hypothesis that labor shortage *encouraged* investment in America in the 19th century and in the UK in the postwar period. On the other hand we have, in business-cycle
theory, the hypothesis that the approach to the full-employment ceiling *discourages* investment and presages the end of the boom. We also have the widely accepted hypothesis
that in the postwar period investment and growth generally were *discouraged* in the UK,
by comparison with countries such as France, Italy, and Japan, by the nonavailability of a
reserve labor force in agriculture.

†It cannot be assumed that the investment projects with the highest MEI are the ones
with the lowest SPOF; so it would be an oversimplification to envisage a monotonically
falling MEI schedule for the economy as a whole matched by a monotonically rising SPOF
schedule. However, for the representative firm the SPOF schedule will be upward sloping, and likewise for any particular category of investment.

The actual level of investment is determined (subject to any quantity constraints such as government controls) by the intersection of the schedules of MEI and SPOF. Investment in one period is liable to affect the forces determining MEI and SPOF in the next, with possibilities of positive or negative feedback: through the level of activity on the one hand and the size of the capital stock on the other (as in Harrod's growth model and in trade-cycle theory) and possibly through other channels as well, such as induced changes in the rate or bias of technical progress.

The MEI schedule is usually understood to describe the functional relationship between the amount of investment (in constant prices) and the rate of return. So defined, it is subject to a trend shift over time as the economy grows. For our purposes, it is more convenient to think of investment in the MEI function, and likewise in the SPOF function, as a percentage addition to the capital stock. With this unit of measurement there is no presumption of a trend shift in the function.

The foregoing analysis in terms of MEI and SPOF is a framework of thought rather than a hypothesis. Its relation to the most generally favored explicit investment function, the modified-acceleration principle, is plain enough. Both incorporate elements relating to the expected rate of growth of output, the initial capital stock, and the desired capital-intensity of production. Analysis in terms of MEI and SPOF can also easily be related to investment functions based on profitability. Actual profitability affects MEI insofar as it affects expected profitability; it may also affect SPOF. It may be noted that though a fall in expected profitability relative to SPOF will tend to depress investment, the same is not necessarily true of a fall in expected profitability that is matched by an equal fall in SPOF. The latter combination may even have a net favorable effect on investment, by increasing the optimum capital-intensity of production.

THE PRINCIPAL TRENDS: DISAGGREGATION BY INDUSTRIAL
SECTORS, ASSETS, AND PUBLIC AND PRIVATE SECTORS

We shall (in Chapter 13) treat fixed investment in three separate classes: industry and commerce; utilities, transport, and public and professional services; and dwellings. Table 11.1 summarizes the chief data and shows the relative importance of those three classes in peacetime periods (along with agriculture, which after the 1870's was a small part of the total). As we see, the industrial and commercial sector made the largest contribution to the rises in the investment-income ratio and in the rate of growth of the capital stock in the postwar period compared with earlier periods. Investment in utilities, transport, and public and professional services was also substantially higher than in the earlier periods. Investment in dwellings rose in the interwar period and stayed up in the postwar period.

Broadly similar results are shown by both of the indicators in Table 11.1, investment as a percent of GNP and the rate of growth of the gross capital stock. But there are certain significant differences. First, a slightly larger proportion of GNP was devoted to investment in dwellings in the postwar period than in the interwar period, though in the interwar period the stock of dwellings grew more rapidly; the explanation lies partly in the much higher cost of dwellings relative to general prices in the postwar period and partly in differences in the initial stocks in the two periods. Second, gross investment in industry and commerce was the same proportion of GNP in the interwar period as in 1874–1913, though the rate of growth of capital in this sector was lower. The main explanation here is that the capital-output ratio was high in the interwar period, because of the depression, so that a given investment-income ratio produced a relatively low rate of growth of the capital stock, but in addition, the retirements were marginally higher in the interwar period (or are assumed to have been; Fig. 5.4), so that a given amount of gross investment meant less new investment. This element of replacement must be borne in mind when considering

TABLE 11.1

Fixed Investment in Principal Sectors in Peacetime Periods, 1856–1973

Category	Agri-culture etc.	Industry and commerce	Utilities, transport, and social capital	Dwellings	Total
Share of gross fixed capital stock in 1973 (percent):	2%	34%	33%	31%	100%
Investment (percent of GNP):[a]					
1857–1873	1.2%	2.8%	3.6%	1.4%	9.0%
1874–1913	0.6	3.2	3.8	1.5	9.1
1925–1937	0.1	3.1	3.6	3.3	10.0
1952–1973	0.6	8.0	6.6	3.7	18.7
Annual growth rates of gross fixed capital (percent):					
1856–1873	0.3%	2.5%	3.0%	1.5%	2.0%
1873–1913	−0.1	2.2	2.4	1.9	2.0
1924–1937	−0.1	1.2	1.6	3.4	1.9
1951–1973	2.3	4.0	3.2	2.7	3.3

Note: Agriculture includes forestry and fishing. Industry and commerce consists of mining and quarrying, manufacturing, construction, and commerce. Utilities, transport, and social capital consists of gas, water, and electricity; transport and communications; and public and professional services.
[a] Average of annual percentages at current prices.

TABLE 11.2

Growth of Gross Domestic Fixed Assets Excluding Dwellings, 1856-1973

(Annual percentage growth rates)

Period	Buildings and works Industrial	Commercial	Other	Plant and machinery Manufacturing	Other	Road vehicles	Ships, aircraft, and railway rolling stock	Total
Peacetime phases:								
1856-1873	2.2%	1.5%	1.8%	4.4%	2.6%	3.6%	3.6%	2.2%
1873-1913	2.1	1.5	1.7	2.9	2.6	4.2	2.1	2.0
1924-1937	1.2	1.5	1.1	0.0	4.4	4.4	-0.9	1.3
1951-1973	2.8	4.8	2.7	3.7	5.1	4.8	1.6	3.5
Wartime phases:								
1913-1924	2.5	0.6	0.4	0.8	1.9	6.4	-0.3	0.9
1937-1951	1.4	0.0	0.1	2.9	1.1	0.9	-0.2	0.9
Post-WWII cycles:								
1951-1955	2.6	2.6	0.7	3.5	3.6	3.6	0.9	2.3
1955-1960	2.5	4.1	1.6	2.8	4.3	3.1	2.8	2.6
1960-1964	3.3	6.1	2.7	4.0	5.4	7.2	0.8	3.5
1964-1968	3.3	5.6	3.8	4.3	7.1	6.4	-0.3	4.5
1968-1973	2.6	5.4	4.4	3.8	5.4	4.5	3.0	4.2

Note: The 1938 break in the capital series has been eliminated.

the slow growth of the capital stock (excluding dwellings) in the interwar period. To the extent that the replacement contributed a quality improvement not allowed for in the statistics, our measures may underrate the contribution of capital investment to the growth of production in this period compared with earlier periods.

Within the postwar period the rate of growth of the gross fixed capital stock underwent a long swing, with a peak in the mid-1960's. This is shown in Figure 11.1 by moving averages that smooth out the shorter four-to-five year cycles.* The long swing was asymmetrical, the rise being much greater than the subsequent fall up to 1973. The movement in the total was, as may be seen, the outcome of substantially different movements within sectors.

The above measures disaggregate investment by industrial sector. This is the most generally useful basis of disaggregation. But investment may also be disaggregated by type of asset or by private and public sectors. The three bases of disaggregation partly overlap.

A breakdown by type of asset is given in Table 11.2. In the interwar period the only classes of fixed assets showing rapid growth (apart from dwellings, not included in this table) were nonmanufacturing plant

*The moving averages in Fig. 11.1 are carried only up to 1974, which was the peak year of investment in that cycle. Capital accumulation declined still further in the ensuing recession years.

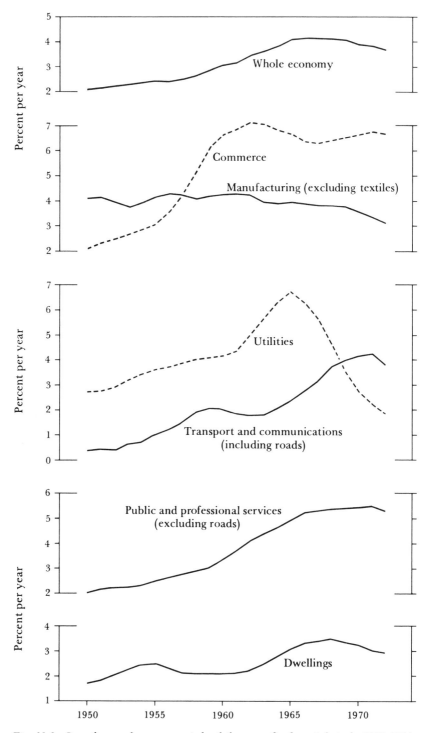

Fig. 11.1. Growth over four-year periods of the gross fixed capital stock, 1948–1974. These are average annual growth rates over four-year periods centered in the years shown; they are approximately equal to four-year moving averages of year-to-year growth rates.

TABLE 11.3

Public-Sector Fixed Investment as a Percentage of
Total Fixed Investment, 1925–1973

(Average of annual percentages at current prices)

Period	Total public-sector investment excluding dwellings		Total public-sector investment	
	Actual	Sometime-public	Actual	Sometime-public
1925–1937	31.4%	51.3%	29.6%	42.9%
1952–1973	43.6	42.8	44.7	44.2
1952–1964	43.7	42.3	45.4	44.3
1965–1973	43.4	43.6	43.7	43.9

Note: Exact estimates of investment in those industries that have at some time been in the public sector are not available. Sometime-public-sector investment is defined here and in Fig. 11.2 as investment in mining and quarrying, utilities, transport and communications (other than shipping), public and professional services, and public-sector housing. It therefore includes investment in some industries that have never been in the public sector (e.g. non-coal-mining and quarrying, private road transport, and private social services, especially education), and it excludes those parts of the iron and steel industry (and other manufacturing industries) that were in public ownership during the postwar period.

and machinery and road vehicles. Growth rates in all other cases were lower than in 1856–1913 except for commercial buildings, where there was no change. In the period 1937–51 the overall rate of investment was, of course, much lower, but there was also a pronounced switch within it, toward manufacturing plant and machinery and to a lesser extent industrial buildings. The rate of growth in these two important groups in 1937–51 was higher than in the interwar period; in the case of manufacturing plant and machinery, appreciably so.

All classes of assets (with the exception of ships, aircraft, and railway rolling stock compared with pre-1914) showed much faster growth rates after 1951 than in 1873–1913, the interwar period, or 1937–51. The biggest postwar increase compared with the interwar period was in manufacturing plant and machinery and commercial buildings. All classes of assets (except ships, aircraft, and railway rolling stock) accelerated up to the early or mid-1960's, but most experienced some slackening in growth rates thereafter.

Table 11.3 shows fixed public-sector investment as a percent of total investment for the interwar and postwar periods. The annual figures for public and private investment at constant prices are plotted in Figure 11.2.

The public sector's nonhousing capital expenditure accounted for some 31 percent of total nonhousing investment from 1925 to 1937. This is substantially less than the average postwar proportion of some 44 percent. These figures, however, are greatly affected by the differences between the two periods in the range of industries falling into the

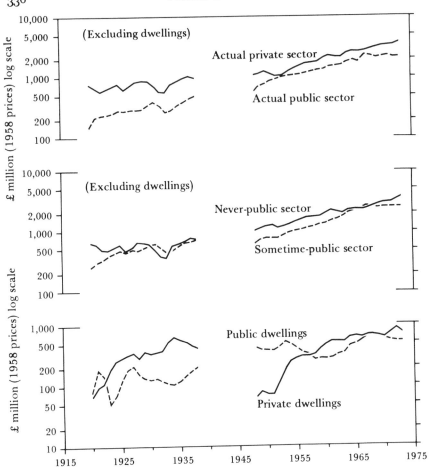

Fig. 11.2. Capital formation at constant prices in the public
and private sectors, 1920–1973

public sector (because of nationalization). If the sometime-public sector is defined so as broadly to comprise those nonmanufacturing industries that were in the public sector in the postwar period,* then over
50 percent of nonhousing investment was undertaken by the sometime-
public sector between 1925 and 1937 — a significantly higher propor-

*The exact coverage of the sometime-public sector is shown in the note to Table 11.3.
The fact that some never-public industries are included in the definition and some
sometime-public ones excluded is unimportant when compared with the benefits of having
the same coverage for both the interwar and postwar periods.

tion than the same industries and services absorbed in the postwar period.

If housing is brought into the picture, the position is rather different. Public sector house-building was a much larger proportion of all house-building in the postwar period than in the interwar period. This offset the decline between the two periods in the sometime-public sector's share in non-housing investment. As a result the sometime-public sector's share in total investment was higher postwar than interwar, by a very small amount.

The postwar period is divided in Table 11.3 into two subperiods, 1952–64 and 1965–73. There was little change between them in the public sector's average share in investment. This apparent stability, however, was the result of fluctuations within both subperiods. In the first the public sector share rose until 1953, when it reached a peak of 56 percent, then steadily decreased until 1961, by which point it had fallen to 39½ percent. After that there was a further change of direction, with the public sector gaining slightly but reaching only 43 percent of the total by 1964. This rise then continued in the second period to reach a peak of 48 percent in 1967, but from there onward the public sector share fell steadily, to stand at only 40 percent in 1973.

THE CAPITAL-OUTPUT RATIO, AGGREGATE AND SECTORAL

There is a presumption that economic growth will be accompanied by an increase in the capital-intensity of production, if that is defined to mean the capital-labor ratio. There is no such presumption about the trend in the capital-output ratio (K/Y). The implication of most models of the investment function or of economic growth is that K/Y will be constant over time unless there are specific forces tending to alter it. Such forces may of course well exist, in the form of the various forces that may cause SPOF not to be constant over time. Moreover, in addition to such cases making for nonconstancy in *desired* K/Y, an observed movement in K/Y may alternatively be a disequilibrium phenomenon, reflecting a divergence between desired and actual K/Y or else the correction of such a divergence.

Since the following chapters make frequent reference to the sectoral behavior of K/Y, especially in manufacturing, let us here consider what determines the capital-output ratio at the sectoral level.

Any presumption of constancy in K/Y for the whole economy does not imply that it will be constant in individual sectors. On the contrary, if technical progress is neutral in all sectors and differs only in its rate, and if competition equates the wage-rental ratio between sectors,

K/Y will fall in sectors with above-average rates of technical progress. Likewise, if K/Y falls generally, it may be expected to fall more in sectors with above-average rates of technical progress. This indeed proves to be the case, both as between broad sectors and as between individual manufacturing industries (see Table 8.3 and Appendix J).

Moreover, the movement of K/Y in the economy as a whole will reflect not only movements in K/Y within individual sectors, but also the effects of shifts in weight between industries of different capital-intensity. Table 11.4 decomposes the changes in the capital-output ratio in each period into three elements: intra-industry, structural (inter-industry), and interaction. It refers to fixed capital throughout, and for the economy as a whole shows a breakdown for both nine sectors and eight (including dwellings and excluding dwellings). The following comments relate to the data *with dwellings excluded*.

Over the whole period the capital-output ratio rose from its initial level in 1856 of some 2.5 by only 0.3. This was the net outcome of divergent movements in the three components. The structural element was positive in all periods and on its own would have raised the ratio by about 45 percent, i.e. from 2.5 to 3.6.

This effect is in accord with theoretical expectation. One would expect that the long-run increase in the capital-labor ratio would lead to a shift toward more capital-intensive industries. However, the data show little relationship in timing between the increase in the capital-labor ratio and the shift to capital-intensive industries. Most notably, in the postwar period capital per man-hour grew much faster than before, but the shift to capital-intensive industries, as measured by the structural term in Table 11.4, was small (and negative, if dwellings are included). Thus, though the long-run tendency of the kind postulated by theory was no doubt present, the extent of the shift to more capital-intensive industries in any one period may be taken to have been determined chiefly by the direction of technical progress and demand (and public policy).

The main factor working to offset the structural effect was the interaction element. This was negative in all periods; sectors with a rising share in GDP tended to have falling capital-output ratios. This can be regarded as part of the general tendency noted above for there to be a correlation across industries between falling costs (rising output per unit of input) and rising output. As such, it too is in accordance with theoretical expectation.

The period when both structural and interaction components were largest was 1873–1913. The chief source of these components in that period was the increase in the weight of two highly capital-intensive

TABLE 11.4
Contribution of Intra-Industry and Structural Changes to Change in the Capital-Output Ratio, 1856–1973

(Absolute changes between end-years)

Period	Total change in K/Y	Components of change		
		Intra-industry	Struc-tural	Inter-action
All sectors:[a]				
1856–1873	0.01	0.09	−0.05	−0.03
1873–1913	0.19	0.18	0.26	−0.25
1913–1924	0.27	0.15	0.17	−0.05
1924–1937	−0.17	−0.11	−0.02	−0.04
1937–1951	−0.25	−0.36	0.21	−0.10
1951–1964	0.01	0.19	−0.13	−0.05
1964–1973	0.48	0.39	0.11	−0.02
1856–1973	0.54	0.53	0.55	−0.54
All sectors other than dwellings:				
1856–1873	0.03	0.01	0.04	−0.02
1873–1913	0.10	−0.12	0.41	−0.19
1913–1924	0.24	0.12	0.17	−0.05
1924–1937	−0.35	−0.32	0.01	−0.04
1937–1951	−0.20	−0.41	0.31	−0.10
1951–1964	0.08	0.09	0.03	−0.04
1964–1973	0.44	0.34	0.13	−0.03
1856–1973	0.34	−0.29	1.10	−0.47
Manufacturing:[b]				
1924–1937	−0.72	−0.63	−0.08	−0.01
1937–1951	0.19	0.25	−0.04	−0.02
1951–1964	−0.04	−0.04	0.00	0.00
1964–1973	0.12	0.19	−0.03	−0.04
1924–1973	−0.45	−0.23	−0.15	−0.07
Manufacturing excluding textiles:				
1924–1937	−0.58	−0.53	−0.03	−0.02
1937–1951	0.17	0.12	0.04	0.01
1951–1964	0.16	0.15	0.06	−0.05
1964–1973	0.14	0.21	−0.03	−0.04
1924–1973	−0.11	−0.05	0.04	−0.10

Note: The definitions are as follows:

Intra-industry $= \sum(y/Y)\Delta(k/y)$

Structural $\quad = \sum[(k/y) - (K/Y)]\Delta(y/Y)$

Interaction $\quad = \sum\Delta(y/Y)\Delta(k/y)$

where y and k denote output and gross fixed capital stock in an individual sector and Y and K denote total output and gross fixed capital stock (all at constant prices, viz. for each period the prices of the first year of that period, except for 1856–73 and 1873–1913, where the constant prices used are those of 1907). The sum of these three is identically equal to the change in the capital-output ratio, $\Delta(K/Y)$.

The change over the whole period is calculated as the sum of the changes in the 7 subperiods shown and is related to the capital-output ratio in 1856 at 1907 prices. Different results would be obtained if one were simply to calculate the change from 1856 to 1973, but this would involve the recalculation of 1973 capital and output at 1907 prices, and so would not necessarily be more meaningful.

[a] 9 sectors: see Table 8.1. Roads are included under transport, unlike Table 8.1.
[b] 13 industries: see Table 8.6.

sectors: transport and utilities. This accounted both for the large positive structural term and for the large negative interaction term, since both sectors, though still highly capital-intensive, were becoming less so in this period. The period 1937–51 also showed substantial structural and interaction components — larger on a per-annum basis than the pre-1914 period. The large structural component in this case was due partly to a continuation of the shift toward the two highly capital-intensive sectors and partly to a new factor: a fall in the proportion of total output contributed by commerce and construction, sectors of low capital-intensity. The size of the interaction component was due largely to an unusually rapid decline in the capital-output ratio in utilities. In the interwar period, and again in the postwar period (particularly 1951–64), both structural and interaction components were small. The movement in the overall capital-output ratio thus corresponded closely to the movements in the intra-industry component.

The effect of this component, intra-industry changes, was to reduce the capital-output ratio over the period as a whole, with particularly large downward movements in 1924–37 and 1937–51, which were partially offset by a moderate rise in the postwar period.* The dominant factor at work is the one already referred to: the downward trend in the capital-output ratio in two very capital-intensive sectors, transport and utilities. In transport the ratio declined by 0.8 over the whole period, in utilities by 0.3, in both cases with a consistent fall in every one of the subperiods. These movements were themselves the result of structural shifts within the two sectors: in the one a shift away form the very capital-intensive railways toward the less capital-intensive road transport and communications industries; in the other, a shift away from the very capital-intensive water industry toward the less capital-intensive gas and electricity industries. In the remaining sectors the general trend in the capital-output ratio was upward, most notably in the postwar period for commerce[1] and for public and professional services.

The intra-industry component is the one that shows the most signs of being influenced by disequilibrium elements as opposed to responses to changes in the equilibrium capital-intensity of production. An obvious example (further discussed in Chapter 13) is the rise in 1964–73.

For manufacturing, it is possible to disaggregate further into 13 in-

---

*The situation is different, however, when dwellings are included. There was a strong and persistent upward trend in the capital-output ration for dwellings (i.e. a fall in the rate of return, since output in this sector is measured by the net rent received). Over the period as a whole this rise in the dwellings sector was more than sufficient to offset the decline in the intra-industry component for all sectors other than dwellings.

dustries for the four subperiods between 1924 and 1973. Over the period as a whole the capital-output ratio in manufacturing fell by 0.45, i.e. by about a fifth from its initial level in 1924 (at 1924 prices) of 2.35. For all manufacturing industries both the intra-industry component and the structural component contributed to this fall, with the largest shift in the former in the interwar period. However, the greater part of this movement is attributable to the changes in the textile industry, and if textiles are excluded (as in the bottom section of Table 11.4), the overall fall in the capital-output ratio for the 12 remaining industries was only 0.1. Here the interwar fall in the intra-industry component was almost offset by the upward trend in each of the three subsequent periods.

This intra-industry rise in the capital-output ratio in manufacturing in the trans–World War II and postwar years was not, however, accompanied by a marked shift toward more capital-intensive industries, and the structural term was small. As for the economy as a whole, the interaction term was negative in the postwar years, indicating that the industries that increased their share of manufacturing output tended to have falling capital-output ratios.

CHAPTER TWELVE

Investment: The Cost and Availability of Finance

TRENDS IN SPOF

Conventional measures of "the rate of interest" need to be supplemented by other indicators, such as the earnings yield on equities and measures of the availability of internal finance. Even so, they show at best only changes in the actual SPOF at prevailing levels of investment; these may or may not betoken shifts in the SPOF schedule, the relevant independent variable. However, a favorable shift in the SPOF schedule between pre-1914 and the postwar period can be inferred from the fact that in the postwar period the rate of capital accumulation was higher despite a much lower profit rate. The interwar position is unclear. Within the postwar period the SPOF schedule can be inferred to have fallen until some time in the 1960's.

INFLUENCES AFFECTING SPOF

The first possible influence on SPOF to be considered is the saving propensity (s). Much of the observed behavior of s was induced, but the rise in personal s within the postwar period and the existence of positive government s in that period were favorable autonomous features.

Before 1914 capital export was a force tending to keep SPOF higher than it would otherwise have been. Some crowding out of domestic investment in the capital market probably resulted, though not to such an extent as might be suggested by the long-swing alternations. The decline in capital exports in the 1930's and the control over capital export in the postwar period were forces tending to keep SPOF down by comparison with earlier periods. Competition between domestic and foreign investment for markets, labor, and entrepreneurship may in some periods (including postwar) have been more important than competition for finance.

An important source of trend reduction in SPOF throughout the period was reduction in capital market imperfections, notably by (1) the development of the joint-stock company and the widening of the equity market and (2) an increase in the size and product range of firms.

Inflationary expectations lowered SPOF in the 1950's and 1960's by increasing the market for equities and causing their prices to rise by more than general prices. Inflation as such increased somewhat the availability of internal finance in the earlier part of the postwar period but had the opposite effect in the 1970's.

The net effect of tax changes across World War II was probably to raise SPOF. In the course of the postwar period tax changes tended to lower SPOF until toward the end of the 1960's and thus helped to sustain manufacturing investment in the face of falling profitability. Tax considerations do not help much to explain the rise in commercial investment during the postwar period.

Inherited wartime liquidity made some small contribution to the supply of finance for investment after World War II. The relaxation of restrictions on bank lending assisted the supply of finance in the course of the postwar period but not to the full extent indicated by the increase in bank lending.

The large rise in the relative price of capital goods across World War II — unique to that period — increases the burden falling on other explanations of the historically high average level of investment in the postwar period. The relaxation of physical controls contributed to the rise of investment in the early 1950's.

Of the various causes making for the favorable shift in the SPOF schedule between pre-1914 and near the end of the postwar period, some operated fairly continuously, others only in certain periods.

TRENDS IN THE SUPPLY PRICE OF FINANCE

The traditional measure of the supply price of capital is the rate of interest on fixed-interest debt. The measure requires radical adjustment as an indicator in the postwar period, because it takes no account of the effect of expected inflation on the real cost of borrowing. That deficiency probably does not matter too much in relation to peacetime periods previous to World War II. Since changes in the general price level were then relatively small and uneven in direction and pace, they are unlikely to have generated sufficiently firm expectations to have an important effect on people's assessment of the real cost of borrowing.

A measure related to the rate of interest is the earnings yield on equities. Investment that is financed by the issue of equities will be in the interests of existing shareholders if the expected rate of return exceeds the expected rate of return on the company's existing assets at their stock market valuation.* The latter can be measured by the earnings yield (current earnings divided by stock market valuation) if it can be assumed that real quasi-rents from existing assets are expected to remain constant over time. However, if a company already has some fixed-interest debt, the market valuation of the equity will be affected by any expected future reduction in the real burden of its debt brought about by inflation. The earnings yield is therefore not an inflation-proof measure.

Because of the opposite biases that expected inflation has on nominal interest rates and earnings yields, a superior measure—which we call the composite measure—is the ratio of total earnings, including debt interest, to total market valuation, including debt. Estimates for this are available for the years after 1960 (Flemming et al. 1976b). As a measure of the cost of capital, the composite measure, like the earnings yield from which it is largely derived,[1] is subject to certain possible biases, unconnected with inflation. In particular, changes in the market's expectations about the relation between present and future quasi-rents on existing assets will alter share prices and earnings yields, without necessarily altering the required yield on new investment. (This is most apparent in the case of a company that is currently running at a loss but retains a positive market valuation because the losses are not expected to be permanent.) Moreover, the managements of companies may not identify completely with existing shareholders; they may, as an extreme example, regard them as if they were debenture-holders and treat the dividend yield (rather than the earnings yield) as the cost of new equity finance.

A further complication is taxation, which, like inflation, is important mainly in relation to the postwar period. To this point, all the measures of profit rate we have considered are before any tax. Of the

---

*In other words, the effect of new investment will be to raise the value per share, as long as the cost of the investment is less than the discounted present value of the expected stream of resulting quasi-rents, where the discount rate is that implicit in the market's valuation of the expected quasi-rents from existing assets.

measures so far mentioned of the cost of capital, the dividend yield and the earnings yield (as usually measured) are calculated before deduction of income tax but after deduction of company taxation, and are thus not fully on a par with the measures of the pre-tax profit rate. The rate of interest on fixed-interest securities and the composite measure are in principle calculated before tax; but movements in the composite measure, at least, are liable to be indirectly affected by tax changes, and the same may be true of the rate of interest.[2] The effects of taxation are so pervasive that for certain purposes it may be best not to attempt any pre-tax measure but instead to focus attention on the cost of capital net of all taxes. In that case, in order to indicate the inducement to invest, the cost of capital has to be set against a corresponding measure of the return from capital, net of all taxes (as is done in Flemming et al. 1976b).

A final possible proxy measure for the cost of capital is the *ex post* rate of profit itself. The two are not the same thing. Even if we accept that in principle firms equate SPOF to MEI, there is no presumption that the current rate of return on existing assets will correspond to MEI, i.e. to the expected rate of return over the lifetime of a new asset. It cannot even be assumed that there will be a constant relationship between them. In the first place, the one is an average concept and the other a marginal concept. Changes in the number of intra-marginal investment opportunities, in industrial structure, and in the average age or rate of growth of capital may all lead to changes in the profit rate on existing assets, even though the profit rate on new investment remains unchanged. In the second place, the *ex post* profit rate may contain disequilibrium elements, positive or negative. Over business cycles, for example, there is no presumption that fluctuations in expected profit rates on new investment have the same amplitude and timing as fluctuations in *ex post* profit rates.

However, the two are not entirely unrelated. Over a period of time, forces making for upward or downward movements in required marginal profitability are likely also to come to be reflected in *ex post* profit rates. *Ex post* profit rates do not therefore need to be entirely disregarded as indicators of the supply price of capital, provided their limitations are understood.

All the measures so far referred to are subject to limitations of one sort or another. But the various limitations do not all apply equally strongly in all periods, and by looking at a combination of them we may be able to derive a fair picture.

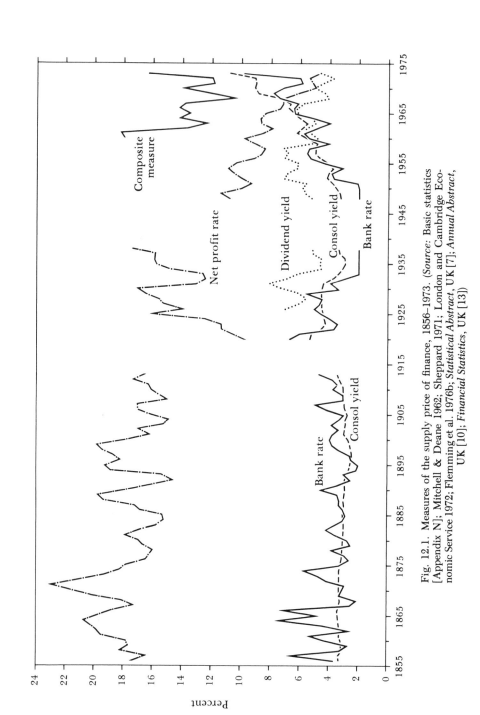

Fig. 12.1. Measures of the supply price of finance, 1856–1973. (*Source:* Basic statistics [Appendix N]; Mitchell & Deane 1962; Sheppard 1971; London and Cambridge Economic Service 1972; Flemming et al. 1976b; *Statistical Abstract, UK* [7]; *Annual Abstract, UK* [10]; *Financial Statistics, UK* [13])

Figure 12.1 shows four types of measures of the interest rate for the peacetime periods between 1856 and 1973 (Bank rate, consol yield, composite measure of cost of capital, dividend yield on equities), along with the domestic non-farm non-rent net profit rate series repeated from Figure 6.4.

All these are measures of the *cost of external* finance. They do not take account of changes in the *availability* of external finance. Such changes were important in some periods and will be referred to below. Nor do these measures give any direct indication of the cost and availability of *internal* finance. Undistributed profits are, in fact, the most important source of finance for investment. Their cost is an imputed cost and cannot be directly measured. It is reasonable to suppose that this imputed cost fluctuates less than the cost of external finance; it is unlikely that firms allow their criteria for internally financed investment projects to fluctuate from month to month with their share prices. Subject to this, we may infer the trend in the imputed cost of internal finance *relative* to that of external finance by looking at movements in the proportion of capital formation financed from the two types of source. Relevant data are shown in Tables 12.1 and 12.2.

In the light of these various indicators, we turn now to consider historical trends in the supply price of capital. It must be understood that these measures relate to the supply price of finance *at the margin*, and movements in them do not necessarily indicate shifts in the *schedule* of SPOF. We shall revert to this.

Since the postwar period is the best documented, it is convenient to work backwards.

Within the postwar period, the downward trend in the pre-tax net profit rate was accompanied in the late 1950's by a steep fall in the dividend yield and the earnings yield (not shown in Fig. 12.1).[3] This fall continued, and is reflected in the composite index, in the 1960's through 1968. The rate of interest on fixed-interest securities, on the other hand, rose. This divergence in trend was, of course, the result of the increasing prevalence of expectations of inflation and of capital gains on equities. Insofar as the fall in equity yields was the result of increasingly optimistic expectations about future real profitability, it did not as such reflect a decline in the standard of profitability to which new investment had to conform; the resulting stimulus to investment came from an increase in the expected return on capital rather than from a decline in the cost of capital (assuming that industrialists and the stock market had similar expectations). However, a consideration of the causes of the rise in equity prices (see below, pp. 362–64) suggests

TABLE 12.1

*Capital Expenditure and Sources of Finance of Industrial
and Commercial Companies, 1952–1973*

Period	Percent of gross trading profits		Percent of capital expenditure[a]					
	Capital expenditure	Savings[b]	Savings[b]	New issues	Banks	Other borrowing	Realization of liquid assets	Other
1952–1955	60%	54%	90%	10%	−1%	2%	−3%	4%
1956–1960	74	60	81	10	7	4	−6	6
1961–1964	81	57	70	11	13	4	−2	5
1965–1968	81	58	72	13	10	3	−5	7
1969–1973	98	60	62	8	33	3	−18	12

Source: BEQB, March 1967; National Income and Expenditure, UK [21], 1964–74.
[a]Includes gross fixed investment, stock-building, cash payments to acquire interests in other companies, change in hire purchase credit extended, overseas investment, and a residual item.
[b]Includes investment grants from 1967.

that at least part of it was of such a nature as to imply a genuine cheapening of finance.

After 1968 the earnings and dividend yields ceased to fall and the rate of interest continued to rise. The composite index accordingly rises. A turning point in the cost of external finance around that time is therefore indicated.

The proportion of capital expenditure financed internally fell during the 1950's and again after 1968 (Table 12.1). The fall was matched by an increase in bank finance and in "other" sources of finance (chiefly overseas sources). Insofar as the increase in bank finance in the late 1950's resulted from less tight government control over lending by banks, it represented an increase in availability of external finance; the decline in the proportion of internal finance did not therefore necessarily imply a rise in its imputed cost relative to the actual cost of external finance. However, there is little reason to doubt that the decline in self-financing after 1968 was caused partly by a decline in profitability and thus did betoken some rise in its relative imputed cost. It therefore reinforces the impression conveyed by the interest rate data that the cost of finance increased at that time, following its previous trend fall.

We consider next the trend in the cost of finance *across World War II*. A rise between the late 1930's and the early 1950's is shown for all interest rate measures,* though the profit rate fell. Was this rise in the cost of external finance offset by an increase in its availability? In the postwar period various steps were taken by the government to improve

---

*Including the earnings yield on equities, which did not fall below the average level of the 1930's till after 1960.

TABLE 12.2

Ratio of Company Savings to Company Investment, 1927–1973

(Percent)

Period	Average of annual ratios	Period	Average of annual ratios
1927–1929	147.1%[a]	1956–1960	126.0%
1936–1938	143.9[a]	1961–1964	106.5
1948–1951	134.3	1965–1968	98.8
1952–1955	176.5	1969–1973	93.0

Source: Feinstein 1972 and the sources used for it; *National Income and Expenditure*, UK [21], *1968, 1964–74*; *Report of the Commissioners of H.M. Inland Revenue*, UK [58], 1948–49: 57–76.

Note: Savings includes additions to dividend, interest, and tax reserves, and investment grants, and excludes stock appreciation. It is measured at current prices. Investment is company gross fixed capital formation and stock-building, at current prices. All companies (industrial, commercial, and financial) are included.

[a] Roughly adjusted to remove savings and investment for the companies that were public corporations in the postwar period.

the functioning of the capital market in areas where it was thought to have been operating imperfectly. Moreover, various new forms of financial intermediation evolved in the private sector. As against these, however, bank finance after World War II was subject to a new set of government restrictions. In view of the quantitative importance of bank finance, this probably more than outweighed the effects of improvements in financial institutions. Interwar company statistics do not permit an analysis of the relative importance of different sources of finance for capital expenditure along the lines of Table 12.1. We can, however, get some indication of the role of internal finance, compared with postwar, by setting estimates of company savings alongside estimates of companies' investment in real capital (Table 12.2; rather than their total capital expenditure, as shown in Table 12.1). These data indicate that companies' savings were quite large relative to their real investment in 1936–38: less large than in 1952–55, but larger than in other phases of the postwar period.*

The evidence thus suggests fairly clearly that the cost of finance was lower in the 1930's than in the 1950's (though probably not than in the 1960's). This relates, it must be understood, to the cost of finance at the margin. It does not necessarily imply that the SPOF *schedule* was lower in the 1930's than in the 1950's, given that investment was so much higher in the 1950's.

The comparison *between the 1930's and the 1920's* is straightforward. Interest rates were considerably higher in the 1920's. The

---

*In Table 12.2 subsequently nationalized parts of the company sector are excluded from the interwar figures. This adjustment is important, because the subsequently nationalized parts of the company sector had, before nationalization, made significantly less use of internal finance than the rest of the company sector.

availability of internal finance in relation to investment appears to have been about the same in the 1920's and the 1930's (Table 12.2), though the underlying data here are very unreliable.[4]

As we go back *before 1914* trends become clouded by institutional changes. The general level of interest rates was remarkably constant, though there was some fall in the 1890's and a rise thereafter. Interest rates were lower than in the 1920's, and the long-term rate was lower even than it was in the 1930's. On the other hand, the profit rate was higher before 1914 than after. The reasons for this apparent anomaly will be considered presently.

Observed changes in SPOF, which we have just reviewed, may be the result either of shifts in the SPOF schedule or of movements along it caused by shifts in the MEI schedule. Only shifts in the SPOF schedule represent independent influences on investment; it is the factors that cause those shifts that we wish to identify.

There is a further complication. Shifts in the SPOF schedule may not be exogenous; they may be caused by shifts in the MEI schedule. One way this may happen is through the multiplier: higher investment makes for higher income, which makes for higher savings. Another way it may happen is through depreciation allowances. It is considered sound business practice to provide for depreciation out of retained earnings, so a fall in the average life of capital is likely to lead to an increase in companies' gross savings, even though the return on replacement investment may actually be lower than it was formerly.

In the light of these considerations, what conclusions can be drawn about shifts over time in the SPOF schedule? The easiest comparison is between pre-1914 and the postwar period. In the postwar period the rate of growth of the capital stock was substantially higher than it was before 1914. On the other hand the profit rate was substantially lower (both the profit rate as conventionally measured and the profit rate measured at constant prices, that is to say, after allowance for change in the relative price of capital goods; Table 6.16). Even when allowance is made for possible changes in the ratio of subjective MEI to *ex post* profitability, the conclusion seems unavoidable that there was a downward shift in the SPOF schedule. Just how much difference a hypothetical shift in the SPOF schedule would have made to investment in either period is another matter. That depends on the elasticity of the MEI schedule. Thus it is possible that if the SPOF schedule had been lower before 1914, the result would have been only slightly more investment and much lower profitability.

It can likewise be concluded that within the postwar period up till some time in the 1960's, the SPOF schedule was tending to shift down, since the rate of capital accumulation was increasing in face of a fall in MEI.

Comparisons with the interwar period are more difficult. Depression and structural change make the *ex post* profit rate an unreliable indicator of MEI, and the depression also made for large multiplier-induced, non-exogenous shifts in the SPOF schedule.

INFLUENCES AFFECTING THE SUPPLY PRICE OF FINANCE

The Propensity to Save

Orthodox Keynesian theory says that if the economy is pressing against the full employment ceiling, an exogenous rise in the propensity to save permits more investment, but that if there is not full employment its main effect is to reduce effective demand and hence income. When dealing with long-run growth, on the other hand, economists tend to assume that the full-employment condition somehow looks after itself. To put it another way, it tends to be assumed that in the long run the market rate of interest adjusts itself to the natural rate, and that a high propensity to save therefore makes for high investment. There is no agreed doctrine, however, about how this happens.

As already noted, changes in the *ex post* propensity to save may be *induced* by changes in investment. To a considerable extent, observed changes in the propensity to save in the British economy (reviewed in Chapter 5) were of the induced class. But two of the observed changes cannot be explained in this way. (1) The rise in personal savings within the postwar period—the main source of the rise in the overall propensity to save—was not traceable in any obvious way to investment behavior. (2) Though a significant part of the excess of the *gross* savings ratio in 1952–73 over 1874–1913 was associated with increased depreciation, and in that sense was related to investment, the increase from 9.0 percent to 11.2 percent between the two periods in the *net* savings ratio was wholly accounted for by the net savings of government, which averaged 2.2 percent of GNP in 1952–73, compared with approximately zero before 1914. It is unlikely that government savings before 1914 would have been significantly affected if investment had been different.

What were the effects of these changes? As far as the postwar period is concerned, the question cannot be separated from the government's management of demand. If personal savings had not risen, stronger government action would have been taken to restrain demand. The effect on investment would have depended on the policy instruments chosen, but it is extremely probable that one of the instruments would have been tighter credit policy. In that sense, without going into the intricacies of financial markets, we can say that the rise in personal savings within the postwar period created conditions favorable to rising investment; likewise with regard to the *average* level of personal savings over the postwar period.

The same holds, in a rather different sense, for government savings in the postwar period. If, say, the government had chosen always to have a balanced budget on current account instead of a surplus, it would have had to have a more restrictive monetary policy. It is unlikely that this would have induced a fully equivalent increase in private savings. So, given the level of income, investment would have been less than it actually was.

This latter point indicates one way in which the Keynesian revolution in fiscal policy may be held to have encouraged investment, in addition to the more obvious encouragement it gave by guaranteeing that there would not be severe slumps. The use of fiscal policy to restrain demand and protect the balance of payments, instead of monetary policy, which alone was available before 1914, helped to raise the overall propensity to save. The quantitative importance of this should not be exaggerated, however. Net government savings were not enormous, except for brief periods immediately after World War II and in 1969–71; moreover, monetary restraints on demand would have had part of their effect on private consumption and so would have increased private savings as a percentage of GNP.

The question whether the rise in the overall propensity to save, comparing the postwar period with pre–1914, helped bring about the rise in investment resolves itself into two questions. The first has just been discussed, namely whether a lower propensity to save would have been prejudicial to investment in the postwar period, and the answer is on the whole affirmative: in general, this effect of the increase that occurred in the propensity to save, insofar as it was autonomous, was to encourage investment rather than to depress activity.* The second question is whether a higher private propensity to save before 1914 would have helped promote investment. This question raises all the Keynesian difficulties, with the added complication that the additional savings might have been devoted primarily to the purchase of overseas assets (in which case they might even have tended to raise the interest rate, by leading to an adverse balance of payments and an outflow of gold). Statistically, there is no clear relationship between the movements in the savings-income ratio and movements in domestic invest-

---

*The increase in government savings in 1969–71 was an exception. It is also possible that the rise in the personal savings ratio *after* 1973 caused the level of activity to be depressed by more than the authorities had intended.

ment between the mid-1870's and 1914, chiefly because the movement in domestic investment was dominated by the long swing.

Be that as it may, the difference of 2.2 percent between the pre-1914 and postwar net savings ratios is much less than the difference between the two periods in the ratio to GNP of gross domestic fixed investment (9.6 percent). The balance of the difference, apart from capital consumption and inventory investment, is accounted for by capital export, to which we now turn.

Capital Export

Capital export (net foreign investment) and domestic investment are alternative outlets for savings. If savings are given, the two are in competition. Was the level of capital export important in determining SPOF and hence domestic investment? This is chiefly a question about the period before 1914, when the proportion of savings devoted to capital export was higher than in any other phase in the history of any major country (Kuznets 1961b: 5, 10–11). Supposing capital export from Britain at that time had been restricted by government, as it then was in Germany and as it has been in Britain in more recent times, would domestic capital accumulation have been higher? Even if what caused capital export was that there were greater opportunities for profitable investment abroad, it could still be held that Britain's disadvantage in not having those opportunities (for whatever reason) was reinforced by the consequent diversion of its savings to assist those other countries' development.* The advantages of the other countries were correspondingly reinforced.

The well-established inverse pattern of the long swings in domestic and foreign investment between 1870 and 1914 establishes a strong prima facie case that the two were in competition.† But that leaves

---

*It is in the light of this that we need to understand the contention that, because other countries' industrial output was growing more rapidly than Britain's, they were bound on average to have capital of more recent vintage and hence higher productivity (Temin 1966). Had the British savings been invested at home instead of abroad, the fact that Britain had slower growth than some other countries and so had less need for widening investment could in principle have permitted more deepening and modernizing investment and so have led to the British worker actually being equipped with a larger and/or more modern set of equipment than his foreign counterpart.

†See Ford 1965. The inverse relationship applied to almost all the principal categories of domestic investment (including manufacturing), not just to investment in dwellings, as has been sometimes supposed. The time pattern, over the long swing, of investment in dwellings and investment in manufacturing was basically the same, with the one exception that investment in manufacturing recovered after 1907 whereas investment in dwellings continued to decline. But investment in manufacturing had still not regained its 1903 level in 1913 in absolute terms, and the rate of addition to the capital stock in 1913 remained much lower than earlier.

open the direction of causation. At points in the long swing when capital export was high, did high capital export raise SPOF and inhibit domestic investment? Or did low domestic investment lower SPOF and drive capital-owners to seek outlets abroad? Was it crowding out of domestic investment or crowding in of overseas investment? Or was it the consequence of causes simultaneously lowering MEI at home and raising it abroad? An obvious example of such causes is the well-known effect on investment in dwellings of waves of emigration, themselves connected with broader alternations of phases of expansion.

Some presumption that the direction of causation went from capital export to domestic investment is created by the observed inverse relation between movements in capital export and movements in British share prices (B. Thomas 1973: 96–99). However, there is reason to suppose that the causation was not in the same direction at all phases. The rise in capital export in the late 1880's, when the domestic profit rate had fallen severely, looks like a case of crowding-in (Habakkuk 1962). But in 1903–13 the profit rate was not declining, and interest rates were rising; here a better case can be made that domestic investment was being crowded out by the rise in capital export. Likewise, the domestic investment boom of the late 1890's originated at a time when interest rates were low and share prices had risen steeply, possibly because capital export was low.

Even if there were *phases* when crowding-out occurred, the question remains whether capital export had a substantial effect on the average level of domestic investment over the whole period, rather than merely on its timing. Most modern writers have concluded that it did not (Kindleberger 1964: 59–58; Landes 1969: 348–52; Cairncross 1973: especially p. 6). They have pointed to the absence of specific complaints about a shortage of finance and have held that the domestic economy would not have been able to absorb much of the savings that went into capital export. This view receives support from the macrodata: Feinstein's new estimates of domestic investment, unlike his earlier ones, show a rate of capital accumulation that was not particularly low, at least in relation to the rate of growth of GNP. Hence they do not provide evidence of a shortage of capital. Indeed, taken in conjunction with the downward trend in the profit rate, they suggest the opposite.

The implication of this line of argument is that in the absence of the outlet provided by capital export, the domestic savings would not have been generated. The savings ratio was in fact about 3 percentage points higher at the foreign investment peaks around 1872 and 1913 than it was at the domestic investment peak around 1900 (Fig. 5.4). If there had been no outlet for funds abroad, the profit rate would certainly have been forced down by more than it was; and in the absence of capital export, exports of goods and hence incomes and savings would have been lower. Maybe this would have reduced savings by the full amount that capital export on average absorbed.

The question is whether *all* the adjustment would have been on the savings side. Even if there was not an actively felt demand for more finance for domestic investment, a plethora of funds might have led enterprising people to develop new domestic outlets, including possibly new financial institutions, as indeed did happen to some extent in the 1890's. As it was, capitalists were able to get an acceptable return on overseas investments without exerting themselves; and industrialists and their children and grandchildren were able to divert their energies from business and become rentiers without undergoing a drastic loss of income.

Reference to financial institutions leads on to a more specific hypothesis: that the capital market before 1914 was biased in favor of overseas issues. Such a bias was held by the Macmillan Committee to have been still present in the 1920's (UK [28]: 171). The reason did not lie in a bias in favor of overseas lending as such.[5] Insofar as there was a bias, it arose from the nature of domestic and overseas financing needs. The development of a well-organized stock exchange antedated the spread of the joint-stock principle throughout industry at large. Railways, on the other hand, financed themselves by the issue of negotiable securities from the first. Hence the staples of the London stock exchange in the nineteenth century were the securities of governments (British and overseas) and of railways and other undertakings of the public utility type. By the late nineteenth century it was the countries of recent European settlement, rather than Britain itself, that were expanding their social overhead capital at the greatest rate and therefore needed this kind of finance. It was therefore overseas investment that the market was institutionally best fitted to finance.[6] The well-organized market for negotiable securities was not meanwhile matched by a correspondingly well-organized system of investment banking, which was developing on the Continent, where by contrast stock exchange facilities were inferior.[7] The lack of investment banking and generally of active participation by banks in industry was regretted by contemporaries (Marshall 1919: 346–48) and has remained a point of difference between British and continental capital markets up till recent times (Lamfalussy 1968). The existence of ample scope for capital export may be held, moreover, to have made this structure persist longer than it would otherwise have done.

There is a good deal of evidence for the view that there was a bias in the capital market.[8] If it is correct, what are the macro-economic implications? Insofar as the bias simply raised SPOF for domestic investment, the removal of the bias would have depressed domestic profit rates, and the arguments recited above about the possible consequences apply. However, insofar as a better-functioning capital market would have meant that domestic investment was better *directed*, domestic investment might have been higher without depressing the rate of return. The bias, if present, then ranks as one of the causes making for slow growth in TFP in the pre-1914 period.

The conclusions so far are therefore as follows. Over the long swing there was some crowding-out of home investment by capital export. Over the period 1870–1913 as a whole the degree of crowding-out was much less. In the absence of capital export, the profit rate would have been further depressed and with it the savings ratio. But *some* increase in domestic investment could scarcely have failed to occur, especially if capital market institutions had adapted themselves.

In recent times the motive for restricting overseas investment has been to protect the balance of payments rather than fear of its direct competition with domestic investment in the capital market. This raises considerations going beyond SPOF, but the subject may conveniently be discussed here.

The purchase of overseas assets is bad for the balance of payments at the time but good for the balance of payments later, when it yields a return. The effect therefore depends on the length of time under consideration. During the 60 or so years before 1914, the proportion of overseas investment to national income remained about constant (averaged over long swings) at around 5 percent (Table 14.7), whereas the trend in income from abroad was upwards, from about 2 percent of national income in the 1850's to over 8 percent in 1913 (Table 6.1). The effect of capital export, on this reckoning, was to make the balance of payments stronger as time went on; even though if at any moment capital export had ceased, the immediate effect on the balance of payments would have been favorable. It is difficult to know what conclusions to draw from this, since capital export had other effects on the balance of payments, helping to finance exports and increasing the supply and lowering the cost of imports, and in any case it is not too clear how prices or output would have been affected, under the gold standard as it then worked, if the long-run trend in the balance of payments had been different. However, no presumption emerges that the effect of capital export on the balance of payments was unfavorable, taking the pre-1914 period as a whole.

The effects of capital exports on domestic investment in later periods can be more briefly treated. The net balance of long-term and short-term capital exports was much smaller in the 1920's than before 1914, but the continuing tendency to long-run capital exports was one of the contributing causes of the balance-of-payments pressure, which in turn was responsible for the dear-money policy. The decline of long-run capital exports in the 1930's helped the balance of payments and facilitated the adoption of cheap money.

The question about the postwar period is the antithesis of the question about the pre-1914 period. Control over capital export was one of the cardinal principles of policy. Net capital export was small. Did this make a significant contribution to the historically high rate of domestic capital formation?

Control over *portfolio* investment was effective, as shown by the persistent dollar premium (the excess of the prices of overseas securities purchasable from other British nationals over their prices on Wall Street). Without control, there would certainly have been a tendency to substantial portfolio investment. This would have added to the balance-of-payments problem at the time of purchase, while lessening it as returns accrued. Apart from that ambivalent effect, would there have been a higher SPOF for domestic investment and crowding-out in the capital market? There would have been less upward pressure on the market for British equities. So domestic investment *would* have been adversely affected, insofar as it was responsive to the earnings yield on equities (see pp. 362–64, below). The behavior of the savings ratio in the postwar period (pp. 139–51, above) gives no particular reason to suppose that this would have been prevented by an induced rise in private savings.

There is fair agreement that controls on *direct* investment (as opposed to portfolio investment) in the postwar period had rather small effects on the amount undertaken. Such effect as the controls had was chiefly on how the direct investment was financed: they encouraged finance by means of borrowing abroad. Their effects were thus more like the effects of control over portfolio investment than appears at first sight. If foreign borrowing had not been induced by the controls and the direct investment had been financed by sterling funds instead, there would have been an immediate adverse effect on the balance of payments and a subsequent favorable one; and there would inevitably have been increased competition in the domestic capital market.

The conclusion therefore follows that control of capital export in the postwar period did tend to keep down SPOF for domestic investment, and that this marked a point of difference from earlier periods, especially the period before 1914. (Whether this was desirable is, of course, another matter.)

Since the amount of direct investment was not, it seems, very much affected by the controls, it is also of some interest to ask how domestic investment would have been affected if control in the postwar period had been *tighter* than it actually was (rather than less tight). The answer depends partly on the form the control would have taken and partly on the consequent adjustments to general macro-economic policy.[9] Less direct investment would probably have meant less overseas borrowing to finance it. It follows that it would not have reduced SPOF by enough to give much stimulus to domestic investment. The main source of any such stimulus would have had to arise from a reduction in different kinds of competition between domestic and direct overseas investment, namely competition due to limitations on the market served by a firm and limitations on the energies of its management. However, the survey evidence collected by Reddaway in the mid-1960's indicated clearly that firms did not view their overseas operations and their domestic ones as being in competition: they viewed them as serving separate markets rather than as alternative locations from which to supply a given market. It is possible that after the mid-1960's this rather surprising conclusion may have become rather less applicable, on account of the increased unification of world markets through trade liberalization.

Let us sum up, taking a rather broader view.

Capital formation in one country, whether undertaken by its own nationals or by foreigners, may tend to be at the expense of capital formation in another insofar as they compete for (1) markets, (2) labor, (3) entrepreneurship, and (4) savings. The last of these is the one most directly connected with capital export; but they are all interrelated.

Markets. In all periods capital formation in some foreign countries encroached on British markets and lowered the British MEI. Capital export did not have much to do with this, except in agriculture, where the building of British-financed railways opened up competition from the new world. Otherwise capital export before 1914 was not chiefly in activities that were in competition with British producers. As for the postwar period, the growth of industrial capacity abroad competitive with Britain's would have gone ahead at much the same pace irrespective of the small contribution made by British direct investment.

Labor. The association of labor migration in the pre-1914 world with booms in countries of recent European settlement, and with the capital export that helped to finance them, is well known. Whether labor shortage inhibited British industrial investment in those periods is doubtful. Emigration did certainly affect investment in dwellings. This is really a case of competition for markets rather than for labor as an input.

Entrepreneurship. The portfolio investment of pre-1914 did not involve any great diversion of entrepreneurial energies as such. However, the return from it may have made (potential) entrepreneurs take things easy. In the postwar world the scope for this kind of competition was greater, though it is not well attested by the survey evidence.

Savings. Before 1914 overseas investment certainly absorbed a lot of British savings. In some phases of the long swing British investment was probably subject to crowding-out. How important this was over the average of the whole pre-1914 period is more doubtful. It depends partly on how far savings rose in response to foreign investment opportunities and partly on how much scope for higher domestic capital formation was allowed by the other constraints. We concluded above that there was some scope, but that the profit rate would have been further depressed. Contrariwise, in the postwar period the restrictions on capital export, portfolio and direct, built a ring-fence around British savings and made them more readily available for the finance of home investment. A similar ring-fence could not be built around markets or entrepreneurship.

Capital Market Imperfections

Reference was made above to the alleged bias of the capital market in favor of overseas issues before 1914 and to the subsequent gradual decline in that bias. This is one aspect of a more general class of consideration.

In principle it is to be expected that continual technical progress will take place in financial intermediation, no less than in other economic activities. The effect of reductions in the real cost of financial intermediation is to narrow the gap between the rate of profit achieved on real capital and the rate of interest that can be earned by the owner of purely financial assets.

There is clear evidence that the gap did become narrower over time. In 1873 the net rate of return on the real capital stock in the non-farm trading sector is estimated to have been 17.3 percent (Table 6.13). The yield obtainable on consols was 3.2 percent. A hundred years later, in 1973, the net profit rate, similarly defined, had fallen to 4.6 percent. The dividend yield obtainable by an individual investor buying the late-twentieth-century equivalent to consols, the *Financial Times* index, was still 3.2 percent (if he bought at the peak in December 1972 — more if bought later). The exact result would, of course, be altered by a different choice of measures, and neither 1873 nor 1973 was a typical year. But any measure would show a large decline over the long period in the gap between the two types of rate.

Improvements in the efficiency of financial intermediation, i.e. reductions in capital market imperfections, have taken a variety of forms. In the 1930's and in the postwar period some of them arose from government initiative; others are described in histories of the capital market. Attention will be called here to two related forces that operated over the whole period.

The first arose from the development of the public joint-stock company and from the widening of the market for equities. In an economy composed mainly of unincorporated businesses, as the British economy was until the last quarter of the nineteenth century, there are likely to be large variations in the rate of return on capital according to whether its ownership is or is not linked to entrepreneurship. Before the advent of the joint-stock company, a large proportion of firms was confined, for the finance of fixed investment, to plowed-back profits and family resources. The return to the owners' capital at the margin in these circumstances was bound to be much higher, on the average, than that available to a rentier, limited in the placement of his funds largely to securities of home and overseas governments and utilities and to mortgages.

In 1880 public joint-stock companies accounted for only a small part of the economy outside railways and other utilities. Major changes took place in the ensuing years, and by 1914 most of manufacturing and some of commerce was organized in joint-stock companies.* Not only was there an increase in the number of public companies, and with it an increase in the number of firms able to tap the resources of the stock

*Between 1885 and 1907 the number of firms in domestic manufacturing and distribution with shares quoted on the London stock exchange rose from 60 to over 600, and provincial stock exchanges were said to be of almost greater importance (Hannah 1976: 21).

market; there was also an improvement in the terms on which companies could raise finance. Early companies had faced suspicion, not wholly unjustified, about their financial soundness and about the probity of their promoters. As the company sector expanded, this suspicion diminished, and the risk premium in equity yields diminished with it. There was an upward trend in the price of equities and a downward trend in their yields between the 1870's and 1914, notwithstanding that the rate of interest on fixed-interest securities was fractionally higher at the end of the period than at the beginning.[10] Correspondingly with this decline in SPOF, the net rate of return on real capital fell.

The transition to the public joint-stock form of organization continued in the interwar period, especially in commerce and in some of the more recently developed branches of manufacturing (the shares of Morris Motors were not put on the market till 1935). By World War II the scope for further change along the same lines had been much reduced. However, there remained scope for the widening of the market for equities. This provided an important further source of reduction in SPOF (as discussed below).

The second of the two related forces making for diminished imperfection of the capital market was the increase in the size of firms. This increase was typically associated with product diversification, which carried with it a reduction in risk. The increase in size improved access to external finance. Perhaps more important, though not easily measurable, was the fact that it enabled firms to operate a wider and hence more efficient internal capital market for their own plowed-back profits. It reduced the need for individual specialized lines of production with good investment opportunities to have accumulated their own profits to finance them. Unlike the transition to the joint-stock form, the increase in the size of firms had not run its course by World War II; on the contrary, the growth of multiproduct firms was particularly characteristic of the postwar period. The increase in the size of firms went on throughout the whole of our period, apart from a pause in the 1930's and 1940's.[11]

Reductions in capital market imperfections thus made for a long-run downward shift in the SPOF schedule, though not necessarily at a steady rate or with equal effect on all sectors of the economy. They were not, it may be noted, confined to the industrial and commercial sector. An important case in point was the improvement in the financial provision for investment in owner-occupied dwellings brought about by the development of Building Societies, especially in the interwar period.

Inflationary Expectations, Inflation, and Share Prices

The matters for consideration under this heading are confined to the postwar period.

In the postwar period up to about 1968, there was little trend variation in the rate of general price increase (Table 10.2). On the other hand, nomimal interest rates rose steadily and substantially (Fig. 12.1). It follows that if the expected rate of price increase had been equal to the actual rate, there would have been a significant rise in the cost of finance.

It is not a reasonable hypothesis that expectations followed this pattern. Had they done so, the yield on equities would have risen in line with the rate of interest. In fact it fell steeply. Hence, either the expected rate of price increase rose during the period, or else there were other powerful forces pushing up share prices, or (as is most likely) both. One might postulate that actual price trends were not extrapolated at all at the beginning of the 1950's and were fully extrapolated by the mid-1960's. On that assumption, the *ex ante* real cost of fixed-interest borrowing remained about constant during that period, for the increase in nominal interest rates in those years was of about the same order (between 3 percent and 4 percent) as the rate of price increase at the end of it. Moreover, the trend rise in interest rates was fairly continuous, so if people were adjusting their price expectations at a steady rate, the *ex ante* real cost of fixed-interest borrowing could be held to have been fairly constant throughout the period, as well as between its end points.

This hypothesis, which is perhaps not too unreasonable, does not, however, explain the behavior of yields on equities; by itself it would lead one to expect yields on equities to have been constant, rather than to have fallen as they actually did.

A number of forces apart from increased awareness of inflation combined to bring about the rise in share prices between the early 1950's and 1968:

(1) The extremely high earnings yields that prevailed up to 1958 made sense only if major changes for the worse were to be expected. The uncertainties inherent in the early postwar period were prolonged for a while by the price fluctuations of the Korean War, but the effects of these receded. There was thus a turn for the better in expectations about *real* prospects.

(2) The takeover boom called attention to the unrealistically low valuation of some companies.

(3) A significant contribution came from the side of company taxation; this is discussed separately below.

(4) The rise in share prices had cumulative effects by calling attention to the advantages (including personal tax advantages) of equities compared with fixed-interest securities in a period of inflation. This led to institutional changes: changes in legislation relating to permitted holdings for trustees, the formation of unit trusts, and so forth. This served to break down the market imperfections that, in earlier periods, had made the yield on equities unduly high relative to the yield on gilt-edged, even in the absence of inflation.

(5) The rise in share prices (which for these reasons was substantially faster than the rise in general prices) assumed some speculative momentum of its own, particularly in the stock exchange booms of 1958–60 and 1966–68.

Insofar as the rise in share prices was due to the first of these causes — greater optimism about real prospects — and insofar as this greater optimism was felt by management as well as by the market, it should be regarded as representing an increase in MEI rather than a decrease in SPOF.* The observed rise in share prices and fall in equity yields thus exaggerate the extent to which SPOF fell over the period 1951–68. However, the other forces enumerated in the previous paragraph *were* such as to betoken a fall in SPOF.

The conclusions are therefore that it is doubtful whether inflationary expectations as such lowered SPOF in the period 1951–68, but that they did cheapen equity finance, both within the period and by comparison with earlier periods, by widening the market for equities and causing equity prices to rise by more than general prices.

Things were different in the final phase, 1968–73. The rate of price inflation increased, and so did the rate of interest on fixed-interest securities, by about the same amount. Assuming that by now price movements were fully extrapolated, this would imply little change in the real rate of interest. But the rate of increase of equity prices greatly slowed down, and the earnings yield, instead of falling as it had previously done, rose significantly.

---

*Greater optimism about real prospects raises the quasi-rents expected to accrue from new investment and thereby increases MEI. It also raises share prices and so cheapens finance derived from new issues. But at the same time it raises the quasi-rents expected from existing assets. So it leaves unaffected the standard of profit to which new investment must conform if it is not to dilute the equity. By contrast, an increase in the expected rate of inflation does not affect MEI as we have defined it (at constant prices). It would lower the cost of finance if the rate of interest did not rise by as much as the expected rate of inflation did — a condition probably not fulfilled in the period 1951–68.

Several of the special forces that earlier had made for rises in share prices had by this time exhausted their effects (the widening of the market for equities, the takeover phenomenon, the disappearance of early postwar uncertainties). So it is not too difficult to understand why the earnings yield should have ceased to fall. This would not explain why it actually rose. The most likely explanation is a reduction in the amount of optimism felt about future real prospects, or at least an increase in uncertainties about them.* Such a change in attitudes could have resulted from the absence in the late 1960's of a cyclical boom comparable to 1955, 1960, and 1964 (the apparent replacement, until 1972–73, of stop-go by stop-stop) and possibly from anxieties created by the speeding-up of inflation itself and from increasing uncertainties about government policy. It is most likely that this weakening of confidence was felt by managements, as well as by the market. Insofar as that was so, it must be regarded as a fall in MEI rather than a rise in SPOF.

What has been said so far about inflation has concerned the effects of expectations of inflation. It remains to note certain effects of inflation itself on the supply of finance.

Inflation, as experienced in the postwar period, did not lead to an increase in profits' share in output. So it did not through that channel increase the availability of self-finance for investment. It did, however, benefit firms' financial position, and hence the *ex post* availability of internal finance, insofar as it reduced the real value of their old debts and the interest due on them. At the very end of the period, on the other hand, when the rate of inflation went up, it posed a financial problem for firms, to the extent that they were unable or unwilling to fix their prices on a replacement-cost basis and hence did not generate the funds needed to finance their stock appreciation (see Flemming et al. 1976a: 43–44).

Taxation

The main points of interest here, as in the preceding section, concern trends within the postwar period.

From the early 1950's till 1966 the amount of taxation paid by companies had no upward trend, even at current prices. Consequently, the proportion of profits taken in tax fell steeply. The ratio of company tax liabilities (i.e. accruals) to total company income arising in the United

---

*Tax considerations are discussed in the next section. In addition to the points there mentioned about company taxation, it is possible that the introduction of capital gains tax had some damping effect on the demand for equities.

Kingdom fell from 36½ percent in 1948–51 to 18 percent in 1961–64; after 1965 there was no further trend decline in the ratio.[12] So though the pre-tax profit rate tended to fall, the post-tax profit rate did not, up till the mid-1960's. The question therefore arises of the extent to which the diminished severity of taxation was the reason why the rate of capital accumulation was sustained and even increased at that time in face of the fall in the profit rate.

A reduction in taxation can encourage investment by raising the *ex ante* net profitability of investment and by increasing the availability of finance. The ways in which these two channels of influence are affected by the various elements in the tax structure are not the same. And the strength of neither is properly measured by the *ex post* proportion of gross profits taken in tax. The decline in this ratio in fact gives an exaggerated picture of the extent to which changes in tax rates and provisions lightened the burden on companies. There were a number of other causes contributing to the decline in companies' tax liabilities. They included a decline in retention rates, in consequence of which income tax payments were attributed to shareholders rather than to companies, and a reduction in the average life of the capital stock and an increase in investment itself, both of which had the effect of increasing depreciation allowances. Nonetheless, there *were* important changes in the real burden of taxation on companies. We consider first the effects on the *ex ante* profitability of investment in the postwar period, then the effects on the availability of finance in the postwar period, and finally how the postwar period compares with the interwar period.

The postwar period: effects on the ex ante profitability of investment. A whole range of investment inducements, with a general trend toward increased generosity, were introduced in the course of the period: initial allowances, investment allowances, and investment grants, with preferential treatment in some parts of the period for development areas. At the same time, there were numerous variations in the form and rates of company taxation (for a summary, see Melliss & Richardson 1976). Allowances and tax arrangements have to be looked at together in order to assess the net effect of tax measures on the *ex ante* profitability of investment. The exact way in which this should theoretically be computed affords room for disagreement, particularly in relation to tax rates.* It is clear, however, that from the early 1950's

---

*Among the questions at issue are whether the relevant rate of tax includes or excludes standard-rate income tax, whether it is the rate on retained profits or the rate on all profits, how far existing tax rates should be assumed to be extrapolated into the future, and what rate of discount should be applied.

to the mid-1960's the trend was substantially favorable, as a result of the increasing generosity of allowances. In the mid-1960's there were major changes in arrangements: in 1965 profits tax was replaced by corporation tax, and in 1966 investment allowances were replaced by investment grants. The net result appears to have been that the ratio of the pre-tax *ex ante* rate of return to the post-tax rate ceased to rise or even fell.[13]

These conclusions are subject to one significant qualification. Survey evidence, too clear-cut to be easily dismissed, indicates that at least until the early 1960's the large majority of firms based their investment decisions on pre-tax profitability and disregarded tax inducements or deterrents. There was apparently an increase in companies' conscious responsiveness to tax incentives after about 1963, stimulated no doubt by the very considerable additional incentives introduced that year. Moreover, the replacement of investment allowances by investment grants in 1966 had as one of its aims to increase the visibility of inducements. A survey in 1970 indicated rather greater responsiveness to fiscal inducement than most earlier surveys had done.[14]

It is difficult to believe that, even before 1963, the fiscal incentives did not to some extent encourage investment through their effects on *ex ante* profitability, even if they did so for only a minority of firms. The survey evidence suggests, however, that the increase in incentives up to the early 1960's may have had less effect then their actual value would lead one to expect; and that in the course of the 1960's there may have been an increase in their effect, even though their actuarial value had ceased to rise.

The postwar period: availability of finance. As already noted, the proportion of profits taken in tax fell until the mid-1960's. Thereafter the trend was less favorable to companies. This is particularly so if profits are reckoned net of stock appreciation: the increase in the rate of inflation from the late 1960's meant that the non-tax-deductibility of stock appreciation became increasingly burdensome.

The survey data do not cast the same doubt on the effect on taxation through availability of finance as they do on its effect through *ex ante* profitability. There is no reason to doubt that reductions in taxation did assist companies to finance rising investment in the 1950's and early 1960's, and that the finance of investment was hampered by the taxation of stock appreciation in the closing years of the period.

In addition to the effects on internal finance, taxation influenced share prices and hence the terms on which external finance could be raised. The reduction in company taxation served to make equities more attractive, both directly, by helping to keep up the post-tax profit rate, and indirectly, by enabling companies to increase the ratio of dividends to retentions without prejudice to the actual amount of retentions (the last point was significant chiefly in the late 1950's). Part of the fall in recorded earnings yields up to the mid-1960's was probably due to these direct and indirect effects of taxation.*

It may therefore be concluded that tax changes did serve to encourage investment to an increasing extent up to some point in the late 1960's, the exact timing of this point being rendered doubtful by the possibility that business reponsiveness to an incentive of given actuarial value increased over time.

The timing of tax effects is thus broadly compatible with the timing of the observed long swing in industrial and commercial investment. But some cautions are needed. Tax effects are more important in explaining why the ratio of investment to output in the earlier part of the postwar period did not fall in face of a falling rate of profit than they are in explaining why the investment-output ratio actually rose. That rise came chiefly in the distributive trades and services rather than in manufacturing. But the tax treatment of the distributive trades and services was not eased in the course of the period to nearly the same extent as it was for manufacturing. Buildings are the largest component in the capital stock in the distributive trades and services, and at no time in the period did commercial buildings qualify for any depreciation allowances at all. Moreover, certain of the other relaxations applied only to manufacturing. The acceleration in investment in the distributive trades and services was no doubt helped by increasing generosity in depreciation allowances on their equipment and vehicles (and also indirectly by the relief on the capital market afforded by generous depreciation allowances in manufacturing). But the main explanation must lie elsewhere.

Postwar period: comparison with the interwar period. Taxation impinged more unfavorably on the supply of finance for investment in the postwar period than it did in the interwar period, because the higher rates of tax prevailing in the postwar period much outweighed other changes. On the side of *ex ante* profitability, however, the more generous depreciation allowances of the postwar period were more

---

*Only part, however. This may be seen from the downward trend until 1968 in Flemming's index of the post-tax cost of capital (Flemming et al. 1976b: 197), which is constructed in such a way that it will be unaffected by an increase in share prices in proportion to an increase in the ratio of post-tax profits to pre-tax profits. The fall in the index is too large to be attributable to the increase in the ratio of dividends to retentions.

than sufficient to outweigh any tendency for inflation to erode the real value of historic cost depreciation. The higher rates of tax, moreover, increased the real value of this accelerated depreciation. The introduction of profits tax (a tax not levied in most of the interwar period) tended to diminish *ex ante* profitability, but not, on the basis of the usual type of calculation, by enough to outweigh the effects of accelerated depreciation.[15]

It appears, therefore, that the effects of taxation on investment were more favorable in the interwar period than in the postwar period as far as finance availability is concerned but less favorable as far as *ex ante* profitability is concerned. As noted above, in the earlier part of the postwar period, firms appear to have paid relatively little attention to the effects of tax on *ex ante* profitability. So the net effect on investment of tax changes across World War II was probably unfavorable. It follows that tax considerations cannot be invoked as an explanation of the increase in investment between the two periods, and that if anything they probably pulled in the other direction.

Monetary Factors

Specifically monetary influences on the cost and availability of finance are in principle those that derive from exogenous changes in the supply of money or other manifestations of monetary policy. But real and monetary forces are closely intertwined, both under a gold-standard system and under a government full-employment policy. We shall not attempt to look deeply into the controversial theoretical issues involved — issues that are more relevant to the study of prices and cycles than to the study of growth — and will merely refer to the chief occasions when specifically monetary forces may be held to have been important.

(1) Increased world gold production in the 1890's certainly contributed to the fall in interest rates that occurred then, and hence presumably facilitated the domestic investment boom.[16] The trend in interest rates was soon reversed, however, as world prices rose. Insofar as the increased gold supply affected British domestic investment in the quarter-century before 1914, the effect thus seems to have been on its timing rather than on its amount.

(2) The monetary experience of the interwar period is well known: the dear-money policy of the 1920's and the cheap-money policy of the 1930's. The fall in gilt-edged yields in the 1930's communicated itself to yields on industrial securities, including both equities and debentures

TABLE 12.3

Liquidity Position of Quoted Companies, 1949–1964

(Average of annual percentages of real capital assets at current prices)

Period	Liquid assets	Net short-term liabilities (excluding liabilities to banks)			
		Tax liabilities	Net trade and other creditors	Other	Total
1949–1951	9.8%	4.9%	−2.3%	1.9%	4.5%
1952–1955	9.3	4.4	−2.8	1.7	3.3
1956–1960	7.4	3.8	−3.0	1.7	2.5
1961–1964	5.8	3.4	−3.8	1.9	1.5

Source: Financial Statistics, UK [13]: Jan. 1966; "Income and finance of quoted companies, 1949–1960," UK [14]; *Board of Trade Journal*, Feb. 11, 1966.

(Nevin 1955: 245–47). It was also reflected in a rise in the quantity of money relative to GNP. In the 1920's monetary conditions were certainly unfavorable to investment.

(3) It is difficult to isolate the effects of monetary policy in the postwar period or to compare that period with earlier ones, because of the changes in general context. The first of these changes was the adoption of a full-employment policy and the use of fiscal and other instruments to regulate demand. This made it possible for monetary policy to be less tight than it might otherwise have been, as argued above. The second change was the chronic rise in prices.

There are two, more specific aspects of the postwar monetary situation that can usefully be discussed here.

(a) Policies adopted during and immediately after the war caused the quantity of money in the early postwar period to be exceptionally high relative to GNP. A counterpart of this was high company liquidity. Did this liquidity encourage investment then or in the subsequent years by making its financial opportunity cost low? Companies' liquid assets actually went on increasing (Table 12.1). But the increase was proportionately less than the increase in their total assets (Table 12.3). Relatively speaking, therefore, they drew on liquid assets to finance capital expenditure, particularly from 1954 onward. According to one reckoning, some 3½ percent of capital expenditures in 1954–63 was financed in this way — not a large proportion, but not negligible.[17] Insofar as the reason why companies reduced their liquidity was that their desired liquidity fell because of other changes in conditions, it is the changes affecting the desired liquidity that should be regarded as having the causal significance rather than the initially high liquidity.

One such change was the decline in their tax liabilities (Table 12.3, second column). Others may have been expectations of inflation and generally improved confidence.* Allowance for these factors makes the overall significance of the inherited high liquidity appear rather small, but does not destroy it altogether.

(b) The increase in the importance of bank finance was the most important single change in the sources of company finance (Table 12.1). As with equity prices, a turning-point came in the upswing of 1958–60. Clearing-bank deposits grew at an annual rate of 4.5 percent from 1958 to 1964, compared with an annual rate of only 1.2 percent between 1948 and 1958. In addition, advances to the private sector grew as a proportion of deposits (28 percent in 1958, 50 percent in 1964). There was also a significant increase, particularly after 1960, in the lending of non-clearing banks.

A principal reason for this change lay in the relaxation of government controls over bank lending. These had been severe up to 1958. In face of this manifest influence on the supply side, it is difficult to tell how far the increased reliance on bank finance was influenced also by a shift in companies' preferences as to the sources of finance—for example, because they were less willing or able to use undistributed profits or draw on liquid assets. Some influences of this sort did probably operate, so not the whole of the increase in bank finance is necessarily to be taken to represent an easing in the supply of finance (see Bank of England 1969: 184). But there is no question that the reduced severity of official restrictions on bank lending in the period 1958–64 was an exogenous force tending to make easier the supply of finance for investment.

A large increase in bank finance in the 1970's was partly the result of the further relaxations on controls on banks that took place under the Bank of England's new policy of Competition and Credit Control. It did represent some genuine increase in the supply of finance. However, the observed increase in bank lending was also partly, and perhaps chiefly, due to causes that did not have that implication. Changes in relative interest rates led nonfinancial companies to engage in purely financial operations ("round-tripping"), which were reflected in large increases in their liquid assets (Table 12.1). Moreover, in a period when interest rates were exceptionally high by historic standards, it

---

*These considerations about changes in desired liquidity make it difficult to say much about the relative extent to which the availability of liquidity helped investment in *different parts* of the postwar period.

was natural for companies to avoid long-term indebtedness and prefer the short-term credit offered by banks.

Capital Goods: Prices, Availability, and Controls

The cost of the services of capital depends not only on the cost of finance, but also on the prices of capital goods relative to the prices of final output—a topic that usually gets much less attention.

The main feature in the historical behavior of p_I/p_Y in the economy as a whole (Fig. 5.5) was its very large rise across World War II. This rise was partly but by no means wholly reversed during the postwar period. Prior to World War II there had been no clear trend. Some of the causes of the peculiar rise across World War II (such as the rise in house prices relative to rents) were not such as to impinge on the industrial and commercial sectors. But even in those sectors the transwar rise was very substantial—some 20 percent in manufacturing and some 15 percent in services—and must have tended to reduce the profitability of investment in the postwar period compared with earlier. The item is not a small one. So, far from helping to explain why investment was high, taking the postwar period as a whole, it increases the amount that falls to be explained by other causes. The main identifiable sources of the rise in p_I/p_Y were the rise in import prices and the fall in productivity in the construction industry across World War II (see Appendix H).

Shortages of capital goods and government controls on investment are in principle similar in their effects to high prices of capital goods. Their effects over time were also similar. Shortages and controls were severe in the early postwar period, and they were then relaxed. There is some difference in that whereas p_I/p_Y throughout the postwar period remained above prewar, controls and shortages had disappeared by the mid-1950's; but delivery dates were probably longer then prewar.

Absolute shortages were most important in the years immediately after World War II. Government controls remained important well beyond that. In the case of building there were direct statutory controls. Investment in plant and machinery was not subject to formal control in the same way, but it was affected by steel allocation and also by a variety of informal rationing arrangements, largely designed to free a sufficient proportion of the output of the engineering industry for exports and (in 1950–52) for defense.[18] Controls inherited from the war had been gradually loosened during the late 1940's, but they were tightened again in 1950 and 1951 on account of the Korean War and rearmament. From 1952 onward they were relaxed again, and by 1955 no significant controls remained on either building or investment in plant and equipment, apart from those related to location of industry and town and country planning policy.

Controls clearly had a significant effect in holding down investment in the early postwar period. The controls were not, of course, arbitrary acts. They were imposed because of real scarcities, both of resources in general and of capacity in the capital goods industries. The shortage of capacity in the capital goods industries, relative to demand, was prolonged beyond the time when it might have been expected to ease by the great expansion in the early 1950's of defense expenditures which competed for the same resources as investment. It was no doubt largely in consequence of this that investment in manufacturing (in real terms) did not continue to rise after the general business cycle peak in 1951, as occurred after other cyclical peaks in the postwar period, but instead showed little upward trend from 1950 through 1954.

Conclusions

(1) A favorable shift in the SPOF schedule between the pre-1914 period and the period after World War II can be inferred from the conjunction of a higher rate of capital accumulation and a lower profit rate. Of the forces considered in the previous pages, the following emerge as exogenous (or partly exogenous) contributions to this shift: (a) diminution in capital market imperfections; (b) decline of capital export; (c) increase in government savings. These forces were more than sufficient to outweigh the adverse effects of the rise in the relative prices of capital goods across World War II.

(2) Both the decline in capital market imperfections and the decline in capital exports were fairly continuous, embracing also the interwar period, but taking different forms in different phases. In regard to capital market imperfections, the benefits from the transition to the joint-stock form were achieved mainly before 1914, at least in manufacturing, but the effects of the increase in the size of firms were continuous, and the widening of the equity market was a postwar feature. The decline in capital exports in the interwar period resulted largely from the lack of opportunities, but its further decline across World War II was the result of controls. The rise in government savings was confined to the postwar period.

(3) Within the postwar period relaxation of government controls affecting physical investment and bank lending, diminished taxation of companies, and increase in personal savings all conduced to an increase

in investment, with somewhat different timing in each case, up to the mid-1960's, but not beyond; the relative price of capital goods declined through almost the whole period. Other apparent manifestations of falling SPOF reflected chiefly changes in confidence and in MEI.

(4) Changes in monetary conditions and policies affected SPOF in various phases without producing any clear long-run trends.

CHAPTER THIRTEEN

Investment: The Forces Determining Investment in the Principal Sectors

INDUSTRY AND COMMERCE

(1) Manufacturing. A fair part of the differences between periods in the rate of capital accumulation can be related to differences in the rate of growth of output, as described by the acceleration principle. This applies to the fall in the rate of capital accumulation between 1856–73 and 1873–1913 and to its historically high rate in the postwar period. Insofar as these differences in growth rates of output were the result of differences in the growth rate of TFP, capital accumulation thus served as a reinforcing factor. The acceleration principle also made some contribution to the long swings in the rate of capital accumulation before 1914 and in the postwar period.

The acceleration principle does not account for the low rate of capital accumulation in the interwar period, when there was not only a steep fall in the capital-output ratio, but also a fall in the capital-labor ratio. The following causes contributed: a capital-saving bias in technical progress, chiefly due to electrification; lack of business confidence, due to the long depression; lack of inducement or ability to substitute labor for capital, due to low profits and hence shortage of internal finance on the one hand and abundant labor supply on the other.

The acceleration principle also leaves unexplained the rise that occurred in both the pre-1914 period and the postwar period in the capital-output ratio in manufacturing. In the pre-1914 period the rise was attributable partly to a trend fall in SPOF, itself due to a reduction in capital market imperfections, and partly (at least in the 1870's and 1880's) to the failure of demand to match expectations. In the postwar period a number of causes contributed: again a fall in SPOF, associated with a widening of the market for equities and with tax encouragements to investment; the effects of full employment and the slow growth of labor supply on the desired capital-intensity of production, combined with some arrears inherited from the interwar period, when opposite conditions had prevailed. This process involved an element of overshooting, with the profit rate falling more steeply at the end of the period, at a time when SPOF was (for other reasons) tending to rise.

A higher level of investment than was actually carried out in the interwar period would have brought good returns, at least in the long run. In the pre-1914 and postwar periods it is difficult to discern signs of a shortage of finance for investment, and a substantially higher level of investment would have been likely to run into diminishing returns unless there had at the same time been an improvement in its quality.

(2) *Commerce.* Investment in commerce had a time pattern considerably different from that in manufacturing. The rate of capital accumulation was low before 1914 and higher in the interwar period. The rise between the interwar period and the postwar period was greater than in manufacturing, and within the postwar period there was no long swing but a sharp rise followed by a plateau. Among the most important points of difference from manufacturing accounting for this were:

(a) Commerce, or at least parts of it, had a tendency to be the residual claimant on the labor force. Hence the continued presence of surplus labor before 1914, and the sharp disappearance of that surplus after World War II, had greater effects on desired capital-intensity than in manufacturing.

(b) The timing of the reduction in capital market imperfections came later in commerce. This made for a stronger trend increase in investment between the successive periods.

(c) Commerce, unlike manufacturing, was not affected by a capital-saving bias in technical progress in the interwar period.

(d) Commerce was less affected than manufacturing by the downward pressure on profitability on account of foreign competition, notably in the late postwar period.

INFRASTRUCTURE

Many of the same general influences affected investment in utilities, transport and communications, and public and professional services as affected investment in manufacturing and commerce: the pace of economic growth, the supply of finance, and so on. These help to explain why postwar investment was higher than interwar investment. But their impact was much complicated by (1) changes in technology; (2) changes in demand structure; (3) the scope for increasing the degree of capital utilization; (4) the dominance of government; and (5) high capital intensity.

(1) Technological change made railways a declining industry and

electricity supply an expanding one. As far as investment is concerned, the decline of the one and the expansion of the other were in the period before 1914 both unduly delayed. The effect was felt all the more strongly in the interwar period. The net result was probably to increase *investment in the interwar period, because of the asymmetric effects on investment of expansion and contraction (though the investment in electricity supply was partly at the expense of investment in manufacturing).*

(2) These industries cater in general for the domestic market rather than exports. Moreover, public utilities, school-building and road construction have close links with house-building, insofar as the latter involves suburbanization or other geographical shifts. They therefore benefited in the 1930's. These links help to account for the decline found in investment of this type in the ten years or so before 1914.

(3) Infrastructure capital, by its nature, is capable of being stretched, even to the point of neglect of maintenance. This happened not only during World War II, but during much of the 1950's as well, notably in the case of transport.

(4) A somewhat different reason why investment could be kept relatively low in the 1950's is that priorities could be and were determined by the government rather than by consumer preferences. It was decided to give relatively low priority to roads, hospitals, and telecommunications. It is difficult to deny that the priorities then accorded and the changes in them in the 1960's and 1970's had a large arbitrary element. However, whether a smoother pattern would have made much difference to the rate of growth of measured GDP is more doubtful. A more blatant error was the one that led to the violent long swing in capital formation in electricity supply in the postwar period.

(5) The relative price and availability of labor and capital impinge less directly on investment decisions in a number of these industries than elsewhere in the economy, because labor is not an important part of cost. They do impinge indirectly, however, through demand for the final product.

DWELLINGS

Though fluctuations in investment in dwellings are complicated and not well understood, trends over broad periods (combining 1913–24 with 1924–37 and 1937–51 with 1951–73, to allow for war arrears) can be quite well explained by the hypothesis that the demand for the occupation of dwellings has a more-than-unit-elasticity with respect to total consumer expenditure and at the same time is responsive to relative costs. The only period when the relative cost of housing fell was be-

tween 1913 and 1937, and it was in this period that the rate of growth of the stock of dwellings exceeded the rate of growth of total consumer expenditure by the largest margin (though there were other contributory causes besides the fall in relative costs). Changes in the relative cost of housing in the several periods had various causes, including productivity trends in construction, interest rates, controls, and subsidies. Between 1937 and 1973 there was a great increase in subsidies but also a great increase in relative (unsubsidized) costs, arising particularly from the fall in TFP in construction across World War II. The effects of subsidies on investment in dwellings in the postwar period were lessened but not eliminated by keeping local authority house-building below the market-clearing level.

COMPETITION BETWEEN CATEGORIES OF
DOMESTIC INVESTMENT

Differences between peacetime periods before World War II in the rate of domestic capital accumulation were much smaller in the aggregate than in individual sectors. Does this imply mutual crowding out or crowding in — which may have continued in modified form in the postwar period, when of course total investment was much higher? Such an idea is not to be pushed too far. But there is some evidence that in periods when industrial investment was low, the cost of finance was eased for investment in dwellings and some forms of infrastructure. It can likewise be argued that chronic downward pressure on investment in manufacturing, arising from international competition, facilitated investment in dwellings and infrastructure, and so explains why Britain has a good housing stock compared with other countries. It is, however, much more doubtful whether investment in manufacturing would have been significantly higher if investment in dwellings or infrastructure had been lower.

INDUSTRY AND COMMERCE

Table 13.1 and Figures 11.1 and 13.1 display some of the principal data for manufacturing (the main constituent of industry as here defined*) and for commerce. Textiles are excluded from manufactur-

*The other constituents are mining and quarrying and construction. For mining and quarrying, see footnote to p. 405 and Fig. 13.4. Investment in the construction industry is a relatively small item.

TABLE 13-1

Annual Growth Rates of Output, Labor, and Fixed Capital, Investment-Output Ratios, and Profit Rates, in Manufacturing and Commerce, 1856–1973

(Percent)

Sector and variable	1856–1913		1924–1973			Post-WWII cycles				
	1856–1873	1873–1913	1924–1937	1937–1951	1951–1973	1951–1955	1955–1960	1960–1964	1964–1968	1968–1973
Manufacturing:										
Output	2.6%	2.0%	3.2%	2.5%	3.4%	4.3%	3.1%	3.2%	2.9%	3.2%
Labor[a]	(0.2)	0.8	1.4	1.0	-0.3	1.8	2.0	-0.3	-1.4	-1.5
Capital	3.2	2.6	0.7	2.9	3.9	3.8	4.2	4.2	3.9	3.4
Capital per man-hour	3.0	1.8	-0.7	1.9	4.2	2.0	4.0	4.5	5.3	4.9
Capital per unit of output	0.6	0.6	-2.4	0.4	0.5	-0.5	1.1	1.0	1.0	0.2
Investment-output ratio[b]	7.8	9.5	6.0	—	13.1	11.8	13.2	13.3	13.3	13.8
Profit rate[c]	—	—	9.7	—	8.6	10.7	9.9	9.0	8.1	5.7
Commerce:										
Output	(2.4)	(2.0)	1.7	-0.2	3.1	2.7	3.2	3.2	2.3	3.6
Labor[a]	(1.0)	1.3	2.3	-3.2	-0.2	0.5	0.2	0.3	-2.0	0.3
Capital	1.6	1.6	2.1	-0.2	5.7	2.7	4.7	7.1	6.4	6.7
Capital per man-hour	0.5	0.3	-0.2	3.0	5.6	2.2	4.5	6.8	8.4	6.4
Capital per unit of output	-0.8	-0.4	0.3	0.0	2.4	0.0	1.5	3.9	4.1	3.1
Investment-output ratio[b]	2.8	2.6	3.6	—	9.8	5.7	8.3	10.7	11.1	13.0
Profit rate[c]	—	—	26.0	—	17.5	19.1	19.2	18.0	16.8	14.5

Note: The manufacturing data exclude textiles after 1951. The comparative figures on the investment-output ratios and profit rates for 1951–73 with textiles included are as follows:

	1951–73	1951–55	1955–60	1960–64	1964–68	1968–73
Investment-output ratio	13.0%	11.6%	13.0%	13.2%	13.4%	13.9%
Profit rate	8.3	10.0	9.4	8.8	8.1	5.7

The growth rates of output, labor, and total capital (fixed and inventories) in manufacturing including textiles are shown in Table 8.3 and Appendix K.

[a] Man-hours (rough estimates for 1856–73).

[b] The average of the annual ratios (excluding the first year shown) of gross domestic fixed capital formation to output, at current prices for 1924–73 and at constant (1907) prices for 1856–1913.

[c] The average of the annual ratios (excluding the first year shown) of gross profits to capital stock (including inventories) at current prices. The profit rate for 1924–37 has been adjusted upward to eliminate the 1938 break in the capital series (see p. 122).

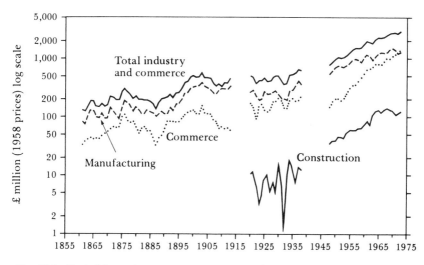

Fig. 13.1. Capital formation at constant prices in industry and commerce, 1861–1973. Total industry and commerce is the sum of manufacturing, commerce, construction, mining, and quarrying.

ing in the postwar period because of statistical difficulties relating to the capital stock (see p. 649, note 17).

The following features may be noted.

(1) The excess of the investment-output ratio in the postwar period, compared with earlier periods, was greater in commerce than in manufacturing.

(2) In manufacturing differences between periods in the rate of growth of the capital stock largely matched those in output, with the conspicuous exception of the interwar period, when the rate of capital accumulation was anomalously low.

(3) The capital-output ratio in manufacturing rose both in the pre-1914 period and after World War II. However, this finding cannot be leant on too heavily for the pre-1914 period because of the unreliability of the data on the capital stock, particularly those on retirements.

(4) The high rate of capital accumulation in both manufacturing and commerce in the postwar period occurred notwithstanding a profit rate that was on average lower than in the interwar period.

(5) In commerce the trend in the *rate of change* in the capital-output ratio was steadily upward: the capital-output ratio fell before 1914 (again a statistically unreliable finding), rose slightly in the interwar period, and rose substantially after World War II.

(6) Manufacturing and commerce differed greatly in the amplitude and timing of the long swing in capital formation after World War II (Fig. 11.1). In manufacturing the swing was mild, especially its upward phase, and the peak came earlier than in any other major sector. In commerce the rate of growth of the capital stock rose steeply during the 1950's and thereafter remained more or less on a plateau.

With these feature in mind, we shall now review the chief forces that influenced the course of investment. The treatment will be analytical but not econometric.[1]

The Pre-1914 Period: Manufacturing

The rate of fixed capital accumulation in manufacturing followed a clear-cut long swing after the early 1870's, with peaks in 1876 and 1903 and a trough in 1891 (Fig. 13.1). Before 1873 its movements were irregular and it was at a higher level than subsequently.

In considering forces affecting MEI, it is natural to look first at output trends. Accordingly, capital accumulation and the growth of output in manufacturing are compared in Tables 13.1 and, by individual business cycles, 13.2. Both were lower in 1873–1913 than in 1856–73. The long swing in the rate of growth of the capital stock after 1873 likewise conformed broadly to the movements of output, subject to a lag and with larger amplitude. The wider amplitude of the movements in capital accumulation may be conjectured to have been the result partly of overshooting, as in ordinary business cycles, and partly of crowding-out (or its opposite) by overseas investment in certain phases.

The trend in the capital-output ratio over the period as a whole was upward: upward till the early 1880's, flat or slightly downward from then until 1899, and then upward again at the second long swing peak. Though the possibility cannot be ruled out that the trend rise in the capital-output ratio was due partly to an increase in the relative weights of industries with high capital-intensity, there is no actual evidence for this.[2] What, then, *was* it due to?

In part it was probably unplanned. After the investment boom of the 1870's, demand notoriously failed to rise as much as had been hoped — partly because of foreign competition and general depression, partly because the investment had simply been based on exaggerated expectations. However, if that had been the only cause, one would expect the trend to have reversed itself, and this did not happen: the reaction in investment in the late 1870's and in the 1880's was not sufficient to reduce the capital-output ratio significantly. Moreover, the hypothesis that the rise in the ratio was unplanned does not apply readily to its

TABLE 13.2

Growth of Output and Fixed Capital Stock in Manufacturing Between
Cycle Peaks, 1856–1907

(Annual percentage growth rates)

Variable	1856–1860	1860–1865	1865–1873	1873–1882	1882–1889	1889–1899	1899–1907
(1) Output	2.5%	1.8%	3.2%	2.3%	1.8%	2.3%	1.6%
(2) Capital (lagged 4 years)	4.3	3.8	3.8	2.3	1.6	2.8	2.7
(3) Excess of (2) over (1)	1.8	2.0	0.6	0.0	−0.2	0.5	1.1

renewed rise in the 1890's and 1900's, when complaints of disappointed expectations were not prominent. The resumption in this period of investment on a substantial scale implies acquiescence in a lower profit rate, since, though the profit rate by then had stabilized, it had not made good its earlier fall.

It appears, therefore, that the explanation must lie in a decline in SPOF. Since interest rates ceased to fall after the mid-1890's, this decline in SPOF must have been due primarily to diminished imperfection in the capital market. The spread of the joint-stock form of organization is indeed known to have been particularly rapid in this period.

The combination of an upward trend in the capital-output ratio and a falling trend in the rate of profit gives little support to the hypothesis that an unduly high SPOF was creating a capital shortage in manufacturing or was itself much of an independent obstacle to growth in that sector. The implication is of a movement downward along the MEI schedule, not due wholly to the fall in the rate of growth of output.

Would the fall in MEI have been less if the investment had been better directed? The rate of growth of TFP was low and falling, and it is natural to conjecture that the direction of investment was insufficiently innovative. As against this, there is evidence that some of the innovative investment that firms in traditional industries were reproached for not doing would not have been worthwhile; and that the profit experience of firms that invested in the newer industries (where it is more difficult to find objective reasons for Britain's lag) was not uniformly favorable (A. J. Taylor 1961; Sandberg 1969; see also Saul 1960, 1962). Yet it remains a paradox, particularly, that the investment boom of the late 1890's and early 1900's was followed by a period in which labor productivity grew more slowly than ever — and this notwithstanding that there was not the same manifest deficiency of demand as there had been in the 1880's. One partial explanation of this paradox may be that the benefits of the investment are understated insofar as it was directed to the production of new goods (bicycles, cars) underweighted in the production indexes. Even allowing for this, however, and for the possibility that other real forces were making it more difficult to increase productivity after 1900, the result remains surprising, and it is difficult to avoid the conclusion that much of the investment was ill-conceived.

The Pre-1914 Period: Commerce

Investment in commerce followed broadly the same long swing pattern as investment in manufacturing (Fig. 13.1); but the average rate of growth of the fixed capital stock was much lower than in manufacturing, both absolutely and relative to the growth of labor input. This difference can be explained in several ways. (1) In many regions, notably in London, there was still a chronic excess supply of labor, making for low-productivity employment in services, in accordance with the usual pattern. (2) Demand was more stable and less subject to foreign competition, so there was less propensity for capital capacity to outstrip demand. (3) It is possible that investment in commerce was more sensitive than investment in manufacturing to crowding-out by capital export, either directly, because it was more dependent on external finance, or indirectly, because it had more links with investment in dwellings. This is suggested by the experience of the years 1907–13, when interest rates were rising, and investment in commerce did not share the recovery manifested by investment in manufacturing.

The Interwar Period: Manufacturing

Investment in fixed capital in manufacturing in the interwar period was remarkably low. Both the investment-output ratio and the rate of growth of the capital stock were lower than before 1914, *notwithstanding that the rate of growth of output was higher.* The capital-output ratio fell steeply, in contrast to its rise before 1914, and by a much greater extent than in any other sector of the economy (Table 8.3). More than this, the capital-labor ratio actually fell (Table 13.1). What explanations can be found for this unusual pattern?

A distinctive feature of the interwar period in a number of industries was the existence of excess capacity, consequent on the failure of output to regain its 1913 level. This is the most obvious explanation for the low investment and for the large fall in the profit rate compared with pre-1914. But though excess capacity certainly played a major role in inhibiting investment in some industries, it cannot serve as the whole explanation for the low level of manufacturing investment. It cannot be held that the expansion of output between 1924 and 1937 was made possible simply by calling back into use old unused capacity in such a way as to make new investment unnecessary. This may be seen from a review of the data.

In industries like cotton and iron and steel, output in 1924 was below the 1913 level, and the amount of excess capacity was large (partly because of overoptimistic investment in the years immediately after the war). But even as early as 1924 there were other industries where the situation was much better. Between 1913 and 1924 manufacturing output as a whole grew at an annual rate of 0.7 percent, and the fixed capital stock in manufacturing is estimated to have grown at an annual rate of 1.5 percent. This rise in the capital-output ratio at a rate of 0.8 percent, distributed very unequally between different industries, was only slightly higher than the trend rate of rise, 0.6 percent, between 1856 and 1913. Between 1924 and 1929 manufacturing output grew quite rapidly, and by 1929 the capital-output ratio was already lower than it had been in 1913. A further sharp fall in the ratio took place between 1929 and 1937. By 1937 output in all but a few manufacturing industries was far above what it had been in 1913 or 1920: as a percentage of 1913, total manufacturing production was 162, the gross fixed capital stock was 128, and the net fixed capital stock was 115.*

It is the steepness of the rise in output in the interwar period that makes the low investment puzzling. The problem has an investment function aspect and a production function aspect; the two are related. Why did manufacturers not choose to do more investment in view of the rise in the demand for their products? And how were they able to increase their output so much from such a slowly growing capital stock?

Part of the answer to the first of these questions lies in the state of confidence and expectations. The damage done to confidence by the generally depressed condition of the economy in the 1920's, followed by the renewed deterioration after 1929, was such that in the early 1930's a return to the 1929 peak was the best that was hoped for in many industries; the concept of long-run growth as the normal state of

---

*The effective capital-output ratio admittedly fell less than the measured capital-output ratio, on account of the trend increase in the intensity of use of equipment (above, pp. 152–54). This increase apparently reflected an increase in planned intensity of use, rather than a rise in demand, since it is observable between the years 1924 and 1930, in which output of manufactures was at about the same level. A similar upward trend occurred in 1937–51 and in the postwar period. We do not know whether it occurred before 1914. If it did, comparison between periods is unaffected. If it did not, the question remains why for the first time it became possible in the interwar period.

affairs is conspicuously lacking in the literature of the period (for example, British Association 1935, 1938). As a result, industry was taken by surprise by the steep rise in demand in 1935–37, and the industries most affected had difficulty in meeting the demand by the end of the period. In the machine tool industry, for example, delivery dates as far ahead as 1940 were being quoted by some manufacturers in 1937 (British Association 1938: 390). The iron and steel industry was another case in point. Here output in 1929 had barely regained its 1913 level, and the industry was taken unawares by the steep increase in demand from 1935. Investment in the industry rose very rapidly in the late 1930's under this stimulus, but because the rise in output was sudden and unexpected, demand outran the increase in the capital stock. Such investment as had been carried out earlier had been designed to improve efficiency rather than increase capacity (Burn 1940: 450–83, especially p. 468). Moreover, not only had industry failed to invest enough to provide in advance for the increase in output, but when the increase in output came, there were fears that it was transitory (because of its dependence on rearmament). This encouraged firms to meet the high demand as far as they could by intensive use of their existing capacity rather than by adding new capacity. Investment and output in manufacturing both rose to new peaks in the late 1930's. However, whereas the rise in output was general across manufacturing industry, the investment boom, such as it was, was mainly confined to the metals and metal-using industries. In the remainder of manufacturing industry investment was only moderately higher in 1937 than in 1929.[3]

Expectations thus helped to explain why the growth of the capital stock was low despite the rapid increase in output and despite a significant recovery in profit rates. But they do not answer the production function side of the question: that is, how it was possible to expand output so much with so little investment. It is remarkable that a fall in the capital-output ratio between 1924 and 1937 is found in every manufacturing industry group without exception, including rapidly growing industries such as vehicles and electrical engineering, where a legacy of old excess capacity can hardly have been important. Falls in the capital-labor ratio were, naturally, less universal, but nonetheless widespread (Table 8.7). The question therefore arises whether there was a technological bias toward capital-saving.

Comparison of trends in manufacturing at the aggregate level between 1924 and 1937 does not give any guidance one way or the other about the presence of a capital-saving bias in technical progress, as theoretically defined.[4] However, it is possible to point to technical developments in this period that had, to a greater extent than most innovations have, the effect of reducing capital costs in manufacturing. The chief of these was the changeover to electricity as a source of power, a development that was accompanied by an increase in the proportion of electricity purchased as opposed to generated within the firm.[5] This had its counterpart in the high rate of growth of output and capital stock in the public utilities sector.

Electrification was a change that extended over the whole range of manufacturing. It meant that the capital required to produce the power used by manufacturing lay increasingly outside manufacturing. Apart from this straightforward capital-saving effect of electrification (as far as manufacturing is concerned), it is likely that a capital-saving effect also resulted because electrification permitted the more flexible and efficient use of any given horsepower. One of these consequences was the extension of the use of (relatively cheap) machine tools. This development was also facilitated by metallurgical advances.[6]

Structural changes among our 13 standard manufacturing industry groups contributed to the reduction in the capital-output ratio, but not to an important extent (Table 11.4). A finer disaggregation might indicate a rather larger contribution from this source. Electrical engineering is a case in point. The flattening-out of the investment program of the electricity supply industry after the completion of the national grid in the early 1930's led to a shift away from heavy engineering toward the labor-intensive production of electrical equipment for cars, radios, and the like.

The foregoing considerations all relate to MEI. The effects of trends in SPOF are more difficult to trace.

(1) Interest rates were high in the 1920's compared with before 1914. When they fell in the 1930's, it is doubtful whether there was much effect on investment in manufacturing, since, as already seen, the rise in investment was mainly in the metal-using sectors, where the exceptional pressure of demand provides an adequate explanation. It is possible, however, that if interest rates had been lower in the 1920's, when confidence had not yet been so undermined by the cumulative effects of prolonged depression, investment would have been more responsive, at least in the newer industries.

(2) The transition to the joint-stock form of organization in manufacturing was largely completed by World War I, so there was less gain to be had in the interwar period from that source of reduction in capital market imperfection and fall in the SPOF schedule.

(3) The supply of *internal* finance at the margin appears to have been fairly adequate (above, p. 349). The margin, however, is defined by the low prevailing level of investment. The substantial fall in the

profit rate compared with before 1914 must have made for difficulty in financing additions to the capital stock from internal sources, had manufacturers been minded to do so on a larger scale. All in all, therefore, it appears that the trend in SPOF was unfavorable, compared with before 1914. The trend is therefore in the right direction to have encouraged the use of labor-intensive methods of production, especially when taken in conjunction with the abundant supply of labor.

The Interwar Period: Commerce

Investment in commerce in the interwar period followed a markedly different path from investment in manufacturing. It was higher than before 1914, both as a proportion of income generated in the sector and as a proportion of its capital stock. There was, it is true, some fall in the capital-labor ratio in commerce, as well as in manufacturing; but it was of smaller extent, and in any case it is less surprising, in view of the abnormal increase in commercial employment on account of the depression. The recorded capital-output ratio rose. It is tempting to explain the contrast with manufacturing by saying that commerce did not take such a knock across World War I as manufacturing did from changes in international competitiveness. But the data on output, for what they are worth, do not support this explanation. Output in commerce is shown as actually having a less favorable trend than output in manufacturing: it was lower absolutely in 1924 than in 1913, and its rise between 1924 and 1937 was no more rapid than in 1873–1913 — in both respects contrasting with manufacturing. The most obvious explanation for the contrasting trend in investment is simply that unlike manufacturing, commerce did not experience a capital-saving bias in technical progress — indeed there may have been some bias in the opposite direction, notably because of the increased use of motor vehicles in commerce. In addition, the large changes in the structure of commercial output may have stimulated investment: there was a decline in commercial activities connected with foreign trade and an increase in, for example, banking and building societies catering for the domestic market; and the shift in population with suburbanization created demand for new shopping facilities. Finally, though this is a matter of speculation, the trend in the supply of finance may have been more favorable for commerce than for manufacturing. Did some of the people driven into commerce by lack of jobs elsewhere bring some capital with them? More important, probably, the spread of the joint-stock form of organization and the resulting trend reduction in the degree of capital market imperfection had proceeded less far by World War I in commerce than in manufacturing, so there was more scope for continuing gain in the interwar period.

The final question that remains to be asked about industrial and commercial investment in the interwar period is the counterfactual one: what would have happened if investment had been higher? The question, clearly, is of interest chiefly in relation to manufacturing. Would there have been a strong tendency to diminishing returns, as was suggested above in regard to the period 1873–1913? Diminishing returns would have been expected insofar as the reason why investment was actually low was that technical progress had a capital-saving character. But though that was part of the reason, it was not the only one. Insofar as the reason for low investment was a lack of confidence, a shortage of internal finance, or the availability of large resources of labor, a higher rate of investment would not necessarily have been attended by much tendency to diminishing returns, at least in the long run. The long run, in this sense, arrived for a limited number of industries in the late 1930's, when capital capacity became a bottleneck, and it arrived for the economy as a whole during World War II. Given the relatively short length of life of much plant and equipment, a higher level of investment in this class of capital in the 1920's or even the 1930's might not by itself have made much difference to the capital stock available during most of the postwar period. But it would have eased the transition to the requirements of the postwar period, both by allowing a higher level of output (and hence savings) in the early part of the postwar period and by facilitating learning from the experience of more capital-intensive techniques of production.

The Postwar Period: Manufacturing

After the peculiar interlude of the interwar period, with its steeply falling capital-output ratio, investment in manufacturing in the postwar period reverted to a pattern that in its statistical aggregates in some ways more resembled the pre-1914 period.* The major difference from the pre-1914 period was, of course, that both output and the capital stock in the postwar period grew much faster. The resemblances between the two periods are that the capital-output ratio rose (at much the same rate: 0.6 percent a year in 1873–1913, 0.5 percent a year in 1951–73), and that the rate of profit had a downward trend.

*Manufacturing in this section refers throughout to manufacturing excluding textiles, for statistical reasons (see p. 649, note 17).

It is not surprising that the pattern should have been different from the interwar pattern, since two of the principal forces that had kept investment down had ceased to apply, the once-for-all capital-saving bias in technical progress, chiefly associated with electrification, and the abnormally depressed state of expectations. However, there remain some important questions to consider about manufacturing investment in the postwar period. Why did the capital-output ratio rise, contrary to what would be expected in a sector with an above-average rate of growth of TFP? Was it because of trends in the MEI schedule or because of trends in the SPOF schedule? Would still higher investment have permitted output to grow at a rate more like that achieved on the Continent?

These and other questions about manufacturing investment in the postwar period as a whole have to be considered in relation to its time pattern within the period. Apart from business cycles, this pattern was one of relative stability by comparison with most other sectors (Fig. 11.1). However, there was a mild long swing, which reached its peak relatively early, around 1960. The downward phase of the long swing was steeper than the upward phase. Another characteristic is apparent in Figure 13.2. The long swing was due essentially to investment in buildings and works. The time pattern in the case of plant and machinery was entirely different, except for the closing years of the period (after 1969), when both classes of capital accumulation fell quite steeply. Prior to that, the trend in the rate of increase in the stock of plant and machinery was either constant or mildly downward, lacking both the upward phase of the long swing in buildings and works and the pronounced falloff in the 1960's. The rate of increase in the stock of plant and machinery was considerably higher than that in buildings and works throughout (as it had been before 1914 but not in the interwar period).[7]

Let us consider first the influence of *the expected growth of output*. Acceleration-principle models, based on the hypothesis that expectations about future output are derived from an extrapolation of past actual trends, have been found quite good predictors of short-run (cyclical) movements in manufacturing investment in the postwar period (Doig 1976; Savage 1977). They do not explain why investment was higher in the postwar period than in the interwar period, since output of manufactures grew at much the same rate in the two periods; but the forces that made the interwar period peculiar have already been explained. Acceleration-principle models could explain why investment was higher in the postwar period than in the period before

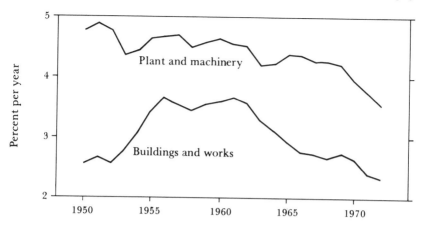

Fig. 13.2. Growth over four-year periods of the gross fixed capital stock in manufacturing (excluding textiles) by asset, 1948–1974. These are average annual growth rates over four-year periods centered in the years shown; they are approximately equal to four-year moving averages of year-to-year growth rates.

1914, but not why the capital-output ratio rose in both periods. Moreover, at least in the postwar period, the effective capital-output ratio rose more than the measured capital-output ratio, on account of the upward trend in utilization (pp. 152–57).

Variations in the actual rate of growth of output go a little way, but not very far, to explain movements of investment in manufacturing *within* the postwar period. The output of manufactures grew fast in the first half of the 1950's and more slowly after that. The lagged effects could help to explain why the rate of capital accumulation rose up to about 1960 and then tailed off. However, after 1955 the rate of growth of output was very stable (apart from cycles), so these effects can scarcely account for the *continuous* falling-off in the rate of capital accumulation that occurred after the beginning of the 1960's.[8]

Expectations about the rate of growth of demand are not necessarily determined exclusively by an extrapolation of the recent past. It was suggested earlier that in the course of the 1950's, postwar prosperity was viewed with increasing confidence as more than just a flash in the pan, and it was also suggested that after the mid–1960's, there was a waning of confidence, due particularly to the apparent feebleness of the cyclical peak of 1968–69. This would be broadly consistent with the observed time pattern of investment. Profitability (in the sense of profits' share) is a further possible influence on producers' expectations about what level of output they can most advantageously produce. Profitability was already declining in the 1950's, so it cannot be invoked to explain the *rising* trend in capital accumulation at that time; but its continued fall in the 1960's, and especially after 1968, is consis-. tent with the downward phase in the long swing in capital accumulation. The downward trend in profits' share in manufacturing in the period 1951–73 was substantial, so it is quite possible that it exercised some downward pressure on producers' expectations about the output that would be most profitable to produce.*

The acceleration principle, broadly interpreted to take account of confidence, profitability, and the known abnormalities of the interwar period, is thus capable of explaining a good deal but not all of the postwar behavior of investment in manufacturing. Can it be extended to explain also the rise in the capital-output ratio and the fall in the profit rate, by postulating that as the postwar period advanced, output fell below expectations to an increasing degree? It was suggested earlier that disappointment of this sort was an element in the similar situation in the 1870's and 1880's. As applied to the postwar period, however, the hypothesis is difficult to reconcile with the absence of any clear trend in the degree of capacity-utilization in the sense measured by the CBI survey data. Also apparently to be rejected is the hypothesis that the rise in the capital-output ratio was due to a structural shift toward industries with above-average capital-intensity (see Table 11.4). So we turn now to other possible explanations.

Arrears. The acceleration principle can be modified to take into account the initial level of the capital stock. The hypothesis could be advanced that one reason why investment in manufacturing in the postwar period was high by historical standards was the need to make up for arrears originating during and before the war. An objection to this is that betweeen 1937 and 1951 the capital-output ratio in manufacturing actually rose.[9] However, some arrears were already present in 1937 on account of the failure of investment to keep pace with the growth of output in the 1930's. Moreover, in the early 1950's investment, particularly in buildings and works, was still to some extent held back by shortages and controls, delaying the elimination of any existing arrears and adding to them (the rate of growth of the stock of manufacturing buildings and works in the early 1950's was considerably less than the rate of growth of manufacturing output).

*The decline in profitability was not nearly as great as it was after 1974. It is natural to suppose that the severe squeeze on profits in 1974 caused more damage to expectations, and led to a greater curtailment of investment plans, than had occurred in the first year of earlier downturns in the output cycle. However, the marked downward trend in investment at the end of the period is apparent already in the moving averages that terminate before 1974. The 1974 observation is not out of trend.

Increase in the desired capital-output ratio on account of labor shortage. Unemployment was much lower in the postwar period than in former periods, and the labor force was growing much less rapidly. A shortage of skilled labor, at least, was a regular feature in manufacturing at cyclical peaks. Labor did not become *increasingly* scarce in the course of the postwar period, so full employment cannot be invoked as an explanation for the *continuous* rise in the capital-output ratio. But the cost of labor continued to increase relative to the cost of capital. This may provide some explanation for the contrasting trends in investment in plant and machinery and investment in buildings and works. Investment in buildings and works probably contains a larger element of investment designed to expand capacity ("widening") and a smaller element of investment designed to substitute capital for labor ("deepening") than investment in plant and machinery. During the whole of the 1960's the rate of growth of the stock of plant and machinery was well maintained,[10] whereas that of buildings and works fell off steeply. Likewise, in the late 1940's and early 1950's investment in plant and machinery was already high, whereas investment in buildings and works was only just beginning to rise. These contrasts are consistent with the notion that investment in buildings and works was chiefly determined by confidence about the rate of growth of output and investment in plant and equipment was largely, if not chiefly, determined by the inducement to substitute capital for labor.* At the end of the period, in the late 1960's and early 1970's, the combination of rising SPOF and diminished profitability discouraged both classes of investment.

The inducement to substitute capital for labor in the postwar period operated even more strongly in commerce than in manufacturing (see below). In both sectors, insofar as investment was stimulated by the low postwar growth of the labor supply (rather than by full employment), capital accumulation acted as a *stabilizer* on growth, compensating for the slow growth in the complementary input.

Movements in SPOF. The movements in SPOF discussed in the preceding chapter are consistent with its having played a part in the long swing within the postwar period. Tax changes tended to lower the SPOF schedule till the mid-1960's, or possibly longer if lagged reactions to tax incentives are allowed for. The widening of the market for

---

*A particular class of investment induced by labor shortage is "amenity investment"—investment that serves exclusively or mainly to improve working conditions and is undertaken to help recruit or retain labor. It was often said by businessmen that this was a significant motive for investment, both in manufacturing and in services, but its magnitude cannot be assessed from macro-economic data.

equities and the relaxation of restrictions on bank finance in the 1950's also tended to lower the SPOF schedule. After about 1968 the SPOF schedule rose, on account of less favorable tax treatment and a reduction in the profits available for self-finance. These movements would by themselves have tended to make for a rather later downturn than actually occurred, but they have to be considered in conjunction with the fall in profitability.

How did SPOF in the postwar period as a whole compare with what it had been in earlier periods? The widening of the market for equities represented a continuation of the long-term trend toward diminished imperfections in the capital market. The same is true of the increase in the size of firms. By comparison with before 1914 the decline in the ability to invest abroad had some tendency to reduce competition for finance.

Since firms did in fact increase their capital stock at a faster rate than formerly, despite a lower and falling profit rate, these long-run influences tending to reduce SPOF must have outweighed the adverse effects of the lower profit rate on the availability of internal finance.

We turn finally, as we did in treating the earlier periods, to counterfactual questions. The answer to these depends on the extent to which there was a downward shift in the MEI schedule in the latter part of the period on account of diminishing returns. In other words, did the (historically) high rate of capital accumulation depress the MEI schedule to a greater extent than it was being raised by the other elements in growth? If so, the long swing can be viewed as having some resemblance in its underlying mechanism to an ordinary business cycle (only without much feedback through the level of demand in the downswing phase, since the rate of growth of manufacturing output between cycle peaks was more or less constant from 1955 to 1973). In the case of widening investment, this would mean that there was overshooting in manufacturing similar to that experienced, on a much more spectacular scale, in electricity supply. In the case of deepening, it would mean that opportunities for substituting capital for labor were being used up faster than new ones accrued.

The macro-economic evidence in favor of this hypothesis is substantial. The capital-output ratio rose (in contrast to what was happening in other countries). Ever-increasing fiscal inducements to investment, extending up to the mid-1960's and with effects lasting possibly longer, failed to prevent a falling-off in investment, especially in buildings and works. The rate of return on capital fell.

Certain objections may be raised to the relevance of the evidence afforded by the fall in the profit rate — and hence also to the evidence afforded by the fall in investment, insofar as that was caused by the fall in the profit rate.

(1) The decline in profitability was at least partly due to causes other than diminishing returns: (a) increased foreign competition, (b) increased labor militancy and/or government restriction of profit margins, (c) historic cost pricing in face of accelerating inflation. Of these, the last two apply only to the years after 1968. They do mean that not too much weight should be attached to the *accelerated* fall in the profit rate in those years as evidence of diminishing returns in the above sense. Whether foreign competition is sufficient to account for the whole of the downward trend in the profit rate in the earlier part of the postwar period is more doubtful (there was also a fall, albeit a smaller one, in the profit rate in services, which were relatively free from foreign competition).

(2) The profit rate may have understated the social return from investment to an increasing extent as the period advanced; the rate of growth of TFP in manufacturing had an upward trend, especially after 1964, and this was partly or wholly due to capital accumulation. Like all hypotheses about externalities, this one is difficult to rule out. However, it is not at all clear that the increase in the rate of TFP growth after 1964 was due to concurrent increases in capital input rather than to a once-for-all shake-out. It may be noted that there is no correlation between the rate of growth of the capital stock (or of capital per unit of labor) and the rate of growth of TFP in cross-section comparisons of manufacturing industries (Appendix J).

Though these objections have a certain amount of force, they do not seem to us sufficient to overturn the presumption created by the macro-evidence that diminishing returns attended postwar investment in British manufacturing. If this is correct, it follows that a higher rate of investment than was actually carried out would, in the absence of other changes, have led to a correspondingly more rapid tendency to diminishing returns. This does not imply that higher investment would not have made a contribution to faster growth, or even that the rate of return on investment was not below the optimum, defined as the social rate of time discount. But it does seem unlikely that a higher rate of investment would by itself have transformed the performance of British manufacturing and led it to achieve a "continental" growth rate.[11]

A more difficult question is how far the diminishing returns were due to lack of demand for the product of manufacturing, and how far to more deep-seated constraints on the supply side. A similar question arises for the pre-1914 period. To any individual firm or industry, the limits to profitable capital accumulation will always seem to be set by demand, but that does not necessarily prove that the same is true for the economy as a whole. This question will arise again in the discussion of the effects of trends in international trade in Chapter 15.

Pursuing the counterfactual question further, we may ask whether there would have been more scope for (privately and socially) profitable investment if investment had been better directed. Mention may be made of some particular hypotheses that have been put forward in this connection.

One set of hypotheses relates to the balance between widening and deepening investment. Some years ago Sargent (1963: 8–12) suggested that manufacturing investment in the earlier part of the postwar period involved too much widening and not enough deepening. He attributed this to an illusion of ample labor supply created by the stop-go cycle (it could also have been attributed to an underestimation of future rises in labor costs). This hypothesis seems less plausible now than it did when it was first put forward. Evidence of a substantial amount of investment having had a deepening character is provided by the large shake-out of labor that proved possible after the middle of the 1960's and by the trend rise in the capital-output ratio combined with the absence of any clear trend in underutilization of capacity at successive cycle peaks. A rather more convincing variant of the hypothesis is that the choice of investment projects did not have sufficient regard to the need to economize on *skilled* manual labor. The proportion of skilled manual labor in the total labor force had a pronounced downward trend (Table 4.5), and skilled labor was persistently the most stringent supply-side bottleneck at cycle peaks (Table 3.22).

The "defensive-investment" hypothesis of Lamfalussy (1961, 1963) relates to a different dimension of investment, a dimension not much considered in conventional capital theory: its complementarity with existing capital. According to this hypothesis, there was an excessive tendency in British manufacturing to devote investment to patching up and improving old plants in circumstances where it would have been better to start completely afresh. This fault was attributed by Lamfalussy to the disadvantages of an early industrial start.* We have not been able to devise a satisfactory test of this interesting hypothesis, and it may have some validity. There is some reason to suppose that any

*In principle, the existence of old assets cannot be an actual disadvantage unless there is a cost of demolishing them to make way for new ones. This is a plausible hypothesis in the case of land-intensive activities like agriculture (David 1971) or central-city commerce, but hardly in the case of manufacturing, since there is normally no need to locate new manufacturing plant on the old site. However, the same effect may be produced by pressure from trade unions or by irrational conservatism in management.

tendency to concentrate on "defensive" investment was mainly a feature of the early postwar years and diminished thereafter.[12]

Yet another hypothesis is that the government's location policy forced or induced firms to carry out investment in areas that were not the most advantageous. This suggestion, like the one about defensive investment, has most relevance to the earliest part of the postwar period, though it has some application to the concluding years as well. Between the mid–1950's and the mid–1960's, location policy was pretty well in abeyance.[13]

The misdirection of investment is barely separable from other managerial or organizational shortcomings. If investment decisions are unscientific, so, probably, are other managerial decisions; if there are restrictive labor practices, they probably affect current labor productivity as well as the inducement to innovative investment; and so on. A case can be made for all the suggestions made in the foregoing paragraphs, and they are best regarded as *examples* of general inefficiency. It is doubtful whether one can conclude that it was *predominantly* in investment decisions that room existed for improving efficiency, or that correction of a few basic and systematic faults in this area would have made all the difference.

The Postwar Period: Commerce

In the case of commerce in the postwar period, we need to consider two questions: why capital accumulation was so high, not only in relation to earlier periods but also in relation to manufacturing in the same period; and what accounted for its time path within that period, viz. a steep rise in the 1950's, followed by the maintenance of a high and slightly rising level until the end of the period—a quite different pattern from manufacturing's (Fig. 11.1).

The high rate of capital accumulation in commerce occurred notwithstanding a substantial fall in the profit rate compared with before World War II (Table 13.1), and notwithstanding the relative absence in the postwar period of the fiscal favors lavished on manufacturing—in particular commercial buildings qualified for no depreciation allowances, accelerated or otherwise, and they form a large part of the capital stock in services. In the period 1937–51 investment in commerce, in contrast to manufacturing, was very low, so arrears were to be expected in the ensuing period. But output in commerce, as measured, was lower in 1951 than in 1937,* so the capital-output ratio did not fall.

*This is not as paradoxical as it seems, because consumption, the main determinant of output in the distributive trades, rose very little between 1937 and 1951, unlike GDP.

Output in commerce grew at a significantly faster rate in the post-war period than in the interwar period. Moreover, commerce did not experience more than a mild squeeze on profits' share in the course of the postwar period, so there was little reason on that account for pro-ducers, in forming expectations about the level of output that would prove most profitable, to take a less optimistic view than that suggested by extrapolation of the recent past. This does not, however, as such ac-count for the rises that occurred in the capital-output ratio and in the capital-labor ratio: both larger than the corresponding rises in manu-facturing.

As far as the capital-output ratio is concerned, it is again not surpris-ing that there should have been some rise, and moreover a larger one than in most of the rest of the economy, for the general reason referred to (pp. 337–38). Productivity grows less rapidly in commerce than in the economy as a whole, and the price of its output (as measured) con-sequently rises relative to other prices, including the prices of capital goods. This does not explain, however, why the capital-*labor* ratio rose more than in manufacturing. Nor does it explain why the volume capi-tal-output ratio in commerce rose by enough to bring about a rise in the value capital-output ratio. The rise in the value capital-output ratio was a larger element in the fall in the profit rate than was the fall in profits' share.

There are grounds for believing that an important part of the expla-nation was that the shortage of labor brought about by the transition to full employment had particularly strong effects in commerce.

In the first place, industries that have a relatively low capital-intensity, as do most of the service industries, are likely to be par-ticularly concerned to find means of economizing labor when it be-comes scarce or dear. This is supported by the data in Table 13.3, which show an inverse relationship between the initial level of capital-intensity and its subsequent increase, comparing parts of the economy that are predominantly or largely in the private sector.*

In the second place, certain features of the labor market are rele-vant. The distributive trades (and also miscellaneous services, though not insurance, banking, and finance) traditionally pay relatively low wages. They are therefore particularly sensitive to the general state of the labor market. If higher-paying jobs in manufacturing or elsewhere

---

*This relationship can be interpreted in various ways. The interpretation here offered is in keeping with Charles Kennedy's hypothesis (1964) of induced bias in technical progress. A different interpretation is put forward by Ulman 1968, and discussed by Matthews 1970 and Caves 1970.

TABLE 13.3

Capital-Output Ratios and Changes in Capital Intensity by Sector, 1951–1973

Sector	K/Q at current prices, 1951	1951–1973	
		$\hat{K} - \hat{Q}$	$\hat{K} - \hat{L}$
Construction	0.7	3.3	5.7
Commerce	2.1	1.5	4.8
Manufacturing	3.2	0.5	4.2
Transport and communications	7.2	−1.0	2.7

Note: K includes inventories. Manufacturing excludes textiles, and transport and communications excludes roads.

are available, people prefer to take them. The inflow of labor into the distributive trades and related service activities in the interwar depression has already been discussed. Across World War II employment in these industries declined drastically. In the postwar period they continued to experience difficulty in recruiting labor, especially in cyclical booms (George 1966: 60–64; George 1969). The shortage of labor manifested itself in non-availability rather than relatively increased wage rates: the ratio of average hourly earnings in the distributive trades to those in manufacturing (excluding textiles) was much the same in 1964 (92 percent) and 1973 (90 percent) as it was in 1937 (91 percent).[14] However, the cost of labor in services was increased by the imposition of the Selective Employment Tax in 1968, by which time labor had become less scarce and the effects of the adjustment to the earlier labor shortage might otherwise have been expected to have run out.

A further possible reason why a labor shortage may have had a stronger effect on investment in commerce than in manufacturing concerns expectations. As was noted in Chapter 11, a shortage of labor has an ambivalent effect on investment, and much depends on producers' expectations about future demand. Manufacturing, being more subject to international competition than commerce, was less able to project a firm rate of growth of output in the expectation that the prices realized could be relied upon to cover the costs. Hence insofar as a labor shortage *was* experienced, as it was with skilled labor, a larger proportion of firms in manufacturing than in commerce may have chosen to acquiesce in a slow rate of growth of output rather than compensate by labor-saving investment.

There were thus at least three reasons making for high MEI, and hence for a high rate of capital accumulation, in commerce in the postwar period: a reasonably high rate of growth of consumption and hence of output; a rise in the relative price of the sector's output; and a scarcity of labor. Profits' share was better maintained by commerce during the postwar period than by manufacturing. The profit rate in commerce did fall significantly across World War II, and it fell again after 1960 (following some rise in the 1950's). But it evidently remained sufficiently high relative to SPOF for investment not to be deterred.

In addition to the reasons already cited, there were others that affected some of the service industries for part or all of the postwar period. Thus the trend to self-service in the distributive trades and the building of supermarkets were encouraged by the diffusion of car ownership and by the shifts of population away from the inner city, as well as by the labor shortage. On the financial side, speculative considerations (the property boom) doubtless influenced office-building toward the end of the period, but it was probably only in the 1970's that this became a force in its own right (rather than a reflection of rising land prices due to real forces). Finally, it may be conjectured that the continued high rate of personal savings after the mid–1960's, when corporate savings were dropping off (Fig. 5.6), helped commerce relative to manufacturing because of its greater dependence for finance on personal savings channeled through financial intermediaries.

The foregoing discussion of the forces affecting investment in commerce over the postwar period as a whole leaves relatively little to add about the reason for its time pattern within the periods. The low rate of investment until the late 1950's was largely attributable to continuing controls, especially on building. This low rate made for arrears and hence for higher investment later. The forces that made for high MEI in the postwar period as a whole also accounted for the long persistence of high investment in the sector between the late 1950's and the early 1970's. The property boom contributed somewhat to the maintenance of high investment in the early 1970's but was not the chief cause.[15]

INFRASTRUCTURE

Infrastructure investment is here defined as investment in utilities, transport and communications, and public and professional services. Not all the capital in these industries is strictly speaking of the infrastructure type, but most of it is. In the postwar period infrastructure investment so defined was equivalent to public-sector investment, excluding dwellings and mining, plus a certain amount of private-sector investment (mainly in shipping and road transport). In earlier periods there was already much public ownership in these industries, and there

TABLE 13.4

Annual Growth Rates of Output, Labor, and Fixed Capital, and Investment–Gross National Product Ratios, in Utilities, Transport and Communications, and Public and Professional Services, 1856–1973

(Percent)

Sector and variable	1856–1873	1873–1913	1913–1924	1924–1937	1937–1951	1951–1964	1964–1973
Utilities							
Output	5.5%	5.1%	3.2%	5.8%	4.2%	5.1%	5.2%
Labor[a]	1.8	3.5	3.8	3.1	1.4	0.5	−3.4
Capital	4.9	3.6	2.8	4.9	0.9	4.0	4.2
Investment-GNP ratio[b]	0.3	0.4	–	1.2	–	2.0	2.1
Transport and communications[c]							
Output	2.9	2.7	1.4	1.5	2.4	2.2	3.5
Labor[a]	2.6	1.8	0.3	0.7	0.5	−0.7	−1.3
Capital	2.9	1.9	0.0	0.6	−0.3	1.4	3.5
Investment-GNP ratio[b]	2.9	2.6	–	1.7	–	2.4	3.3
Public and professional services							
Capital	2.7	3.9	0.4	1.9	1.2	3.0	5.3
Investment-GNP ratio[b]	0.4	0.8	–	0.7	–	1.4	2.3

[a]Labor is measured in man-years for 1856–1924, in man-hours for 1924–73.
[b]The average of the annual ratios (excluding the first year shown) of gross domestic fixed capital formation to GNP at current prices.
[c]Capital and investment include roads.

was also much public regulation of the parts in private ownership, such as the railways. The industries share the characteristic that they are in general highly capital-intensive and their products are not directly exportable or subject to international competition, apart from shipping and aviation.

Summary statistics are shown in Tables 13.4 and 13.5, and annual data on fixed capital formation in Figures 13.3–13.6.[16] As was shown in Table 11.1, the postwar rate of growth of infrastructure capital as a whole exceeded the interwar rate, but the excess was a good deal smaller than in manufacturing and a fortiori in commerce. The excess, moreover, was to a considerable extent the consequence of a shift in weights to more rapidly growing industries. The capital stock in electricity (Table 13.5) and in utilities as a whole grew more slowly in the postwar period than in the interwar period, even though in contrast to manufacturing capital formation had been severely restricted in World War II.

TABLE 13.5
Growth of Output, Labor, and Fixed Capital in Public
Corporation Industries, 1924–1973
(Annual percentage growth rates)

Industry	1924–1937	1937–1951	1951–1964	1964–1973
Gas				
Output	1.6%	3.3%	– 0.7%	8.4%
Labor[a]	1.2	0.6	– 1.6	– 3.1
Capital	2.6	– 0.2	3.6	6.5
Electricity				
Output	10.8	6.6	7.7	4.6
Labor[a]	7.2	2.7	1.7	– 3.8
Capital	9.9	2.0	5.8	4.5
Railways				
Output	0.4	1.1	– 1.4	– 0.4
Labor[a]	– 0.9	– 0.3	– 2.5	– 5.8
Capital	0.1	– 1.0	0.0	– 0.6
Post Office				
Output	3.0	2.2	3.5	5.7
Labor[a]	1.8	2.0	0.6	1.1
Capital	6.7	3.4	4.2	6.9

Source: Basic statistics (Appendix N) and sources quoted there; B. C. Brown 1954; Deakin & Seward 1969; communication from Deakin; Ministry of Power *Statistical Digest*; Cambridge University Department of Applied Economics 1974; communication from Central Statistical Office.
[a]Man-hours.

Utilities

Electricity supply is the industry of chief interest here. Water and (till the very end of the period) gas grew relatively slowly. Electricity already dominated investment in utilities in the interwar period.[17] Its development falls into three phases. In the 30 or so years before 1914 its growth (from a start of virtually zero) was rapid in proportionate terms; but the growth occurred later and was slower than in other countries, and this was a subject of criticism. In the interwar period the lost time was made up, and electricity was the typical growth industry. By the postwar period the diffusion of the innovation was more or less completed. Output and the capital stock in the industry continued to grow considerably more rapidly than GNP, but their growth rates were lower than in the interwar period.

A number of explanations have been offered for the relatively tardy growth before 1914 (Byatt 1979): the entrenched position of gas lighting and steam power (seen by some as a rational reason for delaying investment and by others as a source of irrational conservatism); disputes between municipalities and private undertakings; and the unsatisfactory state of the law. The slowness of the initial start in the 1880's was no doubt due to these causes. In the period immediately before 1914, crowding-out by capital export was probably also significant. The 1904 peak was not surpassed till after World War I (Fig. 13.4). The external mode of financing in this sector made it directly competitive with overseas capital issues, and some complaints of a shortage of finance were heard in this period.

In the interwar period the mutually reinforcing effects of delayed diffusion, institutional improvements, and reductions in cost made the electricity supply industry immune from the problems of excess capacity and lack of confidence that beset much of manufacturing. The industry was relatively little affected even by the depression of the early 1930's. The flattening-out of investment in the 1930's reflected not a falloff in demand, but the completion in 1932 of major nonrecurrent work on the construction of the national grid. Since the grid permitted the use of larger-scale generating plants, it considerably reduced capital costs. Even before that, much progress had been made through area schemes for the exploitation of economies of scale. These develop-

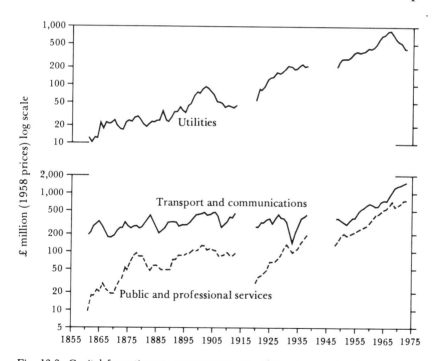

Fig. 13.3. Capital formation at constant prices in utilities, transport and communications, and public and professional services, 1861–1973

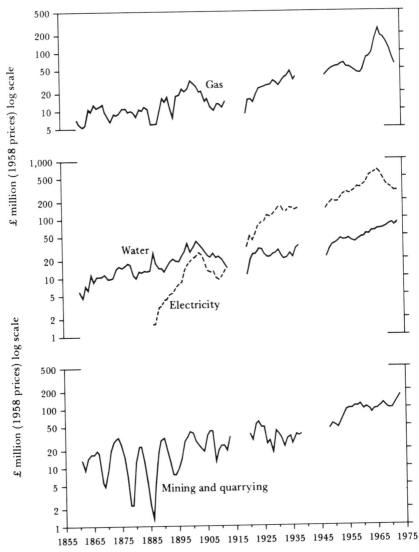

Fig. 13.4. Capital formation at constant prices in gas, electricity, and water, and mining and quarrying, 1861–1973

ments in centralization were facilitated by an enabling act in 1919, which was followed by the Act of 1926 setting up the Central Electricity Board (Ballin 1946). The legal obstacles that had been largely responsible for uneconomically small-scale operation before 1914 were thus removed. Economies of scale in the generation of electricity reduced costs and promoted consumption, and also led to an increase in the proportion of electricity purchased from the public supply.

Demand continued to rise across World War II, but investment was kept down. It was possible to go on increasing output by stretching the existing capacity, but this could not be continued indefinitely. A fuel crisis in 1947, due to lack of generating capacity as well as to coal shortages, persuaded the authorities not to delay expansion any longer. Investment and the capital stock rose rapidly thereafter until 1966, with pauses imposed by government restraint in 1951–52, 1956–57, and 1960–61.

This expansion was partly to make up for wartime arrears and partly to keep pace with the growth in electricity consumption associated with growing national income. By the end of the war electricity was completely dominant as a source of industrial power, as well as lighting. Though other domestic uses increased, diffusion at the expense of other sources of power was no longer the major source of growth that it had been earlier. The rate of growth of output was less rapid than in the interwar period, notwithstanding the more rapid rise in GNP. This was matched by a slower rate of growth of the capital stock.

The long swing in capital formation in the postwar period was more prominent in electricity than in any other sector (Figs. 11.1 and 13.4). Investment rose rapidly until 1966, then fell off steeply, until in 1973 it was less than half of what it had been at the peak—a long downswing similar to the one that had occurred after 1904 (Fig. 13.4). Some flattening-out of the rate of investment in the industry was probably inevitable. It may be conjectured that if the future had been correctly foreseen, the flattening-out would have occurred early in the 1960's, yielding a mild long-swing pattern corresponding in timing to that of the metals and metal-using industries. As it was, the exceptional violence of the upswing, and the timing of its peak, reflected the ill-founded expectation, prevailing at the time of the National Plan of 1965, that the consumption of electricity would increase at a more rapid rate than before.*

*Investment in the gas industry showed an even more violent cycle (see Fig. 13.4), but for a different reason, namely once-for-all expenditure on North Sea gas.

Labor costs are a small proportion of total costs in electricity supply; in electricity *generation* they are a very small proportion. Reduction in capital costs and fuel costs are therefore more important than reduction in labor costs, and research effort is directed accordingly. This helps explain why the capital-output ratio continued to fall in the postwar period, even continuing to do so slightly between 1964 and 1973.* Capital *per man-hour* did increase, but taking the period up to 1964, including the war, the rate of increase was less than in the interwar period. Even including the years 1964–73, the rate of increase in capital per man-hour over the period 1937–73 (3.3 percent a year) exceeded that in the interwar period (2.7 percent a year) by only a modest amount, much less than happened in manufacturing or commerce. Capital-labor substitution within the industry in response to changes in factor prices therefore does not appear as an important stimulus to investment in the postwar period. The effect of the postwar labor shortage on investment in electricity worked more indirectly, by increasing the demand for electricity as part of the process of increasing the capital-labor ratio in consuming industries.

Though the rates of growth of output and capital in electricity supply were lower in the postwar period than in the interwar period, reflecting the industry's approach to maturity, investment in electricity was a considerably larger item relative to GNP in the postwar period, reflecting the increasing importance of the industry in the economy. Despite the slowdown in the industry's own rate of growth, its high capital-intensity meant that its growth relative to the rest of the economy tended to raise the capital-intensity of the economy. In this way it contributed to the increase in total investment and absorbed, and possibly elicited, savings.

Transport and Communications

The effect of technical change in the transport and communications sector was to diminish its capital-intensity. Road transport is less capital-intensive than rail transport (partly, of course, because private cars are not treated as capital).† Despite this, investment in this sector

---

*The slowdown in the rate of fall in the capital-output ratio after 1964 was due partly to over-investment and also partly to the extremely high capital-intensity of nuclear power stations.

†In the present context, where we are discussing investment, roads are included in the capital stock in transport, so as not to obscure the consequences of the transition from rail to road. (In Chapter 8, where we were concerned with productivity, roads were not in-

remained a large item — larger than investment in utilities even in the postwar period. Movements of the components are shown in Fig. 13.5.

Before 1914 over three-quarters of investment in this sector was in railways and shipping. Since the main railway network was complete by 1881, it may seem surprising than the capital stock in transport grew as rapidly as it did between then and 1914 (Table 13.4). The explanation is partly that railway investment, though its great days were over, was still enough to keep the railway capital stock growing at almost the same rate as GNP; partly that investment in shipping was high; and partly that there was quite a rapid growth already in urban road transport (urban transport — the underground and suburban systems — also contributed to railway investment).[18] In the interwar period investment was much lower in all categories except roads and the Post Office.

The scope for using the existing infrastructure more intensively and also for neglecting, for a time, the replacement of equipment was particularly apparent during World War II, when the capital stock in transport (including railway rolling stock) was allowed to run down, but the volume of traffic increased considerably. In contrast to electricity, where similar war arrears accumulated, investment was not resumed on a large scale in the early postwar years. Railway renovation, road-building, and the extension of the telecommunications system were considered by the authorities to have low priority. In all three cases a high level of investment was not achieved till the late 1950's (see Fig. 13.5). In the case of railways this was followed by a sharp falling-off.* The net outcome was that total investment in transport and communications grew quite rapidly over the postwar period

---

cluded in transport, because no output is directly attributed to them.) We exclude not only private cars, but also road vehicles owned by firms engaged primarily in activities other than transport. Inclusion of the latter would increase the rate of growth of the capital stock in transport by 0.6 percentage point in the interwar period and by 0.4 percentage point in the postwar period. These changes are significant but are not large enough to alter qualitatively the conclusions stated in the text. They would not, moreover, have a corresponding effect on trends in the capital-output and capital-labor ratios, since for comparability the output and labor data would have to be adjusted to include in transport the parts of value-added and employment in manufacturing, the distributive trades, etc. that stem from the operation of producers' own vehicles.

*The timing of investment in coal mining followed the same pattern in the postwar period, for much the same reason. Coal mining more closely resembled railways in its investment behavior than manufacturing or commerce. Annual investment in mining and quarrying is shown in Fig. 13.4. The rise at the very end of the period reflects the North Sea gas and oil installations.

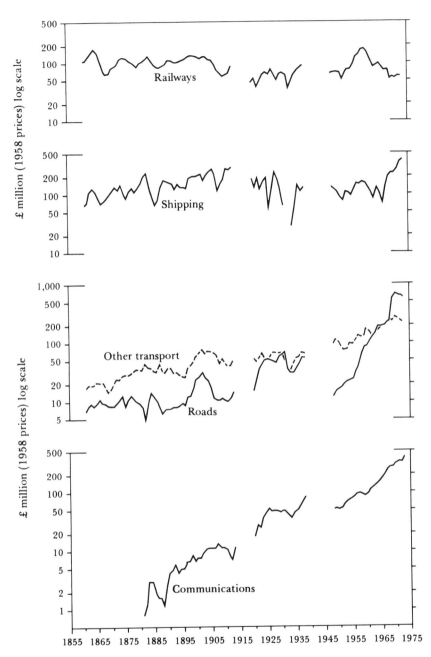

Fig. 13.5. Capital formation at constant prices in transport and communications, 1861–1973. Gross domestic capital formation in ships was negative in 1932 and 1933 because the depreciated value of ships scrapped or sold exceeded purchases, and the estimates cannot therefore be shown on a semi-log figure. (See Feinstein 1965: 175–76 for the definition of gross capital formation in ships.)

up to 1973, having previously shown no upward trend at all for three-quarters of a century (Fig. 13.3).

Both the timing and the magnitude of postwar public investment in transport and communications were largely determined by varying political decisions on what it was thought that the nation could afford and on what constituted an acceptable rate of return on public investment. The link between capital infrastructure and the volume of measurable output is less direct and obvious in transport than in electricity, and a good deal of the benefit from improved infrastructure consists of unmeasured amenities. Moreover, the pressure to substitute capital for scarce labor was weakened by the fact that in the case of roads the capital and the labor are paid for by different agencies (the public purse on the one hand and road haulage firms on the other). It is not surprising, therefore, that the economic forces tending to affect investment in the rest of the economy in the postwar period were felt less directly in this sector. Of course the political decisions were a good deal affected by the overall balance of supply and demand. In this way, for example, investment in the late 1950's was helped by the rise in savings, as was investment elsewhere in the economy.

Shipping stands apart from the rest of transport. It is not in the public sector, it is not a social overhead, and it is directly subject to international competition.* Investment in shipping has some of the characteristics of capital export (not only in the obvious sense that the inclusion of shipping in the national capital depends on ownership rather than location, but also in the sense that British capital is not necessarily cooperating with British labor).[19] Before 1914, when capital export was a major part of British capital formation, so too was investment in shipping; it was, moreover, a classic case of cyclical instability. In later periods the cyclical instability remained, but the rate of increase of the capital stock greatly declined. The causes of the decline, accompanying as it did a steep decline in the British share of world shipping, had a good deal in common with the causes of the decline in the less-successful export industries.†

*Air transport is in some degree similar. Even at its peak this was a small item quantitatively, responsible for only about 10% of total GFCF in transport and communications (1% of national GFCF).

†However, after World War II some small part may have been played by restrictions—finally removed in 1956—on the purchase or construction abroad of ships for British ownership. Sturmey (1962: 296) concludes that the decline in the British share of world shipping up to 1929 can be explained largely by external factors, notably the effects of World War I and the decline in the British share of world domestic trade, but that its further decline after 1929 was due to "internal constraints," i.e. competitive weakness.

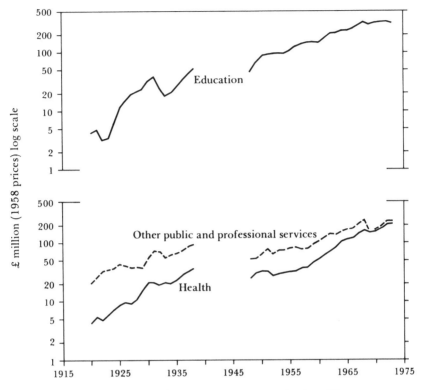

Fig. 13.6. Capital formation at constant prices in public
and professional services, 1920–1973

Public and Professional Services

Investment in social capital, that is to say, in public and professional services, tended to rise as a proportion of GNP between periods (Table 13.4). Likewise, the stock of capital grew at a more rapid rate than GNP in all peacetime periods — by a rather smaller amount in the postwar period than before 1914. Within the postwar period the pattern resembled that in transport and communications; the rate of growth of the stock of social capital was low in the early part of the postwar period and increased steadily almost the whole way up to 1973.

Education is much the largest constituent item, followed by health. Figure 13.6 shows a contrast in the postwar period between education and health similar to that found between electricity and transport. The steep rise in investment in education began in the 1940's and continued

TABLE 13.6

Growth of Stock and Investment in Dwellings, 1860–1973

Period	Annual percentage growth rates of stock of dwellings at constant prices[a] (1)	Investment as percent of GNP[b]		
		Total (2)	Public (3)	Private (4)
1860–1913	1.8%	1.5%	0.0	1.5%
1860–1870	1.2	1.3	0.0	1.3
1870–1884	2.2	1.8	0.0	1.8
1884–1895	1.4	1.2	0.0	1.2
1895–1907	2.5	1.9	0.0	1.9
1907–1913	0.9	1.0	0.0	1.0
1920–1938	3.2	3.0	0.9	2.1
1920–1927	3.1	2.5	1.0	1.5
1927–1938	3.6	3.3	0.8	2.5
1947–1973	2.7	3.6	2.0	1.6
1947–1951	1.9	3.0	2.5	0.5
1951–1955	2.6	3.9	2.7	1.2
1955–1960	2.2	3.2	1.4	1.8
1960–1964	2.9	3.6	1.4	2.2
1964–1968	3.7	4.2	2.0	2.2
1968–1973	3.2	4.0	1.7	2.3

[a]Average of growth rates of gross and net stock.
[b]The average of the annual ratios (excluding the first year shown) of gross investment in dwellings to GNP, at current prices.

strongly thereafter, though checked at intervals by government deflationary measures (as it had been in the 1930's). Investment in hospitals
and other fixed assets in the health service, on the other hand, remained at a nearly constant level until 1959, when government policy
changed and a rapid rise began.*

DWELLINGS

The stock of dwellings, in common with the rest of the capital stock,
grew a good deal more rapidly in the postwar period than over the
average of the previous century (Table 11.1). But in contrast to other
classes of capital, it grew at a slower rate after World War II than between the wars. Investment in dwellings was a considerably lower proportion of total fixed-capital formation in 1951–73 than in 1924–37. It
was, however, a rather larger proportion of GNP on account of the rise
in its relative unit cost.

Investment in dwellings takes place partly in the public sector and
partly in the private sector. The markets served by privately owned

*Investment in universities, however, conformed to the health service timing, not start-
ing to rise steeply till the end of the 1950's.

housing and publicly-owned housing overlap, though they are not the same. We therefore consider investment in dwellings as a whole in this chapter. Before World War I virtually all house-building was in the private sector. In the 1920's local authority house-building became significant. Thereafter the relative importance of private and public building varied with changes in governments and their policies, as well as with the inducements to private building arising from causes other than government action (Table 13.6, columns 3 and 4). The spectacular rise of house-building in the 1930's came from the private sector, but local-authority building remained substantial. During World War II practically no new houses were built. In the early postwar period public house-building accounted for more than half the total; but the private sector's share increased under the Conservative governments of 1951–64, and from 1958 onward it was the larger item.

The forces affecting house-building, especially in the short period, are complex and not perfectly understood. Before 1914 house-building was the prime example of the long cycle in domestic investment, which alternated with the long cycle in capital export. Evidence of this cycle may be seen in the alternation of low and high figures in the pre-1914 periods distinguished in Table 13.6. The nature and causes of this cycle have been much debated among economic historians.[20] After 1914 and especially after 1939, house-building was affected by an elaborate array of government measures that affected not only building as such, but also the housing market and the supply of finance for building. Within the postwar period there was some tendency, in much milder form, to a movement like the long swing of earlier times, with a peak in 1951–55 and another, substantially higher, in 1964–68. This movement arose almost entirely from public-sector house-building (Fig. 11.2).*

Housing differs from other kinds of capital in that it yields services to consumers without the need for any current labor input (apart from maintenance). The flow of services is proportional to the stock, and there is therefore no point in looking at capital-output or capital-labor ratios. The natural way to look at the relationship between the growth of the housing stock and the growth of the economy as a whole is by reference to consumption. The trend over time in the stock of houses,

*These swings corresponded broadly, but only broadly, to alternations between Labour and Conservative administrations. Peaks were in 1953 and 1968; troughs in 1958 and 1972. The peak in 1953, two years after the Conservatives took office, was the result of the Macmillan housing drive. The subsequent turning points preceded the changes in government that might have been expected to be responsible for them. This perhaps reflected the tendency for governments in their later years in office to move in the direction of policies more commonly associated with their political opponents.

TABLE 13.7

*Growth of Dwellings and Consumption at Constant Prices,
and of the Relative Price of the Occupation of
Dwellings, 1870–1973*

(Annual percentage growth rates)

Variable	1870–1913	1913–1937	1937–1973
(1) Dwellings[a]	1.9%	2.3%	2.1%
(2) Consumers' expenditure	1.7	1.0	2.0
(3) Ratio of price of occupation of dwellings to price of consumption[b]	0.5	−0.3	0.4

Source: Basic statistics (Appendix N); J. P. Lewis 1965: Appendix 13 (for Weber's and Cairncross's indexes of rent).

[a] Average of growth rates of gross and net stock.

[b] The price of occupation of dwellings is based on the implicit price deflator of occupation of dwellings for 1913–73, and on Weber's and Cairncross's indexes of rent for 1870–1913.

taken as an indicator of the consumption flow it yields, may be compared with the trend in total consumption of goods and services.

Rows 1 and 2 of Table 13.7 accordingly show the rates of growth of the housing stock and consumption over three long periods.* To allow for the effects of the arrears built up over the wars, we treat the war and postwar periods 1913–37 and 1937–73 as a whole, disregarding our usual benchmark years 1924 and 1951. Row 3 shows the rate of change in the cost of occupation of dwellings relative to the cost of consumption in general, i.e. the relative price of accomodation, which might be expected to affect the demand for it.

Dwellings grew at a faster rate than consumption in all three periods. This happened notwithstanding a rise in the relative cost of the occupation of dwellings in 1870–1913 and 1937–73. In 1913–37 the relative cost fell, and the rate of growth of dwellings exceeded that of consumption by a much larger margin than in the other two periods. These results suggest that the consumption-elasticity of demand for dwellings exceeded unity, and that the price-elasticity of demand for dwellings was significant. Such an inference is not, of course, firmly based unless the changes in relative cost were externally given and were not themselves determined by the rate of growth of the stock of dwellings, but this assumption, which will be discussed below, appears broadly justified.

It is possible to find values for income- and price-elasticities that fit

*The housing stock is measured as the value of dwellings at constant prices. Its rate of growth is therefore not necessarily the same as the rate of growth in the *number* of dwellings.

TABLE 13.8
Relative Prices of Dwellings, the Occupation of Dwellings,
and Consumption, 1870–1973
(1964 = 100)

Ratios	1870	1913	1937	1973
(1) Price of occupation of dwellings to price of consumption (p_o/p_c)	84	103	95	111
(2) Price of dwellings to price of consumption (p_d/p_c)	66	71	73	102
(3) Price of occupation of dwellings to price of dwellings (p_o/p_d)	127	145	130	109

Source: Same as Table 13.7.
Note: p_d is the implicit price deflator of investment in dwellings; p_o is the implicit price deflator of occupation of dwellings for 1913–73, and is based on Weber's and Cairncross's indexes of rents for 1873–1913; and p_c is the implicit price deflator of consumers' expenditure.

the three periods. However, it is not really reasonable to suppose either that the same elasticities persisted over a century of economic growth and institutional change in the housing market or that there were no other forces at work. In particular, it is likely that the high rate of investment in dwellings in the interwar period was due partly to other causes (see below), and that the price-elasticity was not therefore as great as the data in Table 13.7 suggest. Any actual estimates of elasticities can only be illustrative.[21] We do suggest, however, that trends in total consumption and in relative costs are sufficient to account for the main long-period trends in the housing stock. The rate of growth of total consumption depended on the general rate of economic growth. The causes of changes in relative costs will now be considered, along with other features of the three periods.

1870–1913. Table 13.8 shows that the rise in the relative cost of accommodation (p_o/p_c) was due to rises both in the relative cost of dwellings (p_d/p_c) and in rents relative to the cost price of dwellings (p_o/p_d). The rise in the relative cost of dwellings (row 2) may reasonably be taken as an exogenous cost change, reflecting the lack of productivity growth in construction (Table 8.3). The rise in rents relative to the cost price of dwellings (row 3) is of about the right order to be explained by the rise in interest rates.[22] In the broadest terms, therefore, the trend in the housing stock between 1870 and 1913 seems to be explicable by exogenous rises in cost, combined with a more-than-unit consumption-elasticity of demand. As an explanation of the actual course of house-building in particular decades this, of course, is inadequate, since it leaves out of account the long swing. Account must be taken of this in the comparison of end-years, 1913 having been at a long-swing trough.[23]

1913–37. In this period there was again some rise in the relative cost of dwellings, p_d/p_c.[24] But this was offset by a much larger decline in p_o/p_d. The reasons for this decline are well known: rent control and subsidies, important chiefly in the 1920's, and the fall of interest rates in the 1930's. These falls in costs are in line with the great excess in the rate of increase of the housing stock over that of consumption. Together with the need to provide for the arrears accumulated during the war, they go much of the way toward explaining the high level of house-building in the interwar period.* It is unlikely, however, that they constituted the whole explanation. The other causes are also well known, notably improved suburban transport and the development of building societies, and their contribution was probably substantial (for details, see Richardson & Aldcroft 1968). Moreover, once under way, the boom acquired cumulative force through the demonstration effect on people's expectations regarding the quality and style of housing.

1937–73. The trends in costs over this period are peculiar. On the one hand a whole battery of housing subsidies was introduced.[25] The trend during most of the postwar period was for these to be reduced. But the average cost (excluding local rates) of housing to the occupier in the early 1970's was still below the economic rent on the capital value of the house by a much larger amount than it had been in the interwar period. This is reflected in the fall in p_o/p_d shown in row 3 of Table 13.8.

On the other hand, the relative cost of dwellings rose by a much greater extent across World War II than over the period 1870–1937. This was due chiefly to the unusually rapid rise in building costs during the war, which was referred to earlier in connection with the rise in the relative cost of capital goods generally—a transwar rather than a postwar phenomenon. In the postwar period, particularly in the later

---

*We do not, of course, mean to suggest that rent controls encouraged the building of rent-restricted houses. But insofar as they increased house occupancy, they increased the demand for housing space in general and so contributed to encouraging other building by local authorities and in the private sector. It is probable, however, that rent controls were partly responsible for the relatively slow start of the increase in house-building in the 1920's. Private building for letting, before 1914 the main part of house-building, was unattractive because of the controls; and the major restructuring toward local-authority building and building for owner-occupation naturally took time.

years, the price of land rose steeply, and this too was communicated to the cost of houses.

The net result of these rises in costs was that by the early 1970's the cost of housing to the occupier was apparently significantly higher relative to the cost of consumption than it was in 1937, despite the enormous increase in subsidies.[26] In the early postwar years, when rent controls were more stringent and applied to a larger proportion of dwellings, the relative cost of housing was much lower than in either 1937 or 1973 (p_o/p_c = 55 in 1951, taking 1964 as 100).

As noted above, explaining the observed movements in the housing stock in terms of demand-side forces, namely total consumption and relative prices, is valid only if consumers are actually on their demand curves (more strictly, if any departure from this position is of constant amount). During the postwar period, however, there were clear manifestations of excess demand, and its amount was not constant. By the early 1970's excess demand had diminished but not disappeared. Local authorities still had waiting lists, though not such long ones as they had earlier in the postwar period, and the overall rate of vacancy was still low, though again not so low as earlier.[27] The reason for the fall in excess demand during the postwar period was no doubt partly that the housing stock was catching up with arrears and partly that the relative cost of housing had risen, following its steep fall across World War II.

It is not clear how far the persistence of some excess demand for housing in the early 1970's reflected the general strength of the demand at prevailing prices, rather than more special causes. A number of special causes have been alleged. One is that the uneven incidence of subsidies, possibly combined with the structure of housing stock (heavily concentrated on four- and five-room houses), caused a misallocation of housing space and thereby increased demand. That inequities existed is beyond question, and there is also fairly convincing evidence of misallocation;[28] but it is not clear that this tended to increase overall demand, however much hardship it caused to those unfavorably placed.[29] Another possibility is that the excess demand apparently indicated by Council waiting lists did not represent true overall excess demand, but rather represented people's desire to move into a class of dwellings enjoying an above-average subsidy. This too is debatable.*

*Council houses were cheaper than uncontrolled private rented accommodation, so tenants in the uncontrolled sector had an inducement to go on Council waiting lists. On the other hand, new Council houses tended to be more expensive, even allowing for quality, than the average of all Council houses. Not all local authorities carried the pooling principle to the full extent, and even if they did it would not have brought about full

Whatever the reason, there *were* manifestations of excess demand for housing throughout the postwar period. The building that would have cleared off this excess demand was delayed by a variety of direct controls. In the early postwar period there existed a range of direct controls on building as such, both private and public. By the end of the period private-sector building for owner-occupation was not subject to any significant controls, though restrictions on land use through planning policy were becoming increasingly felt; but throughout the postwar period the funds available through building societies were frequently curtailed because of credit squeezes. Local authorities were prevented from building enough to get rid of their waiting lists by the central government's control of their borrowing as well as by considerations of cost.

Government policy toward housing in the postwar period had thus some tendency to take with one hand what it gave with the other. But it took less than it gave. The net effect was to increase house-building. In the absence of the various kinds of subsidy, the rise in costs compared with prewar would inevitably have tended to reduce the amount of building.[30]

In the owner-occupied sector the pressure of demand (given the subsidies) made itself felt directly through market forces. In the public sector it made itself felt indirectly through the political effects of waiting lists on the central government and local authorities. The effect of these pressures was persistent. The extent to which government permitted house-building to respond to them in particular phases of the postwar period was, however, affected by its view on the overall pressure on resources and the balance of payments.

In this chapter rather little attention has been paid to the demographic factors — number and size of households and so on — that are normally emphasized in discussion of long-run trends in housing. Our explanation has been in narrowly economic terms. Likewise, by taking as our central measure the constant-price value of the housing stock, we have sidestepped questions about numbers of houses or numbers of rooms, and have treated all forms of improvements in the quantity and quality of the housing stock as equivalent. This is not to deny that demographic and other factors are important. Thus the increase in the married proportion of the population and the reduction in household

---

equalization at the national level, because the authorities that did the most building tended to have a housing stock of below-average age and hence of above-average historical cost. The above-average cost of new Council houses operated to discourage people from seeking to move from private rent-controlled accommodation to Council houses.

size probably accounted in part for the housing stock growing faster in
the interwar and postwar periods than before 1914.* Demographic
and physical factors also influenced the government actions that in
later parts of the period composed a major element in the economic
forces affecting the housing market.

COMPETITION BETWEEN CATEGORIES OF DOMESTIC INVESTMENT

The overall rate of domestic fixed-capital formation varied remarkably little between peacetime periods before World War II, despite
substantial variations within each of the broad sectors we have been
considering: industrial and commercial; infrastructure; and dwellings
(Table 11.1). This could be taken to indicate some systematic tendency
to mutual offsetting—crowding-in or crowding-out. Moreover, even in
the postwar period, when there certainly was a rise in the total, and a
large rise in the industrial and commercial sector, there was much less
rise in investment in infrastructure and dwellings—indeed there was
no change in the rate of growth of the capital stock if the war period is
included.[31] This could be taken as an indication that these sectors were
being relatively crowded out. The offsetting tendency should not, of
course, be exaggerated. In the first place, the total *was* higher in the
postwar period than earlier; in the second place, though total domestic
capital accumulation in the interwar period proceeded at about the
same rate as before 1914, it did not make up for the great fall in capital
export, so that there was both a deficiency of demand and a reduction
in the rate of growth of total assets (Table 5.1); and in the third place,
there was some downward trend in the rate of capital accumulation in
the pre-1914 period, which does not show up in the comparison of our
standard periods 1856–73 and 1873–1913 because of the timing of the
long swing.† There is thus no question of the rate of domestic capital
accumulation having been rigidly fixed (say by an exogenously given
propensity to save). There was, however, sufficient tendency to offsetting to warrant discussion.

The tendency to offsetting was most apparent in investment in
dwellings. Investment in dwellings, as we have seen, was sensitive to

---

*There is in all periods a strong and systematic negative relation between the size of
household and the amount of housing space per head (Hole and Pountney 1971: 9).

†Dividing the period instead at 1886 (the low point in the long swing of domestic investment) yields annual growth rates of the gross fixed capital stock of 2.1% in 1856–86
and 1.9% in 1886–1913. The main difference between these periods was that there were
two phases of high investment in the first, the mid-1860's and the mid-1870's, but only one
in the second around 1900 (see Fig. 5.2).

costs. Cost includes the cost of finance. The relevance of this is well known in relation to the particularly pronounced inverse relationship between house-building and overseas investment during pre–World War I swings (though finance was not the only factor); but the time pattern suggests that house-building was also affected by competition for funds from other classes of *domestic* investment. The rate of growth of the stock of dwellings was higher in 1873–1914 than in 1856–73 and, moreover, was somewhat higher at the long-swing peak of the 1890's than at the long-swing peak of the 1870's, in both respects contrasting with most other classes of investment. Most obviously, house-building was high in the interwar period when other investment was low. The forces, including diminished international competitiveness, that depressed industrial investment in these various phases may have helped to encourage house-building by crowding-in.

A similar point may be made in regard to international comparisons. The lower level of industrial investment in Britain compared with some other countries, whatever its cause, may be part of the reason why Britain is well supplied with dwellings by comparison with most other industrial countries (UN 1965: Map 1).

Crowding-out and crowding-in are less apparent in relation to investment in infrastructure. However, it was obviously crowded out in wartime; and in the postwar period public investment programs were consciously seen as in competition both with one another and with other claims on national resources. This helps to account for the relatively slow growth of infrastructure capital between 1937 and 1973.

It has sometimes been argued that British economic growth would have been faster if there had been less investment in dwellings and in some forms of infrastructure, so as to free resources for investment in other sectors, especially manufacturing. Particularly in relation to the postwar period, attention has been drawn to the low rate of return and favorable terms of finance available for public investment in infrastructure and dwellings.[32] It can also be argued that in the early and mid-1960's and in the 1920's an inappropriate exchange rate made the private return on investment in foreign-trade-oriented manufacturing less than its social return, by comparison with investment in infrastructure and dwellings serving a protected domestic market.*

*In a somewhat similar sense it could be held that there was a tendency for investment to be too oriented to the protected sectors of the home market in the investment boom around 1900, insofar as income from abroad enabled the exchange rate to be held at a level that ceased to be viable (consistent with full employment) after World War I—that is to say, within the lifetime of some of the capital that might have been, but was not, invested in the unprotected sector.

The fact that investment in manufacturing was, by historical standards, unusually high in the postwar period by comparison with other classes of investment creates some supposition that the above argument, insofar as it has any validity, applied at least as much to earlier periods. Indeed, low rates of return on infrastructure capital and dwellings were no postwar novelty. Admittedly, in parts of the postwar period investment in infrastructure and dwellings was carried out on favorable terms because of government policy; but the same had been true in earlier periods, on account of the structure of the capital market. In the case of dwellings, public subsidies *were* larger than in earlier periods, but they were not allowed to have their full effect on investment.

Much turns on whether a lower level of investment in infrastructure or dwellings would in fact have caused investment in manufacturing to be significantly higher. This must be considered doubtful, since there were in each period good reasons on the MEI side why manufacturing investment was no higher than it was. On this reckoning, lower investment in infrastructure and dwellings would not have helped to speed up economic growth—though if *other circumstances* had made for higher manufacturing investment, and infrastructure investment and house-building had been consequently crowded out to some degree, the result might well have been higher growth.

A somewhat different question may conveniently be mentioned in conclusion. Was there a misallocation of investment within the public sector in the postwar period, *because* it was public? Certainly, it is difficult to believe that the wide discrepancies in timing between the various sorts of public capital expenditure represented an optimum allocation of resources. Public investment was, moreover, particularly liable to be leant on in the interests of macro-policy, sometimes with wasteful consequences for the programs concerned. Convincing criticisms can also be made of individual programs: the decisions on railway electrification and aircraft development, overexpansion of electricity generating capacity in the 1960's, policy toward nuclear energy, overconcentration on three-bedroom houses and on tower blocks, and so on. Public investment, being centrally determined, offers opportunity for errors on a grander scale than private investment. Errors in the areas referred to were part of the shortfall below optimum efficiency prevalent throughout the economy, though elsewhere less prominent because more diffused. It may be that on average the quality of investment was worse in the public sector than in the private sector; but we hesitate to infer that.

Summaries of the conclusions relating to the various classes of investment were given in the synopsis at the beginning of this chapter (pp. 374–76). A more general summary and assessment of the role of investment in British economic growth is contained in the concluding chapter — Chapter 17.

CHAPTER FOURTEEN

International Aspects: Introduction

THEORETICAL CONSIDERATIONS

The question is to what extent trends in Britain's international trans-actions — volumes, values, and capital movements — were the cause or the consequence of its rate of economic growth. This section explains the approach to be adopted in Chapter 15. The first step is to consider the relative importance of the different influences responsible for trends in the country's international transactions: (1) the domestic growth rate itself, together with the domestic real forces affecting it; (2) real trends abroad; and (3) international and domestic monetary institu-tions and policies. Then we ask what effects trends in international transactions had on the growth rate, the possible channels being the amount and composition of demand, prices of goods and factors, and "learning." After allowance for feedback, we are thus in principle able to say how forces exogenous to the British economy affected British growth and also how international transactions amplified or damped the effects of domestic forces on the growth rate. In practice there are, of course, many obstacles to arriving at clear-cut answers.

THE MAIN TRENDS IN INTERNATIONAL TRADE AND PAYMENTS

Tables 14.1–14.8 and Figures 14.2–14.9 provide a statistical review of the main trends in Britain's international transactions as a back-ground for a period-by-period discussion in Chapter 15 of their rela-tionship to the country's economic growth.

THEORETICAL CONSIDERATIONS

In this chapter and the one that follows we consider the relationship between trends in Britain's foreign trade and payments and the rate of economic growth. Did the causation run from the growth rate to the international position, or the other way around, or both, or neither? Was there a consistent pattern over the long period?

The balance of payments has commonly been seen as *the* problem of the British economy in the postwar period and the principal obstacle to much faster growth. More generally, the international position has been invoked to explain differences between earlier periods in the British growth rate and to explain the general tendency for growth in Britain to be slower than in other countries. Thus the decline in the rate of growth of exports and the increase in foreign competition in the 40 years before 1914 can be invoked to explain the decline in the overall rate of growth in that period compared with the period before 1873 (Conrad & Meyer 1965; Phelps Brown & Browne 1968: 192–95; W. A. Lewis 1978); obviously the troubles of the 1920's arose mainly from foreign trade; and the improvement in the 1930's can be attributed to the adoption of protection and the abandonment of the gold standard.

However, there are contrary hypotheses. Trade problems may have been the *result* of slow growth, and slow growth the result of other forces. It is also possible to regard the problem of growth and the problem of the balance of payments as largely separate.

The flows of international trade and payments are not themselves independent variables. They are the result of the simultaneous working of the equations describing the world economy. Strictly speaking, if one asks how far such and such a phenomenon was *due* to foreign trade, one is asking how differently things would have turned out in a closed economy — not an interesting question for such an open economy as Britain's. A more appropriate question is how the rate of growth was affected by those influences on international transactions that were themselves independent of real supply-side forces operating within Britain. A further question concerns the significance of feedbacks from the rate of growth to international transactions and back again to the rate of growth.

Figure 14.1 provides a simple way of structuring the various interactions involved. The two right-hand boxes at the top shows the forces that are exogenous with respect to the real performance of the British economy but influence its international transactions (links *c* and *d*). International transactions are also influenced by exogenous real trends in

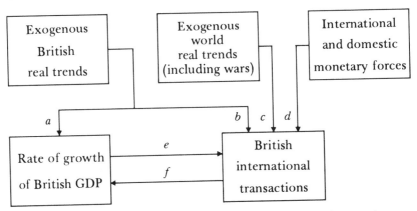

Fig. 14.1. Model of relationships between growth and international economic transactions

the British economy and by the actual rate of growth itself (links *b* and *e*). International transactions affect the rate of growth (link *f*). If links *e* and *f* are both strong and have the same sign, a cumulative vicious or virtuous circle can result.

On this model, the net effect on the growth rate, through international transactions, of the forces independent of real trends within Britain depends on the strength of links *c* and *d*, as transmitted through link *f*, and possibly augmented through feedback via link *e*. In addition, feedback through links *e* and *f* could amplify (or dampen) the influence on the rate of growth of real trends within Britain.

The ideal aim would be to produce "reduced-form" estimates of the net effects on the growth rate of the various exogenous forces operating through international transactions. It is possible to do this only in the most qualitative manner.

We shall use this way of structuring the relationship as a framework for this chapter and the next one, without adhering to it rigidly. It is of course a crude model, and many alternatives could be devised involving other and more complicated linkages. It is designed for our particular purpose, namely the explanation of the rate of growth, not as a general model of international trade and payments. It has also to be noted that feedbacks may exist *within* certain of the boxes, notably the international transactions box: one category of the international transactions may affect the others.* We shall revert to this later.

*The existence of such feedbacks is the basis of the monetarist objection to the traditional "top-downwards" treatment of the balance-of-payments accounts.

The link from British international transactions to the rate of growth of British GDP (link *f*) is obviously crucial; without it, the other linkages would not affect the rate of growth. This link has a number of different strands.

(1) International transactions can affect total demand through direct (Keynesian) injections into the circular flow of incomes or through monetary consequences of surpluses or deficits in the balance of payments as a whole. In both cases the effect can be either on the average level of demand or on the rate of growth of demand. The further critical question is whether demand affects the long-run rate of growth of real output. In some models of international trade (e.g. extreme versions of global monetarism) it is *assumed* that it does not, and that its effect is only on prices. The more usual view is that some effects on the level of output are likely, at least in the short run. The hypothesis that the long-run growth rate of output is affected is a stronger one and requires that demand should affect the rates of growth of factor input or productivity.

(2) The existence of international transactions causes the structure of demand for domestic output to be different from what it would be in their absence. This may affect the rate of growth of output by affecting the weight in the economy of sectors where the level or rate of growth of productivity is different from average. (These effects are not the same as the "gains from trade" as analyzed in traditional trade theory. The latter include effects arising from changes in the terms of trade, which affect the disposable income concept of national income [see pp. 27–29] but not real GDP in the conventional sense.)

(3) Associated with the foregoing, international trade is likely to affect the relative prices of goods and of factors of production. Effects on the profit rate are liable to affect domestic investment. Domestic investment is also liable to be affected by international capital movements. A question important in relation particularly to the period before 1914 is whether or not the property income from abroad that resulted from capital export compensated, in its effect as GNP, for any adverse consequences capital export had on GDP by depressing domestic investment; the effect of capital export on domestic investment has already been discussed in Chapter 12. International labor movements affect the national accounts differently from international capital movements. The income of emigrants is not treated as part of GNP except insofar as it is remitted home. Emigration thus tends unequivocally to lower GDP, though it does not necessarily lower welfare or lower GDP per head.

(4) Other strands in link f include "learning." An increase in international transactions is likely to improve the transmission of knowledge about foreign innovations. Such knowledge is, of course, likely also to be transmitted directly, not through international flows of goods or factors — one of the influences of exogenous world trends on British growth not shown in Figure 14.1.

Different aspects of international transactions are relevant to these various categories of influence on the domestic growth rate. It is therefore not possible to simplify the analysis by focusing on a single variable, such as the balance of payments or the rate of growth of exports. This is important, because values and volumes of exports and imports, the current balance, and the overall balance by no means always behaved in the same way.

Let us now consider the other links in Figure 14.1.

Exogenous British real trends affect international transactions directly (link b) and through their effects on the growth rate (link a + link e). These channels are closely related and may be considered together. The rates of growth of factor input and productivity determine the rate of growth of the productive potential from which exports are supplied. Slow growth in productivity is therefore likely to mean slow growth in exports and an unfavorable trend in the share of world exports. It may also encourage the emigration of capital and labor. At the same time, if income is growing slowly, the demand for imports is also likely to be growing slowly. The net effect on the balance of payments is therefore ambiguous. The most usual view has been that the favorable effects of growth on the balance of payments tend to preponderate. On this reckoning, slow growth may have been the cause of balance-of-payments troubles rather than the other way around. A rather similar conclusion is reached by reasoning in an entirely different theoretical tradition. Slow growth means a slow increase in the demand for real balances. If international reserves provide the base of the domestic money supply, then slow growth relative to other countries may necessitate a net outward movement of reserves.

The effects of *exogenous world real trends* (link c) are largely the mirror-image of the above. An important hypothesis in this connection is that because fast growth abroad caused other countries first to catch up with Britain and then to overtake it, the industries in which Britain had a comparative advantage kept changing, and the consequent adjustments created strains and costs. Quite separate from these long-term trends are the effects of the two world wars, which led to some major discontinuities in Britain's international economic position.

International and domestic monetary institutions and policies (link *d*) is a rather broad category. It includes the effects of British exchange-rate policy, traditionally held to have been the source of troubles in the 1920's and 1960's. Also included are the intended and unintended effects of demand-management policies at home and abroad on international transactions. Whether world business cycles and long swings should properly be included under this heading or under the preceding one depends, strictly speaking, on the view taken of their causes; later in this chapter we generally include them under exogenous world trade trends, but this is just a matter of convenience. There are also questions on the more strictly institutional side about the effects on the British economy of the various different international monetary regimes that prevailed in different periods and the changing position of sterling as an international currency.

Finally, movements in world prices will affect domestic prices and, through their effects on the balance of payments and real money balances, domestic demand. These mechanisms are mainly discussed here in terms of the effects of a rise in world prices on domestic prices. The prices of British exports and import-substitutes will tend to rise, by competition. We may distinguish three cases, as follows:

(1) There is simultaneously and independently a rise in British domestic demand. It will then be difficult to distinguish domestic and external sources of the rise in domestic prices (p_y). There will be an increase in demand pressure in goods markets.

(2) There is no independent rise in British demand, but the rise in world demand and prices leads to an improvement in the balance of payments. Under the gold standard the inflow of gold raises the domestic money supply. The rise in p_y in sympathy with world prices can therefore be accommodated without difficulties on the monetary side. The rise in p_y will be less than the rise in foreign trade prices (p_{ft}), because not all domestic goods are in competition with foreign goods.

(3) There is no independent rise in British demand, and the rise in world prices leaves the British balance of payments unchanged or worse (because the British price-elasticity of demand for imports and/or the world income-elasticity of demand for British exports are low). Then the rise in p_{ft} will tend to lead to a shortage of real money balances. This subjects p_y to conflicting pressures, domestic monetary pressure tending to push it down and sympathy with foreign prices tending to push it up. If prices were perfectly flexible, the prices of non-tradables would fall to offset the rise in p_{ft}. Normally, however, this will not happen to a sufficient extent, if at all, and there will be a

reduction in the pressure of demand in the goods market unless there is an accommodating increase in the money supply.

One way of trying to arrive at conclusions about the relative importance of the various exogenous forces is by scrutiny of the comparative movements of quantities and prices in international transactions. Thus in the case of exports, if their prices relative to GDP prices (p_x/p_y) move in the opposite direction from their volume relative to GDP (q_x/q_y), this suggests prima facie a *shift* of the supply curve of exports, such as might be due, for example, to more rapid growth of TFP in the production of exportables than in the production of non-exportables; whereas if p_x/p_y and q_x/q_y move in the same direction, this suggests prima facie a movement *along* the supply curve of exports, such as might be due to cyclical or long-run shifts in world demand.

Such price-quantity data are helpful to some extent. There are, however, considerable difficulties in drawing inferences from them. (The difficulties apply both to domestic price measures, like p_x/p_y, and to comparisons of prices or costs in different countries.) In the first place, there are the usual identification problems, compounded by having to look at supply and demand abroad as well as at home. In the second place, observed trends may represent *either* equilibrium relationships, of the sort analyzed in the pure theory of foreign trade (like the above example about differences between sectors in the rate of growth of TFP) *or* disequilibrium relationships, that is to say, movements along Marshallian short-run supply curves. The latter, it may be noted, are the chief subject of the literature on "competitiveness" (Enoch 1978). In the third place, such disequilbrium movements may themselves arise either from real forces (e.g. the process of adjustment by British industry to the growth of the foreign supply of British exportables) or from monetary forces (e.g. devaluation). There is thus usually more than one explanation that will fit the observed patterns of price-quantity relationships.

Two further points should be made before we conclude this section.

(1) In the British economy, the long-swing phenomenon has been most promimently manifested in the country's international transactions. Explanations of the long swing as such fall outside our scope, just as explanations of the ordinary business cycle do. However, long swings were the medium through which some of the long-run trends were experienced, and to that extent they must command our attention.

(2) Throughout this book our subject is the comparison of different phases of British economic growth, rather than the comparison of Brit-

ish economic growth with growth in other countries. This remains true of the present chapter. However, a large proportion of the literature on British international trade and payments is concerned with the second subject, and this will inevitably be reflected to some extent in our treatment.

This section provides a summary statistical view to serve as a background to the next chapter, in which frequent reference will be made to the tables and charts here given.

Exports and Imports of Goods and Services

Figure 14.2 shows the movements over time of the volume of exports and imports of goods. Outstanding features are the downward displacements across wars, especially World War I in the case of exports and World War II in the case of imports. The corresponding growth rates are shown in Table 14.1. Imports grew more rapidly than exports over the period 1856–1973 as a whole and in each individual period except 1937–51. The postwar period was thus not abnormal historically in this respect. Also shown in Table 14.1 are the growth rates of the

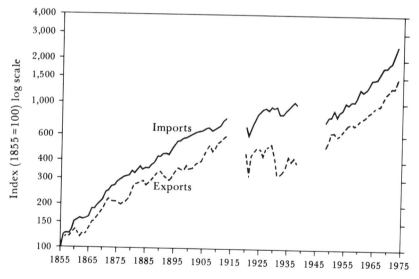

Fig. 14.2. Volume of imports and exports of goods, 1855–1973

TABLE 14.1

Growth of Trade and Gross Domestic Product, 1856–1973

(Annual percentage growth rates)

Period	Exports		Imports		GDP[a]
	Goods and services	Goods	Goods and services	Goods	
Peacetime phases:					
1856–1873	3.6%	3.4%	4.6%	4.7%	2.2%
1873–1913	2.6	2.7	2.7	2.8	1.8
1924–1937	−0.8	−1.1	1.7	1.6	2.2
1951–1973	4.3	3.9	4.7	4.8	2.8
Wartime phases:					
1913–1924	−1.8	−2.3	1.4	1.0	−0.1
1937–1951	2.6	2.9	0.1	−0.8	1.8
Post-WWII cycles:					
1951–1955	3.4	1.9	3.3	2.9	2.8
1955–1960	2.7	2.6	4.4	4.4	2.5
1960–1964	3.1	3.5	3.5	3.9	3.4
1964–1968	5.3	4.9	4.3	5.0	2.6
1968–1973	6.9	6.6	7.5	7.3	2.6
1856–1973	2.2%	2.1%	2.8%	2.7%	1.9%

Note: The growth rates for exports and imports exclude re-exports through 1964.
[a]GDP at factor cost, measured as the geometric mean of estimates from the income, output, and expenditure sides.

volume of exports and imports of goods and services. The inclusion of services does not greatly alter the picture shown by goods along (except in one period, 1937–51). About half of the exports of services consisted of shipping earnings, which themselves largely depended on the volume of commodity exports.

Similar information is expressed in different form in Figures 14.3 and 14.4. Exports and imports of goods at constant prices are expressed as proportions of, respectively, Gross Domestic Product and Gross National Product at constant prices, to provide a measure of the general scale of the economy. GDP is a measure of the productive capacity out of which exports are supplied; GNP is a measure of the total income available for purchasing imports. The long-run tendency for the volume of imports of goods to rise relative to GNP in constant prices was interrupted by the major downward displacement across World War II. The volume of exports relative to GDP moved more irregularly, though it too had some upward trend in peacetime periods other than the interwar period.

The movement of the four main constituents of goods imports (food, beverages, and tobacco; materials; manufactures; and fuel) is shown in

Figure 14.5 and Table 14.2. As with the total, there is no substantial fall in volume relative to GNP in any peacetime period except the 1930's, and big falls were registered across World War II, except in fuel. Over the whole period there was no tendency for imports of food and materials to rise relative to GNP, but imports of fuel and manufactures rose relatively rapidly. The penetration of imported manufactures was most severe before 1914 and in the postwar period, though the starting point after World War II was exceptionally low.

The index-number difficulties involved in comparisons over a period as long as a 100 years limit the usefulness of ratios of export and import volumes to GDP and GNP as measures of very long-run trends. A more appropriate measure of the importance of exports and imports in the national economy is given by the current-price ratios. Comparison of the constant- and current-price ratios yields an implicit index of the prices of exports or imports relative to the prices of GDP or GNP as a whole. Since this is subject to the same index-number difficulties as the constant-price measures, one cannot attach too much significance to the relative levels of the price index at widely separated dates. Its

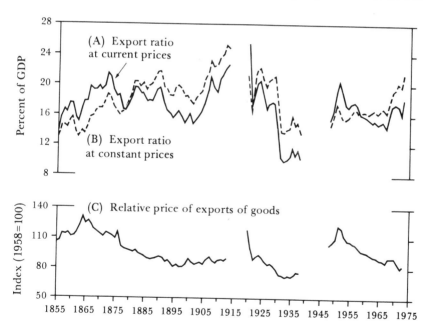

Fig. 14.3. Ratio of exports of goods to gross domestic product at current and constant prices, and relative price of exports of goods, 1855–1973. Exports of goods exclude re-exports.

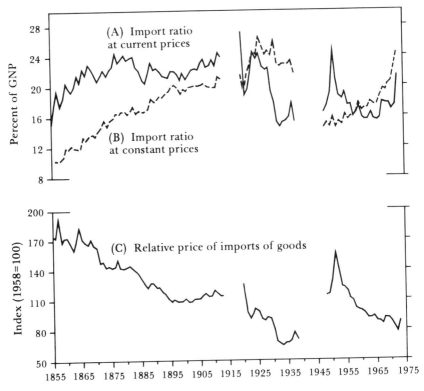

Fig. 14.4. Ratio of imports of goods to gross national product at
current and constant prices, and relative price of imports of
goods, 1855–1973. Imports of goods exclude re-exports.

movements over short periods, however, reveal some points of interest
and may not be too misleading.

The ratio of exports of goods to GDP at current prices and the implicit export-GDP price index for goods are shown in Figure 14.3, and the
actual figures for benchmark years are given in Table 14.3, together
with the current-price ratio of exports of goods and services to GDP. In
the great majority of peacetime years, the trend in p_x/p_y (series C in
Fig. 14.3) was downward. Some downward trend in this ratio is to be
expected, on account of the faster growth of TFP in sectors producing
exportables (chiefly manufactures) than in the economy as a whole.
However, as will be seen in the next chapter, the pressure of foreign
competition appears to have contributed to the trend in some periods,
leading to downward pressure along short-run supply curves.

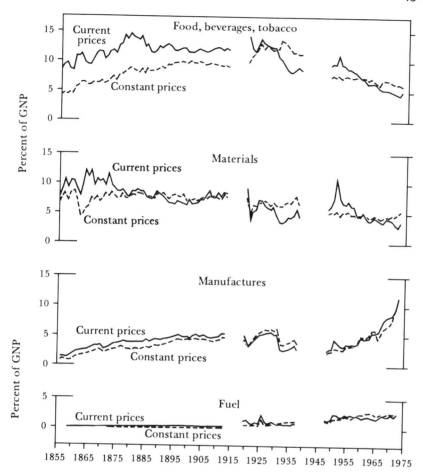

Fig. 14.5. Ratio of retained imports to gross national product at current and constant prices by commodity group, 1855–1973

The effects of wars in raising p_x/p_y are obvious from Figure 14.3 — not only the two world wars, but also the American Civil War (with the associated cotton famine) and the Korean War. Wars raise world demand for tradables or reduce world supply, or both. Only the Korean War did not also reduce the *British* supply of tradables, and only in it was the rise in p_x/p_y accompanied by a rise in q_x/q_y. In peacetime medium-term movements in p_x/p_y tended to be associated with movements in the same direction in q_x/q_y, which suggests that demand-side forces of some kind were at work: 1870–1900 compared with

TABLE 14.2

Ratio of Imports to Gross National Product by Commodity Group, 1856–1973

(Percent)

Price basis and commodity group	1856	1873	1913	1924	1937	1953[a]	1964	1973
Current prices:								
Food, beverages, tobacco	9.2%	11.8%	11.8%	14.0%	9.0%	9.4%	6.3%	5.1%
Materials	9.0	9.7	8.4	7.2	6.0	6.8	4.3	3.5
Manufactures	1.3	2.9	5.3	5.0	3.4	3.2	5.7	11.6
Fuel	—	0.1	0.4	1.0	1.0	2.1	2.0	2.7
Total[b]	19.5	24.5	25.9	27.2	19.4	21.5	18.3	23.0
Constant (1958) prices:								
Food, beverages, tobacco	4.5	7.4	9.1	13.0	11.1	7.5	6.5	6.0
Materials	7.6	8.4	7.7	6.8	7.9	5.1	4.6	5.4
Manufactures	1.0	2.4	4.8	5.2	4.4	2.7	6.0	11.8
Fuel	—	—	0.2	0.6	1.1	1.7	2.9	2.7
Total[b]	12.2	17.5	21.5	25.7	24.5	17.0	20.0	25.9

Note: Imports are imports of goods c.i.f., less re-exports of goods f.o.b. GNP is measured at factor cost from the expenditure side.

There are three breaks in the series, 1 in 1920 resulting from the change in territory and 2 in 1913 and 1951 resulting from changes in classification. Estimates on 2 bases in each of the overlap years are as follows:

Price basis and commodity group	1913 1855–1913 basis	1913 1913–1951 basis	1920 Including So. Ireland	1920 Excluding So. Ireland	1951 1913–1951 basis	1951 1951–1973 basis
Current prices:						
Food, etc.	11.8%	11.9%	13.0%	14.2%	11.1%	11.1%
Materials	8.4	8.0	9.0	9.3	11.4	11.2
Manufactures	5.3	5.5	4.9	5.1	4.2	4.4
Fuel	0.4	0.5	1.1	1.2	2.4	2.4
Total	25.9	25.9	28.0	29.8	29.1	29.1
Constant prices:						
Food, etc.	9.1	9.2	9.0	9.8	7.9	7.9
Materials	7.7	7.4	7.5	7.8	5.5	5.4
Manufactures	4.8	4.9	4.2	4.4	2.9	3.0
Fuel	0.2	0.2	0.4	0.4	1.7	1.7
Total	21.5	21.5	20.9	22.2	18.0	18.0

[a]The usual benchmark year at the beginning of the postwar period, 1951, is unrepresentative because of the unusually high level of import prices. The figures for 1951 are shown in the note above.

[b]The totals shown in this table differ from those shown in Table 14.4 and plotted in Fig. 14.5 because they include the cost of insurance and freight on total imports. Estimates of insurance and freight are available for all commodity groups together but not individually. In the case of the estimates at constant prices the figures for all commodities in this table do not necessarily equal the sums of the figures for each commodity group. This is because the estimates for all commodities were made in the same way as those for each commodity group, namely by linking the import-GNP ratios for 1855–1913 at 1900 prices, for 1913–48 at 1938 prices, and for 1964–73 at 1970 prices, to the ratios for 1948–64 at 1958 prices.

TABLE 14.3
Ratio of Exports to Gross Domestic Product at Current and Constant Prices,
and Relative Price of Exports, 1856–1973
(Percent)

Year	Export of goods ratio at con- stant prices (1)	Export ratio at current prices		Relative price of exports of goods (1958 = 100) (2) ÷ (1) (4)
		Goods (2)	Goods and services (3)	
1856	14.6%	15.6%	21.5%	107
1873	18.3	21.0	28.5	115
1913	25.0	22.5	30.1	90
1924	22.2	20.5	26.6	92
1937	15.0	11.4	16.3	76
1953[a]	15.5	17.4	24.1	112
1964	16.3	14.9	20.5	92
1973	21.6	18.1	26.1	84

Note: The export figures exclude re-exports. GDP is measured at factor cost estimated from the expenditure side. Comparability between 1913 and earlier years on the one hand and 1924 and later years on the other is affected by the change in geographical coverage in 1920. Estimates for 1920 on both bases are:

	(1)	(2)	(3)	(4)
Including Southern Ireland	19.5%	23.3%	31.2%	120
Excluding Southern Ireland	21.4	25.7	33.9	120

[a]The usual benchmark year at the beginning of the postwar period, 1951, is unrepresentative because of the unusually high level of export prices and to a lesser extent, export volumes. The figures for 1951 are (1) 16.9%; (2) 20.7%; (3) 27.9%; (4) 123%.

1900–1913, 1950–65 compared with 1965–73, and the whole of the interwar period.

Exports contain an import content. GDP does not. The ratio of exports to GDP therefore overstates the proportion of domestic output exported. The import content of exports of goods, at current prices, fell considerably between 1870 and 1935; there was a further small fall between 1935 and 1963, offset by a rise between 1963 and 1972.[1] Consequently, the fall in the proportion of domestic output exported between the pre-1914 period and the 1930's was considerably less than the fall in the ratio of exports of goods to GDP at current prices shown in Figure 14.3 (series A). Probably more than half of the fall in the import content of exports of goods over the period from 1870 to 1964 was accounted for by the improvement in the terms of trade, in the sense of the decline in the price of the imports embodied in exports relative to the price of the domestic resources embodied in them. Shifts in the structure of exports toward commodities with a lower import content, especially the decline in textiles' share, were also important.

The movements of imports relative to GNP, when both are measured in current prices, are markedly different from the movements in volume. (See Figures 14.4, series A, and 14.5, and, for benchmark years, Table 14.4.) Very broadly speaking, imports of goods as a proportion of GNP at current prices rose till the late 1870's, were constant until the late 1920's, and then fell by 7 or 8 percentage points. They remained not far from this historically low level for most of the postwar period — an important change from the half-century or so before 1930. Imports of services grew at much the same rate as imports of goods in peacetime periods, but at a much faster rate across the two wars. As a result, imports of goods and services as a proportion of GNP at current prices did not fall as much from the pre-1914 level in the interwar and early postwar periods as did the proportion of imports of goods alone (Table 14.4).

The long-run movement in the price of imports of goods relative to the GNP price deflator (Fig. 14.4 and Table 14.4) is downward in most peacetime years. Five secular phases can be distinguished, with the possibility of a sixth beginning at the very end: 1855–95, falling; 1895–1921, constant; 1921–33, falling; 1933–51, rising; 1951–72, falling; 1972–?, rising. There is a tendency for these long-run movements to be in the opposite direction from those in the corresponding quantity

TABLE 14.4

Ratio of Imports to Gross National Product at Current and Constant Prices, and Relative Price of Imports, 1856–1973

(Percent)

Year	Import of goods ratio at constant prices (1)	Import ratio at current prices Goods (2)	Goods and services (3)	Relative price of imports of goods (1958 = 100) (2) ÷ (1) (4)
1856	10.3%	17.7%	19.6%	172
1873	15.5	22.3	24.6	143
1913	21.0	23.9	26.2	114
1924	24.6	24.7	28.3	100
1937	23.3	17.8	20.7	77
1953ᵃ	15.2	18.7	24.8	123
1964	17.9	16.5	22.4	92
1973	24.4	21.3	28.5	87

Note: The import figures exclude re-exports. GNP is measured at factor cost estimated from the expenditure side. Comparability between 1913 and earlier years on the one hand and 1924 and later years on the other is affected by the change in geographical coverage in 1920. Estimates for 1920 on both bases are:

	(1)	(2)	(3)	(4)
Including Southern Ireland	20.0%	25.2%	28.9%	126
Excluding Southern Ireland	21.6	27.1	30.9	126

ᵃThe usual benchmark year at the beginning of the postwar period, 1951, is unrepresentative because of the unusually high level of import prices. The figures for 1951 are (1) 16.0%; (2) 25.4%; (3) 32.4%; (4) 159%.

TABLE 14.5

The United Kingdom's Share of World Exports of Manufactures Compared with Six Other Industrial Countries, 1881–1973

(Percent, based on values in U.S. $ at current prices)

Year	UK	U.S.	Germany[a]	Italy	France	Japan	Sweden
1881– 1885[b]	43.0%	6.0%	16.0%	2.0%	15.0%	0.0%	1.0%
1899	34.5	12.1	16.6	3.8	14.9	1.6	0.9
1913	31.8	13.7	19.9	3.5	12.8	2.5	1.5
1929	23.8	21.7	15.5	3.9	11.6	4.1	1.8
1937	22.3	20.5	16.5	3.7	6.2	7.4	2.8
1950	24.6	26.6	7.0	3.6	9.6	3.4	2.8
1964	14.0	20.1	19.5	6.2	8.5	8.3	3.4
1973	9.1	15.1	22.3	6.7	9.3	13.1	3.3

Source: Hilgerdt 1945; Maizels 1970; *National Institute Economic Review; Board of Trade Journal,* Sept. 30, 1970; *UN Yearbook of International Trade Statistics.*

Note: Total for world exports excludes exports from small manufacturing countries and the postwar Soviet bloc.

[a]For 1881–1937 estimates are 71% of contemporary Germany.

[b]The comparability between the estimates for 1881–85 and those for later years is imperfect.

index, suggesting movement along the demand curve. Before 1880 the long-run movement in the volume ratio was larger than that in the price index. Hence the value of imports relative to GNP followed the volume ratio; that is, it rose. From 1880 to 1929 volume and price movements roughly offset each other. After 1929 the movement in the price index was usually the stronger and therefore communicated itself to the value ratio. There were exceptions to these patterns: in the early 1930's both the price and the quantity index fell; and in the early postwar years both rose.

Despite the historically quite rapid rise in exports in the postwar period, Britain's share in world exports of manufactures fell. This is shown in Table 14.5, which relates to values at current prices. Apart from short-run fluctuations, the fall was at a fairly even rate after 1951, and this rate was (proportionally) faster than in earlier parts of the twentieth century.[2] The postwar fall has to be seen against the background of the exceptional rise in Britain's share that took place immediately after World War II, due to the absence of war-devastated countries, especially Germany, from the competitive scene. This rise was reflected on the import side in the very low imports of manufactures (Fig. 14.5). As a result, Britain's share in 1950 was much above the historical trend, and it remained above that trend for most of the 1950's. By 1973, however, Britain's share had fallen to well below that to be obtained by extrapolating pre–World War II trends.

There was a change over time in the countries to which Britain's share was being lost. Up till 1929 by far the greater part of the loss was matched by the gain of the United States. The United States also had a temporary increase after World War II, similar to that enjoyed by the United Kingdom, but thereafter its share fell steeply. The chief gainers were Germany, Japan, and to a lesser extent Italy. Germany's gain was in part a reversion to the larger share it had in 1913, after a decline in the interwar period. France's share fell up till World War II. In contrast to the United Kingdom, this decline was especially rapid in the interwar period. Within the postwar period France's share remained approximately constant.

To a large extent, the long-run decline in Britain's share in world exports of manufactures was no more than a reflection of the decline in its share of total output of manufactures. Since there were good reasons why at least some other countries should have experienced a more rapid increase in the output of manufactures than Britain did, it would not be reasonable to expect the British share of world exports to have remained constant. However, the fall in Britain's share in world exports of manufactures was greater than the decline in its share in world output (Table 14.6, rows 1 and 2). This was so in most periods, but particularly in 1950–64.

TABLE 14.6

The United Kingdom's Export and Output Ratios at Constant Prices, for Totals and Manufactures, Compared with Other Industrial Countries, 1899–1973

Category	Actual 1929 figure[a]	Index: 1929 = 100						
		1899	1913	1929	1937	1950	1964	1973
Manufacturing: Exports and output								
(1) Exports of manufactures: UK relative to sum of other industrial countries (X_m^{UK} / X_m^{OIC})	28%	223	169	100	92	129	51	35
(2) Output of manufactures: UK relative to sum of other industrial countries (Q_m^{UK} / Q_m^{OIC})	13	189	138	100	128	113	85	67
(3) Export-output ratio in manufacturing, UK (X_m^{UK} / Q_m^{UK})	48	114	132	100	59	72	59	79
(4) Export-output ratio in manufacturing, other industrial countries (X_m^{OIC} / Q_m^{OIC})	21	97	107	100	82	63	98	153

TABLE 14.6 *continued*

Category	Actual 1929 figure[a]	Index: 1929 = 100					
		1899	1913	1929	1937	1950	1964	1973
Total exports and output								
(5) Total exports: UK relative to sum of other industrial countries (X^{UK} / X^{OIC})	22%	163	156	100	98	125	60	41
(6) Total output: UK relative to sum of other industrial countries (Q^{UK} / Q^{OIC})	13	185	146	100	109	94	78	66
(7) Export-output ratio, UK (X^{UK} / Q^{UK})	17	87	119	100	71	83	77	102
(8) Export-output ratio, other industrial countries (X^{OIC} / Q^{OIC})	10	99	111	100	80	63	100	164
Manufactures' share in total output and exports								
(9) Manufactures' share in total output, UK (Q_m^{UK} / Q^{UK})	29	79	84	100	115	119	125	129
(10) Manufactures' share in total output, other industrial countries (Q_m^{OIC} / Q^{OIC})	31	77	89	100	98	100	115	120
(11) Manufactures' share in total exports, UK (X_m^{UK} / X^{UK})	82	103	94	100	96	104	95	100
(12) Manufactures' share in total exports, other industrial countries (X_m^{OIC} / X^{OIC})	62	76	86	100	101	100	112	119

Source: Basic statistics (Appendix N); Maizels 1970; *UN Statistical Yearbook*; *UN Yearbook of National Accounts*; OECD [3], [10]; IMF, *International Financial Statistics.*

Note: Other industrial countries here means Belgium, Canada, France, Germany (West Germany from 1950), Japan, Italy, Luxembourg, the Netherlands, Sweden, Switzerland, and the U.S. X = exports; Q = output; the subscript m = manufactures; and the superscript OIC = the sum of the other industrial countries. The underlying figures are taken from Maizels 1970, brought up to 1973, except for X^{UK}, Q^{UK}, and Q_m^{UK}, and they are at 1955 dollar prices. Thus the figures for the UK here do not necessarily correspond to those elsewhere in the book, partly because of the use of Maizels' X_m^{UK} series and partly because of the difference between a ratio at constant 1955 dollar prices and the same ratio at 1958 sterling prices.

[a]At 1955 dollar prices; hence not comparable to figures given elsewhere in this book at constant sterling prices.

Rows 1–4 of Table 14.6 compare British and world output and exports of manufactures; rows 5–8 do the same for total output and exports of goods; and rows 9–12 compare manufactures with the total. The long-run fall in the proportion of British manufactures exported (row 3) was greater than the fall in the proportion of British GDP exported (row 7). This is accounted for by the rise in the output of manufactures relative to GDP (row 9). Rather surprisingly, this rise between

1899 and 1950 was of greater extent in Britain than in the world as a whole (row 10). In the postwar period, however, this trend altered; the output of manufactures grew only slightly faster than GDP in Britain, but considerably faster than GDP in other countries.

Foreign Trade Prices and the Terms of Trade

Broadly speaking, the long-run movements in export and import prices relative to GDP (or GNP) prices were similar.* (See Figs. 14.3 and 14.4, series C; the average of the two series is plotted in Fig. 14.6). They both fell from the 1860's to the end of the nineteenth century; rose slightly up to 1913; fell between the 1920's and 1930's; rose across World War II to a pronounced peak in 1951; and fell away during the postwar period, with some recovery at the end of it. Part of the explanation for the similar movement in export and import prices lies in the import content of exports (import prices do not enter into the price of GDP). If one assumes that import prices are determined exogenously, about a third to a half of the major swings in export prices relative to GDP prices is accounted for by the movements in import prices. The remaining correlation between export and import prices is presumably the result of their both being determined by similar demand and supply forces.

There was a regular tendency for the GDP price (p_y; see Fig. 10.1) to move in the same way as the ratio of foreign trade prices to the GDP price (p_{ft}/p_y). In other words p_{ft} not only moved in the same way as p_y, but did so by a greater extent. The only major exception was the postwar period: from 1950 to the early 1970's p_y rose, but p_{ft}/p_y fell. (The old relationship was resumed in 1973, and after, when p_{ft}/p_y rose and the rise in p_y accelerated.)

If movements in export and import prices were *identical*, their ratio, the terms of trade, would be constant. But, as can be seen from Figure 14.6, the terms of trade were far from constant. The size of the long-swing fluctuations makes it difficult to identify trends. Disregarding the abnormally favorable interwar period, there was some general upward trend. The improvement in the terms of trade between the 1850's and 1873 only partially reversed the substantial deterioration that had occurred during the first half of the nineteenth century. On the measure 1880 = 100, the terms of trade fell from an average of 190 in 1801-10 to an average of 97 in 1851-60; in 1900, which was the peak year between 1850 and 1913, they were only 120 (Imlah 1958: Table 8

*Unless otherwise specified, export and import prices in this section refer to the prices of exports and imports of goods excluding re-exports.

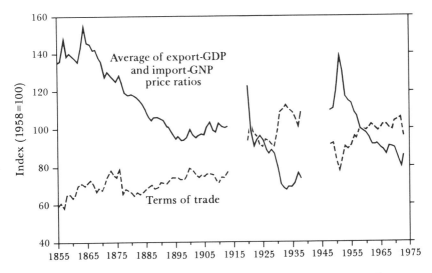

Fig. 14.6. Terms of trade and relative price of traded goods, 1855–1973

and Chapter 4). The early-nineteenth-century deterioration, which was associated with the fall in the prices of cotton textiles, was much larger than the falls in later periods (ignoring, that is, short-term fluctuations), and it was more prolonged.

A striking feature of Figure 14.6 is the inverse relationship between the foreign trade–output price ratio and the terms of trade in all periods after the 1880's, with the exception of the 1920's. Typically, export and import prices moved in the same direction compared with GDP prices, but import prices more so. Presumably, the causal links between import prices and GDP prices were weaker than those between export prices and GDP prices. In these circumstances, it is not surprising that movements in the ratio of foreign trade prices to GDP prices were typically larger than the matching movements in the terms of trade.

The measures of the terms of trade discussed so far relate to the relative prices of merchandise exports and merchandise imports. For most purposes the relative prices of exports and imports of all goods and services would be the more relevant measure. Only for the postwar period, however, are independent estimates available of the terms of trade on services and hence on goods and services together. The terms of trade on services deteriorated throughout the period, slowly in the 1950's and more rapidly in the 1960's. The terms of trade on goods and

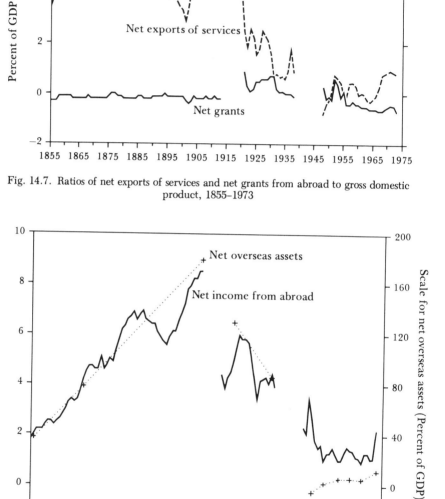

Fig. 14.7. Ratios of net exports of services and net grants from abroad to gross domestic product, 1855-1973

Fig. 14.8. Ratios of net overseas assets and net income from abroad to gross domestic product, 1855-1973. The crosses indicate the ratio of net overseas assets to GDP in benchmark years, the only years for which estimates are available.

services together therefore improved less rapidly during the 1950's than those on goods alone, and ceased to show any further upward trend after 1958.

The Balance of Payments on Current Account

The current account of the balance of payments is the sum of exports less imports of goods and services, net property income (interest, profits, and dividends) from abroad, and net grants received from abroad.* Net exports of services and net grants as a proportion of GDP are shown in Figure 14.7, and net property income and net overseas assets as a proportion of GDP are shown in Figure 14.8. The crosses in Figure 14.8 show the ratio to GDP of net overseas assets in benchmark years.[3] The scales are chosen so that the ratio of net income from abroad to GDP coincides with the ratio of net overseas assets to GDP when there is an average rate of return of 5 percent.

Up to the end of World War II changes in the level of property income from abroad were the result mainly of changes in the size of overseas assets. The chief movement shown by the assets figure, and likewise by that for income from abroad, is a single gigantic cycle with its peak in 1913. In that year net overseas assets were 1.8 times as high as GDP, and the income derived from them contributed 8.5 percent of GDP.[4] These ratios probably represent an all-time high not merely for Britain, but for any major country. The falloff after that time was essentially due to the wars; changes within the interwar and postwar periods were small by comparison. As a result, income from abroad was much lower relative to GDP in the interwar period than before 1914, and much lower again in the postwar period. There was no significant trend in the ratio of net income from abroad to GDP in the interwar period, or in the postwar period after the cycle that peaked in 1950 had subsided.

Though the size of net overseas assets is the major determinant of net property income from abroad, the rate of return (or at least the relationship between the rates of return on gross assets and on liabilities) accounts for some of its movements. A remarkable feature of the whole period up to World War II was the relative stability of the average rate of return (in the sense of the ratio of *net* property income from abroad to *net* overseas assets) at around 5 percent in our benchmark years (see Fig. 14.8). The main exception was 1924, when the rate of return was

---

*Except where otherwise stated, interest, profits and dividends, whether gross or net, are measured after the deduction of taxes paid in the country in which they are earned.

TABLE 14.7

Ratio of the Balance of Payments on Current Account to Gross Domestic Product, 1855–1973

(Average of annual percentages)

Period	Exports of goods (1)	Imports of goods (2)	Net services (3)	Balance of trade and services (1) − (2) + (3) (4)	Net income from abroad (5)	Net investment and grants[a] (4) + (5) (6)
Peacetime periods:						
1855–1873	17.9%	20.9%	4.7%	1.7%	2.8%	4.5%
1874–1890	18.4	23.9	5.1	−0.4	5.4	5.0
1891–1913	17.7	23.8	4.3	−1.8	6.8	5.0
1921–1929	18.2	23.3	2.2	−2.9	5.1	2.2
1930–1938	10.9	16.9	0.9	−5.1	4.2	−0.9
1952–1964	16.6	17.5	0.2	−0.7	1.3	0.6
1965–1973	16.3	17.3	0.6	−0.4	1.3	0.9
Post-WWII cycles:						
1948–1951	17.9	20.1	−0.4	−2.6	2.6	0.0
1952–1955	17.8	19.5	0.5	−1.2	1.5	0.3
1956–1960	16.7	17.1	0.2	−0.2	1.3	1.1
1961–1964	15.2	16.0	−0.1	−0.9	1.3	0.4
1965–1968	15.2	16.2	0.2	−0.8	1.1	0.3
1969–1973	17.3	18.3	0.9	−0.1	1.4	1.3

Note: Exports and imports of goods exclude re-exports. GDP is measured at factor cost estimated from the expenditure side. Comparability between pre-1914 periods and post-1920 periods is affected by the change in geographical coverage in 1920. Estimates for 1920 on both bases are:

	(1)	(2)	(3)	(4)	(5)	(6)
Including Southern Ireland	23.3%	26.3%	4.1%	1.1%	4.3%	5.4%
Excluding Southern Ireland	25.7	28.3	4.3	1.7	4.3	6.0

[a] Net investment abroad (as shown in Fig. 14.9) is defined as the sum of the balance of trade and services and net income from abroad, less net grants paid abroad (shown in Figs. 14.7–14.9). This column is the sum of the first two components only, and represents the net outflow of capital funds and current grants.

TABLE 14.8

Interperiod Changes in the Ratio of the Balance of Payments on Current Account to Gross Domestic Product, 1855–1973

(Changes in averages of annual percentages)

Changes between:	Exports of goods (1)	Imports of goods (2)	Net services (3)	Balance of trade and services (4)	Net income from abroad (5)	Net investment and grants (6)
1855–1873 and 1874–1890	0.5	3.0	0.4	−2.1	2.6	0.5
1874–1890 and 1891–1913	−0.7	−0.1	−0.8	−1.4	1.4	0.0
1891–1913 and 1921–1929[a]	−1.2	−2.1	−2.2	−1.3	−1.7	−3.0
1921–1929 and 1930–1938	−7.3	−6.4	−1.3	−2.2	−0.9	−3.1
1930–1938 and 1952–1964	5.7	0.6	−0.7	4.4	−2.9	1.5
1952–1964 and 1965–1973	−0.3	−0.2	0.4	0.3	0.0	0.3

Source: Table 14.7.
[a] The estimates for 1921–29 were adjusted onto the same geographical basis as those for 1891–1913 using the estimates for 1920 on both bases, as given in Table 14.7.

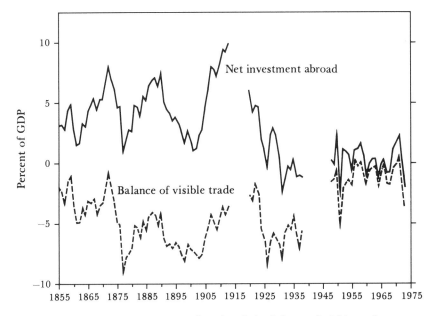

Fig. 14.9. Ratios of net investment abroad and the balance of visible trade to gross domestic product, 1855–1973

affected by the intergovernment loans incurred during and immediately after World War I. The average rate of return on net overseas assets was considerably greater than 5 percent after World War II because of the structure of net assets.[5] A much higher proportion of gross assets than of liabilities was in the form of relatively high-yielding direct and other private long-term investment in the postwar period than in earlier periods.

Net investment abroad, identically equal to the current account surplus, is shown in Figure 14.9 as a proportion of GDP at current prices. Figure 14.9 also shows the balance of visible trade relative to GDP (the balances of the various invisible items were shown in Figs. 14.7 and 14.8). Figures for each of the main components of the current balance are given in Table 14.7; the period 1874–1913 is here divided into two, the point of division being chosen so as to eliminate as far as possible the effects of long swings. First differences between periods are shown in Table 14.8.

The general picture, abstracting from the very large fluctuations, is one of a high level of foreign investment relative to GDP before 1914, a rapid decline in this level during the interwar period with disinvestment in the later years, and on average little net investment or net dis-investment in the postwar period. This is broken by the two world wars, when net overseas assets were run down. From the 1850's to the 1950's the United Kingdom always had a deficit on visible trade, usually offset by net invisible earnings, at least up to the 1930's.[6]

CHAPTER FIFTEEN

The Relationship Between International Transactions and Economic Growth

Each section of this chapter deals first with the forces affecting Britain's international transactions and then with the effects of international transactions on growth.

THE PRE-1914 PERIOD

The rate of growth of exports was less in 1873–1913 than in 1856–73. In the case of textiles – an important part of the total – this was largely because of an unavoidable decline in the scope for TFP improvement after about 1860. The reason why other industries did not take the place of textiles was partly that, for domestic reasons, TFP did not grow in those industries as rapidly as it had grown in textiles and partly that markets had increasingly to be shared with foreign competitors. The resulting trend deterioration in the balance of trade as a proportion of GNP was offset by a trend rise in income from abroad, which (along with coal exports) may also have been an active force in pushing down the competitiveness of British manufactures. Large fluctuations in the balance of trade could be accommodated, partly because long-term capital movements were subject to the same forces as the balance of trade and partly because confidence in the currency made short-term capital movements highly interest-elastic.

International transactions contributed less to the growth of demand in 1873–1913 than in 1856–73. Augmented after 1900 by the adverse real-balance effect of rising world prices, they caused the average pressure of demand to be rather lower after 1873 than before. They did not produce a cumulative increase in unemployment, but they did have an adverse effect on the growth of TFP – more pronounced in agriculture than in manufacturing – and on capital accumulation. At a guess, half of the decline in the rate of growth of TFP between 1856–73 and 1873–1913 had international origins. The growth of real disposable income was further depressed by the effect of foreign competition on export prices.

THE 1913–1937 PERIOD

The main forces responsible for changes on the international front across World War I and in the interwar period were exogenous, though doubtless the outcome would have been different if domestic productivity trends had been other than they were; the unusually rapid rise in wage costs across World War I may also have played some part. The exogenous forces were: war-induced shocks leading to depression in most of Northern Europe in the early 1920's; continued industrialization in overseas markets; a changed phase of the long swing; and the world depression of the 1930's. These contributed to and were compounded by a change in the position of London as a financial center. The return to gold at the prewar parity made matters worse, but probably no policy would have produced a satisfactory outcome.

The main effects on growth were through demand and hence industrial investment. The reduction in demand relative to supply between 1913 and 1924 was chiefly due to exogenous international forces. Between 1924 and 1937 demand rose rather faster than it had done on average between 1873 and 1913, but its rise was not mainly due to foreign trade and was anyway not enough to take up the slack already present in 1924. The improvement in the rate of growth of TFP in most sectors compared with 1873–1913, apparent in both the 1920's and the 1930's, was not attributable in any obvious way to trends in international transactions.

THE 1937–1973 PERIOD

World War II reduced income from abroad, as World War I had done. In other respects changes in the international position were more favorable to GDP across World War II than across World War I, though with an offset to disposable income from worse terms of trade. These differences reflected (1) the greater setback to competitors in World War II, which gave Britain (along with the United States) a temporary ascendancy in world markets reminiscent of the third quarter of the nineteenth century; (2) the absence of a postwar slump; (3) the different long-swing standings of 1937 and 1913. Trends in British foreign trade within the postwar period are mainly explicable by the relative growth of real supply at home and abroad, though exchange-rate policy made matters worse for a while, in the 1960's, as it had in the 1920's.

The balance of payments does not appear in retrospect to have been either so bad absolutely or so great a constraint on growth as was believed at the time. However, the diminished position of sterling *made fluctuations in the balance more difficult to accommodate than formerly, and the resulting stop-go cycles, despite their mildness, may have had some psychological ill-effects on the growth of TFP and capital accumulation on account of their peculiar time pattern. Taking the postwar period as a whole, world real trends, in the shape of fast-growing demand, increased scope for learning from the foreigner, and the absence of export-led slumps, were more favorable than in earlier periods, making for stronger demand and faster TFP growth. However, increasing foreign competition made for a slowdown in the growth of demand within the postwar period. The matching slowdown on the supply side arose from the supply of labor and cannot be attributed to international forces to the same extent as the forces that made for retardation on the supply side in 1873–1913. However, in the late postwar period more favorable trends in foreign trade would have permitted more capital accumulation in manufacturing and probably also rather faster TFP growth, and so helped to offset the effects of the decline in the rate of growth of labor input.*

THE PRE-1914 PERIOD: FORCES AFFECTING BRITAIN'S
INTERNATIONAL TRANSACTIONS

The questions to be considered first are those that relate to links b, c, and d in Figure 14.1, together with the joint effects of links a and e.

We may summarize the chief trends before 1914 as follows:

(1) The volume of exports grew more slowly in 1873–1913 than in 1856–73, and the rate in 1856–73 was lower than in the preceding decades (Table 14.1, also Table 15.1). The tendency apparent for most of the period 1856–1913 for exports of goods to rise faster than the rest of output was a continuation of a trend that had been in existence much longer, and indeed had been more pronounced in 1820–50 than it was later (Deane & Cole 1962: 309–12). There was a significant increase in imports of manufactures, as well as of food (Fig. 14.5), as a proportion of GNP in 1856–1913.

(2) The balance of trade, as a percentage of GDP, was deteriorating (Table 14.7).

(3) Notwithstanding this, there was no trend deterioration in the balance of payments on current account. This was because of the rise in income from abroad. The ratio of the favorable current balance (capi-

TABLE 15.1
Growth of Volume of Exports and Net Exports of
Manufactures, 1830–1913
(Annual percentage growth rates)

Category	1830–1857	1857–1873	1873–1913
Exports:			
Cotton textiles	5.1%	3.0%	1.7%
Other textiles	5.7	3.1	0.3
Other manufactures	6.4	3.3	3.4
Total manufactures[a]	5.6%	3.1%	2.0%
Exports minus imports (net of re-exports):			
Textiles	5.4	2.5	0.7
Other manufactures	6.7	2.1	2.8
Total manufactures	5.7%	2.4%	1.4%

Source: Schlote 1952: Tables 9, 10, 13, 15.
Note: Textiles are assumed to have constituted the same proportion of re-exports of manufactures as of imports of manufactures. 1857 is used as a benchmark year (instead of our standard date 1856) because it was the cycle peak for exports and net exports of manufactures.
[a]The figures are not directly comparable to those for total exports in Table 14.1 because different constant-price weights are used.

tal export) to GDP was on average at the high level of about 5 percent, without any clear trend up or down (Table 14.7). In addition to this emigration of capital, there was a net emigration of labor.

(4) There were very marked long swings in net overseas investment, with peaks in 1873, 1890, and 1913 (Fig. 14.9). They were matched by long swings in exports and to some extent, especially after 1890, by long swings in income from abroad, in imports, in the ratio of foreign trade prices to the price of GDP, in the terms of trade (inversely), and in emigration (Figs. 14.3, 14.4, 14.6, 14.8, Table 3.1).

The features that have most often been invoked as responsible for the slowing down of the economy's overall rate of growth during the period are the decline in the rate of growth of exports and the decline in the balance of trade (particularly the balance of trade in manufactures) as proportion of GDP. Explanations have been variously offered in terms of three categories of forces distinguished earlier: domestic real, overseas real, and monetary. The influence of these forces on Britain's international transactions will now be considered in turn.*

*The division between the categories contains some rather arbitrary elements, because they were often intertwined. Thus the long swing, discussed below under the "real trends abroad" heading, could from some points of view be regarded as monetary; and the effects of income from abroad on the balance of trade, treated below under the monetary heading, could alternatively be regarded as an effect going on inside the box labeled British international transactions in Fig. 14.1, rather than as an effect on it from the outside.

Exogeneous British Real Trends

The rate of growth of productivity, and also of production, was lower in 1873–1913 than in 1856–73. It also tended to decline within the period 1873–1913 (Fig. 2.1). Which way did the causal connection run between this and the decline in the rate of growth of exports?[1]

The effect of productivity trends on exports requires consideration of the course of events in certain individual industries.

Much the most important industry in which productivity trends were both exogenous (i.e. originating on the supply side) and significant for foreign trade was textiles. In the 1850's textile exports, of which cotton textiles were the largest part, amounted to over half of all exports. The slowdown in their expansion made an important contribution to the slowdown in exports as a whole. Indeed, after 1873 there was no slowdown in the rate of growth of exports of manufactures other than textiles (Table 15.1, row 4); the same is true of net exports (Table 15.1, last row).

As Table 15.1 shows, the decline in the rate of growth of export of cotton textiles began before 1873. The rate of growth, which had been very high in the late 1850's, was scarcely higher in 1860–73 than in 1873–1913. The very rapid increase in productivity in the second quarter of the century had led to steep reductions in price (Table 15.2) and hence permitted movements along the demand curves of overseas buyers. A consequence had been a sharp deterioration in the terms of trade, brought about mainly by falling export prices rather than rising import prices (Imlah 1958: 91–110) — an event never subsequently repeated in British economic history — so that growth in real disposable income benefited less than growth in GDP at constant prices. The sharp slowdown in productivity growth in the cotton textile industry after 1860 seems to have been the principal explanation of the reduction in the rate of growth of the industry's exports, though the effect may have been augmented by import-substitution in some foreign markets.[2]

Reference to the technology of the industry leaves little room for doubt that the decline in the rate of productivity growth was itself primarily exogenous and not a consequence of lagging demand. The very fast productivity growth in the second quarter of the century was the result of the progressive replacement of manual power by steam power. This process was completed in weaving by the 1850's, with the virtual extinction of handloom-weaving, and in spinning by the 1860's, with the completion of the transition to the self-acting mule (S. J. Chapman 1904: 70).[3] A slowing down then became inevitable. It is

TABLE 15.2

Growth of Total Factor Productivity and Prices in
Cotton Textiles, 1834–1885

(Annual percentage growth rates)

Period	TFP	Price of grey cloth
1834–1856	4.8%	− 2.5%
1856–1885	0.5[a]	− 0.3

Source: Blaug 1961.
[a] The figure for output in 1885 used for calculations of TFP is trend, not actual, to allow for that year being a year of recession (the unadjusted figure for 1856–85 is 0.1).

true that in the late nineteenth and early twentieth centuries the Lancashire cotton industry was slow in adopting certain innovations (notably ring-spinning and automatic looms), and this was held to be partly the *consequence* of its slower growth (*ibid.*, p. 33; Sandberg 1974: 61). But even if these innovations had been energetically adopted, productivity growth at the rate experienced earlier in the century would not have been possible.[4]

Similar considerations apply to the woollen industry, but the role of foreign competition was greater there. The mechanization process was completed a generation later in the woollen and other textile industries than in cotton, and fast growth of exports continued rather longer, up to the 1870's. The fall thereafter was more severe than in cotton, largely because of import substitution by the growing U.S. woollen industry (the U.S. market had never been important for cotton textiles). The volume of woollen exports was lower absolutely in 1913 than in 1873.

The case of the cotton industry is clear because there was a specific technical reason for productivity growth to slow down, and this (through the concomitant slowdown of price reduction) was bound to lead to a slowdown in the growth of the quantity demanded. The issue is less clear with iron and steel, cotton's successor as the leading growth industry. As in cotton, the falloff in the rate of increase of exports began well before 1873. Some slowing down of productivity growth may have been inevitable after the early inventions that made cheap steel available for the first time. But world demand went on rising rapidly for a long time after that, and the British share in world exports fell substantially — unlike cotton textiles, where the share was well maintained (Saul 1960: 33–35). It is a matter of debate among historians how far the shortcomings of the British steel industry in the late nineteenth century were technically unavoidable (Burn 1940;

Temin 1966; McCloskey 1973; Allen 1979). It can be argued that whatever slowdown there may have been in the rate of productivity growth was a consequence of increasing international competition. Hence, though exogenous elements, both technical and entrepreneurial, very possibly did cause a retardation of productivity of growth, we cannot say this with as much confidence as we can for textiles.

Rather clearer is the case with the principal "new" industries of the late nineteenth and early twentieth centuries, especially chemicals, motor vehicles, and electrical engineering. Here Britain was never in the lead, either in production or in exports, and it is difficult to attribute this to foreign competition. For in general these industries in each country developed first on the basis of a domestic market. In this phase, therefore, we may identify a weakness on the supply side as an independent factor restricting the growth of exports.

The conclusions are therefore these. A decline in the rate of growth of productivity, originating on the supply side, did have an effect on the rate of growth of exports in the pre-1914 period. Up to the 1860's the effect was more than just what would be expected from a *general* slowdown in the rate of growth of productive potential, since the slowdown was particularly great in the main export sector, textiles. In that sector the main source of the slowdown was technological. In other sectors there was no trend fall in the rate of growth of exports after 1873. However, the question remains whether weaknesses on the productivity side hindered other industries from making up for the inevitable falloff in textile exports. There are good reasons to suppose that this did happen in certain sectors, notably the "new" industries, and it may have happened more generally to some degree. But it does not provide a complete explanation. Account has to be taken also of increasing foreign competition, to which we now turn.

Exogenous Real Trends Abroad

The clearest account of trends in British exports in terms of the effects of overseas industrialization is Sayers 1965. Sayers distinguishes complementary and competitive effects (corresponding broadly to income effects and substitution effects in foreign demand). A rise in overseas incomes tended to increase the demand for imported goods, and so helped British exports. The opposite effect was produced insofar as the foreign growth was concentrated on goods competitive with British exports, leading first to import substitution, then to competition in third markets, and finally to competition in the British market. In the third quarter of the nineteenth century, the rise in incomes on the Continent and in the United States and other countries of recent European settlement, not as yet based mainly on industrial development, led to an enormous world demand for British textiles and iron and steel, both in those countries themselves and in primary producing countries, which enjoyed rises in incomes because of the increased world demand for their produce, not least demand from Britain itself. The pattern of events changed after the American Civil War and the European wars that followed it. After 1870 growth in Western Europe and in the United States was based increasingly on industrialization, a natural process but hastened by protection. The earliest phases of overseas industrialization increased the demand for imported capital goods, and there was still a favorable income effect, including an indirect effect via the incomes of primary producers. But the competitive element in the process became increasingly strong.

Evidence in support of this interpretation comes from the changes in the destination of British exports. British exporters progressively retreated from markets in advanced and industrializing countries and turned instead to unindustrialized countries. The value of British exports to the United States was actually lower in 1913 than in 1873. The proportion of total exports going to Britain's two most important industrial competitors, the United States and Germany, fell from 24 percent in 1873 to 13 percent in 1913, and the proportion going to Asia and Africa rose from 17 percent to 31 percent.

The hypothesis that foreign industrialization had competitive effects is also consistent with the decline that appears to have occurred in the late nineteenth century in the rate of growth of world trade as a whole (A. J. Brown 1965). There was relatively less international division of labor than there had been when Britain was the only important industrial country. This can be related to what has already been said about textiles. The characteristic industrial product cycle made it natural that the rate of productivity growth in textiles should tail off in the third quarter of the nineteenth century. The chief innovations in this period were in iron and steel and related industries. Why did they not give the same boost to world trade, and especially to British trade, as textiles had done earlier? This was where the overseas industrialization came in. Britain had increasingly to share the growing market in iron and steel products with foreign competitors, both in their domestic markets and in third countries; the near-monopoly that Britain once enjoyed in cotton textiles lasted much less long in heavy industry (with the partial exception of shipbuilding), so exports of iron and steel products never came to have a position comparable to those of cotton textiles in their heyday. Even if the British iron and steel industry had not been guilty of technical conservatism at the end of the century, it could only have been one of several major national producers; it would not have enjoyed the scope for expansion in world markets that had previously been available to the cotton industry.

For these reasons, a slowdown in the rate of growth of exports was unavoidable. Permanent maintenance of the mid-nineteenth-century position was not a possibility. The rapid growth of exports depended in large part on the rapid growth of foreign incomes, and that could only be sustained in the long run by industrialization, which in turn increased competition in British export markets.

This competition had an effect on prices and profitability. The fall in the price of exports relative to the price of GDP (Fig. 14.3) — a fall of more than 1 percent a year in the last quarter of the nineteenth century — was much more than can be accounted for by differences in the rate of growth of TFP between sectors (Table 8.3). Some of it was doubtless due to a fall in the prices of the import content of exports, but it is difficult to account for it all in that way. It follows that there must have been some downward pressure along the short-run supply curve of exportables, making for lower relative prices and profitability (though this downward pressure was not strong enough to offset the forces that were still making for some trend rise in the volume of exports relative to GDP).[5]

The difference in the competitive environment for British exports before and after 1873 can largely account for the less favorable trend in the terms of trade. This owed more to movements in export prices than to movements in import prices, as may be seen from the following tabulation of annual percentage rates of change in the prices of exports and imports relative to the price of GDP:

Period	Exports	Imports	Terms of trade
1856–1873	0.4%	− 1.1%	1.5%
1873–1913	− 0.6	− 0.6	0.0

The foregoing implies that changes in the prices of exports relative to the price of GDP were due to rather different forces in the period before 1850 and in the period 1856–1873–1913. The fall in the pre-1850 period was due chiefly to domestic productivity and cost trends. The contrast between the rise in 1856–73 and the fall in 1873–1913 was more largely due to the strength of foreign competition relative to demand.

Our discussion so far has related mainly to exports. Industrialization abroad had similar effects on imports of manufactures, which rose quite rapidly during the period (Fig. 14.5). The growth of food imports, with its devastating effects on British agriculture, was a more extreme consequence, resulting from a different aspect of growth abroad.

Though the growth abroad had some adverse long-run effects on British exports, they naturally benefited in the short run from periods of fast foreign growth associated with the business cycle. They also benefited from upward phases of the long swing. The long swing was a complicated phenomenon, involving the interaction of a number of elements: investment opportunities, absolute and relative price changes, migration of capital and labor, and monetary movements. To a large extent long swings were cycles in the pressure of world demand relative to supply. Primary products were affected more than prices of manufactures. Consequently, the fluctuations were more pronounced in primary producing countries in the New World than in Britain. Hence, in the upswings the British economy became more externally oriented: exporting became relatively more profitable, and the inducement to capital export increased. The movements in the downswings were the reverse. Since the rapid growth in long upswings was most prominent in primary producing countries, the elements complementary to British exports were to the fore relative to the competitive elements.

For this reason, long upswings do not provide a criterion of the effect of fast foreign growth generally on British trade in this period. They do, however, show in strong form the effects of overseas growth on long-term capital movements. As seen above (Chapter 12, p. 355), capital export was associated not so much with industrialization abroad as with infrastructure development, this being the type of activity that the London capital market was adapted to finance.

The same circumstances, namely booms in the countries of the New World, fostered both the acquisition of overseas assets and the exports of British goods. In addition, long upswings tended to raise the cost of imports and to increase income from abroad. There were thus forces tending to stabilize the overall balance of payments over the long swing, though the canceling-out was not necessarily complete.

In some respects long swings are rather a distraction in the study of trends in foreign trade in this period. They were, after all, cycles that tended to reverse themselves. However, they are too prominent to ignore, and they were the medium through which one of the major effects of overseas growth on British international transactions, namely capital export, was chiefly felt. They are, moreover, of interest in that rather similar long movements, intertwined with trend forces, continued in the interwar and postwar periods — accompanied, however, by some changes in pattern that we shall note in due course.

International and Domestic Monetary Influences

A principal hypothesis for discussion here is a less familiar one than those so far considered. It is that the deterioration in Britain's balance of trade was an induced phenomenon, brought about by the need to effect the transfer of the growing property income from abroad so as to maintain equilibrium in the overall balance of payments. Net property income from abroad grew from less than 2 percent of GDP in 1855 to over 8 percent in 1913.

It would be easier to assess this hypothesis if we had a better understanding of how balance-of-payments equilibrium was maintained under the pre-1914 gold standard. We know that in the short run an important part was played by short-term capital movements induced by interest-rate differentials (we revert to this below). What is not so clear is how equilibrium was maintained over longer periods. The machinery of classical gold-standard theory, with its induced adjustment of relative incomes and price levels, is not easy to observe in operation in the way that short-term capital movements are. But this does not necessarily mean that it was not functioning under the surface.

The hypothesis is that the rise in income from abroad tended to give Britain an increasingly favorable balance of payments, and that this in turn tended to raise British prices and incomes and/or to depress prices and incomes abroad. This made British exports become relatively less competitive and exporting relatively less profitable to British producers.[6]

The argument can be supplemented as follows. There was a rapid rise in exports of coal.[7] This powerful source of increasing export earnings strengthened Britain's balance of payments and kept up the British price level, so making the developments of other export lines more difficult and less profitable. Both income from abroad and coal proved unmaintainable sources of foreign exchange after World War I, and their damaging effects on the development of net exports of manufactures were then painfully felt. There is a close analogy to the fears expressed in the 1970's about the "Dutch disease" — the likely effects of North Sea oil on exports of British manufactures.

Pressure on the competitiveness of exports for the above reasons would have similar implications for relative prices and costs as pressure on competitiveness arising from exogenous increases in the foreign supply of British exportables — a fall in the price of exports relative to the

price of GDP, a rise in British export prices relative to those of competitors, and so on.[8] Reference to price data therefore does not help
much to discriminate between the two hypotheses, which are in any
case not incompatible. However, the Dutch-disease hypothesis does not
explain the contrast in price movements before and after 1873 — the rise
in export prices relative to the price of GDP before 1873, the fall after
1873 — since the trend rate of increase of income from abroad as a percentage of GNP was much the same in the two periods. This suggests
that it was at most one element in the story.

At the least we can say that there was (from the balance-of-payments
point of view) a fortunate coincidence that income from abroad rose at
the same time as the trade balance deteriorated. It remains a matter of
conjecture whether the strengthening of the overall balance due to the
rise in income from abroad was an active agent in making the trade
balance deteriorate.

We have been discussing a rather specific "monetary" hypothesis,
relating to trends in the balance of trade before 1914. Some reference
needs also to be made to the more general effects of the international
monetary arrangements prevailing before 1914. This is relevant to
comparisons with later periods, rather than to trends within the
pre-1914 period itself.

The central question is why there were not, before 1914, more frequent and severe short-term balance-of-payments crises of the kind
that became so familiar and so disruptive in later periods. There was
no major "crisis" after 1866.* This was notwithstanding that the Bank
of England's reserves were equivalent to only about two weeks'
imports — much less than in the post–World War II period.

The immediate explanation was short-term international capital
movements. The *net* amount of these movements was not great, taking
one period with another, but variations in them were the normal way
by which short-term disequilibrium in the balance of payments was
corrected.[9] Short-term capital movements also acted as a buffer against
variations in the domestic demand for cash (see Goodhart 1972: Chapters 14–15) — the "internal drains" that, under the Bank Charter Act of
1844, could be no less of a threat to the Bank's reserves than external
drains.

Small movements in interest rates were able to swing the balance of
short-term capital movements because Britain's predominance in

*That was the last occasion when a "Chancellor's letter" had to be issued promising the
Bank of England indemnity if it allowed its reserves to fall below the level required to
cover the note-issue. It was also the last occasion before 1914 when Bank Rate was raised
to 10%.

world trade made sterling the chief international currency. Why did sterling enjoy the confidence necessary for it to play this role? To say that the confidence arose from "the basic underlying strength" of the currency is hardly helpful, since though Britain had very large overseas assets and also a large volume of sovereigns in internal circulation, the Bank of England did not have any way to mobilize them. To a large extent it appears to have been a psychological self-perpetuating phenomenon, supported of course by the fact that the long-term adjustment forces, whatever they were, prevented any *permanent* downward trend in reserves. The possibility of changes in the exchange rate was never seriously in the public mind, and the only contingency to be feared was that the Bank of England would cease to be able to pay out gold. In assessing the likelihood of this, people did not look at the ratio of the Bank's reserves to the country's imports;* they looked rather at the ratio of the Bank's reserves to its own liabilities. Under the provisions of the Bank Charter Act of 1844, the relevant ratio was "the Proportion"—the proportion of the reserves in the Banking Department (the total gold reserves minus the excess of the note issue over the Fiduciary issue) to the liabilities of the Banking Department (chiefly bankers' balances). The proportion was not particularly low—rarely below a third, often over a half[10]—and the possibility of legislation to reduce the required cover for the note-issue provided a further reserve, for use in extreme emergencies.

The logic of looking at matters in this way depended on the assumption that in the last resort the Bank would be willing to defend its own reserves by allowing a fall in its holdings of bankers' deposits, i.e. a fall in the quantity of high-powered money. It may be doubted whether the Bank would, in fact, have carried out this policy in its full rigor in the absence of the defense provided by short-term international capital movements. But the belief that it would represented the triumph of the principles of the Currency School as enshrined in the 1844 Act.

The absence of balance-of-payments crises, made possible by short-term capital movements and by the unquestioned role of sterling, did not of course mean that there were not periods of monetary pressure. These were apparently most prone to occur in periods of high or rising world prices, i.e. in long upswings, whether because the net outcome of the above-mentioned offsetting effects of those prices on the balance-of-payments tended to be somewhat adverse or because of their effects on real balances. But they took a less abrupt and violent form than in later periods.

*Except in consideration of the need for a "war-chest" (Pressnell 1968: 223–24).

THE PRE-1914 PERIOD: THE EFFECTS OF INTERNATIONAL
TRANSACTIONS ON GROWTH

We turn now to the effects appearing as link f in Figure 14.1.

The Effects on Demand

The proximate effects on demand of movements in exports and imports were rather more than sufficient to account for the retardation of growth between 1856–73 and 1873–1913 (Table 10.10).* Within the period 1873–1913, the proximate contribution of foreign trade to the growth of demand did not tend to diminish, but rather the contrary. Trends are difficult to identify because of the enormous magnitude of long swings; but if 1890 is taken as a benchmark, broadly comparable in its place in the long swing to 1873 and 1913, it turns out that the contribution of foreign trade to growth, calculated in the same way as in Table 10.10, was greater in 1890–1913 than in 1873–90, though still considerably smaller than in 1856–73.† In other words, there was a sharp jolt to foreign trade's contribution to the growth of demand in the 1870's, followed by an incomplete recovery, all much punctuated by long swings.

As noted above, the approach embodied in these calculations is most suited to a model in which growth is determined entirely by demand, unconstrained by supply limitations. On this reckoning, one would conclude from the above that foreign trade accounted for the retardation in growth in 1873–1913 compared with 1856–1873 but not for the further retardation that appears to have occurred within 1873–1913, especially after 1900. In a model in which growth is entirely determined by the supply side, calculations of this sort have little relevance, since it is a matter of secondary interest which class of demand bears the brunt of adjustment to supply limitations.

The demand-dominated model of growth, in its simplest form, implies that a deficiency in the growth of demand manifests itself in an increase in unemployment. This does not fit the present case. Measured unemployment was, it is true, slightly higher on the average in 1874–1913 than in 1856–73 (4.7 percent compared with 3.7 percent);

*The fall in the rate of growth of GDP between 1856–73 and 1873–1913 was 0.3 percentage point. This compares with a fall between the two periods of 0.4 point in the sum of the three foreign-trade-and-payments items in Table 10.10. A significant part of this fall came from the behavior of the terms of trade.

†The terms of trade were again important in bringing this about: having improved up to the mid-1870's, they then took a single steep step down, followed by a long gradual recovery (Fig. 14.6).

but there was not a cumulative increase in unemployment, such as would be required on the foregoing model, and in any case the trend in the unemployment statistics in this period may well be subject to an upward bias (above, p. 83). The case was, on any reckoning, not comparable to that of the interwar period, when influences from the side of foreign trade manifestly had a major effect in increasing unemployment.

However, calculations on the level of demand (Table 10.5) suggest that insofar as there *were* forces tending to make demand lower relative to supply in 1873–1913 than in 1856–73, they did come from the side of foreign trade. (This applies to the average of all years, but not to the peaks.) The rise in income from abroad, which lacks a first round in the multiplier process, was not, according to these calculations, quite large enough to offset the lower proportion of exports to full-employment income and the higher propensity to import. So though it cannot be held that deficient growth of demand from foreign trade after 1873 caused unemployment to pile up cumulatively, it is possible that foreign trade, especially in cyclical recessions, had the effect of making demand somewhat lower relative to supply than it had been previously. This may have had some influence on the decline in the profit rate, referred to below.

The foregoing relates to the direct (Keynesian) effect of international transactions on the circular flow of incomes. In modern times at least as important have been their indirect effects, felt through pressure (or its opposite) on the balance of payments. As in modern times, pressure on the Bank of England's reserves in the pre-1914 period was usually felt at or around cycle peaks. It is doubtful, however, whether this should be taken to mean that the balance of payments was acting as a constant brake inhibiting the achievement or maintenance of full employment. The cyclical amplitude of fluctuations in imports was not especially great (Table 10.7). The pressure on reserves at cycle peaks was largely connected with increased internal demand for money, rather than with international transactions. There does not seem to have been any general trend for cyclical (or other) pressure on the reserves to become more severe over time. It does appear, however, that rather more financial pressure than usual was experienced in 1900–1913, operating through a real-balance effect. Domestic prices rose, but output and employment both rose less than previously; the unemployment in the cycle-peak year 1907 was unusually high. The annual percentage growth of real balances was somewhat lower than in the previous period, chiefly because of the rise in the price level, though there was also little upward trend in the quantity of high-powered money.[11] There was a rise in interest rates and in the velocity of circulation. These data are consistent with the hypothesis that the rise in world prices had a deflationary monetary impact on the British economy.* This period thus seems to conform to pattern (3) noted in Chap. 14 (pp. 425–26). The adverse real-balance effect was a long-swing phenomenon, rather than a trend phenomenon; but it may have helped to depress activity in that period. Apart from this, it does not seem that conclusions drawn from consideration of the direct (Keynesian) effects on demand, in comparing the periods 1856–73 and 1873–1913, require any significant modification on account of indirect effects of international transactions through the balance of payments.

Given that the decline in the rate of growth of demand generated by foreign trade did not simply lead to a pile-up of unemployment, it is necessary now to consider how the rate of growth of supply may have been affected by the country's international transactions: not only through their effect on the growth of demand but also through any other effects they may have had. In other words, what effect did international transactions have on the rate of growth of TFP and on capital accumulation?†

The Effects on Total Factor Productivity

The effects on TFP raise considerations about structure similar to those discussed in Chapter 9. The late-nineteenth-century decline in the growth of exports meant *ceteris paribus* a less rapid increase in manufacturing's share of output. The estimates in Table 9.10 showed that trends in the balance of trade were favorable to manufacturing in 1856–73 but slightly unfavorable in 1873–1913. We can use these figures to try to estimate what would have been the purely structural effects on productivity growth, if the balance of trade had affected manufacturing's share in output in 1873–1913 as it had in 1856–73. By

*Deflationary effects were not in evidence in the boom of 1899–1900, despite an absolute fall in real balances from 1898 to 1900. A lagged effect has therefore to be postulated. It is not possible to say whether similar effects were felt in the period of rising world prices in the third quarter of the 19th century, since money-stock data are available only from 1880. During that period interest rates were relatively high, suggesting the possibility of deflationary pressure. On the other hand, unemployment at cycle peaks was low, and the rate of growth of output relatively high, which suggests that the monetary system may have adapted more successfully than it did after 1900.

†Effects on the third component of supply, labor input, are taken to be unimportant in the present context. The rate of growth of the labor force in the long run was determined predominantly by demographic forces, though, within the long swing, variations in the amount of net emigration were of course important.

purely structural effects is meant the effects of shifts of factors to industries where either the level or the growth rate of productivity is above average.

The calculation cannot be done exactly. But it is immediately obvious that the effects so calculated would be quite trivial. In the first place, the average wage in manufacturing was slightly *lower* than in the rest of the economy, so there would be no positive labor quality-shift. In the second place, the annual percentage rate of growth of TFP in manufacturing in 1873–1913 exceeded that in the rest of the economy by only quite a small absolute margin, 0.6 percent compared with between 0.1 percent and 0.2 percent (Table 8.3); so the hypothetical rise of about 5 percentage points between 1873 and 1913 in manufacturing's share in output, which is what is in question, would have raised the annual rate of growth of TFP by only about 0.01 over the period as a whole. This is characteristic of the small effect of such structural changes.*

However, this approach scarcely does justice to the case. In the first place, it does not take account of Verdoorn effects, which were noted by contemporaries in relation to the cotton industry and which might have helped other industries if international competition had not prevented them from fully taking cotton's role. In the second place, the effects of changes in the structure of demand can scarcely be separated from the effects of the growth of demand in the aggregate. It could be contended that if there had been further growth in the net export demand for manufactures, the necessary resources would have come from uses where their marginal product was low or zero. In other words, there would have been a reduction in disguised unemployment. On the extreme assumption that not merely any additional exports of manufactures but also any other multiplier-induced increase in output could have been produced at virtually zero net cost, the whole of the demand effect discussed above could obviously have been accommodated.

There is clearly some substance in this line of argument. There certainly was disguised unemployment. More favorable conditions on the foreign trade side would have raised TFP growth in the period 1873–1913 by more than the minimal amount implied by the strict structural measures referred to above; they would, moreover, probably have had

---

*It is likely that the second quarter of the 19th century was an exception, and that there was then a substantial positive structural effect from the growth of manufacturing, chiefly cotton textiles. The rate of productivity growth in textiles was extremely high (Table 15.2), no doubt much higher than in the rest of the economy, and the increase in the industry's share of GDP was substantial.

a further effect by stimulating investment. However, the rate of growth of TFP in manufacturing itself was lower in 1873–1913 than it had been in 1856–73. This would not as such have been corrected by the shift of resources from low-productivity uses. Verdoorn effects might have helped but would not have removed the strictly technological sources of slowdown referred to above in connection with textiles.

So much for manufacturing. Even more severely affected by foreign competition in the last quarter of the nineteenth century was agriculture, still an important sector in the early 1870's (Table 8.1). Economists have been so preoccupied with manufacturing that they have tended to lose sight of the quantitative importance of the agricultural depression. Agricultural output fell absolutely between 1873 and 1913, and the annual rate of growth of TFP in 1873–1913 was only 0.4 percent, compared with 0.9 percent in 1856–73 (Table 8.3). Agriculture, in fact, made a considerably greater contribution than manufacturing to the shortfall in the rate of growth of TFP in the economy as a whole in 1873–1913 compared with 1856–73. Most of this was to be attributed to the effects of foreign competition.

A word may be said about the only important nonmanufacturing export industry, coal-mining, and its effects on productivity growth in the period 1873–1913. As already noted, exports of coal grew rapidly in this period, and so did the proportion of the labor force in coal-mining. Labor productivity in the industry fell absolutely. Since the exporting of coal was found profitable, and since, moreover, the diminishing returns in the industry were internalized, there is no presumption of a misallocation of resources (save insofar as the labor proved immobile later on, when the exports declined). But the growth of measured GDP at constant prices was damaged (1) by the allocation of more resources to an industry where productivity was not growing, and (2) by intensifying the operation of diminishing returns within the industry and so reducing its rate of productivity growth. The reconciliation between the profitability of the industry and its damage to measured productivity growth is partly that the export of coal had a favorable effect on the terms of trade and partly that it was achieved at the cost of unrecorded capital consumption, i.e. using up the more accessible coal deposits. To measure the effect, one has to say what would have happened otherwise. An extreme hypothesis is that if exports of coal had not risen, productivity would have grown at the same rate in coal-mining as in the rest of the economy (in which case average intra-industry growth would have been independent of coal-mining's share in employment). Allowing for some loss of quality-shift gain (p. 263), productivity in the economy as a whole would then have grown by about 0.05 percent a year more than it did.

A remaining point to be mentioned about the effects of international transactions on TFP growth in this period concerns learning. Industrialization abroad, especially in the United States and Germany, meant that the scope for learning from the foreigner increased in the course of the period. There was certainly increasing awareness in British industry of foreign innovations. Moreover, by the early years of the twentieth century foreign firms, chiefly American, were beginning to participate directly in the British economy itself. Such forces facilitating the adoption of foreign innovations of course operate in the opposite direction from that required to explain observed trends in TFP growth. To the extent that they were significant, retardation from other sources must have been correspondingly greater.

The fall in the annual rate of TFP growth between 1856–73 and 1873–1913 was 0.6 of a percentage point if account is taken of changes in labor quality (Table 7.4). From what has been said above about disguised unemployment and about Verdoorn effects, it is obvious that one can only guess how much of this fall between the the two periods was due to differences between them on the side of international transactions. Perhaps 0.3 of a point (0.15 from agriculture, 0.05 from manufacturing, 0.05 from mining, and 0.05 from elsewhere)? The chief arguments against setting the figure higher are the technological element in textiles, the slow development of new industries mainly dependent on the domestic market, and the especially poor productivity performance after 1900, which cannot readily be attributed to international transactions, since it was accompanied by an unusually fast growth of exports.

The Effects on Domestic Capital Accumulation

There remains to consider the effects of international transactions on the growth of the domestic capital stock. One aspect, the effects of capital export, was dealt with in Chapter 12 (pp. 353–59). It was there noted that capital export probably did have some long-run depressing effect, but not a very large one, on domestic investment, and that it also had an effect in limiting the extent of the fall in the profit rate. Reference was made also to the diversion of entrepreneurial talents associated with the external orientation of the British economy, of which capital export was one manifestation. These considerations apply to the whole of the period 1856–1913, averaged over long swings; they do not mark a major point of difference between the periods before and after 1873.

Insofar as changes in the international environment made for a slow-down in the rate of growth of TFP in the course of the period 1856–1913, they must also have had a tendency to discourage investment, thus magnifying the effect on the growth of productive potential. Suppose that the international environment had not taken a turn for the worse, and that, as a result, the rate of growth of TFP had been 0.3 percentage point higher in 1873–1913 than it actually was. Suppose too that the capital-output ratio had had the same trend as it actually had, and that the capital-elasticity of output had not been significantly affected. Then the rate of growth of the capital stock would have been 2.4 percent (instead of 1.9 percent), and the rate of growth of output would have been 2.3 percent (instead of 1.8 percent).

Could this higher rate of capital accumulation have been achieved consistently with the constraints on savings? Probably the increased investment in manufacturing, the sector chiefly affected, would have been partly offset by rather less investment in dwellings, which, as things were, was to some extent crowded in by lack of industrial investment opportunities. (Probably too there would have been rather less capital export, which in some phases also gave signs of being crowded in.) The hypothetical effects on GDP described in the last paragraph therefore need to be shaded down, but not very much—doubtfully if enough to show at the first decimal point—especially in view of the relatively low measured rate of return on dwellings.

A further point concerns the terms of trade. The change in the terms of trade added 0.2 percent to the annual rate of growth of real disposable income in 1856–73 but had no net effect in 1873–1913 (Table 2.4). The difference between the two periods arose more from the price of exports than from the price of imports (Tables 14.3, 14.4). It thus indicates the effects of competitive pressure on the prices of British exports in 1873–1913.

On this reckoning, the exogenous effects of foreign trade can, with reasonable figures, be made to explain the whole of the fall of 0.4 percentage point in the annual rate of growth of GDP between the periods 1856–73 and 1873–1913 (and likewise the fall in the rate of growth of real disposable income). This is notwithstanding that we are postulating that even in the absence of unfavorable influences from foreign trade there would still have been a lower rate of growth of

TF_QP in 1873–1913 than in 1856–1873 (0.3 percent compared with 0.6 percent). The explanation for the apparent inconsistency is twofold: (1) the rate of growth of the quality-adjusted labor input was 0.3 of a point higher in 1873–1913 than in 1856–73, and (2) the rate of growth of the capital stock was higher relative to the growth of output (both actually and in the hypothetical case) in 1873–1913 than in 1856–73.[12] If there had been *no* fall in the rate of growth of TF_QP between the two periods, those two factors would have caused output to rise *faster* in 1873–1913 than in 1856–1873. (Moreover, the rate of growth of output in that case would have been just about sufficient to keep GDP per head rising in pace with its rise in the United States; see Table 2.5.) The effects of autonomous decline in the rate of growth of TFP and the effects of foreign trade thus *both* remain of importance in explaining the course of events.*

1913–1937: FORCES AFFECTING BRITAIN'S
INTERNATIONAL TRANSACTIONS

The chief features of Britain's international transactions in the interwar period were these:

(1) The volume of exports fell absolutely across World War I, fell again in the early 1930's, and did not regain the 1913 level in any interwar year (Fig. 14.2 and Table 14.1).

(2) The value of exports fell as a proportion of GDP both across World War I and in the course of the interwar period (Fig. 14.3).

(3) The trend deterioration in the balance of trade and services compared with pre-1914 was no greater than the trend deterioration within

---

*The arithmetic may be set out explicitly as follows. We have

$$\hat{q} = \alpha\hat{n} + (1 - \alpha)\hat{k} + \hat{x}$$

Suppose that in each period the trend in the capital-output ratio is taken as given, so that $\hat{k} = \hat{q} + \delta$. Then

$$\hat{q} = \hat{n} + \frac{1 - \alpha}{\alpha}\delta + \frac{\hat{x}}{\alpha}$$

Let Δ refer to the excess of 1873–1913 over 1856–73. Disregard $\Delta\alpha$ as second-order. Let $\Delta\hat{x}_1$ refer to changes in $\hat{x}$ due to foreign trade and $\Delta\hat{x}_2$ refer to changes in $\hat{x}$ due to other causes. Then the components of $\Delta\hat{q}$ are as follows (the figures in parentheses show the values of the various magnitudes on the assumptions made in the text):

$$\Delta\hat{q} = \Delta\hat{n} + \frac{1 - \alpha}{\alpha}\Delta\delta + \frac{\Delta\hat{x}_1}{\alpha} + \frac{\Delta\hat{x}_2}{\alpha}$$
$$(-0.4)\quad(0.3)\quad(0.3)\quad\quad(-0.5)\quad(-0.5)$$

the pre-1914 period as a proportion of GDP and only slighly greater as a proportion of full-employment GDP (Table 14.8).[13] The deterioration continued between the 1920's and 1930's, at a faster pace.

(4) There was an improvement in the terms of trade, both across World War I and in the 1930's, of a much larger extent than anything that had occurred before 1914 (Fig. 14.6).

(5) Net income from abroad fell as a proportion of national income across World War I (Fig. 14.8, Table 14.7). There was a further fall between the 1920's and 1930's (Table 14.8).

(6) Net capital export remained quite substantial in the 1920's, though much lower than before 1914. It became slightly negative in the 1930's (Table 14.7, column 6).

(7) Considerable difficulty was experienced in reestablishing and maintaining the pre-1914 exchange rate, and short-term interest rates were kept at an unprecedentedly high level in the 1920's. The overall balance-of-payments situation eased in the 1930's after the decision to go off gold.

Exogenous Real Trends at Home and Abroad

The fall in the volume of British exports between 1913 and the 1920's was spectacular. Forces similar to those of the pre-1914 period continued to reduce Britain's share in world exports at a rather more rapid rate than before, and at the same time there was a great reduction in the rate of growth of world trade. As may be seen from Table 15.3, the difference between 1899–1913 and 1913–29 in the rate of growth of British exports of manufactures was due more to the decline in the rate of growth of world trade than to an acceleration in the decline of Britain's share, though both were significant.*

The causes of the slowdown in the growth of world trade were complicated. In the first place, there was some slowdown in the growth of world output of manufactures. The source of this lay in Europe, and the concomitant slowdown in the growth of incomes reacted back on the purchasing power of primary producers. This was particularly important in the early 1920's, when severe unemployment was experienced not only in Britain, but also in Germany and most of Northern Europe. There was a recovery in the late 1920's, but even so the annual growth rate of manufacturing production over the period 1913–29 in

*The decline in the growth of world trade would appear even more important relatively if 1924 were taken as the benchmark year instead of 1929. Evidence presented to the Balfour Committee at that time suggested there had been little, if any, fall in Britain's share in world exports.

TABLE 15.3

Growth of British Exports of Manufactures and of World Trade in Manufactures, 1899–1929

(Annual percentage growth rates)

Period	British exports	World trade	British share (residual)
1899–1913	2.8%	4.9%	– 2.1%
1913–1929	– 0.5	2.9	– 3.4
Difference	– 3.3	– 2.0	– 1.3

Source: Maizels 1970: Table A4.

Europe was only 1.0 percent (Svennilson 1954: 54). This can be regarded as in a sense the consequence of the disruption caused by the war, but the form it took was largely a straightforward deficiency of demand.

In the second place, world trade in manufactures grew less rapidly than world output of manufactures. The reasons here were the following. (1) The increase in world output and income was concentrated disproportionately in the United States, which was more self-sufficient than other industrial countries. (2) Industrialization had proceeded more rapidly than previously in some of the less-industrialized countries, under the stimulus of the nonavailability of industrial imports during the war, and these industries developed further in the 1920's, helped by protection. In addition, there was an increase in protection in already industrialized countries. (3) The terms of trade were much more favorable to manufactures relative to primary products than they were before 1914. This was partly a consequence of the relatively depressed level of income in some of the chief importing countries, notably Britain itself, and to that extent was not an independent cause. But the slowdown in the rate of population growth in consuming countries was also important.[14] (4) 1913 and the immediately preceding years had themselves been somewhat out of trend. They were a foreign-trade-oriented world boom, especially strong in primary-producing countries.

The slower growth in world trade within the interwar period was associated with a fall in world prices, especially prices of primary products. This was transmitted to domestic prices, which also fell (Figs. 10.1, 14.6). The movement in domestic prices was also influenced by the domestic pressure of demand, itself partly the result of external developments (see below).

From the British point of view, one of the causes of the slowdown in the growth of world trade, import substitution in foreign markets, represented a more extreme continuation of what had gone before, only this time in different countries, especially India. The swing back from the unrepresentatively high level of foreign trade in 1913 likewise resembled earlier long-cycle swings. But the postwar disruption and demand-deficiency that brought about the decline in the growth rate of world output were not continuations of earlier trends. Also a novelty, and largely the result of the war, was the rise in imports of services relative to GDP as British shipping and financial services suffered an erosion of their monopoly position.

Further breaks from past experience occurred in the 1930's, with the unprecedented magnitude of the world depression, the retreat into protectionism, and the abandonment of the gold standard.

The fall in the real value of income from abroad between the pre-1914 period and the 1920's was the direct result of the war. It represented a break from past trends. Indeed, it was a much bigger break than the deterioration in the balance of trade (Table 14.8). In the pre-1914 period the trend deterioration in the balance of trade and services was offset by a trend increase in income from abroad (both as a proportion of GDP). The trend *increase* in income from abroad resulted from net investment abroad that was *positive* but roughly constant as a proportion of GDP (apart from fluctuations) between 1856 and 1913. If net investment abroad grows, along with GDP, at a steady rate, income from abroad will exceed annual lending, so long as the interest rate exceeds the percentage rate at which the assets are being added to. This broadly speaking describes the British case in most of the years between 1875 and 1913. The country was in the position of a rentier plowing back part, but not all, of his receipts of interest. Moreover, the excess income from overseas assets over annual lending was increasing faster than GDP, thus permitting the trade balance to deteriorate relative to GDP. There was no reason in principle why this trend should not have continued, provided that the country had been willing to devote a rising proportion of the national income to overseas investment. It is a matter of speculation how long it would have continued, had not the more drastic disruptions that followed World War I brought it to an end.

The pre-1914 pattern of steady deterioration in the balance of goods and services required a continual increase in income from abroad to sustain it. Since the balance on goods and services continued to become less favorable across World War I (Table 14.7), the overall balance on current account would have deteriorated even if income from abroad had merely remained constant as a proportion of GDP. As it was, it actually fell, and the deterioration in the balance on current account was correspondingly worse.

No one suggests that productivity trends *within* the interwar period were the source of trouble in foreign trade. Productivity in manufacturing grew considerably faster than before 1914; moreover, its growth compared favorably with that abroad. Productivity grew at just about the same pace in export industries as in manufacturing as a whole (this was also true of the periods 1937–51 and 1951–64).[15] In a more general way, the productivity weaknesses of the period before 1914 were still felt, indeed in more acute form, especially in the slowness of the buildup of new industries. But after 1920 supply was not a constraint on exports in the principal industries, except in a few cases in the late 1930's.

Industrialization in semi-industrialized countries, hastened by the war, contributed by import-substitution to the diminished growth of world trade as a whole. Moreover, the encouragement given by the war to import-substitution was prolonged by continued shortages of supplies from traditional exporters in 1919–20 (League of Nations 1942). The pace and character of development abroad also contributed to the decline in Britain's share of exports, in several ways:

(1) The American economy had grown rapidly during the war. The U.S. share in world exports increased substantially, at the expense not only of Britain, but of Europe as a whole. The United States also began to encroach on Britain's monopoly as an international commercial and financial center.

(2) Britain suffered from the process of import substitution more than other countries, because in 1913 semi-industrialized countries accounted for about 40 percent of its exports of manufactures, compared with some 10–15 percent for other industrial exporters (Maizels 1963: 228–31).

(3) Britain's share in world trade was unrepresentatively high in 1913. This was mainly the consequence of the character of the 1913 boom, in which the "complementary" effects of overseas economic growth were strong relatively to the "competitive" effects. These conditions no longer prevailed after the war.

International and Domestic Monetary Influences

We discussed above the hypothesis, based on classical gold-standard theory, that before 1914 the strengthening of the balance of payments due to the increase in income from abroad tended to move relative prices to the disadvantage of Britain's trade. As a result of World War I, income from abroad fell as a proportion of GDP, instead of progressively increasing, as it had previously, and the balance of services worsened. This was a radical change and called for a correspondingly radical change in the trend of the other components of the balance of payments on current account. If the gold standard had worked completely according to the book, the decline in income from abroad after the war would correspondingly have led to a reduction in British relative prices and would have promoted an offsetting improvement in the trade balance. But the hypothesis about the pre-1914 situation, insofar as it holds at all, relates to slow adjustments over a long period; it does not imply that sudden sharp disequilibria could easily be corrected in that way, or that they were so corrected before 1914.* In order to achieve the required relative price change quickly in response to the large disequilibrium that appeared across World War I, a different mechanism would have been required, namely exchange-rate adjustment. Money wage rates in Britain did fall, absolutely and relative to other countries, in the 1920's, but not by enough to restore competitiveness.[16] By returning to $4.86 the authorities were maintaining relative prices at a level that had been appropriate before the war but had now ceased to be; they were acting as if income from abroad were still high and increasing.

However, the decision to return to gold at the old parity was not the *initiating* source of the trouble. The great fall in export volume compared with 1913 was already apparent in the early 1920's, when the exchange rate was still floating. Even in the boom year 1920 (when the exchange rate averaged $3.66), the volume of exports was less than three-quarters of what it had been in 1913. Admittedly, supply limitations directly affected exports in 1920 itself; but not after. The trend in exports from 1922 on was upward, though not at a rapid rate. The question about the return to gold in 1925 is thus not whether it was the *cause* of the fall in exports, but whether a different policy in 1925 would have facilitated recovery in the late 1920's. So posed, the question is of rather less interest, relating as it does to only a short period— for the further decline in exports in the 1930's was due to other causes. A more general question is how events *before* 1925 would have turned out if a different exchange-rate policy had been adopted, since the ex-

---

*Thus the quite sharp reduction in income from abroad as a percentage of GDP in the 1890's was offset, not by an improvement in the balance of trade, but by a decline in capital export.

pectation that there would be a return to the prewar parity influenced the rate while it was still free to fluctuate.

There is no doubt that the prices of British exports were high relative to those of other countries in the 1920's, and that Britain's share of world trade suffered in consequence. It is extremely unlikely, however, that a moderate difference in the exchange rate would have been sufficient to eliminate the depression in exporting industries (an *immoder-* ate difference would have raised the possibility of retaliation).* Moggridge (1969: 91–96), using estimates of trade elasticities at the lower end of those estimated for other countries and periods, estimates that an exchange rate of $4.38 (10 percent below $4.86) would have raised the volume of exports at the end of the 1920's some 9 percent. This would have left them in 1929 still nearly 10 percent below the 1913 level. There would thus still have been a need for a major structural realignment of the economy.[17] Moggridge's figures also suggest, however, that with an exchange rate of $4.38 the overall balance of payments would have improved sufficiently to pay for near-full-employment imports. On this admittedly conjectural reckoning, the improvement in the terms of trade compared with before the war and the reduction in overseas lending would have been sufficient to offset the effect on the balance of payments of the reduction in exports and in income from abroad.

This has to be considered in relation to the question of the role of real wages. The assumptions about the prices of imports and exports underlying Moggridge's calculations imply that if the exchange rate had been $4.38, real wages would have been about 3 percent lower than they actually were (the loss to real wages being matched partly by a gain to profits and partly by a deterioration in the terms of trade). If this relative decline in real wages had been resisted, i.e. if the hypothetically higher sterling prices of imports and exports had resulted in a higher level of money wages, the gain to exports and the balance of payments would have been correspondingly less.

Real wages are also relevant on the supply side. The exceptionally rapid rise in real wages immediately after World War I was noted in Chap. 10 (pp. 314–15). A difference in the exchange rate of the amount considered by Moggridge would not have been nearly enough to restore profitability to its pre-1914 level. There remains a question, therefore, whether the relative unprofitability of production would have stood in the way of the hypothetical increase in exports. Likewise, more

---

*This applies particularly to the franc. The French franc (and hence the Belgian franc) was undervalued as a deliberate act of policy.

generally, it is possible that the unprofitability of production, connected with the earlier fast rise in real wages, contributed to the poor performance of exports throughout the 1920's, even before the return to gold (though it cannot be blamed for the slow growth of world trade). This consideration is probably less important in relation to the traditional export staples, where there was manifestly excess supply but demand was possibly not very elastic, than it is in relation to newer lines of exports that would have required more active efforts to develop.

In any event, it is plain that the problem of the traditional export industries was more intractable than the problem of the overall balance of payments. There was no possibility of getting the old export industries back on their pre-1914 footing; moreover, if attempts *had* been made to do this, say by a very large devaluation, it would have left the economy extremely vulnerable in the face of the further decline of world trade that came in the 1930's. It is possible, however, that a *modest* stimulus to exports would, by its multiplier effects and by removing the need to protect the balance of payments by high interest rates, have permitted the economy in the 1920's to launch itself earlier into a domestically oriented boom of the type that developed in the 1930's (and had occurred in the 1890's).

The volume of imports of manufactures, as a proportion of GNP, continued to rise in the 1920's along much the same trend line as before 1914. The import component of the balance of trade in manufactures thus did not experience an adverse shift across World War I comparable to that experienced by exports, though it did not improve either. The measures of protection introduced already during World War I may have been among the forces preventing imports from rising more rapidly.

We turn now to the causes of capital movements in the interwar period. Net capital export in the pre-1929 period was a much smaller proportion of GNP than before 1914 (Table 14.7). It remained quite substantial, however, equal to about two-thirds of the capital exports of the United States, the chief lender of that period (UN 1949). The British capital market retained much the same attitude to foreign lending as it had had before 1914, concentrating on investment in infrastructure and primary production in non-European countries. There was no British counterpart to the large movement of American capital to Germany in the late 1920's. Gross capital export by Britain was considerably higher than net; for there was not only a significant amount of direct investment in Britain, as in other European countries, by the

United States, but also a large inflow of short-term capital, especially from France, attracted by high interest rates. This inflow had no parallel as a *sustained* movement before 1914. Its reversal in 1931 played an important part in the collapse of that year.

The reduction in net lending compared with before 1914 thus came about partly because the investment it traditionally financed was not undergoing such a boom and partly because the weak balance-of-payments position led to high interest rates. There was some official discouragement of capital export in the 1920's, but it was halfhearted and ineffective (Atkin 1970).

There were several reasons for the sharp further decline in capital export in the 1930's. Most important, the world depression, emanating from outside Britain, destroyed the incentive to invest abroad. Informal controls over capital export were strengthened, especially in relation to countries outside the sterling area. Some increase took place in the balances held in London by sterling-area countries (Oppenheimer 1966). The behavior of the overall balance of payments in the 1930's thus resembled in more acute form what occurred in the pre-1914 long-cycle downswings in foreign trade: the current balance worsened, but net capital exports also tended to decline, and to a rather greater extent. It was therefore possible to maintain interest rates at a much lower level than in the 1920's.

Conclusions

The fall in exports across World War I was due largely to a continuation of the long-existing trend of increasing foreign competition. This trend, however, was hastened by the war; and an important part was also played by certain other factors, notably the depression of demand in Northern Europe in the early 1920's and the reduction in the purchasing power of primary producers brought about by the deterioration in their terms of trade. The general fall in profit margins, associated with the large postwar rise in wages, may also have played some part. Some decline in exports from their 1913 peak would probably have occurred even without the war, because 1913 was a long-swing peak, and the change in the terms of trade across the war had some of the characteristics of a long-swing downturn. The return to gold at $4.86 was not the initial cause of the decline in exports, nor was it responsible for the further decline in the 1930's, but it hampered recovery in the late 1920's.

The decline in income from abroad and the balance of services as a proportion of GDP, due directly to the war, was a major cause of the difficulties experienced in the overall balance of payments. The attempts to deal with these difficulties by maintaining high interest rates and attracting short-term funds was less successful than it had been before 1914, when it had been used for the correction of temporary disequilibria rather than a chronic imbalance; and the large short-term balances built up in consequence of this policy proved a major source of instability after 1929.

The balance of payments was relieved during the 1930's by a steep decline in capital exports—a phenomenon parallel to what had occurred in the foreign trade downswing of the 1890's, but strengthened in the 1930's by special forces.

Whether the British balance of payments was in "fundamental" disequilibrium in the 1930's is doubtful. Imports were, of course, kept down by a domestic demand-deficiency, as well as by production, but exports were kept down by a *foreign* demand deficiency. The question is impossible to answer because of the all-pervasive consequences of the world depression, including its effects on the terms of trade and on the inducement to overseas investment.

1913–1937: THE EFFECTS OF INTERNATIONAL TRANSACTIONS ON GROWTH

The Effects on Demand and Domestic Capital Accumulation

It is no surprise to find that the expenditure flows arising directly from foreign trade and payments, including the fall in the real value of income from abroad,[18] had a heavily negative effect on the growth of demand across World War I and, correspondingly, that they were the prime source of the lower level of demand relative to supply in the interwar period compared with the pre-1914 period (Tables 10.4, 10.5). The direct effects were strengthened in the 1920's by the monetary stringency associated with the adverse balance of payments, as well as by accelerator effects. The direct effects were worse than ever in the 1930's, but the indirect effects through the balance of payments were greatly mitigated and disappeared toward the end of the decade, partly because of the further reduction in net capital export (aided by the inflow of sterling balances) and partly by the abandonment of a fixed exchange rate.

International transactions made some contribution to the growth of demand *within* the interwar period (Table 10.10) on account of the fall in the import propensity at current prices, which in turn was due primarily to the fall in import prices and, to a less extent, to a fall in the volume of imports relative to GDP, doubtless associated with protection (Fig. 14.4). However, the contribution to the growth in demand arising from international transactions was small by historical standards, and the main source of growth in demand was domestic investment.

Since the interwar period, especially the 1930's, had some of the characteristics of the trough phases of the pre-1914 long swings in exports and overseas lending, the question may be asked why the depression of exports was not matched by an offsetting domestic investment boom as in the 1890's. The answer is that the trouble with exports and the balance of payments in the 1920's was not *merely* the sort of trouble experienced previously in long swings. The other sources were enumerated above: the war had speeded the displacement of British exports, so that the decline in exports across the war was more than in proportion to the decline in capitalists' desire to buy overseas assets; the loss of income from abroad, in contrast to its previous rise, created an additional weakness in the balance of payments; and short-term international capital movements could no longer be so easily elicited by small interest differentials to offset payments deficits arising from other sources. Thus, not merely was the hole created by the fall in exports a bigger one for domestic investment to fill than it had been in pre-1914 long swings, but also the bad state of the overall balance, and the resultant monetary pressure, hindered domestic investment from filling it.

In the 1930's, when the overall balance of payments had been more nearly set to rights, the situation did rather more resemble the 1890's. But in the meanwhile industrial expectations had been damaged, and the rise in domestic investment was largely confined to house-building. So though the rise in domestic investment did offset the further damage to exports done by the world depression of the 1930's and bring about a rate of growth of demand that was respectable by historical standards, it was not sufficient to make good the decline in exports that had already taken place before that, and unemployment remained high.

The Effects on Total Factor Productivity

International transactions did not contribute in any obvious way to bringing about the increase in the rate of growth of TFP in the interwar period compared with pre-1914. That phenomenon was common to all sectors of the economy except commerce. The absolute decline in TFP in commerce, insofar as it was attributable to underemployment deriving from general demand deficiency, *can* be traced indirectly to international transactions; but not the improvement in the other sectors, with the possible exception of coal-mining, where the decline in output may have reversed previously existing tendencies to diminishing returns. In manufacturing the improvement in the rate of growth of TFP compared with 1873–1913 was substantial (1.9 percent compared with 0.6 percent). It was common to most if not all manufacturing industries;[19] it was not due to shifts of weight in favor of more progressive industries. The faster rate of growth of output of manufactures — a possible source of help to TFP growth — in 1924–37 compared with 1873–1913 was attributable to domestic absorption, not foreign trade. Differences in trends in foreign trade between the 1920's and the 1930's may have accounted in part for TFP in manufacturing growing faster in the 1930's than in the 1920's; but its growth was already substantially faster in the 1920's than in the pre-1914 period.

The comparison of the 1920's and the 1930's in this regard is of interest because of the role some would accord to protection in the 1930's in improving the performance of British industry (Kaldor 1979: 22–23). The scope for such claims is limited, inasmuch as output and TFP in the economy as a whole grew less rapidly in the 1930's than in the 1920's, not more rapidly (see Appendix M). So let us examine the case of manufacturing, where output and TFP did grow more rapidly in the 1930's than in the 1920's.

The comparison is rather complicated. In the period 1924–37 as a whole foreign trade made a negative contribution to the change in manufacturing's share of output (Table 9.10). However, this negative contribution came entirely before 1929, and foreign trade's contribution after 1929 was slightly positive. It is tempting to identify here a causal element in the recovery of the 1930's, namely the reduction in imports of manufactures brought about by protection. It turns out, however, that the difference between 1924–29 and 1929–37 was entirely due to textiles, at this stage still dominated by the traditional textile industries (rayon accounted for less than 10 percent of textile output in 1923). Textile exports fell very sharply in the 1920's and then stabilized. The balance of trade in manufactures excluding textiles actually deteriorated more in 1929–37 than in 1924–29. Productivity in textiles did indeed do substantially better in the 1930's than in the 1920's (Table M.3), and textiles accounted for a major part of the improvement in the rates of growth of production and productivity in manufacturing as a whole in the 1930's compared with the 1920's. The improvement in productivity in textiles in the 1930's was no doubt helped by the faster rate of growth of output, and this in turn owed much to the improved trend in the industry's balance of payments. However, the industry's improved productivity performance was due in part to another cause, viz. "rationalization." This is reflected in the fact that employment in textiles fell in the 1930's, after a slight increase in the 1920's.

The conclusion is therefore that changes in the balance of trade, influenced by protection, did contribute to raising the rate of growth of productivity in manufacturing in the 1930's, but that their main beneficial impact was on one industry, of a traditional rather than innovative kind, and was there reinforced by other causes.

It appears, therefore, on the face of it, that the improvement in the rate of growth of TFP in most sectors of the economy in the interwar period occurred despite trends in foreign trade, rather than because of them. In order to sustain an opposite view, one would have to rely on very general hypotheses. One such hypothesis is that the shake-up to traditional export industries and hence to the economy as a whole brought about by the change in the foreign trade position had a favorable net effect on the efficiency of management or labor. Another is that, in the 1930's particularly, the reduced profitability of overseas operations and of capital export directed entrepreneurial energies to domestic production, with good effect. Such hypotheses may well contain an element of truth. But it is difficult to test them, or to discriminate between then and the hypothesis that the improved rate of TFP growth was due to more strictly technological factors, as suggested by the parallel rise in the rate of growth of TFP in the United States after World War I, or to the increase in the scope for catching up with other countries.

1937–1973: FORCES AFFECTING BRITAIN'S INTERNATIONAL TRANSACTIONS

The effects of World War II and its aftermath on Britain's balance-of-payments position were in some respects even more unfavorable than those of World War I. The movements across the two wars were similar in the decline, relative to GDP, in income from abroad and in net exports of services (Figs. 14.7, 14.8). Net overseas assets were reduced, Britain's lead as a provider of services was eroded, and after World War II, there was an increase in government expenditure abroad. However, there was a great fall across World War I in private overseas investment. This cushioning of the effects of the unfavorable trends in the current balance was not available across World War II; in the 1930's there had not been any net overseas investment, so there was nothing to reduce. Moreover, the terms of trade deteriorated across World War II, instead of improving as they had done across World War I (Fig. 14.6).

The unfavorable trends across World War II were, in the outcome, offset by an enormous and unprecedented improvement in the balance of trade due to a rise in the volume of exports relative to the volume of imports (Figs. 14.2, 14.9). Britain's share in world exports rose, contrary to trend (Table 14.5). The prices, both of exports and of imports, rose by unprecedentedly large amounts relative to the price of GDP, encouraging exports and discouraging imports (Figs. 14.3, 14.4, 14.6). A similar movement had taken place immediately after World War I but was reversed in 1921. Across World War II there was a great fall in the volume (though not the value) of imports relative to GNP. The improvement in the balance of trade exceeded the deterioration in services and income from abroad, so the overall current balance was better than in 1930's (Tables 14.7, 14.8).

The main causes of the differences in the movements across the two wars are not far to seek.

(1) The destruction of productive capacity among Britain's industrial competitors on the Continent and in Japan in World War II was greater than it had been in World War I, when the fighting, though intense, had been concentrated in a relatively small geographical area. It was not matched by a corresponding reduction in demand, because of Marshall Aid and the avoidance of a recession like that of 1921.

(2) Britain's competitive position deteriorated relative to that of the United States, as had happened after World War I. After World War II, however, this was offset by the devaluation of 1949, which was chiefly a devaluation against the dollar. This no doubt accounted for the different trend in foreign trade prices relative to GDP prices.

(3) Industrial trends in the interwar period and during World War II itself left Britain with an industrial structure that was more suited to meeting world demand than it was after World War I, when there was still heavy reliance on a limited range of export industries in which Britain had decisively lost its comparative advantage.* This helped to

---

*We are indebted to W. W. Rostow for the interesting suggestion that the two wars had different effects on account of the differences in the nature of the fighting. The hypothesis is that whereas World War II stimulated electronics and other new industries, the stationary trench warfare of World War I mainly encouraged the production of crude objects like barbed wire and army uniforms and boots. To test this hypothesis we would require data on production at a finer level of disaggregation than are available. It receives some confirmation, however, from the existing data. Neither chemicals nor electrical engineering did particularly well during World War I. On the other hand, there were three industries that reached a wartime maximum production well above the 1913 level but then fell back and never regained the 1913 level in the interwar period. They were (maximum wartime output as percent of 1913 and year in parentheses): shipbuilding (107%, 1918), textiles (113%, 1915), and leather (146%, 1918).

make the devaluation of 1949 more successful than a devaluation would have been after World War I.

(4) Transwar movements were affected by the different standings of 1913 and 1937 relative to trend. In 1913 world trade was above trend; in 1937 it was abnormally low.

The result of all these differences was that by comparison with the interwar period, the postwar foreign trade problem was less a problem of the export industries and more a problem of the balance of payments. There was not a problem of decaying staple industries; but the shock to the balance of payments brought about by World War II was in some ways even more severe than the shock brought about by World War I.

So much for movements across World War II. We now turn to the postwar period itself.

The balance of payments was a central preoccupation of British policy-makers throughout the postwar period. It regularly appeared as the chief obstacle to faster growth; and the direction of government effort and exhortation was persistently such as to imply an enormous premium in the shadow value of foreign exchange.

The relationship between foreign trade and growth in the postwar period raises questions about the direction of causation, as the pre-1914 period does. By comparison with the past, both British growth and British foreign trade (at least British exports) showed a better performance, though there was little correlation between export and output growth in individual post–World War II cycles. By comparison with other countries, performance in both trade and output was worse. Moreover, there was a general tendency, too pronounced to be plausibly regarded as coincidental, for countries like Germany and Japan, with the highest growth rates, to perform best in foreign trade as well.

What were the principal trends in Britain's international transactions in the postwar period?

(1) The rate of growth of exports (in volume) was high by historical standards and increased during the period (Fig. 14.2). Up to the devaluation of 1967, exports' share in output (in volume) was constant; thereafter it increased (Fig. 14.3). Britain's share in world exports fell throughout, from its abnormally high level in the early 1950's — not itself particularly disturbing or surprising, since Britain's share in world output was also falling (Tables 14.5, 14.6). However, export's share in output (at current prices) fell up to 1967, in contrast to what was happening in the world as a whole and in all the other principal industrial countries except the United States. After 1967 exports' share in

output at current prices rose, and Britain's share in world exports compared more nearly to its share in world output. In both 1964 and 1973 the proportion remained higher in the United Kingdom than in the industrial world as a whole, even excluding the United States.

(2) The volume of imports rose faster than GNP (following the very steep fall in imports of goods across World War II; Fig. 14.2). This trend had occurred in earlier periods as well. Unlike the trend in exports, it was not perceptibly affected by the devaluation of 1967, and indeed tended to accelerate. In terms of value, however, imports' share in GNP followed a long cycle of large amplitude, with sharp peaks in 1951 and 1973 (Fig. 14.4), food and materials being the most important in 1951 and manufactures in 1973. The trough was in the early 1960's. Imports of manufactures, but not total imports, tended to rise more rapidly relative to the rise in GNP than in other countries.

(3) There was not much trend change in net exports of services or in property income from abroad as percentages of GDP — except for a sharp rise in income from abroad in the year 1973 (Fig. 14.8).

(4) The overall balance of payments on current account was on average positive and only slightly lower as a proportion of national income than in other European countries.[20] It had very regular cyclical fluctuations, rising in recession and falling in the boom, whereas previously it had usually been the other way around. It had little trend over the period as a proportion of national income. There was, it is true, some trend deterioration in the 1960's; but this movement was tiny compared with earlier trend movements (Fig. 14.9), and in any case it was reversed after the devaluation of 1967.*

Despite certain unfavorable features noted under points 1 and 2, the above recital does not suggest a particularly bad performance; indeed, at first sight it raises the question why it is held that there was trouble at all. There was not on average over-absorption in the sense of a current account deficit, nor, apart from a period in the 1960's, was there

*The above relates to the years through 1973. The very large deficits in the years 1974–76, which lie outside our purview, were the result of the enormous deterioration in the terms of trade caused by the rise in the price of oil (and to a less extent other primary products). The volume of exports in those years was higher relative to the volume of imports than before 1973. The adverse balances of payments during those years are therefore to be regarded not as a continuation of the effects of previously existing trends (except insofar as the balance of payments in the single year 1973 was already affected to some extent by the prices of primary products other than oil), but as the result of the failure to adapt to entirely new circumstances. In their nature these new circumstances resembled, in greatly exaggerated form, earlier long-swing peaks, with the difference that the newly enriched primary producers had a much lower marginal propensity to import — and *a fortiori* a lower marginal propensity to import from the UK — than primary producers had had in earlier long swings. The suddenness of the change resembled the effects on the balance of payments of the two world wars.

any trend toward it within the period. However, there is a certain amount of substance in the contention that such a trend was avoided only by keeping the economy relatively depressed, since there was probably some downward trend in the overall pressure of demand in the United Kingdom and some upward trend in most other major industrial countries. (See, in addition to Table 3.23 and pp. 299–300, above, McCracken et al. 1977: 82–99.)

The trouble, as it presented itself to successive governments, was largely a financial one. Though net national overseas assets increased, these assets were not at the disposal of governments to deal with short-run deficits. The trend in the reserves over the period was almost flat in current prices. The reserves therefore declined in real terms and as a percentage of GNP. The failure to build up reserves was in contrast to what happened in most other industrial countries, apart from the United States. At the same time it was not easy to attract private short-term capital to bridge the quite small and temporary balance-of-payments deficits, as it had been before 1914, when sterling occupied the international position held in most of the postwar period by the dollar. Consequently, temporary deficits frequently had to be met by troublesome emergency recourse to official international sources, and pains had to be taken to prevent other short-term capital movements from actually swelling the deficit (instead of balancing it), as a result of loss of confidence.

Exogenous Real Trends at Home and Abroad

On the side of foreign real trends, the outstanding feature was the unusually rapid growth, especially on the Continent and in Japan, relative both to the United Kingdom and to the past performance of the countries concerned (Table 14.6). Three elements can be distinguished here:

(1) Recovery from abnormally low levels of output in war-devastated countries, largely complete by the early 1950's.

(2) Continuation of unusually fast growth after the early 1950's in already well-industrialized countries such as France and Germany.

(3) Industrialization in semi-industrial countries, notably Japan and Italy.

The third of these represented a continuation of a familiar long-run trend that edged Britain out of traditional markets in earlier periods as well. The second was a novelty historically.

On the side of domestic real trends, the historically fast and accelerating growth rate of productivity was a permissive cause of the historically fast and accelerating rate of growth of British exports. It is more difficult to maintain that it was an initiating cause, since the rate of growth of TFP in manufacturing up to the mid-1960's was no higher than it was in the interwar period, and the bulk of exports are manufactures. The slow rate of growth of productivity by *international* standards, taken in conjunction with the absence of any large amount of underemployment of resources, would have made it difficult for exports to grow much more rapidly than they did. However, the question of course remains, as it does for 1873–1913, to what extent this slow productivity growth by international standards was exogenous and how far it was influenced by the conditions of foreign trade.

If these foreign and domestic real trends are regarded as exogenous, they can go a long way to explain the observed trends in trade and payments.

The rapid growth in world output and demand was plainly a major factor making for a historically fast rate of growth of British exports. Its effect was augmented by the tendency for world trade to grow faster than world output. As far as the United Kingdom was concerned, matters were helped by the historically unusual conjunction for most of the postwar period of rapidly growing world trade and declining relative prices of primary products.* When this trend was reversed, at the end of the period, the balance of payments became much more favorable. A similar tendency had been observable in earlier periods, though for rather different reasons.†

The distinctive features of world growth in the postwar period also led to some changes in the *character* of British foreign trade. There was an important change in the historical trend in the geographical distribution of British exports. The progressive retreat toward markets in less-developed countries, apparent up till World War II, was reversed. The proportion of exports going to the Continent increased, and losses were most severe in the markets where the British share had initially been highest, notably in relatively unindustrialized countries in the overseas sterling area (Major 1968). The growth of trade, in both directions, with countries at a comparable stage of development, viz. those

---

*The nearest parallel is the short period 1925–29, when there was a world boom but a fall in primary product prices. The absolute prices of primary products fell in the early 1950's and had a horizontal trend from then until the end of the 1960's.

†In the 1970's the rise in primary product prices affected the balance of payments simply by increasing the cost of imports. Before 1914, the net effect of the increased cost of imports was much less important, because primary producers had a much higher marginal propensity to import from the UK than they had in the postwar period; insofar as high primary product prices in that period tended to put pressure on the balance of payments, it was because they encouraged capital export.

of continental Europe, also had the consequence that British exports no longer had such a tendency as before 1914 to be concentrated in relatively unsophisticated products, though some such tendency apparently remained by comparison with other industrial exporters.[21]

Since productivity was growing less rapidly in Britain than elsewhere, it was inevitable that its share in world exports of manufactures should tend to fall. A rapid increase in productivity permits a rapid increase in production and in capacity to export, and this capacity will be made effective by the development of competitive advantage in one form or another. From this point of view, studies of the exact nature of Britain's lack of competitiveness have perhaps been rather overdone. Competitive advantage is the *dual* of more rapidly growing output, and it is a matter of secondary interest whether it takes the form of lower prices, better quality, earlier or more reliable delivery dates or whatever. The hypothesis that underlying trends in supply were responsible for the decline in Britain's share in world exports also helps to explain the well-known fact that Britain's share tended to decline most rapidly in years when world trade was growing particularly fast. It is to be expected that supply constraints should be most felt in boom years, and that they should be more important then relative to other factors (such as traditional trading relationships) than they are in years when demand is pressing less strongly against the ceiling.[22]

This simple point explains a lot. But it does not explain everything. Most important, it does not explain why there was trouble with the *balance of payments*, as manifested by the decline in the real value of the reserves (and by the latent tendency to deficit implicit in the tight restrictions on capital export), for as a first approximation a country with a lower rate of growth than other countries might be expected to have a correspondingly slow growth in imports as well as in exports. Nor does it explain why Britain's share in world exports of manufactures fell by a larger proportion than its share in world output of manufactures, especially until the mid-1960's.

Three types of explanation have been offered. All have counterparts in relation to earlier periods. The first type is in terms of real causes, the second and third in terms of monetary causes.

The first hypothesis, in the broadest terms, is that the competitive effects of fast growth abroad preponderated over the complementary effects. In particular, it has often been held that rapid productivity growth is systematically associated with quality improvements that are difficult to combat by price competition, it being well known that product innovations have become increasingly important relative to process innovations, especially in the more sophisticated industries where Britain might be expected to have a comparative advantage. This in turn is related to the hypothesis of Posner (1961) that comparative advantage resides to a large extent in temporary technical leadership rather than in static cost differences. The general idea is that a country that is being overtaken or left behind in the productivity race is chronically in a defensive posture; it must continually adjust the structure of its production in response to outside impulses. Even if in theory the necessary adjustments can be procured by relative prices changes, the process takes time, and in the meanwhile the balance of payments is under pressure. This is one form of the theory of the disadvantage of an early start. With respect to the postwar period, the disadvantage of Britain's (ancient) early start in industrialization was renewed by the temporarily favorable position it occupied in the immediate postwar period before the rest of Europe and Japan had recovered from the war.

This argument can be reinforced by reference to long-term capital movements, since these were related to trends in real growth. Net export of capital was not large by the standards of the 1920's or earlier. However, Britain was the only industrial country, apart from the United States, to be a significant net exporter of private long-term capital in the early postwar period. Even in the 1960's it was a major exporter of direct investment.[23] This was influenced by relative rates of growth and the investment opportunities they created. Insofar as German industry, for example, had lower costs or produced goods of better quality than British industry, there was less incentive for German companies to build up production in subsidiaries abroad. Direct investment by British companies abroad was partly offset by substantial investment by U.S. companies in Britain. This was considerably larger than American investment in any other European country. But the reasons for that appear to have been in large part historical: in 1950 America's stake in Britain was larger than its stake in the rest of Europe put together. As the postwar period proceeded, U.S. companies allocated an increasing proportion of their direct investment to the Continent rather than to Britain (Dunning 1970: 273). Both inward and outward private long-term capital movements increased, but the balance remained outward.

How much weight one attaches to these real forces in the explanation of Britain's balance-of-payment troubles depends largely on how one assesses the ability of relative price changes to bring about the necessary offsetting adjustments. "Market optimists" are inclined to dismiss such explanations on the grounds that even if the forces referred to did operate, they would have been quickly offset in their effect on the over-all balance unless there was something wrong with total absorption (or domestic credit expansion) or with relative prices. "Market pessimists" agree that in principle adverse real forces could be offset if absorption were kept sufficiently low or the price of tradables relative to the price of non-tradables sufficiently high; but they would hold that strong measures would have been required to achieve this, and that in view of the understandable difficulties of adopting them, the real forces had a direct relevance to the overall balance of payments.

International and Domestic Monetary Influences

The first of the alternative monetary explanations of the trouble was, until recently, the prevailing view among economists. It is that the combination of quite rapidly rising wages and an inflexible exchange rate up to 1967 made British goods relatively expensive and impaired competitiveness.

The evidence on costs and prices is as follows.[24]

In the early 1950's, up to about 1959, domestic unit costs rose faster in Britain than among its principal competitors, because their higher productivity growth was not being offset by correspondingly higher rates of growth of money wages (except for France, where it was offset by devaluations in 1957 and 1958 — the actions commonly cited as an example of what Britain should have done). From 1959 to 1964 the productivity growth differential remained, but money wages abroad moved ahead of those in Britain at a more rapid rate than before. As a result, unit costs in Britain grew less fast than in France, Germany, Italy, or Japan, though faster than in the United States. From 1964 to 1967 British relative costs went ahead again. Over the period 1954–67 as a whole unit cost grew faster in Britain than in other countries. Devaluation in 1967 naturally brought about a substantial change for the better. The benefit had been largely but not wholly eroded by 1972, and it increased again in 1973.

The foregoing relates to *costs*. The most usually quoted national data on export *prices* are not helpful; they are subject to margins of error and to lack of comparability that prevent them from being usable to measure trends in competitiveness. The very careful study by Kravis and Lipsey (1971) however, shows that British export prices did rise rather more than those of other countries up to 1964 or so.[25] This is reflected in the rise in the price of British manufactured exports relative to the price of world manufactured exports in 1950–64 implied by the movements of Britain's share in world exports of manufactures at constant and current prices (Tables 14.5, 14.6). In 1964–73, however, the relative price of British exports fell. But the differences between the changes in British and world export prices were extremely small. It would appear that competition left little room for divergent trends in the prices actually charged, and that the effect of divergent trends in costs was felt in a different way, namely on the supply side. It is well known that the rise in costs relative to world prices had made exports much less profitable than domestic sales for British producers by the mid-1960's.[26] In the 1950's the price of exports resumed its long-run tendency to fall relative to the price of GDP, putting into reverse the large and untypical rise across World War II, which had helped to encourage exporting in the late 1940's (Fig. 14.3).

The postwar period differed from earlier peacetime periods in the behavior of world prices and the interaction between foreign trade and domestic prices. As noted above, the prices of primary products fell despite the unusually rapid growth in world trade. The ratio of foreign trade prices (p_{ft}) to domestic prices (p_y) also fell, but in contrast to other periods, p_y moved in the opposite direction (Figs. 10.1, 14.6). For once foreign trade prices were not leading the way. This suggests that domestic forces, in the form of high demand pressure or trade union militancy, were more important relative to world forces in bringing about the trend in prices than they had been in earlier periods. The tendency for deceleration in p_y up to the mid-1960's, however, may well have been due to the moderating influence of p_{ft}. In addition, Ball and Burns (1976) suggest that an upward pressure on British prices in world markets arose because the devaluation of 1949 was excessive and pulled British prices below the world level[27] — the converse of the suggestion sometimes made about the downward pressure on prices created by the over-high exchange rate established in 1925, an effect on prices arising from foreign trade relationships, though not from current trends in world prices.

The period 1968–72 is interesting. The rise in world prices (in U.S. dollars) tended to speed up, and foreign trade prices in sterling rose even more rapidly on account of the devaluation of 1967. This was matched by an acceleration in p_y, notwithstanding relatively low pressure of domestic demand. However, in contrast to what had happened in earlier times, p_{ft}/p_y continued to fall, after an initial rise following devaluation. Here again there are signs of a new relationship: the "sympathetic" rise in p_y more than matched the exogenous rise in p_{ft}; domestic demand in money terms more than fully accommodated the rise in p_{ft}. This accommodation was, of course, facilitated by the move to floating exchange rates. Something nearer the earlier type of relationship was restored in 1973–74, when the further acceleration in p_{ft} was accompanied by a further acceleration in p_y, but not to the same extent, so that p_{ft}/p_y at last rose.*

The implication of the hypothesis about costs and prices is that Britain's foreign trade troubles were due, or partly due, to the failure to devalue before 1967. The chronology is favorable to that conclusion in some respects, unfavorable in others. It is difficult to maintain that sterling was overvalued in the early 1950's, at least in relation to the dollar, following the enormous devaluation of 1949. Moreover, Britain's share in world trade continued to decline at an undiminished rate between 1959 and 1964, when movements in domestic costs relative to costs abroad had apparently ceased to be unfavorable; indeed, the overall current balance showed more tendency to deteriorate in this peroid than in the 1950's. Trends in those years resemble those in 1873–1913, when the movement in relative costs was apparently in Britain's favor, yet the balance of trade deteriorated. The paradox in 1959–64 is a degree more marked in that the countries whose relative costs were rising experienced an upward trend in the ratio of exports to output, whereas the United Kingdom did not, a contrast not present before 1914.† However, there is no doubt that exporting had become very unprofitable by the mid-1960's; and there are good grounds for believing that devaluation, when it was ultimately done, helped significantly (Artus 1975). Thus is may be concluded that the behavior of wages and prices, in conjunction with the exchange rate, contributed significantly to the tendency for the balance on current account to deteriorate in the mid-1960's and to improve after 1967. It is more

---

*The deflation in domestic real demand following the oil-price rise in 1974 had something in common with the deflation of domestic real demand in 1900–1913 (and also with occasions earlier in the 19th century when a rise in wheat prices due to a bad harvest had deflationary effects).

†A possible explanation is that the trends in relative costs in the 1950's had lagged effects. Foreign producers may have had sufficient slack in their profit margins at the end of the 1950's to give them an inducement to go on competing energetically in export markets even though the trend in costs had moved against them. A different kind of lagged effect is in consumers' tastes and in marketing organization. These were molded in favor of British goods, especially in the overseas sterling area, by a variety of historical circumstances: Britain's original economic and political predominance; imperial preference in the 1930's; and lack of supplies from competitors in the early postwar years. It took time for them to be altered. The fact that Britain's loss of market shares was greatest in the sterling-area countries suggests that these historical links had a significant effect on the extent and on the timing of the loss in shares. Similar considerations apply to the domestic British market.

doubtful how far it explained the chronic tendency throughout the postwar period for the balance to be less favorable than the authorities would have liked.

The alternative monetary hypothesis is quite different. It is that the trouble with the balance of payments arose from a chronic tendency to excess absorption, i.e. too high a level of demand.*

As already noted, there will presumably always be some level of absorption that will procure balance-of-payments equilibrium, however unfavorable the real trends or relative prices may be. Hence in one sense this hypothesis is always bound to be true. To be significant as a hypothesis in its own right, it is necessary to hold that absorption was high by some absolute standard. If the postwar period is considered as a whole, it is not at all evident that the pressure of demand was on average higher in Britain than in other countries (pp. 94–95). If, in order to maintain a satisfactory balance of payments, it was necessary for Britain to have a *lower* average pressure of demand than other countries, the question arises why, and that brings us back to the hypotheses already considered.

It could be argued that though there was not de facto excess absorption on average, there was a *tendency* to excess absorption, checked only by the restrictions imposed by government at cycle peaks to protect the balance of payments. Some support is given by the fact that the cyclical amplitude of imports was higher than in the past relative to the cyclical amplitude of income (Table 10.7), suggesting a greater tendency than in the past for demand to spill over into imports at cycle peaks, though there are other possible explanations.† It is of course true that in many years balance-of-payments considerations caused governments to keep demand at a lower level than they would otherwise have wished. But insofar as the pressure of demand was, on average, apparently much the same as in other countries, the question comes back to that considered above.

*The hypothesis of the Global Monetarist School comes to much the same in the present context, though it is not logically identical. According to their hypothesis, balance-of-payments deficits are traceable to an excessive rate of domestic credit expansion, which creates a tendency for the supply of money to increase faster than the demand for it, with the result that the excess money is ejected through the balance of payments. In the circumstances of the postwar British economy, where overseas investment by British nationals was tightly controlled, this ejection would have had to take the form of excess net imports of goods and servcies, i.e. excess absorption.

†Compared with the past, there was a greater variety of overseas suppliers. Cycles were shorter, and stock-building played a greater part. Excess demand at cycle peaks may have arisen from the suddenness of growth in cyclical upswings and represented temporary adjustment problems rather than fundamentally excessive absorption. (Brechling & Wolfe 1965; Oppenheimer 1966.)

A more specific hypothesis about excess absorption concerns the early postwar period. It is generally agreed that a smooth transition of British exports from the world of postwar shortages was hampered by the diversion into rearmament of the resources of the potential export industries in the years 1950–53, at much the same time as rapid growth was occurring in industrial countries that had temporarily been unable to compete because of war disruptions (Nurkse 1956). In addition to weakening the balance of payments at the time, this may well have had a more long-lasting unfortunate effect, by failing to provide producers with the necessary incentive to develop export markets at a critical time and, more generally, by prolonging the wartime era of shortages, weakening the urge to be competitive.

Conclusions

The main trends in Britain's international transactions in the postwar period can be adequately explained by the trends in productive potential at home and abroad. The rapid growth of world income and demand helped permit a (historically) rapid growth of exports, especially since this growth was accompanied by an increase in the international division of labor, in contrast to the interwar period and also to some extent the pre-1914 period. The difference, to Britain's disadvantage, in the rate of growth of productivity compared with other countries was the main reason for the decline in the British share of world exports. It is likely that it also put some pressure on the balance of payments. The balance of payments was helped in the 1950's by the improvement in the terms of trade; when the terms of the trade moved in favor of primary products in the early 1970's, the balance of payments became much worse. Movements in relative money costs put pressure on the balance of payments in the years leading up to the devaluation of 1967, but did not lie at the heart of the problem: the failure to devalue earlier was rather like the return to gold in 1925, in that its main effects were confined to a fairly brief period (the mid-1960's in the one case, 1925–29 in the other). In the early 1950's there was excess demand on potential export industries, brought about by rearmament; otherwise, the significance of excess demand is more doubtful, save in the tautological sense that a lower level of demand would always have tended to help the balance of payments. Throughout the postwar period deficits in the basic balance that were transitory, and quite small by historical standards, were much more disruptive than they had been in previous periods, especially before 1914, because of the changed international position of sterling.

The questions relate to comparisons with earlier periods, to comparisons between parts of the postwar period, and to counterfactual comparisons. As in previous sections, we consider them in relation to the various channels of influence in turn.

The Effects on Demand

On any reckoning, foreign trade played a significant part in maintaining income nearer the full-employment *level* in the postwar period than it was in the interwar period (Tables 10.4, 10.5). The part played by foreign trade in this result was, however, much less for cycle-peak years than it was for the average of all years. This reflects the great reduction, compared with earlier times, in the cyclical amplitude of fluctuations in exports. The major way in which foreign trade contributed to the high level of demand in the postwar period was through the avoidance of export-led slumps.

The contribution of foreign trade to the *growth* of demand was, as would be expected, higher within the postwar period than it was within the interwar period (Table 10.10, sum of the columns relating to exports, income from abroad, and import propensity). It was not, however, higher than it was in 1873–1913, when the rate of growth of total demand was of course much less. The explanation (in these terms) of the difference in the rate of growth of demand between 1873–1913 and 1951–73 thus lay on the investment-savings side, rather than on the side of foreign trade. Within the postwar period there was a sharp difference between 1951–64 and 1964–73 in the *source* of the contribution to the increase in demand originating in foreign trade: in the early years it came mainly from the fall in the import propensity (at current prices), in the later years it came more than wholly from the rise in exports. The total foreign trade contribution was markedly less in 1951–64 than in 1964–73 (1.1 percent compared with 1.9 percent).

Deflationary action by the authorities to protect the balance of payments was the prominent feature of the postwar stop-go cycle. It was less severe on average than the monetary contraction of the 1920's, but it was a feature absent in the pre-1914 period, when short-run deficits had been more easily dealt with by the attraction of international capital. It did not of course prevent the level of activity from being higher on average than in earlier periods, but since it was particularly stringent between 1966 and 1971, it contributed to the slight downward trend in the pressure of demand within the postwar period.

Both direct and indirect effects of international transactions on the pressure of demand as such, i.e. on the degree of utilization of resources, have a rather different significance for the postwar period compared with earlier periods. In the postwar period the trend rate of growth of output was manifestly limited by supply constraints, in a way that it certainly was not in the interwar period, at least. The main question is therefore how far these demand movements originating from foreign trade *influenced* the supply constraints. Earlier in this chapter we considered a similar question in relation to the decline in the rate of growth of output in 1873–1913 compared with 1856–73. On the supply side, the decline in the rate of growth between those two periods came from a decline in the rate of growth of TFP; so it is a reasonable hypothesis that demand trends may have been partly responsible. The same cannot on the face of it be said of the (relatively small) decline in the rate of growth of GDP between the two parts of the postwar period, 1951–64 and 1964–73. That was much more than wholly attributable to a decline in the rate of growth of labor input, a decline that cannot be mainly ascribed to demand. The rates of growth of TFP and the capital stock were actually higher in 1964–73 than in 1951–64, though declining somewhat at the end of the period. This, however, does not settle the question of how they were affected by international transactions, which remains relevant for the comparison with earlier periods and for counterfactual comparisons.

The Effects on Total Factor Productivity

In certain general respects the effects of international transactions on the growth of TFP were favorable by comparison with earlier periods. They were favorable insofar as they made for more buoyant demand on the average and insofar as trade liberalization facilitated the international transmission of knowledge—for which there was more scope than there had been in former times when Britain's relative productivity standing had been higher. In addition, strictly structural (quality-shift) effects were of some significance across World War II, though not within the postwar period.[28]

The above effects are straightforward. Much more difficult to assess are the counterfactual issues.

The combination of the relatively weak underlying balance-of-payments position and the commitment to seek full employment was probably chiefly responsible for the peculiar pattern of the postwar British business cycle, with its short duration and its particularly short upswings (pp. 294–97). Denison (1974: 169) has suggested that the business-cycle pattern most conducive to growth is one of predominantly strong demand, punctuated by short sharp recessions to clear away dead wood. This was conspicuously not the pattern in postwar Britain. Indeed, it was not the pattern in Britain in any period; but the short duration of postwar cycles meant that upswings were shorter than formerly; moreover (a postwar novelty), the upswings were on average rather shorter than the downswings. It is perhaps rather far-fetched to suppose that postwar cycles were on balance less conducive to growth than the longer but larger cycles of earlier times. However, it is certainly arguable that long-run ill-effects on the growth of TFP followed from the increased preponderance of downswing years over upswing years that occurred after 1964 (even though TFP for the time actually rose faster, partly because of shake-out). It is also certainly arguable that more favorable results for growth ensued from the cycle pattern in other countries, where fluctuations, though not smaller in overall amplitude, conformed more nearly to the pattern recommended by Denison.*

The other aspect of the counterfactual question relates to Verdoorn effects. The contribution of foreign trade to the growth of output of manufactures diminished after the initial postwar period. Indeed, by the end of the period it was negative. If different real trends abroad or a different exchange-rate policy had permitted a faster growth of net exports, no doubt there would have been some induced gain in TFP. The question is how much. The magnitude of the depressing effect of foreign trade on the growth of output in manufacturing should not be exaggerated. Two calculations illustrate this (based on Table 9.10). If output of manufactures had risen between 1954 and 1972 at the same

---

*Cross-section comparison of manufacturing industries in the postwar period (using our standard breakdown) gives only very limited support to the hypothesis about the significance of the shape of the cycle. True enough, in those industries in which output grew at 1% below trend rate or lower in only a relatively few years, the postwar rates of growth of TFP exceeded interwar rates by more than in other industries. But their absolute rate of TFP growth in the postwar period was not above average. There was no significant difference, either absolutely or compared with the interwar period, in the rate of TFP growth between industries classified according to the relative number of years when output grew at a higher or lower rate than its trend rate. One industry group — food, drink, and tobacco — was far less affected by fluctuations in output than any other, and its rate of growth of TFP was below the average and below its own interwar rate. Cross-section comparisons are, of course, not the ideal test of the hypothesis and might in any case come out differently with a finer industrial breakdown.

rate as domestic absorption of manufactures, its annual percentage rate of growth would have been higher than it was by 0.4 of a point. Alternatively, if the balance of trade had added as large a proportion of base-year value-added in manufacturing between 1954 and 1972 as it had done between 1937 (when it was barely above zero) and 1954, the annual growth rate of output would have been 0.6 of a point higher in 1954–72 than it actually was. Even on the limiting assumption that Verdoorn effects had been so great that this extra growth in output could have been achieved costlessly, the effect on the annual percentage growth rate of GDP would in neither case have exceeded 0.2. Larger results could of course be derived from more extreme counterfactual assumptions; but the above are extreme enough, in the absence of any assumption about *exogenous* forces making for higher TFP growth.

The Effects on Domestic Capital Accumulation

Many of the same considerations apply as to the effects on TFP. International transactions helped promote a high level of investment insofar as they contributed to the buoyancy of demand compared with earlier periods. In addition, by comparison with before 1914, the low level of capital export left room for more domestic investment. The upward trend in the rate of increase in the capital stock over most of the postwar period cannot be attributed to causes on the international side. Arguably, the pattern of the stop-go cycle discouraged investment, especially widening investment, and so made it more difficult to meet demand when the next peak arrived.

It is fairly clear that increasing international competition had a depressing effect on the trend of *manufacturing* investment in the course of the postwar period. In addition to making for a slowdown in the rate of growth of output after the early postwar years, it depressed profitability. The rate of growth of the capital stock in manufacturing in the postwar period exceeded that in earlier periods by a rather larger margin than elsewhere in the economy; but it had a tendency to fall off from the early 1960's, sooner than in other sectors (as well as being, of course, lower than in other countries). Had exogenous forces on the foreign trade side been more favorable, manufacturing investment in the late postwar period would no doubt have been higher. The extra investment in manufacturing would probably have been partly at the expense of investment in other sectors, but not wholly and probably not mainly. Granted that, in that contingency, manufacturing investment would have been higher, the likely effect on output — in other words, the marginal product of the investment — brings us back to the question of TFP, already discussed. If there had been no induced increase in the rate of growth of TFP, diminishing returns would have resulted — as they showed signs of doing in any case — since there was no substantial reserve of unused labor to call on. In that case, there would have been some increase in output as a result of the total investment, and some further increase insofar as investment was switched to manufacturing from sectors where it had a lower return, but the increase would have been limited.

In considering the effects of international transactions on supply, we have dealt with TFP and capital accumulation. The main proximate source on the supply side making for slowdown in the rate of growth within the postwar period actually lay in neither of these, but rather in the supply of labor. The accelerating fall in labor input, measured in man-hours, cannot be attributed to international transactions. However, more favorable international influences on TFP and on capital accumulation might have helped to offset it, if only to a limited extent.

PART FIVE

An Overall View

CHAPTER SIXTEEN

The Rate of Growth and the Proximate Sources of Growth

This chapter and the next summarize some principal conclusions, review their relation to one another, and consider unanswered questions. For the benefit of readers in a hurry, we have tried to make them self-contained in substance, though not in methodology or documentation.

A summary of trends in the rate of growth and its proximate sources between 1856 and 1973 is given in Tables 16.1–16.4. These tables bring together some of the principal findings discussed more fully in Chapters 2, 3, 4, 5, and 7. Growth rates over the standard phases used in this book are shown in the top half of these tables, with wartime phases italicized. These are followed by a view over longer periods: here 1856–1913 is treated as a single period, and war and postwar phases are amalgamated (this irons out a tendency to opposite movements in certain variables between periods of war and peace). Our main story starts in 1856, but rather less reliable data relating to 1800–1860 (for Great Britain only) are given for comparison in Table 16.1; statements made in the text do not embrace that period except where indicated.

A pictorial representation is given in Figure 16.1. The growth rates here shown relate to the standard periods, except that 1873–1913 is divided into subperiods at 1899, and the postwar period is divided at 1964.*

OUTPUT AND INCOME

The rates of growth of GDP and GDP per head followed a roughly U-shaped pattern over the period 1856–1973 (Table 16.1): a long intermediate period of slow growth separated initial and terminal periods of

---

*Growth rates for the subperiods 1873–99 and 1899–1913 are unreliable, because large discrepancies exist between the growth rates yielded by the income, output, and expenditure measures of GDP (see Appendix L).

TABLE 16.1

Growth of Gross Domestic Product and Growth of Gross Domestic Product and Real Disposable Income per Head of Population, 1800–1973

(Annual percentage growth rates)

			Contribution of:		
Period	GDP (1)	GDP per head (2)	Income from abroad (3)	Terms of trade (4)	Real disposable income per head[a] (2) + (3) + (4) (5)
Standard phases:					
1856–1873	2.2%	1.4%	0.1%	0.2%	1.7%
1873–1913	1.8	0.9	0.1	0.0	1.0
1913–1924	*−0.1*	*−0.6*	*−0.1*	*0.3*	*−0.4*
1924–1937	2.2	1.8	0.0	0.3	2.0
1937–1951	*1.8*	*1.3*	*−0.3*	*−0.3*	*0.7*
1951–1973	2.8	2.3	0.0	0.1	2.5
Combined periods:					
1800–1860[b]	2.6	1.3	0.0	−0.2	1.1
1856–1913	2.0	1.1	0.1	0.0	1.2
1913–1937	1.1	0.7	0.0	0.3	0.9
1937–1973	2.4	1.9	−0.1	0.0	1.8
1856–1973	1.9%	1.2%	0.0%	0.1%	1.3%

Source: Tables 2.4, 3.17; Feinstein 1978.
Note: Transwar periods are shown in italics in the tables in this chapter.
[a] Readjusted to market prices. The readjustment affects the following periods: 1924–37 (−0.1); 1913–37 (−0.1); 1951–73 (0.1).
[b] Data for Great Britain.

faster growth. The differences in rates of growth between periods were not enormous, but neither were they trivial. In no period did the rate of growth approach that achieved in the postwar period by France and West Germany, let alone Japan. However, the range between periods was of the same order of magnitude as the *average* difference over the long run between the British growth rate and U.S. or continental growth rates. By all criteria, growth in the postwar period was higher than in any earlier period. When the postwar period is amalgamated with the transwar period, 1937–51, the extent of its superiority over earlier periods is reduced but remains substantial by comparison with all other periods after 1873.

The bottom point of the U was reached in the first quarter of the twentieth century. Growth in the period 1899–1913 was significantly slower than in 1873–99 (Fig. 16.1), and across World War I real GDP did not rise at all.

The rate of growth per head in the United Kingdom was persistently lower than in most other industrial countries from the 1870's onward, by an average margin of about 1 percent a year (Table 2.5). It is difficult to generalize about which were the periods of greatest short-fall, since the timing of periods of more or less rapid growth differed considerably between other industrial countries, especially between the United States and continental Europe. The British U-shaped pattern is not prominent in most other countries, though all enjoyed faster growth in the postwar period than earlier.

The persistent shortfall in the British growth rate meant, of course, that the level of income in the United Kingdom declined steadily relative to that in other countries. This, together with the associated decline in Britain's share in world trade, is the basis of the popular notion of continuous deterioration in British economic performance. That notion is not warranted by comparison of the domestic growth rate in successive periods. Are other symptoms discernible of continuous deterioration in the United Kingdom's performance? One might so consider the trend decline in the balance of payments on current account as a percentage of GNP (Table 14.7). This decline was not a steady one; it took place mainly across World War I and in the interwar period. It is not self-evident in what sense it is a measure of economic performance, but it could be regarded, at the least, as posing a threat. Another feature that might be regarded as ominous was the trend decline in the rate of profit per unit of capital (Tables 6.12, 6.13). The timing of that

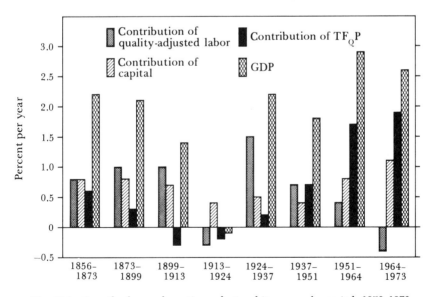

Fig. 16.1. Growth of gross domestic product and its sources by period, 1856–1973

decline was complicated by the wars and the interwar depression, but the underlying trend appears to have been fairly steadily downward for over a hundred years. The effect on the profit rate of the decline in profits' share was augmented by a rise in the capital-output ratio (measured gross, at current prices). Contrary to what might have been expected, however, the large decline in the profit rate was not accompanied by any trend decline in the rate of capital accumulation.

The broad pattern of differences between periods in the rate of growth of real disposable income was due to corresponding differences in the rate of growth of GDP. However, changes in the other two elements affecting real disposable income — property income from abroad and the terms of trade — were also important in some phases (Table 16.1, columns 3 and 4). The most striking instance was the change between 1924–37 and 1937–51, when a reduction in the annual percentage rate of growth of GDP per head of 0.5 was transformed into a reduction of 1.3 in the rate of growth of real disposable income per head. Also noteworthy was the effect of changes in income from abroad and the terms of trade in raising the rate of growth of disposable income per head in 1856–73 over what it had been in 1800–1860.

THE PROXIMATE SOURCES OF GROWTH

The growth-accounting method (discussed in Chapter 1) divides the proximate sources of growth of GDP additively into growth of total factor input (TFI) and growth of total factor productivity (TFP). This division is a convenient way of classifying information; it does not prejudge issues about ultimate causes. TFI in turn contains two elements, labor input and capital input, which are weighted in accordance with their distributive shares in GDP. The figures are shown in Table 16.2. These figures relate to the variants of the TFI and TFP concepts that we have denoted by $TF_Q I$ and $TF_Q P$, that is to say, quality improvements in labor (defined below) are included in TFI, not in TFP. At various points later in this chapter we shall have occasion to use alternative concepts, $TF_Y I$ and $TF_H I$, and correspondingly $TF_Y P$ and $TF_H P$, in which the labor component in TFI is measured respectively in man-years and man-hours, without adjustment for quality.

A corresponding division of the sources of growth on a per-head-of-population basis is shown in Table 16.3. Abstracting in this way from the effects of population growth serves, of course, to reduce the rates of growth of TFI and its components, while leaving unaffected the rate of growth of TFP.

We now consider in turn the rates of growth of labor input, capital input, TFI, and TFP.

TABLE 16.2

Growth of Labor, Capital, Total Factor Input, and Total Factor Productivity, 1856–1973

(Annual percentage growth rates)

Period	Quality-adjusted labor (1)	Capital (2)	Contributions to TF_QI of: Quality-adjusted labor (3)	Capital (4)	TF_QI (5)	TF_QP (6)
Standard phases:						
1856–1873	1.4%	1.9%	0.8%	0.8%	1.6%	0.6%
1873–1913	1.7	1.9	1.0	0.8	1.8	0.0
1913–1924	*− 0.4*	*0.9*	*− 0.3*	*0.4*	*0.1*	*− 0.2*
1924–1937	2.1	1.8	1.5	0.5	2.0	0.2
1937–1951	*1.1*	*1.1*	*0.7*	*0.4*	*1.1*	*0.7*
1951–1973	0.1	3.2	0.1	0.9	1.0	1.8
Combined periods:						
1856–1913	1.6	1.9	1.0	0.8	1.8	0.2
1913–1937	0.9	1.4	0.5	0.5	1.0	0.1
1937–1973	0.5	2.4	0.3	0.8	1.1	1.3
1856–1973	1.2%	2.0%	0.7%	0.7%	1.4%	0.5%

Source: Tables 4.7, 7.1, 7.4.

TABLE 16.3

Growth of Labor, Capital, and Total Factor Input per Head of Population and Growth of Total Factor Productivity, 1856–1973

(Annual percentage growth rates)

Period	Quality-adjusted labor per head (1)	Capital per head (2)	Contributions to TF_QI per head of: Quality-adjusted labor (3)	Capital (4)	TF_QI per head (5)	TF_QP (6)
Standard phases:						
1856–1873	0.6%	1.1%	0.3%	0.5%	0.8%	0.6%
1873–1913	0.8	1.0	0.5	0.4	0.9	0.0
1913–1924	*− 0.9*	*0.4*	*− 0.6*	*0.2*	*− 0.4*	*− 0.2*
1924–1937	1.7	1.4	1.2	0.4	1.6	0.2
1937–1951	*0.6*	*0.6*	*0.4*	*0.2*	*0.6*	*0.7*
1951–1973	− 0.4	2.7	− 0.3	0.8	0.5	1.8
Combined periods:						
1856–1913	0.7	1.0	0.5	0.4	0.9	0.2
1913–1937	0.5	1.0	0.3	0.3	0.6	0.1
1937–1973	0.0	1.9	0.0	0.6	0.6	1.3
1856–1973	0.5%	1.3%	0.3%	0.4%	0.7%	0.5%

Source: Tables 3.17, 7.1, 16.2.

Inputs: Labor

The rate of growth of quality-adjusted labor input is equal to the sum of the rates of growth of man-hours and labor quality (Table 16.4). The rate of growth of man-hours was on balance negative after 1913. It can in turn be divided into contributions from population growth, participation rates and unemployment, and hours of work (Table 16.4, columns 1–3). The rate of growth of labor quality, which was always positive, is here defined to consist of changes due to the following: education; age-sex composition; diminution in the weight of Ireland (before 1914); and increases in the intensity of work associated with reductions in hours per man (Table 4.7). Other sources of change in labor quality are included, not in TFI, but in TFP.

The measures of man-hours are reasonably firm statistically. The same cannot be said of the measures of labor quality. This applies particularly to the items relating to education and the intensity of work. The inclusion of the item relating to the intensity of work serves to mitigate the effects of changes in hours of work on the measure of labor input; the extent of changes in hours of work differed greatly between periods, and some mitigation is certainly appropriate, but the amount is largely a matter of guesswork. The unreliability of the item relating to education probably matters less for comparison of periods than it does for the relative rates of growth attributed to TFI and TFP over the period as a whole. The quantity of schooling embodied in the labor force grew at a fairly even rate after 1880; unevennesses in the rate of growth between successive age-cohorts were largely damped out in the labor force as a whole. Any substantial differences between periods in the contribution of education would therefore have to have arisen from unmeasured changes in the quality of education. However, the estimate of the absolute magnitude of the contribution made by education to improvement over time in the quality of the labor force is subject to a very wide margin or error. Using conventional methods, we have estimated it at 0.5 percent a year on average, an estimate that may err on the high side. If a lower estimate were adopted, the rate of growth of TFP in 1873–1913 would no longer be zero, though it would still be lower than in other peacetime periods.

Given these definitions and measures, with all their imperfections, what picture emerges? The rate of population growth underwent a once-for-all fall from around 0.9 percent a year before 1914 to around 0.5 percent a year after that. This was not the only source of decline in the rate of growth of labor input. The rate of growth of labor input per

TABLE 16.4

Sources of Growth of the Labor Input, 1856–1973

(Annual percentage growth rates)

Period	Population (1)	Man-years in employment per head of population (2)	Man-hours per man-year in employment (3)	Total man-hours (1) + (2) + (3) (4)	Quality adjustment per man-hour (5)	Quality adjusted labor input (4) + (5) (6)
Standard phases:						
1856–1873	0.8%	0.1%	−0.9%	0.0%	1.4%	1.4%
1873–1913	0.9	0.0	0.0	0.9	0.8	1.7
1913–1924	*0.5*	*−0.9*	*−1.9*	*−2.3*	*1.9*	*−0.4*
1924–1937	0.4	0.8	0.3	1.5	0.6	2.1
1937–1951	*0.5*	*0.3*	*−0.7*	*0.1*	*1.0*	*1.1*
1951–1973	0.5	−0.1	−0.9	−0.5	0.6	0.1
Combined periods:						
1856–1913	0.9	0.0	−0.3	0.6	1.0	1.6
1913–1937	0.4	0.0	−0.7	−0.3	1.2	0.9
1937–1973	0.5	0.0	−0.8	−0.3	0.8	0.5
1856–1973	0.7%	0.0%	−0.5%	0.2%	1.0%	1.2%

Source: Tables 3.10, 3.17, 4.7.

head of population actually declined more than the rate of population growth: from 0.7 percent a year in 1856–1913 to 0.0 in 1937–73 (Table 16.3, column 1). The main single source of this was a speeding-up in the rate of decline of hours of work. In none of the three combined periods — 1856–1913, 1913–37, and 1937–73 — was there any net change in participation rates: the trend rise in the female participation rate was offset by the trend increase in the duration of education, earlier retirement, and a less favorable age-distribution.

Over a very long period the trend was thus a decline in both the rate of growth of labor input and the rate of growth of labor input per head of population. Over the shorter time spans of our standard periods, these movements were not smooth. There were violently discrepant movements in 1913–24 and 1924–37. Labor input per head of population fell steeply between 1913 and 1924, mainly on account of abnormally large reductions in hours and the rise in unemployment; the effects of these reductions were of about the same size, after allowance for an intensity offset to the reductions in hours. Between 1924 and 1937, on the other hand, labor input per head of population rose greatly, chiefly on account of an increase in the proportion of those of working age. This was the deferred and temporary result of the once-for-all reduction in the rate of population growth: there were fewer children, but the elderly still belonged to cohorts substantially smaller than those of working age. The weighted contribution to the growth of real disposable income per head in the interwar period made by increase in labor input per head, as here estimated, was 1.2 percent a year, exceeding the average over the period 1856–1973 as a whole by 0.9 of a percentage point (Table 16.3, col. 3). It is interesting to note that this abnormal contribution of 0.9 was three times as great as the contribution made by the improvement in the terms of trade, the item most commonly cited as a special factor making for rising real income in that period.

Within the period 1937–73 the rate of growth of quality-adjusted labor input per head fell substantially, as well as being lower on average than in earlier periods. In 1937–51, 1951–64, and 1964–73, respectively, the annual percentage rates were 0.6, 0.1, and −0.9. Between 1951 and 1973 total quality-adjusted labor input scarcely rose at all, and total man-hours worked (without quality-adjustment) fell significantly—a point of contrast both with earlier peacetime experience in Britain and with the postwar experience of most other advanced industrial countries. The historically high rate of growth of GDP was thus achieved despite the trend in labor input, not because of it.

Inputs: Capital

The movements over time in the rates of growth of the capital stock and the capital stock per head of population conformed after a fashion to those in GDP (Tables 16.2, 16.3). They were notably higher in the postwar period than in earlier periods. However, differences between the combined periods 1856–1913, 1913–37, and 1937–73 were not enormous, and they are further scaled down in the calculation of the contribution to the rate of growth of TFI, where they are multiplied by a coefficient of less than a half (capital's distributive share). The increase in capital's contribution to the rate of growth of TFI in the postwar period partly offset the decline in the contribution from the labor side. The rate of growth of the capital stock was lower in transwar periods than in peacetime periods, as would be expected. Rather more surprisingly, variations between peacetime periods were smaller than in the case of labor input.

Within the postwar period the rate of growth of the capital stock, and its estimated contribution to growth, followed a pronounced long swing, rising up to about 1968 and then falling (Fig. 11.1). This long swing is reminiscent of the long swings in domestic capital formation before 1914, but the order of magnitude of the upward phase of the postwar long swing was altogether greater. It would require a future downward phase of unprecedented severity and duration to reduce the postwar rate of capital accumulation to the long-term historical average. Thus, in order for the long-term rate of capital accumulation, even starting from 1937, to be reduced to its historical average, it would be necessary for the annual percentage rate of increase of the capital stock to be at its war-period rate (1.0) for over 20 years from 1973.

The Weights of Labor and Capital in Total Factor Input

The growth-accounting measure weights the contribution of labor and capital in TFI according to their distributive shares in GDP.

Over the period 1856–1973 as a whole there was a downward trend in property's share in national income and in the profit rate. The downward trend was not equally rapid in all periods, but from the 1870's onward it was persistent and large. Property's share in GNP fell from nearly half in the early 1870's to barely more than a quarter in 1973. This fall was not due to rent, whose share fell steeply across the wars but rose enough to compensate in peacetime; nor was it due to income from abroad, whose share in 1973 was almost the same as it had been in 1856, after a huge intermediate rise and fall. The fall was due predominantly to profit's share in trading income. The consequence of the fall in property's share in GDP is that a considerably lower weight in the measure of TFI is given to capital in the postwar period than in the nineteenth century.

The postwar period is the only one in which the weighting makes a significant difference in the measurement of TFI. In earlier peacaetime periods the rates of growth of quality-adjusted labor and capital were quite close to each other, so any weighting would give much the same result. In 1951–73 the rate of growth of $TF_{\varrho}I$, as measured, was 1.0 percent a year; had pre-1914 weights been used, it would have been 1.4 percent. This is not a negligible difference, but it does not alter the general picture.

Whether it is appropriate to give capital input a diminishing weight over time in this way depends on what caused the decline in profits' share — itself of course a question of much interest. There are two possible types of explanation: (1) a neoclassical type of explanation, in terms of a less-than-unit-elasticity of substitution between labor and capital (or else a capital-saving bias in technical progress, the two being difficult to distinguish, as is well known), combined with a willingness of investors to continue capital accumulation in face of a falling profit rate; (2) an explanation in terms of an increase over time in labor's bargaining power, possibly due to a trend increase in labor shortage, constituting a change favorable to labor in the degree of monopoly in labor and product markets, taken together. Both types of causes appear to have played a part, and they interacted with each other.*

Insofar as the explanation lay in changes in the degree of monopoly, it did not necessarily betoken a corresponding change in the relative marginal products of labor and capital. It is possible, therefore, that the rate of growth of TFI in the postwar period is somewhat under-estimated relative to earlier periods.

Total Factor Input and Total Factor Productivity

Over the period 1856–1913 as a whole growth of TFI contributed 1.4 percent a year to the growth of GDP and growth of TFP contributed 0.5 percent a year. Their contributions to the growth of GDP per head were more nearly equal: 0.7 percent from TFI per head and 0.5 percent from TFP. However, there was virtually no increase at all in TFP between 1873 and 1937, a period of nearly two-thirds of a century. This does not mean, of course, that there was no technological advance during that period. Certainly there was. What it *does* mean is that the whole of the net increase in labor productivity over that period is capable, according to the present measures, of being attributed to increases in the capital stock and improvements in the quality of labor (both of which had, as one effect, the promotion of technical advance). Other sources of improvements were in net offset by tendencies inimical to productivity. Some of these operated in particular sectors, such as commerce and mining, other perhaps more generally.

Some of the changes between periods in the rate of growth of TFI were quite large, but they did not follow any regular pattern, nor were they related in any regular way to changes in the rate of growth of GDP. Only in the trans–World War I recession, and to a lesser extent in the interwar period (as compared with 1873–1913), did change in the rate of growth of TFI make a major contribution to the change in the rate of growth of GDP. The decline in the rate of growth of GDP in the period before 1914 was due to TFP, not TFI. So was the historically high rate of growth of GDP in the postwar period. Variations in the rate of growth of GDP, and in particular the U-shaped pattern, thus arose more from TFP than from TFI.

The U-shaped pattern in the rate of growth of TFP was a smooth one, *including* war periods (Fig. 16.1). Moreover, estimates for years

---

*The possible effects of a third cause, foreign trade, are discussed below, p. 529.

before 1860 indicate that the downward phases of the U had already begun early in the nineteenth century; and, at the other end of the story, the rate of TFP growth continued to increase within the postwar period up to 1973 (though not beyond). The complications caused by wars, depressions, and statistical deficiencies make it impossible to say whether the U-shaped movement was really a continuous one or whether the underlying phenomenon consisted rather of a limited number of steps — downward at some point in the second quarter of the nineteenth century and again in the first quarter of the twentieth century, upward in the interwar period and after World War II. The low point in Table 16.2 is located in the period 1913–24, when TFP growth (measured, it must be remembered, excluding the effects of improvements of labor quality) was actually negative. When 1899–1913 is taken as a separate period, as in Figure 16.1, instead of being incorporated in 1873–1913, as in Table 16.2, it comes out fractionally worse than 1913–24. On any reckoning, the low point in the rate of growth of TFP came in the first quarter of the twentieth century.

In the foregoing we have reviewed trends in the rates of growth that actually occurred and their proximate sources in the sense used in growth-accounting. It remains to consider causes and consequences in a more fundamental sense.

Causes and Consequences of the Growth of Total Factor Input and Total Factor Productivity

THE QUESTIONS TO BE ASKED

Why is it necessary to go beyond the enumeration of the proximate sources of growth, as described in the preceding chapter?

There is no presumption that the rates of growth of labor, capital, and TFP are ultimate independent variables. The need to consider their *causes* is therefore plain enough. Those causes may be endogenous to the growth process, or they may be of a kind that can reasonably be treated as exogenous. The latter, by definition, mark the end of the road for this investigation. Insofar as the growth of TFI or TFP was endogenous, it was part of the mechanism of the growth process. That mechanism determined the ultimate impact on growth of the exogenous forces, whether those impinged directly on the variable concerned or on one of the other variables.

It is perhaps a little less obvious why it is necessary to consider further the *consequences*, for the growth of output, of growth in labor, capital, or TFP; for the growth-accounting identity may appear to have already answered that question. However, this is not really so. There are quite a number of complications. Any consideration of the consequences means consideration of counterfactual alternatives — of which interperiod comparisons are one case. Growth-accounting is concerned with the counterfactual consequences of alternative overall rates of growth of labor, capital, and TFP, irrespective of their causes. But one may instead wish for some purposes to consider the counterfactual consequences of some particular exogenous influence on TFI or TFP. In an extreme case, a change in one of these could produce no change at all in actual TFI or TFP; for example, a demographically induced rise in the labor supply could lead merely to an equal increase in unemployment. Whatever counterfactual question is asked, the working of the whole system has to be taken into account. It cannot be assumed, for example, that variations in the rate of growth of the labor input will leave unaffected the rates of growth of capital and TFP. Moreover — a more technical point — the coefficients in the growth-accounting identity, even supposing they correctly identify marginal products at the points observed, cannot be assumed to remain valid if one is contemplating the effects of a different rate of growth of an input over a substantial period.

These considerations can be made more concrete by relating them to theoretical models of economic growth.

Take the elementary neoclassical model. In this model supply creates its own demand (business cycles being allowed as a possible exception). The underlying supply-side variables are population growth and technical progress. These are exogenous. They determine the long-run equilibrium rate of growth of output — the "natural" rate in the sense of Harrod. Investment is a function of income, and the rate of capital accumulation is therefore primarily an endogenous variable, though the ratio of investment (savings) to income is exogenous.

This model contains important elements of truth. The rate of growth of supply does have at least *some* tendency to communicate itself to the rate of growth of demand. There are at least *some* exogenous elements in the rates of growth of the labor supply and technical knowledge and in the savings ratio. It is part of the task of the economic historian to identify them.

But there are important qualifications, particularly in regard to demand. It cannot be taken for granted that demand wholly accommodates itself to supply, even in the long run. Equally, it cannot be taken for granted that the rates of growth of labor and TFP are wholly exogenous; they may be influenced by endogenous forces, including the pressure of demand. These questions require investigation, as do the forces determining demand itself. Because of the role of demand, the treatment of the effects of increase in labor input and the effects of increase in capital input cannot be fully symmetrical: both contribute to the growth of supply, but expenditure on capital accumulation direcly generates demand in a way that an increase in the size of the labor force does not.

Further complications result from relaxing the assumption of a closed economy made in the neoclassical model in its elementary form. It is not just that the exogenous elements affecting the rate of growth of TFP must now be defined to include innovations originating abroad. In addition, foreign trade may affect the rate of growth of TFP by affecting the relative size of sectors, since sectors may differ in their suscep-

tibility to productivity improvements. Moreover, if capital is interna-
tionally mobile, domestic savings are no longer identically equal to
domestic investment, and insofar as savings are a function of income
the link between domestic investment and income is weakened.
Finally, the self-balancing forces in the balance of payments do not
work perfectly or instantaneously. Hence foreign trade and payments
provide a further reason why the rate of growth of output may from
time to time diverge from the natural rate.

These considerations are important. They indicate that the rate of
growth is not necessarily to be explained exclusively, or even primarily,
by exogenous supply-side forces. Attention has to be given to the interaction of those with demand—its growth, level, and structure. Investment and foreign trade and payments are the principal elements of demand in this connection.

We may nonetheless organize the discussion by continuing to focus
on the growth-accounting categories. We shall accordingly consider in
turn the causes and consequences of the rates of growth of labor,
capital, and TFP, taking due account of the various interactions mentioned. An alternative, equally valid, way of structuring the discussion
would be in terms of categories of exogenous influences, irrespective of
whether their impact was on labor, capital, or TFP, or on all of these.
It is convenient to do this in the case of international trade and payments. This is dealt with in a separate section, which therefore comple-
ments the sections on the growth-accounting categories.

In the light of the foregoing, the following are among the principal
questions to which we must address ourselves in considering the British
experience:

(1) How exogenous was the rate of growth of the labor input? Did it
communicate itself to the rate of growth of demand and output?

(2) How endogenous was investment? How did variations in investment, whether endogenous or exogenous, affect the rate of growth of
output through their effects on (a) the supply of capital capacity, and
(b) demand?

(3) Did foreign trade cause demand to grow at other than the "natural" rate? Did it affect supply by its effects on the rate of growth of
TFP or on the rate of capital accumulation?

(4) What were the domestic or foreign exogenous forces affecting the
rate of growth of TFP? How much was the rate affected by demand?
How far was the growth of TFP itself communicated to demand?

The foregoing enumeration of questions matches the arrangement of
the next four sections, which deal in turn with labor, capital, foreign

trade and payments, and TFP. We then conclude the main part of this chapter by looking at matters chronologically and reviewing the principal forces that affected the rate of growth of output in each period.

THE GROWTH OF LABOR INPUT

Causes

The proximate sources of growth of labor input were summarized in the preceding chapter (Table 16.4; see Tables 3.17 and 4.7 for a fuller breakdown). The main sources of differences in the growth rate between periods were demographic change and changes in hours of work. War losses were important in World War I, as were the rise in unemployment across World War I and its fall across World War II. Changes in age- and sex-specific participation rates largely canceled out.

In the light of this, how far is the rate of growth of the labor input to be deemed to have been determined by exogenous forces and how far was it a function of the demand for labor?

Changes in the rate of natural increase, together with their effects on age distribution, both of which were important, plainly rank as exogenous (save in the broadest and most long-run sense). At the other extreme, changes in unemployment were plainly endogenous. One might expect the rate of net migration to be an endogenous variable, but it was in fact mainly determined by conditions abroad and, latterly, by social policy. It would probably have been affected, but only to a minor extent, had the domestic demand for labor been other than it was. Changes in participation rates—more married women working, earlier retirement, and longer schooling—were in part sensitive to the demand for labor. However, to a large extent they reflected social change and the *existence* of economic growth, rather than its precise rate in any particular period. Much the same may be said of the progressive improvement in the quality of labor brought about by education.

Changes in hours of work were of major importance, both for the long-run trend in labor input and for its variation between periods. Their status regarding exogeneity is peculiar. Reduction in hours of work did not take place at a steady rate but were concentrated, with ratchet effects, in phases when the bargaining power of labor was strong: in the early 1870's, in 1919, in 1948–49, and in the postwar period. Their timing resembled that of the rise in *money* wages rather than that of the rise in real wages. There was some very long-run trend for the rate of reduction of hours to speed up, and this too is consistent with labor's bargaining power having been an important influence. The bargaining power of labor was in turn a function largely (though not wholly) of the demand for labor. Long-run changes in hours were thus endogenous, but in a perverse direction (in contrast to the normal rise and fall in hours over the business cycle). This, it should be understood, is a description of what actually occurred, not a statement of a general law. The bargaining power of organized labor is not solely a function of the pressure of demand, and if it had been — or were to be in the future — strong for other reasons, it could be used to push down hours of work during a period of low demand.

The major observed rises and falls between periods in the rate of growth of labor input thus did not occur in response to changes in the same direction in the demand for labor. Counterfactually, higher demand for labor would have elicited higher supply through some channels, but the net outcome would have been uncertain on account of the tendency to a perverse response in hours of work.

Consequences

No one would maintain that variations in the rate of growth of labor input were the principal causes of the variations in the rate of growth of GDP. The single most important change in the rate of growth of labor — its fall, chiefly due to demographic causes, from about 1 percent a year in 1856–1913 to about half of 1 percent a year in 1913–73 — was in fact accompanied by scarcely any change in the rate of growth of GDP between those very broad periods. But one pair of observations is no basis for generalization, and the question remains what effects growth in labor supply had or might counterfactually have had in various periods, both on GDP and on GDP per head of population.

This raises extremely general and controversial theoretical questions about whether there is an inherent long-run tendency to full employment, and if so what the mechanism is.

One hypothesis regarding the mechanism is that cyclical upswings have (or sometimes have) an anti-damped or unstable tendency that brings them up against a full-employment ceiling. Hence the faster that ceiling rises, the faster the long-run rate of growth. This is easily understandable. Insofar as growth presses against a labor shortage, labor is a constraint, and the rate of growth of the labor supply directly affects the rate of growth of output.

Was the labor supply a constraint on growth or would it have been if its growth rate had been lower than it was? Assuming that the rate of growth of labor productivity is taken as given, labor supply was obviously a constraint in the period 1937–73, when there was full employment at cycle peaks. This is not refuted by the occurrence at postwar cycle peaks of another constraint, in the form of the balance of payments, since balance-of-payments difficulties may well have reflected underlying supply constraints. It is consistent with the slight decline in the rate of growth of GDP between 1951–64 and 1964–73, accompanying a less rapid growth of labor input (itself due mainly to demographic causes and to trends in hours of work). In this connection, it is interesting to speculate on how the trend in output might have been affected if government had not chosen, for social reasons, to impose restrictions on immigration in the early 1960's, thus preventing the domestic labor force from being augmented by immigrants to the extent that it was in West Germany and France.

A full-employment ceiling can scarcely be said to have been reached, even at cycle peaks, before World War II, except in a few sectors and possibly more generally on one or two occasions (1872–73, 1920). Labor supply was not in general a constraint on output in the interwar period, apart from certain sectors affected by rearmament in the late 1930's; but the question can still be asked whether it would have been a constraint if the rate of growth of the labor supply had not been so exceptionally high. The increase in employment (3 million between 1924 and 1937) much exceeded the number of unemployed at the end of the period (1.8 million in 1937). So if there had been *no* increase in the labor supply, GDP could not have risen as much as it did. Likewise, output could scarcely have risen as much as it did if the labor force had risen only at the same rate as population (even leaving aside hours of work); it would then have been some 1.8 million less in 1937 than it actually was, a difference equal to the entire number of the unemployed. However, it was not a necessary condition of the observed GDP growth, on this reckoning, that the labor force should have risen *faster* in 1924–37 than in 1873–1913. If the number of workers had instead risen at the same rate as in 1873–1913, there would have been only some 0.7 million fewer than they actually were, and the difference could surely have been made up by drawing on the pool of unemployed. A similar conclusion probably holds in relation to the period before 1914. Given the existence of concealed unemployment and the extent of emigration at that time, it is difficult to believe that labor would have become a constraint on growth if the rate of growth of the labor force had been less by a moderate amount than it actually was. But labor would have become a constraint if its supply had not increased at all.

In view of what was said earlier about exogeneity, these conclusions do not need to be much qualified on account of the possibility of induced changes in the labor supply. However, there is more ground for objecting to the *ceteris paribus* assumption about labor productivity. There is certainly reason to suppose that shortage of labor in the postwar period was partly responsible for the high rate of capital accumulation, and possibly of TFP as well. We revert to this below.

In periods when the labor supply was not directly a constraint on output, did the rate of growth of the labor supply nonetheless influence the rate of growth of output in other ways? In order for it to have done so, it would have needed to influence the rate of growth of demand for output; otherwise its effect would merely have been on unemployment (or underemployment), and the change in the labor *supply* would not have resulted in any actual change in labor *input*. Possible channels are through effects on the real wage, or on the efficiency wage (in the case of improvements in labor quality), or on the money wage and hence on international competitiveness and/or real balances. These effects cannot easily be traced. But they cannot be precluded. There is reason to suppose that changes in the supply of labor due to changes in hours of work had a more direct effect on the demand for labor and hence on output than did changes in the supply of labor due to changes in numbers, because reductions in hours of work tended more directly to affect costs. Indeed, they may have reduced the demand for labor by more than they reduced the supply; the large reductions in hours in the 1870's, and in 1919 were followed by unusually severe unemployment. Since these reductions were themselves largely the lagged consequence of high demand, there was here a factor making for oscillations. It is possible that a similar cyclical effect has, since 1973, attended the large reduction in hours of the postwar period.

Our general conclusions about the role of the labor supply in the several periods are these. In the postwar period and in 1937–51 the slow growth of the labor force was a constraint on growth, subject, however, to offsets in the shape of induced increases in capital accumulation and TFP, to be discussed below. It is doubtful whether the abnormally high rate of growth of the labor supply in the interwar period, by previous standards, was either a necessary condition for the growth of GDP that occurred or a direct influence in promoting it. But if the labor supply had grown only at the same rate as population in the interwar period, a labor bottleneck could have been encountered. Moreover, given that the interaction of forces on the supply side and on the demand side caused GDP in the interwar period to grow at the rate it did, the increase in labor input per head of population did permit a correspondingly rapid increase in income *per head*, and in that sense our conclusions in Chapter 16 about the importance of this source of growth in the interwar period stand. In regard to the period 1913–24, the great reduction in hours of work, which was one of the principal sources of the fall in labor input, did contribute to the reduction in the demand for labor and the setback to output. Finally, before 1914, a complete absence of growth in the labor supply would certainly have affected the growth of GDP. Moreover, improvements in education probably increased the employability of labor. But the rate of growth of GDP would probably not have been affected much if the labor supply had grown at a moderately faster or slower rate than it did.

Where does this leave "labor's contribution to GDP growth," as measured by the growth-accounting conventions of Table 16.2? It is perhaps not too bad as an indicator of the effects of labor-force growth in the very long run and in certain periods, including the postwar period. But exogenous changes in the labor supply cannot be assumed to be translated automatically into changes in the demand for labor. Nor can they be assumed to leave unaffected the rates of growth of the capital stock or of TFP. Hence "labor's contribution to GDP growth" is not a good measure of the extent to which differences between periods in exogenous sources of labor-supply growth were the causes of differences between periods in the rate of growth of GDP. Nor is it a good counterfactual measure of the likely effects of alternative rates of growth of the labor supply in particular periods. However, nothing that has just been said invalidates it as an indicator of labor's contribution to growth *on the production function side*, and hence as an indicator of the contributions to growth, *given* the demand for final output, that must have come from the other elements on the supply side, namely growth of the capital stock and growth of TFP.

THE GROWTH OF CAPITAL INPUT

Causes

The constancy in the rate of growth of the domestic capital stock in broad peacetime periods before World War II is remarkable. The annual percentage rates were 1.9 in 1856–73, 1.9 in 1873–1913, and 1.8 in 1924–37 (along with an estimated 2.0 in 1830–60; Feinstein 1978: 86).

This constancy up to the postwar period did not reflect immutability in the components of the Harrod identity (growth rate of the capital stock equals the savings-income ratio divided by the capital-output ratio). Overseas investment made for important divergences between savings and domestic investment. In the interwar period the depression caused the savings-income ratio to be lower and the capital-output ratio higher than before 1914, but the adverse effects of those movements on the rate of domestic capital accumulation were almost completely compensated for by the reduction in the proportion of savings devoted to overseas investment. In the postwar period the savings-income ratio was somewhat higher than it had been before 1914 (and *a fortiori* higher than in the interwar period); but compared with the pre-1914 period it was the lower rate of overseas investment that was, in the arithmetic of the Harrod identity, the most important source of the higher rate of domestic capital accumulation. This higher rate occurred notwithstanding a significantly higher current-price capital-output ratio, brought about by a once-for-all rise in the relative price of capital goods across World War II.

One would expect the rate of capital accumulation to be more endogenous to the growth process than the rate of growth of labor input and less influenced by outside forces (apart from wars). However, the distinction between induced and exogenous movements in the labor supply has some counterpart in the distinction between influences on capital formation arising from the side of the schedule of the marginal efficiency of investment (MEI) and influences arising from the side of the schedule of the supply price of finance (SPOF). Changes in investment due to changes in MEI are likely to reflect and reinforce other influences making for growth. Changes arising from the side of SPOF have more claim to rank as independent influences on the rate of growth.

The effects of these two classes of changes are best considered separately for the three broad sectors distinguished in Table 17.1. The trend in each was different, and only in the case of industrial and commercial investment was the rate of growth of the fixed capital stock, averaged over the trans–World War II and postwar periods, higher than the average for earlier periods.

The conclusion reached in Chapter 13 was that differences between broad periods in the rate of growth of *industrial and commercial* fixed capital chiefly reflected movements in MEI. There were some important trends in the SPOF schedule (see below); but it is doubtful whether the MEI schedule in industry and commerce was sufficiently elastic in the long run for movements in SPOF by themselves to have been capable of causing large changes in investment (as opposed to changes in the profit rate).

TABLE 17.1

Growth of the Gross Domestic Fixed Capital Stock in Three Broad Sectors, 1856–1973

(Annual percentage growth rates)

Sector	1856–1873	1873–1913	1913–1937	1937–1973
Industry and commerce[a]	2.5%	2.2%	1.2%	3.1%
Infrastructure[b]	3.0	2.4	1.2	2.1
Dwellings	1.5	1.9	2.3	2.0

Source: Table 11.1; basic statistics (Appendix N).

[a]Manufacturing, mining, construction, distributive trades, finance, and miscellaneous services.

[b]Gas, electricity, water, transport, communications, and public and professional services.

There was some downward trend in the rate of growth of the industrial and commercial capital stock running through the long swings of the pre-1914 period. It was attributable to a decline in the rate of TFP growth and a decline in international competitiveness. There was a more substantial reduction in the interwar period: apart from the obvious effects of the depression, including its important psychological effect in preventing investment in many sectors of industry from responding much to the recovery of GDP in the 1930's, there was apparently in this period some capital-saving bias in technical progress. The rate of growth of the capital stock in the postwar period exceeded that in earlier times by a greater margin in industry and commerce than in infrastructure or dwellings. The causes responsible for this historically high rate of industrial and commercial investment included improved confidence, faster output growth, and labor shortage, particularly in commerce. The response of investment to faster output growth was a reinforcer of other sources of growth; its response to labor shortage (itself caused partly by full employment and partly by slow growth of the labor force) was not a reinforcer of another source of high growth, but an offset to a potential source of low growth.

Shifts in the SPOF schedule appear to have had less effect on differences between periods in the rate of growth of industrial and commercial fixed capital than they had on differences within periods, that is to say, between phases of the long swing before 1914 and between parts of the postwar period. In the early 1950's some classes of investment were still held up by shortages and controls, themselves the result of government's perception of pressures on the economy, and thus a manifestation of a high SPOF, interpreting that concept broadly. From then until the late 1960's SPOF in manufacturing was reduced by increasingly generous tax treatment. These changes in SPOF within the

postwar period strengthened a long-swing tendency that would probably have existed anyway on account of trends in MEI.

Investment in *infrastructure and dwellings* likewise largely reflected
and reinforced the general trends in the economy, while also being
influenced by certain Schumpeterian elements (the falloff in investment in transport after the main railway-building period of the mid-
nineteenth century; the growth of the electricity supply industry;
suburbanization in the 1930's). The influence of SPOF was greater,
however, than in the case of industrial and commercial investment.
The demand for dwellings was responsive to its cost, and its cost was in
turn affected not only by productivity in the construction industry, but
also by the rate of interest and government policy. The increase in the
rate of growth of the stock of dwellings in 1873–1913 compared with
1856–73 and its further and larger increase in 1913–37 compared with
1873–1913 were opposite to the trends in industry and commerce and
in infrastructure, and it is possible that they reflected partly a taking-
up of slack in the supply of finance — crowding-in. In the postwar period the amount and timing of investment in transport and in social
capital such as schools and hospitals were chiefly determined by the
government's perception of pressures on the economy. The steep decline in these classes of investment in wartime was a more extreme example of the crowding-out manifested to some extent in parts of the
postwar period.

In two senses adjustments in SPOF, if not in the SPOF schedule,
were necessary conditions of the observed movements in investment. In
the first place, the savings had to be forthcoming to match the investment. How was this achieved? Before 1914 the link between savings
and domestic investment was not close, because capital export was
large and variable. In the interwar period savings were reduced by the
depression. This was reversed in the postwar period. For more obscure
reasons, there was a rise within the postwar period in the personal savings ratio, and this helped to finance the rising ratio of investment to
income. Finally, government savings were a much higher proportion of
GNP in the postwar period than previously. This must be ranked,
along with restrictions on capital export, as an autonomous factor,
serving to increase the availability of finance for domestic investment
compared with earlier periods.

In the second place, some explanation is needed of the following
paradox. The rate of profit on trading capital underwent a long-run
decline, and though the particular steps in this decline were matched
for the time being by falls in investment (in the 1870's and 1880's, the

1920's, and the 1970's), the long-run decline itself was not accompanied by a decline in the rate of capital accumulation, but rather the contrary. There must therefore have been a trend reduction in the acceptable rate of return on investment. In part this may be taken to mean simply that suppliers of finance had no choice but to put up with whatever rate of return was available. Also of substantial significance, however, was a trend reduction in the degree of imperfection in the capital market, attributable chiefly to the increase in the proportion of the economy in the hands of public joint-stock companies, to the increase in their size, and to the expansion of the equities market. This reduced the gap between the supply price (actual or imputed) of finance to the enterprise and the yield available to the rentier.

It may be noted that the maintenance of investment in face of the declining trend in profitability is not to be explained by an increase in public investment relative to private investment. Leaving aside dwellings, investment in the never-public sector was a significantly *higher* proportion of total investment in the postwar period than in the interwar period.*

Consequences

The rate of capital accumulation can influence the rate of growth of GDP in two separate ways: through its effect on demand and through its effect on productive capacity. We consider these in turn.

Effect on demand. As noted earlier, the existence of this (Keynesian) effect deriving from investment expenditure is a feature of increases in the capital input that does not have a parallel in the case of increases in the other factor, labor.

The effect was particularly apparent in the postwar period. High investment (itself largely endogenous in origin) was the major source of the high level of demand, and the high demand in turn not only en-

---

*A related question may be asked here in parentheses. Was the downward trend in the profit rate the principal reason for the trend increase in the size of the public sector (as, for example, in Italy in the 1930's, when the bankruptcy of much of industry brought it under the aegis of the state?) The answer is, on balance, no. A fall in profits was, it is true, the main reason for the nationalization of the railways (and, after the end of our period, of the firms taken over by the National Enterprise Board). It was also the cause of the decline in the private rented sector of the market for dwellings; but there the fall in profitability was of the government's own making through rent control. Declining profitability was not the main reason for the nationalization of utilities, coal-mining, steel, and aviation, or for the expansion of education and health. Moreover, certain industries that suffered severe reductions in profitability in one phase or another remained in the private sector — agriculture, building, and the bulk of manufacturing. Most of the public sector, it may be noted, enjoys natural protection from foreign competition, and is therefore sheltered from pressure on profitability from that source.

sured high employment, but also contributed to the growth of TFP (see below). Conversely, in the interwar period output would have grown faster if demand had been higher, and demand would have been higher if investment had not been depressed by other forces making for slow growth.

The Keynesian effect of high investment did not operate in all circumstances. It was certainly present in some degree in the period before 1914, but its operation then is clouded by the long-swing alternation of domestic investment and capital export. In the postwar period, at least one of the influences on SPOF favorable to investment, namely the historically high government saving propensity, was not such as in net to make for higher demand. In several periods high MEI in one sector meant high SPOF to another sector, damping the overall result, as noted above in the case of dwellings. And of course if investment had been *higher* than it was in the postwar period, there would have been at least some crowding out of other classes of expenditure, since the economy was in general near to full employment.

Effect on productive capacity. This is what is in principle measured by "capital's contribution to GDP growth," in growth-accounting. That measure provides a starting point. It indicates that if, in the postwar period, the capital stock had grown at only the same rate as it did in the interwar period, the annual rate of growth of GDP would have been lower than it was by 0.4 percentage point: quite a large part of the difference between the two periods in the rate of growth of GDP (0.6), but quite a small part of the difference between them in the rate of growth of GDP per man-hour (2.6).

That measure is subject to a good many qualifications. Apart from any more fundamental objections, it takes the capital-elasticity of output as given, an assumption that is not necessarily justifiable if one is considering what the consequences would have been had the rate of growth of the capital stock been higher or lower than it actually was over a substantial number of years. The measure does not therefore dispense with the need to look at the circumstances of individual periods.

It is a reasonable conjecture that if the rate of capital accumulation in the postwar period had really been kept down to what it was between the wars, the detriment to the rate of growth of productive capacity would have been greater than just indicated, on account of the need to embody at least parts of the historically high rate of growth of TFP in new equipment.

The opposite contingency has been the subject of much controversy. What would have happened in the postwar period if, say, firms had been generally more optimistic and their investment plans had not been discouraged by stop-go, i.e. by the peculiar pattern of the British postwar business cycle, with its relatively short upswing phases? In manufacturing, the sector of chief interest in this connection, there was a rising capital-output ratio and a falling trend in the profit rate. Prima facie these features suggest diminishing returns rather than any capital shortage; they suggest that if extra investment had been undertaken, it would as such have yielded only limited benefit. In some industries, indeed, over-investment as it was led to blatant excess capacity, though the prime example was not in manufacturing but in electricity supply.

This macro-evidence is not decisive. Inadequate expansion of capacity may ultimately lead to the under-use of even what capacity there is, if customers become discouraged by supply difficulties. Hence a rising capital-output ratio does not *necessarily* betoken diminishing returns. Moreover, greater confidence or greater availability of funds for capital investment might conceivably have caused the investment to have been of higher quality, and so conduced to faster growth in TFP. However, cross-section evidence within manufacturing does not indicate a positive correlation between the rate of capital accumulation and the rate of growth of TFP (Appendix J).

The period 1873–1913 has points in common with the postwar period. Then too the trend of the capital-output ratio was upward, and that of the profit rate downward. There is therefore a presumption that if the rate of domestic investment had been higher, say, on account of a more domestically oriented capital market, the potential gain to output would have been no more than limited.

The answer is less doubtful in the case of the interwar period. Though the profit rate was not particularly high, it did not have a downward trend, nor was the capital-output ratio rising. If industrial investment had not been depressed by the state of confidence, output could have expanded more in the late 1930's, when bottlenecks were encountered in some sectors; moreover, industry would have been better placed to take advantage of its opportunities in the early postwar years.

To conclude. Trends in the rate of capital accumulation in the British economy were mainly determined by trends in the marginal efficiency of investment and were thus endogenous to the growth process. They served, by their effects on both supply and demand, to magnify the effects on output created by variations in the rate of growth of TFP. They likewise served to amplify the effects of variations in demand arising from other sources, and they were a channel by which demand affected the rate of growth of supply. These sources of feedback were somewhat reduced, but by no means eliminated, by a certain tendency for high MEI in one sector to crowd out investment in other sectors.

Capital accumulation did not, apparently, serve to magnify the effects on output of variations in the rate of growth of the labor supply, but rather at least in the interwar and postwar periods to offset them, though less than completely. It is doubtful whether investment would have been stimulated by a faster rate of growth of labor input than actually occurred, at least if it had taken the form of greater quantity rather than improved quality. It is also doubtful whether a higher level of investment, due to exogenous causes such as greater availability of finance, would, in the absence of other changes, have made a major difference to the growth rate of GDP over most of the period.

THE ROLE OF INTERNATIONAL TRADE AND PAYMENTS

Discussion so far in this chapter has focused on the causes and consequences of the rates of growth of labor and capital, the constituents of TFI. Before we go on to treat TFP similarly, as we do in the next section, it is convenient at this point to adopt a different and complementary approach, focusing attention, not on one of the growth-accounting categories, but on a class of exogenous influences and structural relationships that affected all of those categories, namely the influences and relationships involved in Britain's international trade and payments.

The effects of international economic transactions were largely on demand: its growth, its level, and its structure. Did they cause the rate of growth of demand to diverge from the "natural" rate, i.e. the rate of growth of supply? Did they affect supply itself by their effects on the rate of capital accumulation? Or by their effects on the rate of growth of TFP?

The main questions here concern the causes and consequences of changes in Britain's relative standing among industrial countries. Also significant, however, were certain other world events exogenous to British economic growth, and we shall deal with those first.

Exogenous World Events

World demand. In the postwar period the high level of world demand helped sustain high demand in Britain. In particular the absence of major world recessions (before 1974) was the main reason why cyclical fluctuations in Britain were milder in the postwar period than previously. In the interwar period demand in Britain was depressed by the world recession of the 1930's and by the recession that affected most of Northern Europe in the early 1920's. These trends in demand affected GDP and its growth directly by affecting the utilization of resources and indirectly by their effects on capital accumulation and TFP.

Primary-product prices. Most of the major movements in Britain's terms of trade were due to movements in primary-products prices, exogenous from the British point of view. They affected real disposable income directly — favorably during the interwar period and unfavorably across World War II — and they also tended to affect it indirectly by their effects on the balance of payments, and hence on demand. The 1950's and early 1960's offered an unusually favorable conjunction of improving terms of trade and strong world demand. (The deterioration in the terms of trade from 1974 was likewise unusually unfavorable in coinciding with a world recession.)

Loss of overseas assets. The influences considered under the two previous headings affected all or many industrial countries, not just Britain. Peculiar to Britain were the effects of the two world wars on the value of overseas assets, and hence on income from abroad. The decline in the value of overseas assets, from the the high point in 1913, was almost wholly due to the wars — partly to war finance and partly to the reduction by wartime inflation in the real value of overseas assets denominated in money terms. The estimated decline amounted to some 15 percent of the total UK net capital stock (domestic and overseas together) in the case of World War I and no less than 28 percent in the case of World War II. These losses put pressure on the balance of payments and affected GNP directly, through the consequent loss of income from abroad. The direct effect on GNP was doubtless less than would have followed from the loss of a corresponding amount of domestic capital (since in that case the average product of the capital lost would have much exceeded the marginal product of a unit of capital). On the other hand, the loss of overseas assets did not have the benefit of creating a *tabula rasa* for new investment, as the destruction of domestic assets might have done.

The foregoing effects were important. They are easy to understand. Much more complex were the effects to be considered under the next heading.

Britain's Relative Standing Among Industrial Countries

The period from 1800 until 1973 may for this purpose be divided schematically into three phases.

(1) In the first half of the nineteenth century Britain was enabled, by exporting, to expand its output of manufactures, chiefly textiles, by much more than would have been justified by the structure of domestic demand. This was achieved largely by sharply increased productivity, which reduced the prices of exports and so allowed Britain to move along foreigners' demand curves. The domestic benefit of the rise in productivity and in GDP was thus subject to an offset due to the deterioration in the terms of trade.

(2) The third quarter of the century was a transitional period in which Britain remained the predominant producer of manufactures and was able to continue to increase its exports at a rapid rate (though less rapidly after 1860 than previously). This was notwithstanding that the prices of exports ceased to fall and even rose. There was in this phase an acceleration in the rate of economic growth abroad; foreigners' demand curves were shifting upward. In this period international transactions had a uniquely favorable effect on the growth of real income in the United Kingdom. Industrialization was being promoted by rapid growth in export demand; the terms of trade were improving; and capital export had already produced a substantial increase in income from abroad.

(3) In the fourth quarter of the nineteenth century and throughout the twentieth century, Britain was no longer the only industrial country; the *proportion* of world demand for manufactures met by Britain became, as it had not been before, no less important than the *level* of world demand for manufactures in determining the demand for British manufactures. Hence Marshall's dictum that after 1870 it is no longer possible to write *British* economic history. After 1870 British economic history has to be understood partly in terms of the theory of the location of industry.

Our interpretation is consistent, subject to some significant qualifications, with the following commonly held characterization of trends in the century after 1870. Industrial production and productivity were growing faster in other countries than in the United Kingdom, whether because they had more arrears of industrial development to make up or because conditions there were more conducive to TFP growth or to capital accumulation. The resulting international competition put pressure on prices and profits in British manufacturing (i.e. in the tradables sector). This discouraged investment in manufacturing, making either for a reduction in total capital formation or for a shift of capital formation into capital exports or into the domestic non-tradables sector. The growth of GDP was thereby retarded, and retarded, moreover, to a heightened extent (a) because the rate of growth of TFP in manufacturing is partly a function of the rate of growth of output of manufactures, and (b) because the needed adjustments in the structure of domestic output tended to occur with a lag, so that there was chronic trouble with the balance of payments, leading to deflationary pressures.

The qualifications to this description are, first, that the quantitative importance of the effects of the processes just described on the British rate of growth is less clear than the direction of those effects, and, second, that those processes did not take place in a uniform manner. We now consider the periods more closely.

Pre-1914. This period exhibits many of the characteristics described. There was a decline in the balance of trade in manufactures as a proportion of GNP, and also in agriculture, a tradable sector that in this period suffered even more from international competition; there was a fall in the profit rate in the 1870's and 1880's, not fully retrieved thereafter; there was a downward trend in the rate of growth of the capital stock in manufacturing, partly offset by an opposite movement in dwellings (a non-tradable sector); and, of course, there were very large capital exports.

Capital exports gave the pre-1914 period some peculiar features. The two great phases in the history of Britain's overseas assets — their rise from 1850 to 1913, their decline from 1913 to 1951 — did not have symmetrical causes. The rise was due to economic conditions; the fall was due to wars. A really high level of capital exports requires two circumstances not usually present together: a strong balance of payments on current account and an inducement to invest a large proportion of the country's savings abroad rather than at home. This unusual combination of circumstances emerged in the third quarter of the nineteenth century, because exports were not yet too much affected by foreign competition and at the same time the expected MEI abroad was high relative to the expected MEI at home because of territorial expansion in countries of recent European settlement. The necessary combination of circumstances persisted in 1873–1913, but now the source of the strength in the balance of payments on current account was to an increasing extent the earnings on the accumulated overseas investment: the earlier strength of the current-account balance was providing a source of continuing strength. The growth of income from abroad allowed overseas investment to remain at an average of 5 percent of GNP, notwithstanding a trend decline in the remainder of the balance of payments on current account as a proportion of GNP. Hence there was in this phase no balance-of-payments aggravation of the ill-effects of declining competitiveness on industrial investment. Indeed it is arguable that the strengthening of the overall balance by the increase in income from abroad was itself a part-cause of the declining competitiveness, through its effects on relative prices ("Dutch disease").

The pattern described contributed to the retardation of growth of real disposable income in the period 1873–1914 compared with 1856–73 through its effects on (1) the terms of trade, which now ceased to improve—not a fortuitous event, but an inherent part of the underlying change, reflecting the increased competition in export markets; (2) the rate of growth of TFP (see below); and (3) to a small extent, the rate of capital accumulation. Because the overall balance of payments was not under pressure, ill-effects through the level of activity were not prominent and had nothing like the importance they had in the interwar period, but they do seem to have been present to some degree.

The ill-effects of international economic relations on the rate of growth in this period should not be exaggerated. The relationship between the foreign trade position and the growth of GDP or TFP was not simple or direct. It is reasonable to suppose that the decline in the rate of growth of net exports of manufactures brought about some reduction in the scope for growth economies. But the timing of changes in the rate of growth of TFP in manufacturing and of changes in the rate of growth of net exports does not suggest a close connection between the two: there was little or no decline in the rate of growth of TFP in manufacturing until the period 1899–1913, and in that period net exports were booming.[1]

Some of the ill-effects of foreign trade were, moreover, inevitable. Britain, as the early starter, could plainly not be expected to complete the process of absorbing surplus labor by industrialization before continental countries had even started to do so. Likewise, it was inevitable that the potential obstacle to world industrialization arising from food supply should have been removed by investment in New World infrastructure rather than by investment in British agriculture. The rate of capital accumulation did decline significantly in manufacturing (and still more in agriculture), but over the economy as a whole the decline was slight, and the nonmanufacturing investment undertaken did yield a return. In Chapter 15 we offered the guess that about half of the decline between 1856–73 and 1873–1913 in the rate of growth of TFP was due to the effects of the country's changed international position, including both changes due to events abroad and the reinforcing effects through international transactions of changes in the rate of growth of TFP originating at home.

World War I and the interwar period. In the interwar period adverse underlying trends in competitiveness continued to be felt, in more acute forms—partly a deferred penalty for the long period of slow TFP growth that had gone before, though World War I speeded up the decline in Britain's share in world markets, in services as well as in goods. As a result of the war income from abroad fell as a proportion of national income, instead of rising, as it had formerly done. The combination of these circumstances led to a balance-of-payments problem of a kind not experienced before 1914. These unfavorable developments on the international front, together with the world depression of the 1930's, were the main cause of the low aggregate demand in the interwar period and its effects in the form of discouragement to industrial investment and declining TFP in sectors affected by the underemployment of labor. However, the main feature of the behavior of TFP in this period—its faster growth in most sectors compared with before 1914—is not explicable by trends in the country's international transactions, unless in the most general sense that changes on the international front were part of a general process of shake-up following the war. The effects of the balance of trade on the demand for manufactures were more unfavorable in the interwar period than before 1914, but whatever ill-effects this may have had on the rate of growth of TFP in manufacturing were outweighed by forces working in the opposite direction.

World War II and the postwar period. Across World War II there was a major break from long-run trends. Britain's share in world exports actually rose; imports declined steeply as a proportion of national income; and the main export sector, manufacturing, experienced an increase in profitability and, for the first time for over a hundred years, a substantial increase in its share of the labor force (the subsequent decline in this proportion, from its high point in the early 1950's, left it still in 1973 well above its historical average). Foreign trade was the main source of the increase in the level of demand compared with the 1930's. All this reflected the temporary absence of competition from war-devastated countries, helped by the devaluation of sterling against the dollar. It produced a short-lived situation with certain resemblances to the third quarter of the nineteenth century. Its erosion resembled what occurred after that period, but with some differences and at a faster tempo. The resemblances were declining competitiveness, pressure on profitability, and hence pressure on capital accumulation in manufacturing, which as in the earlier period reached its peak before capital accumulation in the rest of the economy. One difference was that in the postwar period pressure was felt through the balance of payments, which on this occasion was not being helped by rising income from abroad on the scale of 1870–1914. There was not (until 1973) any substantial adverse trend in the actual balance of payments on current account as a proportion of national income, but an underlying tendency to one can be held to have been present, inasmuch as the trend in the pressure of demand during the 1960's was downward in the United Kingdom and upward in most of the rest of the industrial world. (The latter fact, incidentally, tells against the hypothesis that the balance-of-payments pressures were the result of a tendency to chronic excess absorption.) Balance-of-payments pressure was largely responsible for the peculiar time pattern of the British business cycle in 1951–73, with downswings on the average longer than upswings, and the whole cycle short and not severe. Another difference from the pre-1914 period was that since the rates of capital accumulation (industrial as well as total) and TFP growth were high by historical standards, any ill-effects from the international side were ill-effects relative to what might have been, not (as they had been before 1914) relative to what had actually occurred earlier.

As in 1870–1914, some erosion of the initial position was inevitable, as other countries made good their arrears. But the erosion would not have continued as long as it did, had there not been other forces making for slower growth in TFP in Britain than abroad. It is not consistent to argue *both* that Britain was at a disadvantage by having been in the lead in the early postwar period while Germany and Japan were able to make a fresh start, *and* that once those countries had taken the lead, the cumulative advantages of that lead made their position impregnable. It is clear enough that in the postwar period foreign competition reduced profitability, MEI, and hence capital accumulation in the tradables sector. The effect on the growth of TFP is less apparent. Whereas in 1870–1914 pressure on the tradables sector from foreign competition can be held to have inhibited the transfer of underemployed labor from agriculture, that is not applicable to the postwar period. We may grant that there was *some* adverse effect, and that it reinforced shortfalls arising from other causes in the rate of growth of TFP compared with abroad. This is, however, a far cry from the view that has sometimes been held of the balance of payments as in itself the dominant or sole constraint on the growth rate.

A word may be said, finally, about two related topics, the effect of foreign trade on trends in profitability and the role of exchange-rate policy in the interwar and postwar periods.

In Chapter 16 reference was made to the long-run downward trend in profits' share and in the profit rate (more fully dealt with in Chapter 6). In most of the phases in which there were substantial movements in profitability (profits' share in trading income), trends in international competitiveness were in the right direction to explain them. This applies to the rise in profits' share in 1856–73; to its falls in the 1870's and 1880's and again after World War I; and to the temporary rise in profitability in manufacturing across World War II and its subsequent decline during the postwar period. It does not apply well to the acceleration in the decline in 1968–73, since in that phase competitiveness, following devaluation, was for a while better than before. Nor does it apply well to the sharp fall of profitability in the services sector across World War II.

It is easily understandable that there should be a relationship between profitability and international competitiveness. Profits accrue as quasi-rents, so in the short-run changes in the world prices of tradables relative to domestic costs impinge mainly on profits. Moreover, insofar as there was *chronic* pressure on competitiveness after 1870, it would account for profitability being chronically below a steady-state equilibrium *level*. It is not clear, however, that declining competitiveness can account for the trend *fall* in profits' share after the 1870's, a fall that, moreover, would have been even more pronounced had capital export not provided an outlet for savings. In the long run one would expect the supply of capital and its allocation between sectors to adjust. Whatever the effect of foreign trade on the level of output or on its structure, it is not obvious why it should as such in the long run affect the distribution of the value of output between labor and capital.* Though foreign trade accounts for much of the *timing* of the trend fall in profitability, other causes have to be sought for the trend itself.

The relationship between profitability and the exchange rate is, of course, that devaluation has as one of its immediate effects an increase in profits' share. The function of exchange-rate changes is to facilitate adjustments called for by underlying circumstances. In addition to its

*To the extent that influences from the side of foreign trade caused TFP and hence GDP to rise less fast than they would have otherwise done, foreign trade must indeed have *tended* to lower the profit rate. But since the rate of growth of TFP was not actually falling in the twentieth century, this cannot be invoked to explain the fall in the profitability that *did* occur.

effects on profits' share, devaluation raises the prices of tradables relative to the prices of non-tradables and usually, though not necessarily, lowers the terms of trade.

A decision to adopt a lower exchange rate than $4.86 in the 1920's would have had these effects. The adjustments needed were large and difficult, on any policy. An increase in the relative price of tradables would have encouraged the growth of newer export industries and helped the balance of payments, but it would not have solved the problems of the old staples. Its effectiveness would, moreover, have depended on public willingness to accept the effects on real wages of a less rapid improvement than actually occurred in labor's share and in the terms of trade. It would also have depended on the response of other countries to the devaluation of sterling.

The decision to devalue in 1949 contrasts with the return to the pre-1914 parity in 1925 and was perhaps the single most important point of difference between postwar and interwar government policy. It facilitated the major break from past trends after World War II in Britain's international trading position. The adjustments required in this period were admittedly easier than the adjustments that had to be made after World War I, because of buoyant world demand and because of the more appropriate structure of manufacturing inherited from the war and the 1930's. No one disputes that further adjustments had become necessary by the mid-1960's. The debate about whether the devaluation of 1967 should have been made earlier or not at all is a debate about whether this particular device sufficiently facilitated adjustment — a similar doubt as may be felt about the alternative policies available in 1925, and one apparently given substance by the continuing balance-of-payments troubles experienced after 1967. These troubles however, were partly the result, not of the intractability of the problem as it existed in 1967, but of the subsequent change, exogenous from Britain's point of view, in the trend in primary-product prices.

Conclusions About the Effects on the Growth Rate

Let us now summarize the answers to the questions that were put at the beginning of this section.

Did international influences cause demand to tend to grow less rapidly than supply and hence cause output to grow at less than the "natural" rate? There are obvious difficulties in defining a "natural" rate of growth for such an open economy as Britain's in abstraction from international trade; but, briefly, the answer is yes, for much of the period. It is plainly so for 1913–24, and also, though to a less degree, for 1873–1913 and the interwar period. For the postwar period, there is no clear answer. On the one hand, high and rapidly growing demand in the rest of the world was a major plus by comparison with almost all earlier periods; on the other hand, the increase in foreign competition made the resultant benefit less than that derived by other countries, to say the least.

Did foreign trade and international capital movements adversely affect supply by their influence on the rate of capital accumulation? Before 1914, not much — less than might have been expected. In the interwar period, certainly. In the postwar period foreign trade affected at least the timing of the fall in profitability in manufacturing and so discouraged investment in that sector. This has to be seen, however, in conjunction with the abnormal stimulus to investment in manufacturing arising from the side of foreign trade at the beginning of the postwar period.

Did foreign trade affect the rate of growth of supply by its effects on the rate of growth of TFP? This is largely related to the first question. Adverse effects can be traced in 1873–1913. The main trends in TFP in the interwar period do not appear to have been at all directly due to foreign trade. The effects in the postwar period are ambivalent. The influence of foreign trade does not go far to explain the U-shape of the very long-run movement in the rate of growth of TFP, which is further discussed in the next section.

THE GROWTH OF TOTAL FACTOR PRODUCTIVITY

TFP is a weighted average of the productivity of labor and the productivity of capital. As noted above, the rate of growth of TFP was the principal proximate source of variations between periods in the rate of growth of GDP per head of population.

The Time Pattern to Be Explained

The rate of growth of TFP was the prime example of the U-shaped time pattern. However, this time pattern, as it was shown in Table 16.2 and Figure 16.1, requires some comment and some qualification. The rate of growth of TFP in 1924–37 and 1937–51 was much affected by its behavior in commerce and by the movements of factors between that sector and the rest of the economy. Both of these were largely reflections of changes in the amount of concealed unemployment. A better indication of the underlying pattern in those periods is given by the rate of intra-industry growth in TFP in the rest of the economy (Table 17.2 , row 2). This was significantly higher in 1924–37 than in

TABLE 17.2

Growth of Total Factor Productivity Including and Excluding Commerce and Quality-Shift, 1856–1973

(Annual percentage growth rates)

Category	1856–1873	1873–1913	1924–1937	1937–1951	1951–1973
(1) Rate of growth of TFP	0.9%	0.5%	0.7%	1.4%	2.3%
(2) Rate of growth of TFP, excluding contributions from commerce and quality-shift	(0.5)[a]	(0.1)[a]	0.7	0.4	1.6
(3) Rate of growth of TFP in manufacturing	0.9	0.6	1.9	0.9	2.4

Source: Tables 7.2, 8.3, 9.7.

Note: The figures do not relate to the same concept of TFP as that used in Table 16.2 and Fig. 16.1, namely TF_QP, because sectoral data on labor quality are not available. The concept of TFP used in this table, namely TF_YP for 1856–1913 and TF_NP for 1924–73, serves to allow for the only part of labor-quality change that has a major effect on comparisons between periods, the 100% increase in intensity of work assumed to have accompanied the reduction in hours in 1856–73. For definitions of the alternative concepts of TFP, see p. 199.

TFP in rows 1 and 2 is based on the average of the GDP estimates from the expenditure, income, and output sides. Commerce and manufacturing in rows 2 and 3 are estimated from the output side.

[a] Quality-shift is assumed to be 0.25.

1873–1913. It underwent a large setback in 1937–51, not surprisingly. It then improved further in the postwar period. This improvement after the two wars, following a decline up to World War I, is the pattern to be considered.

Trends in the rate of growth of TFP, excluding commerce and quality-shift, exhibit broadly the same pattern as trends in manufacturing, also shown in Table 17.2. These trends were pervasive throughout the economy (with the exception of the period 1937–51). TFP grew more rapidly in 1924–37 than in 1873–1913 in every sector except commerce, and it grew more rapidly in 1951–73 than in 1924–37 in every sector without exception. This pervasiveness of trends between broad periods — less pronounced within periods — is a characteristic to be borne in mind in seeking explanations. The rate of growth of TFP in individual sectors was the dominant influence on the rate of growth of TFP in the economy as a whole. The effects of shifts of weights between sectors with different levels or rates of growth of TFP were small by comparison, both in absolute amount and in their contribution to differences between periods.

Causes

We now turn to an analysis of the forces responsible for the U-shaped pattern in the rate of growth of TFP. Four broad categories are considered: (1) the rate of growth of demand (including one aspect of economies of scale); (2) the level of demand; (3) the introduction of new technology; (4) the sociocultural factors reflected in the attitudes of labor and the quality of management. There is some overlap between them, as well as between them and the effects of foreign trade, already discussed.

The rate of growth of demand. Fast growth of demand, at least for a single industry and maybe for the economy as a whole, conduces to rapid growth of TFP by facilitating embodied technical progress, opening the way for enterprise (great generals are not made in peacetime) and lessening labor resistance to change. A special case of this relationship is that put forward in the Kaldor-Verdoorn hypothesis, according to which the tendency operates in manufacturing only but extends to the economy as a whole because of manufacturing's importance; the effect can then result from a switch in demand to manufacturing, typically because of foreign trade, as well as from rapid growth in demand in the economy as a whole.*

The period in which this effect was most apparent was 1873–1913. Trends in foreign trade then affected adversely the rate of growth of TFP in some manufacturing industries and still more so in agriculture. Perhaps surprisingly, the effect in agriculture had considerably greater impact on TFP in the economy as a whole than did the effect in manufacturing. Output in agriculture fell absolutely between 1873 and 1913. At the same time the rate of decline of the agricultural labor force diminished somewhat, no doubt largely because there were less opportunities for employment elsewhere in the country. The result was a fall in the rate of growth of TFP in agriculture that accounted for about a third of the fall between 1856–73 and 1873–1913 in the rate of growth of TFP in the economy as a whole.

The trouble with the Kaldor-Verdoorn hypothesis as applied to later periods is not that it is necessarily wrong as a counterfactual proposition, but that it is largely irrelevant to the explanation of interperiod differences in the rate of growth of TFP in the United Kingdom. The rate of growth of output of manufactures was the same in the interwar period and in the postwar period, and therefore does not help to explain why TFP grew more rapidly in the postwar period. Similarly, since the rate of growth of output of manufactures was the same in the two parts of the postwar period, 1951–64 and 1964–73, it does not help to explain why TFP grew more rapidly in the second of these. The output of manufactures did grow faster in 1924–37 than in before 1914, so

---

*An alternative version of the hypothesis, relating productivity growth in manufacturing to the growth of inputs rather than of production, must be considered refuted by the empirical evidence both on the UK time-series and on international comparisons.

the hypothesis works in the right direction to explain the rise between those periods in the rate of growth of TFP. But in this instance it explains too much, since in manufacturing the increase in TFP growth was greater than the increase in output growth, so the hypothesis implausibly implies negative marginal costs; moreover, the increase in the rate of output growth arose from domestic absorption rather than from the balance of trade, the most likely source of an *exogenous* change of demand. Cross-section studies of manufacturing industries do give some indication of the presence of a Kaldor-Verdoorn relationship. The most reasonable conclusion is that the growth of output did make some contribution, though not the sole contribution, to the higher rate of growth of TFP in manufacturing achieved in the interwar period compared with before 1914; and that, though change in the rate of growth of manufacturing output does not explain why TFP grew faster in the postwar period than in the interwar period, the lack of such change between those periods may have been part of the reason why TFP growth increased *less* in manufacturing than in most other sectors.

As a counterfactual proposition, the Kaldor-Verdoorn hypothesis is less attractive for the postwar period than for 1873–1913. In the postwar period there was less slack in the economy, and faster growth in the demand for manufactures would have had more tendency to be halted by supply-side bottlenecks before it could begin to generate dynamic economies of scale.

The level of demand. Like rapidly growing demand, a high level of demand may conduce to a high rate of growth of TFP, and for much the same reasons. It may enable enterprising new men to come to the fore; facilitate mobility; dispel restrictive labor practices by reducing fear of technological unemployment; and induce innovations to overcome labor shortages. On the other hand, it may enable inefficient firms to survive; destroy labor discipline; weaken the inducement to cut costs; and defer needed changes in industrial structure or attitudes. Any of these effects may be important. They are not trivial matters. But the net outcome cannot be predicted *a priori*, nor is it easy to test empirically. Some of the above effects do not seem to have been significant in Britain: neither the extent of labor restrictive practices nor labor mobility bore any clear relationship to the prevailing level of demand. The relationship between the level of demand and the growth of TFP is not necessarily monotonic. The pattern Denison has conjectured as the most conducive to economic growth — predominantly strong demand, punctuated by short sharp recessions — was not the pattern of British business cycles in *any* period. If Denison is right, it could help to explain why TFP generally rose less rapidly in Britain than elsewhere.

However, the evidence suggests that the high level of demand in the postwar period had a net favorable effect, and a substantial one, on the growth of TFP (as well as being favorable to capital accumulation). Certainly this was so in the important commercial sector. In one sector, construction, full employment appears to have had an adverse effect on the level of TFP (if not on its growth rate). The sector was not large enough for the movement of TFP there to have much effect on the movement of TFP in the economy as a whole; however, the fall in TFP in construction across World War II had some significance in raising the price of capital goods and reducing the profit rate earned on them.

Though the high level of demand in the postwar period thus had a positive effect on TFP growth, Kendrick's finding (1973: 41–51) that the depression of the 1930's led to a slowdown, not subsequently made good, in the growth of TFP in the United States does not hold for the United Kingdom. On the contrary, as already noted, TFP grew more rapidly in 1924–37 than in 1873–1913 in every sector other than commerce. Was this *notwithstanding* the uniquely low level of demand, or was it, partly, *because* of it? Did the favorable effects on TFP of low demand in that phase preponderate over the unfavorable ones? Schumpeter saw the business cycle as a wave of creative destruction, upswing and downswing both playing their part, and this idea could be extended to the longer alternations represented by the interwar and postwar periods. Good effects exercised by the depression on the growth of TFP are more dubious and were certainly smaller than the good effects of the high level of demand in the postwar period; moreover, the depression had some deferred ill-effects, such as discouraging the training of skilled labor, as well as direct and immediate ill-effects on the utilization of resources and capital accumulation. However, it would not be inconsistent to suggest that, as far as the growth of TFP is concerned, both the high demand of the postwar period and the low demand of the interwar period had *some* good effects.

The introduction of new technology. It is helpful to draw a distinction here between innovations that originated in Britain and those that where wholly or largely initiated abroad and taken up in Britain after some delay.

In the first half of the nineteenth century only the domestic source of innovation was important to Britain, and the increase in TFP up to about 1860 was largely dependent on the mechanization of the textile industries and the construction of the railways. When this process was completed, the effect was sufficient to bring about an appreciable deceleration in the growth of TFP. The second half of the century brought no new domestic innovations with effects comparable to the earlier advances in textiles. Some key improvements were not widely taken up in Britain, most notably the Gilchrist-Thomas process in the production of basic steel and the use of electricity as a source of motive power.

As industrial leadership passed from Britain, so the possibilities increased for adopting innovations pioneered abroad. Both *a priori* reasoning and empirical evidence (Table 2.5, Fig. 2.2) create a presumption of international convergence in productivity levels. The further a country lags behind the leading country or countries, the greater the scope for catching up and the faster the rate of growth of TFP that can be expected, other things being equal. In principle, an increase over time in the rate of growth of TFP in the British economy would be expected on this account.

The catching-up hypothesis has to be considered in conjuction with the hypothesis of the disadvantage of an early start. That asserts that the existence of old-vintage capital, non-human and human, slows down the adoption of innovations, because the old capital is not itself adaptable to the new methods and has demolition costs, physical or social. This hypothesis has been applied in many contexts. One is the explanation of Britain's technological lag in the last quarter of the nineteenth century. Another relates to more recent times, when West Germany, it is claimed, was able to renew its status as late starter because of the destruction of old capital by bombing.* The hypothesis has a good deal of plausibility—especially in its most general applications, that is to say, the persistence of outdated attitudes among labor and management, often reinforced by common-interest groups—and it has relevance to the general problem of Britain's slow rate of growth. It is not directly antithetical to the catching-up hypothesis, and indeed to some extent concerns a different point (old age brings disadvantages, whether or not new ideas are being introduced by the younger generation). It does mean, however, that the existence of a technological gap provides less easy scope for increasing TFP in an old industrial country than in a new one, and thus helps to explain why the convergence phenomenon is less apparent in the British case than in others. Only on extreme assumptions, however, does it remove altogether (or reverse)

*Other cases in which the early-start hypothesis has been invoked include, for the pre-1914 period, gas delaying electricity, mules delaying ring-spindles, Bessemer converters delaying the open-hearth process, and the Leblanc process delaying the Solvay process in soda-making, as well as the logically different and simpler case of the depletion of the most accessible mineral deposits; and for the postwar period, the dispersed location of the motor industry, the over-defensive orientation of early postwar investment (above, pp. 394–95) and, at a regional level, the less rapid growth of industry in traditional locations, like Merseyside and Glasgow, than in newer ones.

the presumption that the opening up of a technological gap increases the scope for innovation. It does not apply, for example, in industries where there is freedom of entry and new firms (or new divisions of multiproduct firms) can set up free from the millstones that encumber the old ones. Let us proceed, then, on the assumption that Britain's international standing in relative productivity did at least to some extent affect the scope for growth in TFP in the manner postulated by the catching-up hypothesis, and consider how it affects the view taken of performance in each period.

Before 1873 the United Kingdom had the world's highest GDP per man-year. In some sectors, possibly in manufacturing as a whole, the United States was already leading, but the scope for catching up by the United Kingdom was still small.

At the beginning of the period *1873–1914* GDP per man-year in the United States was equal to Britain's. In the course of the period the United States progressively moved ahead of Britain. So did Germany in some sectors. There was thus increasing scope for catching up by the United Kingdom. The decline over time in the British rate of growth of TFP after 1873 therefore implies a *greater* decline in the rate of growth of TFP relative to what might have been expected. It leaves correspondingly more to be explained.

World War I widened the productivity gap between the United Kingdom and the United States. Some improvement in the rate of growth of TFP in *1924–37* was therefore to be expected, compared with earlier. The improvement that did occur, however, was larger than can easily be accounted for by the increase in the scope for catching up; the increase in the scope for catching up was part of a continuous process, whereas the improvement in the rate of growth of TFP was abrupt and already in evidence in the 1920's. On this reckoning, there must have been domestically originating sources of improvement as well.

1951–73 is the most difficult period to characterize. World War II increased the productivity gap between Britain and the United States, as World War I had done. Moreover, the postwar rate of growth of productivity in the United States was faster than before, betokening a more rapid extension of the production frontier. The improvement in the UK growth rate compared with the prewar rate more than matched the improvement in the United States: for the first time since the Civil War, the British rate of growth of productivity was not below the American. Thus the United Kingdom shared in whatever was the source of the U.S. improvement, and rather more besides. As in the interwar period, the improvement appears to have been more than can be accounted for by the increase in the size of the initial gap (though this must be a subjective judgment), and domestic sources have to be sought. However, other countries showed a much greater break from their past. In particular, the gap separating France and Germany from the U.S. level of productivity, which proportionally had changed little before World War II, now narrowed rapidly, and those countries overtook the United Kingdom. The experience of those countries does not negate the evidence for domestic sources of improvement in Britain, but it implies that those countries had much stronger sources of domestic improvement.

Some of the specific advances to which this hypothesis of technological lag and catching up might apply are the use of electricity for power, the internal combustion engine, the production of synthetic dyestuffs and other chemicals, the development of the basic process and the open-hearth furnace in steel making, the spread of mechanization, and the use of automatic machinery.[2] These are all areas in which Britain fell behind its competitors on the Continent and in the United States in the period after 1870, and even if there were often sound economic reasons for the reluctance of British management to introduce new technology, the effect was seen in the slow growth of TFP. Conversely, some part of the improvement in TFP growth in the interwar period can be attributed to a belated introduction and extension of these innovations.

In the early 1950's the scope for technological catching up by Britain was again large. In the subsequent period the pace of world technological advance was more rapid than in earlier periods. Innovation took place on a wide front throughout the industrial world (including Britain), and the increase in the number of countries at a comparable stage of technological development facilitated international learning. Outstanding innovations of the period came in electrical engineering and electronics (including computers and the use of automated machinery), in aircraft, in the development of synthetics, antibiotics, and other products by the chemical industry, and in the peaceful application of nuclear power. Mention may also be made of new managerial techniques, such as stock control, largely derived from operations research, which (like many of the above) had its origins in World War II; these techniques were akin to technological advance, rather than the consequence of changes in the personal qualities of management of the kind to be considered under the next heading.

Neither technological innovation nor catching up is, of course, an inevitable or automatic process.[3] The extent to which other factors facilitated or obstructed them must be analyzed. These factors include the level and rate of growth of demand, already considered, and the socioeconomic forces of labor and management, to which we now turn. Changes in the attitudes of labor and in the quality of management are the most truly exogenous and least quantifiable of the possible causes of TFP change. They are thus not very well suited for study from the macro-economic data on which this book is based. So in a sense our inquiry ends with a question mark. Certain observations can, however, be tentatively made.

Attitudes of labor and quality of management. British workers have been said for over a hundred years to be more adverse to change, to flexibility in working practices, and to a fast tempo of work than their foreign counterparts, this aversion being expressed both through trade unions and, informally, through the attitudes of individuals and groups. Even allowing for frequent exaggeration, the testimony to this effect is too strong to be dismissed. The origins of the phenomenon have been sought in numbers of causes: the tradition of craft unionism and the slow rate of growth in industrial employment, both related to the country's early start on the path of industrialization; the absence, by comparison with the United States, of a flow of immigrants of mixed nationalities; the absence, by comparison with Germany and Japan, of traumatic setbacks to the standard of living that forced the practice of each-man-for-himself. *Changes over time* in labor attitudes in the United Kingdom have some, but only limited, relevance to the explanation of changes over time in the rate of growth of TFP. For reasons that are not entirely clear, industrial relations markedly deteriorated in the 20 years before World War I, and the rate of growth of TFP reached its nadir at the same time. The decline in labor militancy after 1926 probably assisted TFP growth. It is unclear whether change in labor attitudes in the postwar period, compared with earlier periods, was on balance such as to contribute to faster growth of TFP or to inhibit it. With a faster underlying rate of technical change, a given degree of labor resistance to change mattered more, labor attitudes and technical progress thus having a multiplicative rather than an additive effect on the growth of TFP.

It is a well-known contention that the quality of entrepreneurship declined in late-Victorian and Edwardian Britain. If true, it would help to explain the decline in the rate of growth of TFP in that period. The argument is that any corps of industrial leadership will deteriorate over time if there is not enough infusion of new talent, and that the values of late-Victorian Britain, reflected and reinforced by the educational system, did not direct enough able people that way: the most successful in business were drawn into the lifestyle of the landed gentry, and the middle classes looked for their careers to the professions, the public service, and jobs in the Empire. The educational system reflected these goals and neglected engineering and chemistry.

Not all the arguments that have been advanced in this regard stand up to examination. However, there is enough direct evidence about motivation, recruitment, and education to justify the inference of some falling off in entrepreneurship in the late nineteenth century, quite apart from indirect evidence afforded by the performance of the economy. Much of this falling off (including that due to the expansion of Empire, a point of difference from other industrial countries) can be traced directly or indirectly to the early start of British economic growth and to the economy's consequent temporary world leadership.

The attitudes and institutions just referred to outlived the circumstances of their origin. However, they did gradually alter. The timing of that gradual and incomplete alteration is consistent with the improvements in the rate of growth in TFP after World War I and again after World War II.

The alteration came about partly because of the jolts administered by the two wars, which upset institutions, compelled a reexamination of attitudes, and led people and firms into activities they would not otherwise have contemplated. The effects of wars and other political upsets have been made the basis of a general theory of economic growth by Olson (1978).* There is no need to go all the way with him in order to recognize that the adverse effects of the wars on the capital stock and the foreign trade position were significantly offset by the shake-up of attitudes and institutions, governmental as well as private.† Jolts may also have been administered (in accordance with the Schumpeterian idea) by the depression of the 1920's *and* by the boom of the postwar period.

Consequences

So much for the causes affecting the rate of growth of TFP. Its consequences can be more briefly treated. The question is, did the rate of growth of TFP affect the rate of growth of GDP?

―――――――

*Olson's theory has particular reference to common-interest groups (cartels and labor unions) that retard growth.

†Changes in government attitudes on aspects of policy indirectly affecting TFP – demand management, health, education, and to some extent science – were probably the most important. Governments throughout the postwar period also concerned themselves more than before with policies designed to improve productivity directly, and there were some successes, but the result of these policies generally fell below expectations, and it is doubtful whether in net they contributed substantially – if indeed at all – to overall growth in TFP.

Insofar as the rate of growth of TFP was a function of the rate of growth of demand, the answer is plainly yes: it was part of an endogenous cumulative process.

More generally, in those periods when demand was pressing against a ceiling of productive potential, anything making for fast or slow growth in TFP was bound to translate itself into the rate of growth of GDP.

The less easy question concerns the effects of changes in TFP due to exogenous causes (technological or sociocultural) or to perversely endogenous ones (low demand stimulating high TFP growth) in periods when the economy was not pressing against a ceiling. The issue resembles the issue about the effects of exogenous changes in the labor supply. However, there are good reasons for supposing that the answer is more straightforward than in that case. TFP growth not only raises the ceiling on output, but it also reduces costs, and so facilitates its own absorption, by improving international competitiveness, as shown by evidence from all periods. Moreover, insofar as it requires to be embodied in new equipment, it contributes directly to demand by stimulating gross investment.

In principle, of course, fast growth in TFP could lead to slow growth in TFI rather than to fast growth in output. To some extent that may have happened in the interwar period, when there was spare labor to draw on and when, moreover, the capital-saving element in TFP growth was prominent and kept down investment in some sectors. Even in that period, however, growth in TFP in the construction industry was an important element in stimulating the building boom. In general, we need not feel much doubt that growth in TFP, whether exogenous or endogenous, was both a necessary and a sufficient condition for growth in GDP, while recognizing that the effect was not in all cases necessarily one for one, and that its magnitude depended partly on the form of the growth of TFP and on its sectoral incidence, especially on the extent to which it generated demand by improving international competitiveness.

CHARACTERISTICS OF THE SUCCESSIVE PERIODS

So far this chapter has considered, one by one, the various factors in British economic growth. Let us now, at the risk of some repetition, review matters from the other angle, chronologically.

The Pre-1914 Period

GDP grew more slowly in 1873–1913 than in 1856–73. This slowdown was not due to any change in the rate of growth of labor input: population and employment grew at a constant rate (cycles and long swings apart), and indeed in 1873–1913 there were less reductions in hours of work and rather more improvement in the quality of the labor force (in education and age composition) than in 1856–73. Nor was there a decline in the rate of domestic capital accumulation; there was admittedly some decline in the rate of investment in industry and commerce, but this was matched by a rise in house-building, and the rising capital-output ratio in industry does not suggest a capital shortage. The decline was in the rate of growth of TFP. TF_QP did not increase at all over the period 1873–1913 as a whole, and it actually declined after 1899.

TF_QP had not grown all that rapidly before 1873 either, and the falloff, at least until 1899, was therefore not so enormous. But comparison with other countries suggests that TFP ought to have increased *more* rapidly after 1873 than before. In that sense, the comparison of successive periods understates the deterioration.

Part of the explanation was the increase in foreign competition. Its most visible effect was on agriculture, which suffered both a decline in the rate of growth of its output and a slowdown in the trend rate of reduction of its labor force, the latter due, presumably, to diminished scope for absorption of labor elsewhere in the economy, itself partly related to the slower rate of growth of net exports. As was argued above (pp. 533–34), the effect of foreign competition on TFP in manufacturing is more doubtful, though there probably was some.

A further part of the explanation lies in certain special factors. In textiles there was already a decline in the rate of growth of TFP some time before 1873, attributable to the exhaustion of the once-for-all effects of the industrial revolution. In mining, where there was an absolute fall in output per man (not merely in TFP), classical diminishing returns played a part. But for the economy as a whole more general explanations must be sought. Deteriorating industrial relations in the latter part of the period were one. Decline in entrepreneurial vitality may have been another. It is possible that both of these were affected (with different timing) by a vicious circle between performance and remuneration, the decline in industrial profit rates in the 1870's and 1880's having harmful effects on the recruitment and motivation of entrepreneurs, and the check to real wages after 1900 souring industrial relations. No offsetting incentive effect could be expected from the concomitant increase in income from abroad.

The surprisingly small part of the falloff in the rate of growth of overall TFP that was attributable to manufacturing appears on the face of it to militate against both the foreign-competition hypothesis, as normally stated, and the entrepreneurial-deficiency hypothesis (though not against the industrial-relations hypothesis); and there remain some puzzling features about the period. These are especially concerned with the timing of movements within it and their relation to long swings. The falloff in the rate of growth of TFP was not continuous but was temporarily arrested in the 1890's. Both in 1873–90 and in 1899–1913 there were elements of demand deficiency, though with different origins: in 1873–90 largely foreign competition, in 1899–1913 the long-swing fall in domestic construction and perhaps an adverse real-balance effect created by the rise in world prices. It is arguable that demand deficiency of one kind or another ultimately accounted for the major part of the falloff in the rate of growth of TFP in the period 1873–1913 as a whole compared with 1856–73 and also for the more severe falloff after 1899. However, demand deficiency cannot explain why the rate of growth of TFP in most sectors was so much lower than it came to be in the interwar period. This *is* indicative of entrepreneurial deficiencies or other supply-side sources, which doubtless interacted with demand.

World War I and the Interwar Period

Such a large gap opened up between supply and demand in the interwar period that it is tempting to regard demand-side forces as the only ones relevant to the explanation of the actual movement of output. However, exogenous trends in supply did contribute as well to the decline in GDP across World War I, and they were the main cause of the better trend performance in the interwar period compared with 1873–1913.

The absolute fall in GDP across the war, not made good till the late 1920's, is one of the most spectacular features of recent British economic history. Its main constituent, from the growth-accounting point of view, was the fall in labor input. Three sources had about equal effects in reducing the annual percentage rate of growth of (quality-adjusted) labor input from 1.7 in 1873–1913 to −0.4 in 1913–24: population growth, hours of work, and unemployment. The causes of the movement in the three were to a large extent independent of each other, and to that extent the magnitude of the movement had a fortuitous element. Population growth (affected by war casualties and the influenza epidemic) and hours of work (affected by immediate postwar labor militancy) were supply-side factors, both much influenced in their different ways by the war itself. Unemployment, of course, was a demand-side factor, though a subordinate part may also have been played by the rapid transwar rise in the real wage (comparable in origin, and indeed partly due to, the reduction in hours).

In regard to the movement of TFP across the war, there is not so much to explain. The performance was bad (TF_QP is estimated to have been lower in 1924 than in 1913); but the trend was not worse than 1899–1913, and the underlying trend was probably somewhat better, since TFP in 1924 was no doubt depressed by below-capacity working.

The importance of the supply constraints was apparent in 1920, when unemployment was extremely low yet GDP was 5 percent below 1913. The ensuing major decline in demand arose from the side of foreign trade. How much of it would have happened if there had not been a war can only be a matter of speculation. The balance of trade would certainly have deteriorated because of foreign competition anyway, very likely to nearly the same extent. But the disappearance of the support formerly given to the overall balance of payments by increasing income from abroad was a new feature, directly attributable to the war. So, doubtless, were the violent price movements and ensuing depression that affected most of Northern Europe in the early 1920's.

The recovery in 1924–37 was not to any large extent due to a reversal of the specific causes responsible for the previous contraction. The balance of payments on current account continued to have a downward trend; unemployment did not diminish; there was only a slight increase in hours of work.

On the supply-side the two new features were an abnormally rapid increase in the proportion of population of working age and a much improved rate of growth of TFP in most sectors — better than in 1873–1913, let alone 1899–1913. The first was purely demographic. In regard to TFP, there is no single simple answer to the question why it took a turn for the better in this period rather than a bit sooner or a bit later. The factors at work included belated adaptation to earlier sources of technical innovation, stimulated by the increase in the size of the productivity gap compared with the United States, by the jolt to the system administered by the war, and possibly also in some sectors by the depression; a decline in labor militancy in the aftermath of the General Strike of 1926, affected also by the growth of indusrry in new regions lacking old traditions of labor relations; and possibly improvements in entrepreneurship, particularly in recruitment.

On the demand-side the main source of growth was investment, chiefly in dwellings and in manufacturing (where investment, though still low absolutely, rose considerably under the influence of rearmament in the 1930's). Some growth in demand originated in foreign trade, but less than in any other peacetime period: the gain from the fall in the import propensity, due mainly to the fall in the prices of primary products, was largely offset by the continuing poor performance of exports.

If exogenous influences on the rates of growth of labor input or TFP had been *much* less favorable in the interwar period – if, for example, TFP had continued to decline at the same rate as in the years before World War I – the actual rate of growth of output would not have been possible. If they had been only *slightly* less favorable, it is not clear, in view of the slack in the economy, that output would have risen more slowly than it did, *provided* demand had risen at the same rate. But it is unlikely that that proviso would have been met, particularly if the difference had been in TFP. Higher real costs would have inhibited the growth of investment (notably in dwellings) and possibly made the balance of trade worse as well. This is quite apart from the importance of the interwar growth of TFI and TFP in establishing the productive potential that more directly constrained output during and after World War II.

World War II and the Postwar Period

There is an extraordinary contrast in respect of demand between the transitions across World War I and World War II. Yet in other respects the two wars had many similar features: large losses of overseas assets and consequent problems for the balance of payments; low domestic investment; jolts to established attitudes and, partly in consequence, improvement after the war in the rate of growth of TFP; increased involvement of government in economic affairs.

Among the many points of contrast between the two transwar phases, four may be singled out.

(1) The pressure of demand on the eve of the war was different. The existence of slack in the economy at the outset of World War II gave a margin from which to satisfy increased aspirations generated during the war.

(2) The scope for increasing exports was greater after World War II, on account of the greater setback to competitors, the more appropriate structure of industry developed before and during the war, and the decision not to adhere to the prewar parity.

(3) Transition from the war economy was smoothed by the much longer continuation of controls after World War II, and this helped

prevent a recurrence of the pattern of violent postwar boom and slump of 1919–21. This, along with the absence after World War II of a *world* recession like 1921, is the difference most directly relevant to the contrasting behavior of demand.

(4) In the aftermath of World War II there was a sense of national unity conspicuously lacking after World War I. Great attention had been paid to morale during the war, the fighting itself had been less traumatic, and a reformist government with a strong majority was elected in 1945. The exact effects of this different mood are difficult to pinpoint. At the least it helped avoid the industrial unrest of 1919. It probably had a more general effect too on the performance of labor and management.

In the postwar period itself growth in the British economy was more rapid than in earlier periods, by a substantial margin, though less rapid than in most other industrial countries (as it had been since 1870). Britain shared, in its fashion, in the outstanding postwar performance of the world economy.

As in earlier periods the rate of growth actually achieved was the result of forces on both the supply side and the demand side, interacting with each other. TFP in the economy as a whole increased much more rapidly than in any previous period (though in manufacturing the improvement over the interwar period was only moderate). In part this represented a catching up of accumulated arrears. In part it resulted from changes in business attitudes, facilitated by the jolt administered by World War II and manifested in increased sophistication in management and some redirection of talent and education. In part it resulted from faster and more broadly based technical progress throughout the world.

The predominantly high level of demand not only ensured that supply was taken up, but also contributed to the rate of growth of supply itself. It did this by encouraging capital accumulation and by stimulating the growth of TFP, particularly in the service sectors. Capital accumulation was a reinforcing element in growth, encouraged both by the rapid *growth* of output (permitting a correspondingly rapid growth of savings and also helping to keep up the marginal efficiency of investment) and by the high *level* of output. The process was a circular one in that the fast rate of growth of output, permitted by supply, was a contributing cause of the historically high rate of investment, which itself was a principal source of high demand (along with the growth in world trade and, probably, government commitment to the goal of full employment). The period thus had some of the characteristics of a business-cycle boom, but augmented and prolonged by an additional source of feedback not present in the textbook model of the business cycle, namely feedback through the supply side. Demand acted as a reinforcer of supply — as it had not done in the interwar period.

The generally buoyant level of world demand made an important contribution to the high average level of demand, compared with the past, and in that respect international trade acted as a benign reinforcer of fast growth. However, at the same time trends in the country's international position probably acted as a malignant reinforcer of the tendency to grow slowly *relative* to other countries: this tendency led to weakened competitiveness; hence to balance-of-payments trouble; hence to the distinctive British postwar cyclical pattern in which downswings (though not severe) lasted longer than upswings; and hence to ill-effects on confidence and on the growth of TFP compared with that enjoyed elsewhere. This ambiguous effect of foreign trade — favorable compared with the past, unfavorable compared with other countries — may be contrasted with its unambiguously adverse effect in the 40 years before 1914, when changes in Britain's competitive position tended to slow down its growth relative to its own past as well as relative to other countries.

GDP grew fast in the postwar period despite a rate of growth of labor input that was, primarily for demographic reasons, not only unprecedentedly low but declining; and the labor input per head of population was declining more rapidly than in earlier periods, with the exception of the period 1913–24. Labor shortage, due to this cause and to full employment, might in theory have either stimulated investment or discouraged it. In the event, it stimulated it. Such a response carried with it an inherent threat of diminishing returns to investment. The rate of capital accumulation did in fact begin to tail off in the course of the 1960's — in manufacturing earlier than in most other sectors — and the capital-output ratio began to show a marked tendency to rise after 1968. Thus indications of an end or at least a slowing down of the postwar boom were apparent well before the world recession that began in the course of 1973.

EPILOGUE: THE PERIOD SINCE 1973

Throughout this book we have deliberately avoided carrying the story beyond the watershed of 1973. Our approach has been based mainly on comparisons of cycle peaks, and there has been none worthy of the name since 1973. We have, moreover, been aware that nothing dates a work of history more surely than an attempt to bring its coverage up to the moment of writing. Let us, however, conclude with some brief and tentative remarks.

The recession since 1973 has been a world phenomenon. The falloff in the rates of growth of production and productivity relative to previous trend has been of the same order in most other industrial countries as in the United Kingdom, though their actual rates of growth have remained higher. Similarities between the United Kingdom and other countries in the impact of the recession on output have been more important than differences between them. Since both the causes and the consequences of the recession were worldwide, systematic discussion of them lies far beyond our scope. We can, however, usefully say something about what the magnitude of the change in the United Kingdom has been and consider how far it suggests that the historically high growth rate of 1951–73 was a flash in the pan.

Since 1973 Britain has suffered the severest setback to output *relative to previous trend* of any peacetime period since the middle of the nineteenth century. Real GDP in the late 1970's fell below the previous trend line by more than it did in the 1870's, the most severe recession before 1914; and a much longer time has passed without substantial signs of recovery than in the 1930's. Only the setback across World War I was more severe — albeit by quite a large margin.

The year 1979 saw the end of the limited upswing that began in 1975, following the absolute fall in real GDP in each of the two previous years. It therefore provides a convenient benchmark for the comparison of rates of growth of TFP, the variable that chiefly distinguished earlier periods from one another.

Between 1973 and 1979 the annual percentage rate of growth of TF_HP in the economy as a whole was about 0.7, compared with 2.3 in 1951–73; it was close to the average figure for the century before 1951 (0.8). Even less favorable is the comparison in manufacturing, where output fell absolutely between 1973 and 1979 and the absolute level of TF_HP remained about constant. The rate of growth of TF_HP in manufacturing averaged over the whole period from 1951 to 1979 was little higher than it was in the interwar period.

These comparisons are too gloomy as indicators of underlying trends in TFP. TFP has always been temporarily below trend in recession years, and 1979 was still a year of recession, as measured not only by unemployment, which may be an unreliable indicator, but also by survey data on the proportion of firms restricted in their output by lack of orders. It is obvious that in all countries the decline in demand played a large part in the setback to TFP, especially in the years immediately after 1973. However, the improvement in productivity in the limited recovery after 1975 was much less than would have been expected on the precedent of earlier postwar recessions. This has been true of most sectors in most countries. Admittedly, there has been no postwar precedent for a recession of such magnitude, and the possibility cannot be ruled out that the slowdown in the rate of growth of productivity in Britain and in other European countries was entirely cyclical in nature. That it was cyclical in *origin* is indeed much the most likely hypothesis. But whether it was cyclical in the sense of being speedily reversible is much less clear; there may have been a downward ratchet. This is suggested not only by the occurrence of certain supply-side bottlenecks, but also by the experience of the United States, where a similar slowdown in productivity growth occurred even though by 1978 unemployment was not abnormally high.

This has been taken to indicate either a decline in the underlying rate of growth of productivity or else a once-for-all reduction in the level of productivity. The reasons for such a change, if it has occurred, remain fundamentally unclear. Denison (1979a, 1979b), who has made the most thorough attempt at quantification of possible causes, found that the sum of the effects of the various possible causes he could identify fell far short of explaining the slowdown in productivity growth in the United States. The same appears to hold for the United Kingdom (Sheriff 1979). The whole matter is thus obscure. Even if it were agreed that the ultimate cause was some kind of downward ratchet effect brought about by the recession, the way in which it affected productivity would remain to be determined.

The exact extent of short-run excess supply in the late 1970's is not entirely relevant to the assessment of the long-run trend in TFP. Short-run bottlenecks have not been unknown in all recessions. Still less does the occurrence of a prolonged and severe recession as such imply a permanent fall in the underlying rate of growth of TFP — though in all bad recessions there have been people who drew this inference. However, prolonged setbacks to the rate of growth of TFP *have* occurred, most notably at the beginning of the twentieth century, so a recurrence cannot be ruled out on grounds of historical precedent.

Prediction is not part of our aim, and we shall not try to evaluate the effects of certain features of the post-1973 period that are completely new, like the rise in energy prices, British membership in the EEC, the exploitation of North Sea oil, or the possibility of persistent high inflation independent of the level of activity. More appropriate in the context of a historical study is to conclude with a few words on which of the principal forces making for historically fast growth in the United Kingdom in 1951–73 appear in the light of subsequent events to have been of a permanent kind, and which of a transitory kind.

(1) There is no convincing evidence that the speedup on the strictly technological side was other than permanent. This holds both for the world as a whole and for the United Kingdom. Though some of the United Kingdom's improvement over earlier periods came from catching up with improvements already in use abroad, the scope for such catching up did not diminish in the course of the postwar period, but if anything the reverse. Nor is there any reason to suppose that the improvement in the quality of management was other than permanent.

(2) The high average level of demand between 1951 and 1973 not only ensured the take-up of supply, but also contributed to the rate of growth of supply. High demand proved compatible with non-accelerating inflation until toward the end of the 1960's. This compatibility now appears to have been transitory. Given the determination of governments to try to stop inflation, it follows that the reinforcement to rapid growth that was derived from high demand (at home and abroad) must regretfully be deemed to have been transitory too. This does not mean that advances in the *level* of TFP achieved under that stimulus were such as to be lost, only that the more rapid trend *rate of growth* due to that cause was once-for-all.

(3) During almost the whole of the postwar period up to 1973 the investment-income ratio was rising. Such a trend could clearly not be maintained indefinitely. It is the feature of the postwar period most manifestly indicative of a long swing, providing some basis for the contention that a growth boom of record proportions, like the postwar one, was likely to be followed by a setback even apart from inflation.

These considerations suggest that part of the excess of the growth rate achieved in the postwar period over that achieved in earlier periods was due to causes that were transitory. They also suggest, however, that not all of it was of that nature, either in respect of the level of productivity attained as a result of the growth or in respect of the continuing growth rate itself.

Appendixes

Alternative Measures of Gross Domestic Product

Changes in real GDP at factor cost can be estimated in three ways: from the expenditure, income, and output sides. The estimates are broadly independent, though certain component series may be common to two or more of the aggregate estimates (e.g., the price series implied by the expenditure series estimated at both current and constant prices is used to deflate the current-price income series). In Feinstein 1972 all three estimates are available for 1870–1964, and the income- and output-side ones for 1855–70. The postwar estimates are those of the Central Statistical Office, published in *National Income and Expenditure*, UK [21], with the estimates for 1964–73 coming from the 1964–74 issue.

Our general policy in this study is to employ whichever estimate is most appropriate in each particular context. Thus, when considering the growth of output in individual sectors (as in Chapter 8), it is appropriate to use the output-side estimate of GDP in comparing the sectoral output indexes, since it derives from them. On the other hand, the growth of the components of final demand are most appropriately compared (in Chapter 10) with the growth of the expenditure-side estimates. Where there is no reason to choose one measure of GDP growth over another (e.g. in the analysis of GDP and GDP per man-year in Chapter 2), the geometric mean of the three measures (for 1856–73, the geometric mean of only the income and output measures) is employed.

The growth of GDP as measured from the three different sides is shown for our usual periods in Table A.1. Generally speaking, the comparison between the periods is qualitatively much the same whichever series is used, though the arithmetical changes differ slightly between the estimates. There is a slight tendency for the income-side estimate to grow more rapidly than the other two, the difference compared with the expenditure-side estimate being greatest in 1913–37, and that compared with the output-side estimate greatest in 1937–68 and before 1873. The differences between the three sets of growth rates tend to be greatest the shorter the period. This suggests that one or more of the underlying series may not estimate annual movements very accurately. There are a number of possible reasons for this. First, stock-building and stock appreciation are notoriously difficult to measure—indeed for the pre–1914 years only a very crude attempt was made to measure stock-building and stock appreciation was

TABLE A.1

Alternative Measures of the Growth of Gross Domestic Product at Factor Cost, 1856–1973

(Annual percentage growth rates)

Period	Expenditure-side estimate (1)	Income-side estimate (2)	Output-side estimate (3)	Geometric mean (4)
Peacetime phases:				
1856–1873	—	2.3%	2.0%	2.2%
1873–1913	1.9%	1.8	1.8	1.8
1924–1937	1.9	2.4	2.3	2.2
1951–1973	2.8	2.8	2.7	2.8
Wartime phases:				
1913–1924	−0.4	−0.1	0.2	−0.1
1937–1951	1.9	1.9	1.5	1.8
War and postwar phases:				
1913–1937	0.9	1.3	1.3	1.1
1937–1973	2.4	2.4	2.1	2.3
Post–WWII cycles:				
1951–1955	2.9	3.0	2.7	2.8
1955–1960	2.4	2.5	2.5	2.5
1960–1964	3.6	3.5	3.1	3.4
1964–1968	2.7	2.7	2.5	2.6
1968–1973	2.5	2.5	2.8	2.6
1856–1973	1.9%	2.0%	1.9%	1.9%

assumed to be zero — and yet they can be important for year-to-year changes in GDP measured from the expenditure and income sides. Second, a certain amount of linear interpolation was necessary for components of all series, especially in earlier periods. Third, some of the methods used to impart a cyclical pattern to certain components of the output series for pre-1914 years are rather speculative.*

There are so many weak elements in all three series that we cannot say unequivocally that one is better or worse than the others. We therefore regard the mean as being the best estimate because it incorporates all the information. It is

*See Feinstein 1972: 18–20 and Fuller 1970 for further discussion of the differences between the three estimates. The growth rates in column 4 of Table A.1 differ from those calculated from the compromise GDP estimate in Feinstein 1972: Table 6, column 4, for two reasons: the use of slightly different base years in combining the output indexes for individual sectors; and the use of the geometric mean rather than an arithmetic mean. The comparison of the growth rates for 1856–73 and 1873–1913 is further complicated by the different link year used for splicing the pre-1870 mean series to the post-1870 series (1873 in the present study, 1870 in Feinstein 1972). Despite these differences, the two estimates yield almost the same annual percentage growth rates of GDP; for the principal phases (six first rows of Table A.1) the only differences are in 1856–73 (2.1 in Feinstein 1972 compared with 2.2 here) and 1937–51 (1.7 in Feinstein 1972 compared with 1.8 here).

even possible that all three series are biased to much the same extent. For example, there might be a similar amount of underestimation of quality improvements in all three measures. Improvements in the quality of capital goods may not be fully reflected in either the index of production for the engineering industry or the real-fixed investment estimates; and the underestimation of the growth of the latter implies the overestimation of the growth of prices, and hence the underestimation of the growth of the income-side estimate of real GDP. Or again there may be a consistent underestimate of output growth because all three series are in effect base-weighted (or Laspeyres) indexes. The income series is actually a current-price series deflated by a current-weighted (or Paasche) price index, which comes to the same thing. No allowance is made for a consistent underestimate of output growth in any of the series.

The differences between the three series do not greatly hinder the analysis, though they are sometimes irritating. The main place where confusion may arise is in Chapter 8, in which output and productivity growth in the whole economy are disaggregated by sector. As noted above, the output series is the only one suitable for making comparisons with growth in individual sectors. But this of course is not always the same as the mean, and so there is an unexplained residual when the mean is regarded as the true estimate.

Another example of how the differences hinder the analysis is provided by the pre-1914 period. The estimates from both the expenditure and income side suggest a marked slowdown in GDP growth around the turn of the century; but such a trend is barely visible in the output-side estimates (Table L.1). The exact location of the so-called climacteric is therefore uncertain. This problem is discussed further in Appendix L.

The Measurement of Trend
Rates of Growth

There is no ultimate truth in the choice between alternative measures of trend rates of growth within periods, or in the demarcation of the periods. If the behavior of the system over time is irregular, there are bound to be different ways of summing it up. Moreover, the same measure is not necessarily appropriate for the two purposes for which economists have commonly used the concept of a trend rate of growth, namely as a summary of the actual behavior of output and as an indicator of the growth of productive potential.

Throughout this study, except where stated otherwise, the trend rate of growth of any series during a particular period is measured as the annual compound rate of growth between the first and last years of the period. This method ignores all the intervening years and therefore depends very heavily on the exact period chosen.

Wherever possible we have chosen periods such that the end-years are roughly comparable from a cyclical point of view. The chosen periods usually begin and end with years of high levels of activity (low unemployment), because the peak years provide the best approximation to productive potential, and are also easy to identify. Some peaks, of course, were stronger than others, and a comparison between peaks of different strength may not provide a very good measure of secular change. Whenever such a distortion might alter the conclusions to be drawn from the data, we have said so in the text, but in general the point can be forgotten.

There are strong practical and analytical reasons for using growth rates between end-years in preference to the alternative method of using growth rates derived by fitting an exponential trend to all the years in the period. In the first place, growth rates between end-years have a clear meaning, whereas fitted trends are a statistical artefact. In the second place, unlike fitted trends, growth rates between end-years allow consistency between the growth rates of disaggregated elements and the growth rates of their total, both for additive disaggregation (the sum of the output of different industries equals GDP) and for multiplicative disaggregation (employment times productivity equals production). And finally, they are, of course, less laborious to calculate.

TABLE B.1
Alternative Measures of the Trend Growth of Gross Domestic Product at Factor Cost, 1856–1973
(Annual percentage growth rates)

Period	Between end-years of period	Exponential trend fitted by least squares	Least squares R^2
Peacetime phases:			
1856–1913	2.0%	1.9%	0.99
1856–1873	2.2	2.1	0.97
1873–1913	1.8	1.8	0.98
1924–1937	2.2	1.8	0.80
1920–1938	1.9	2.0	0.88
1951–1973	2.8	2.8	0.99
1948–1973	2.8	2.8	0.99
Wartime phases:			
1913–1924	−0.1	−1.3	0.24
1937–1951	1.8	1.1	0.30

However, growth rates between end-years are not ideal measures, for the reasons stated above, and if substantial differences exist between them and fitted trend rates, their use requires to be justified. In the rest of this appendix we therefore compare the two types of measure.

Growth rates calculated in the two ways are shown in Table B.1, together with the corrected coefficient of determination of the least-squares trend. The GDP series is the mean of the output-, income-, and expenditure-side estimates, as in Table 2.1. The most obvious point that emerges is the great difference between peacetime and wartime phases. In the peacetime phases the growth rates calculated in the two ways are similar, and the fit of the least squares is good. In the wartime phases the fitted trend growth rates are much lower than the peak-to-peak rates, and the fit is poor.

The explanation for the wartime results is that in both cases the war occurred nearer the beginning of the period than the end. Since GDP as measured includes military expenditure, the level of GDP during the war years was high,* and this pulls up the fitted trend toward the beginning of each period. The result is that the first years of both phases, being prewar, are below the fitted trend, and the last years are above, thus causing the growth rates between end-years to be higher than the fitted trend rates.

In this study we are not really concerned with what happened during the wars, except insofar as postwar economic growth was affected. Growth over the transwar periods is interesting, not because of what was happening during those periods, but because it indicates the position of the economy at the beginning of

*Real GDP was higher throughout World War I than in 1924; and in World War II it was higher in one year (1943) than in 1951.

the ensuing peacetime periods compared with its position at the end of the previous peacetime periods. For this purpose, the growth rates between end-years are more suitable since they are not affected by abnormal wartime events, which are anyway only approximately reflected in the rough statistical estimates covering the war years.

Let us turn, then, to the peacetime phases. It can be seen from Table B.1 that comparisons between the phases lead to very similar conclusions whichever set of growth rates is used. The two measures are closest for the pre–World War I and post–World War II periods, for which the fits of the least-squares trends are very good. For the 1856–73 period the peak-to-peak rate of growth was slightly higher than the fitted-trend rate. Since 1873 is known to have been a stronger peak than 1856, 2.1 percent may be a better measure of the secular rate of growth in 1856–73 than 2.2 percent. For the 1873–1913 period there is, for all practical purposes, no difference between the two measures; in 1856–1913 as a whole the 0.1 percentage point difference associated with the weak peak of 1856 appears again.

Similarly, there is no difference to speak of for the postwar phase. Two sets of growth rates are shown: in addition to the one for the usual peak-to-peak period, 1951 to 1973, we show the rate for 1948 to 1973, since 1948 is the first year reasonably free of wartime distortions for which data are available. The end-to-end growth rates are the same for the two periods, even though 1948 was not a peak year. They are also the same as the fitted-trend growth rate. Furthermore, the $\bar{R}^2$'s are very high, indicating that the fluctuations were not severe, and the cycles are known to have been fairly regular. The 1951–73 peak-to-peak rate can therefore be held to be a good measure of postwar growth.

Two possible periods are used to represent "the interwar phase": 1924 to 1937, which begins and ends in years with similar levels of economic activity, and 1920 to 1938, which are the first and last interwar years for which reliable data exist. For 1924–37, the fitted-trend rate turns out lower, probably because the cyclical downswing of the 1930's tends to pull the trend line down. However, whereas the end-to-end rate of growth is lower for 1920–38 than for 1924–37, because 1920 was a boom year and 1938 was not, the use of fitted-trend growth rates makes 1920–38 appear to have been a period of more rapid growth than 1924–37. The explanation for this is probably that the inclusion of the period of fairly rapid growth from the recession of 1921 until 1924 more than compensates for the inclusion of the two years of 1920 and 1938 and tends to increase the slope of the trend line.

There are thus three reasonable alternative measures of the trend rate of growth in the interwar period: the fitted rate 1924–37, the fitted rate 1920–38, and the end-to-end rate 1924–37. (The end-year rate of growth between 1920 and 1938 cannot be considered reasonable, because the two years are not cyclically comparable.) Which is the best? The interwar period was marked by greater fluctuations than the other peacetime periods shown in Table B.1; this is reflected in the lower $\bar{R}^2$'s. Furthermore, there was only one major cycle, with a peak in 1929 and a trough in 1932, and this gives a rather lopsided appearance to the period and pulls down the fitted trend. The 1924–37 peak-to-peak growth rate is not affected by the cycles, and so probably represents more satisfactorily the secular rate of growth.

To sum up, differences between end-to-end growth rates and fitted growth rates are substantial only for the war periods. For our purposes, the end-to-end growth rates are the more appropriate ones for those periods. As far as concerns the small differences found for peacetime periods, the evidence of the fitted trends suggests that the end-to-end growth rate for 1856–73 is too high by 0.1 of a percentage point. No amendment is indicated for 1873–1913, 1924–37, or 1951–73.

It obviously follows from this that as far as total output is concerned we can use the end-to-end measures with a clear conscience. We have not repeated the exercise for all the other series we shall be considering, and no doubt there are cases when the end-to-end growth rates give a faulty indication of underlying trends. In the course of the study we try to avoid misleading ourselves and our readers in such cases by supplementing growth-rate data with charts of annual data and other summary measures.

The Total and Economically Active Populations of Great Britain, 1881-1973

This appendix presents the underlying population data for the analysis in Chapter 3 of the sources of changes in the economically active population (see especially Tables 3.5–3.8). Table C.1 gives a breakdown of the total population by age, sex, and (for females only) marital status for the census years from 1881 through 1966 and for 1973. Data on the economically active population, broken down in the same way (but with more detailed age groups), are shown in Table C.2 for the same years.* Finally, in Table C.3 age-, sex-, and (for females only) marital-specific participation rates are given.

The primary source of the 1881–1966 data was the *Census of Population*. Since the data refer to Great Britain, both the census of England and Wales and the census of Scotland were required. Four minor adjustments were made to the census estimates:

(1) The economically active population estimates for 1881–1911 were adjusted so that the totals agreed with those in Feinstein 1972: Table 11.8, column 1. This involved excluding farmers' daughters and other female relatives, and (in 1891 only) 100,000 other unoccupied women who were incorrectly classified as being in domestic service (see Feinstein 1972: 223 for details).

(2) The economically active population estimates for 1921 and 1931 were adjusted to arrive at the same age groups used in other years. This required splitting the 14–15 age group into separate groups, and (in 1931 only) splitting the 18–20 age group into 18–19 and 20 groups. Rough assumptions about the distribution of the economically active population within the larger groups were necessary for this exercise.

(3) The economically active population estimates for 1961 were adjusted for bias, using factors derived from the *British Labour Statistics Historical Abstract* (UK [48]: Table 109).

(4) Only a sample census was taken in 1966, and the resulting estimates of population and economically active population are commonly believed to have a downward bias. We therefore raised all data by 1.3 percent to roughly offset

---

*In the *Census of Population*, from which the estimates are derived, the economically active population was called the occupied population in 1881–1951.

this (following the correction adopted by the Department of Employment; see "Fall in the labour force," UK [44]). In order to bring the estimates for the 0–14 age group on to the same basis as those for other age groups (from the Census of Population Economic Activity Tables), estimates of visitors (from the Census of Population Usual Residence Table 4) had to be subtracted from estimates of enumerated population (and the resulting figures were then raised by 1.3 percent).

The 1973 figures, though not drawn from a census, are comparable. The economically active population data from "Labour force projections, 1976–1991," UK [46]: Table 3 were adjusted to include persons under 16 years old and to exclude members of the armed forces stationed abroad.

The population census estimates of economically active population differ from the central concept of the working population used in this study, which was derived from the population censuses in years up to 1914, from a variety of sources including the population censuses for interwar years, from the number of National Insurance cards in the postwar period up to 1971, and from the annual censuses of employment from 1971 on. The main differences are (1) the exclusion from the population census of members of the armed forces, seamen, and fishermen abroad on the day of the census and (2) the exclusion from the population census of students and irregular workers who did not work in the week preceding the census, but who carried insurance cards. The discrepancy because of these two differences was especially severe in 1961, and it makes it difficult to compare growth rates based on the two series over periods that begin or end in 1961. The population census estimates for 1961 are therefore not used in Chapter 3, and they appear in Tables C.1–C.3 for completeness only.

TABLE C.1

The Total Population of Great Britain by Age, Sex, and (Females Only) Marital Status, 1881–1973

(Thousands)

Age, sex, and marital status	1881	1891	1901	1911	1921	1931	1951	1961	1966	1973
Males:										
0–14	5,420	5,805	6,021	6,304	6,011	5,466	5,588	6,109	6,314	6,634
15–24	2,737	3,098	3,521	3,593	3,618	3,834	3,108	3,403	3,852	3,887
25–64	5,669	6,411	7,611	8,943	9,691	10,733	12,567	12,958	12,944	13,037
65 and over	613	689	749	914	1,103	1,425	2,187	2,317	2,480	2,862
Total	14,439	16,003	17,902	19,754	20,423	21,458	23,450	24,787	25,590	26,420
Married females:										
15–24	484	490	529	475	551	546	863	1,038	1,175	1,266
25–64	4,274	4,755	5,584	6,544	7,410	8,310	10,275	10,771	10,906	10,928
65 and over	241	275	295	374	474	636	1,093	1,261	1,388	1,620
Total	4,999	5,720	6,408	7,393	8,435	9,492	12,230	13,070	13,469	13,814
Unmarried Females:										
0–14	5,414	5,799	6,020	6,284	5,930	5,359	5,359	5,814	6,001	6,294
15–24	2,376	2,792	3,207	3,327	3,393	3,410	2,387	2,345	2,611	2,493
25–64	1,961	2,303	2,773	3,226	3,583	3,820	3,376	2,801	2,559	2,425
65 and over	521	611	690	847	1,006	1,256	2,053	2,468	2,646	2,940
Total	10,272	11,505	12,690	13,684	13,912	13,845	13,175	13,428	13,817	14,152

Source: Census of Population (for England and Wales and for Scotland), UK [52] (1881–1966); *Annual Abstract*, UK [53], *1974*: Tables 11, 14; supplemented by *British Labour Statistics Historical Abstract*, UK [48]: Table 109; R.C. on Population, 1950, UK [81]: 190–91, 203–4 (1881–1931).

TABLE C.2

The Economically Active Population of Great Britain by Age, Sex, and (Females Only) Marital Status, 1881–1973

(Thousands)

Age, sex, and marital status	1881	1891	1901	1911	1921	1931	1951	1961	1966	1973
Males:										
0–14	361	471	409	347	268	167	0	0	0	0
15–19	1,328	2,910	3,334	1,730	1,772	1,713	1,265	1,350	1,486	1,047
20–24	1,244			1,657	1,601	1,853	1,518	1,465	1,619	1,717
25–44	3,585	6,176	7,346	5,725	5,618	6,099	7,017	6,587	6,468	6,648
45–64	1,883			2,950	3,746	4,275	5,168	6,104	6,045	5,892
65 and over	451	452	460	520	650	683	681	565	584	532
Total	8,852	10,009	11,549	12,929	13,655	14,790	15,649	16,071	16,202	15,836
Females:										
0–14	236	290	227	197	165	144	0	0	0	0
15–19	1,011	2,034	2,288	1,297	1,415	1,456	1,229	1,256	1,354	908
20–24	780			1,154	1,203	1,343	1,106	1,002	1,078	1,142
25–44	1,146	1,927	2,085	1,829	1,910	2,167	2,659	2,744	3,104	3,431
45–64	577			739	860	1,000	1,802	2,537	3,170	3,464
65 and over	137	140	132	140	148	155	165	201	272	297
Total	3,887	4,391	4,732	5,356	5,701	6,265	6,961	7,740	8,978	9,242
Married females:										
15–24	—	—	—	57	70	102	316	428	512	591
25–64	—	—	—	635	643	833	2,312	3,417	4,540	5,289
65 and over	—	—	—	18	20	18	30	41	77	112
Total	—	—	—	710	733	953	2,658	3,886	5,129	5,992
Unmarried females:										
15–24	—	—	—	2,394	2,548	2,697	2,019	1,830	1,920	1,459
25–64	—	—	—	1,933	2,127	2,334	2,149	1,864	1,734	1,606
65 and over	—	—	—	122	128	137	135	160	195	185
Total	—	—	—	4,646	4,968	5,312	4,303	3,854	3,849	3,250

Source: Census of Population (for England and Wales and for Scotland), UK [52]; supplemented by "Labour force projections, 1976–1991," UK [46]; Table 3 (for 1973); *British Labour Statistics Historical Abstract*, UK [48]; Table 109. What we call the economically active population the censuses called the occupied population in 1881–1951.

TABLE C.3

Participation Rates by Age, Sex, and (Females Only) Marital Status, 1881–1973

(Percent)

Age, sex, and marital status	1881	1891	1901	1911	1921	1931	1951	1961	1966	1973
Males:										
0–14	6.7%	8.1%	6.8%	5.5%	4.5%	3.1%	0.0%	0.0%	0.0%	0.0%
15–24	94.0	93.9	94.7	94.3	93.2	93.0	89.5	82.7	80.6	71.1
25–64	96.4	96.3	96.5	97.0	96.6	96.6	97.0	97.9	96.7	96.2
65 and over	73.6	65.6	61.4	56.9	58.9	47.9	31.1	24.4	23.5	18.6
Total	61.3	62.5	64.5	65.5	66.9	68.9	66.7	64.8	63.3	59.9
Females:										
0–14	4.4	5.0	3.8	3.1	2.8	2.7	0.0	0.0	0.0	0.0
15–24	62.6	62.0	61.3	64.5	66.4	70.7	71.8	66.7	64.2	54.5
25–64	27.6	27.3	24.9	26.3	25.2	26.1	32.7	38.9	46.6	51.6
65 and over	18.0	15.8	13.4	11.5	10.0	8.2	5.2	5.4	6.7	6.5
Total	25.5	25.8	24.8	25.4	25.5	26.8	27.4	29.2	32.9	33.0
Married females:										
15–24	—	—	—	12.0	12.7	18.7	36.6	41.2	43.6	46.7
25–64	—	—	—	9.7	8.7	10.0	22.5	31.7	41.6	48.4
65 and over	—	—	—	4.8	4.2	2.8	2.7	3.3	5.5	6.9
Total	—	—	—	9.6	8.7	10.0	21.7	29.7	38.1	43.4
Unmarried females:										
0–14	—	—	—	3.1	2.8	2.7	0.0	0.0	0.0	0.0
15–24	—	—	—	71.9	75.1	79.1	84.6	78.0	73.5	58.5
25–64	—	—	—	59.9	59.4	61.1	63.7	66.6	67.8	66.2
65 and over	—	—	—	14.4	12.7	10.9	6.6	6.5	7.4	6.3
Total	—	—	—	34.0	35.7	38.4	32.7	28.7	27.9	23.0

Source: Calculated from Tables C.1 and C.2; economically active as percentage of total population.

APPENDIX D

Hours Worked

New estimates of hours worked in 11 benchmark years were prepared for this study. They refer to the hours actually worked after allowing for overtime, short-time, and part-time working; holidays; sickness; and strikes. The estimates and their sources are shown in Tables D.1 and D.2, and the methods used to arrive at them are outlined in this appendix.

We believe that the estimates of average hours worked per year are accurate enough to indicate the broad changes that have taken place over a number of years. However, some of the detailed components of the estimates are unreliable, and no doubt improvements could be made. This is especially true of the estimates for pre–World War I years.

The estimation of total hours worked required the separate estimation of seven variables:

	Variable	Column in Table D.1
(a)	Total in employment	(1)
(b)	Average hours worked per week by full-time workers	(2)
(c)	Percentage of part-time workers in the total in employment	(3)
(d)	Average hours worked per week by part-time workers	(4)
(e)	Average weeks lost per year due to holidays	(6)
(f)	Average weeks lost per year due to sickness	(7)
(g)	Average weeks lost per year due to strikes	(8)

Total hours worked can then be calculated in the following stages:

(h) Average hours worked per week
by all workers
$$(5) = \big[(2) \times [1 - (3)] + (4) \times (3)\big]/100$$
(i) Average weeks worked per
year
$$(9) = 52 - (6) - (7) - (8)$$
(j) Average hours worked per year $\quad (10) = (5) \times (9)$
(k) Total hours worked $\quad (11) = (1) \times (10)$

The definition of each of these variables should be clear from the name. One detail might be noted here. Absenteeism is in principle allowed for in the

565

TABLE D.1
The Total in Employment and Total Hours Worked per Year, 1856–1973

Year	Total in employment (Thousands) (1)	Average full-time hours per week (2)	Percentage of part-timers (3)	Average part-time hours per week (4)	Average hours per week (5)	Average weeks lost per year due to: Holidays (6)	Sickness (7)	Strikes (8)	Average weeks per year (9)	Average hours per year (10)	Total hours per year (millions) (11)
1856	12,170	65.00	–	–	65.00	–	–	–	49.00	3,185	38,760
1873	14,100	56.00	–	–	56.00	–	–	–	49.00	2,744	38,690
1913	20,310	56.40	–	–	56.40	1.42	1.70	0.07	48.81	2,753	55,913
1924	18,238	47.00	1.8%	24.50	46.60	2.11	2.19	0.08	47.62	2,219	40,475
1937	21,272	48.60	1.5	25.40	48.20	2.31	2.11	0.03	47.55	2,293	48,786
1951	23,589	45.63	4.1	20.15	44.59	3.13	2.45	0.01	46.41	2,071	48,856
1955	24,347	45.88	6.1	20.18	44.32	3.45	2.31	0.02	46.22	2,051	49,941
1960	24,823	44.75	8.6	20.89	42.69	3.56	2.35	0.02	46.07	1,969	48,879
1964	24,999	43.85	10.9	19.96	41.24	3.54	2.34	0.01	46.11	1,904	47,591
1968	24,854	42.16	12.8	19.85	39.31	3.84	2.31	0.03	45.82	1,804	44,832
1973	25,030	41.40	15.5	19.88	38.06	4.67	2.29	0.06	44.98	1,715	42,926

Source:

(1) See Appendix N.

(2) Principally *Department of Employment Gazette*, largely reprinted in *British Labour Statistics Historical Abstract*, UK [48]. Also, for 1856–1913: Clapman 1932: 667–68; Chief Inspector of Factories, UK [26], *1910*; R.C. on the Civil Service, UK [82], *1914*: 37 and Q. 36, 105–15; R.C. on the Coal Industry, UK [84]: 166; Select Committee on Early Closing of Shops, UK [91], especially Q. 629, 2568–73, 114–19. *For 1924–37, Fuel and Power Digest*, especially 1953, Table 30; Balfour Committee, UK [31]: 111–12; 19th *Abstract of Labor Statistics*, UK [64]; Select Committee on Shop Assistants, UK [92]; H. L. Smith et al. 1930–35; Klingender 1935: 89. *For 1951–73, New Earnings Survey*, UK [47]; *Digest of UK Energy Statistics*, UK [49]; *Time Rates of Wages and Hours of Work*, UK [68]; R.C. on the Civil Service, UK [83], *1955*; National Board for Prices and Incomes, UK [74], [75], [76]; Civil Service Clerical Association (n.d.); Industrial Society 1966; G. S. Bain 1970.

(3) *For pre-1914*, there were assumed to be no part-timers. *For 1924–37*, Chapman 1952. *For 1951–73*, estimates from *Census of Population*, UK [52], *1961, 1966*, and census of employment (for 1968, 1973) in *Department of Employment Gazette* and *British Labour Statistics Year Book*, UK [39].

(4) *For pre-1914*, there were assumed to be no part-timers. *For 1924–37*, Chapman 1952. *For 1951–73*, estimates from *Census of Population*, UK [52], *1961, 1966*, and *New Earnings Survey*, UK [47].

(6) *Manual workers: For pre-1914, Report of an Enquiry by the Board of Trade*, 1906, UK [51]. *For 1924–37*, rough estimates from various sources, including *Ministry of Labour Gazette*, March 1938, pp. 86–87, and Committee on Holidays with Pay, UK [30]. *For 1951–73, Time Rates of Wages and Hours of Work*, UK [68]. *Non-manual workers: New Earnings Survey*, UK [47]; Cameron 1965: 273–99; G. S. Bain 1970: 63–68.

(7) *For pre-1914*, A. L. Bowley 1919: 28. *For 1924–37*, rough estimates from *Report by the Government Actuary, 1955–56*, UK [97]: Table 7. *For 1951–73, Social Security Statistics*, UK [51]; Ministry of Pensions and National Insurance, UK [69], various years; and UK [70], *1964*: Tables A13, B13; *Report by the Government Actuary*, UK [97], [98], and others.

(8) *For 1893–1973, British Labour Statistics Historical Abstract*, UK [48]: Table 197.

Note: The definition of the working population changed in 1951 and 1964 (see Appendix N); the estimates of the total in employment (column 1) and total hours worked (column 11) are consistent with later years but not with earlier years. For the total in employment, the 1951 and 1964 estimates comparable with earlier years are 23,748 and 25,541, respectively. For the total hours worked, the comparable estimates are 49,110 and 48,559. Other columns are not significantly affected by the change in definition.

TABLE D.2

Total Hours Worked per Year, by Industry, 1924–1964

(Millions)

Industry	1924	1937	1951[a]	1951[b]	1955	1960	1964[c]	1964[d]	1968	1973
Sector										
Agriculture, forestry, fishing	3,288	2,829	3,013	2,745	2,658	2,362	2,014	2,216	1,779	1,426
Mining, quarrying	2,492	1,930	1,775	1,781	1,778	1,451	1,249	1,226	859	627
Manufacturing	13,333	16,054	18,473	17,152	17,984	17,867	17,520	16,687	15,611	14,430
Construction	1,819	2,858	3,332	3,368	3,515	3,685	4,123	3,997	3,788	3,710
Gas, electricity, water	438	652	791	791	821	788	847	853	798	627
Transport, communications	3,474	3,779	4,058	3,954	3,831	3,673	3,626	3,625	3,435	3,212
Distributive trades	5,023	6,984	5,074	5,456	5,925	6,297	6,384	6,157	5,466	5,192
Insurance, banking, finance	767	975	869	871	930	1,030	1,126	1,407	1,495	1,721
Professional and scientific services	1,790	2,245	3,612	3,241	3,453	3,739	4,006	4,038	4,444	4,645
Miscellaneous services	6,042	7,956	3,583	5,097	4,791	4,412	4,388	4,050	3,767	3,970
Public administration and defense	2,009	2,524	4,530	4,400	4,255	3,575	3,276	3,335	3,390	3,366
All sectors	40,475	48,786	49,110	48,856	49,941	48,879	48,559	47,591	44,832	42,926
Manufacturing										
Food, drink, tobacco	1,367	1,729	1,775	1,562	1,648	1,627	1,582	1,515	1,422	1,357
Chemicals and allied	475	588	1,004	963	1,026	1,065	995	932	876	845
Iron and steel	780	888	966	976	998	997	978	985	869	744
Electrical engineering	382	756	1,166	1,149	1,416	1,540	1,697	1,563	1,485	1,412
Mechanical eng., shipbuilding	1,621	1,876	2,822	2,942	3,194	3,165	3,142	2,844	2,805	2,470
Vehicles	901	1,349	2,232	1,558	1,883	1,886	1,770	1,752	1,557	1,483
Other metal industries	926	1,246	1,591	1,305	1,350	1,402	1,417	1,452	1,388	1,299
Textiles	2,747	2,645	2,236	2,250	2,001	1,745	1,562	1,463	1,249	1,061
Clothing and footwear	1,685	1,784	1,416	1,245	1,164	1,085	1,008	936	805	751
Bricks, pottery, glass, cement	492	701	727	727	761	731	744	713	650	597
Timber, furniture	589	761	716	694	679	660	641	626	633	644
Paper, printing, publishing	861	1,114	1,088	1,063	1,138	1,230	1,234	1,192	1,163	1,049
Leather and other manufacturing	507	617	734	718	726	734	750	714	709	718
All manufacturing	13,333	16,054	18,473	17,152	17,984	17,867	17,520	16,687	15,611	14,430

Source: See Table D.1.

[a]Comparable with interwar years.

[b]Comparable with 1955–64: there was a change in 1951 in both the definition of the economically active population (Table D.1) and the SIC.

[c]Comparable with 1951–60.

[d]Comparable with 1968–73: there was a change in 1964 in both the definition of the economically active population (Table D.1) and the SIC.

estimates of the average number of hours worked per week (both full-time and part-time), and not in the estimates of the average number of weeks worked per year.

The estimates for the three earliest years, 1856, 1873, and 1913, were made for the whole economy only; those for the two interwar years, 1924 and 1937, were broken down by industry; and those for the six postwar years, 1951, 1955, 1960, 1964, 1968, and 1973, were broken down by industry and sex. The industrial breakdown of total hours worked in 1924–73 is shown in Table D.2. The seven primary variables for each industry and, in postwar years, for each sex, are not shown here, but they have been used for some of the tables in the text (e.g. Table 3.13).

The following notes briefly outline the methods used for the seven primary variables.

(a) *Total in employment.* See Appendix N.

(b) *Average hours worked per week by full-time workers.* Separate estimates were made for broad groups of workers, and then weighted averages were obtained. The hours worked by full-time manual workers were estimated from Ministry of Labour inquiries, supplemented by information on a few specific industries (agriculture, coal mining, and railways). There were no satisfactory inquiries in the years before 1914, and so the actual hours worked by full-time manual workers were assumed to be two hours per week longer than the normal hours.* The full-time hours of non-manual workers were estimated on the basis of various scanty pieces of information relating to shop assistants, civil service clerks, and other categories of non-manual workers.

The main source for estimates of hours worked is the *Department of Employment Gazette.* Most of the relevant information is reprinted in *British Labour Statistics Historical Abstract 1886–1968.* Other sources used are shown in Table D.1.

The weights for combining the estimates of the average weekly hours worked by various groups of full-time workers were derived from the *Census of Population* either directly or indirectly using data in Routh 1965.

This method underestimates the average hours worked per week by full-time workers to the extent that there was any double job-holding, or moonlighting, to use the American term. No attempt was made to allow for moonlighting at any stage of the estimation of total hours worked per year, and hence our estimate of the total labor input is biased downward in all years on this account.

The bias is likely to be small, but only an order of magnitude can be indicated because of the conflicting evidence provided by three different sources. In the 1966 *Census of Population* 3.3 percent of males in employment in Great Britain, and 1.7 percent of females, were found to have a second job (as cited in Alden

---

Normal weekly hours represent the period recognized, in agreements or by custom, as the basis for the payment of the weekly wage rate. It is exclusive of mealtimes. *Actual* weekly hours may exceed or fall below this according to the amount of overtime or short-time working.

1971: Table 2; the census estimate was not officially published). In a survey in Midlothian in 1968, Alden found a proportion of 5.8 percent (males and females together); he suggests (p. 104) that part of the discrepancy between this figure and the 2.7 percent found in the 1966 census resulted from a higher rate of admission among moonlighters in the Midlothian survey. It was estimated from the Family Expenditure Survey that 6.2 percent of males and 9.1 percent of females had second jobs in 1970.* Finally, the *General Household Survey* found that multiple-job holders were 3.1 percent of all workers in 1971 and 1972 (3.5 percent for males and 2.6 percent for females in 1972), and 4 percent in 1974 (4 percent for males and 3 percent for females). (UK [77]; the relevant question was not asked in the 1973 survey.) It is difficult to believe that the discrepancies between the various sources are all due to changes over time. More likely than not, they are due to inaccurate responses and to differences in definition (for example, the census recorded only moonlighting that occurred in the week ending April 23, 1966, whereas the Midlothian and Family Expenditure surveys in principle recorded moonlighting at any time during the year).

To illustrate the order of magnitude of the bias arising from the exclusion of moonlighting, we assume that in 1964 5 percent of males and 7.5 percent of females had second jobs. We assume further that on average moonlighters worked eight hours per week at their second jobs.† These assumptions imply that our estimate of total hours worked per year in 1964 should be raised by 0.9 percent for males and 1.7 percent for females. ‡ In the absence of any information referring to years before 1966 it is not possible to make similar estimates for earlier years.

The failure to allow for moonlighting in the estimates of total hours worked may bias the interperiod comparison of labor input growth. Though the evidence is inadequate, most writers believe that moonlighting expanded during the postwar period, at least until the 1960's, after which there may have been little change. The biggest error from this source in our measure of the growth of labor input is probably therefore in the period 1951–64. However, there are two reasons for believing that this point is not important quantitatively at the economy-wide level. (1) As shown in the preceding paragraph, the underestimate of the total labor input in the mid-1960's on this account was probably little more than 1 percent. Assuming there had been no moonlighting in 1951, the downward bias in the 1951–64 growth rate would be only 0.1 percent per

*UK [45]: Table 1. An estimate for males and females together for 1969 of 7.1% is also given (Table 3), for comparison with the 1970 figure for males and females together of 7.4%.

†In the Midlothian survey 38.7% worked 0–5 hours, 16.1% 11–15 hours, and 6.3% over 15 hours (Alden 1971: Table 12). In the Family Expenditure Survey 70.2% of males and 77.9% of females in 1969 worked 1–8 hours, 25.2% of males and 14.7% of females 9–20 hours, and 4.6% of males and 7.4% of females over 20 hours (UK [45]: Table 8).

‡These figures were calculated by multiplying the proportion of moonlighters by the ratio of eight hours to the average hours worked per week by all workers (both full- and part-time) in 1964.

year. And (2) it is not even obvious that there was less moonlighting in 1951 than in 1964. On the one hand, full-timers worked fewer average hours in 1964 than in 1951, and there were more part-timers, so that on both accounts workers had more time in which to do a second job. On the other hand, real incomes were higher, so that there was less financial incentive (unless income *aspirations* were even higher) to seek a second job.

Moonlighting tends to be concentrated in a few sectors. In Midlothian in 1968, for example, Alden (1977: Table 7) found that almost 60 percent of second jobs were as teachers (19 percent), in entertainment (29 percent), or as painters and decorators (10 percent). In the United Kingdom in 1969, 43 percent of second jobs were in the distributive trades, 11 percent in professional services, and 24 percent in miscellaneous services ("Family expenditure survey," UK [45]: Table 5; these figures refer only to workers who were employees [not self-employed] in their main jobs). The bias might therefore be more serious in particular sectors. But even if one assumes that 50 percent, for example, of moonlighters in 1964 were in the distributive trades, the downward bias in that sector is only 4.4 percent. The 1951–64 growth rate of the labor input in the distributive trades would be underestimated by at most 0.3 percent, and in other sectors the bias would be less.

The failure to allow for moonlighting in the labor statistics carries over to the output statistics in those sectors, such as professional and miscellaneous services, where output growth is measured by employment growth. Productivity growth is therefore less likely to be estimated inaccurately in these sectors on this account than output growth or employment growth.

(c) *Percentage of part-time workers in the total in employment.* Because the *Census of Population* concept of part-time work is broader than that employed for Ministry of Labour inquiries,* the present estimates of average hours worked per week for years up to 1964 may be biased downward to the extent that the estimates of average hours worked per week by full-time workers have already been reduced by the inclusion in the samples on which the estimates were based of workers who would be classified as part-time workers according to the *Census of Population* concept. No attempt has been made to correct for this potential source of bias, but rough tests suggest that it is not serious.

(d) *Average hours worked per week by part-time workers.* The same assumptions about the relationship between the hours worked by part-time workers and those worked by full-time workers as were made by Chapman (1952) were used for the estimates for 1924 and 1937. As with the estimate of average full-time hours, no allowance was made for the holding of second jobs by part-timers.

(e) *Average weeks lost per year due to holidays.* The holiday entitlements of manual workers covered by collective agreements were published for the post-

*In the population censuses of 1961 and 1966 part-time appears to mean anything that is not normally full-time; in the 1968 *New Earnings Survey* it means working less than 30 hours per week (see *British Labour Statistics Historical Abstract*, UK [48]: Table 143).

war years by the Ministry of Labour. For interwar years the information is less complete, and some rough estimation from various sources was required. No comparable figures for non-manual workers were available, but it appears that their holidays were normally longer than those of manual workers, and that they benefited from longer holidays to the same extent. (*New Earnings Survey*, UK [47]; Cameron 1965: 273–99; G. S. Bain 1970: 63–68.) For pre-1914 years there was only a single estimate for manual workers derived from a Board of Trade inquiry. This was assumed to apply to 1913. For 1856 and 1873, since there was also no information on time lost due to sickness and strikes, it was assumed that the total time lost due to all three causes was slightly less than in 1913: 3 weeks, as compared with 3.2 weeks.

(f) *Average weeks lost per year due to sickness.* The basic source of sickness data was National Insurance statistics. Time lost due to accidents or prescribed diseases qualified for Industrial Injury Benefit, and statistics were available in the annual *Reports* of the Ministry of Pensions and National Insurance. Time lost due to other sickness qualified for Sickness Benefit, and statistics were taken from Government Actuary sources. Again the information was less satisfactory for interwar than for postwar years, and again the only pre–1914 estimate, referring to sickness among members of a benevolent society in 1910, was assumed to apply to 1913.

The figures of time lost due to other sickness exclude absences of less than four workdays. The inaccuracy introduced by this omission is probably not too serious because the Ministry of Labour estimates of actual hours worked by manual workers — used for the estimates in (b) above — exclude time lost through sickness (or absenteeism) if the person is absent for only part of the week. A short illness of only a few days will therefore be reflected in our figures in a shorter working week rather than under sickness.

(g) *Average weeks lost per year due to strikes.** Use was made of the Ministry of Labour's annual series of the total number of working days lost per year due to industrial disputes. The series commenced in 1893, and so it was possible to estimate the average number of weeks lost due to strikes in 1913, but not in 1856 or 1873.

*For convenience the reference is to strikes; in fact the desired concept, and that which the statistics measure, is all industrial disputes (including lock-outs, etc.).

The Educational Level
of the Labor Force

AVERAGE YEARS OF SCHOOLING

Estimates of the average number of years' schooling (AYS) of the labor force (Table E.1) have been constructed by estimating the number of years' schooling of each cohort (Table E.2) and multiplying this by the cohort's representation in the labor force. The estimates relate to males in England and Wales, but for certain cohorts data had to be used that relate to the schooling of females as well.

Data on the terminal education age of cohorts born in 1877 and later are available form the censuses of 1951 and 1961. These have been translated into estimates of AYS in an unpublished paper by Mrs. Rose Knight, kindly made available to us by the author. We use Mrs. Knight's estimates, adjusted (see below) for attendance rates, for those cohorts. In Figure 4.1 and Table E.2, interpolations are used to give a breakdown into five-year bands for cohorts born in the 1877–1916 period. In calculating the AYS of the labor force, data based on the 1951 census are used except for 1961, where the 1961 census data are used.

For pre-1877 cohorts our estimates are based on the data (of varying degrees of reliability), available from sources indicated in Table E.1, on the numbers in school in given age-bands at particular dates. These are converted into AYS figures by assuming that the average number of years' schooling received between ages m and n by cohorts born in years $t - n$ through $t - m$ is equal to the proportion of children aged m through n in school in year t relative to the total number of children aged m through n in year t, multiplied by $(n - m + 1)$. (This method involves assuming that the proportion of a given cohort in school at year t is constant between year $t - (n - m)/2$ and $t + (n - m)/2$; it also disregards any differences between the number of children aged $m, m + 1, \ldots n$ in year t.)

For the pre-1881 cohorts, attendance at Sunday school was given one-fifth weighting for persons attending Sunday school only, and zero weighting if they also attended day school.

All figures are adjusted for any daily attendance rate below 90 percent (taken as full attendance).

TABLE E.1

Average Number of Years of Schooling of Males in England and Wales by Birth Cohort, 1800–1946

Birth year	Years of schooling[a]	Birth year	Years of schooling[a] (1951 census)	(1961 census)
1805 or before	2.3[b]	1877–1886	7.2	—
1806–1815	2.7[b]	1887–1896	8.3	8.6
1816–1825	3.6[b]	1897–1906	9.1	9.1
1826–1835	4.2[b]	1907–1916	9.4	9.5
1836–1845	4.7	1917–1921	9.6	
1846–1851	5.0	1922–1926	9.6	9.8
1852–1856	5.2	1927–1931	9.7	10.1
1857–1861	5.3	1932–1936	9.9[c]	10.5
1862–1866	5.4	1937–1941	—	10.6
1867–1871	6.1[b]	1942–1946	—	10.3[c]
1872–1876	6.6[b]			

Source: Years of schooling, Committee of Council on Education, UK [27]; *Scholars in England and Wales*, UK [55]; *Table on General State of Education*, UK [56]; census of England and Wales for 1851, 1861, 1871; Knight 1966. Attendance, *Statistical Abstract*, UK [7], *1900–1937*; Committee of Council on Education, UK [27]; R.C. on the State of Popular Education, UK [85]; R.C. on the Working of the Elementary Education Acts, UK [87].
Note: The 1806–15 and 1826–35 figures are interpolations.
[a]Adjusted for attendance.
[b]Males and females.
[c]Affected by non-completion of education at census date.

TABLE E.2

Average Number of Years of Schooling of the Male Labor Force of England and Wales, 1871–1961

Year	Years of schooling	Year	Years of schooling
1871	4.21	1921	7.41
1881	4.69	1931	8.14
1891	5.32	1951	9.21
1901	6.02	1961	9.78
1911	6.75		

Source: See Table E.1 and text.

UNIVERSITY GRADUATES

Data on the number of graduates in 1921–61 were taken from the Robbins Committee report (UK [29]). Data for 1908–20 were derived from returns of individual universities. Graduations have been assigned to birth cohorts on the basis of estimates of the normal age of graduation. To minimize the difficulty of allotting to age cohorts the graduations in the early postwar period (affected by war and national service), the cohorts born in the 15-year period 1917–31 have been taken together. The figures in the second column of Table 4.4 are the proportion of graduates to the total number in a cohort reaching the normal age of graduation (not the proportion of graduates to the number of births in the cohort). The figures in the fourth column of Table 4.4 were obtained by multiplying the proportion of the age group in the labor force by the cohort graduation percentages, adjusted to allow for the fact that the percentage of graduates *in the working force* in cohorts below the graduation age is zero, not the graduation percentage for the cohort. (This last adjustment explains how it is possible for the proportion of graduates in the labor force in 1931 to be below any of the cohort graduation percentages.) The estimates derived by this method for the proportions of graduates in the labor force in 1951 and 1961 may be compared with the Robbins estimates (p. 126) of 1.7 percent for 1951 and 2.3 percent for 1961. The differences arise mainly because the Robbins estimate relate to the proportion of graduates in the labor force of age 20 or over, not the proportion of graduates in the entire labor force. There are also minor differences of definition and coverage.

The Measurement of the Capital Stock

The problem is how to weight heterogeneous capital goods in calculating the total at any point in time. This is related to more general problems about the production function, which are discussed in Chapter 7 and Appendix I.

The choice of measure depends on the purpose. In the present context the chief purpose is to measure the contribution of increases in capital to increases in production. The principle is therefore as far as possible to weight different capital goods according to their efficiency in production in the base year, so that the hypothetical removal or addition of one unit of capital, so measured, would have had the same effect on output whatever physical form the one unit took. Capital goods of the same physical type but of different ages should be treated as different capital goods and separately weighted, if age affects efficiency. The weight attributed on this principle to a capital good of given type and age conforms to the rental it could have earned in the base year. Distortions of the ordinary index-number kind arise insofar as the relative efficiency of different capital goods of given age differs between the current year and the base year; these can be minimized by constructing the index of capital on a chain basis (Champernowne 1953–54).

None of the actually available measures of capital corresponds perfectly to this description, and it is a question of which comes nearest to it and what the biases are likely to be. There are two principal measures available.

The *gross* stock, G, is defined as the aggregate, for all assets, of the flows of gross fixed investment in each type of asset, measured at constant base-year prices, cumulated over a period equal to the assumed life of the asset. No allowance is made for wear and tear, obsolescence, or age. Assets thus remain in the stock at their original (constant-price) valuation until the end of their assumed lives, at which date they are assumed to be scrapped (retired) and are removed from the stock. As with any index using constant prices, the results are liable to be affected by the choice of the base year. For series covering a long period of time, the use of a single base year is inappropriate. The series is therefore chained together out of series for subperiods, each using different base years. The constant base-year prices refer in principle to the cost of production of the different classes of capital goods in the base year.

The *net* stock, N, is measured by deducting from accumulated gross investment the accumulated amount of depreciation (including obsolescence, etc.) that has been written off assets still in the capital stock. Depreciation has to be estimated on the basis of assumptions about the life of the assets and of some conventional method for spreading the total over this life.

The two measures G and N thus differ in the relative weight given to capital of different ages. The assumption implied in using the gross stock as a measure of input is that the asset makes the same contribution to output throughout its allotted life. For some assets, such as buildings or roads, this may be a broadly reasonable assumption, even though the asset will require increased expenditure on maintenance and repairs as it gets older, thus reducing profits but not output (value-added).* For other assets, such as machinery or vehicles, it would probably be more appropriate to assume that the contribution to output diminishes over time because of physical deterioration. Such a diminution is implied by the deduction of depreciation, as in N.

This is, however, quite an arbitrary measure for the purpose of allowing for deterioration. The accountant's concept of depreciation is designed to give an estimate of the net value of an asset corresponding to the present value of the unexpired services that it is expected to yield in the future. This way of valuing an asset is appropriate for certain purposes, such as calculating the rate of profit, but there is no presumption that the value of an asset so calculated will decline over time at the same rate as its current usefulness as an input in production. In fact there is some presumption that it will not, since the decline in an asset's value over its life is partly due to the decline in the number of years for which it is expected to remain in service, and this is irrelevant to the value of its current contribution to production. It may just happen, however, that the depreciation conventions used—straight line or diminishing balance—do give a roughly appropriate measure of the contribution of two assets that had the same (base-year) cost of production but are of different ages; or at least they may give a better measure than is had by assuming that the contributions of the two assets are equal, as is assumed by the gross stock measure of capital. This would provide a case for preferring N as a measure to G.

Physical deterioration is not the only reason for which it may be appropriate to give a higher relative weight to newer capital than is done in G. The price deflators used in the series for investment at constant prices may have a systematic tendency to understate the reduction in cost and/or improvement in the quality of capital goods that occurs over time. One possible source of error is statistical. The price indexes may simply be biased. The bias arises most plainly where price indexes of capital goods are derived from the unit cost of labor and materials and therefore fail to take account of improvements in productivity in the capital goods industries. The same bias arises in cases where there is an im-

---

*Where the repair work is done by an outside contractor, value-added will be reduced in the industry owning the asset, but increased by a corresponding amount in the contracting industry.

provement over time in the average quality of the capital goods produced, and the higher quality goods are more expensive to produce than the lower quality ones in the base year, and therefore should be more heavily weighted, but the price data relate to units, such as tons of machinery, that do not distinguish higher and lower quality goods. Another possible source of error is conceptual. The relative cost of two types of capital goods will not necessarily conform to their relative efficiencies unless they are both actually being produced and sold. A new type of capital good may supersede an old one, so that the old one ceases to be produced. The (hypothetical) *cost* of producing the old one in the base year then overestimates its *efficiency*, and the proper measure is not its cost of production, but the price it would fetch, which will be lower.

The capital-stock data derived by accumulating investment at supposedly base-year prices may thus underestimate the increases in the capital stock that have taken place in the later years, and a correction will then be required. In order to meet this problem, in particular as it relates to quality improvements, Solow (1960) has proposed an alternative measure of capital, J, differing from both G and N. This "vintage" concept of the capital stock is derived by multiplying each year's gross investment by a term that increases over time at a rate corresponding to the estimated rate of quality improvement ("embodied" technical progress) and then accumulating the resulting augmented gross-investment series, subject to deduction in respect of physical deterioration of assets over time. There is, naturally, no way of directly estimating the appropriate augmentation factor, which in principle should measure, not the rate of quality improvement as such, but the extent of the quality improvement that fails to be captured by the available constant-price investment data. The estimates of J that have been produced for the United States have been admittedly based on arbitrary assumptions.

Since J cannot be calculated, the question may be asked how far N captures the features that J was designed to bring out. N and J are alike in giving more weight to more recently constructed capital goods than to older ones. N does this by writing down assets as they grow older; J does it by writing down older assets for physical deterioration and writing up the value of the more recent years' investment for improvement in quality. If the rate at which capital is depreciated in the calculation of N is equal to the rate of decline in its efficiency due to deterioration and obsolescence combined, it can be shown that in principle J and N give the same relative weight as each other to capital of different vintages, but that J grows more rapidly over time at a rate reflecting the rate of embodied technical progress.* Write t = current date; v = date of construction of capital (vintage); θ = rate of depreciation used in calculating N; δ = rate of

---

*This assumes that depreciation is calculated on the declining-balance method, as is most consistent with the concept of an exponential rate of embodied technical progress. In practice most of our data on N calculate depreciation on the straight-line method, as mentioned below. For further discussion of the concept of J, see Solow 1962; and for its relation to N, see Hickman 1965; Conlisk 1966.

physical deterioration of capital; λ = rate of embodied technical progress, defined such that $e^{\lambda v}$ units of equipment of v are equivalent in efficiency to $e^{\lambda(v+\epsilon)}$ units of equipment of vintage $(v - \epsilon)$. Then

$$N(t) = \int_{-\infty}^{t} e^{-(t-v)\theta} I(v) \, dv$$

$$J(t) = \int_{-\infty}^{t} e^{-(t-v)\delta + \lambda v} I(v) \, dv = e^{\lambda t} \int_{-\infty}^{t} e^{-(t-v)(\delta+\lambda)} I(v) \, dv$$

If $\theta = \delta + \lambda$, then $J(t) = e^{\lambda t} N(t)$.

Thus, whereas J as a measure takes account of changes in the efficiency of the capital stock due to changes in its average vintage (date of construction), N takes account of changes in efficiency due to changes in capital's average age (number of years since date of construction). In steady growth the average vintage becomes more recent, but the average age does not change; J therefore rises more rapidly than N, but G and N rise at the same rate. As far as the rate of growth of the capital stock is concerned, it will then not make any difference whether N or G is used as a measure, so long as the economy is in steady-state growth. But outside steady growth — in other words in the normal real-life situation — significant changes in the average age may take place, and these will be reflected in changes in the ratio of N to G. Broadly speaking, the more rapid the rate of growth, the greater the proportion of the capital stock that is of recent origin and therefore relatively little depreciated; the greater, therefore, the ratio of N to G.

Assume that all assets have the same life, T years; that gross investment grows at a steady proportional annual rate g; and that depreciation is calculated on the straight-line principle. Write t = current year, N = net stock of capital, G = gross stock of capital, A = average age of gross capital stock.

Then it can be shown that, for values of $gT < 2$, which cover the relevant range, approximate values of N/G and A are given by

$$\frac{N}{G} = \frac{1}{2} + \frac{gT}{12}$$

$$A = T \left(1 - \frac{N}{G} \right) = T \left(\frac{1}{2} - \frac{gT}{12} \right)$$

N/G is thus an increasing function of g, and A is a decreasing function of g. N/G and A are both increasing functions of T. (Goldsmith 1962: 17–28, 71–73, 100–104.)

In the more general case, where g is not constant and T differs between classes of assets and over time, the results are likely to be much more complicated. It follows from the definition of N and G that

$$R_t > R_{t-1}$$

if

$$\frac{I_t - D_t}{N_{t-1}} > \frac{I_t - S_t}{G_{t-1}}$$

where D = depreciation and S = scrapping. Since $N < G$, a high level of I will raise N proportionately more than G, and so will raise R, unless $D > S$ by a sufficient extent to compensate.

If the average age of capital is falling, the rate of growth of G will underestimate the rate of increase of the productive capacity of the capital stock, if the difference in age is accompanied by an improvement in quality. There is no presumption that, by taking the rate of growth of N instead, we shall be getting the right degree of adjustment, but the difference between the rates of growth of N and G will indicate the direction in which the adjustment should be made.

Insofar as both G and N underrate quality improvement, our series will underestimate the rate of growth of K, overestimate the rate of increase in the prices of capital goods, and overestimate the rate of growth of TFP; they will also transfer to consumer goods industries increases in TFP that properly belong to capital goods industries.

To sum up. It is unclear whether G or N gives a better measure of the rate of growth of the capital stock in efficiency units. Both measures have therefore been referred to where appropriate. Data on G have been referred to much more frequently than data on N, because they are available in much more detail. The merit of N is that it takes account, albeit in a rather arbitrary fashion, of changes in the average age of capital. This is useful because the direct data available on average age are very limited. Neither G nor N, however, properly takes account of quality improvements not allowed for in the underlying data.

Another possible measure of the capital input should be mentioned. Given correct foresight, the expected relative efficiencies of assets, which entrepreneurs equate at the margin to relative costs at the time when the assets are acquired, are a discounted average of relative efficiencies over the lifetimes of the assets. But they are not necessarily equal to the relative contributions to the productive process made by the assets at any given point of time, and it is the latter that is relevant to TFP. More specifically, long-lived assets will have a higher capital value (cost) in relation to current contribution to production in any one year than short-lived ones. On these grounds, Griliches and Jorgenson (1966) have proposed that capital input should be measured, not by G or N, but by "capital services," in which assets are weighted according to their gross earnings (including depreciation) in the base year. This is sound in principle, but only very crude approximations can be made from the available data to the earnings attributable to different classes of assets. Chiefly for this reason, we have not adopted this procedure. Such data as are available suggest it would not greatly alter the measured growth rate of the capital stock. Estimates of total domestic capital were in fact constructed by weighting separately in this manner four main classes of capital, namely, dwellings; other buildings and works; plant, machinery, and vehicles; and inventories. The growth of the resulting index did not differ significantly from that of our usual capital index in which these classes of capital are weighted by their values.

There are two possible refinements to the above procedure for measuring the capital input:

(1) The one-hoss-shay assumption that an asset is retired at the end of its expected service life might have been replaced by the assumption that retirements are distributed in some way around the average expected life. This is now done by the Central Statistical Office and incorporated in the Blue Book estimates of the gross stock used in the present study for 1964–73 (Griffin 1975). A comparison of the revised and original estimates suggests that the differences between capital stock estimates based on alternative retirement assumptions are negligible, and a similar conclusion follows from U.S. experience (Creamer 1972). Accordingly, no attempt was made to apply this alternative procedure to the pre-1964 estimates.

(2) Alternative formulas for estimating depreciation and hence the net capital stock might have been attempted. There is something to be said for the declining-balance formula rather than the straight-line formula underlying our estimates, because the former implies the reasonable assumption that an asset's ability to contribute to output decreases most rapidly in absolute terms near the beginning of its service life. Again the U.S. evidence indicates that alternative formulas would make little difference in practice (Creamer 1972: 68).

The Age of the Capital Stock

As noted in Chapter 5, average age of the gross fixed capital stock is a function of the assumed lives of the assets and of the rate of growth of investment. The growth of the stock was discussed in Appendix F. The lengths of lives assumed for the principal types of assets are shown in Table G.1.

In principle it is possible to calculate the average age of the gross fixed capital stock when it has been estimated by aggregating capital-formation series over the assumed service lives of the assets, and this has been done for 1938 and the postwar years. The age distribution of the gross capital stock in manufacturing (excluding textiles) and construction at the ends of 1938, 1948, and 1962 is shown in Table G.2. (A similar age distribution of the stock in the other main sectors of the economy at the end of 1961 is given in Dean 1964: Table 9.) The implied average ages of the stocks at those dates are given in Table G.3.

TABLE G.1

Assumed Life of Principal Types of Asset, 1856–1973

(Years)

Type of asset	1856–1913	1920–1938	1948–1973
Buildings and Works			
Dwellings, public buildings, and railway permanent way	100	100	100
Industrial and commercial buildings	80	80	80
Agricultural buildings and works	50	100	
Other buildings and works	60 or 80	60 or 80	63[a]
Plant, vehicles, ships, etc.			
Plant and machinery	30	30	33[b]
Ships	20 or 30	20	20 or 25
Road vehicles	8	8	10

Source: Dean 1964; *Sources and Methods*, 1968 UK [20]: 386; Feinstein (forthcoming).

[a] The weighted average (in 1958) of lives of 40, 60, and 75 years assumed for separate categories.

[b] The weighted average (in 1958) of lives of 16, 19, 25, 34, and 50 years assumed for separate types of plant and machinery in manufacturing, construction, and the distributive trades and other services (see Dean 1964: 346). For all plant and machinery the weighted average in 1958 was 30.

TABLE G.2

Age Distribution of the Gross Fixed Capital Stock in Manufacturing
(Excluding Textiles) and Construction, 1938, 1948, and 1962

(Percent)

Period in which capital was invested	Buildings, plant, and machinery[a]			Plant and machinery[a]		
	1938	1948	1962	1938	1948	1962
1850–1859	0.1%					
1860–1869	2.6	0.2%				
1870–1879	4.6	3.3				
1880–1889	3.3	2.1	0.8%	0.6%		
1890–1899	7.7	2.7	1.4	7.3	0.3%	
1900–1909	10.4	5.3	2.3	8.5	2.3	
1910–1919	15.9	7.8	3.1	17.2	5.6	0.9%
1920–1929	26.7	17.2	5.6	29.9	17.1	2.4
1930–1939	28.7	25.5	12.4	36.5	29.9	12.4
1940–1949		35.9	21.8		44.8	24.9
1950–1959			36.7			41.8
1960–1962			15.9			17.6
Total	100.0%	100.0%	100.0%	100.0%	100.0%	100.0%
Value of year-end stock in £ billions at 1958 prices	8.03	11.17	19.81	4.51	6.54	12.60

Source: Dean 1964 and other data.
[a]Excluding vehicles.

TABLE G.3

Average Age of the Gross Fixed Capital Stock in
Manufacturing (Excluding Textiles) and Construction,
1938, 1948, and 1962

(Years)

Year	Buildings, plant, and machinery[a]	Plant and machinery[a]
1938	22.8	16.5
1948	20.2	13.8
1962	17.4	13.2

Source: Calculated from Table G.2.
[a]Excluding vehicles.

A similar calculation covering the period 1960–74 is given in Table G.4. These estimates are derived from the latest Central Statistical Office perpetual inventory model (Griffin 1975).

The average age of the manufacturing gross capital stock fell both across World War II and in the early postwar period. As can be seen in Table G.2, 29 percent of the gross fixed stock was over 29 years old in 1938, against only 21 percent in 1948. Similarly, in comparing 1962 with 1948, it can be seen that there was relatively less old capital and relatively more new capital in 1962. The

TABLE G.4

Analysis by Age of the Gross Fixed Capital Stock in Manufacturing, 1960–1974

(Percent)

Age in years	1960	1965	1970	1974
5 or less	23%	24%	24%	22%
6–10	18	19	19	19
11 or more	59	57	57	59
Total	100%	100%	100%	100%

Source: Griffin 1976a: Appendix C.
Note: Gross capital stock here covers all fixed assets.

TABLE G.5

Classification of Iron and Steel Plant, 1955, 1960, and 1965

Year	Thousands of tons	Percentage classified as:			Unclassified
		A	B	C	
1955	57,180	32.2%	45.6%	19.3%	2.9%
1960	75,890	49.8	38.3	10.2	1.7
1965	113,165	69.1	22.4	5.7	2.8

Source: Iron and Steel Board 1964: 66.
Note: Data relate to plant in operation in 1955 and 1960 and plant expected to be in operation in 1965. The categories are defined as follows.
Category A: First-class large-scale modern plant in a good location. Most of the plants in this category would have been built or extensively reconstructed in the previous 15 years, but it includes older plant that is still of modern design (e.g. continuous wide-strip mills and continuous billet mills).
Category B: Efficient though older plant that is likely to be useful for many years, and smaller-scale modern plant.
Category C: Old plant that might be capable of some years of useful life in conditions of high demand but is otherwise of doubtful viability.
Unclassified: Mainly alloy and special steelmakers.

main explanation for these changes in average age is that levels of capital accumulation in manufacturing industry were higher across World War II and after 1948 than they had been before 1938. From 1960 to 1974 (Table G.4) there was practically no change in the age composition of the stock of capital.

The estimates of the average age of the capital stock given in Table G.3. relate to the gross capital stock concept used in this study, and hence are largely dependent on the exact assumptions made about the average lives of particular assets and the instant scrapping at the end of these lives. Very little direct information on the age of the capital in use is available, but there are three surveys that provide useful statistics.

The first of these relates to the plant used for iron making, the production of crude steel, and the various finishing processes in the iron and steel industry in the postwar period, and is summarized in Table G.5. It is evident that there was a major improvement in the quality of the plant: by 1965 more than two-thirds was classified as first class and modern, compared with only one-third ten years earlier.

TABLE G.6

Age of Machine Tools in 1961

		Percentage aged		
Category	Thousands of tools	Less than 10 years	10–20 years	21 years or more
Machine tools				
Mechanical engineering	397.8	40%	36%	24%
Electrical engineering	191.4	46	33	21
Shipbuilding and marine engineering	41.2	13	42	45
Motor vehicle manufacturing	204.8	43	40	17
Aircraft manufacturing	60.8	53	30	17
Other metal industries	337.7	44	33	23
Total	1,233.7	41%	37%	22%
Ancillary equipment (all industries)	250.7	58	31	11
Total	1,484.4	44%	36%	20%

Source: Metalworking Production 1961.

The second survey relates to the number of metal-cutting and metal-forming tools and ancillary items (such as heating and welding equipment or industrial trucks) owned by various industries in 1961, and is summarized in Table G.6. The results are broadly consistent with figures in Dean 1964: Table 6, which show 50 percent for the proportion at the end of 1961 of the gross stock of plant and machinery in the metal-using industries acquired after 1948. But the census shows a rather lower proportion for the 10-to-20-year-old category (covering mainly the war years) and a higher proportion for equipment more than 20 years old: 20 percent for machine tools of pre-1941 vintage compared with Dean's estimate of 10 percent for plant and machinery of pre-1938 vintage. It may be, therefore, that Dean's series slightly overstates the rate of scrapping of old equipment. The survey does not permit any comparison of the change in age composition over time, but it is relevant perhaps to note here an estimate in *Metalworking Production* that a 1960 vintage machine tool was about 40 percent more productive than one of 1950 vintage.

A third set of statistics covers electricity generating plant and is particularly useful in that it also shows how the capacity (and thus the efficiency) of the sets has increased over the years (Table G.7). As of March 31, 1949, 14 percent of the installed capacity was under 5 years old and 53 percent under 15 years, and the average capacity per set in these two age groups was just over 30 MW. By March 31, 1960, the plant was more modern relatively, in the sense that 34 percent was less than 5 years old and 66 percent less than 15 years old; and it was also more efficient absolutely with an average capacity per set of 15 years or less of 50 MW.

TABLE G.7

Age Distribution and Capacity Rating of Steam-Driven Generating Sets, 1949 and 1960

Period in which installed	Continuous maximum rating of installed capacity (MW)						Totals		
	Less than 4	4 and under 8	8 and under 16	16 and under 32	32 and under 64	64 and over	No. of sets	Capacity in MW	Percent of capacity
As of March 31, 1949									
1899–1913	64	1	–	–	–	–	65	50	–
1914–1923	121	58	32	15	–	–	226	1,270	10%
1924–1933	134	80	91	72	18	4	399	4,700	37
1934–1943	10	8	9	94	34	4	159	4,980	39
1944–1949	–	1	3	38	15	–	57	1,850	14
Total	329	148	135	219	67	8	906	12,850	100%
As of March 31, 1960									
Before 1925	64	33	25	8	–	–	130	743	3
1925–1934	68	45	67	52	21	4	257	3,587	13
1935–1944	5	8	9	85	41	4	152	4,870	18
1945–1954	3	3	2	53	137	6	204	8,802	32
1955–1960	–	–	3	30	83	41	157	9,436	34
Total	140	89	106	228	282	55	900	27,438	100%

Source: British Electric Authority 1949; Central Electricity Generating Board 1960.

The Rise in Capital Goods
Prices, 1938-1948

As noted in Chapter 5 (p. 136), the sharp rise in the relative price of capital goods between 1938 and 1948 must create suspicions of statistical bias. This appendix considers the evidence.

Table H.1 compares the price indexes of the different classes of capital goods that are used to arrive at the overall index of the price of capital goods with some independent evidence on costs. It may be seen that though the correspondence between the indexes of cost and the price indexes in rows 1–4 is far from exact, the differences are not systematically in one direction. Moreover, the cost increases, like the price increases, are much larger than the increase in the GDP implicit price deflator (p_Y). In the case of plant and machinery, the cost increase is less than the increase in the general wholesale price index, but this itself is considerably larger than the increase in p_Y.

The cost figures may, of course, themselves be biased, e.g. by insufficient allowance for reductions in material requirements per unit of output or for improvements in the quality of the product in the measures of productivity change. Supposing they are not, it next requires to be explained why costs and prices of capital goods rose more rapidly than p_Y. (It will be noted that differential increases in labor earnings do not appear to help toward the explanation.)

The implicit price deflator for GDP, p_Y, is an index of the cost of domestic production, and excludes any effects of changes in import prices. In 1948 import prices stood at a much higher level as a percentage of 1938 than did p_Y (287 compared with 180). Consequently, the implicit price deflator for total final expenditure stood at a significantly higher level (200) than p_Y. Since the capital goods price indexes are measures of actual prices, they are more appropriately compared with the total final expenditure price deflator than with the GDP price deflator.* This would account for 20 points out of the 58 points difference between p_Y and p_K in 1948 (p_Y = 180, p_K = 238). (A more exact calculation would of course have to estimate the direct and indirect import content of

---

*A further complication is that p_K is at market prices and p_Y at factor cost. However, indirect taxes have only a very small effect on p_K, being limited to tax on commercial road vehicles.

TABLE H.1

Costs and Prices in 1948 as a Percentage of 1938

Category	Earnings	Output per man	Labor cost	Material prices	Overheads and profits	Direct costs	Total costs	Prices
Dwellings	197%	76%	258%	257%	287%	257%	260%	263%
Other buildings and works	197	70	281	215	295	241	246	233
Plant and machinery	180	102	176	220	—	207	—	221
Vehicles	194	78	249	220	—	230	—	237
Wholesale prices	—	—	—	—	—	—	—	219
GDP	205	105	200	—	—	—	—	180

Source: Basic statistics (Appendix N); *Annual Abstract*, UK [10]; Girdwood Committee, UK [63]; Working Party on Building Operations, UK [73].

capital goods and take account of the price movements of the specific imports concerned.) It is interesting to note that the timing of the movement of p_K/p_Y — rising sharply across World War II, continuing to rise to 1952, and thereafter falling but remaining above its 1938 level — closely parallels that of import prices relative to p_Y (Fig. 14.4).

As shown in the table, productivity in construction is estimated to have fallen substantially between 1938 and 1948, whereas productivity for the economy as a whole rose fractionally. Assuming this is correct, it represents an increase in the real cost of one major class of capital goods relative to GDP. By itself it would account for between 15 and 20 points of the 58 points difference to be explained. The fall in productivity in construction across the war probably reflects in part the disorganization of the industry in a persisting environment of material shortages in 1948 and the neglect of training of skilled labor for the industry during the war. In the United States there has been a *long-run* tendency for construction prices to rise relative to other prices, partly because productivity grows more slowly in construction. In the United Kingdom productivity per man-hour in construction did rise more slowly than in the economy as a whole before 1914 and in the postwar period, but this was not the case in the interwar period. However, it is possible that some such long-run tendency does exist and contributed to the transwar movement.* Some cyclical element was probably also present. Before World War II there was a clear tendency for p_K/p_Y to fluctuate with the cycle and in particular with the level of domestic investment. On this precedent the rise in the level of activity between 1938 and 1948 could have been expected to raise p_K/p_Y. Insofar as the cyclical effect worked by raising the relative level of earnings in the investment industries, its operation between 1938 and 1948 is not confirmed by the figures quoted above. Its effect,

*On this reckoning the tendency must either have ceased after 1948 or have been marked by recovery from the temporary disorganization of the industry at the end of the war.

however, was probably partly through productivity (e.g. shortage of skilled labor in construction during booms), and such a consequence of the general increase in the pressure of demand between 1938 and 1948 may have contributed to the fall observed in productivity in construction.

Price controls still covered a wide range of products in 1948 (see Worswick 1952). This served to raise p_K/p_Y insofar as capital goods prices were less severely controlled than others. The most important case in point is rent control, which had a significant effect in limiting the rise in p_Y. Rent of dwellings and government non-trading property accounted for 6 percent of GNP in 1938; between then and 1948 most house rents did not increase at all. Apart from rents, the prices of consumer goods, especially food, were in general more closely controlled than capital goods prices, though some capital goods prices (such as iron and steel) were also subject to control. It is difficult to estimate the size of the effect of this on p_K/p_Y. Comparable data on profits by industry for 1938 and 1948, which might show the squeeze of price controls on profit margins, are not available. To some extent, too, producers of consumer goods reacted to price controls by reducing quality; it is possible that these quality changes are not fully taken account of in the data, in which case there will be a downward bias in p_Y (instead of the more commonly alleged upward bias in p_K). Rent control by itself would account for about 5 points of the difference to be explained between the increases of p_Y and p_K between 1938 and 1948. Other price controls also certainly worked in the same direction, operating less severely but over a wider field.

The unexplained residual left in the 1938–48 movement of p_K/p_Y after these three considerations have been taken account of is not large. They are not, perhaps, quite sufficient to account for the rise in the prices of machinery relative to p_Y, and for this class of asset there may be some bias due to the underestimation of quality improvements. But the evidence does not point sufficiently clearly to a significant bias to justify rejecting or amending the figures.

The trend of p_K/p_Y after 1948 is consistent with the hypothesis that the three considerations mentioned above were mainly responsible for the rise in p_K/p_Y between 1938 and 1948. After 1948 import prices relative to p_Y fell, but remained higher than in 1938; productivity in construction increased slightly faster than in GDP, but by 1964 had still not made good the effects of the wartime differential; and price controls were dismantled, but rent continued to be a much smaller proportion of GDP than in 1938. These movements would tend to lower p_K/p_Y, while still leaving it above its 1938 level, and this is what happened.

Total Factor Productivity and the Production Function

In this appendix we consider (1) certain technical aspects of the relation between TFP and possible underlying production functions and (2) certain problems that arise in the measurement of TFP in individual sectors of the economy.

TOTAL FACTOR PRODUCTIVITY AND THE PRODUCTION FUNCTION

Consider the most general form of production function relating the real value of output (q) to total factor productivity (x), labor (n), and capital (k):

$$q = \phi(x, n, k) \tag{1}$$

So long as the function is continuously differentiable, the proportional rates of change (denoted by circumflexes) over infinitesimal periods are related by the equation

$$\hat{q} = \phi_x \frac{x}{q} \hat{x} + \phi_n \frac{n}{q} \hat{n} + \phi_k \frac{k}{q} \hat{k} \tag{2}$$

where $\phi_i = \partial q/\partial i$. The units in which x is measured are arbitrary, so we may define x in such a way that $\phi_x x/q = 1$, giving

$$\hat{q} = \hat{x} + \phi_n \frac{n}{q} \hat{n} + \phi_k \frac{k}{q} \hat{k} \tag{3}$$

If the factors n and k are paid the value of their marginal products, as defined by $\partial q/\partial n$ and $\partial q/\partial k$, (3) is equivalent to

$$\hat{x} = \hat{q} - \alpha\hat{n} - (1 - \alpha)\hat{k} \tag{4}$$

where α is labor's share in national output. This corresponds to the measure of $\hat{x}$ used in the text.

The requirement that factors are paid their marginal products implicitly excludes non-constant returns to scale in k and n. If there are increasing returns to scale, factors cannot be paid the values of their marginal products without over-exhausting the total product. In this case (4) will lead to an overestimate of $\hat{x}$; or to put it another way, the part of growth that is due to scale economies is in-cluded in $\hat{x}$.

The requirements that are needed in order for (4) to be valid for infinitesimal changes are thus: a production function that is continuously differentiable in n and k; constant returns to scale; marginal productivity factor pricing; and, of course, factors of production that can without bias be aggregated under the two headings n and k. These are formidable requirements. It is to be noted, however, that it is not required that the production function should be Cobb-Douglas or of any other specific form.

If $\hat{x}$, $\hat{n}$, and $\hat{k}$ are not independent of one another, the three terms $\hat{x}$, $\alpha\hat{n}$, and $(1 - \alpha)\hat{k}$ will not correctly measure the direct and indirect contributions to $\hat{q}$ made by *exogenous* changes in $\hat{x}$, $\hat{n}$, and $\hat{k}$. (This is familiar from the simplest neoclassical growth model, with a constant savings ratio and no technical prog-ress. In the steady state, population growth is the only exogenous source of growth in output. But q grows at a rate equal to n, not at the lower rate αn that corresponds to "the contribution to growth made by the increase in n." The reason is that the increase in n, through its effect on q, leads to an increase in k.) This is an important point, but it affects the interpretation of (4) rather than its formal validity.

In practice we are not dealing with infinitesimal changes. We shall now con-sider what difference that makes.

Let us assume that there are constant returns to scale and Hicks-neutral technical progress. The production function can then be written

$$q = fx \tag{5}$$

where f is total factor input. f is a function of n and k such that if x is held con-stant at the arbitrarily measured level of unity, then $q = f$.

Given $x = 1$,

$$f = q = \psi(n,k) \tag{6}$$

where ψ defines the production function.

Then, writing $\hat{}\prime$ to denote proportional changes over non-infinitesimal periods, and assuming marginal productivity factor pricing, using Taylor's expansion

$$\Delta f = \left(\frac{\partial q}{\partial n}\, \Delta n + \frac{\partial q}{\partial k}\Delta k \right)$$

$$+ \frac{1}{2!} \left(\frac{\partial^2 q}{\partial n^2}\, (\Delta n)^2 + 2\, \frac{\partial^2 q}{\partial n\, \partial k}\, \Delta n \Delta k + \frac{\partial^2 q}{\partial k^2}\, (\Delta k)^2 \right)$$

$$+ \text{ higher-order terms}$$

That is to say,

$$\hat{f}' = \frac{\Delta f}{f} = [\alpha\hat{n}' + (1 - \alpha)\hat{k}']$$

$$+ \frac{1}{2f} \left(\frac{\partial^2 q}{\partial n^2} (\Delta n)^2 + 2 \frac{\partial^2 q}{\partial n \partial k} \Delta n \Delta k + \frac{\partial^2 q}{\partial k^2} (\Delta k)^2 \right)$$

$$+ \text{ higher-order terms} \tag{7}$$

If the production function were linear in k and in n (taken separately), the second- and higher-order terms would disappear. This is also true of a linear homogeneous production function in the special case where $\hat{n}' = \hat{k}'$, because $\hat{f}'$ can then be written:

$$\hat{f}' = \frac{\psi[n(1 + \hat{n}'), k(1 + \hat{k}')]}{\psi(n,k)} - 1 = (1 + n') \frac{\psi(n,k)}{\psi(n,k)} - 1$$

$$= \hat{n}' = \hat{k}' = \alpha\hat{n}' + (1 - \alpha)\hat{k}'$$

When $\hat{n}' \neq \hat{k}'$, and the production function is convex, the second-order term in (7) will be negative and the second- and higher-order terms together will usually sum to less than zero. That the second-order term will be negative follows mathematically from the fact that convexity implies that the signs of the principal minors of the hessian matrix H alternate, and hence the quadratic form that is the second-order term in (7) is negative definite, where H is given by

$$H = \begin{bmatrix} \dfrac{\partial^2 q}{\partial n^2} & \dfrac{\partial^2 q}{\partial n \partial k} \\ \dfrac{\partial^2 q}{\partial k \partial n} & \dfrac{\partial^2 q}{\partial k^2} \end{bmatrix}$$

For most common convex production functions the negative second-order term will determine the sign of all second- and higher-order terms taken together. In economic terms the negative second- and higher-order terms reflect the diminishing returns to the factor that has increased most rapidly.

It follows that, on the normal assumtions (viz. diminishing returns and $\hat{k}' > \hat{n}'$) the measure adopted in the text for $\hat{f}'$, namely $\alpha\hat{n}' + (1 - \alpha)\hat{k}'$, will be an overestimate.

From (5), we have

$$\hat{q}' = \hat{f}' + \hat{x}' + \hat{f}'\hat{x}' \tag{8}$$

$$\hat{x}' = \frac{\hat{q}' - \hat{f}'}{1 + \hat{f}'} \tag{9}$$

TABLE I.1

Growth of Total Factor Productivity: Alternative Estimates Showing Effects of Measurement over Non-Infinitesimal Periods

(Percentage change over the period)

Estimate	Length of period (years)		
	13	40	117
Present estimate[a]	19.8	74.4	408.7
Cobb-Douglas estimate	19.5	73.2	398.2
CES ($\sigma = 0.5$) estimate	20.3	83.4	624.1
Difference between present estimate and Cobb-Douglas, as percent of latter	1.5%	1.6%	2.6%
Difference between present estimate and CES estimate, as percent of latter	-2.5%	-10.8%	-34.5%

Note: The annual growth rates of output, labor, and capital are assumed to be 3%, 1%, and 3%, respectively. The first year factor shares are assumed to be 0.7 (labor) and 0.3 (capital).

[a] The average annual rate of growth of TFP, $\hat{x}$, for each period was calculated using the equations of Chapter 7:

$$\hat{x} = \hat{q} - \hat{f} \qquad (1)$$
$$\hat{f} = \alpha\hat{n} + (1-\alpha)\hat{k} \qquad (2)$$

where the circumflexes denote the average annual rate of change between two benchmark years, x is TFP, f is TFI, q is output, n is labor, k is non-human capital, and α is the weighting term, taken as equal to the share of labor income in the first year. The percentage change over a period of t years was derived from $(1 + \hat{x})^t$.

The interaction term $\hat{f}'\hat{x}'$ in (8) reflects the fact that the increase in x increases the productivity of any additional factor input as well as that of the original factor input. It is apparent from (9) that if $\hat{f}'$ were correctly measured, the measure of $\hat{x}'$ used in the text, namely $\hat{q}' - \hat{f}'$, would be an overestimate, since normally both $\hat{x}'$ and $\hat{f}' > 0$. However, as we have just seen, our measure of $\hat{f}'$ will itself normally be an overestimate, and this will tend to make our measure of $\hat{x}'$ an underestimate. Thus the biases introduced by neglect of diminishing returns on the one hand and neglect of the interaction effect $\hat{f}'\hat{x}'$ on the other have opposite effects on $\hat{x}'$, and the net direction of bias cannot be determined *a priori*. It will depend on the exact form of the production function and on the magnitudes of $\hat{x}'$, $\hat{n}'$, and $\hat{k}'$.

Over a period of only a year, the shortest period we are interested in, the biases are negligible in practice. To illustrate this, take growth rates that have been fairly rapid by historical standards (3 percent for output and capital, and 1 percent for labor), and assume first year factors shares of 0.7 (labor) and 0.3 (capital). The growth of TFP calculated according to (1) and (2) is then 1.4 percent, which overestimates the "true" growth rates implied by the Cobb-Douglas production function (1.382 percent) and the CES production function with $\sigma = 0.5$ (1.386 percent). In both cases the bias is small and does not affect the estimate of $\hat{x}'$ to the nearest tenth of a percentage point.

When the period of years under consideration is longer, the biases become larger absolutely and as a percentage of the growth rate between end years. This may be seen from Table I.1. The bias remains slight even over the longest period in the Cobb-Douglas case, but it becomes substantial in the CES case. If the growth rates are decompounded into annual percentage rates of growth, the bias in the Cobb-Douglas case is unaffected by the number of years (present estimate 1.40 percent per year, Cobb-Douglas estimate 1.38 percent per year). In the CES case, the bias so calculated increases with the number of years (present estimate 1.40 percent per year regardless of duration, CES estimates 1.43, 1.53, and 1.71 percent per year for 13, 40, and 117 years, respectively). In both cases the biases are not serious over 13 years, the approximate length of our standard twentieth-century periods (if the postwar period is divided at 1964).

Thus if the underlying production function were of the type described by (5), the possibility of significant bias cannot be ruled out if the period under consideration is long, but in practice the problem does not appear to be too bad. Much more seriously open to question is the propriety of assuming that the production function is of this type (or indeed of any specific type) over the range of its length relevant to comparisons over longer periods. We cannot really pretend to know what the shape of the production function is in a single year for factor proportions that are greatly different from those actually found in that year.

Both types of problem can be avoided by a different interpretation of annual compound interest growth rates. This is the interpretation that we adopt (in common with other authors, though they have not always made it clear). We regard the percentage annual growth rates derived from estimates of $\hat{f}'$ and $\hat{x}'$ as measuring the increase in f and x between *each successive year* within the period. For one-year periods the bias is likely to be very small, as seen above. Thus the statement that in the period 1951–73 the annual rates of growth of TFI and TFP, respectively, were 0.5 and 2.3 is to be interpreted to mean that the observed movement between 1951 and 1973 is *as if* there had been rises of 0.5 percent in f and 2.3 percent between 1951 and 1952, between 1952 and 1953, and so on. We are thus comparing not end-year production functions but hypothetical production functions in successive years.[*] We are not purporting to say what q in 1973 would have been with 1951 f and 1973 x, or with 1973 f and 1951 x. If for any purpose we did wish to make such a direct comparison between 1951 and 1973, the importance of second-order effects would require to be recognized.

The "as if" interpretation means that the use of the base year α is not strictly justified unless α remains constant throughout the period, as it would do with the Cobb-Douglas production function. (As between periods we do allow for changes in α.) But in practice the changes in α within each period are small, and the results would not be significantly different if we used instead, say, an average of the α's prevailing in the opening and closing years. This is shown in Table I.2. Only for 1913–24 are the differences apparent to the nearest tenth of a percentage point. This of course was the period when labor's share rose most rapidly (see Chapter 6), from 62 percent in 1913 to 70 percent in 1924. Despite this, the use of the average of the α's prevailing in the opening and closing years makes no significant difference to comparisons one might make with other periods.

---

[*] It is because of the distortions introduced by the business cycle that we do not choose to measure interannual growth rates directly (even in periods where annual data are available).

TABLE I.2

Alternative Measures of the Growth of Total Factor Input and
Total Factor Productivity Calculated with Weights of
Different Years, 1856–1973

(Annual percentage growth rates)

Period	Opening year a		Average of opening and closing year a's	
	TFI	TFP	TFI	TFP
1856–1873	0.8%	1.4%	0.8%	1.4%
1873–1913	1.3	0.5	1.3	0.5
1913–1924	−1.1	1.0	−1.2	1.1
1924–1937	1.5	0.7	1.5	0.7
1937–1951	0.4	1.4	0.4	1.4
1951–1973	0.5	2.3	0.5	2.3

Note: TFI and TFP are based on man-hours of labor and the gross capital stock.

MEASUREMENT OF TOTAL FACTOR PRODUCTIVITY BY SECTOR

There are three aspects of the measurement of TFP in individual sectors of the economy (as in Chapter 8) that we need to consider: (1) the use of single-indicator measures of output; (2) the effect of changes in quality; (3) the use of sectoral factor shares to weight the inputs of labor and capital.

(1) Single indicators for sectoral output. A possible bias in the comparison of TFP growth in individual sectors is created by the use of single-indicator measures of output change in all sectors and industries (except agriculture) rather than the conceptually preferable double-deflation measures. The double-deflation method of measuring the growth of real net output is from a value-added series derived as the difference between gross output revalued at constant prices and intermediate inputs also revalued at constant prices. Comprehensive series on a double-deflation basis are not available, except for agriculture.* Though *conceptually* preferable to single indicators, the double-deflation measures may not be more accurate *in practice* because of the compounding of errors that results from having to revalue at constant prices two series instead of just one. For a full discussion of this problem, see Hill 1971.

Most of the single indicators are based on gross output. (In the official output-based index of GDP, gross output indicators account for 77 percent of the total weight: *Index of Industrial Production*, UK [15]: 2. In the index of industrial production covering the years 1958–64, gross output indicators accounted for 83 percent of the total weight; *Sources and Methods*, UK [20]: 85.) In industries where there has been material-saving progress, a gross output measure will

*Estimates for a few postwar years have been made by Gupta (1963) and the Cambridge University Department of Applied Economics (1974). The same broad differences between the output growth rates of different industries are revealed by these estimates and by our single-indicator measures, though the ranking is not identical: the rank correlation coefficients between the two measures of output growth are 0.57 (8 major sectors, 1954–63), 0.49 (12 manufacturing industries, 1948–54), and 0.81 (12 manufacturing industries, 1954–63).

underestimate the growth of value-added and hence of the desired concept of TFP; and the opposite will occur in material-using industries. We noted in Chapter 7 (p. 205) that for the economy as a whole material saving through technical progress was roughly offset by the substitution of materials (made relatively cheaper through technical progress in the supplying industry) for labor. This does not necessarily apply in individual industries, however. In electricity, for example, which dominates the public utility sector, the efficiency of power stations in the utilization of primary fuel inputs has risen steadily throughout this century (except during World War II).* Salter (1966: 118, 134–35, 204) found that there was a tendency for the industries that experienced the most rapid increases in output per head to be those that achieved the greatest reduction in raw materials costs per unit of gross output. This finding receives confirmation from our own estimates of a high correlation between the growth of total productivity and the extent of real material saving.† It follows that our TFP growth measures for industries where single gross output indicators dominate, and where rapid growth is measured, tend to underestimate the desired TFP growth measure, and there is an overestimation for industries with slow measured TFP growth. In other words, the true dispersion between industries in TFP growth is likely to be greater than is suggested by our estimates.

Some of the single indicators are based on employment. For some services in particular it is often difficult to obtain any kind of output measure, and this is a well-known weakness of estimates of GDP growth from the output side. (See, e.g., *Sources and Methods*, 1968, UK [20]: 79; Hill 1971; A. D. Smith 1972.) However, by no means all of the output indicators in commerce and services are based on employment. The industrial orders within those sectors can be classified into three groups (percentage shares of GDP in 1973 in parentheses):

Mainly quantity indicators: distributive trades (10.6), insurance, banking, and finance (8.7); ownership of dwellings (5.8)

Both quantity and employment indicators: miscellaneous services (7.7)

Mainly employment indicators: professional services (10.1); public administration and defense (7.9)

Thus perhaps half of the output of commerce and services in 1973 is measured by employment indicators, and a quarter of GDP. Before 1913 the correspond-

---

*The average thermal efficiency (the total calorific value of the electricity sent out expressed as a percentage of the calorific value [gross as fired] of the total fuel consumed) of steam stations (excluding nuclear stations) in Great Britain rose from 8.7% in 1920 to 21.7% in 1938, and from 21.6% in 1951 to 27.6% in 1964 and 29.9% in 1973. It was 23.7% in 1954 and 27.5% in 1963. (*Digest of UK Energy Statistics*, UK [49].)

†The product-moment correlation coefficients between the growth of material savings and the growth of TFP are 0.87 for the 12 manufacturing industries, and 0.84 for the 12 manufacturing industries plus 4 nonmanufacturing sectors (excluding only commerce). Material-saving growth is defined as the difference between the annual growth rates between 1954 and 1963 of gross output and intermediate inputs, and TFP growth is defined as the difference between the annual growth rate of value-added in 1954–63, and that of TFI in 1951–64. With the exception of the latter growth rates, all the data came from Cambridge University Department of Applied Economics 1974.

ing proportions were broadly similar: employment indicators were more widely used, but public and professional servivces were less important. There must be a presumption that employment indicators underestimate the growth of output because they do not take account of improvements in productivity.* Account is taken of this possible bias wherever it may cause us to misinterpret the data.

(2) *Allowance for changes in quality.* The failure to allow for an improvement in the quality of a product that is the output of one industry and the input of another will bias the comparison growth rates in the two industries (Carter, Reddaway & Stone 1948; Nicholson 1967; *Index of Industrial Production*, UK [15]: 3; Griliches 1971.) If output is measured by the double-deflation method, growth in output and productivity will be underestimated in the first industry and overestimated in the second. This would also tend to occur if the measure is a single gross output indicator, assuming that other biases did not happen to offset this one. An example is provided by the increased sophistication of the packaging of manufactured goods, especially those intended for distribution to consumers through supermarkets and other self-service stores. It is likely that output and TFP growth in manufacturing in the postwar period are in consequence underestimated, with a corresponding overestimation in distribution. If these biases could be corrected, part of the overall improvement in TFP growth between the interwar period and the postwar period would be attributable to manufacturing and a smaller part to commerce than is suggested by the figures in Table 8.3. There may be a similar tendency for productivity growth arising from the increased use of more efficient fertilizers and pesticides to be attributed to agriculture rather than to chemicals. Some account is, however, taken of quality improvements on the input side of the double-deflation agriculture index. (See "New index of agriculture net output," UK [23], where it is stated that inputs of 11 different types of fertilizers are measured.)

(3) *The use of sectoral factor shares as weights.* The weights used in each sector or industry to combine the growth rates of labor and capital are the shares of labor and capital in the total income of the particular sector in the first year of the period. This requires some justification. In the first section of Chapter 7 it was argued that the appropriate measure of $(1 - \alpha)$, the weight for k, was the marginal productivity of capital times the capital-output ratio, both in respect of the first year of the period. If the marginal productivity is measured by the average gross profit rate per unit of capital, then $(1 - \alpha)$ is the share of gross profits in total income. However, it was also pointed out that the average profit rate does not necessarily equal the marginal productivity of capital in a perfectly competitive world. The marginal rate will exceed the average rate if the profits from obsolescent capital decline without capital itself being written down to the same extent. It is also possible for the average rate to exceed the marginal rate; this may occur if the profits earned on existing assets include elements of

---

*In the pre-1914 estimates, output in finance and in public, professional, and miscellaneous services was based on employment indicators with an assumed increase in output per head of 0.5% per year. No productivity increase was assumed for defense, catering, or domestic services. (See W. A. Lewis 1978: 264.)

economic "rent," properly attributable to entrepreneurship, location, monopoly power, etc., but statistically attributable to capital. For the economy as a whole this problem was ignored, chiefly because there is no other satisfactory way of estimating the marginal profit rate. However, there is an alternative for individual sectors and industries, and we consider it now.

The alternative is to continue to assume that the average profit rate is a good estimate of the marginal productivity for the economy as a whole, and in addition to assume that marginal profit rates net of depreciation are the same in all industries. So instead of using the gross profit rate in a particular sector in calculating the weight of capital TFI growth in that sector, one may use the net profit rate in the whole economy plus the depreciation rate in the sector.* Differences between marginal profit rates in different sectors, as estimated, will then reflect only differences in depreciation rates, and not differences in the degree of divergence between average and marginal profit rates, which we wish to exclude. However, this measure also excludes permanent differences between sectors in net rates of return that occur on account of the immobility of capital, different degrees of riskiness and of oligopoly, and divergences in pricing policies, none of which could occur under a narrowly defined state of perfect competition. It is not appropriate to exclude differences of this kind, and hence the proposed alternative estimate of sectoral marginal profit rates is not necessarily better than the original one.

Which measure is better depends on whether the errors arising from divergences between average and marginal rates of return within a sector or an industry are greater or less than the errors arising from inequality between sectors or industries in the net output rate. In some industries, such as railways and textiles, the existence of much old and unprofitable capital probably means that the average profit rate is below the marginal one. On the other hand, there are clearly industries where the risks are greater, as for example, chemicals, or where profit rates (both marginal and average) differ from the national average because of pricing policy. Electricity and water supply fall into the latter group. It is not possible to say that one measure of the marginal profit rate, and hence of the weights of labor and capital, is preferable to the other in all circumstances. We have decided to use the average profit rate measure for individual sectors as well as for the whole economy, partly because the depreciation data available to us to calculate the alternative measure are unreliable and not comprehensive. Fortunately, our choice does not matter too much, because the rate of growth of TFP in most sectors is likely to come out much the same either way. This is demonstrated in Table I.3, which gives the comparative figures by industry in the interwar period. Only in the case of gas, electricity, and water do the two measures of the rate of growth of TF_HP differ by more than 0.2 of a percentage point. A similar comparison for manufacturing industries is given in Table I.4.

*This is, broadly speaking, the method used in Reddaway & Smith 1960 for the comparison of different industries and in Jorgenson & Griliches 1967 for the comparison of different classes of assets.

TABLE I.3

Alternative Measures of the Growth of Total Factor Productivity by Sector Calculated with Sectoral and with Constant Net Profit Rates, 1924–1937

| | Weight of $\hat{k}$ based on: | | Annual percentage growth rate of TF$_n$P | |
| | Sectoral profit rate | Constant net profit rate | | |
Sector	(1)	(2)	Using (1)	Using (2)
Agriculture, forestry, fishing	0.391	0.564	2.1%	1.9%
Mining, quarrying	0.139	0.137	1.2	1.2
Manufacturing	0.257	0.255	1.9	1.9
Construction	0.121	0.053	1.3	1.1
Gas, electricity, water	0.524	0.791	1.8	1.4
Transport, communications	0.259	0.746	1.0	1.2
Commerce	0.408	0.161	−0.5	−0.5
Ownership of dwellings	1.000	1.000	−1.5	−1.5
Total (including public and professional services)	0.299	0.299	0.7%	0.7%

TABLE I.4

Alternative Measures of the Growth of Total Factor Productivity in Manufacturing Calculated with Sectoral and with Constant Net Profit Rates, 1924–1937

| | Weight of $\hat{k}$ based on: | | Annual percentage growth rate of TF$_n$P | |
| | Sectoral profit rate | Constant net profit rate | | |
Industry	(1)	(2)	Using (1)	Using (2)
Food, drink, tobacco	0.466	0.249	1.5%	1.6%
Chemicals	0.418	0.382	1.4	1.5
Iron and steel	0.139	0.521	2.0	1.8
Electrical engineering	0.405	0.262	2.0	2.4
Mechanical engineering and shipbuilding	0.180	0.195	0.7	0.7
Vehicles	0.083	0.158	3.1	2.9
Other metal industries	0.234	0.149	2.3	2.4
Textiles	0.231	0.408	1.9	2.0
Clothing	0.142	0.084	1.4	1.5
Bricks, pottery, glass, cement	0.250	0.295	2.5	2.5
Timber, furniture	0.068	0.091	2.9	2.8
Paper, printing, publishing	0.341	0.224	0.8	1.0
Leather and other	0.250	0.241	2.7	2.7
Total manufacturing	0.257	0.257	1.9%	1.9%

Correlations Among Manufacturing Industries

We present here the results of a simple correlation analysis performed on the growth rates of output, labor, etc. and on the absolute values of other variables for 12 manufacturing industry groups (the 13 discussed in Chapter 8, with the exclusion of textiles, for which the data are unsatisfactory). The analysis is in two parts: (1) correlation coefficients between two different variables in the same period (calculated for 1924–37, 1951–64, and 1964–73), and (2) correlation coefficients between the same variables in successive periods. Nineteen variables, listed in Table J.1, were used, and throughout there were 12 observa-

TABLE J.1

Variables Used in the Correlation Analysis

Variable	Abbreviation
Annual percentage growth rates of:	
Output	$\hat{q}$
Labor	$\hat{n}$
Capital	$\hat{k}$
TFI	$\hat{f}$
TFP	$\hat{x}$
Labor productivity	$\hat{q} - \hat{n}$
Capital per man-hour	$\hat{k} - \hat{n}$
Capital per unit of output	$\hat{k} - \hat{q}$
Buildings	$\hat{b}$
Plant and machinery	$\hat{m}$
Implicit output prices	$\hat{p}$
Average hourly earnings (first year of period)	w
Average hourly earnings (last year as percent of first year)	$(1 + \hat{w})^t$
Average profit rate (first year of period)	r
Average profit rate (last year as percent of first year)	$(1 + \hat{r})^t$
Capital per man-hour (first year of period)	k/n
Output per man-hour (first year of period)	q/n
Capital-output ratio (first year of period)	k/q
Proportion of output exported in value-added term	
(intermediate years)[a]	e

[a]The years used, which were dictated by the availability of input-output tables, were as follows: 1935 was used for the 1924–37 period; 1954 for 1951–64; and 1968 for 1964–73.

TABLE J.2

Within-Period Correlation Coefficients for Twelve

Variable	$\hat{n}$	$\hat{k}$	$\hat{f}$	$\hat{x}$	$\hat{q}-\hat{n}$	$\hat{k}-\hat{n}$	$\hat{k}-\hat{q}$	$\hat{b}$	$\hat{m}$
$\hat{q}$	0.82*	0.52	0.88*	0.81*	0.52	-0.45	-0.80*	0.46	0.26
	0.67*	0.60*	0.71*	0.57	0.65*	0.07	-0.48	0.50	0.29
	0.59*	0.66*	0.74*	0.81*	0.88*	0.37	-0.69*	0.61*	0.71*
$\hat{n}$		0.35	0.97*	0.36	-0.06	-0.75*	-0.70*	0.31	0.08
		0.59*	0.86*	-0.07	-0.13	-0.25	-0.12	0.50	0.18
		0.68*	0.80*	0.16	0.13	0.04	-0.11	0.59*	0.60*
$\hat{k}$			0.54	0.31	0.38	0.36	0.10	0.84*	0.85*
			0.87*	-0.18	0.20	0.63*	0.41	0.78*	0.82*
			0.91*	0.17	0.40	0.75*	0.10	0.75*	0.90*
$\hat{f}$				0.43	0.09	-0.59*	-0.64*	0.50	0.22
				-0.17	0.07	0.21	0.14	0.69*	0.60*
				0.21	0.44	0.52	-0.10	0.71*	0.85*
$\hat{x}$					0.88*	-0.14	-0.72*	0.25	0.22
					0.83*	-0.15	-0.84*	-0.10	-0.29
					0.90*	0.09	-0.91*	0.27	0.30
$\hat{q}-\hat{n}$						0.32	-0.35	0.33	0.34
						0.36	-0.52	0.16	0.21
						0.44	-0.77*	0.39	0.51
$\hat{k}-\hat{n}$							0.78*	0.29	0.52
							0.61*	0.45	0.82*
							0.23	0.49	0.69*
$\hat{k}-\hat{q}$								0.06	0.29
								0.28	0.57
								-0.08	-0.07
$\hat{b}$									0.58*
									0.56
									0.83*
$\hat{m}$									
$\hat{p}$									
w									
$(1-\hat{w})'$									
r									
$(1-\hat{r})'$									
k/n									
q/n									
k/q									

Source: Basic statistics (Appendix N); Barna 1952; *Input-Output Tables*, 1954, 1968, UK [9], [16].
Note: The first figure in each cell refers to 1924–37, the second to 1951–64, and the third to 1964–73. An asterisk refers to a correlation coefficient significantly different from zero at the 5% level (the critical value is ± 0.576).

Manufacturing Industries, 1924–1937, 1951–1964, and 1964–1973

$\hat{p}$	w	$(1+\hat{w})^r$	r	$(1+\hat{f})^r$	k/n	q/n	k/q	e	Variable
−0.30	−0.08	−0.21	−0.20	0.40	−0.18	−0.15	−0.15	−0.01	$\hat{q}$
−0.60*	0.52	0.07	−0.19	−0.11	0.52	0.47	0.40	0.31	
−0.73*	−0.01	−0.15	0.48	0.23	0.06	0.32	−0.19	0.13	
0.03	−0.14	0.20	0.14	0.16	0.01	0.17	−0.03	−0.02	$\hat{n}$
−0.07	0.64*	−0.12	0.00	−0.22	0.28	0.46	0.22	0.44	
0.02	−0.18	0.16	0.18	0.24	−0.24	−0.08	−0.35	−0.30	
−0.39	0.07	−0.24	0.10	0.12	−0.34	−0.08	−0.46	−0.15	$\hat{k}$
−0.09	0.69*	0.13	−0.01	−0.33	0.66*	0.70*	0.56	0.60*	
−0.31	−0.25	0.10	0.51	0.07	−0.10	0.17	−0.29	−0.24	
−0.06	−0.07	0.13	0.07	0.22	−0.08	0.11	−0.13	0.00	$\hat{f}$
−0.10	0.70*	0.10	0.04	−0.33	0.65*	0.76*	0.53	0.54	
−0.39	−0.05	0.09	0.37	0.45	0.11	0.37	−0.11	−0.20	
−0.50	−0.07	−0.54	−0.47	0.49	−0.25	−0.41	−0.13	−0.01	$\hat{x}$
−0.73*	−0.09	−0.03	−0.33	0.53	−0.03	−0.23	−0.06	−0.21	
−0.72*	0.03	−0.37	0.37	0.29	−0.01	0.15	−0.19	−0.02	
−0.56	0.07	−0.66*	−0.55	0.46	−0.33	−0.51	−0.21	0.02	$\hat{q}-\hat{n}$
−0.73*	0.04	0.21	−0.26	0.37	0.42	0.16	0.31	−0.05	
−0.90*	0.09	−0.29	0.48	0.14	0.22	0.43	−0.03	0.01	
−0.30	0.19	−0.37	−0.07	−0.08	−0.25	−0.23	−0.30	−0.09	$\hat{k}-\hat{n}$
−0.04	0.22	0.26	−0.02	−0.18	0.52	0.39	0.45	0.29	
−0.44	−0.18	0.01	0.53	−0.12	0.08	0.30	−0.09	−0.06	
0.08	0.15	0.07	0.30	−0.38	−0.03	0.11	−0.15	−0.10	$\hat{k}-\hat{q}$
0.58*	0.17	0.06	0.20	−0.48	0.12	0.23	0.15	0.31	
0.66*	−0.23	0.37	−0.14	−0.23	−0.17	−0.27	−0.03	−0.05	
−0.25	0.28	−0.24	0.07	0.14	−0.23	0.03	−0.38	0.01	$\hat{b}$
0.12	0.40	0.26	0.04	−0.11	0.47	0.46	0.55	0.37	
−0.18	−0.04	0.17	0.48	0.26	−0.20	0.12	−0.31	−0.15	
−0.41	−0.07	−0.38	0.11	0.05	−0.40	−0.24	−0.49	−0.39	$\hat{m}$
−0.01	0.43	0.27	0.28	−0.41	0.60*	0.66*	0.38	0.34	
−0.43	−0.18	−0.16	0.61*	0.22	−0.09	0.23	−0.28	−0.19	
	0.35	0.85*	−0.17	0.40	0.46	0.24	0.51	0.39	$\hat{p}$
	−0.41	0.23	0.08	0.11	−0.23	−0.29	0.02	−0.01	
	−0.25	0.46	−0.23	0.21	−0.54	−0.65*	−0.32	−0.22	
		0.29	−0.48	0.36	0.71*	0.52	0.62*	0.34	w
		−0.18	0.05	−0.66*	0.43	0.71*	0.20	0.66*	
		−0.01	−0.65*	−0.33	0.78*	0.76*	0.81*	0.65*	
			−0.11	0.19	0.41	0.33	0.40	0.30	$(1-\hat{w})^r$
			−0.07	0.18	0.48	0.25	0.53	0.09	
			−0.05	−0.22	−0.18	−0.09	−0.12	−0.13	
				−0.68*	−0.13	0.37	−0.35	−0.28	r
				−0.47	−0.23	0.25	−0.52	−0.30	
				0.55	−0.54	−0.21	−0.72*	−0.60*	
					0.06	−0.28	0.24	0.19	$(1-\hat{f})^r$
					−0.20	−0.62*	0.06	−0.36	
					−0.59*	−0.36	−0.68*	−0.52	
						0.79*	0.92*	0.39	k/n
						0.82*	0.87*	0.46	
						0.90*	0.95*	0.59*	
							0.52	0.07	q/n
							0.52	0.46	
							0.76*	0.40	
								0.50	k/q
								0.50	
								0.67*	

tions corresponding to the 12 industry groups. In this appendix we do no more than present the results and draw attention to some of the more significant figures. Some of the correlation coefficients are quoted elsewhere to support or refute particular hypotheses.

The within-period correlation coefficients are shown in Table J.2. The more interesting facts are as follows.

(1) Output growth was correlated both with input growth and with the growth of labor productivity (Verdoorn law).

(2) There was an inverse correlation between output growth and the growth of output prices, more pronounced in the postwar period than in the interwar period.

(3) There was no significant correlation between the growth of TFI (or of capital or labor) and the growth of TFP. This tends to refute the hypothesis that there were economies of scale associated with inputs. Nor was the growth of TFP correlated with the growth of capital per unit of labor.

(4) The growth of TFP was positively correlated with the growth of both labor productivity and capital productivity. The other input did not, as it were, fully account for inter-industry differences in one input's productivity.

(5) The growth of output prices was inversely correlated with both the growth of labor productivity and the growth of TFP. In the interwar period and to a lesser extent in the postwar period, there was also a positive correlation between the rate of growth of prices and the rate of growth of wages.

(6) There was a tendency for those industries with high capital intensity (relative to either labor or output) and high absolute labor productivity, all of which were related, to have high average earnings of labor, as well. On the other hand, there was no tendency for industries with rapidly increasing labor productivity to have rapidly increasing wages; indeed, in the interwar period, the opposite was the case.

(7) There was a positive correlation between capital intensity and the proportion of output exported.

(8) In 1951–64, but not in 1964–73 or in the interwar period, industries with rapidly growing output, labor input, and capital input had high wages.

(9) In 1951–64, but not in 1964–73 or in the interwar period, the rate of growth of TFI was positively correlated with capital intensity.

(10) In the interwar period the rate of growth of TFI was inversely correlated with the *increase* in capital intensity. In the postwar period the tendency was in the opposite direction.

Between-period correlations are shown in Table J.3. There was a tendency for the same industries to have high capital intensity, high labor productivity, high wages, and high export proportions in all periods. The between-period correlations of the variables referring to growth rates are in general remarkably low. There is no growth-rate variable that gets an asterisk in both columns, though there is a moderately high correlation in output growth in both. In general, though not without exceptions, there was more resemblance between the two parts of the postwar period than between the interwar period and 1951–64.

TABLE J.3
Between-Period Correlation Coefficients for Twelve Manufacturing
Industries, 1924–1937, 1951–1964, and 1964–1973

Variable	Between 1924–37 and 1951–64	Between 1951–64 and 1964–73	Variable	Between 1924–37 and 1951–64	Between 1951–64 and 1964–73
$\hat{q}$	0.46	0.55	$\hat{p}$	−0.14	0.47
$\hat{n}$	0.85*	0.12	w	0.50	0.76*
$\hat{k}$	−0.21	0.08	$(1-\hat{w})^{r}$	−0.08	0.29
$\hat{f}$	0.61*	0.20	r	0.14	0.49
$\hat{x}$	0.10	0.57	$(1-\hat{r})^{r}$	−0.07	0.00
$\hat{q}-\hat{n}$	0.10	0.55	k/n	0.88*	0.94*
$\hat{k}-\hat{n}$	−0.15	0.40	q/n	0.68*	0.81*
$\hat{k}-\hat{q}$	−0.35	0.65*	k/q	0.50	0.84*
$\hat{b}$	−0.05	0.47	e	0.90*	0.93*
$\hat{m}$	−0.64*	0.36			

Source: Same as Table J.2.
Note: An asterisk refers to a correlation coefficient significantly different from zero at the 5% level (the critical value is ±0.576).

Thus there was a tendency for the same industries to have high rates of growth of TFP in both parts of the postwar period, but not in 1924–37 and 1951–64. There was a surprising *negative* correlation in the growth of plant and machinery ($\hat{m}$) between 1924–37 and 1951–64: those industries where the stock of machinery grew relatively rapidly in 1924–37 had a relatively slow rate of growth in machinery in 1951–64. On the other hand, the growth of labor (and hence of TFI) was strongly correlated between 1924–37 and 1951–64 but not between 1951–64 and 1964–73 (see Chapter 8, pp. 242–43).

Sectoral Growth Rates
in Postwar Cycles

TABLE K.1

Growth of Output, Labor, Capital, Total Factor Input, and
Total Factor Productivity by Sector in Postwar Cycles, 1951–1973

(Annual percentage growth rates)

Variable and sector	1951– 1955	1955– 1960	1960– 1964	1964– 1968	1968– 1973
Output:					
Agriculture, forestry, fishing	1.3%	3.2%	3.2%	1.4%	3.4%
Mining, quarrying	0.3	– 2.2	0.4	– 3.2	– 3.4
Manufacturing	3.8	2.8	3.1	2.9	3.1
Construction	3.5	3.1	5.0	3.2	0.7
Gas, electricity, water	5.4	4.6	5.6	5.2	5.2
Transport, communications	1.6	2.1	3.0	2.3	4.4
Commerce	2.7	3.2	3.2	2.4	3.6
Public and professional services	(1.3)	(0.9)	(2.1)	(2.6)	(1.9)
Ownership of dwellings	1.4	2.0	1.9	2.8	2.4
GDP	2.7	2.5	3.1	2.5	2.8
Labor:					
Agriculture, forestry, fishing	– 0.8	– 2.3	– 3.9	– 5.3	– 4.3
Mining, quarrying	0.0	– 4.0	– 3.7	– 8.5	– 6.1
Manufacturing	1.2	– 0.1	– 0.5	– 1.7	– 1.6
Construction	1.1	0.9	2.9	– 1.3	– 0.4
Gas, electricity, water	0.9	– 0.8	1.8	– 1.7	– 4.7
Transport, communications	– 0.8	– 0.8	– 0.3	– 1.3	– 1.3
Commerce	0.5	0.2	0.3	– 2.0	0.3
Public and professional services	0.2	– 1.0	– 0.1	1.5	0.5
GDP	0.5	– 0.4	– 0.2	– 1.5	– 0.9

TABLE K.1 *continued*

Variable and sector	1951–1955	1955–1960	1960–1964	1964–1968	1968–1973
Capital:					
Agriculture, forestry, fishing	1.2	1.4	1.8	2.9	3.6
Mining, quarrying	4.3	4.9	0.5	2.1	1.3
Manufacturing	3.4	2.9	3.7	3.7	3.0
Construction	5.6	5.8	7.6	7.4	5.6
Gas, electricity, water	3.2	3.8	5.0	6.2	2.5
Transport, communications	0.6	1.5	1.1	1.9	3.3
Commerce	0.3	4.3	6.6	5.9	6.1
Public and professional services	2.2	2.5	4.3	5.5	6.0
Ownership of dwellings	2.4	2.1	2.5	3.4	3.1
GDP	2.3	2.6	3.4	4.1	3.7
TF_HI:					
Agriculture, forestry, fishing	-0.1%	-0.9%	-1.7%	-1.5%	-1.0%
Mining, quarrying	0.3	-3.1	-3.1	-6.5	-4.7
Manufacturing	2.0	0.8	0.0	0.0	-0.3
Construction	1.5	1.5	3.5	-0.1	0.6
Gas, electricity, water	1.8	1.2	3.5	2.8	-0.4
Transport, communications	-0.4	-0.2	0.1	-0.4	0.0
Commerce	0.4	1.6	2.4	0.3	1.9
Public and professional services	(0.8)	(-0.1)	(1.2)	(2.6)	(2.0)
Ownership of dwellings	2.4	2.1	2.5	3.4	3.1
GDP	1.0	0.4	0.9	0.1	0.4
TF_HP:					
Agriculture, forestry, fishing	1.4	4.1	4.9	2.9	4.4
Mining, quarrying	0.0	0.9	3.5	3.3	1.3
Manufacturing	1.8	2.0	2.3	2.9	3.4
Construction	2.0	1.6	1.5	3.3	0.1
Gas, electricity, water	3.6	3.4	2.1	2.4	5.6
Transport, communications	2.0	2.3	2.9	2.7	4.4
Commerce	2.3	1.6	0.8	2.1	1.7
Ownership of dwellings	-1.0	-0.1	-0.6	-0.6	-0.7
GDP	1.7	2.1	2.2	2.4	2.4

Productivity Trends Within the Period 1873-1913

We have dealt with this subject at greater length elsewhere (Feinstein, Matthews & Odling-Smee 1981) and confine ourselves here to a brief summary.

It has long been debated whether the "climacteric" came in the 1870's or at the end of the 1890's. The question cannot be resolved decisively because of the divergences between the output, expenditure, and income estimates of GDP (Table L.1). The rate of growth of TF_rI varied little between periods, so changes between periods in the rate of growth of TF_rP are dominated by those in GDP. (TF_rP is used as the measure of TFP because it is the only one available on a sectoral basis.)

The output measure shows a comparatively small retardation in GDP and TFP over the whole period from 1856 to 1913, and the retardation is of much the same extent before and after 1899. The other two measures, and hence the compromise measure, show a much sharper falling-off after 1899.

The compromise index is, on balance, probably the most reliable indicator. On this assumption, the conclusion is that retardation was of very limited extent before 1899 but became much more severe thereafter. Data on individual business cycles (not here reproduced) indicate that there was significant retardation in the cycle 1873–82, but that this was largely offset by a recovery in the two ensuing cycles, 1882–89 and 1889–99.

Sectoral data are shown in Table L.2. Agriculture and mining were the most important sources of such retardation in TFP as took place before 1899; there was no retardation in TFP in manufacturing during that phase. On the other hand, manufacturing does appear as the most important single source of retardation after 1899. The sectoral breakdown of the incidence of retardation after 1899 is inevitably unsatisfactory, however. The sectoral data are, of course, based on output indicators, and these, as already stated, show much less retardation in TFP in the economy as a whole than do the other indicators of GDP.

TABLE L.1

Alternative Measures of the Growth of Output, Inputs, and Total Factor Productivity, 1856–1913

(Annual percentage growth rates)

Category	1856–1873	1873–1899	1899–1913
GDP:			
Income measure	2.3%	2.2%	1.1%
Expenditure measure	—	2.2	1.3
Output measure	2.0	1.9	1.7
Compromise measure	2.2	2.1	1.4
Inputs:			
Labor	0.9	0.9	0.9
Capital	1.9	2.0	1.8
TF_rI	1.3	1.4	1.3
TF_rP:			
Income measure of GDP	1.0	0.8	−0.2
Expenditure measure of GDP	—	0.8	0.0
Output measure of GDP	0.7	0.5	0.4
Compromise measure of GDP	0.9	0.7	0.1

Note: Labor is measured in man-years; capital is measured as gross fixed capital plus inventories.

TABLE L.2

Growth of Total Factor Productivity by Sector, 1856–1913

(Annual percentage growth rates)

Sector	1856–1873	1873–1899	1899–1913
Agriculture, forestry, fishing	0.9%	0.5%	0.4%
Mining, quarrying	1.4	0.0	−0.3
Manufacturing	0.9	0.9	0.3
Construction	0.8	0.8	−1.2
Gas, electricity, water	0.6	1.1	2.6
Transport, communications	0.5	0.3	1.2
Commerce	(0.6)	(0.8)	(0.6)

Note: Labor is measured in man-years; capital is measured as gross fixed capital.

Productivity Trends Within the Period 1924-1937

The experience of the 1920's and the 1930's differed in many respects, not least in government policy, and it is therefore interesting to compare the behavior of productivity in the two periods 1924–29 and 1929–37 (1929 being the relevant cycle peak). Unfortunately, there are several obstacles:

(1) Data on hours of work are not available for 1929, since the relevant survey appears not to have been conducted in that year. TFI must therefore be calculated on the basis of man-years, not man-hours, and TFP likewise. The growth of TFP is consequently overstated for either 1924–29 or 1929–37, or both, since between 1924 and 1937 hours of work increased somewhat.

(2) More important, there are large divergencies between the alternative indicators of GDP (see Table M.1.). The output measure shows the 1930's in a much less unfavorable light relative to the 1920's than the income and expenditure measures, and hence the compromise measure. This requires to be borne in mind in studying sectoral measures, which necessarily come from the output side.

(3) Revisions are not available of the estimates in Feinstein 1965 of the interwar capital stock for individual manufacturing industries, consistent with his revision for total manufacturing.

(4) In addition to the above statistical problems, there are problems of interpretation. Though the unemployment rate was much the same in 1924, 1929, and 1937, none of those years had anything near to full employment, and there were substantial differences between industries in the time patterns of the movement of demand relative to supply. It cannot be assumed that the effects of these differences on productivity were neutral even at the aggregate level. Some of the observed sectoral differences in the rate of growth of productivity between 1924–29 and 1929–37 undoubtedly reflected cyclical-type forces rather than long-run trends. This applies in some degree to 1924–37 as a whole, but not so much.

With these qualifications in mind, the following conclusions from Tables M.1–M.3 may be noted.

(1) TFP in the economy as a whole grew faster in 1924–29 than in 1929–37 (Table M.1).

TABLE M.1

Alternative Measures of the Growth of Output, Inputs, and Total Factor Productivity, 1924–1937

(Annual percentage growth rates)

Category	1924–1929	1929–1937
GDP:		
Income measure	3.1%	1.9%
Expenditure measure	2.3	1.7
Output measure	2.3	2.2
Compromise measure	2.6	2.0
Inputs:		
Labor	1.2	1.2
Capital	1.9	1.8
TFI	1.4	1.4
TFP:		
Income measure of GDP	1.7	0.5
Expenditure measure of GDP	0.9	0.3
Output measure of GDP	0.9	0.8
Compromise measure of GDP	1.2	0.6

Note: Labor is measured in man-years, not man-hours, and hence TFI and TFP for these periods are not the same as in text tables on 1924–37.

(2) The rate of growth of TFP (compromise measure) in 1929–37 was about the same as it had been in 1873–1913 (making an allowance for an assumed increase in hours of work).

(3) The relations between the rates of growth of TFP in the two periods 1924–29 and 1929–37 differed greatly between sectors (Table M.2). Agriculture, mining, construction, and transport did substantially better in 1924–29, commerce and manufacturing in 1929–37. These output-side measures are probably biased in favor of 1929–37, as noted above, but this could scarcely affect the differences between sectors. In most of the sectors where there were large differences in TFP growth between the two periods, there were similar differences in output growth, no doubt due to demand (commerce and mining were exceptions).

(4) The worst of the effects of general unemployment on TFP in commerce came in the 1920's rather than in the 1930's.

(5) Within manufacturing (Table M.3) the majority of industries did better in 1929–37 than in 1924–29, but some did much worse. As at the sectoral level, the major differences were associated with corresponding differences in output trends. By far the largest improvement in TFP growth in 1929–37 occurred in textiles.

It is plain that the main increase in the rate of growth of TFP between 1873–1913 and 1929–37 occurred between 1873–1913 and 1924–29 rather than between 1924–29 and 1929–37. This is true even of manufacturing, where the rates of growth of TFP in 1873–1913, 1924–29, and 1929–37, respectively, were 0.6 percent, 1.8 percent, and 2.4 percent. The unusually large and divergent

TABLE M.2
Growth of Total Factor Productivity by Sector, 1924–1937
(Annual percentage growth rates)

Sector	1924–1929	1929–1937
Agriculture, forestry, fishing	4.0%	0.9%
Mining, quarrying	3.3	1.1
Manufacturing	1.8	2.4
Construction	4.2	0.3
Gas, electricity, water	1.7	2.0
Transport, communications	1.7	0.6
Commerce	− 1.1	0.0
Public and professional services	(− 0.4)	(− 0.5)
Ownership of dwellings	− 1.6	− 1.4
GDP	0.9	0.8

Note: See note to Table M.1.

TABLE M.3
Growth of Total Factor Productivity in Manufacturing, 1924–1937
(Annual percentage growth rates)

Sector	1924–1929	1929–1937
Food, drink, tobacco	1.4%	1.9%
Chemicals	0.1	2.3
Iron and steel	1.0	3.1
Electrical engineering	0.4	3.4
Mechanical engineering and shipbuilding	3.1	− 0.5
Vehicles	2.5	3.8
Other metals	2.9	2.6
Textiles	− 0.9	4.4
Clothing	2.4	1.3
Bricks, pottery, glass, cement	3.0	2.8
Timber and furniture	5.4	2.0
Paper, printing, and publishing	0.7	1.1
Other manufacturing	1.7	3.6

Note: See note to Table M.1. The figures are based on unrevised capital stock data, and hence not consistent with Table M.2. For manufacturing as a whole, revision of the capital stock data lowers the rate of growth of TFP by 0.2 in 1924–29 and by 0.4 in 1929–37.

sectoral and industrial changes in the rate of growth of TFP between the two parts of the interwar period, dominated by demand movements, were a natural feature of a period of a general deficiency of demand. TFP continued to grow faster in the 1930's than in the pre-1914 period (except in commerce), but it is difficult to discern in the 1930's evidence of a further trend improvement in the rate of growth of TFP over the 1920's, independent of demand. Some such trend improvement may have been present in parts of manufacturing. It is also possible that 1924–29 still contained some abnormal elements of recovery (from World War I, the ensuing reduction in hours of work, and the recession of 1921), and that consequently any underlying tendencies of acceleration in TFP growth within the interwar period are understated by the statistics.

Basic Statistics: Sources and Methods

The following statistical series are considered in this appendix:
(1) Gross domestic product and the main national income accounting sub-aggregates (e.g. income from employment, consumers' expenditure)
(2) Income, output, and factor shares by industry
(3) The total in employment and hours worked by industry, and the total working population
(4) The gross fixed capital stock; inventories and gross fixed capital formation by industry, sector, and asset; and net overseas assets and the net fixed capital stock in the whole economy
(5) Imports and exports of goods and services
Except where otherwise indicated, all data refer to the contemporary area of the United Kingdom.

With one major exception, the industrial classifications used are identical to those in Feinstein 1972, to which reference should be made for further details. The exception is that the rent from non-trading property owned and occupied by the central government and local authorities is treated as the income of the public administration and defense sector, rather than as the income of insurance, banking, and finance. In general, the classification for 1920–48 follows the 1948 Standard Industrial Classification, that for 1948–64 the 1958 Standard Industrial Classification, and that for 1964–74 the 1968 Standard Industrial Classification. There are therefore breaks in classifications in 1948 (in the capital stock series, for which the classification is anyway not very precise, the break occurs in 1938) and 1964. The classification for 1855–1920 corresponds approximately to the 1948 Standard Industrial Classification.

GROSS DOMESTIC PRODUCT AND SUBAGGREGATES

The two sources for nearly all the data are Feinstein 1972, for 1855–1964, and *National Income and Expenditure, 1964–74*, UK[21], for 1964–73. Additional detail was obtained from the working papers and sources used for Feinstein 1972 and, for 1948–64, *National Income and Expenditure, 1968*.

The estimates in Feinstein 1972 are consistent with those in *National Income and Expenditure, 1968*. But the latter are not necessarily consistent with the estimates in *National Income and Expenditure, 1964–74*, because of data revisions. In a number of series, adjustments were made to either the 1948–64 or 1964–73 series to enable comparisons to be made.

The reliability of the historical estimates is discussed in Feinstein 1972: Chapter 1. The following reliability gradings are attached to the current- and constant-price series of GDP:

1855–1889	C	1924–1938	A
1890–1913	B	1939–1947	C
1914–1923	C	1948–1973	A

where the corresponding margins of error are A, ± less than 5 percent; B, ± 5–15 percent; and C ± 15–25 percent.

The differences between the alternative estimates of real GDP over our usual periods are discussed in Appendix A.

INCOME, OUTPUT, AND FACTOR SHARES BY INDUSTRY

The main sources are Feinstein 1972 and working papers, and *National Income and Expenditure, 1964–74*.

Additional sources for income by industry are as follows:

W. A. Lewis 1978: Table A.3, for 1907

A. L. Chapman 1952, for additional detail of income from employment in 1920–38

Inland Revenue Statistics, UK [57], for PAYE (Pay as you earn) statistics used to allocate income from employment between professional services and miscellaneous services in postwar years

Input-output Tables for the postwar years (UK [9], [16], [17])

A variety of sources for estimates of end-year inventories at current prices, from which stock appreciation estimates were obtained, including Feinstein 1965; *Economic Trends* (e.g. October 1968, Table M); *Sources and Methods*, 1956, UK [22]: 321, and 1968, UK (20): 400; and *Board of Trade Journal* (e.g. issue of Feb. 23, 1968, for motor repairers and catering)

Forestry Commission, *Annual Reports; Trading Accounts and Balance Sheets*, UK [96]; *Inland Revenue Statistics*, UK [57] (to isolate agriculture from forestry and fishing in the postwar period)

National Income and Expenditure, 1958 and 1959 issues, for estimates of the effects of the change in Standard Industrial Classification

Sources and Methods, 1968, UK [20]: 91–93, for the weights of industries in GDP in 1958

All real output indicators were derived from the same sources as (and for individual industries and sectors they agree with) those in Feinstein 1972: Tables 8, 51–53, and *National Income and Expenditure, 1964–74*, UK [21]: Table 15. For aggregates (e.g. manufacturing and GDP) the agreement is not exact for periods after 1913 because the individual industry indicators were combined using different base years, as follows:

Period	Base year	Period	Base year
1913–37	1924	1955–60	1955
1937–51	1937	1960–64	1960
1951–55, 1951–64,	1951	1964–68, 1964–73	1964
1951–73		1968–73	1968

This system of first-year weighting (except for 1913–24) was adopted to permit some of the calculations in Chapter 9. In principle, it is not so accurate as that employed in Feinstein 1972 (see his Chapter 10, especially Table 10.1), where the base year was changed more often. But the growth rates of the aggregate series do not differ significantly from those of the Feinstein series, except across the wars, as the estimates of the growth of GDP in Table N.1 show.

Labor income is the sum of income from employment and an estimate of labor income from self-employment, and property income is the residual from total income. The method of estimating labor income from self-employment is explained in Chapter 6. In addition to the main sources, those cited above for estimating total income, and those in Chapter 6, note 7, estimates of the numbers of self-employed and of employees in employment are required. They are discussed in the next section.

THE TOTAL IN EMPLOYMENT AND HOURS WORKED BY INDUSTRY, AND THE TOTAL WORKING POPULATION

The main sources for the total in employment are Feinstein 1972: Table 59, for 1920–64; and the *Department of Employment Gazette*, March and October 1975 and December 1976, for 1964–73.

A minor adjustment to Feinstein's estimates for agriculture and hence all industries in 1920–38 was made to exclude some casual and part-time workers, mostly female. On pre-World War I and post-World War II definitions, these workers would not have been included in the labor force, and so they are excluded to permit transwar comparisons. Even so, the interwar and postwar seires are not strictly comparable because of a further discrepancy in the coverage of casual workers in agriculture, and a difference in coverage of seamen abroad. A further break in the concept of the total in employment occurs in 1964, after which the new census of employment concept is used. These breaks are summarized below in the paragraph on the working population. In tables and figures the series have been spliced at 1951 and 1964 where it would have been misleading not to do so. To do this, a separate estimate for 1951 had to be made on a basis exactly comparable with the interwar estimates. This required an adjustment to agriculture (because the interwar concept of the total in employment was *still* broader than the postwar one, even after the minor adjustment of Feinstein's data noted above), an adjustment to shipping (because again the interwar concept was broader than the postwar one), and a general reclassification (because the interwar statistics are classified according to the 1948 Standard Industrial Classification, and the postwar statistics according to the 1958 Standard Industrial Classification).

TABLE N.1

Alternative Estimates of the Growth of Gross Domestic Product, 1913–1973

(Annual percentage growth rates)

Period	Present estimates[a]	Alternative estimates[b]	Period	Present estimates[a]	Alternative estimates[b]
1913–1924	0.2%	0.0	1951–1955	2.7%	2.7%
1924–1937	2.3	2.3	1955–1960	2.5	2.5
1937–1951	1.5	1.3	1960–1964	3.1	3.1
1951–1973	2.7	2.7	1964–1968	2.5	2.6
			1968–1973	2.8	2.7

[a]From Table A.1, column 3.
[b]Calculated from Feinstein 1972: Table 6, column 1; *National Income and Expenditure*, 1964–74, UK [21]: Table 15.

The source for the total in employment in the whole economy in 1856–1920 is Feinstein 1972: Table 57. Estimates by industry for benchmark years before 1914 were obtained by interpolation between the decennial estimates derived from *Census of Population* data in Feinstein 1972, Table 60, and a comparable estimate made for 1851. Uniform rates of unemployment (as in Feinstein 1972: Table 57) were applied to all industries.

The totals in employment by industry in 1920–73 were disaggregated by sex (postwar only) and employment status (employees and self-employed) on the basis of data in the *Gazettes* cited above and the working papers and sources used for Feinstein 1972: Tables 57–59. The total self-employed in 1911 in Feinstein 1972: Table 7.17 was disaggregated into seven sectors on the basis of rough backward extrapolations from 1921 (for Great Britain and Northern Ireland) and 1926 (for Southern Ireland, from Saorstát Éireann, *Census of Population, 1926*). For 1861–1901 it was assumed that the self-employed were the same proportion of working population in each of the seven sectors as in 1911.

New estimates of hours worked in 11 benchmark years were prepared for this study. They refer to the hours actually worked after allowing for overtime, short-time, and part-time working; holidays; sickness; and strikes. Their sources and methods are summarized in Appendix D.

The sources for the total working population are Feinstein 1972: Table 57, for 1855–1964, and the *Department of Employment Gazette*, March and October 1975 and December 1976, for 1964–73. The minor adjustment described above for the total in employment in 1920–38 was also made for the total working population. Our definition of the working population changes twice in the whole period. For years from 1951 a slightly narrower concept is employed than for earlier years. Some casual workers in agriculture and some seamen abroad are excluded: they numbered 115,000 and 44,000, respectively, in 1951. The census of employment that replaced the National Insurance card estimates in 1971 excludes employees who worked for part of the year but who had jobs during census week, and private domestic workers, and includes the secondary jobs of multiple job holders. In practice we switch onto the census of employment concept in 1964 or 1966, depending on the context. In most of the tables, especially those showing growth rates, the series on different bases have been spliced according to their ratios in overlapping years.

CAPITAL

The main sources for the fixed capital stock, gross and net, are Feinstein (forthcoming) for 1856–1938; Feinstein 1965 for individual manufacturing industries in 1920–38; Feinstein 1972 and associated working papers, as amended by Chapter 5, note 1, for 1938–64; and *National Income and Expenditure, 1964–74*, UK [21], for 1964–73, with additional detail kindly supplied by the Central Statistical Office. The same sources were used for gross fixed capital formation except that Feinstein (forthcoming) was used for 1860–1920 and Feinstein 1965 and 1972 for 1920–64.

Gross capital stock by sector (i.e. unincorporated, other never-public, and sometime-public sectors) was estimated by allocating industries to sectors. First, the sometime-public sector was defined to comprise mining and quarrying, iron and steel, gas, electricity, and water, and transport and communications (excluding shipping). Then capital in manufacturing, construction, and commerce was divided between the unincorporated and corporate sectors on the basis of the two sectors' shares of depreciation allowances given in *Inland Revenue Statistics* (UK [57]). The unincorporated sector's capital stock consists of capital in the unincorporated parts, together with capital in professional services. Other never-public sector capital consists of shipping capital, and capital in the corporate parts of manufacturing (other than iron and steel), construction, and commerce.

The main sources for inventories are for 1856–1920, Feinstein (forthcoming), whole economy and agriculture only; for 1920–38, Feinstein 1965; for 1938–51, *Agricultural Statistics*, UK [60], for agriculture; for 1951–73, a variety of sources including *National Income and Expenditure, 1968* and *1964–74* and the works cited in the list on p. 613.

The estimates of the growth in constant prices for aggregates (e.g. manufacturing and the whole economy) were obtained by summing the series for individual industries at the prices of the base years shown in the tabulation on p. 615. As with output, this system of first-year weighting is necessary for some of the calculations in Chapter 9.

The fixed capital stock estimates for 1920–73 might be graded C and D (margin of error ± more than 25 percent) for earlier years. The fixed capital formation estimates might be graded as follows: 1856–90, C; 1891–1919, B/C; 1920–73, B.

The estimates of net overseas assets were built up from a variety of sources, of which the most important are these:

1856–1913, Morgan 1952: 331–34, 342–43; Imlah 1958: 68–80

1924–37, Kindersley 1929–39; *Finance Accounts*, UK [93]; London and Cambridge Economic Service 1972: Table N; *Reserves and Liabilities*, UK [94]

1951–73, Conan 1952: Appendix 1; *UK Balance of Payments*, UK [25]; Radcliffe Committee, 1959, UK [32]: 264; Bank of England, *Quarterly Bulletin* and *Statistical Abstract* 1970, 1975; *Midland Bank Review*; London and Cambridge Economic Service 1972

IMPORTS AND EXPORTS OF GOODS AND SERVICES

The main sources are Feinstein 1972 and working papers; *National Income and Expenditure, 1968* and *1964–74*, UK [21]; and *UK Balance of Payments, 1968* and *1964–74*, UK [25]. For 1855–70, the sources used for Feinstein 1972, especially Imlah 1958, were used. For re-exports, the following sources were also used: Imlah 1958; *Board of Trade Journal*; *Annual Abstract*, UK [10]; London and Cambridge Economic Service 1972.

A variety of sources were used for estimates of imports by main commodity group. The most important, in addition to those above, are Schlote 1952; Scott 1963: Appendix II; *Statistical Abstract*, UK [7]; *Annual Abstract*, UK [10]; *Annual Statement of Trade*, UK [2]; *Trade and Navigation Returns*, UK [8]; *Report on Overseas Trade*, UK [6]; *Board of Trade Journal*; and Mitchell & Deane 1962. The classification into the four commodity groups is, as far as possible, that of Scott 1963: Appendix II, pp. 210–13.

Notes

Notes

For abbreviations used in these Notes, see the References, p. 675.

CHAPTER 1

1. For the UK, see below, pp. 221–25; for other countries, Kuznets 1966: 106–7, 131–33, and (for the postwar period) Brown & Sheriff 1979.

2. Some national-accounting estimates are available for the 18th and early 19th centuries; in particular, for real product and national income in Deane & Cole 1962: 40–82, 154–73, and Deane 1968; and for capital stock in Feinstein 1978. Though these estimates are valuable, the foundations on which they rest are very unreliable, and the series are not comprehensive, not available on an annual basis, and not fully comparable with those for 1856 onward. For a critical comment on the 18th-century estimates, see Crafts 1976.

3. Hendry (1980) summarizes the list of problems first given by Keynes (1939b) in a comment following his review of Tinbergen's work in business cycles, and then adds another six problems to it.

4. Comparing the policy implications of analysis based on different models of the UK economy in the 1960's and 1970's, Goodhart (1978: 188) says: "Looking at exactly the same economy, and even using on occasions very similar structural equations, different modellers come to totally different policy conclusions because of their fundamental perceptions about the working of the economy. Econometrics has not, at least so far, provided any alternative for basic judgement, only some quantitative dressing and support for such judgements."

5. See in particular Reddaway & Smith 1960, Salter 1966, and Wragg & Robertson 1978 for industry-by-industry data; and Denison 1967, Panic 1976, and Christensen, Cummings & Jorgenson 1978 for international comparisons. (This list is not exhaustive.) The estimates given by these authors differ in various respects from one another and from ours in regard to coverage, method, and choice of data.

6. Most early work on growth accounting pointed to the predominance of TFP. This was challenged in later work, notably by Jorgenson and his associates. See Jorgenson & Griliches 1967; Denison 1969; Denison's exchange with Jorgenson and Griliches (1972); Christensen, Cummings & Jorgenson 1978.

CHAPTER 2

1. Except where stated otherwise, a geometric mean of the three estimates of GDP from the expenditure, income, and output sides is used. The main differences between the three series are discussed in Appendix A.

2. Real GDP per employed worker does not necessarily move in the same ways as real GDP per head of population, because the ratio of employed workers to total population may change, either because of changes in the average participation rate or because of changes in unemployment. These changes are dealt with in Chapter 3.

3. There are two reasons for this: (1) the basic statistics are more reliable for years late in the 19th century than for earlier years, and (2) 1856 and 1873 are not strictly comparable years between which to measure growth rates (see Appendix B); they were chosen because 1856 is the first peak year for which consistent data exist, and 1873 is the most appropriate year to compare with 1913.

4. The years 1856, 1873, 1913, 1937, 1951, and 1973 were at or near cyclical peaks; 1924 was not exactly a cyclical peak, but the level of unemployment was approximately the same as in 1937. (Comparisons between either 1924 or 1937 and years before 1914 or after World War II are, however, affected by the higher level of unemployment that existed throughout the interwar period.) See Appendix B for a discussion of the method of measuring secular growth by compound rates of growth between cycle peaks.

5. The political division actually occurred in December 1922, but 1920 is the dividing year used in this study.

6. Southern Ireland's share of the UK population was 18.7% in 1851 and 6.9% in 1911. The distinctive feature of the Southern Irish economy up to 1914 was the absolute decline of population.

7. The highest annual rate of growth of GDP between cycle peaks in the second half of the 19th century was 2.5%, the lowest 1.8% (see Fig. 2.1).

8. Going back into the 18th century, Deane and Cole (1962) found growth rates that were considerably lower but accelerated in the 1780's and 1790's, and then accelerated again in the early 19th century to the figures quoted above.

9. These six years are not perfectly comparable, though they all rank as cyclical peaks; in particular, 1960 was a weaker boom than 1955, and 1968 was a much weaker boom than 1973. But the differences are not enough to invalidate the conclusions drawn in the text.

10. See Appendix L for a discussion of the evidence.

11. Conventionally, income from abroad at constant prices is derived by deflating income from abroad at current prices by the prices of imports.

12. For a further discussion, see Stuvel 1959. The most recent issues of the National Income Blue Book give data on this concept, under the heading Gross National Disposable Income. See Hibbert 1975a.

13. The other six countries are those for which there are similar studies of long-term economic growth to our own, also supported by the (American) Social Science Research Council. We have tried in all cases to use estimates consistent with those studies.

14. This is true not only of the countries in the table, but also of the smaller industrial countries; see Kuznets 1956: 64–65; Maddison 1964: Table 16; Maddison 1977: Table 3. Only Australia, Belgium, the Netherlands, and Switzerland have had a low long-term rate of growth near to the UK's.

15. The data underlying Figure 2.2 were obtained by extrapolating estimates of absolute GDP per man-year for 1970 using the indexes from which the Table 2.5 growth rates were calculated.

The 1970 GDP estimates were derived from Kravis, Heston & Summers 1978a, except for Sweden. The geometric mean of the ratio of each country's GDP per capita to U.S. GDP per capita at that country's prices and the same ratio at U.S. prices, from Table 5.31, was multiplied by the ratio of the country's population to the U.S. population from Table 1.2, to obtain relative GDP. The ideal index was chosen as an approximation to a multilateral index covering the seven countries in the comparison, as opposed to the multilateral index covering, in principle, the whole world, which Kravis et al. 1978a estimate. The figures that they provide in Table 3.4 suggest that the ideal index might not be a bad estimator of such a multilateral index. A multilateral index is to be preferred to a binary one because it permits comparisons between any pair of countries, not just between each country and the U.S.

GDP per man-year in Sweden relative to the U.S. was estimated from data given in Kravis, Heston & Summers 1978b: Table 4. Their preferred approximation to a multilateral index for the whole world was adjusted in order to produce an estimate of a multilateral index covering the seven countries alone.

Employment in all countries in 1970, and population in Sweden, were taken from OECD [6].

16. The main problem is that the national indicators of GDP used for extrapolating backwards from 1970 are based on national rather than international prices. Ideally one would wish to redo the exercise of Kravis, Heston, and Summers (1978a) for benchmark years back to the 1870's. The resulting figures would not necessarily be the same as those in Figure 2.2. Note, for example, that their estimates of the 1970 GDP of France, Germany, Italy, and the UK relative to the U.S. are higher than those obtained by an extrapolation with national indicators of the 1950 estimates of Gilbert & Kravis 1954 (Kravis, Kenessey, Heston & Summers 1975: 8–9; see also Hibbert 1975b for a correction to allow for the difference between GNP and GDP). If this pattern were maintained in extrapolations back to the 1870's, our estimates of absolute GDP per man-year in the U.S. in the 19th century would be too low relative to the UK. More speculatively, the gap in the 1870's between the UK and the other European countries and Japan may be exaggerated in Figure 2.2.

17. Maddison 1977: Table 1 shows that the smaller industrial countries fit into the same pattern.

CHAPTER 3

1. No special significance attaches to the much greater absolute extent of the decline in the SMR compared with the crude death-rate over the period shown in Figure 3.2 as a whole. This is as to be expected, since a progressive fall in mor-

tality increases the size of the age groups with a high mortality rate. The (reciprocal of the) expectation of life, which measures the mortality to be expected from cohorts of equal initial size, declined at a rate much more nearly resembling that of the crude death-rate than that of the SMR. However, it continued to decline after 1921–30, thus showing that the absence of a fall in the crude death-rate was due partly to changes in cohort size.

2. Logan 1950. Some difficulties are created by changes in classification over time, as medical knowledge and diagnosis improved, but these difficulties are not too serious if attention is confined to broader categories of disease.

3. Typhus, enteric fever, simple continued fever, 23%; scarlet fever, 20%; diarrhea, dysentery, cholera, 9%; smallpox, 6%; accompanied by an *increase* of 5% due to measles, diphtheria, and whooping cough (McKeown & Record 1962).

4. At first due exclusively to declines in infectious diseases and deaths classified as infantile convulsions, and then to declines in all the chief causes of death.

5. The importance of general economic conditions receives confirmation from the substantial differences between social classes that persisted throughout the period in certain forms of mortality. Thus infant mortality in the lowest social class, Registrar General's Occupational Group V, remained between two and three times that in the highest class, Group I, throughout the period (Office of Health Economics 1964: 17–28).

6. See Schofield 1977, reviewing McKeown 1976. Insofar as such changes occurred and were related to increased internal migration, they did have a relationship, albeit a very long-run one, with economic development.

7. The difficulty in explaining the timing of the fall in the death-rate is not, perhaps, too surprising in view of the difficulty experienced in explaining the large regional and national differences that exist in both general mortality and mortality from specific diseases.

8. For further references and for documentation of some of the points made in the text, see Habakkuk 1972: 53–74. For an exhaustive survey of earlier literature, see UN 1953: Chapter 5.

9. Some relationship between movements in the two might also be expected because of causal effects running in the opposite direction. One such effect works through changes in the age structure of the population, given the above-average mortality of infants; this is not important in explaining the pattern before World War I, since, as shown in Figure 3.2, the movement of the SMR closely paralleled that of the crude death-rate. Another possibly more important causal effect running from lower birth-rates to lower death-rates operates through the effects of smaller family size on the health of the mother and other children.

10. Surviving family size cannot be estimated reliably for marriage cohorts earlier than that of 1881, because data are not available on the dates of births to earlier marriage cohorts. But since the reduction in infant mortality did not begin till the 20th century, it cannot have affected the surviving family size for pre-1881 marriage cohorts; hence we can be confident that the reduction in

family size between cohorts of 1861–69 and the cohort of 1881 was accompanied by a fall in surviving family size.

11. For example, in the U.S. the time pattern of the movement in the death-rate was similar to Britain's, but the U.S. birth-rate, as we have seen, fell throughout the 19th century, and Britain's did not. For further discussion of the death-rate hypothesis, see Habakkuk 1972, and the authors cited in UN 1953: 81; and for an interesting older article, Yule 1925.

12. The greatest use of non-appliance methods was by the marriage cohort of 1920–24 (Lewis-Faning 1949: 54).

13. There was also a large increase in nuptiality and a decline in the age at marriage compared with the pre–World War II period. But the effect of this on the crude birth-rate was partly offset by the decline in the population share of the 15–44 age group.

14. Jones & Smith 1970: 5. There was some compensatory increase in immigration from Europe after restrictions had been imposed on immigration from the New Commonwealth (*ibid.*, p. 15).

15. Two statistical points should be borne in mind in interpreting the table. The first is that the measured relative importance of age-distribution changes and specific-participation-rate changes depends on the actual age and sex groups used in the calculations. What might appear as a participation-rate change for a broad group might appear mainly as an age structural shift if the group were disaggregated into narrower age bands. This is less likely to occur the more homogeneous with respect to participation rates are the groups chosen. The eight groups distinguished in our calculations (see Table 3.5) separate out those sections of the population that have significantly different from average participation rates (thus men and women, children and the elderly, are in different groups), but a more detailed age breakdown might lead to different estimates of the relative importance of age distribution and specific participation changes. Comparisons between periods are likely to be more reliable than the absolute figures for a particular period.

The second statistical point refers to the coverage of the data that were used to estimate the sources of working population growth. They relate to Great Britain rather than the UK, which probably does not make much difference, and, more seriously, they are out of necessity based on the *Population Census* concept of the economically active population (see Table 3.4). Thus movements in the average participation rate implied by these data (Table 3.4, column 2) do not exactly correspond to those in the UK average participation rate (Table 3.4, column 1), which is our central interest. The main divergences can be seen when comparing 1931 with 1951, when the rate for Great Britain falls while the UK rate rises. Because of the downward bias in the 1966 sample census, some care must be exercised when interpreting the absolute figures in Table 3.5 of growth between 1951 and 1966, but the relative importance of the different items will be broadly correct.

16. Young adults are the main class of migrants. High emigration therefore tends initially to increase the proportion of children in the population. The

unusually steep rise in the proportion of population of working age between 1891 and 1901 probably reflected the low level of emigration in that decade. It is also possible that the sharp change from net emigration in the 1920's to net immigration in the 1930's contributed to the continued steep reduction in the proportion of children that occurred in the 1930's, when the birth-rate was flattening out.

17. We have not commented in the text on fluctuations in specific participation rates in the period before 1914. Some tendency may be observed for inverse movements between specific participation rates and the proportion of population of working age, especially in 1891–1901 (Table 3.5). This might be taken to suggest that in periods when the proportion of working population was rising especially rapidly, the pressure of supply on the labor market forced out marginal members of the labor force. This is not necessarily inconsistent with the fact that the fall in specific participation rates in 1891–1901 owed much to the 0–14 age group: better school attendance could have resulted from less availability of jobs. The conclusion is, however, to be accepted with some reserve, since the apparent inverse movement may in part be due to imperfect consistency between periods in the statistical breakdown of the sources of growth in the working population.

18. Two hypotheses about the fall in elderly workers' participation can be dismissed: (1) that it was the result of the rising average age of the over-64 group (male participation rates fell steadily after 1931 within each over-64 age group, 65–69, 70–74, and 75 and over); and (2) that employers were reluctant or unable to accept an increased proportion of elderly workers (the proportion of elderly males in the working population fell between every census after 1921, suggesting that supply factors were more important than demand factors).

19. Though high by historical standards, the participation rate of married women in Great Britain in the 1960's was not especially high by international standards. Of the six other countries for which information is given in Fogarty, Rapoport & Rapoport 1971: 517–18, Table III 1 (ii), three (France, West Germany, and the U.S.) had higher rates, and three (Ireland, Norway, and Sweden) lower rates. It is possible also that the rates for married women were significantly higher in Eastern European countries, as those for all women certainly were (UN 1969: Table 28).

20. See G. Thomas 1944, 1948; Leser 1955–56; James 1962; Beckerman 1963; Routh 1965: 43–49; Williams 1965; Galambos 1967; A. Hunt 1968; Bowers 1970.

21. "It must be emphasized that we have received very striking evidence not only from employers but also from some of the Trade Unions, which is confirmed by the testimony of Government inspectors and costing experts, that in certain occupations in which both men and women are employed—notably the gauging, sorting and adjusting of minute components, the running of automatic lathes, and certain kinds of weaving—the average woman produces over a long period a larger output than the common run of men, with greater docility, and a more contented mind, involving less 'worry' to the management" (B. Webb 1919: 281).

22. Despite the increase in female employment during World War I, there was still considerable opposition to it, as is illustrated by the following quotation: "In many districts to state that you go out to work after marriage is to a certain extent to confess your marriage a failure, which a women does not readily do, even on an official return," (Women's Employment Committee, UK [27]). World War II was probably much more important in changing attitudes. No doubt the difference in the employment situation after the two wars largely explains their different impact on attitudes.

23. The average hourly earnings of female manual workers (18 years and over) in manufacturing industry as a percentage of those of male manual workers (21 and over) in the UK were as follows:

1938	1951	1964	1973
83.9%	100.0%	94.7%	100.6%

(See *British Labor Statistics Historical Abstract*, UK [48]: Tables 46–48; the data relate to October in each year.) The slower rate of growth of women's than men's earnings in the earlier part of the postwar period suggests that there may have been sufficient women prepared to work in manufacturing without their having to be attracted by especially high wages.

24. The proportion of women workers who were part-timers was as follows (G. Thomas 1944; worksheets for Appendix D):

1943	1951	1964	1973
7%	12%	29%	35%

25. Bowers (1970: 52) notes that in 1961 there were regional differences in female participation rates even after allowing for the different industrial structures that provide the main explanation for measured differences in participation. The remaining variations are "positively associated with the female-employing bias of the industrial structure and with the bias towards employment implicit in the wage and marital structure of the female population of the regions. This suggests that the provision of female employment has effects both on the demand for female workers in other industries within the region, and on the number of female workers forthcoming."

26. The well-known fact that female participation rates were positively associated with the level of demand over postwar cycles (see Hunter 1963; Galambos 1967) is not inconsistent with the rejection of the *pure* demand explanation of the trend increase in female participation. Supply schedules can be approximately steady (relative to demand schedules) over the cycle while moving slowly during a longer period.

27. There were demand-induced variations in the amount of overtime worked between peak and trough phases of postwar cycles, but these do not affect the comparison between the benchmark years, which are all cyclical peaks.

28. There had been little change in the 1870's; in one or two industries there were then actually increases in hours, as the bargaining power of labor declined (Clapham 1932: 447–50).

29. It is unlikely that the proportion of male part-timers in 1937 was lower

than the 1951 level (0.3%), given that many of the part-timers in 1937 (e.g. those in agriculture and public administration) are known to have been men.

30. The proportion of part-timers among males aged 65 or over rose from 4% in 1951 to 31% in 1964 and 52% in 1973.

31. Hours worked by women as a percentage of total hours worked (the two 1964 figures reflect a change in the concept of employment in that year, the first being comparable with 1951, the second with 1973):

1951	1964	1964	1973
28.8%	28.7%	28.0%	30.4%

32. As noted earlier, apropos of Table 3.7, there was a decline after 1966 in the rate of growth of the participation rate of married women, attributed to less strong demand for labor. This does not appear in Table 3.17 in the comparison of 1951–64 and 1964–73, partly because of the difference in the year used to divide the periods in the two tables (the female participation rate rose strongly between 1964 and 1966) and partly because the increase in the proportion of women working part-time was less pronounced in the late postwar period.

33. Beveridge's remark (1930: 69) has often been quoted: "Has there ever, in the big towns at least, been a time when employers could not get practically at a moment's notice all the labourers they required?" See also the conclusion of the Poor Law Commission (Webb & Webb 1909: 173): "Distress from want of employment, though periodically aggravated by depressions of trade, is a constant feature of industry and commerce as at present administered." The work of the Commission is a main source of information on this question. The conclusion quoted was not a matter of disagreement between the majority and minority reports. See also R.C. on Labour, UK [79].

34. One of the many vivid pieces of evidence given to the Poor Law Commission may be quoted. " 'There is always such a plentiful supply of men eager for work,' deposed the general foreman of a large building firm, 'the trouble is having to refuse applicants who attend early morning and throughout the day, delaying the foreman at every turn. . . . They will follow a builder's cart should it have material until they find out where the job is, and also report same to Trade Unions, so that on going onto an entirely vacant site to commence operations you will often find it surrounded by men of all trades.' " (Webb & Webb 1909: 173.)

35. The view that trend forces were making for increased regularity of employment in the late 19th century is expressed in Marshall 1920: 687–88; 1926: 92–101. Marshall here compares the kind of industrial unemployment reflected in the trade union figures with the much more severe unemployment and underemployment prevailing in a town he was familiar with (Palermo) in an underdeveloped country.

36. Changes in relative male participation rates do not reflect only changes in the relative demand for labor. They are also caused by changes in age composition and educational levels, among other things. Female participation rates are also considered to be an indicator of the demand for labor in the postwar period, but for present purposes male participation rates are preferred because

they do not show the same wide divergences between regions resulting from different occupational and industrial structures and different traditions of female employment.

37. According to the Local Government Board (UK [59]: 67), percentage rates of pauperism in different classes of Poor Law Unions in 1907 were as follows:

Wholly rural	2.9%	Mixed rural and urban	
Wholly urban, excluding London	2.0	Less than 75% urban	2.6%
London	2.6	More than 75% urban	1.9

Pauperism was thus higher in rural areas than in London, but substantially higher in London than in other towns. A detailed map in the same source (p. 48) shows systematically more pauperism in the southern half of the country, especially the South Midlands and the eastern region, than in the North. These data are of only limited value as indicators of unemployment because the class of paupers whose numbers were directly related to unemployment, namely the able-bodied, accounted for less than a quarter of total pauperism, and the importance of the aged in the total causes regional figures to be much influenced by age composition. (Likewise, trends over time in pauperism are of little value as an indicator, both for this reason and because of substantial changes in administrative practice.) They are, however, consistent with the other evidence. On agricultural wages, see Bowley 1921: 170–71; and for a discussion relating them to underemployment, E. H. Hunt 1967.

38. See Lee 1971 for further details of the different regional patterns of development.

39. Apart from statistical biases, there is a problem of principle in that the responses relate to the expected availability of labor *to the firm*. They therefore reflect not merely the degree of overall shortage, but the extent to which employers think that additional labor can be competed away from other employment.

40. The other component, fluctuations in population, does not vary systematically over the cycle. Some small interaction effects also enter the calculation.

41. It is not meaningful to give quantitative estimates of the relative importance of the fluctuations in participation rates and unemployment in pre-1914 years because the interpolation method used to estimate the working population assumes away most of the cyclical movements in participation.

42. For a balanced statement to this effect by a leading member of the "explaining-away" school, see Brittan 1975: 80.

43. For years after 1959 it is possible to make use of the U.S. Department of Labor's adjustments, which are designed to make national unemployment rates consistent with U.S. concepts (see, for example, Sorrentino 1972). Similar rough proportionate adjustments are made to the estimates for 1952–58. Though no adjustments to national unemployment rates were made for the pre–World War II years, it seems likely that the UK and U.S. rates are approximately comparable. Those for Germany and Sweden in the interwar period are probably overestimates.

CHAPTER 4

1. In the case of intersex differences in marginal productivity, the changes in the proportion of females in the labor input were so small that, even if the use of relative earnings leads to considerable overestimation, no significant sex-quality change is recorded. It should also be noted that much of the discrimination against women seems to have taken the form of job discrimination (preventing women from doing certain jobs) rather than pay discrimination (paying women less than men for equivalent work). Job discrimination reduces output below what it would be if women were free to choose the best-paid jobs, but it does not in itself imply that differences between male and female earnings do not reflect differences in marginal productivity.

2. Two historical series of relative earnings exist: (1) those derived from official inquiries into the weekly earnings of full-time manual workers, and (2) those constructed by Routh (1965) relating to the annual earnings of all full-time workers. The first series separates males from females, and young persons from adults; the second only separates the sexes. Both series are shown in the accompanying table.

3. One further statistical reservation attaches to these figures. They are derived from hourly earnings calculated from weekly earnings and the number of hours worked per week. They do not therefore take into account differences between age-sex groups in the number of weeks worked per year. There are known to be differences between men and women, and between elderly persons and the rest, in the number of weeks lost through sickness. In 1949–52 the average number of weeks of incapacity due to sickness and injury per employed

TABLE TO NOTE 2

Relative Earnings of Full-Time Workers by Age and Sex, 1886–1973

(Percent of earnings of men)

Year	Men (21 and over)	Youths and boys (under 21)	Women (18 and over)	Girls (under 18)
(1) Weekly earnings of full-time manual workers				
1886	100.0%	39.5%	51.5%	29.4%
1906	100.0	36.0	44.4	23.3
1938	100.0	37.8	47.1	26.8
1951	100.0	41.6	54.1	34.9
1964	100.0	45.1	49.4	32.9
1973	100.0	51.4	51.7	37.0
(2) Annual earnings of all full-time workers[a]				
1913–14	100.0		54.0	
1922–24	100.0		57.0	
1935–36	100.0		56.0	
1955–56	100.0		50.0	
1960	100.0		54.0	

Source: (1) 1886, Board of Labor, UK [1]; 1906, *British Labour Statistics Historical Abstract*, UK [48]: Table 37 (the figures were roughly adjusted to obtain averages for all industries — using 1911 population data from *BLSHA*, Table 102 — and the required age distribution between men and youths and boys); 1938–73, *ibid.*, Tables 40–42, 49, and *Labour Statistics Yearbook*, UK [39], *1973*: Table 26. (2) Routh 1965: 105.

[a] All age groups.

man was as follows for each age group (*Report by the Government Actuary*, UK [97]: Table 17):

15–19	1.01	35–39	1.59	50–54	3.19
20–24	1.21	40–44	1.85	55–59	4.39
25–29	1.31	45–49	2.39	60–64	6.33
30–34	1.42				

In 1954–55 and 1955–56 the average number of weeks for which sickness benefit was claimed was (*ibid.*, UK [98]: Tables 2, 3):

Employed men	2.04
Employed single women	2.26
Employed married women	3.46

There may also be differences in length of holidays. The adjustment of the figures in Table 4.1 that would be necessary to make an allowance for this point is likely to be small when compared with the large differences shown in the table between male and female earnings, and between young people's earnings and average earnings.

4. Many of the sources quoted in Appendix D in connection with the estimates of hours of work in 1951 and 1964 provide figures for each age group, so that estimates of the total hours worked by each age group could have been built up. However, extensive manipulation of the data is required, and bold assumptions would have to be made to fill some of the remaining gaps in the age-specific information. The benefits, in terms of increased accuracy, of undertaking such an operation did not seem to us to be great enough to justify it.

5. The (correct) use of total man-hours for the sex-quality calculation after 1951 picks up the postwar move toward female part-time working, and so no error stems from this source in the postwar estimates.

6. See Feinstein 1972: 10 for data on labor income in Great Britain and Ireland. Ireland's output was about 6½% of Great Britain's in 1907; and the Irish working population was about 12% the size of Great Britain's in 1901 and about 10% in 1911 (*ibid.*, p. 212, footnote 2, and Table 11.8).

7. The separation of the 26 counties in 1922 does not as such produce any change in quality because of the splicing of series.

8. In exceptional circumstances, the offset may actually exceed one. Thus Chapman (1909: 356) concluded: "I have found no instance in which an abbreviation of hours has resulted in a proportionate curtailment of output. . . . In some cases the product, or the value of the product, has actually been augmented after a short interval."

9. Webb & Cox 1891; Rae 1894. See also Wood 1902; Chapman 1909; and for a careful discussion of the effects on productivity of the fall in hours in 1919 and 1920, Dowie 1975: 441–45.

10. Chief Inspector of Factories, UK [26], *1918*: 2–7, *1919*: 90, *1920*: 150; Florence 1924; Myers 1926; Viteles 1933; Vernon 1934, 1943; Medical Research Council 1942. Some American studies are summarized in Brinberg & Northrup 1950; and D. G. Brown 1965.

11. See Denison 1967: 59–64 for a review of the literature and for a more extended discussion of some of the issues.

12. Unfortunately, figures on the same basis cannot be given for birth cohorts later than 1941 or for the whole labor force for a year later than 1961, because the relevant question was not included in the 1971 census. See p. 111 and note 26, below, for rough estimates.

13. Apart from the difficulty of inferring from cross-section data conclusions applicable to time-series (a point we shall come to shortly), the main objection to the use of relative earnings as a measure of relative marginal productivities is that the higher earnings associated with higher educational levels are not the result *only* of more education. They may also reflect, among other things, the greater intelligence of those who receive more education, or the advantages enjoyed by children of rich or well-educated parents in obtaining both more education and a more remunerative job. In order to eliminate the effects on earnings associated with but not caused by education, Denison (1967: 83–84) assumes that three-fifths of earnings differentials are "due" to differences in education.

Griliches (1970: 92–104) has argued that it may not be necessary to make any significant reduction in earnings differentials to remove elements not caused by education, because many of them — for example, differences in ability — require education to make them operative.

More recently economists have become interested in the "filter" hypothesis of education, according to which the content of education contributes nothing to earnings; it merely provides society with a means of separating out individuals who are likely to be more productive (and hence command higher incomes) for reasons not associated with the amount of education they have had. See Blaug 1972; Arrow 1973; Wiles 1974. If the "filter" hypothesis is correct, the contribution of education to the quality of labor cannot be measured from earnings differentials (because Denison's three-fifths would become zero, i.e. no quality improvement). An alternative method must therefore be devised for estimating the contribution that education makes through its allocative function, through directing the right people to the jobs where their output is maximized.

An empirical study by Taubman and Wales (1973) concludes that roughly half of the extra earnings of U.S. graduates (calculated without reference to other personal attributes) can be explained in terms of the "filter" hypothesis. This suggests that the assumption that the marginal social productivity of schooling approximates to three-fifths of the difference between the earnings of people with different amounts of education may not be too far from the truth.

14. The only available studies of the relation between earnings and education in the UK measure the return from prolonging education beyond the primary level, and hence they are not directly relevant to the problem of measuring the return from extra years of primary schooling (see text below). The main studies are Henderson-Stewart 1965; Blaug, Peston & Ziderman 1967; Selby-Smith 1970; *Survey of Earnings of Qualified Manpower*, UK [38]; Morris & Ziderman 1971.

15. Adjusted for differences in earnings due to factors associated with but not caused by differences in educational attainments. Denison's "European weights" are based on data for France, which are the fullest available.

16. The increase in the quality of the labor force between 1951 and 1961 thus calculated (0.34% per year) may be compared with Denison's figure of 0.45% for 1950–62 (Denison 1967: 89, Table 8-6). Denison's figure is based on the frequency of distribution of years' schooling in the labor force and ours on the average. Frequency distributions can be calculated for 1951 and 1961 but not for earlier years.

17. *15–18*, UK [61]: 10–15. The proportion of 16-year-olds in school rose from 18.9% in 1954 to 28.6% in 1963 (*Statistics of Education*, UK [37], *1966*: vol. 1, p. 32).

18. See Morris & Ziderman 1971: Table B, where mean lifetime earnings for male holders of first degrees only (B.A.s and equivalent) are shown to be 1.7 times those of males with only the pre-university qualifications represented by "A" levels. On the Denison assumption that 0.6 of the difference in earnings is attributable to education (1967: 84), this implies that at the university level each extra year produces an additional 14% of earnings.

19. Crude calculations based on the earnings data in Morris & Ziderman 1971 suggest that the improvement in the quality of the labor force resulting from university education averaged at most 0.04% a year between 1931 and 1961. The slowdown in the rate of growth of AYS after 1931, on the assumption used in the text, lowered the rate of improvement in the quality of the labor force by about 0.06% a year.

20. For information on types of technical training and further education, see *15–18*, UK [61]: Part 6; Williams 1957, 1963; Cotgrove 1958; Nesbitt-Hawes 1966; Blaug, Peston & Ziderman 1967; R.C. on Trade Unions and Employers' Associations, UK [89]: 85–93; Keene 1969: 133–65.

21. The official figures, published in the *Ministry of Labor Gazette*, are probably rather too high (Croft 1960: 2).

22. Routh 1965: 11. (The decimal point in Routh's table is misprinted.)

23. An exact calculation is not possible because data on occupational distribution in 1961 and 1971 are on a different basis from Routh's.

24. The numbers for the four most important classes of technical qualifications in benchmark years are shown in the table on p. 634.

25. Earnings data in Morris & Ziderman 1971: Table B suggest that male workers with technical qualifications earn about 1.6 times as much in their lifetimes as those with no qualifications. Assuming an average training period of five years, and Denison's three-fifths rule, this implies that each extra year of training produces an additional 7% of earnings. The 0.17 of a year increase in training between 1931 and 1951 is therefore equivalent to a 1% quality increase, or 0.05% per year. Adjusting this to exclude university and other full-time schooling, and to include improvements in the quality of technical education, might raise this figure to about 0.1%. If one further assumes that most of this improvement occurred after 1938, and that it continued during the postwar

TABLE TO NOTE 24

Numbers of Workers Acquiring Technical Qualifications

(Thousands)

Year	City and Guilds Institute		Ordinary National Certificate	Higher National Certificate
	Craft certificate	Technician's certificate		
1929	—	—	1.2	0.5
1938	—	—	3.3	1.1
1951	18.6	9.0	11.0	5.6
1964	47.7	37.9	23.0	12.8
1973	183.2	131.0	21.6	15.1

Source: City and Guilds Certificate data kindly made available by the City and Guilds of London Institute; National Certificates, *Statistics of Education*, UK [37].

period, one arrives at a figure of about 0.2% per year for the improvement in the quality of the labor force between 1937 and 1973 resulting from technical education.

26. In Appendix E we have not provided estimates of AYS for years before 1871 on account of lack of adequate statistics of the age distribution of the labor force. However, approximate estimates can be made, and these underlie the figure for 1856–73 given in Table 4.6. Data on changes in AYS are not available for 1964–73, but it appears that the increase was rather less rapid than in 1951–64. The figure given in the text for 1964–73 reflects this.

27. An additional potential source of error is introduced when the estimates of quality growth resulting from changes in the age-sex distribution are added to those resulting from changes in the educational level. If the distributions of earnings by age-sex groups are not independent of those by educational classes, there is some danger of double-counting. This is, however, likely to be negligible quantitatively.

28. Improvements in nutrition and in the working environment lead to an increase in the intensity of work, and the fall in the proportion of self-employed to a decrease, assuming that motivation and hence intensity of work is lower among employees than among the self-employed. See Denison 1967: 109–16 for further discussion of some of these points.

29. Webb & Webb 1902: 392–429; Marshall 1919: 103, 136–37, 213, 639–42; Hilton et al. 1935; Zweig 1951; Phelps-Brown 1959, 1971: 116–20; Fox 1960; Levine 1967: 79–110; R.C. on Trade Unions and Employers' Associations, UK [88], [90]; Ulman 1968; Phelps-Brown & Browne 1968: especially 186–90.

30. "Restrictive practices imposed by trade unions are actually fewer than they were, and of less importance. Employers in a number of industries have referred to conditions in their fathers' or grandfathers' time, and have admitted that, comparatively, their own grounds for complaint are small." (Hilton et al. 1935: 335.)

31. As such it has been challenged by American econometric historians, in relation to the period 1873–1913, on the ground that there is nothing to explain

(see McCloskey & Sandberg 1971, and literature cited there, in rebuttal of the views advanced by such authors as Aldcroft 1964, Levine 1967, and Landes 1969). The argument of the cliometricians has been based chiefly on studies of individual industries, which suggested that Britain's failure to adopt certain specific innovations was not irrational. The contention is, however, more about imagination and energy than about rationality, and here the defenses are less convincing (as recognized by Sandberg 1974: 134–35). The finding of *zero* change in TFP (after allowing for labor quality) in 1873–1914 makes it difficult to believe that there is nothing to explain. (See also Chapter 15, pp. 449–51.)

32. What follows draws in particular on Cotgrove 1958; Reader 1966; Coleman 1973; Rubinstein 1977; and, for later developments, Postan 1967: Chapter 11, and the references cited there.

CHAPTER 5

1. Feinstein 1972: Chapter 9, Tables 43–46; *National Income and Expenditure*, UK [21], *1964–74*. We made minor revisions to the published gross capital stock estimates at current prices for 1948–64 and 1938 (estimate comparable with the postwar estimates) in Feinstein's Table 46 in order to use price indexes consistent with those used elsewhere in the study. The revised figures for those cases where the revisions exceeded 1 percent are (in £ billion) *1938*, other buildings and works, 7.84; plant and machinery, 3.86; vehicles, ships, and aircraft 1.23; and total 18.25; *1952–55*, other buildings and works, 1952, 23.99; 1953, 24.31; 1954, 24.62; 1955, 26.74; and *1964* vehicles, ships, and aircraft, 7.43.

We also made new estimates of net capital stock in 1938 on a basis comparable with those for postwar years (£ billion):

	Dwellings	Other buildings and works	Plant, vehicles, etc.	Total
At 1958 prices	13.3	12.1	8.9	34.3
At current prices	3.5	3.7	2.5	9.7

No comparable estimates appear in Feinstein's Tables 43 and 46.

2. Feinstein has substantially revised his 1972 estimates in this work. The revisions to the gross and net stock of fixed capital are particularly large for 1856–73. For further discussion of these revisions, see the newer study.

3. For some estimates, notably ships, agricultural buildings, hospitals, and assets other than vehicles in the textile industry, scrapping in the postwar period was not estimated in this way; either direct estimates of scrapping were used (ships, textiles) or rough assumptions were made (agricultural buildings, hospitals). See Appendix G for the lengths of lives actually assumed.

4. See Feinstein 1972: 199–200 and (forthcoming) for a brief discussion on consistency and reliability.

5. There is no entirely satisfactory way of dealing with this problem. If the capital estimate for the gross stock comparable with pre-1938 years is too low, the earlier figures need to be scaled up; if the figure comparable with postwar years is too high, the postwar figures need to be scaled down. By either accept-

ing the figures as they stand or chaining them together, we are assuming that they are consistent within pre-1938 and within post-1938, respectively. But this is not necessarily correct, because it cannot be taken for granted that the error, on whichever side it is, affects the capital estimates to an equal proportionate extent within either period. One important context in which care has to be exercised in interpreting the figures is the comparison of pre-1938 and post-World War II capital growth: whichever of the two estimates is correct, our procedures must overestimate the change in growth rates between prewar periods and postwar periods because the growth rates are calculated from consistent (over time) gross investment estimates that are combined with inconsistent capital stock estimates. Fortunately, the difference is not so large as to alter the conclusions qualitatively where movements over substantial periods of time are being considered. See Feinstein (forthcoming) for further discussion of the difference between the two 1938 estimates. There is also a break in 1920 because of the exclusion thereafter of Southern Ireland. This is allowed for in the calculations that follow.

6. Current price estimates can be compared with book values in years that have served as the base years for the constant price estimates (in £ million):

Year	Book values	Current prices	Ratio
1958	9,025	8,977	1.005
1963	11,099	10,973	1.011
1970	17,468	17,034	1.025

7. The two estimates of stocks and work-in-progress at current prices at the end of 1938 are (in £ million):

	Agriculture	All sectors
Comparable with pre-1938 years	411	1,743
Comparable with postwar years	262	1,594

See also Feinstein 1972: 203, footnote 2, where it is noted that end-1938 stocks estimated by subtracting the increase in book values in 1939–48 from end-1948 stocks are *larger* than the estimate that is comparable with pre-1938 years. The estimate based on working backwards from 1948 is, however, very unreliable and can be ignored.

8. For 1856–70, the Sauerbeck-Statist Index (published in the *Journal of the Royal Statistical Society*); for 1871–1920, the Board of Trade Wholesale Price Index.

9. See Feinstein 1972: 204–5 for a comparison between census-type estimates and accumulated net investment abroad; and *BEQB* (various issues, e.g. 10.3, Sept. 1970) for the methods used in estimating figures for recent years and for a consideration of the limitations of the estimates. Revell & Roe 1971: 8–19 provides estimates of net overseas assets in 1957–66 revalued at current market prices. In principle this is the valuation required for our purposes, but it did not seem worth making use of it, given the unimportance of an error in the net overseas assets estimates in years when they were relatively insignificant,

especially when compared with the error resulting from the absence of market valuations of the estimates for earlier years. See Table 5.2 note a for a comparison of the present estimates for 1964 with those of Revell and Roe.

10. Inventories are measured as for Table 5.3. GDP at 1938 prices is based on the compromise index in Feinstein 1972: Table 6, and the base-year value on Table 4, col. 5, of that work. The fall in the pre-1914 ratio mainly reflects the relatively high inventory-output ratio for agriculture at the beginning of the period and the decline in agriculture's share in GDP over the period.

11. For the years before 1920 the assumption that non-farm inventories were 25% of total final expenditure renders pointless any independent analysis of inventories. Trans-World War II changes are very unreliable because of unsatisfactory price indicators and different bases of estimation before and after the war.

12. In Germany the ratio of net to gross stock rose over the period 1950–60 from 57.4% to 65.5%, and the average age fell from 25.0 years to 21.8 years (Denison 1967: 147, 420, Tables 12-5 and J-S). In the UK the ratio of net to gross was 50.9% at the end of 1948 and 59.3% at the end of 1962.

13. In the period 1913–24 net overseas assets at current market prices may have risen by more than the present estimates, which are mostly valued at nominal values. However, the predominance of fixed-interest securities (four-fifths of the total in 1913), and the absence of a spectacular increase in the rate of return on gross overseas assets in the period (it rose from 4.8% in 1913 to 5.0% in 1924), suggest that the excess of the increase in current market values over that in nominal values cannot have been large.

14. In 1924 the assets and liabilities arising out of intergovernment war loans were £1.8 billion and £1.1 billion, respectively. By 1931 the UK had repaid more principal than it had received, so the net grant implied by repudiation was in fact slightly greater than the original net loan.

15. Implicit GDP prices rose by about 110%. The sterling devaluation of 1949 would also have increased the value of dollar securities and other assets that were valued in foreign currency. The estimate of the extent of the appreciation is based on a comparison of the difference between estimated investments at end-1937 and end-1951, and the identified net flows in 1938–51. It therefore includes all the errors and omissions in both series, as well as the valuation errors of the stock estimates, and is thus very approximate.

16. Stock appreciation data broken down by sector are not available for the interwar period. Government stock appreciation was probably close to zero, and the remainder should be allocated between the personal and corporate sectors. Total stock appreciation averaged 0.5% of GNP in 1935–38, ranging from −2.1% in 1936 to +2.1% in 1938 (Feinstein 1972: Table 1).

17. The principal component was receipts of aid under the European Recovery Program; other items included were the settlement of debts and claims arising out of the war and sales of surplus war stores held abroad. Total capital transfers averaged 1.5% of GNP in 1948–51 and 0.1% in 1952–55.

18. The shares in GNP of total personal income and its components in 1937 and 1951 were as follows:

Year	Total	Employment income	Self-employ- ment income	Rent, divi- dends and net interest	National insurance grants, etc.	Other transfers
1937	100.1%	59.2%	12.8%	22.4%	5.4%	0.3%
1951	92.2	65.6	10.2	9.8	6.1	0.5

19. The 1973 figures on personal savings as a percentage of personal disposable income in the major industrialized countries are as follows (OECD [9]: Table 9):

Sweden	5%	Canada	10%	Belgium	18%
Denmark	7	W. Germany	13	Italy	20
UK	7	France	16	Japan	25
U.S.	9	Netherlands	16		

(The figures for the different countries are approximately comparable, but the definitions of personal disposable income differ from those employed in the text, and both savings and disposable income are net of depreciation.)

20. For the postwar shares of all the components in total personal income excluding stock appreciation, see the table below.

21. The 45–59 age group constituted 24.5% of the male population over 14 in 1951 and 26.9% in 1961. On the basis of Lydall's estimates of savings propensities by age group, the 1951 and 1961 age structures imply average propensities of 1.2% and 1.5%, respectively.

22. Two other explanations may be mentioned. Stone (1964) explains the rise in the personal savings ratio as a consequence of a fall in the personal wealth-income ratio. His wealth data, however, are based essentially on nominal values. Though the fall in the real value of government debt held by individuals is undeniable, it is doubtful whether, if account could be taken of the increase in the prices of equities and of house property, the personal wealth-income ratio in real terms would show any fall at all in the postwar period. The Stone hypothesis, therefore, depends on a form of money illusion. Dow (1964: 271–75) suggests that the rapid increase in savings comes from the unincorporated business part of the personal sector rather than from households. If this were so, one

TABLE TO NOTE 20

Year	Employment income	Self-employ- ment income	Rent, divi- dends, net interest	National insurance grants, etc.	Other transfers
1951	71.2%	11.2%	10.6%	6.6%	0.5%
1955	72.1	10.4	9.8	7.1	0.6
1960	71.2	9.3	11.1	7.8	0.6
1964	71.3	8.2	11.8	8.1	0.5
1968	69.3	8.3	11.7	10.1	0.6
1973	69.0	10.1	10.1	10.3	0.5

Source: National Income and Expenditure, UK [21], *1968, 1964–75.*

would expect gross fixed capital formation by unincorporated businesses to show a similar rapid rise, since they normally reinvest their profits. However, fixed investment by the non-farm unincorporated sector, though it rose at a reasonable rate, was not large enough to explain a significant part of the overall rise in the propensity to save.

23. It has already been noted that there is some evidence to suggest that the personal propensity to save out of disposable income did not rise by as much in the postwar period as Figure 5.7 shows, if it rose at all. Of course, it is not so difficult to find explanations for a small or nonexistent upward trend as it is to explain the strong upward trend in the statistics.

In addition to the studies cited in this section, readers may consult the following for empirical work on personal savings in the UK: Radice 1939; Klein 1958; various articles in the *Bulletin of the Oxford University Institute of Statistics* reporting on the Oxford Savings Survey and cited in Lydall 1955 and Klein 1958; Stone & Rowe 1962; *BEQB* 1966, 1976; Stone 1966, 1973; McMahon & Smyth 1971; Common 1972 (also, in the same issue, a reply by McMahon and Smyth and a rejoinder by Common).

24. As noted, the corporate sector is defined as consisting of both companies and public corporations. Post-tax income is defined as total pre-tax income, less payments of UK tax, less taxes paid abroad; and savings as post-tax income, less payments of dividends and interest, less profits paid abroad, less current transfers to charities. From 1967 onward, investment grants are included in savings and in post-tax income (see Table 5.7, note c). Stock appreciation is included in income and savings for the 1933–38 period only.

25. The percentages for the postwar period are as follows (Fig. 5.8; *National Income and Expenditure*, UK [21], *1964–74*):

Category	1965–68	1969–73
Corporate propensity to save	51.6%	49.3%
Post-tax income as proportion of pre-tax income	84.7	81.5
Pre-tax income as proportion of GNP	25.1	25.1
Corporate savings as proportion of GNP	11.0	10.1

26. The proportion of corporate gross trading profits to GNP fell somewhat before 1968 and more sharply thereafter, but there was an offsetting rise in the share of corporate non-trading income, including income from abroad.

27. The standard rate of income tax averaged 25% in 1935–38 and 46% in 1948–51. The National Defence Contribution (the forerunner of the profits tax) was introduced as from April 1, 1937, at a rate of 5%. In 1948–51 profits tax on company income (excluding public corporations) averaged 15½%.

28. There is a large body of literature on corporate taxation and savings behavior. Among the more important empirical works relating to the UK are Walker 1954; R.C. on Taxation, UK [86]; Prais 1959; Rubner 1964; Stone 1964; Feldstein 1967, 1970, 1972; Hart et al. 1968; King 1971, 1972, 1977.

29. For a more detailed analysis of changes in the distribution of income, see Chapter 6, especially (for post-tax incomes) pp. 191–94.

30. Even if structural changes were unimportant, the observed increases in the ratio of actual to potential electricity consumption may not reflect increases in the degree of physical capital utilization. There might have been an increase within industries in the use of electricity for purposes other than the provision of power, such as heating or lighting. If so, then the use of a constant grossing-up factor in Table 5.8 to obtain total installed wattage from electric motor wattage is incorrect, and the figures in the table exaggerate the extent to which electrical equipment was being used more intensively. No satisfactory evidence on how this factor might have changed exists. (In 1924 electricity used for power in all manufacturing industries accounted for about 80% of the total electricity consumption whose end-use was identified (*Census of Production*, UK [4], *Final Report 1924*: vol. 5, Appendix Table 12), which compares with the 1961 proportion of electric motor wattage to total wattage of about 64%. But this does not necessarily mean that the grossing-up factor increased, because the degree of utilization of electric motors may always be higher than that of other electrical devices.) But even if the grossing-up factor did increase over time, it is difficult to imagine that it can have done so to the extent that the corrected ratio of actual to potential electricity consumption would fail to rise substantially in all industries between 1930 and 1951, and in chemicals, iron and steel, and other metal-using industries within the postwar period. Conceivably, the shift toward the use of electricity as a fuel was more rapid in the postwar period than earlier, so that the true postwar rise in relative consumption may not have been more rapid than the transwar rise.

31. A similar lack of trend before 1958 is shown in the data for industries that carried out their own surveys. On pig-iron and crude steel capacity and output, see OECD [4] and earlier issues, and OECD [5]. On cement capacity and output, see OECD [2]: Tables 1, 5, and earlier issues.

32. Notably, that given by the National Institute's annual Industrial Inquiries, reported periodically in the *National Institute Economic Review* (with additional material for some years in the National Institute's press releases).

CHAPTER 6

1. In fact for large parts of the period 1856–1973 the measure of the growth rate of TFI in the British case is not very sensitive to distributive shares, since the rates of growth of labor and capital do not differ by a very wide margin, especially if labor is measured after adjustment for quality change.

2. The distinction between wages and salaries used here is described in more detail in Feinstein 1972: 31. It does not correspond exactly to certain other distinctions sometimes made: e.g., between fixed and variable labor costs, or manual and nonmanual workers, or union and non-union; or according to degree of training or skill, level of average income, or periodicity of payment.

3. Part of the fall in the proportion of wage-earners may be due to changes over time in the classification of certain occupations. This is particularly true of comparisons between 1911 and later years because it is difficult to distinguish accurately between salary-earners and the self-employed in pre–World War II

censuses. Such comparisons are also hindered by the fact that the 1911 data in Table 6.2 include Southern Ireland. However, figures given in Routh 1965: Table 1 for manual workers in Great Britain as a percent of all gainfully occupied employees show a broadly similar picture of the growing relative importance of salary-earners:

1911	85.8%	1931	82.5%
1921	82.8	1951	73.3

4. The number of office workers in employment grew at an average annual rate of 2.4% between 1951 and 1964, whereas the total of all other workers (including the self-employed) grew at only 0.4%. For further details over a longer period of time, see *Growth of Office Employment*, UK [65].

5. Another possible explanation for the relatively slow rate of increase of salaries would be that the proportion of part-timers, with lower average incomes, increased more rapidly among salary-earners than among wage-earners. Data are not available to test this hypothesis, though it does not appear promising in view of the apparently lower proportion of part-timers among salary-earners than among wage-earners toward the end of our period. (In 1961 in Great Britain the proportion of part-timers in the three occupational groups XXI, Clerical Workers, XXIV, Administrative and Managers, and XXV, Professional and Technical Workers, Artists, etc., which roughly correspond to the salaried group, was 7.5%; in all other groups, including the armed forces, it was 9.0%. (*Census of Population*, UK [52], *1966*: Tables 31, 34.)

6. Employers' contributions as a percentage of GNP in benchmark years were as follows:

	1913	1924	1937	1951	1964	1973
State programs	0.4%	0.9%	1.1%	1.6%	2.3%	3.2%
Private programs	0.6	1.2	1.4	2.2	2.7	3.4

7. Estimates of the self-employed in 1911 were found by extrapolating backwards estimates for the early 1920's. The 1911 ratios of the self-employed to the total working population in seven sectors (excluding agriculture and forestry) were then applied to working-population estimates for 1861, 1871, 1881, 1891, and 1901. The implied estimates of the total in employment were then used, together with estimates of income from employment by sector derived from the total income from employment and the 1911 ratios of average income from employment in each sector to the average for all sectors (based on Bowley 1919: 25, Table 4), to give average earnings in each of the seven sectors. With estimates of the self-employed and their average earnings, labor income from self-employment was easily derived, first for census years, and then for all other years by interpolation. Labor income from self-employment in agriculture was derived from the estimates of the numbers of farmers and farm employees in Bellerby 1958, and the estimates of employee remuneration in Feinstein 1972: Table 23.

8. Further reasons for preferring the first method are given in Kuznets 1966:

177–80. Estimates of the overall trend in distribution between labor and property are less sensitive to the choice of assumption on self-employment income in the UK than in countries with a large peasant agriculture.

9. The number of farmers in pre-World War I census years was as follows (estimates from F. D. W. Taylor 1955, based on data in population censuses):

Year	G.B. (000's)	Ireland (000's)	Year	G.B. (000's)	Ireland (000's)
1851	302.9	403.8	1891	277.9	417.0
1861	312.1	440.9	1901	277.7	399.4
1871	305.2	423.6	1911	279.4	383.2
1881	279.2	441.9			

10. For the purpose of calculating the real cost of labor relative to the price of the product, it would be appropriate to include in the wage and in the price of the product the cost of the Selective Employment Tax, net of Employment Premiums, which in the national accounts (and in our tables) is treated as an indirect tax, not as part of net employee compensation. Adjustment for this would alter the growth rate of the real wage by + 0.1 percentage point in 1964–68 and − 0.1 point in 1968–73.

11. In the national accounts when trading concerns own the property they occupy, their trading profits are assumed to include income arising from the property, and no rental income is imputed. When they do not own the property, the rent that they actually pay is classified as rent. Hence any change in the extent of owner-occupation among trading concerns results in a change in the ratio of rent to profits as measured, though it does not reflect a change of much economic importance. The inclusion of this kind of rent with profits removes a possible source of confusion. In agriculture the crude indicators of average rents, and the need to estimate profits as a residual, ensure that separate series for rent and profits provide very little more information than the two together provide, and they may even mislead.

12. The percentage shares in GNP of the two components of rent for benchmark years are shown in the table below.

13. Summaries of the legislation since 1915 are available in Hemming & Duffy 1964; and Greve 1965: 14–18.

14. The rent accruing to owner-occupiers is imputed on the basis of the ratable value of owner-occupied dwellings (see, for example, *Sources and Methods*, UK [20]: 162–63), and these values are in turn based on the rents of

TABLE TO NOTE 12

Year	Dwellings	Government non-trading property	Year	Dwellings	Government non-trading property
1856	4.6%	0.2%	1937	5.4%	1.0%
1873	4.9	0.3	1951	2.9	0.5
1913	5.5	0.9	1964	4.2	0.8
1924	4.6	0.7	1973	5.6	1.0

Ownership	1924	1937	1951	1964	1973
Local authorities and central government	0.2%	0.5%	0.8%	1.1%	1.4%
Private sector	4.4	4.9	2.1	3.1	4.2
Private landlords	–	–	0.6	1.0	0.8
Owner-occupiers	–	–	1.5	2.1	3.4

Note: The rental income of local authorities from dwellings is imputed on the basis of the interest and depreciation charges on the capital involved. It exceeds the actual rents received less the cost of repairs and other expenses by an amount that is treated as a subsidy. Insofar as the loan charges are related to the original cost of the houses and not to their current replacement cost, the imputed rent is different from the full economic rent.

rented accommodation. To the extent that the latter have been held below the free market level by rent-control legislation, imputed rents therefore underestimate the real return from owner-occupation. This underestimate, if it exists, affects not only rent from dwellings, but also GNP and the share of rent in GNP.

15. The percentage shares in GNP of rent from dwellings classified by ownership after World War I are shown in the table above.

16. The fall in the share of agricultural income in GNP can be compared with the fall in the real share of agricultural output, and with relative prices:

	Agricultural income as per- cent of GNP	Agricultural output as per- cent of real GNP (based on 1913 prices)	Ratio of agricultural to GNP prices (1913 = 100)
1856	22.5%	19.5%	116
1873	14.7	13.7	108
1913	6.1	6.1	100

17. Ireland contributed about 27% to total British agricultural output in 1907, compared with an average of under 5% for the other industries and services. With about one-third of GDP originating in agriculture in 1907, Ireland was a predominantly agricultural country (Feinstein 1972: 212–13). Net agricultural output in Great Britain and Ireland was £114 million and £41 million, respectively, in 1870–76 and £108 million and £38 million in 1911–13, all measured at 1911–13 prices (*ibid.*, Table 10.3).

18. Farm rents and farm profits as a percent of GNP were:

Year	Farm rents	Farm profits	Total
1856	7.3%	2.8%	10.1%
1873	4.9	2.3	7.2
1913	1.9	0.5	2.4

19. The shares of property in 1856 were agriculture, 44.7%; GNP, 42.2%; and GDP, 40.9%.

20. In agriculture, rents before 1914 accounted for over two-thirds of farm property income (note 18), and though we do not know what exact proportion of the rent involved land rather than buildings, it was presumably the greater part. By contrast, land is taken by Feinstein (1965: 15) to account for only 7% of

the value of buildings and sites (and hence a smaller percentage of all capital) in the main nonagricultural sectors of the economy.

21. The corresponding measure for agriculture (Table 6.7, last column) resembles the measure for the non-farm sector in showing substantial decline between 1873 and 1913 but, unlike it, has no further trend decline after 1913. The corresponding measures for the other two classes of property income, income from abroad and rent, are by definition always equal to unity.

22. The denominator in Tables 6.9 and 6.10 is total trading income throughout. Data are not available on the trading income of the never-public and sometime-public sectors separately.

23. Iron and steel was the only industry in the sometime-public sector in which the rate of growth of profits transwar (in money terms) was substantially higher than the rate of growth of profits in the never-public sector.

24. The rise in public-sector profits shown in Tables 6.9 and 6.10 would be larger (by about 0.6% of trading income) if subsidies to public corporations were included, as they are, following Blue Book practice, in Table 6.1. They are included here because the rise in subsidies occurred chiefly as a result of a change in government policy, by which, from 1960 onward, these subsidies were treated as government subsidies to the product rather than as deductions from the profits of the public corporations. Since this is regarded as an accounting change rather than a real one, the figures for the shares of profits and property in GNP in Table 6.1 and the other data given earlier in this chapter are somewhat overstated for the years after 1960; and the decline in the share of property in GNP within the postwar period is correspondingly understated.

25. Profits' share fell across World War II in each of the sectors comprising commerce as here defined: distributive trades; insurance, banking, and finance (IBF); miscellaneous services. There was, in addition, a shift in weight, in terms of output at current prices, toward the low-profit miscellaneous services sector away from the high-profit IBF sector. Given that employment and output grew in IBF and fell in miscellaneous services, this shift implies a substantial change in relative prices (the fall in interest rates may have contributed to this in the case of IBF).

26. Profits, output, and capital refer to the domestic non-farm trading sector of the economy: i.e. gross profits equal gross property income less net income from abroad, non-trading rent and farm rent, and profits; net profits equal gross profits less capital consumption in the non-farm trading sector; gross output equals GDP less agricultural income less non-trading rent; net output equals gross output less capital consumption in the non-farm-trading sector; gross capital equals the gross domestic fixed capital stock excluding agriculture, dwellings, roads, and public and social capital, plus non-farm inventories. Profits, output, and capital are measured at current prices.

27. The absolute level of the gross rate of profit on capital in the sometime-public sector, which comprised in 1964 about 38% of the total capital stock excluding agriculture, dwellings, roads, and public and social services, was very much lower than in the never-public sector—about 3% on average over the

period 1952–73, compared with about 9%. This relationship is not much different from what it was before World War II, when many of the sometime-public sector industries were still in private ownership, so it cannot be regarded as a consequence of nationalization as such. Changes within the postwar period of the sometime-public sector's profit rate did, however, reflect to some extent changes in their price and output policies, which stand apart from the normal processes of profit determination.

28. In both cases we are concerned strictly speaking with the price of the flow of services rather than with the price of the stock, but for brevity we shall refer to the price of capital, just as we refer to the price of labor.

29. The national debt amounted to £812 million in 1853, £650 million in 1914, and £7.832 billion in 1920 (Hargreaves 1930: 291).

30. The scope of the private sector changed considerably between 1937 and 1951 as a result of the nationalizations of the postwar Labour government, and about one-third of the fall in property's private share is attributable to the reallocation of some trading profits to the public sector. The share of sometime-public sector property income in GNP fell from 6.0% in 1937 to 2.9% in 1951 (compare with Table 6.18, row 1).

31. Measured in Table 6.18 before allowing for depreciation. The increase in depreciation (see Table 6.1, capital consumption) accounts for part of the transwar increase.

32. Part of the increase in direct taxes on labor income consists of increases in national insurance contributions, which (notionally) are used to pay the national insurance benefits that comprise the greater part of "grants." However, the increase in grants was much less than the increase in direct taxes on labor, and the statement in the text would remain true even if grants were treated as a negative tax on labor.

33. Phelps Brown & Browne 1968: 341 refers to the same phenomenon in the U.S. and Germany.

34. Phelps Brown & Browne 1968 is the most sophisticated account of the interaction of labor-market and product-market pressures on the distribution of income. However, Phelps Brown's explanation of the long-run forces affecting distribution, in his final summing up (pp. 333–43), is much more akin to the neoclassical hypothesis than to the market-power hypothesis.

CHAPTER 7

1. Other references are available in two survey articles: Nadiri 1970 and Kennedy & Thirlwall 1972. See also *The Review of Income and Wealth* for March and June 1972.

2. Griliches & Jorgenson (1967) put forward this line of argument and at first maintained that relatively simple adjustments to conventional measures of TFI were sufficient to eliminate TFP change. They were subsequently obliged to retreat from this position (Denison 1969, and the further exchange of views in Jorgenson, Griliches & Denison 1972). But that does not affect the theoretical point.

3. The measurement of the inputs is explained in the next section. For a more detailed discussion of the classification of the sources of output growth into TFI and TFP growth, see Denison 1972. Denison lists all the factors that he believes contribute to output growth, whether measurable or non-measurable (and hence part of the residual).

4. The data requirements are consistent constant price estimates of gross output, value-added, and intermediate inputs. No official estimates exist. Unofficial estimates for the years 1954, 1960, and 1963 only have been made by the Cambridge University Department of Applied Economics (1974). Estimates for manufacturing industries for 1948 and 1954 are available in Gupta 1963.

5. Cambridge University Department of Applied Economics 1974. Output and inputs are measured at factor cost (i.e. they exclude indirect taxes less subsidies). The total for all sectors excludes some service activities, namely public administration and defense, public health and education services, domestic services, etc. to households, and ownership of dwellings.

6. The statistical reasons for not using net measures in calculating the growth of the capital and labor inputs are twofold: (1) since all estimates of capital consumption contain a large arbitrary element, the resulting net measures are less reliable than the gross measures; and (2) estimates of capital consumption are not available on a sufficiently disaggregated basis to measure the net concepts of output and TFI growth by industry.

7. The growth of TFP in the interwar period is discussed in Appendix M.

CHAPTER 8

1. The justification for this procedure is discussed in Appendix I.

2. Because output in public and professional services is measured almost entirely by a weighted employment index, improvements in labor productivity resulting either from an increased capital input or from increases in TFP are not reflected in the output index. It follows that it is not possible to estimate TFP growth as the residual output growth, since not only the TFP element but even the effects of the capital input are by definition excluded from output growth.

A separate problem arises in the measurement of TFI in public and professional services. A large proportion of the capital in this sector — schools, hospitals, roads — does not earn any profit. Actual distributive shares in the sector would therefore underweight capital input. Instead, as an approximation, overall distributive shares in GDP are used in the calculation of TFI in this sector in Table 8.3 (though not, for the sake of consistency with aggregates, in the figures for the total intra-industry change in TFP in the last section of the table).

Output in the ownership-of-dwellings sector consists of the services provided by the capital input. The growth in TFP is therefore the decrease in the measured capital-output ratio (negative in the periods shown in Table 8.3).

Though the figures for output, TFI, and TFP in these sectors are thus not very meaningful, they necessarily enter the aggregates for the economy as a whole.

TABLE TO NOTE 4

Distribution of the Labor Force in Great Britain, 1801–1861

(Percent of the total occupied population)

Census year	Agriculture, forestry, fishing	Manufacture, mining, industry	Trade and transport	Domestic and personal	All other sectors
1801	35.9%	29.7%	11.2%	11.5%	11.8%
1811	33.0	30.2	11.6	11.8	13.3
1821	28.4	38.4	12.1	12.7	8.5
1831	24.6	40.8	12.4	12.6	9.5
1841	22.2	40.5	14.2	14.5	8.5
1851	21.7	42.9	15.8	13.0	6.7
1861	18.7	43.6	16.6	14.3	6.9

We therefore include the figures for output and TFI growth in these sectors for completeness in Table 8.3, and their TFP growth is included in the total intra-industry growth of TFP in the last section of the table. The reservations relating to these data should, however, be borne in mind. It should also be noted that for 1856–1913 the estimation of output in some components of commerce (finance, catering, domestic and miscellaneous services) is based largely on employment indexes, and so the measure of TFP contains a larger arbitrary element in 1856–73 and 1873–1913 than in later periods.

3. These results are affected in some cases by changes over time in output-mix within sectors. In utilities the most capital-intensive industry, water, constituted a much lower proportion of the sector at the end than at the beginning.

4. Satisfactory data for years before 1861 do not exist. However, Deane and Cole (1962: 142) have made rough estimates (including retired persons and the unemployed) for Great Britain from the censuses, as shown in the accompanying table. These estimates suggest that the proportion of the labor force in manufacturing rose very steeply up to 1831, but not very much after that. But even in 1801 it was quite high—far higher than in the typical underdeveloped country of the present day. See Clark 1957: Chapter 9 for comparative data on many countries.

5. Falls in 1920–21 and 1929–31 reflected unemployment, which affected manufacturing more than most other sectors. But the census figure for 1931 is also substantially lower than that for 1921, showing that workers had in the meanwhile left the sector.

6. The early-19th-century data shown in the Table to Note 4 are extremely uncertain, and we cannot be at all confident about the relative magnitude of the increases in the decades between 1801 and 1841.

7. The total figure is from Deane & Cole 1962: Table 31; the others are from Booth 1886: Appendixes B.1–B.2; and Matthews 1954: 146, note 1. The effects of excluding domestic workers from the 1841 labor force are even more striking in the case of the UK because of the widespread cottage spinning and weaving industry in Ireland. But since this had largely disappeared by 1881 (Booth 1886:

345–46), a more representative picture of changes in the second half of the century is provided by the figures for Great Britain.

8. Clark (1957: 500–501) points out that the proportion of the British labor force in mining between 1911 and 1921 was the highest of any country *ever*, apart from one or two exceptional cases, like South Africa.

9. See note 2, above. The pre-1914 data for commerce are also very arbitrary as measures of output and productivity.

10. The decline of 0.2 of a percentage point in the rate of growth of TFP for the economy as a whole between 1856–73 and 1873–1913, shown in Table 8.3, is to be regarded as an underestimate of the unfavorable trend. The decline shown in Table 7.4, last column, is 0.6. Half of the discrepancy arises from a difference in 1856–73 between the growth rates shown by the compromise estimate of GDP (used in Table 7.4) and by the output-side estimate of GDP (used in Table 8.3 for consistency with the sectoral figures). The other half of the discrepancy arises because Table 7.4 deducts from TFP growth the effects of the significant increase estimated (Table 4.7) to have taken place between 1856–73 and 1873–1913 in the rate of improvement in the quality of labor from sources other than intensity of work (an increase that *is* implicitly allowed for in Table 8.3; see the footnote to p. 230).

11. This fall would probably be still more marked if changes in the degree of utilization of capital were treated as part of changes in TFI, since there is some evidence that the trend rate of increase in the degree of utilization declined in the course of the postwar period (see Chapter 5, especially Table 5.8).

12. They did, however, have rather more significance than a random shift in the relative productivity of different industries, since (as we saw in Chapter 5) the rise in the relative cost of building across World War II substantially increased the proportion of national income that had to be saved in order to achieve a given amount of real capital accumulation.

13. Productivity in construction was also lower than prewar in the short-lived boom of 1919–20 (M. Bowley 1967: 128). By 1924, however, productivity appears to have made a substantial recovery.

14. Feinstein revises his 1965 sectoral figures for the interwar capital stock, in one case substantially, in his forthcoming work, but he has not prepared revised estimates for subsectors. The old and new estimates of the annual percentage growth rates of the gross capital stock in the relevant sectors are:

Sector	Old	New
Manufacturing	0.9%	1.0%
Commerce	1.3	2.0
Transport and communications	0.2	0.2

In manufacturing, where the difference is small, we use the old figures for subsectors (hence a small discrepancy between Tables 8.3 and 8.7). We also use the old figures for subsectors in transport and communications, where there is no change. For commerce, no data for subsectors are available on either basis, so we confine our attention to labor productivity.

15. If weights based on the assumption of a constant net marginal profit rate are used instead, the estimates of TF$_H$P growth in 1924–37 are hardly affected. See Appendix I.

16. One of the exceptions, textiles, would disappear on an alternative basis of calculation. See next note.

17. The capital-stock data are not adjusted for the degree of utilization, and so the rate of growth of utilized capital will differ from our estimate of the rate of capital growth to an extent dependent on the change in the degree of utilization. Textiles is probably the only industry where a serious discrepancy between the growth of capital in use and the growth of capital in place existed. The data in Table 5.8, Chapter 5, suggest that there was about 30% more excess capacity in 1951 than in 1964. If allowance is made for this, the 1951–64 growth rates for textiles in Table 8.7 would be −0.3% for capital, −1.7% for TFI, and 1.8% for TFP. Because these figures differ considerably from those in the table, we have omitted textiles from the correlations in Appendix J. However, it should be borne in mind that minor errors may arise from this source in other industries.

18. See Dean 1964: 333, Table 1. A considerable margin of error must be attached to the transwar capital-stock figures, and to the assumption that privately financed investment during the war years had the same industrial distribution as government-financed investment (*ibid.*, p. 334). Cambridge University Department of Applied Economics 1974 makes a different assumption from Dean's about the proportion of assets that were acquired during the war by the engineering and metal-using industries and not converted back to peacetime uses. The authors assume much less conversion, and on this assumption lower rates of growth of capital in electrical engineering, mechanical engineering and shipbuilding, vehicles, and other metal industries between 1937 and 1951 would be obtained; they would be in the range of 5.0%–5.5%.

19. The IBF category includes the privately owned real estate industry, which controls a very large capital stock. Strictly, of course, this capital should be classified according to the industry that uses it (e.g. distributive trades in the case of shops and warehouses, miscellaneous services in the case of restaurants), and it is because our data do not enable us to do this that we are unable to disaggregate the capital of the whole commerce sector. An additional problem is that buildings may "move" from one industry to another without the change being recorded; a shop may become a bank, or a restaurant a shop.

20. The data in Table 8.11 are unsatisfactory in two respects. First, it is not possible to estimate the shares of labor and capital in each industry, and so the shares for the whole sector were used to weight the growth rates of labor and capital in calculating TFI growth for each industry. Second, the output of the part of the road goods industry that is not owned by road haulage contractors is included in our output series, but the vehicles and drivers that produce the output are not in the capital and labor series. Furthermore, as already noted, roads are not included in the capital stock. If allowance were made for these points, it is unlikely that the conclusions in the text would need to be altered very much.

CHAPTER 9

1. The weighted dispersion is

$$\Sigma \frac{q_i}{q} \bigg/ (\hat{q}_i - \hat{q})$$

where as throughout this chapter, symbols with subscripts relate to individual industries, and symbols without subscripts to totals. Using prime (′) and double prime (″) for industries growing faster and slower, respectively, than the average, this is approximately equal to

$$\Sigma \frac{q'_i}{q} \hat{q}'_i - \Sigma \frac{q''_i}{q} \hat{q}''_i$$

It is exactly equal to it if

$$\Sigma \frac{q'_i}{q} = \Sigma \frac{q''_i}{q}$$

which is not true in general because $\hat{q}$, being measured in average annual terms, is not given by

$$\hat{q} = \Sigma \frac{q_i}{q} \hat{q}_i$$

2. Similar conclusions are reached if we add two other industries to these three: paper, which grew fast before 1914 and again after World War II but not in the interwar period, and utilities, the fastest growing nonmanufacturing industry.

3. The decompounding term is the consequence of calculating the average annual growth rates of output, labor, and capital for an aggregate (i.e. GDP or manufacturing) by decompounding the change in the aggregate series over the period rather than by taking the weighted average of the decompounded individual industry average annual growth rates, the weights being the first year shares. It would, of course, be possible to eliminate it by redefining the average annual growth rate in the latter way, but this would be introducing an artificial and less easily intelligible definition that differs from the one used elsewhere.

We denote the average annual growth rates of output, labor, capital, TFI, and TFP in industry i by $\hat{q}_i, \hat{n}_i, \hat{k}_i, \hat{f}_i$, and $\hat{x}_i$; and the absolute values in the first year of output, labor, capital, the wage, the profit rate, and labor's share in industry i by q_i, n_i, k_i, w_i, r_i, and α_i. S is the weighted sum of labor quality-shift and capital quality-shift. Variables without subscripts refer to totals for all industries.

From equations (1) and (2) of Chapter 7,

$$\hat{x} = \hat{q} - \hat{f} = \hat{q} - [\alpha\hat{n} + (1 - \alpha)\hat{k}]$$
$$\hat{x}_i = \hat{q}_i - \hat{f}_i = \hat{q}_i - [\alpha_i\hat{n}_i + (1 - \alpha_i)\hat{k}_i]$$

Assuming for the moment that there is no decompounding problem, so that

$$\hat{q} = \frac{\Sigma q_i}{q}\hat{q}_i, \quad \hat{n} = \frac{\Sigma n_i}{n}\hat{n}_i, \quad \text{and} \quad \hat{k} = \frac{\Sigma k_i}{k}\hat{k}_i$$

then

$$\hat{x} - \frac{\Sigma q_i}{q}\hat{x}_i = \frac{\Sigma q_i}{q}\hat{q}_i - \left[\frac{\alpha \Sigma n_i}{n}\hat{n}_i + (1 - \alpha)\frac{\Sigma k_i}{k}\hat{k}_i\right]$$

$$- \frac{\Sigma q_i}{q}\hat{q}_i + \left[\frac{\Sigma q_i}{q}\frac{w_i n_i}{q_i}\hat{n}_i + \frac{\Sigma q_i}{q}\frac{r_i k_i}{q_i}\hat{k}_i\right]$$

$$= - \left[\frac{\alpha \Sigma n_i}{n}\hat{n}_i + (1 - \alpha)\frac{\Sigma k_i}{k}\hat{k}_i\right]$$

$$+ \left[\frac{wn}{q}\frac{\Sigma w_i n_i}{wn}\hat{n}_i + \frac{rk}{q}\frac{\Sigma r_i k_i}{rk}\hat{k}_i\right]$$

$$= \frac{\alpha \Sigma n_i}{n}\hat{n}_i\left(\frac{w_i}{w} - 1\right) + (1 - \alpha)\frac{\Sigma k_i}{k}\hat{k}_i\left(\frac{r_i}{r} - 1\right) = S$$

Hence

$$\hat{x} = \frac{\Sigma q_i}{q}\hat{x}_i + S$$

When there is a decompounding problem, the above expressions for $\hat{q}$, $\hat{n}$, and $\hat{k}$ do not exactly hold, and in deriving $\hat{x}$ it is necessary to add a further term given by

$$- \left[\frac{\Sigma q_i}{q}(\hat{q}_i - \hat{q}) - \left(\alpha \frac{\Sigma n_i}{n}(\hat{n}_i - \hat{n}) + (1 - \alpha)\frac{\Sigma k_i}{k}(\hat{k}_i - \hat{k})\right)\right]$$

4. Denison (1967: 211–14) gives quantitative expression to this view by postulating that a 1% reduction in the agricultural labor force reduces output in agriculture by only a third of 1% in the UK, the U.S., and Denmark (and only by a quarter of 1% in other European countries), whereas a rise of 1% in employment in the nonagricultural sector, due to movement out of agriculture, raises output there by four-fifths of 1%.

5. It would be preferable to include education rather than occupation as a broad proxy for the general skill level of the labor force. However, data limitations do not permit the estimation of inter- and intra-industry components of educational-quality change, even in the postwar period. The estimated effect of changes in occupational quality should therefore be thought of as a crude ap-

proximation to the desired concept of the change in the general skill level of the labor force.

6. Deane and Cole's (1962) five sectors are agriculture, industry (mining, manufacturing, construction, and utilities), trade and transport, domestic and personal services, and public and professional services. From their Tables 30 and 34, after making allowances for the self-employed, we made rough estimates of the wage of employees in 1871 and 1911, and these were used to weight the growth of the labor force in 1871–1911 and 1911–24, respectively. Deane and Cole's average wage data refer to Great Britain, and the labor force data to the UK (including Southern Ireland in 1871–1911), which probably has the effect of slightly underestimating the quality-shift in the UK; the only significant difference between the relative wages of two would have been a lower relative wage in agriculture in the UK than in Great Britain, and agriculture was the only sector in which employment was not rising.

7. These figures may be too high, because if the exercise is redone for 1911–24 using relative wages based on data in A. L. Bowley 1919: Table 4, quality-shift is estimated to be about 0.05 percent per year less. The extremely high estimate of the relative wages in public and professional services given by Deane and Cole is rather suspicious.

8. Similar considerations led Jorgenson and Griliches (1967) to use as a measure of capital input their concept of "capital services," which weights different items in the capital stock according to their gross rates of return. Their method assumes that the net rate of return is the same on all classes of assets, and that gross rates differ solely on account of different depreciation. It therefore eliminates by assumption any pure correction-of-misallocation effect.

9. In the service sectors the basis of disaggregation is five sectors for labor quality-shift and two sectors for capital quality-shift. Consistency with the total has been obtained by calculating intra-industry growth in the service sectors, for the purpose of Table 9.7, by deducting from intra-industry growth in the two sectors, as shown in Table 8.3, the additional labor quality-shift that results from disaggregating into five sectors rather than two, weighted by labor's distributive share.

10. One would like to know whether quality-shift measured on the basis of a finer industry breakdown, or even with data at the plant level, would turn out to be greater or smaller than the present estimates. Unfortunately, neither casual empiricism nor enlightened guessing suggests the direction in which the difference might lie. Some limited reassurance that finer disaggregation would not entirely transform the result may be drawn from the findings of Wragg and Robertson (1978). They disaggregate manufacturing into 83 industries. Using a measure based on average labor productivity, not quality-shift as here defined, they arrive (p. 50) at results similar in order of magnitude to those in Table 9.3. Salter (1966), using the same method, found a larger structural contribution in 1924–50 — as we do, though not to the same extent as Salter. The difference in underlying concepts prevents the findings of Wragg and Robertson and Salter from being directly comparable with ours.

11. Quality-shift before 1914 cannot be inferred by deducting the weighted sum of estimated sectoral TFP-growth rates from the total, since in this period, these rates are not derived from actual sectoral distributive shares, as the method requires. The approximation that was used instead is probably adequate for the general picture of sectoral performance, but it will not serve for the more refined calculation needed to separate the contributions of intra-industry growth and quality-shift in total TFP growth.

12. *The measure we use for TFP change in industry i is $\hat{x}_i = \hat{q}_i - \hat{f}_i$*, where $\hat{f}_i$ is the rate of growth of TFI in industry i. Strictly speaking, however, allowing for second-order effects, the underlying concept of the relationship between TFI and TFP, viz., $q_i = x_i f_i$, leads to

$$\hat{x}_i = \frac{\hat{q}_i - \hat{f}_i}{1 + \hat{f}_i} = (\hat{q}_i - \hat{f}_i)\left(1 - \frac{\hat{f}_i}{1 + \hat{f}_i}\right)$$

Our measure of $\hat{x}_i$ thus already incorporates a covariance term in $(\hat{q}_i - \hat{f}_i)\hat{f}_i$, which is a structural effect and should in principle be eliminated to give the true $\hat{x}_i$. See Appendix I.

13. It is generally held that the Selective Employment Tax also played a part (Reddaway et al. 1970, 1973). See also below, p. 315.

14. The figures in Table 8.3 suggest an even higher proportion. The statement in the text is based on a rough prorating of the discrepancy between the output-side estimate of GDP, used in Table 8.3, and the compromise index of GDP used for the calculation of TFP in the economy as a whole in Table 7.2 and elsewhere.

15. It appears quite strongly in the comparisons of individual manufacturing industries in Appendix J.

16. Salter 1960: 114–27 (one of the first discussions of the productivity-production relationship); Caves et al. 1968: 297–98. A similar issue in an international trade context appears in Stigler 1961.

17. An equivalent specification in terms of labor productivity and input was used by Cripps and Tarling (1973). It received some support in Kaldor's earlier writings, but he later repudiated it (Kaldor 1975).

18. Kaldor (1975) offers the following: "A sufficient condition for the presence of static or dynamic economies of scale is the existence of a statistically significant relationship between employment and output with a regression coefficient which is significantly less than 1." Whatever the merits of this as a statement of the underlying relationship on the production side, it is not satisfactory as a statistical resolution of the identification problem, since the stated result could also come about if the exogenous change were in productivity and the elasticity of demand for output were greater than one.

19. A two-stage least-squares model for cross-industry comparisons was attempted by Wragg and Robertson (1978). It suggested that part of the Verdoorn relationship was to be explained by dynamic economies of scale. But it also suggested that these economies were at least as strong in retailing, the only service sector for which data were available, as they were in manufacturing. If this

were true of the rest of nonmanufacturing, a structural shift from nonmanufacturing to manufacturing would not bring about an increase in the rate of growth of TFP in the economy as a whole.

20. In the statistics that follow, the effect of the foreign balance is in fact calculated as a residual, so it will also contain any errors due to rounding or second-order terms. The best way of measuring the proportion of the change in q/Q "due to foreign trade" is open to some debate, particularly in regard to the proper treatment of $(\hat{A} - \hat{Q})$ and $(\hat{B} - \hat{Q})$. The measure given here seemed the best, but the data in Table 9.10 enable alternative measures to be calculated if desired.

21. A half is roughly the ratio of value-added to gross output in manufacturing industry in the postwar period, and though the ratio was probably lower in the 19th century, the error thus introduced would not be very large because the proportion of value-added due to the net foreign balance was fairly low. A more serious error might have been caused by ignoring changes in industrial structure. However, a rough check for the period 1873–1913 using the 1935 input-output table suggested that $\hat{a}$ would not be altered by more than 0.2 of a point if it were possible to do the exercise completely.

22. The exact figures might be altered by a slightly different choice of periods, but this could not remove the major variations.

23. A rough attempt to divide the 1937–54 period at 1948 suggested that absorption in manufacturing grew less rapidly than total absorption between 1937 and 1948, but more rapidly between 1948 and 1954. The decrease in manufacturing's share in 1937–48 reflected partly the increase in the importance of defense (a nonmanufacturing industry) in GDP.

CHAPTER 10

1. In making long-period comparisons, the relative unreliability of the annual data for GDP before 1914 has to be borne in mind. A comparison based on industrial production suggests a rather greater difference between 1951–64 and 1873–1913 in the size of fluctuations (see facing table).

2. An index of conformity defined as var $\sum_i w_i x_i$ / $\sum_i W_i$ var x_i was constructed, where x_i is the ratio of output to trend output in industry i, w_i is the output weight in the base year, $W_i = w_i^2$ / $\sum_i w_i^2$, and the variances are measured over all years in the period. The index varies between zero and unity; it tends to zero as the covariances between pairs of industry x's become small and, in some cases, negative; it tends to unity as the covariances increase. The values of the index of conformity in industrial production for various peacetime periods are as follows:

1865–1882	0.19	1920–1937	0.20
1882–1899	0.23	1951–1964	0.45
1899–1913	0.21	1964–1973	0.36

3. When the level of demand is measured by output relative to trend output, the implicit assumption is that supply increases according to this trend. No

TABLE TO NOTE 1

	Industrial production		GDP	
Period	Amplitude of fluctuation	As percent of 1951–64	Amplitude of fluctuation	As percent of 1951–64
1873–1913	6.2%	206%	2.7%	148%
1920–1937	10.9	366	4.5	244
1951–1964	3.0	100	1.8	100

secular tendency toward excess supply or demand is permitted. In the more sophisticated model of Godley and Shepherd (1964), a quadratic trend in supply, or productive potential, per man-year was assumed, and the parameters were estimated from the data, given some additional assumptions about the short-run employment function. Again this implies no secular trend in the level of demand. More recently, Artus (1977) has estimated potential output in manufacturing by using regression analysis to fit a Cobb-Douglas production function that includes a time-trend for technical change, a term for the mean age of the capital stock to take account of embodied technical progress, and cyclical variables to represent the differences in the intensity of use of labor and capital. Finally there is the method of the Wharton School (Klein & Summers 1966), which assumes zero excess demand and supply at peaks, and steady (linear or exponential) growth in supply between peaks.

4. *Engineering:* ratio of the average of orders on hand (in volume terms) at the beginning and end of the year to the volume of deliveries during the years; for 1958–64, from *Board of Trade Journal*, various issues, beginning July 22, 1960; for 1955–57, deliveries estimated by the index of industrial production extrapolated backwards from 1958, and net new orders from *Board of Trade Journal*, Jan. 26, 1962. *Metal-working machine tools:* ratio of the average of the value of orders on hand at the beginning and end of the year to the value of deliveries during the year, from *Annual Abstract of Statistics*, *Board of Trade Journal*, and *Monthly Digest of Statistics*, various issues.

5. The proportion of firms in the CBI survey referring to a shortage of materials or components rose to 49% in Oct. 1973 and averaged over 50% through 1974, making it the most important single factor limiting output. In 1964–65 it had been relatively unimportant, averaging 9%.

6. The ratio of manufacturers' stocks of materials and fuel to output at the end of 1971 equaled its all-time low, notwithstanding that output was at a cyclical trough (*Economic Trends Annual Supplement*, UK [12], *1975*: Table 64). Exacerbating factors were (1) serious strikes in the coal industry at the beginning of the upswing (1972 I) and soon after its peak (1974 I); (2) an unusual degree of synchronization in the business cycle between countries, which made it difficult to draw on surplus capacity abroad; and (3) a buildup of speculative stocks stimulated by the world boom in commodity prices.

7. $\bar{Y}$ is defined as $Y/(1-u)$, where u is the unemployment rate. The exact values of $\bar{Y}$ do not much affect the conclusions, since any reasonable measure of $Y/\bar{Y}$ would lead to the same ranking of the periods (except possibly 1856–73

and 1874–1913), and our prime concern is the relative importance of different components of demand in bringing about this ranking.

8. For earlier estimates of the absolute and percentage contributions of amplitudes of cycles in components of GDP at *constant* prices to the amplitude of GDP cycles, see Matthews 1968.

9. Data for standard periods are shown in Table 10.8 below. The average annual growth rate in the money supply (M_1) in 1964–69 was practically the same (3.0%) as in 1951–64 (2.9%).

10. See Worswick 1971 for a review and critique of some of the literature. This literature seeks to compare the effects of actual government policies with those of some hypothetical neutral policy. In our present context the comparison is rather different, namely of actual policies with the policies pursued in the past.

11. The annual percentage growth rates of military and nonmilitary P.A.C.E. are shown in the table below (no breakdown available for years before 1924).

12. The overall annual growth rates of P.A.C.E. at GDP prices are as follows:

1913–73	1913–24	1924–37	1937–51	1951–64	1964–73
3.6%	1.2%	4.1%	4.6%	2.7%	3.8%

13. The mixed additive and multiplicative expression for Y given in the text means, of course, that the average annual growth rates are not *exactly* additive. However, it was found that, with the following two approximations, an additive relationship that was correct to the nearest tenth of a percentage point could be obtained: (1) the annual rate of growth of the expression for Y was approximated by the difference between the annual growth rates of the numerator and the denominator; and (2) within the numerator, the annual growth rates of I, X, and A were weighted by their relative importance as measured by the geometric mean of their values in the first and last years of the period; and a similar technique was used to weight the terms s and m in the denominator.

14. Relative price movements enter largely into several of the figures in Table 10.10, especially in 1937–51 and 1951–64 (see facing table). The decline between the two periods in the contribution of exports to growth was thus entirely due to the price element, as also was the rise in the (positive) contribution of the import propensity. Volumes and relative prices are, of course,

TABLE TO NOTE 11

Period	Military	Nonmilitary	Period	Military	Nonmilitary
Phases since 1924			Postwar cycles		
1924–1937	6.9%	1.9%	1951–1955	3.2	1.5
1937–1951	4.9	3.9	1955–1960	−3.7	2.8
1951–1973	−0.9	3.3	1960–1964	1.7	3.0
			1964–1968	−0.4	4.5
			1968–1973	−3.4	4.3

TABLE TO NOTE 14
Contributions to Growth of GDP

Component	1937–1951	1951–1964	Component	1937–1951	1951–1964
Real GDFCF	0.5%	2.6%	X (total)	3.0%	0.3%
p_K/p_Y	0.7	−0.3	Real m	1.3	−0.5
I (total; includes			p_m/p_y	−3.1	2.2
half stock-building)	1.4	2.0	m (total; includes		
Real X	1.2	1.6	half stock-building)	−1.6	1.6
p_x/p_Y	1.8	−1.3			

determined jointly, and it can by no means be assumed that volume movements would have been the same if price movements had been different.

CHAPTER 11

1. The estimates, it will be recalled, relate to ownership of assets. In the postwar years, in particular, part of the increased stock of buildings owned by commerce may in fact have been used by manufacturing industry.

CHAPTER 12

1. Our composite-measure series was derived by dividing the figures in Flemming et al. 1976b for pre-tax earnings of industrial and commercial companies, net of capital consumption stock appreciation and overseas earnings, by the estimates of the market valuation of the earnings on those companies' domestic physical capital. (We are indebted to the Bank of England for supplying us with the underlying data on pre-tax earnings.) This is a less sophisticated concept than either of Flemming's own two proposed measures of the pre-tax cost of capital (p. 205), but it is closer to the ordinary notion of an interest rate.

2. The composite measure will tend to be lowered relative to the rate of interest by any of the following: a reduction in the rate of corporation tax or profits tax; more generous tax provision for depreciation; a reduction in capital gains tax (under inflation); or an increase in income tax (under inflation). If the rate of interest is given, such fiscal changes will lower the yield shown by the composite measure. However, one cannot rule out the possibility that at least part of their effect will be to raise the rate of interest.

3. The earnings yield series for the second half of the 1950's is as follows (London and Cambridge Economic Service 1972: Table M):

1955	12.85%	1958	14.96%
1956	15.92	1959	10.82
1957	15.04	1960	9.02

4. R. F. Henderson 1951: 31 gives statistics suggesting that there was less internal finance in the 1920's. If correct, this would strengthen the conclusion indicated by the comparison of interest rates.

5. The rate of return on *comparable types* of securities, such as government or railway bonds, was rather higher for overseas than for British ones (Cairncross 1953: 230–31).

6. Simon 1967 estimates that 69% of the overseas issues in the London capital market in 1865–1914 were for the finance of social overhead capital.

7. It may be conjectured that the root cause of the superiority of the British capital market for negotiable securities goes right back to the beginning of the 19th century, if not earlier. The stability of the British government during the Napoleonic War and its aftermath encouraged investment in the Funds, hence a capital market geared to it, hence a capacity for dealing with the issues of overseas governments and the fixed-interest securities of large public companies like railways. On the Continent, on the other hand, experience with government securities at the beginning of the 19th century was less satisfactory, savers developed a greater preference for cash, and this served to encourage the growth of investment banks, pioneered in Belgium in the 1820's and later developed on a much larger scale in France and especially Germany. In addition, the concentration of early British industrial development on small-scale textile firms enabled a tradition to be established of self-finance for fixed capital, supported by external finance for working capital, whereas the greater part played by heavy industry in early continental industrialization made external finance for fixed investment more essential from the beginning.

8. The view that there was a bias in the capital market has not gone unchallenged. Edelstein 1971 has suggested that critics of the financial facilities available to British industry have devoted too much attention to the London capital market and have neglected well-functioning provincial financial arrangements. An agnostic view is expressed in Goldsmith 1969: 404–8.

9. See Reddaway et al. 1967, 1968. Reddaway assumes that balance-of-payments effects are offset by compensatory international flows, and that the government maintains the same level of aggregate demand. He therefore postulates that domestic investment is reduced only by the amount needed to release resources to produce the additional commodity exports stimulated by the direct investment abroad.

10. See Mitchell & Deane 1962: 455–60 for rates on fixed-interest securities; Smith & Horne 1934 for a share-price index (see also B. Thomas 1973: 96–99, 403); and Edelstein 1976 for yields on equities (Edelstein's data include capital gains and exclude retentions).

11. Hannah 1976: especially p. 105; Prais 1976. The pause in the 1930's and 1940's was established by Evely and Little (1960). This pause, insofar as it led to the subsequent *more* rapid resumption of the trend to concentration, may have given some extra force to the fall in SPOF in the 1950's and hence to the long-swing rise in investment in that decade.

12. Our own calculations (not here reproduced). These results are broadly confirmed by King 1975.

13. Melliss and Richardson (1976: 41) show little trend after 1963. Flemming et al., using a different method of calculation, show a significant fall in 1965 and a further fall to 1970, followed by a rise to about the 1965 level in 1972 (see

BEQB 1977b: 156, Table B, ratio of third column to second column, being a revision of the data in Flemming et al. 1976a).

14. Unpublished Ministry of Technology survey, described in Lund 1976: 247. For evidence on earlier periods, see Carter & Williams 1957: 148–49; Committee on Turnover Taxation, UK [34]: 77–78; Neild 1964; *Investment Incentives*, UK [36]: 6, based on a CBI survey; and other surveys cited by Lund.

15. The most usual measure of the combined effect of taxation and allowances on the cost of capital is $(1 - A)/(1 - u)$, where A is the present value of tax savings from allowances and u is the rate of taxation (Hall & Jorgenson 1967). If an income tax rate of 25% (the average of the relevant rates in 1935–38) is used, profits tax is assumed to be zero (the National Defence Contribution, the forerunner of the profits tax, was introduced effective April 1, 1937, at a rate of 5%), and a discount rate of 5% (as compared with the rate of 8%, to allow for inflation, in the postwar period) is taken, we arrive at the figures shown in the accompanying table for the end of the interwar period, set alongside those for 1953 (the low point in the postwar period, after which depreciation allowances became more generous). The data are percentages of the cost of the asset.

Income tax is here included in the calculation of A but not in u, following the practice that is normal though debatable. If income tax were included in u, the figures for $(1 - A)/(1 - u)$ would be substantially *higher* in 1953 than prewar, thus reversing the statement in the text, but reinforcing the general conclusion in the following paragraph in the text.

16. For the effects of the gold inflow, see Clapham 1944: 349–50. An important additional source in this period, besides increased production, was gold outflow from the U.S. The complex interaction of real and monetary forces in this period making for a decline in capital import into the U.S., and hence for its loss of gold, is discussed in Friedman & Schwartz (1963): 142–49.

17. Quoted companies' liquid assets in 1954 were £600 million more than they would have been if the liquidity ratio had been the same as in 1963. £600 million is 3½% of their capital expenditure over the period (6% of their gross fixed capital formation). An alternative measure, which naturally comes out higher (£1 billion), is the shortfall of 1963 liquid assets below what they would have been at the 1954 liquidity ratio. The former measure is preferred, on the grounds that it was the 1954 ratio, not the 1963 one, that was abnormal.

18. For discussions of controls on investment and their effectiveness, see P. D. Henderson 1962 and Dow 1964: 149–53. Dow suggests that the effects of

TABLE TO NOTE 15

Category	Machinery		Industrial buildings	
	Prewar	1953	Prewar	1953
Present value of allowances	78.8%	79.1%	33.1%	33.7%
Present value of tax savings (A)	19.7	44.8	4.9	19.1
$(1 - A) / (1 - u)$	80.3	62.5	95.1	91.6

controls on investment in plant and equipment may have been no less than they were on building, despite the looser legal framework. The competitive relationship between investment and exports in connection with the engineering industry is discussed more generally in Nurkse 1956.

CHAPTER 13

1. A number of models of the UK investment function have been produced in recent years: Lund & Holden 1968; Smyth & Briscoe 1969, 1971; Agarwala & Goodson 1969; Burman 1970; Hines & Catephores 1970; Junankar 1970; Nobay 1970; Feldstein & Flemming 1971; Boatwright & Eaton 1972; Rowley 1972; Doig 1976; Lund 1976; Savage 1977. We at one time hoped that the answers to the long-run questions we are interested in could be obtained from these studies or from similar work. We have now become convinced that this is unlikely, at least in the present state of the art, for the reasons explained in Chapter 1. So we shall not report in detail on econometric findings, though we shall refer to them in certain places.

2. Data on the capital stock in individual manufacturing industries do not exist for this period. The sources quoted by Feinstein 1978, however, do not indicate above-average capital-intensity in 1860 for the industries that subsequently grew fast.

3. The figures for gross fixed investment in manufacturing at 1930 prices are as follows (from Feinstein 1965: Table 8.01, adjusted to exclude construction and to include railway engineering workshops; in millions of £):

Category	1929	1937
Metals and metalworking	21.2	51.5
Other	52.6	57.1
Total	73.8	108.6

4. The profit rate rose absolutely, and the capital-output ratio fell. The profit rate rose more than the wage rate and the capital-labor ratio fell. Nothing can therefore be inferred about divergence from either Harrod-neutrality or Hicks-neutrality. The increase in the profit rate between 1924 and 1937 was probably due partly to a reduction in the degree of underutilization and partly also to an increase in the degree of monopoly (cartel arrangements in the 1930's). Allowance for changes in underutilization might also alter the direction of the trend in the capital-labor ratio, though hardly that in the capital-output ratio. We cannot say whether adjustment for these factors would be sufficient to establish a capital-saving bias.

5. According to Census of Production data, electricity provided 53% of the horsepower in manufacturing in 1924, 66% in 1930, and 91% in 1951. No figure is available for the late 1930's, but the trend in electricity consumption suggests that the change shown between 1930 and 1951 occurred most rapidly in the 1930's. The percentage of electricity purchased, as opposed to generated, rose from 47 in 1924 to 56 in 1935.

6. It is interesting to note that the Census of Production shows that horse-

power per worker in manufacturing increased very considerably (by 21% between 1924 and 1930), much more than the capital stock per worker at constant prices. For discussions of electrification and other technical advances in this period, see Sayers 1950, 1967: Chapter 5. A similar hypothesis about the capital-saving effects of electrification in manufacturing in the U.S. has been put forward by du Boff 1966. There the capital-output ratio in manufacturing rose till 1909 and fell thereafter. The period of most rapid transition to electric power was between 1909 and 1929. Du Boff notes that horsepower per unit of capital rose steeply after 1909.

7. This feature made for a trend increase in the ratio of retirements and capital consumption to capital stock, plant and machinery having a shorter life than buildings and works. Hence it made for an upward trend in measures of capital accumulation based on GFCF relative to the measures based on the rate of growth of the capital stock on which attention is here focused. (See Fig. 5.4.)

8. Different trends in output did, natually, explain a fair part of the difference in investment trends between manufacuring industries. A positive correlation between $\hat{k}$ and $\hat{q}$ is shown in Appendix J. The same is true for differences between groups of manufacturing industries. Significant differences in trends occurred between the groups of industries that may be classified as metallurgical (iron and steel, engineering and allied) and others. Output in the metallurgical industries grew very rapidly in 1951–55 and at a much slower and somewhat diminishing rate in subsequent cycles; output in other manufacturing industries grew slowly in 1951–55 and at a much more rapid and roughly constant rate after that. Consistent with this, the peak rate of capital accumulation came considerably earlier in the metallurgical industries than in the other industries. Even so, the conformity in timing between the rate of growth of output and the rate of capital accumulation was by no means complete. In particular the peak rate of capital accumulation in the nonmetallurgical industries occurred fully ten years after the rate of growth of their output had flattened out — too long an interval to be explained as an ordinary lag.

9. There is a qualification that the usefulness for peacetime production of wartime investment in manufacturing may be overstated by the weight given to it in our capital stock statistics (see Dean 1964).

10. This applies particularly to nonmetallurgical industries, where the rate of growth of the stock of plant and machinery reached its postwar peak in the middle and late 1960's, later by one business cycle than the peak in buildings and works. In the metallurgical industries, where there was more tendency to decline in the rate of growth of output, the two classes of investment moved more nearly in parallel after the mid-1950's, apart from an abnormal peak due to high investment in plant and machinery in the steel industry around 1960.

11. A similar conclusion has been reached by many authors. See, for example, the well-known article by Hill (1964).

12. An indirect measure of "defensive" investment may be provided by comparing data on square footage of industrial buildings completed with data on GFCF in buildings and works in manufacturing at constant prices. The square

footage data (in *Monthly Digest*) relate to buildings requiring an industrial development certificate (IDC), viz. buildings or extensions of more than 5,000 square feet. It may be conjectured that defensive investment would typically include an above-average proportion of buildings or extensions too small to require an IDC. Comparison of the trends in the square footage data and in the GFCF series might on this reckoning be used to indicate trends in the proportion of defensive investment. Between 1948 and 1957 and between 1965 and 1971 square footage completed rose considerably more rapidly than the GFCF series, indicating a diminishing proportion of defensive investment. Between 1957 and 1965 the two series appear to move about in parallel, but comparison is hampered by a major change in 1960 in the definitions underlying the IDC data. The measure is, of course, a very imperfect one, since the relative trends in the series could be due to other factors, e.g. structural shifts in investment between industries with different costs of buildings per square foot; thus high investment in the steel industry around 1960 may have been the reason why the relative trends in the two series were different at that time from the periods before or after.

13. See McCrone 1969: 106–48; Hunt Committee, UK [35]: 102–6; A. J. Brown 1972. In the years 1945–47 over half of all industrial investment took place in the development areas. After a fall in the intermediate period, the proportion in 1965–71 was 40%.

14. However, in 1951 wages in the distributive trades were 116% of those in manufacturing. This could be taken as a consequence of shortage. It was probably due partly to the special factor of National Service, which reduced the supply of young workers. The distributive trades normally employ great numbers of young workers, both male and female, who move on to other jobs as they get older. For a discussion of this phenomenon, see Sleeper 1972.

15. The rise in GFCF in commerce between 1964 and 1973 was in fact considerably smaller, both proportionally and absolutely, in buildings and works than it was in plant and machinery. This remains true even if some allowance is made for plant and machinery leased to manufacturing and wrongly credited to commerce in the statistics, estimated at over £100 million in 1975 but probably considerably less in earlier years.

16. In 1973 the gross capital stock in transport and communications formed 43% (of which roads accounted for 9%, shipping 6%, and other industry groups 28%) of the total in this broad sector. Utilities (gas, electricity, and water) accounted for 27% and public and professional services for 30%.

17. Electricity accounted for 34% of GFCF in utilities in 1887–1913, 69% in 1921–28, 75% in 1948–64, and 67% in 1965–73. As late as 1924 over half of the *capital stock* in utilities was in water undertakings. Water is much the most capital-intensive of the utilities. The decline in its share in the total is partly but not wholly responsible for the long-run decline in the capital-output ratio in utilities.

18. The increase in the capital stock in transport and communications between 1873 and 1913 is made up roughly of 49% railways, 21% shipping, 31%

other. Other comprises roads, buses and taxis, tramways and trolleys, Post Office, and harbors, docks, and canals.

19. In the interwar period about 30 % of the labor force in the British merchant fleet was non-British (Mogridge 1962).

20. The fluctuations have been variously attributed to interaction with the American economy, through changes in flows of capital and labor (see especially B. Thomas 1973); and to domestic factors such as local industrial conditions and transport improvements (see Habakkuk 1962; Saul 1962). A full explanation would almost certainly involve both internal and external forces, with the international factors possibly predominant in periods when building was depressed, as in the 1880's and the years preceding 1914, and the domestic factors playing a large part in determining the upswings.

21. Allowance must be made for some excess supply of dwellings in 1913, a year of deep recession in house-building, and for some excess demand in 1973, as manifested in waiting lists. If each of these is estimated at 5 %, for the sake of illustration, an income-elasticity of 1.55 and a price-elasticity of -1.84 fit the observations for the three periods exactly. For other estimates of elasticities of demand for housing, see Clark & Jones 1971; Whitehead 1971; and on the U.S., Reid 1962. Clark and Jones, recognizing the large margin of error in any estimates, conclude cautiously (p. 61) that "there is room in the data as presented for the view that the income-elasticity is at least 1.2 and the price-elasticity at least 0.6." Cross-section studies of the UK housing market have generally yielded lower estimates of income-elasticity, between 0.6 and 0.75 (*Housing Policy*, UK [50], Technical Volume 2: 47–48 and references cited there). This is not necessarily inconsistent, since time-series and cross-section comparisons measure different things.

22. The price of dwellings, p_d, is based on building costs, not selling prices. The rise in the relative cost of accommodation, p_o/p_d, appears, however, to have been matched by a rise in rents relative to selling prices, as measured by the decrease in the number of years' purchase of houses shown in Cairncross 1953: Chapter 6.

23. The approach adopted in the text is not applicable to movements within the long swing, since movements of p_o/p_c over the long swing cannot always be regarded as independent variables determined by costs. Thus in 1897, at the beginning of the building boom of the 1890's, p_o/p_c was very high, yet the relative price of dwellings had risen little, and interest rates were low. Evidently what happened was that the long period of low building preceding 1897 had caused rents to rise — part of the long-swing phenomenon. On the other hand, rises in costs and interest rates *can* be invoked to explain why in the years before 1913 rents were established at a level that caused the building boom to tail off so steeply. Following, as they did, a period of high building, those years might have been expected to show a *low* level of rents, rather than the high one that they actually did.

24. This rise was confined to the transwar period. No change took place between 1924 and 1937.

25. There were five principal forms of housing subsidies:

(1) The pooling system of local authorities, that is to say, their practice of reckoning the economic rent as the amount that would enable them to break even on their housing stock as a whole valued at historical costs. The low historical costs of their older houses enabled them to charge rents much lower than the replacement cost. This was equivalent to transferring to Council tenants as a class the benefits of past capital gains on the Council's houses. This form of subsidy did not occur before the war because there was no inflation.

(2) The reduction, in real terms, and subsequent abolition of Schedule A income tax, formerly charged to owner-occupiers on the imputed values of their dwellings. This also represented a new feature compared with prewar.

(3) Direct subsidies by central and local government in respect of Council houses. These did exist before the war (and for a while in the 1920's private building could also qualify for a subsidy). But the average expenditure on subsidies in the interwar period as a percent of national income was only about half of what it was in 1961. (Interwar housing subsidies amounted on average to between £9 million and £10 million a year; Heales & Kirby 1938: 100). The increase was due mainly to an increase in the number of subsidized houses, the average subsidy per house as a proportion of building cost being not greatly different between the two periods.

(4) Rent controls on privately owned dwellings. The proportion of the housing stock subject to control was lower in the postwar period than in most of the interwar period (interwar data are in Stone et al. 1954: Chapter 15). But the permitted level of rents fell much further below the economic rent in the postwar period. The permitted level of rent in the interwar period was, broadly speaking, 140% of the 1914 rent; building costs, in contrast, had risen by a factor of rather less than two.

(5) Subsidies for improvements to existing dwellings in the private sector. This was a postwar innovation, with no counterpart in the interwar period.

For a fuller discussion of these various subsidies, see Hemming & Duffy 1964; *Housing Policy*, UK [50], Technical Volumes 2 and 3: Chapters 5, 6, 8, 9.

26. We say the relative cost of housing was "apparently" significantly higher because measuring the price of the occupation of dwellings presents a special problem in the postwar period, on account of the treatment of owner-occupied dwellings. The problem is worse than in earlier periods partly because of the increased importance of owner-occupation: the number of owner-occupied dwellings rose from 10% of the total in 1914 to 32% in 1938 and 53% in 1971 (*Housing Policy*, UK [50], *Consultative Document*: #38). A further reason why the problem is worse than in earlier periods is the difficulty of measuring the true annual cost of owner-occupied dwellings under conditions of inflation. Any measure of the cost of an owner-occupied dwelling has to be an imputed one. In theory, the appropriate measure is the interest on the market price of the house, adjusted for the nonliability to tax of such interest (since the abolition of Schedule A), minus the expected capital appreciation of the house. The latter

item involves a subjective element that cannot be directly measured. In any case the foregoing is probably not the way that most owner-occupiers look on the cost of their accommodation. Alternative measures — e.g. actual mortgage interest paid or annual interest and repayment for a first-time buyer — can produce widely discrepant results (see *ibid.*, Technical Volume 2: 1–23, 52–65). The official data underlying Table 13.7 are based, in the case of owner-occupied dwellings, on ratable values. This plainly contains a considerable element of arbitrariness, but it is not obvious in which direction it is biased, and it has the advantage of not giving undue weight to violent short-period movements in house prices, such as occurred in 1972–73. (The figures for 1973 used in Tables 13.7 and 13.8, as far as concerns owner-occupiers, should therefore be taken as an indication of trends, rather than as a measure of true imputed cost in that highly abnormal year.)

The assertion that the price of the occupation of dwellings relative to the price of consumption was higher in the early 1970's than it was in 1937 may seem paradoxical, since it is known that the rents paid by at least one class of tenant, viz. those in the private rented sector, fell as a proportion of earnings (*ibid.*, Technical Volume 1: 43). However, this relates rents to pre-tax earnings, not to consumption; and there was a major switch of tenure from the private rented sector to the public rented sector and to owner-occupation, in both of which costs were higher than in the private rented sector.

27. The vacancy rate of houses was 1.1% in 1951, 2.2% in 1961, and 4.1% in 1971. This may be compared with a rate of around 6% reported in most of the 19th-century British censuses (H. W. Robinson 1939: Appendix 1) and also in the U.S. in modern times. A decline within the postwar period in the amount of excess demand is consistent with the demographic data, which show a steady increase in the number of dwellings relative to the number of households (*Housing Policy*, UK [50], *Consultative Document*: 10). Evidence of a further decline by the mid-1970's is to be found in the emergence for the first time on a significant scale of a problem of "difficult-to-let" local-authority property in some areas.

28. Examples often cited, such as elderly people continuing to occupy quarters that were too large for them, were not peculiar to Britain or to the postwar period. It is striking, however, that in Britain, in constrast to all other countries for which data are available, the average number of persons living in a dwelling in the mid-1960's was practically the same, whatever the size of the dwelling (UN 1965: Table 5).

29. The question is whether an unequal subsidy caused the overall demand for housing space to be larger than an equal subsidy of the same average size would have done.

30. The subsidies themselves owed much to accident and inertia: thus the rents charged for local-authority houses built after the war could not be allowed to be too much higher than the controlled rents that still prevailed in the private sector; Schedule A tax was abolished partly because with the rise in prices it had

become more and more unrealistically low; and the subsidy afforded by the local-authority pooling system was a by-product of inflation. This is not to say, of course, that the subsidies were necessarily ill-advised.

31. The annual percentage growth rates of the gross stock of fixed capital including the wartime periods were as follows:

	1856–1937	1937–1973
Industrial and commercial	2.0%	3.1%
Infrastructure and dwellings	2.1	2.1

32. These arguments and counterarguments are surveyed in Shepherd 1968. Capital quality-shift (Chapter 9) is a measure of the gain actually achieved *ex post* by a shift to higher-yielding classes of investment.

CHAPTER 14

1. This statement on the trends in the import content of exports of goods is based on a calculation relating to five years for which input-output tables are available (1907, 1935, 1954, 1963, 1972), together with a similar calculation for 1870 assuming the same input-output relations as in 1907. The figures, which are very rough, especially for 1870 and 1907, are shown in the accompanying table.

2. The *proportional* rate of decline of the share in world exports is the most appropriate indicator, as measuring the difference between the rate of growth of British exports and the rate of growth of world exports.

3. For a discussion of the statistical basis of the estimates of net investment abroad and net grants from abroad, see Chapter 5, pp. 123, 127. They do not necessarily correspond to the accumulated sum of capital exports because, quite apart from errors in both series, we have made some attempt in these estimates to allow for the appreciation and depreciation of certain existing assets.

4. Gross overseas assets were, of course, even larger — nearly twice GDP in 1913. Gross income from abroad (including taxes paid in the UK by foreign residents) was 9.6% of GDP (Feinstein 1972: Table 15).

5. The concept of an average rate of return on net overseas assets is of course not very meaningful in circumstances such as prevailed after World War II, when positive net income was earned by negative overseas assets.

6. In the first half of the 19th century there were about six years when this was not true, the last being 1822 (Imlah 1958: 94). The next year of positive trade balance was 1956.

TABLE TO NOTE 1

Category	1870	1907	1935	1954	1963	1972
Gross ratio, X/GDP	19	21	11.6	17.1	15.4	16.1
Value-added ratio, X'/GDP	(12)	15	9.3	13.7	12.6	12.7
Import content of exports, $(X - X')/X$	(35)	29	20.0	19.6	18.4	21.1

Note: X = exports of goods; and X' = exports of goods less import content of goods and services.

CHAPTER 15

1. Though both output and export declined between 1856–73 and 1873–1913, the correlation between them disappears over individual business cycles, as the following growth rates show:

	1856–1860	1860–1865	1865–1873	1873–1882	1882–1889	1889–1899	1899–1907	1907–1913
Exports of goods	3.4%	0.1%	5.6%	3.2%	2.6%	1.0%	4.0%	3.0%
GDP	1.8	2.0	2.4	1.9	2.2	2.2	1.2	1.6

Alternating long swings in exports and investment are the main explanation for this.

2. The trend rate of TFP growth in cotton textiles after 1885 appears to have been about the same as in the previous quarter-century. G. T. Jones (1933) found *no* increase in TFP between 1885 and 1913, but his calculations have been criticized by Sandberg (1974: 93–119). Sandberg (p. 96) shows an annual percentage rate of increase of *labor* productivity of 0.8 between the two cyclically comparable years 1890 and 1913.

3. Deceleration in productivity growth after the middle of the century was greatest in weaving, on account of the completion of the transition from cottage industry to factory industry; but it was also quite pronounced in spinning, where cottage industry had disappeared at a much earlier date (Blaug 1961: 366).

4. Sandberg 1974: 113 shows an annual rate of growth of labor productivity in the U.S. cotton textile industry between the cyclically comparable years 1885 and 1912 of 1.4%, still far below the mid-19th century rate of TFP growth in the UK.

5. The hypothesis of increasing competitive pressure is not inconsistent with the evidence on international price relativities (Lipsey 1963: 25–29; Knapp & Lomax 1964; Phelps Brown & Browne 1968: 126–32). The data, such as they are, suggest that the prices of British exports rose slightly relative to those of other industrial countries, as would be expected if British export prices were tending to be undercut by competition. On the face of it, it is more surprising that British unit labor costs appear to have fallen relative to those in other countries, at least till 1900. This can be explained, following Phelps Brown, by postulating that at the beginning of the period profit margins in some of the UK's industrializing competitors, particularly Germany, were above equilibrium and fell as their output expanded.

6. It makes no difference whether the argument is couched in terms of the rise in income from abroad or in terms of the rise in the excess of income from abroad over capital export, since capital export, as a proportion of GNP, was roughly constant over the period, averaged over long swings (Table 14.7).

7. The annual rate of growth of coal exports (tons) in 1873–1913 was 4.6%. Coal exports in 1913 amounted to 2.3% of GDP and 10.2% of total exports, at current prices. (Mitchell & Deane 1962: 121, 303–6.)

8. It would not *as such* explain why British unit costs fell more than German unit costs (note 5), but it is not necessarily incompatible with that trend if there were other forces, internal to Germany, tending in that direction.

9. "When Bank Rate was raised, it was for the purpose of influencing the international capital position. . . . It was not the Bank's purpose thereby to discourage trade and industrial activity, either directly or through any contraction in the supply of bank money. Market operations were directed only at stiffening rates in the London bill market, not at denuding commercial bank reserves for such a purpose as the enforcement of general reduction of credit." (Sayers 1976: 43.)

10. Monthly statistics for 1890–1914 are given in Goodhart 1972: Appendix VA.

11. Data on money stock are in Sheppard 1971. See also Chapter 10, pp. 316–19, above.

12. This is related to the timing of the investment boom in the mid-1870's rather than to the years before 1873; some of the effect on investment of the increase in output between 1856 and 1873 took place after 1873.

13. The change between 1874–90 and 1891–1913 in the ratio of the balance of trade and services to GDP was -1.4%; that between 1891–1913 and 1921–29 was -1.3%. Say that in the interwar period the shortfall of GDP below the full-employment level exceeded the shortfall before 1914 by an amount equal, as an approximation, to 5% of GDP. Taking 105% of GDP as the denominator in calculating exports (and net services) in the 1920's, the figure for change in the balance of trade and services between 1891–1913 and the 1920's is -2.2 percentage points (instead of -1.3 in Table 14.8). This is a fractionally greater deterioration than between the two earlier periods, but the difference is small.

14. Hilgerdt 1945: 18; W. A. Lewis 1949: 149–55; Maizels 1963: 82–84. Lewis argues that the reduced demand for primary products in the 1920's compared with 1913 was sufficient by itself to account for the low level of world trade in manufactures. However, the diminution in the rate of growth in 1913–29 compared with 1899–1913 was of almost identical extent in the trade in manufactures between industrial countries and in exports of manufactures to primary producers (data in Maizels 1963: 89). In the case of UK exports, there was significant reduction in the share of the total going to semi-industrialized countries (including India) between 1913 and 1929; but this was about matched by a rise in the share of non-industrialized countries (Maizels, p. 426).

15. This is shown by comparing TFP growth in manufacturing (1) with industries weighted as usual by output, and (2) with industries weighted instead by exports (the export weights include direct and indirect exports and are derived from the input-output calculations in Chapter 14). See the following table. There is no significant difference between the two columns in any period. The results are based on our usual 13-industry breakdown of manufacturing, and might, of course, be different with finer disaggregation.

TABLE TO NOTE 15

Growth of Total Factor Productivity in Manufacturing, Output-
Weighted and Export-Weighted, 1924–1973

(Annual percentage growth rates)

Period	Output-weighted	Export-weighted
1924–1937	1.74%	1.80%
1937–1951	0.74	0.72
1951–1964	1.88	1.89
1964–1973	3.10	3.02

Note: Base years for weights: *1924–37*, 1935; *1937–51*, growth rates shown are averages of those at 1935 weights and those at 1954 weights; *1951–64*, 1954; *1964–73*, 1968. These base years are chosen on account of the availability of input-output data, and the output-weighted figures are therefore not identical with those given in Chapter 8.

16. The movements in relative wage rates and costs in the 1920's were extremely complex, each of the principal countries having its own peculiarities (Phelps Brown & Browne 1968: 218–34).

17. Convincing arguments against setting too much importance on the return to gold are contained in Sayers 1960: 313–27.

18. For asset owners as a class the reduction in income from abroad was offset largely by the rise in national debt interest (Chapter 6, pp. 191–94). But the debt interest had to be paid for out of taxation. For a discussion of this aspect of the 1920's, see Schumpeter 1939: 731.

19. We do not have data on TFP in individual manufacturing industry groups before 1914, but the rate of TFP growth in 1924–37 in *each* of the 13 manufacturing industry groups was higher than the rate for manufacturing as a whole in 1873–1913 (Tables 8.3, 8.7).

20. Current account (goods, services, property income, and private transfers) surplus as a percent of GNP (1950–65 data from UN 1972: Table 2.5; 1966–73 data from OECD [1], [10]):

	1950–58	1959–65	1966–73
United Kingdom	0.7%	0.3%	0.6%
Industrial Western Europe (including UK)	0.5	0.6	0.9

21. Analysis of the characteristics of different countries' exports in 1965 shows those of the UK as skill-intensive, modern, and subject to a high degree of product differentiation (Hufbauer 1970: 155). However, there is evidence that *within* industry groups, relatively low-valued goods preponderated among British exports by comparison, particularly, with those of West Germany (National Economic Development Office 1977: 13, 26–28).

22. Several studies have suggested that relative productivity trends were the main explanation of different countries' shares in world trade. Most striking is the finding of Gross and Keating (1970), in their study of engineering products,

TABLE TO NOTE 23
Average Annual Net Export of Private Capital from Selected Industrial Countries, 1951–1973
(Millions of U.S. dollars)

Country	1951–1964, all investment	1965–1973 All investment	1965–1973 Direct investment
United States	1,903	4,244	5,736
United Kingdom	389	– 138	640
Switzerland	170	–	–
Belgium/Luxembourg	65	233	– 232
West Germany	36	– 746	– 236
Japan	20	1,512	375
Netherlands	– 20	145	16
France	– 40	210	– 77

Source: 1951–64, Dunning 1970: 30; *1965–73,* OECD [1]. The figures for the two periods are not comparable.

that productivity change was the *only* factor explaining market shares, with cost and price measures having explanatory power only insofar as they were proxies for productivity. A similar conclusion is suggested by the data in Ray 1972.

23. Estimates of the average annual net export of private long-term capital are shown in the accompanying table.

24. The following text draws on Panic & Seward 1966; "International comparisons of costs and prices," UK [18]; Phelps Brown & Browne 1968: 296; Gross & Keating 1970; Kravis & Lipsey 1971. Evidence on the period after 1967 is conveniently summarized in National Economic Development Office 1977, which also contains a survey of the literature.

25. British export prices rose by 3 percentage points relative to U.S. export prices and by 4 points relative to EEC export prices over the period 1953–64, that is to say, by about a third of a percentage point a year.

26. Survey data relating to pre-devaluation and post-devaluation (1966 and 1968) are analyzed in Gribbin 1971. We are indebted to Mr. Gribbin for the information that in 1966 the average profit rate of the firms in the survey was 20.7% for domestic sales and 13.8% for exports. "Profit rate" was defined by the firms in widely varying ways, so the absolute figures are not very significant, but the difference between domestic sales and exports is clearly established.

27. The evidence adduced is that in the early 1950's the purchasing power of the pound over consumer goods was unusually high, at current exchange rates, by comparison with the purchasing power of the dollar.

28. There was a significant shift of resources to manufacturing across World War II, and it was largely due to foreign trade. The substantial labor quality-shift gain over the same period was not mainly due to manufacturing, but the capital quality-shift was (Chapter 9). Trends in foreign trade on this account contributed between 0.1 and 0.2 of a point to the annual percentage rate of growth of 1.1 in TFP across World War II—a small but not negligible contribu-

tion. However, it was probably just about balanced by the loss of productivity due to the shifts of resources into diminishing-returns agriculture and mining — shifts motivated largely by the balance of payments. Within the postwar period there continued to be capital quality-shift gains due to manufacturing, but these cannot be attributed to foreign trade, since foreign trade was tending to reduce manufacturing's share in output (Table 9.10). However, even if foreign trade's effect on manufacturing's share of output had been higher, the extra gain to TFP growth would only have been of the order of 0.1 percentage point, assuming changes of reasonable dimensions.

CHAPTER 17

1. Annual percentage rates of growth of net exports of manufactures were as follows: 1857–73, 2.4; 1873–99, 0.6; 1899–1913, 2.9 (Schlote 1952). Rates of growth of TFP in manufacturing are given in Appendix L.

2. On Britain's record in technological innovations in these and other fields, see M. Frankel 1955; Habbakuk 1962; Saul 1962, 1967; Kindleberger 1964; Levine 1967; Aldcroft 1968; Landes 1969; McCloskey 1971, 1973; Byatt 1979.

3. On the factors influencing the diffusion of technology, see Mansfield 1968; Rosenberg 1976. See also Peck 1968.

References

References

The following abbreviations are used in the Notes and the References:

BEQB	Bank of England Quarterly Bulletin
EcHR	Economic History Review
EJ	Economic Journal
ET	Economic Trends
JRSS	Journal of the Royal Statistical Society
MS	Manchester School of Economic and Social Studies
NIER	National Institute Economic Review
REStud	Review of Economic Studies

Abramovitz, M. 1956. "Resource and output trends in the United States since 1870," *American Economic Review*, 46.2 (May): 523.

Agarwala, R., and G. C. Goodson. 1969. "An analysis of the effects of investment incentives on investment behaviour in the British economy," *Economica*, 36. 144 (Nov.): 377–88.

Aldcroft, D. H. 1964. "The entrepreneur and the British economy, 1870–1914," *EcHR*, 17.1 (Aug.): 113–34.

————, ed. 1968. *The Development of British Industry and Foreign Competition*. London.

Alden, J. H. 1971. "Double-jobholding: A regional analysis of Scotland," *Scottish Journal of Political Economy*, 18.1 (Feb.): 99–112.

Allen, R. C. 1979. "International competition in iron and steel, 1850–1913," *Journal of Economic History*, 39.4 (Dec.): 911–37.

Arrow, K. J. 1973. "Education as a filter," in K. Lumsden, ed., *Efficiency in Education: The La Paz Papers*. Amsterdam.

Artus, J. R. 1975. "The 1967 devaluation of the pound sterling," *IMF Staff Papers*, 22.3 (Nov.): 595–640.

————. 1977. "Measures of potential output in manufacturing for eight industrial countries, 1955–1978," *IMF Staff Papers*, 24.1 (March): 1–35.

Atkin, J. 1970. "Official regulation of British overseas investment, 1914–1931," *EcHR*, 23.2 (Feb.): 324–35.

Bain, G. S. 1970. *The Growth of White-Collar Unionism*. Oxford, England.

Bain, J. S. 1965. *Barriers to New Competition: Their Character and Consequences in Manufacturing Industry* (Cambridge, Mass.)

Bairoch, P., et al. 1968. *The Working Population and Its Structure*, Vol. 1 of *International Historical Statistics*. Brussels.

Ball, R. J., and T. Burns. 1976. "The inflationary mechanism in the U.K. economy," *American Economic Review*, 66.4 (Sept.): 467–84.

Ballin, H. H. 1946. *The Organization of Electricity Supply in Great Britain*. London.

Bank of England. 1970. *Statistical Abstract*, vol. 1. London.

———. 1975. *Statistical Abstract*, vol. 2. London.

Bank of England Quarterly Bulletin. 1966. "Personal saving and financial investment: 1951–65," 6.3 (Sept.): 246–56.

———. 1967. "Company finance, 1952–65," 7.1 (March): 29–42.

———. 1969. "The U.K. banking sector, 1952–67," 9.2 (June): 176–200.

———. 1976. "The personal saving ratio," 16.1 (March): 53–73.

———. 1977a. "The personal sector, 1966–1975," 17.1 (March): 27–33.

———. 1977b. "Economic commentary, supplementary note: Company profitability and the cost of capital," 17.2 (June): 156–60.

Barna, T. 1952. "The interdependence of the British economy," *JRSS*, Series A, 115.1: 29–77.

Beckerman, W. 1963. "Married women at work in 1972," *NIER*, 23 (Feb.): 56–60.

———. 1980. "Comparative growth rates of 'measurable economic welfare': Some experimental calculations," in R. C. O. Matthews, ed., *Economic Growth: Trends and Factors*, vol. 2 of *Proceedings of the Fifth World Congress of the International Economic Association*. London.

Beckerman, W., et al. 1965. *The British Economy in 1975*. Cambridge, England.

Bellerby, J. R. 1958. "The distribution of manpower in agriculture and industry, 1851–1951," *The Farm Economist*, 9.1: 1–11.

Berman, L. S. 1967. "A note on contractual saving in the United Kingdom," *ET*, 166 (Aug.): ix–xvii.

Beveridge, W. H. 1930. *Unemployment: A Problem of Industry*. London.

———. 1937. "An analysis of unemployment," *Economica*, n.s., 4 (May): 168–83.

———. 1944. *Full Employment in a Free Society*. London.

Bienefeld, M. A. 1972. *Working Hours in British Industry: An Economic History*. London.

Blaug, M. 1961. "The productivity of capital in the Lancashire cotton industry during the nineteenth century," *EcHR*, 13.3 (April): 358–81.

———. 1972. "The correlation between education and earnings: What does it signify?," *Higher Education*, 1: 53–76.

Blaug, M., M. Peston, and A. Ziderman. 1967. *The Utilisation of Educated Manpower in Industry*. Edinburgh.

Boatwright, B. D., and J. R. Eaton. 1972. "The estimation of investment functions for manufacturing industry in the United Kingdom," *Economica*, 39. 156 (Nov.): 403–18.

Booth, C. 1886. "On occupations of the people of the United Kingdom, 1801–81," *JRSS*, 49 (June): 314–435.

Bowers, J. 1970. *The Anatomy of Regional Activity Rates* (National Institute of Economic and Social Research Regional Papers 1), Cambridge, England.

Bowley, A. L. 1919. *The Division of the Product of Industry: An Analysis of National Income Before the War*. Oxford, England.

———. 1921. *Prices and Wages in the United Kingdom, 1914–20*. Oxford, England.

Bowley, M. 1966. *The British Building Industry*. Cambridge, England.

———. 1967. *Innovation in Building Materials*. London.

Brechling, F., and J. N. Wolfe. 1965. "The end of stop-go," *Lloyds Bank Review*, 75 (Jan.): 23–30.

Brinberg, H. R., and H. R. Northrup. 1950. *The Economics of the Work Week* (National Industrial Conference Board Studies in Business Economics 4). New York.

British Association. 1935. *Britain in Depression* (Research Committee of the Economic Service and Statistics Section). London.

———. 1938. *Britain in Recovery* (Research Committee of the Economic Service and Statistics Section). London.

British Electric Authority. 1949. *First Report and Accounts, August 1947–1949*. London.

Brittan, S. 1975. *Second Thoughts on Full Employment Policy*. London.

Brown, A. J. 1965. "Britain in the world economy," *Yorkshire Bulletin of Economic and Social Research*, 17.1 (May): 46–60.

———. 1972. *The Framework of Regional Economics in the United Kingdom*. Cambridge, England.

———. 1976. "UV analysis," in G. D. N. Worswick, ed., *The Concept and Measurement of Involuntary Unemployment*. London.

Brown, B. C. 1954. "Industrial production in 1935 and 1948," *London and Cambridge Economic Bulletin*, n.s, 12 (Dec.): v–vi.

Brown, C. J. F. and T. D. Sheriff. 1978. "De-industrialization: A background paper," in F. T. Blackaby, ed., *De-industrialization*. London.

Brown, D. G. 1965. "Hours and output," in C. E. Dankerk, F. C. Mann, and H. R. Northrup, eds., *Hours of Work*. New York.

Brown, M., ed. 1967. *The Theory and Empirical Analysis of Production* (National Bureau of Economic Research Studies in Income and Wealth 31). New York.

Burman, J. P. 1970. "Capital utilisation and the determination of fixed investment," in D. F. Heathfield and K. Hilton, eds., *The Econometric Study of the United Kingdom*. London.

Burn, D. L. 1940. *The Economic History of Steel Making, 1867–1939*. Cambridge, England.

_____. ed. 1958. *The Structure of British Industry*. Cambridge, England.

Byatt, I. C. R. 1979. *The British Electrical Industry, 1875–1914: The Economic Returns to a New Technology*. Oxford, England.

CBI, *see* Confederation of British Industry.

Cairncross, A. K. 1953. *Home and Foreign Investment, 1870–1913: Studies in Capital Accumulation*. Cambridge, England.

_____. 1973. *Control of Long-Term Interntional Capital Movements*. Washington, D.C.

Cambridge University Department of Applied Economics. 1974. *Structural Change in the British Economy 1948–1968*, no. 12 in *A Programme for Growth*. London.

Cameron, G. C. 1965. "The growth of holidays with pay in Britain," in G. L. Reid and D. J. Robertson, eds., *Fringe Benefits, Labour Costs and Social Security*. London.

Carré, J.-J., P. Dubois, and E. Malvinaud. 1975. *French Economic Growth*. Stanford, Calif.

Carter, C. F. 1958. "The building industry," in D. L. Burn, ed., *The Structure of British Industry*. Cambridge, England.

Carter, C. F., and B. R. Williams. 1957. *Industry and Technical Progress*. Oxford, England.

Carter, C. F., W. B. Reddaway, and R. Stone. 1948. *The Measurement of Production Movements*. Cambridge, England.

Caves, R. E. 1970. "Second thoughts on Britain's economic prospects," in A. K. Cairncross, ed., *Britain's Economic Prospects Reconsidered*. London.

Caves, R. E., et al. 1968. *Britain's Economic Prospects*. Washington, D.C.

Central Electricity Generating Board. 1960. *Report and Accounts for the year 31st March 1960*. London.

Chamber of Shipping of the United Kingdom. Various years. *Annual Reports*.

Champernowne, D. G. 1953–54. "The production function of the theory of capital: A comment," *REStud*, 21(2).55: 112–35.

Chapman, A. L. (assisted by R. Knight). 1952. *Wages and Salaries in the United Kingdom, 1920–1938*. Cambridge, England.

Chapman, S. J. 1904. *The Lancashire Cotton Industry*. Manchester, England.

_____. 1909. "Hours of labour," *EJ*, 19 (Sept.): 353–73.

Christensen, L. R., D. Cummings, and D. W. Jorgenson. 1978. "Productivity growth, 1947–73: An international comparison," in W. Dewald, ed., *The Impact of International Trade and Investment on Unemployment*. Washington, D.C.

Civil Service Clerical Association. N.d. *Compendium*.

Clapham, J. H. 1932. *Free Trade and Steel*, vol. 2 of *An Economic History of Modern Britain*. Cambridge, England.

_____. 1944. *The Bank of England*. Cambridge, England.

Clark, C., 1957. *The Conditions of Economic Progress*. 3rd ed. London.

Clark, C., and G. T. Jones. 1971. "The demand for housing," *Centre for Environmental Studies, University Working Paper II*, September.

Coleman, D. C. 1973. "Gentlemen and Players," *EcHR*, 26.1 (Feb.): 92–116.

Commercial History and Review. Various years before 1914. Annual publication of *The Economist*.

Common, M. S. 1972. "A further re-examination of Stone's post-war expenditure function," *MS*, 40.3 (Sept.): 269–81.

Conan, A. R. 1952. *The Sterling Area*. London.

Confederation of British Industry (CBI). Various dates. *Industrial Trends Survey*. Three times a year.

Conlisk, J. 1966. "Unemployment in a neo-classical growth model," *EJ*, 76.303 (Sept.): 550–66.

Conrad, A. H., and J. Meyer. 1965. *Studies in Econometric History*. London.

Coppock, D. J. 1956. "The climateric of the 1890's: A critical note," *MS*, 24.1 (Jan.): 1–31.

Corry, B. A., and J. A. Roberts. 1970. "Activity rates and unemployment: The experience of the United Kingdom, 1951–66," *Applied Economics*, 2.3: 179–201.

Cotgrove, S. F. 1958. *Technical Education and Social Change*. London.

Crafts, N. F. R. 1976. "English economic growth in the eighteenth century: A re-examination of Deane and Cole's estimates," *EcHR*, 29.2 (May): 226–35.

————. 1979. "Victorian Britain did fail," *EcHR*, 32.4 (Nov.): 553–37.

Creamer, D. 1972. "Measuring capital input for total factor productivity analysis: Comments by a sometime estimator," *Review of Income and Wealth*, 18.1 (March): 66–68.

Cripps, T. F., and R. J. Tarling. 1973. *Growth in Advanced Capitalist Economies, 1950–1970*. Cambridge, England.

Croft, M. 1960. *Apprenticeship and the "Bulge"* (Fabian Society Research Series 216). London.

Crossman, R. H. S. 1975. *The Diaries of a Cabinet Minister*, vol. 1. London.

Cubbin, J. S., and K. Foley, 1977. "The extent of benefit-induced unemployment in Great Britain," *Oxford Economic Papers*, 29.1 (March): 128–40.

David, P. A. 1971. "The landscape and the machine," in D. N. McCloskey, ed., *Essays on a Mature Economy*. London.

Deakin, B. M., and T. Seward. 1969. *Productivity in Transport*. Cambridge, England.

Dean, G. A. 1964. "The stock of fixed capital in the United Kingdom in 1961," *JRSS*, Series A, 127.3: 327–51.

Deane, P. 1968. "New estimates of gross national product for the United Kingdom, 1830–1914," *Review of Income and Wealth*, 14.2 (June): 95–112.

Deane, P. M., and W. A. Cole. 1962. *British Economic Growth, 1688–1959*. Cambridge, England.

Denison, E. F. 1962. *The Sources of Economic Growth in the States and the Alternatives Before Us* (Committee for Economic Development). New York.

Denison, E. F., (assisted by J.-F. Poullier). 1967. *Why Growth Rates Differ*. Washington, D. C.

_____. 1968. "Economic Growth," in R. E. Caves et al., *Britain's Economic Prospects*. Washington, D. C.

_____. 1969. "Some major issues in productivity analysis: An examination of estimates by Jorgenson and Griliches," *Survey of Current Business*, 49.5, part 2 (May): 1–27.

_____. 1972. "Classification of sources of growth," *Review of Income and Wealth*. 18.1 (March): 1–26.

_____. 1974. *Accounting for United States Economic Growth, 1929–1969*. Washington, D.C.

_____. 1979a. *Accounting for Slower Growth: The United States in the 1970s*. Washington, D.C.

_____. 1979b. "Explanations of declining productivity growth," *Survey of Current Business*, 59.8, part 2 (Aug.): 1–25.

Dewald, W., ed. 1978. *The Impact of International Trade and Investment on Employment*. Washington, D.C.

Doig, M. 1976. "Investment and the cost of capital – Part two", unpublished Treasury internal working paper.

Dow, J. C. R. 1964. *The Management of the British Economy, 1945–60*. Cambridge, England.

Dowie, J. A. 1975. "1919–20 is in need of attention," *EcHR*, 27.3 (Aug.): 429–50.

du Boff, R. B. 1966. "Electrification and capital productivity: A suggested approach," *Review of Economics and Statistics*, 48.4 (Nov.): 426–31.

Dunning, J. H. 1970. *Studies in International Investment*. London.

Edelstein, M. 1971. "Rigidity and bias in the British capital market, 1870–1913," in D. N. McCloskey, ed., *Essays on a Mature Economy*. London.

_____. 1976. "Realized rates of return on U.K. home and portfolio investment in the age of high imperialism," *Explorations in Economic History*, 13.3 (July): 283–329.

Elton, G. R. 1967. *The Practice of History*. London.

Enoch, C. A. 1978. "Measures of competitiveness in international trade," *BEQB*, 18.2 (June): 181–95.

Evely, R., and I. M. D. Little. 1960. *Concentration in British Industry*. Cambridge, England.

Feinstein, C. H. 1963. "Production and productivity, 1920–1962," *London and Cambridge Economic Bulletin* in *The Times Review of Industry and Technology*, Dec.

_____. 1965. *Domestic Capital Formation in the United Kingdom, 1920–1938*. Cambridge, England.

_____. 1968. "Changes in the distribution of the national income in the United Kingdom since 1860," in J. Marchal and B. Ducroz, eds., *The Distribution of National Income*. London.

_____. 1972. *National Income, Expenditure and Output of the United Kingdom, 1855–1964*. Cambridge, England.

———. 1978. "Capital accumulation and economic growth in Great Britain, 1760–1860," in vol. 7 of *Cambridge Economic History of Europe*. Cambridge, England.

———. N.d. "Capital accumulation in the United Kingdom, 1860–1938," in C. H. Feinstein and S. Pollard, eds., *Capital Formation in Britain, 1750–1938*. Oxford, England. Forthcoming.

Feinstein, C. H., R. C. O. Matthews, and J. C. Odling-Smee. 1981. "The timing of the climacteric and its sectoral incidence in the U.K., 1873–1913," in G. diTella and C. P. Kindleberger, eds., *Economics in the Long View: Essays in Honour of W. W. Rostow*. London.

Feldstein, M. S. 1967. "The effectiveness of the British differential profits tax," *EJ*, 77.308 (Dec.): 947–52.

———. 1970. "Corporate taxation and dividend behaviour," *REStud*, 37(1).109 (Jan.): 57–72.

———. 1972. "Corporate taxation and dividend policy: A reply and extension," *REStud*, 39(2).118 (April): 235–40.

Feldstein, M. S., and J. S. Flemming. 1971. "Tax policy, corporate saving and investment behaviour in Britian," *REStud*, 38(4).116 (Oct.): 415–34.

Flemming, J. S., et al. 1976a. "Trends in company profitability," *BEQB*, 16.1 (March): 36–52.

———. 1976b. "The cost of capital, finance, and investment," *BEQB*, 16.2 (June): 193–205.

Florence, P. Sargent. 1924. "The 48-hour week and industrial efficiency," *International Labour Review*, 10.5 (Nov.): 729–58.

Fogarty, M. P., R. Rapoport, and R. N. Rapoport. 1971. *Sex, Career and Family*. London.

Ford, A. G. 1965. "Overseas lending and internal fluctuations," *Yorkshire Bulletin of Economic and Social Research*, 17.1 (May): 19–31.

Forestry Commission. Various years. *Annual Report*. London.

Foss, M. 1963. "The utilisation of capital equipment," *Survey of Current Business*, 43.6 (June): 8–16.

Fox, A. 1960. *Industrial Sociology and Industrial Relations* (Royal Commission on Trade Unions and Employers' Associations Research Paper 3). London.

Frankel, H. 1945. "The industrial distribution of the population of Great Britain in July 1939," *JRSS*, 108, part 3–4: 392–422.

Frankel, M. 1955. "Obsolescence and technological change in a maturing economy," *American Economic Review*, 45.3 (June): 296–319.

Friedman, M., and A. J. Schwartz. 1963. *A Monetary History of the United States, 1868–1960*. Princeton, N.J.

Fuà, G. 1971. *Formazione, Distribuzione e Impiego del Reddito dal 1861*. Rome.

Fuller, M. F. 1970. "Some tests on the compatibility of historical series of national accounts estimates," *Bulletin of the Oxford University Institute of Economics and Statistics*, 32.3 (Aug.): 219–30.

Galambos, P. 1967. "Activity rates of the population of Great Britain, 1951–1964," *Scottish Journal of Political Economy*, 14.1 (Feb.): 48–69.

Galenson, W., and A. Zellner. 1957. "International comparison of unemployment rates," in *The Measurement and Behavior of Unemployment* (National Bureau of Economic Research). Princeton, N.J.

George, K. D. 1966. *Productivity in Distribution*. Cambridge, England.

_____. 1969. "Productivity in the distributive trades," *Bulletin of the Oxford University Institute of Economics and Statistics*, 31.2 (May): 67–72.

Gilbert, M., and I. B. Kravis. 1954. *An International Comparison of National Products and the Purchasing Power of Currencies* (Organization for European Economic Cooperation). Paris.

Gillion, C., and I. Black. 1966. "Some characteristics of unemployment," *NIER*, 37 (Aug.): 33–38.

Glass, D. V. 1970. "The components of natural increase in England and Wales," in *Towards a population policy*, supplement to *Population Studies* (May): 11–24.

Glass, D. V., and E. Grebenik. 1954. "The Trend and Pattern of Fertility in Great Britain: A Report on the Family Census of 1946, Part I: Report," in vol. 6 of Royal Commission on Population, *Papers*. London.

Godley, W. A. H., and J. R. Shepherd. 1964. "Long-term growth and short-term policy," *NIER*, 29 (Aug.): 26–38.

Goldsmith, R. W. 1962. *The National Wealth of the United States in the Post-War Period* (National Bureau of Economic Research). Princeton, N.J.

_____. 1969. *Financial Structure and Development*. New Haven, Conn.

Goodhart, C. A. E. 1972. *The Business of Banking, 1891–1914*. London.

_____. 1978. "Monetary policy," in M. Posner, ed., *Demand Management*. London.

Gordon, R. A. 1961. "Differential changes in the prices of consumers' and capital goods," *American Economic Review*, 51.5 (Dec.): 937–57.

Greve, J. 1965. *Private Landlords in England* (Occasional Papers on Social Administration 16). London.

Gribbin, J. D. 1971. *The Profitability of U.K. Exports* (Government Economic Service Occasional Papers 1). London.

Griffin, T. J. 1975. "Revised estimates of the consumption and stock of fixed capital," *ET*, 264 (Oct.): 126–29.

_____. 1976a. "The stock of fixed assets in the United Kingdom," paper given to a conference at Southampton University, July 1976.

_____. 1976b. "The stock of fixed assets in the United Kingdom: How to make best use of the statistics," *ET*, 276 (Oct.): 130–43.

Griliches, Z. 1970. "Notes on the role of education in production functions and growth accounting," in W. L. Hansen, ed., *Education, Income and Human Capital* (National Bureau of Economic Research Studies in Income and Wealth 35). New York.

_____. ed. 1971. *Price Indexes and Quality Change*. Cambridge, Mass.

Griliches, Z., and D. W. Jorgenson. 1966. "Sources of measured productivity change: Capital input," *American Economic Review*, 56.2 (May): 50–61.

Gross, R., and M. Keating. 1970. "An empirical analysis of competition in export and domestic markets," *OECD Economic Outlooks, Occasional Studies* (Dec.): 3–38.

Gupta, S. 1963. "Input and output trends in British manufacturing industry, 1948–54," *JRSS*, Series A, 126.3: 433–45.

Habakkuk, H. J. (1962), "Fluctuations in house-building in Britain and the United States in the nineteenth century," *Journal of Economic History*, 22.2: 198–230.

————. 1972. *Population Growth and Economic Development Since 1750*. Leicester, England.

Hall, R. E., and D. Jorgenson. 1967. "Tax policy and investment behaviour," *American Economic Review*, 57.3 (June): 391–414.

Hannah, L. 1976. *The Rise of the Corporate Economy*. London.

Hargreaves, E. L. 1930. *The National Debt*. London.

Hart, P. E., et al. 1968. "Econometric analyses of profit, dividends and business saving," part 4, vol. 2, of Hart, ed., *Studies in Profit, Business Saving and Investment in the United Kingdom, 1920–1962*. London.

Hartog, F. 1956. "Wirtschaftliche Probleme der Arbeitszeitverkurzung," *Zeitschrift für die gesamte Staatswissenschaft*, 112.4: 671–84.

Heales, H. C., and C. H. Kirby. 1938. *Housing Finance in Great Britain*. London.

Heathfield, D. F. 1972. "The measurement of capital usage using electricity consumption data for the U.K.," *Journal of the Royal Statistical Society*, part 2, 135: 208–20.

Hemming, M. F. W., and H. Duffy. 1964. "The price of accommodation," *NIER*, 29 (Aug.): 39–59.

Henderson, P. D. 1962. "Government and industry," in G. D. N. Worswick and P. H. Ady, eds., *The British Economy in the Nineteen-Fifties*. Oxford, England.

Henderson, R. F. 1951. *The New Issue Market and the Finance of Industry*. Cambridge, England.

Henderson-Stewart, P. 1965. Appendix to M. Blaug, "The rate of return on investment in education in Great Britain," *Manchester School of Economic and Social Studies*, 33.3 (Sept.): 252–61.

Hendry, D. F. 1980. "Econometrics — alchemy or science? An inaugural lecture," *Economica*, 47.188 (Nov.): 387–406.

Hibbert, J. 1975a. "Measuring changes in the nation's real income," *ET*, 255 (Jan.): xxviii–xxxv.

————. 1975b. "International comparisons on the basis of purchasing power parities," *ET*, 265 (Nov.): Appendix 2.

Hickman, B. G. 1965. *Investment Demand and U.S. Economic Growth*. Washington, D.C.

Hicks, J. 1979. *Causality in Economics*. Oxford, England.

Hilgerdt, F. 1945. *Industrialization and Foreign Trade* (League of Nations). Geneva.

Hill, T. P. 1964. "Growth and investment according to international comparison," *EJ*, 74.294 (June): 287–304.

_____. 1971. *The Measurement of Real Product* (Organization for Economic Cooperation and Development). Paris.

Hilton, J., et al. 1935. *Are Trade Unions Obstructive?* London.

Hines, A. G. 1964. "Trade unions and wage inflation in the United Kingdom 1893–1961," *REStud*, 31.4 (Oct.): 221–52.

_____. 1969. "Wage inflation in the United Kingdom, 1948–62: A disaggregated study," *EJ*, 79.313 (March): 66–89.

Hines, A. G., and G. Catephores. 1970. "Investment in U.K. manufacturing industry, 1956–1967," in D. F. Heathfield and K. Hilton, eds., *The Econometric Study of the United Kingdom*. London.

Hoffman, W. 1955, *British Industry, 1700–1950*. Tr. W. O. Henderson and W. H. Chaloner. Oxford, England.

Hole, W. V., and M. T. Pountney. 1971. *Trends in Population, Housing and Occupancy Rates, 1861–1961*. London.

Houthakker, H. S. 1960. "An international comparison of personal savings," *Bulletin de l'Institut Internationale de Statistique*, 38.2: 55–69.

Hufbauer, G. C. 1970. "The impact of national characteristics and technology on the commodity composition of trade in manufactured goods," in H. M. Vernon, *The Technology Factor in International Trade* (National Bureau of Economic Research). New York.

Hunt, A. 1968, *A Survey of Women's Employment*, vol. 1.1: *Report* and vol. 2: *Tables* (Government Social Survey). London.

Hunt, E. H. 1967. "Labour productivity in English agriculture," *EcHR*, 20.2 (Aug.): 280–90.

Hunter, L. C. 1963. "Cyclical variations in the labour supply: British experience, 1951–60," *Oxford Economic Papers*, 15.2 (July): 140–54.

Imlah, A. H. 1958, *Economic Elements in the Pax Britannica*. Cambridge, Mass.

Industrial Society. 1966. "Survey of the comparative terms and conditions of employment of manual and non-manual workers." *Industrial Society Information*, Survey and Report Series 133.

Iron and Steel Board. 1964. *Development in the Iron and Steel Industry, Special Report*. London.

James, E. 1962. "Women at work in twentieth century Britain," *MS*, 30.3 (Sept.): 283–99.

Jones, G. T. 1933. *Increasing Returns*. Cambridge, England.

Jones, K., and A. D. Smith. 1970. *The Economic Impact of Commonwealth Immigration* (National Institute of Economic and Social Research). Cambridge, England.

Jones, Stedman G. 1971. *Outcast London*. Oxford, England.

Jorgenson, D. W., and Z. Griliches. 1967, "The explanation of productivity change," *REStud*, 34(3).99 (July): 249–84.

Jorgenson, D. W., Z. Griliches, and E. F. Denison. 1972. *The Measurement of Productivity* (Brookings Institution Report 244). Washington, D.C.

Junankar, P. N. (1970), "The relationship between investment and spare capacity in the United Kingdom, 1957–1966," *Economica*, 37.147 (Aug.): 277–92.

Kaldor, N. 1966. *Causes of the Slow Rate of Growth of the United Kingdom* (Inaugural Lecture, Cambridge University). Cambridge, England.

――――. 1967. *Strategic Factors in Economic Development* (Frank Pierce Memorial Lecture, Cornell University). Ithaca, N.Y.

――――. 1975. "Economic growth and the Verdoorn law: A comment on Mr. Rowthorn's article," *EJ*, 85.340 (Dec.): 891–96.

――――. 1979. "Comment," in F. Blackaby, ed., *Deindustrialisation*. London.

Kalecki, M. 1938. "The determinants of distribution of the national income," *Econometrica*, 6.2 (April): 97–112.

Keene, N. B. 1969. *The Employment of Young Workers*. London.

Kendrick, J. W. 1961. *Productivity Trends in the United States* (National Bureau of Economic Research). Princeton, N.J.

――――. 1973. *Postwar Productivity Trends in the United States, 1948–69* (National Bureau of Economic Research). New York.

Kennedy, C. 1964. "Induced bias in innovation and the theory of distribution," *EJ*, 74.295 (Sept.): 541–47.

Kennedy, C., and A. P. Thirlwall. 1972. "Technical progress: A survey," *EJ*, 82.325 (March): 11–72.

Kennedy, W. P. 1973–74. "Foreign investment, trade, and growth in the United Kingdom, 1870–1913," *Explorations in Economic History*, 11.4: 415–44.

Keynes, J. M. 1939a. "Relative movements of real wages and output," *EJ*, 49.193 (March): 34–51.

――――. 1939b. "Professor Tinbergen's method," *EJ*, 59.195 (Sept.): 558–68.

Kindersley, R. 1929–39. "British overseas investment," *EJ*. Published annually for 11 years.

Kindleberger, C. P. 1964. *Economic Growth in France and Britain, 1851–1950*. Cambridge, Mass.

King, M. A. 1971. "Corporate taxation and business behaviour: Comment," *REStud*, 38(3).115 (July): 377–80.

――――. 1972. "Corporate taxation and business behaviour: A further comment," *REStud*, 39(2).118 (April): 231–34.

――――. 1975. "The United Kingdom profits crisis: Myth or reality?," *EJ*, 85.337 (March): 33–54.

――――. 1977. *Public Policy and the Corporation*. London.

Klein, L. R. 1958. "The British propensity to save," *JRSS*, Series A, 121.1: 60–96.

Klein, L. R., and R. Summers. 1966. *The Wharton Index of Capacity Utilization* (University of Pennsylvania Studies in Quantitative Economics 1). Philadelphia.

Klingender, F. D. 1935. *The Conditions of Clerical Labour in Britain*. London.

Knapp, J., and K. Lomax. 1964. "Britain's growth performance: The enigma of the 1950's," *Lloyds Bank Review*, October, pp. 1–24.

Knight, R. 1966. "The educational stock of the population." Unpublished paper.

Kravis, I. B., and R. E. Lipsey. 1971. *Price Competitiveness in World Trade* (National Bureau of Economic Research). New York.

Kravis, I. B., A. W. Heston, and R. Summers. 1978a. *International Comparisons of Real Product and Purchasing Power*. Baltimore, Md.

_____. 1978b. "Real GDP per capita for more than one hundred countries," *EJ*, 88.350 (June): 215–42.

Kravis, I. B., Z. Kenessey, A. W. Heston, and R. Summers. 1975. *A System of International Comparisons of Gross Product and Purchasing Power*. Baltimore, Md.

Kuznets, S. 1956. "Levels and variability of rates of growth," *Economic Development and Cultural Change*, part 1, 5 (Oct.): 5–94.

_____. 1961a. *Capital in the American Economy* (National Bureau of Economic Research). Princeton, N.J.

_____. 1961b. "Quantitative aspects of the economic growth of nations," part 6: "Long-term trends in capital formation proportions," *Economic Development and Cultural Change*, 9.4, part 2 (July): 1–24.

_____. 1966. *Modern Economic Growth: Rate, Structure and Spread*. New Haven, Conn.

Lamfalussy, A. 1961. *Investment and Growth in Mature Economies*. London.

_____. 1963. *The United Kingdom and the Six: An Essay on Economic Growth in Western Europe*. London.

_____. 1968. *Les Marchés financières en Europe*. Paris.

Landes, D. S. 1969. *The Unbound Prometheus*. Cambridge, England. (Originally published in 1965 as "Technological change and development in Western Europe, 1750–1914," chap. 5, part 2, vol. 6 of *The Cambridge Economic History of Europe*.)

Laslett, R. A. 1978. "A measure of the full employment rate of unemployment in the U.K.," in M. FG. Scott with R. A. Laslett, *Can We Get Back to Full Employment?* London.

League of Nations. 1942. *Economic Fluctuations in the United States and the United Kingdom, 1918–1922*. Geneva.

Lee, C. H. 1971. *Regional Economic Growth in the United Kingdom since the 1880s*. London.

Leibenstein, H. 1979. "A branch of economics is missing: Micro-micro theory," *Journal of Economic Literature*, 17.2 (June): 477–502.

Leser, C. E. V. 1955–56. "The supply of women for gainful work in Britain," *Population Studies*, 9 (Nov.): 142–47.

Levine, A. L. 1967. *Industrial Retardation in Britain, 1870–1914*. London.

Lewis, J. P. 1965. *Building Cycles and Britain's Growth*. London.

Lewis, W. A. 1949. *Economic Survey, 1919–1939*. London.

———. 1978. *Growth and Fluctuations, 1870–1913*. London.

Lewis-Faning, E. 1949. *Family Limitation and Its Influence on Human Fertility During the Past Fifty Years*, vol. 1 of Royal Commission on Population, *Papers*. London.

Liepmann, K. 1960. *Apprenticeship*. London.

Lipsey, R. G. 1963. *Price and Quantity Trends in the Foreign Trade of the United States* (National Bureau of Economic Research Studies in International Economic Relations 2). Princeton, N.J.

Logan, W. P. D. 1950. "Mortality in England and Wales from 1848 to 1947," *Population Studies*, 4 (Sept.): 132–78.

Lomax, K. C. 1959. "Production and productivity movements in the United Kingdom since 1900," *JRSS*, Series A, 122.2: 185–210.

London and Cambridge Economic Service. 1972. *The British Economy: Key Statistics, 1900–1970*. London.

Lund, P. J. 1976. "The econometric assessment of the impact of investment incentives," in A. Whiting, ed., *The Economics of Industrial Subsidies*. London.

Lund, P. J., and K. Holden. 1968. "Study of private sector gross fixed capital formation in the United Kingdom, 1923–1938," *Oxford Economic Papers*, 20.1 (March): 56–73.

Lundberg, E. 1968. *Instability and Economic Growth*. New Haven, Conn.

———. 1971. "Simon Kuznets' contribution to economics," *Swedish Journal of Economics*, 73.4 (Dec.): 444–61.

Lydall, H. F. (1955), *British Incomes and Savings*. Oxford, England.

McCloskey, D. N. 1970. "Did Victorian Britain fail?," *EcHR*, 23.3 (Dec.): 446–59.

———. 1973. *Economic Maturity and Entrepreneurial Decline: British Iron and Steel, 1870–1913*. Cambridge, Mass.

———. 1974. "Victorian growth: A rejoinder," *EcHR*, 27.2 (May): 275–77.

———. 1979. "No it did not: A reply to Crafts." *EcHR*, 32.4 (Nov.): 538–41.

———, ed. 1971. *Essays on a Mature Economy*. London.

McCloskey, D. N., and L. G. Sandberg. 1971. "From damnation to redemption: Judgments on the late Victorial entrepreneur," *Explorations in Economic History*, 9.1 (Fall): 89–108.

McCracken, P., et al. 1977. *Towards Full Employment and Price Stability* (Organization for Economic Cooperation and Development). Paris.

McCrone, G. 1969. *Regional Policy in Britain*. London.

McKeown, T. 1976. *The Modern Rise of Population*. London.

McKeown, T., and R. G. Record. 1962. "Reasons for the decline in mortality in

England and Wales during the nineteenth century," *Population Studies*, 16 (Nov.): 94–122.

McKeown, T., R. G. Brown, and R. G. Record. 1972. "An interpretation of the modern rise of population in Europe," *Population Studies*, 26 (Nov.): 345–82.

McKeown, T., R. G. Record, and R. G. Turner. 1975. "An interpretation of the decline in mortality in England and Wales during the twentieth century," *Population Studies*, 29.3 (Nov.): 391–422.

McMahon, P. C., and D. J. Smyth. 1971. "Saving, income and wealth: A reexamination of Stone's post-war expenditure function," *MS*, 39.1 (March): 37–44.

Maddison, A. 1964. *Economic Growth in the West*. London.

_____. 1967. "Comparative productivity levels in the developed countries," *Banca Nazionale del Lavoro Quarterly Review*, 20 (Dec.): 295–315.

_____. 1977. "Phases of capitalist development," *Banca Nazionale del Lavoro Quarterly Review*, 121 (June): 103–37.

_____. 1979. "Long-run dynamics of productivity growth," *Banca Nazionale del Lavoro Quarterly Review*, 128 (March): 3–43.

Maizels, A. 1963. *Industrial Growth and World Trade*. Cambridge, England.

_____. 1970. *Growth and Trade*. Cambridge, England.

Major, R. L. 1968. "Note on Britain's share in world trade in manufactures, 1954–66," *NIER*, 44 (May): 50–56.

Maki, D. R., and Z. A. Spindler. 1975. "The effect of unemployment compensation on the rate of unemployment in Great Britain," *Oxford Economic Papers*, 27.3 (Nov.): 440–54.

Mansfield, E. 1968. *The Economics of Technical Change*. New York.

Marris, R. L. 1964. *The Economics of Capital Utilisation: A Report on Multiple-Shift Work*. Cambridge, England.

Marshall, A. 1919. *Industry and Trade*. London.

_____. 1920. *Principles of Economics*. 8th ed. London.

_____. 1926. *Official Papers of Alfred Marshall*, ed. A. C. Pigou. London.

Massell, B. F. 1961. "A disaggregated view of technical change," *Journal of Political Economy*, 69 (Dec.): 547–57.

Matthews, R. C. O. 1954. *A Study in Trade Cycle History*. Cambridge.

_____. 1964. "Some aspects of post-war growth in the British economy in relation to historical experience," *Transactions of the Manchester Statistical Society*, Nov.

_____. 1968. "Why has Britain had full employment since the war?," *EJ*, 78.311 (Sept.): 555–69.

_____. 1969. "Post-war business cycles in the United Kingdom," in M. Bronfenbrenner, ed., *Is the Business Cycle Obsolete?* New York.

_____. 1970. "The role of demand management," in A. K. Cairncross, ed., *Britain's Economic Prospects Reconsidered*. London.

_____. 1973. "Foreign trade and British economic growth," *Scottish Journal of Political Economy*, 20.3 (Nov.): 195–209.

———. 1976. "British economic growth 1951–1973: success or failure?," Ninth Geary Lecture, Economic and Social Research Institute, Dublin.

Medical Research Council, Industrial Health Research Board. 1942. *Hours of Work, Lost Time and Labour Wastage*. London.

Melliss, C. L., and P. W. Richardson. 1976. "Value of investment incentives for manufacturing industry, 1946 to 1974," in A. Whiting, ed., *The Economics of Industrial Subsidies*. London.

Metalworking Production. 1961. "First census of machine tools in Britain," *Metalworking Production*, Dec. 29, 1961. London.

Midland Bank Review. Various dates. Quarterly.

Mitchell, B. R., and P. Deane. 1962. *Abstract of British Historical Statistics*. Cambridge, England.

Moggridge, D. E. 1969. *The Return to Gold, 1925*. Cambridge, England.

Mogridge, B. 1962. "Labour relations and labour costs," in S. G. Sturmey, *British Shipping and World Competition*. London.

Morgan, E. V. 1952. *Studies in British Financial Policy, 1914–1925*, London.

Morris, V., and A. Ziderman. 1971. "The economic return on investment in higher education in England and Wales," *ET*, 211 (May): 20–28.

Myers, C. S. 1926. *Industrial Psychology in Great Britain*. London.

Nadiri, M. I. 1970. "Some approaches to the theory and measurement of total factor productivity," *Journal of Economic Literature*, 8.4 (Dec.): 1137–77.

National Economic Development Office. 1976. *Cyclical Fluctuations in the U.K. Economy*. London.

———. 1977. *International Price Competitiveness, Non-Price Factors and Export Performance*. London.

National Institute of Economic and Social Research, *National Institute Economic Review*. Quarterly.

Neild, R. R. 1963. *Pricing and Employment in the Trade Cycle*. Cambridge.

———. 1964. "Replacement policy," *NIER*, 30 (Nov.): 30–37.

Nerlove, M. 1967a. "Recent empirical studies of the CES and related production functions," in M. Brown, ed., *The Theory and Empirical Analysis of Production* (National Bureau of Economic Research Studies in Income and Wealth 31). New York.

———. 1967b. "Notes on the production and derived demand relations included in macro-econometric models," *International Economic Review*, 8 (June): 223–42.

Nesbitt-Hawes, R. 1966. *The Training of Youth in Industry: Engineering*. London.

Nevin, E. 1955. *The Mechanism of Cheap Money: A Study of British Monetary Policy, 1931–1939*. Cardiff, Wales.

Nicholson, J. L. 1967. "The measurement of quality changes," *EJ*, 77.307 (Sept.): 512–30.

Nobay, A. R. 1970. "Forecasting manufacturing investment — some preliminary results," *NIER*, 52 (May): 58–66.

Nordhaus, W., and J. Tobin. 1972. "Is growth obsolete?," in *Economic*

Research, Retrospect and Prospect: Economic Growth (Fiftieth Anniversary Colloquium V, National Bureau of Economic Research). New York.

Nurkse, R. 1956. "The relation between home investment and external balance in the light of British experience, 1945-55," *Review of Economics and Statistics*, 38 (May): 121-54.

Odling-Smee, J. C. 1973. "Personal saving revisited: More statistics, fewer facts," *Bulletin of the Oxford University Institute of Economics and Statistics*, 35.1 (Feb.): 21-29.

Office of Health Economics. 1964. *Infants at Risk*. London.

Ohkawa, Kazushi, and Henry Rosovsky. 1973. *Japanese Economic Growth: Trend Acceleration in the Twentieth Century*. Stanford, Calif.

Olson, M. 1978. "The political economy of comparative growth rates," in *U.S. Economic Growth from 1976 to 1986: Prospects, Problems and Patterns*. Washington, D.C.

Oppenheimer, P. M. 1966. "Monetary movements and the international position of sterling," *Scottish Journal of Political Economy*, 13.1 (Feb.): 89-135.

Organization for Economic Cooperation and Development (OECD) [1]. *Balances of Payments of OECD Countries, 1960-1977*. Paris, Jan. 1979.

_____ [2]. *The Cement Industry: Statistics 1971, Trends 1972* Paris, 1972.

_____ [3]. *Industrial Production Historical Statistics, 1955-1971* and *1960-1975*. Paris, 1973, 1976.

_____ [4]. *The Iron and Steel Industry: Annual Statistics 1971*. Paris.

_____ [5]. *The Iron and Steel Industry in 1968 and Trends in 1969*. Paris, 1969.

_____ [6]. *Labour Force Statistics, 1963-1976*, Paris, 1978.

_____ [7]. *Manpower Statistics, 1950-1962*. Paris, 1963.

_____ [8]. *National Accounts of OECD Countries*. Paris, 1952.

_____ [9]. *National Accounts of OECD Countries*, vol. 2. Paris, 1975.

_____ [10]. *National Accounts of OECD Countries, 1953-1977*, vol. 1. Paris, 1979.

Paige, D. C. 1961. "Economic growth: The last hundred years," *NIER*, 16 (July): 24-49.

Panic, M. 1976. *United Kingdom and West German Manufacturing Industry* (National Economic Development Office Monograph 5). London.

Panic, M., and P. Seward. 1966. "The problem of U.K. exports," *Bulletin of the Oxford Institute of Economics and Statistics*, 28.1 (Feb.): 19-32.

Peck, M. J. 1968. "Science and technology," in R. E. Caves et al., *Britain's Economic Prospects*. Washington, D.C.

Phelps Brown, E. H. 1959. *The Growth of British Industrial Relations*. London.

_____. 1970. "Labour policies: Productivity, industrial relations, cost inflation," in A. K. Cairncross, ed., *Britain's Economic Prospects Reconsidered*. London.

Phelps Brown, E. H., and M. H. Browne. 1968. *A Century of Pay*. London.

Phelps Brown, E. H., and S. J. Handfield Jones. 1952. "The climacteric of the 1890's," *Oxford Economic Papers*. 4.3 (Oct.): 266-307.

Phelps Brown, E. H., and P. E. Hart. 1952. "The share of wages in national income," *EJ*, 62.246 (June): 253–77.

Posner, M. V. 1961. "International trade and technical change," *Oxford Economic Papers*, 13.3 (Oct.): 323–41.

Postan, M. M. 1967. *An Economic History of Western Europe, 1945–64.* London.

Prais, S. J. 1959. "Dividend policy and income appropriation," in B. Tew and R. F. Henderson, eds., *Studies in Company Finance.* Cambridge, England.

_____. 1976. *The Evolution of Giant Firms in Britain.* Cambridge, England.

Pratten, C. F. 1971. *Economies of Scale in Manufacturing Industry.* Cambridge, England.

Pratten, C. F., R. M. Dean, and A. Silberston. 1965. *The Economies of Large-scale Production in British Industry* (University of Cambridge Department of Applied Economics Occasional Paper 3). Cambridge, England.

Pressnell, L. S. 1968. "Gold reserves, banking reserves and the Baring Crisis of 1890," in C. R. Whittlesey and J. S. G. Wilson, eds. *Essays in Banking in Honour of R. S. Sayers.* Oxford, England.

Prest, A. R. 1954. *Consumers' Expenditure in the United Kingdom, 1900–1919.* Cambridge, England.

Radice, E. A. 1939. *Savings in Great Britain, 1922–1935.* Oxford, England.

Rae, J. 1894. *Eight Hours for Work.* London.

Ray, G. F. 1972. "Labour costs and international competitiveness," *NIER*, 61 (Aug.): 53–58.

Reader, W. J. 1966. *Professional Men: The Rise of the Professional Classes in Nineteenth Century England.* London.

Reddaway, W. B., and A. D. Smith. 1960. "Progress in British manufacturing industries in the period 1948–54," *EJ*, 70.277 (March): 17–37.

Reddaway, W. B., et al. 1967. *Effects of U.K. Direct Investments Overseas: Interim Report.* Cambridge, England.

_____. 1968. *Effects of U.K. Direct Investments Overseas: Final Report.* Cambridge, England.

_____. 1970. *Effects of the Selective Employment Tax: First Report: The Distributive Trades.* London.

_____. 1973. *Effects of the Selective Employment Tax: Final Report.* Cambridge, England.

Reid, M. G. 1962. *Housing and Income.* Chicago.

Revell, J., and A. R. Roe. 1971. "National balance sheets and national accounting—a progress report," *ET*, 211 (May): 8–19.

Reynolds, L. 1956. *Labor Economics and Labor Relations.* 2nd ed. Englewood Cliffs, N.J.

Richardson, H. W. 1967. *Economic Recovery in Britain, 1932–39.* London.

Richardson, H. W., and D. H. Aldcroft. 1968. *Building in the British Economy Between the Wars.* London.

Robinson, H. W. 1939. *The Economics of Building.* London.

Robinson, J. 1933. *Economics of Imperfect Competition.* London.

Rosenberg, N. 1976. "On technological expectations," *EJ*, 86.343 (Sept.): 523–35.

Routh, G. 1965. *Occupation and Pay in Great Britain, 1906–60*. Cambridge, England.

Rowley, J. C. R. 1972. "Fixed capital formation in the British economy, 1956–1965," *Economica*, 39.154 (May): 177–89.

Rowthorn, R. E. 1975. "What remains of Kaldor's Law?," *EJ*, 85.337 (March): 10–19.

Rubenstein, W. D. 1977. "The Victorian middle classes: Wealth, occupation and geography," *EcHR*, 30.4 (Nov.): 602–23.

Rubner, A. 1964. "The irrelevancy of the British differential profits tax," *EJ*, 74.294 (June): 347–59.

Salter, W. E. G. 1960. *Productivity and Technical Change*. Cambridge, England.

————. 1966. *Productivity and Technical Change*. 2nd ed., with an addendum by W. B. Reddaway. Cambridge, England.

Sandberg, L. G. 1969. "American rings and English mules: The role of economic rationality," *Quarterly Journal of Economics*, 83.1.330 (Feb.): 25–43.

————. 1974. *Lancashire in Decline*. Columbus, Ohio.

Saorstát Éireann, Department of Industry and Commerce. 1928. *Census of Population, 1926*. Dublin.

Sargent, J. R. 1963. *Out of Stagnation* (Fabian Tract 343). London.

Saul, S. B. 1960. *Studies in British Overseas Trade, 1870–1914*. Liverpool.

————. 1962. "The motor industry in Britain to 1914," *Business History*, 5 (Dec.): 22–44.

————. 1967. "The market and the development of the mechanical engineering industries in Britain, 1860–1914," *EcHR*, 20.1 (April): 111–30.

Savage, D. 1977. "A comparison of accelerator models of manufacturing investment," unpublished National Institute of Economic and Social Research Discussion Paper 9 (August).

Sayers, R. S. 1950. "The springs of technical progress in Britain, 1914–1939," *EJ*, 60.238 (June): 275–91.

————. 1956. *Financial Policy, 1939–45* (History of the Second World War, United Kingdom Civil Series). London.

————. 1960. "The return to gold 1925," in L. S. Pressnell, ed., *Studies in the Industrial Revolution*. London.

————. 1965. *The Vicissitudes of an Export Economy: Britain Since 1880* (R. C. Mills Memorial Lecture). Sydney, Australia.

————. 1967. *A History of Economic Change in England, 1880–1939*. Oxford, England.

————. 1976. *The Bank of England, 1891–1944*, vol. 1. Cambridge, England.

Schlote, W. 1952. *British Overseas Trade from 1700 to the 1930's*. Westport, Conn.

Schofield, R. 1977. Review of T. McKeown's *The Modern Rise of Population*, *Population Studies*, 1.1 (March): 179–80.

Schumpeter, J. A. 1939. *Business Cycles*. New York.

Scott, M. FG. 1963. *A Study of UK Imports*. Cambridge, England.

Selby-Smith, C. 1970. "Costs and benefits in further education: Some evidence from a pilot study," *EJ*, 80.319 (Sept.): 583–604.

Shepherd, W. G. 1968. "Alternatives for public expenditure," in R. E. Caves et al., *Britain's Economic Prospects*. Washington, D.C.

Sheppard, D. K. 1971. *The Growth and Role of U.K. Financial Institutions, 1880–1962*. London.

Sheriff, T. D. 1979. "The slowdown of productivity growth," unpublished National Institute of Econmic and Social Research Discussion Paper 30.

Simon, M. 1967. "The pattern of new British portfolio investment, 1856–1914," in J. H. Adler, ed., *Capital Movements and Economic Development*. London.

Sleeper, R. D. 1972. "Inter-Industry Labour Mobility in Britain, 1959–68," unpublished D.Phil. thesis, Oxford University.

Smith, A. D. 1972. *The Measurement and Interpretation of Service Output Changes* (National Economic Development Office). London.

Smith, K. C., and G. F. Horne. 1934. "An index number of securities, 1867–1914," *London and Cambridge Economic Service Bulletin*, Special Memorandum 37 (June).

Smith, Sir H. Llewellyn, et al. 1930–35. *The New Survey of London Life and Labour*. 9 vols. London.

Smyth, D. J., and G. Briscoe. 1969. "Investment plans and realisations in United Kingdom manufacturing," *Economica*, 36.143 (Aug.): 277–94.

———. 1971. "Investment and capacity utilisation in the United Kingdom, 1923–1966," *Oxford Economic Papers*, 23.1 (March): 136–43.

Solow, R. M. 1957. "Technical change and the aggregate production function," *Review of Economics and Statistics*, 39.3 (Aug.): 312–20.

———. 1960. "Investment and technical progress," in K. J. Arrow, ed., *Mathematical Methods in the Social Sciences, 1959*. Stanford, Calif.

———. 1962. "Technical change, capital formation, and economic growth," *American Economic Review*, 52.2 (May): 78–86.

Sorrentino, C. 1972. "Unemployment in nine industrialised countries," *Monthly Labour Review*, 95.6 (June): 29–33.

Stigler, G. J. 1961. "Economic problems in measuring changes in productivity," with "Comment" by R. M. Solow, in *Output, Input, and Productivity Measurement* (National Bureau of Economic Research Studies in Income and Wealth, vol. 25, Conference on Research in Income and Wealth). Princeton, N.J.

Stolnitz, G. J. 1955. "A century of international mortality trends: I," *Population Studies*, 9 (July): 24–55.

Stone, R. 1964. "Private saving in Britain, past, present and future," *MS*, 32.3 (May): 79–112.

———. 1966. "Spending and saving in relation to income and wealth," *L'Industria*, 4: 471–99.

_____. 1973. "Personal spending and saving in postwar Britain," in H. C. Bos, H. Linneman, and P. de Wolff, eds., *Economic Structure and Economic Development: Essays in Honour of Jan Tinbergen*. Amsterdam.

Stone, R., and D. A. Rowe. 1962. "A post-war expenditure function," *MS*, 30.2 (May): 187–201.

Stone, R., et al. 1954. *The Measurement of Consumers' Expenditure and Behaviour in the United Kingdom, 1920–1938*. Cambridge, England.

Sturmey, S. G. 1962. *British Shipping and World Competition*. London.

Stuvel, G. 1959. "Asset revaluation and the terms-of-trade effects in the framework on the national accounts," *EJ*, 69.274 (June): 275–92.

Svennilson, I. 1954. *Growth and Stagnation in the European Economy* (United Nations Economic Commission for Europe). Geneva.

Taubman, P., and T. Wales. 1973. "Earnings: Higher education, mental ability and screening," *Journal of Political Economy*, 81.1 (Jan.–Feb.): 28–55.

Taylor, A. J. 1961. "Labour productivity and technological innovation in the British coal industry, 1850–1914," *EcHR*, 14.1 (Aug.): 48–70.

Taylor, C. T. 1978. "Why is Britain in a recession?," *BEQB*, 18.1 (March): 38–47.

Taylor, F. D. W. 1955. "UK: Numbers in agriculture," *The Farm Economist*, 8.4: 36–41.

Taylor, J. 1971. "A regional analysis of hidden unemployment in Great Britain, 1951–1966," *Applied Economics*, 3.4 (Dec.): 291–303.

Temin, P. 1966. "The relative decline in the British steel industry, 1880–1913," in H. Rosovsky, ed., *Industrialisation in Two Systems*. New York.

Thomas, B. 1973. *Migration and Economic Growth: A Study of Great Britain and the Atlantic Economy*, 2nd ed. Cambridge, England.

Thomas, G. 1944. *Women at Work* (Wartime Social Survey). London.

_____. 1948. *Women and Industry* (The Social Survey). London.

Ulman, L. 1968. "Collective bargaining and industrial efficiency," in R. E. Caves and associates, *Britain's Economic Prospects*. Washington, D.C.

[The place of publication for all the following UK publications is London.]

United Kingdom, Board of Labour [1]. *First Abstract of Labor Statistics*. 1886.

_____, Board of Trade [2]. *Annual Statement of the Trade of the United Kingdom*.

_____, _____ [3]. *Board of Trade Journal*. Weekly.

_____, _____ [4]. *Census of Production*. From 1907; annually from 1970.

_____, _____ [5]. *Report of an Enquiry by the Board of Trade into the Earnings and Hours of Labour of Workpeople in the United Kingdom in 1906*. *Parliamentary Papers*, 1909–1912/13.

_____, _____ [6]. *Report on Overseas Trade*. Monthly.

_____, _____ [7]. *Statistical Abstract for the United Kingdom*. Annual.

_____, _____ [8]. *Trade and Navigation Returns*. Monthly.

_____, Board of Trade and Central Statistical Office [9]. *Input-Output Tables for the United Kingdom, 1954*. Studies in Official Statistics 8, 1961.

_____, Central Statistical Office [10]. *Annual Abstract of Statistics*.

_____, _____ [11]. *Economic Trends*. Monthly.

_____, _____ [12]. *Economic Trends Annual Supplement*.

_____, _____ [13]. *Financial Statistics*. Weekly.

_____, _____ [14]. "Income and finance of quoted companies, 1949–1960," *ET*, 102 (April 1962): ii–xvii.

_____, _____ [15]. *The Index of Industrial Production and Other Output Measures*. Studies in Official Statistics 17, 1970.

_____, _____ [16]. *Input-Output Tables for the United Kingdom, 1963*. Studies in Official Statistics 16, 1970.

_____, _____ [17]. *Input-Output Tables for the United Kingdom, 1972*. Business Monitor, PA 1004, 1976.

_____, _____ [18]. "International comparisons of costs and prices," *ET*, 163 (May 1967).

_____, _____ [19]. *Monthly Digest of Statistics*.

_____, _____ [20]. *National Accounts Statistics: Sources and Methods* (ed. R. Maurice). Studies in Official Statistics 13, 1968.

_____, _____ [21]. *National Income and Expenditure*. Annual.

_____, _____ [22]. *National Income Statistics: Sources and Methods*. 1956.

_____, _____ [23]. "The new index of agriculture net output," *ET*, 77 (March 1960): viii–xii.

_____, _____ [24]. *Social Trends*. Annual.

_____, _____ [25]. *United Kingdom Balance of Payments*. Annual.

_____, Chief Inspector of Factories and Workshops [26]. *Annual Report* for *1910* (Cd. 5693, 1911); *1918* (Cmd. 340, 1919); *1919* (Cmd. 941, 1920); and *1920* (Cmd. 1403, 1921).

_____, Committee of Council on Education (England and Wales) [27]. *Reports* in *Parliamentary Papers*, 1881–99.

_____, Committee on Finance and Industry [28]. *Report*. Cmd 3897, 1931. (Chairman: Macmillan)

_____, Committee on Higher Education [29]. *Report* and *Appendices*. Cmd. 2154, 1963. (Chairman: Robbins)

_____, Committee on Holidays with Pay [30]. *Report*. Cmd. 5724, 1938.

_____, Committee on Industry and Trade [31]. *Final Report*. Cmd. 3282, 1929. (Chairman: Balfour)

_____, Committee on the Working of the Monetary System [32]. *Report*. Cmnd. 827, 1959. (Chairman: Radcliffe)

_____, Committee on the Working of the Monetary System [33]. *Principal Memoranda of Evidence*, I, 1960.

_____, Committee on Turnover Taxation [34]. *Report*. Cmnd. 2300, 1964.

_____, Department of Economic Affairs [35]. *The Intermediate Areas* (committee report; Chairman: Hunt). Cmnd. 3998, 1969.

————, ———— [36]. *Investment Incentives*. Cmnd. 2874. 1966.

————, Department of Education and Science [37]. *Statistics of Education*. Annual (Formerly Ministry of Education)

————, ———— [38]. *Statistics of Education Special Series No. 3: Survey of Earnings of Qualified Manpower in England and Wales, 1966–67*. 1971.

————, Department of Employment [39]. *British Labour Statistics Year Book*. Annual.

————, ———— [40]. "The changed relationship between unemployment and vacancies," *Department of Employment Gazette*, 84.10 (Oct. 1976).

————, ———— [41]. *Changes in the Industrial Distribution of Employment, 1931–1971*. Unpublished Unit for Manpower Studies paper, 1975.

————, ———— [42]. *Changes in the Occupational Distribution of the Labour Force in Great Britain*. Unpublished Unit for Manpower Studies paper, 1975.

————, ———— [43]. *Department of Employment Gazette*. Monthly.

————, ———— [44]. "The fall in the labour force between 1966 and 1971," *Department of Employment Gazette*, 81.11 (Nov. 1973).

————, ———— [45]. "Family expenditure survey: Subsidiary occupations," *Department of Employment Gazette*, 80.6 (June 1972).

————, ———— [46]. "Labour force projections, 1976–1991, Great Britain and the regions," *Department of Employment Gazette*, 83.12 (Dec. 1975).

————, ———— [47]. *New Earnings Survey*. Annual.

————, Department of Employment and Productivity [48]. *British Labour Statistics Historical Abstract, 1886–1968*. 1971.

————, Department of Energy [49]. *Department of Energy Digest of United Kingdom Energy Statistics*. Annual from 1974. (Formerly *Department of Trade and Industry United Kingdom Energy Statistics* and *Ministry of Power Digest of Energy Statistics*.)

————, Department of the Environment [50]. *Housing Policy*, 4 vols.: *A Consultative Document; Technical Volumes 1, 2, and 3*. 1977.

————, Department of Health and Social Security [51]. *Social Security Statistics*. Annual.

————, General Register Office [52]. *Reports* and *Tables* of the *Census of Population*. 1851–1971.

————, ———— [53]. *The Registrar General's Annual Abstract of Statistics*.

————, ———— [54]. *The Registrar General's Statistical Review of England and Wales*. Annual. (Formerly *Annual Report of Registrar General*.)

————, Home Office [55]. *Summary of Number of Scholars in England and Wales. Parliamentary Papers*, 1835, vol. XLIII.

————, ———— [56]. *Table on General State of Education in England, Wales, and Scotland. Parliamentary Papers*, 1820, vol. XII.

————, Inland Revenue [57]. *Inland Revenue Statistics*. Annual.

————, ———— [58]. *Report of the Commissioners of H.M. Inland Revenue*. Annual.

————, Local Government Board [59]. *Statistical Memoranda and Charts* prepared by the Local Government Board relating to Public Health and Social Conditions. Cd. 4671, 1909.

————, Ministry of Agriculture and Fisheries [60]. *Agricultural Statistics, United Kingdom.* Annual.

————, Ministry of Education [61]. *15–18.* Report of the Central Advisory Council for Education, England. 1959. (Chairman: Crowther)

————, Ministry of Finance, Northern Ireland [62]. *Northern Ireland Digest of Statistics.* Twice yearly.

————, Ministry of Health [63]. Reports of the Committee of Enquiry appointed by the Minister of Health into the Cost of Housebuilding. *First Report,* 1948; *Second Report,* 1950. (Chairman: Girdwood)

————, Ministry of Labour [64]. *Abstract of Labour Statistics.* 22 issues in *Parliamentary Papers,* 1893–1936.

————, —————— [65]. *Growth of Office Employment.* Manpower Studies 7, 1968.

————, —————— [66]. *Ministry of Labour Gazette.* Weekly.

————, —————— [67]. *Occupational Changes, 1951–61.* Manpower Studies 6, 1967.

————, —————— [68]. *Time Rates of Wages and Hours of Work.* Annual.

————, Ministry of Pensions and National Insurance [69]. *Report.* Annual.

————, —————— [70]. *Report of an Enquiry into the Incidence of Incapacity for Work,* vol. 2. 1964.

————, Ministry of Power [71]. *Statistical Digest.* Annual.

————, Ministry of Reconstruction [72]. *Report of the Women's Employment Committee.* Cd. 9239, 1919.

————, Ministry of Works [73]. *Report* of the Working Party on Building Operations. 1950.

————, National Board for Prices and Incomes [74]. *Pay and Conditions of Service of British Railways Staff.* Report 8, Cmnd. 2873, 1966.

————, —————— [75]. *Pay and Conditions of Service of Engineering Workers.* Report 49, Cmnd. 3495, 1977.

————, —————— [76]. *Pay of Workers in the Retail Drapery, Outfitting and Footwear Trades.* Report 27, Cmnd. 3224, 1967.

————, Office of Population Censuses and Surveys [77]. *The General Household Survey* for *1971; 1972;* and *1974.*

————, —————— [78]. *Population Projections, 1974–2014.* 1976.

————, Royal Commission on Labour [79]. *Fifth and Final Report. Parliamentary Papers* (C. 7421), 1894, vol. XXXV.

————, Royal Commission on Population [80]. *Report.* Cmd. 7695, 1949.

————, —————— [81]. *Papers,* vol. 2: *Reports and Selected Papers of the Statistics Committee.* 1950.

————, Royal Commission on the Civil Service (Chairman: MacDonnell) [82]. *Fourth Report.* Cd. 7338, 1914.

————, Royal Commission on the Civil Service (Chairman: Priestly) [83]. *Report.* Cmd. 9613, 1955.

———, Royal Commission on the Coal Industry [84]. *Report*. Cmd. 2600, 1925.

———, Royal Commission on the State of Popular Education in England [85]. *Report. Parliamentary Papers* (C. 2794), 1861, vol. XXI, part 1. (Chairman: Newcastle)

———, Royal Commission on the Taxation of Profits and Income [86]. *Final Report*. Cmd. 9474, 1955.

———, Royal Commission on the Working of the Elementary Education Acts [87]. *First Report, Parliamentary Papers* (C. 4863), 1886, vol. XXV. *Second Report, Parliamentary Papers* (C. 5056), 1887, vol. XXIX. *Third Report, Parliamentary Papers* (C. 5158), 1887, vol. XXX. *Final Report* and *Statistical Reports, Parliamentary Papers* (C. 5458), 1888, vol. XXXV. (Chairman: Cross)

———, Royal Commission on Trade Unions and Employers' Associations [88]. *Productivity Bargaining*. Research paper 4.1, 1967.

———, ——— [89]. *Report, 1965–1968*. Cmnd. 3623, 1968.

———, ——— [90]. *Restrictive Labour Practices*. Research paper 4.2, 1967.

———, Select Committee of the House of Lords on Early Closing of Shops [91]. *Minutes of Evidence. Parliamentary Papers* (HC. 369), 1901, vol. XVI.

———, Select Committee on Shop Assistants [92]. *Report. Parliamentary Papers* (HC. 148), 1930–31, vol. IX.

———, Treasury [93]. *Finance Accounts of the United Kingdom*. Annual.

———, ——— [94]. *Reserves and Liabilities, 1931–1945*. Cmd. 8354, 1951.

———, ——— [95]. "Short-term economic forecasting in the United Kingdom," *ET*, 130 (Aug. 1964).

———, ——— [96]. *Trading Accounts and Balance Sheets*. Annual.

———, ——— National Insurance Acts [97]. *Fifth Interim Report by the Government Actuary for the Year Ended 31st March 1955. Parliamentary Papers* (HC. 274), 1955–56, vol. XXII.

———, ———, ——— [98]. *Report by the Government Actuary on the Second Quinquennial Review. Parliamentary Papers* (HC. 220), 1959–60, vol. XVII.

United Nations. 1949. *International Capital Movements During the Inter-War Period*. New York.

———. 1953. *The Determinants and Consequences of Population Trends* (Department of Social Affairs, Population Division). New York.

———. 1965. *A Statistical Survey of the Housing Situation in European Countries Around 1960* (Economic Commission for Europe). New York.

———. 1969. *The European Economy in 1968* (Economic Commission for Europe). New York.

———. 1972. *The European Economy from the 1950's to the 1970s* (Economic Commission for Europe). New York.

United States. 1960. *Historical Statistics of the United States: Colonial Times to 1957* (Department of Commerce, Bureau of the Census). Washington, D.C.

_____. 1965. *Historical Statistics of the United States: Continuation to 1962 and Revisions* (Department of Commerce, Bureau of the Census). Washington, D.C.

_____. 1979. *International Comparisons of Unemployment* (Bureau of Labor Statistics). Washington, D.C.

Vernon, H. M. 1934. *The Shorter Working Week*. London.

_____. 1943. *Hours of Work and Their Influence on Health and Efficiency* (British Association for Labour Legislation). London.

Viteles, M. S. 1933. *Industrial Psychology*. London.

Walker, D. 1954. "Some economic aspects of the taxation of companies," *MS*, 22.1 (Jan.): 1–36.

Webb, B. 1919. Minority Report to the *Report of the War Cabinet Committee on Women in Industry* (Cmd. 135). London.

Webb, S., and H. Cox. 1891. *The Eight Hour Day*. London.

Webb, S., and B. Webb. 1902. *Industrial Democracy*. London.

_____. 1909. *The Public Organisation of the Labour Market: Being Part Two of the Minority Report of the Poor Law Commission*. London.

Whitehead, C. M. E. 1971. "A model of the U.K. housing market," *Bulletin of the Oxford University Institute of Economics and Statistics*, 33.4 (Nov.): 245–66.

Wiles, P. J. F. 1974. "The correlation between education and earnings: The external-test-not-content hypothesis (ETNC)," *Higher Education*, 3: 43–58.

Williams, G. 1957. *Recruitment to Skilled Trades*. London.

_____. 1965. *The Changing Pattern of Women's Employment* (Eleanor Rathbone Memorial Lecture). Liverpool.

Wilson, T. 1966. "Instability and the rate of growth," *Lloyds Bank Review*, July, pp. 16–32.

_____. 1969. "Instability and growth: An international comparison, 1950–65," in D. H. Aldcroft and P. Fearon, eds., *Economic Growth in 20th Century Britain*. London.

Wood, G. H. 1902. "Factory legislation considered with reference to the wages, etc., of the operatives protected thereby," *JRSS*, 65: 284–320.

Worswick, G. D. N. 1952. "Direct controls," in G. D. N. Worswick and P. H. Ady, *The British Economy, 1945–50*. Oxford, England.

_____. 1971. "Fiscal policy and stabilization in Britain," in A. K. Cairncross, ed., *Britain's Economic Prospects Reconsidered*. London.

Wragg, R., and J. Robertson. 1978. *Post-war Trends in Employment* (Department of Employment Research Paper 3). London.

Yule, G. Udny. 1925. "The growth of population and the factors which control it," *JRSS*, 88 (Jan.): 1–58.

Zweig, S. 1951. *Productivity and Trade Unions*. Oxford, England.

Index

Index

Abramovitz, M., 199

Absorption, domestic: effect on composition of output, 278–83, 654; effect on balance of payments, 488–89

Acceleration principle, 327–28, 331, 388–89, 390. *See also* Capital-output ratio

Agriculture: TFP, 16, 229–37 *passim*, 462, 553, 604–5, 606–7, 610: share of inputs and output, 222, 225, 227; output, 228, 230–31; inputs, 228f, 231, 235; outflow of labor, 252–53, 254–55, 284; and quality shift, 260–62, 266, 268; diminishing returns in, 274–75; investment, 332; and imports of food, 454, 525. *See also* Farm income

Aldcroft, D. H., 635

Allen, R. C., 451

Arrears, wartime: in output, 23–24, 25; in investment, 125, 390, 395

Balance of payments: trends in current account, 130, 440–44, 447–48, 479–80, 499, 669; and foreign investment, 356–57; effects on growth, 459, 479, 480–81, 490–91. *See also* Foreign trade and payments

Ball, R. J., 486

Bank finance, 348–49, 370–71, 392

Bank of England: pre-1914 operations, 456–57

Beckerman, W., 18

Bienefeld, M. A., 71

Birth-rate: trends in, 41–42; causes of decline, 45–49, 78, 624–25

Bricks, pottery, glass, cement: output, inputs, and TFP, 239–43, 610; inter-industry correlation analysis, 599–603

Building, *see* Construction

Burn, D. L., 450

Burns, T., 486

Business cycles, *see* Cyclical fluctuations

Cairncross, A. K., 354

Capital accumulation, *see* Investment

Capital deepening, 391, 394

Capital goods: prices, 134, 135–36, 189–91, 371, 412–13, 586–88; supplies, 371–72; controls on, 371–72, 372–73, 559–60

Capital input: concept, 206–7; growth rates, 207–9, 210, 501; weights in TFI, 208, 210, 505–6; sectoral growth rates, 227–30, 231–32, 604–5; sub-sectoral growth rates, 238–47, 648–49; contribution to GDP growth, 499–501, 520; per-capita growth, 501. *See also* Capital stock

Capital intensity, *see* Capital-output ratio

Capital-labor ratio: aggregate and sectoral trends, 232, 378; effect on investment, 326, 338, 384; and investment in commerce, 382, 386, 396–97; and investment in manufacturing, 391, 394, 397

Capital markets: imperfections and direction of investment, 355–56, 359–61, 372, 519, 658

Capital movements, short-term international, 455, 456–57, 472–73, 668. *See also* Investment, foreign

Capital-output ratio: and growth of capital, 131–34; aggregate and sectoral trends, 135–37, 337–41, 378–79; and growth of total assets, 137–39; and profit rates, 184–91; actual and desired, 327–28; and investment in manu-